YEARBOOK
OF INTERNATIONAL CO-OPERATION ON
ENVIRONMENT AND DEVELOPMENT
2002/2003

YEARBOOK
of International Co-operation on Environment and Development
2002/2003

an independent publication from the Fridtjof Nansen Institute, Norway

Editors
Olav Schram Stokke and Øystein B. Thommessen

Assistant Editor
Claes Lykke Ragner

EARTHSCAN

Earthscan Publications Ltd,
London and Sterling, VA

First published in the UK in 2002 by
Earthscan Publications Ltd

10th edition. Yearbooks before 1998 published as *Green Globe Yearbook*

A catalogue record for this book is available from the British Library

ISBN: 1 85383 929 9 *hardback* (available world-wide)
ISBN: 1 85383 934 5 *paperback* (available only in the Indian subcontinent, sub-Saharan Africa, the Philippines, the Caribbean, and Latin America)
ISSN: 1500-6980

Page design and typesetting by the Fridtjof Nansen Institute
Maps by Torstein Olsen, GRID-Arendal
Printed and bound by Bell & Bain Ltd, Glasgow
Cover design, layout, and paste-up by Morten Mathiesen, M&M Design, Oslo
Cover illustration: NPS/Images

***Yearbook* website: http://www.greenyearbook.org**

For a full list of publications, please contact:
Earthscan Publications Ltd
120 Pentonville Road
London N1 9JN
Tel: +44 (0)20 7278 0433
Fax: +44 (0)20 7278 1142
email: earthinfo@earthscan.co.uk
http://www.earthscan.co.uk

22883 Quicksilver Drive, Sterling, VA 20166-2012, USA

Earthscan is an editorially independent subsidiary of Kogan Page Ltd
and publishes in association with WWF-UK and the
International Institute for Environment and Development

Acknowledgements

First and foremost we are deeply honoured by the fact that Dr Gro Harlem Brundtland, Director-General of the World Health Organization (WHO) and Chair of the Commission on Environment and Development, has contributed a preface to this tenth anniversary edition of the *Yearbook*. Our sincere appreciation is extended to WHO's Communications Adviser, Jon Lidén, for his effective intermediate role in this regard.

In preparing this edition of the *Yearbook* we have benefited from and relied on, as before, both practical and professional assistance from quite a number of actors. Several of them deserve special mention.

We want to express our sincere appreciation to Earthscan Publications for their continuing interest, support, and smooth co-operation, and especially to the Publishing Director, Jonathan Sinclair Wilson, and Publishing Manager, Frances MacDermott. As previously, Earthscan Publications has offered us the services of Caroline Richmond, our unmatched copy-editor. Due to her experience and patience, she has been a key actor, ensuring the quality of this edition. We are also indebted to Earthscan's Marketing Executive, Helen Rose, and her marketing staff and to the co-operating distributors for promoting and supplying the *Yearbook* world-wide.

We extend our thanks to the contributors to the analytic Current Issues and Key Themes section in this edition for conscientiously respecting our deadlines, while at the same time following up suggestions both from us and from the peer reviewers. In the peer review process we have benefited from the expertise of Adil Adjam, Calestous Juma, Richard Kenchington, John Lanchbery, and Sebastian Oberthür. In addition we have received useful assistance from our Advisory Panel in the preparation of this section.

Thanks are also due to an extensive network of officials at international organizations and secretariats. Their enduring interest and support, and their positive responses to our drafts and queries, are indispensable in ensuring the quality of contents for the reference sections in the *Yearbook*.

As earlier, we have relied on the continuing support of the staff at the Fridtjof Nansen Institute. We are especially grateful for the perpetual enthusiasm and active editorial support of its Executive Director and Co-chair of the *Yearbook*'s Advisory Panel, Willy Østreng. The moral support we receive from Helge Ole Bergesen, founding editor and Co-chair of the Advisory Panel, is also much appreciated. As previously we have benefited from both editorial and legal advice from Davor Vidas for several entries in the Agreements section. We are also indebted to Maryanne Rygg for her dedicated editorial and administrative assistance in the production of this edition. The same appreciation is due to Rigmor Hiorth, Erling Hagen, Ivar Liseter, Kari Lorentzen, Morten Sandnes, and Henning Simonsen for their administrative support. We have once more drawn on the expertise and professional advice of our consultant in China, Zhu Rong-fa, based on his overall quality control of the Chinese version of the *Yearbook*.

Special thanks are due to our old hands at dealing with technical aspects of the *Yearbook*, that is Morten Mathiesen at M&M Design for his highly experienced handling of the design, graphics, and paste-up, and Torstein Olsen at the UN Environment Programme (UNEP)'s centre GRID-Arendal, who has been responsible for technical support in producing maps and tables both for the *Yearbook* and its web directory. Their assistance in the final stages of production remains essential.

We are further indebted to UNEP's GRID-Arendal for their valuable support in hosting the *Yearbook*'s web directory on their web server. The staff at Konsis Grafisk also deserve mention for technical support in producing film.

Finally, we acknowledge the financial support provided for this edition, and the respect maintained for our editorial independence, by the Norwegian Ministry of Foreign Affairs. The *Yearbook* was established with financial support from the Research Council of Norway, the Norwegian Agency for Development Co-operation (NORAD), the Norwegian Ministry of the Environment, and the Norwegian Ministry of Foreign Affairs.

The Editors

Advisory Panel to the Yearbook

Homero Aridjis, President,
Grupo de los Cien Internacional, Mexico DF,
Mexico

Alicia Bárcena, Senior Advisor,
UNEP Regional Office for Latin America and the Caribbean, Mexico DF,
Mexico

Helge Ole Bergesen, Senior Research Fellow and Co-chair of the Panel,
Fridtjof Nansen Institute (FNI), Lysaker,
Norway

Leif E. Christoffersen, Senior Fellow,
Noragric, Agricultural University of Norway, Ås,
Norway

Michael Zammit Cutajar, Former Executive Secretary,
Climate Change Secretariat (UNFCCC), Bonn,
Germany

Bruce W. Davis, Professor and Honorary Fellow,
Institute of Antarctic and Southern Ocean Studies (IASOS), University of Tasmania, Hobart,
Australia

Raimonds Ernšteins, Director,
Centre for Environmental Science and Management Studies (CESAMS), University of Latvia, Riga,
Latvia

Julie Fisher, Program Officer,
The Kettering Foundation, Dayton, Ohio,
USA

Susan George, Associate Director,
Transnational Institute, Amsterdam,
The Netherlands

Ernst B. Haas, Professor,
University of California, Berkeley, California,
USA

Calestous Juma, Special Advisor,
Center for International Development,
Harvard University, Cambridge, Massachusetts,
USA

Roger Kohn, Former Head,
Information Office,
International Maritime Organization, London,
United Kingdom

Martin Khor, Director,
Third World Network (TWN), Penang,
Malaysia

Geoffrey Lean, Environment Editor,
Independent on Sunday, London,
United Kingdom

Adil Najam, Assistant Professor,
Department of International Relations and Center for Energy and Environmental Studies,
Boston University, Boston, Massachusetts,
USA

Magnar Norderhaug, Director,
Worldwatch Norden, Tønsberg,
Norway

Amulya K. Reddy, Professor and President,
International Energy Initiative (IEI), Bangalore,
India

Bruce M. Rich, Senior Attorney and Director,
International Program,
Environmental Defense, Washington, DC,
USA

Peter H. Sand, Lecturer,
Institute of International Law, University of Munich,
Munich, Germany

Richard Sandbrook, Professor,
Centre for International Studies, University of Toronto,
Toronto, Canada

Lawrence Susskind, Ford Professor,
Department of Urban Studies and Planning,
Massachusetts Institute of Technology (MIT),
Cambridge, Massachusetts,
USA

Alexey V. Yablokov, Professor and Chairman,
Center for Russian Environmental Policy, Moscow,
Russian Federation

Farhana Yamin, Director,
Foundation for International Environmental Law and Development (FIELD),
University of London, London,
United Kingdom

Willy Østreng, Director and Co-chair of the Panel,
Fridtjof Nansen Institute (FNI), Lysaker,
Norway

Foreword

Dr Gro Harlem Brundtland
Director-General of the World Health Organization

A decade after the 1992 Earth Summit in Rio de Janeiro, the notion of sustainable development is universally accepted. We have seen some significant progress on environmental issues, including new global conventions, reduced pollution in many countries, and greater awareness of the value and importance of sound environmental policies. As the long list of agreements in this *Yearbook* testifies, a legal international framework for environmental protection is slowly but surely being built.

We can all agree that progress is too slow. The signs of environmental degradation and abject poverty are constantly urging us to move faster. The clock is ticking, giving us no rest. We are still far from the point where human activity is adjusted to the limits of what our global environment can support. We have still not reached a point where we can fulfil our needs in a world free from poverty without compromising future generations' ability to do the same.

During my 30 years in national and international decision making, two principles have stood out as crucial to achieving results: the need for unbiased, scientific evidence, and the need for collaboration that reaches across traditional barriers to bring together unorthodox partners. Only arguments that are based on solid evidence are able to withstand the tough scrutiny and confrontation that form the political process. And only broad collaborations and commitments from several parties can turn political decisions into productive results.

This is what makes the *Yearbook of International Co-operation on Environment and Development* such an important tool for researchers and decision makers alike. It is a child of the spirit and determination of the Rio Conference ten years ago to make a difference. It aims to present a clear overview of ongoing international collaboration in the field of sustainable development. In addition, it provides thoughtful analysis and assessment of the progress made to date. It demonstrates the international community's position on specific problems. It outlines the obstacles to effective international solutions and it charts the way to overcome them.

As we renew our commitments to our common future at this year's World Summit on Sustainable Development in Johannesburg, the emphasis must be on results. The *Yearbook* will continue to be a valuable assessment of the extent to which we succeed in this endeavour.

Contents

Intergovernmental Organizations (IGOs)

Non-Governmental Organizations (NGOs)

Contributors to this Yearbook

Michael Bowman is Senior Lecturer in Law at the University of Nottingham and Director of the University's Treaty Centre. He is also Rapporteur of the International Law Association's British Branch Committee on International Environmental Law. He is co-author or editor of various works, including *Multilateral Treaties: Index and Current Status* (1984, and numerous cumulative supplements, with D. J. Harris), *International Law and the Conservation of Biological Diversity* (1996, with C. J. Redgwell), and *Environmental Damage in International and Comparative Law* (in press, with A. E. Boyle). He has published widely in the form of journal articles in the areas of negligence liability, international environmental law, and the law and practice of treaty making.
E-mail: maureen.welch@nottingham.ac.uk.

Richard Herr is a Reader in Political Science at the University of Tasmania. He has taught in the field of international relations and international organizations. He earned a PhD in political science from Duke University, and during his academic career he has published widely on aspects of South Pacific affairs, Antarctic politics, parliamentary democracy, elections, and marine resource policy. Herr has held visiting appointments in New Caledonia, New Zealand, the United States, and the USSR. He has undertaken consultancies for regional organizations and governments of the South Pacific. Recent publications include the edited volumes *Sovereignty at Sea: From Westphalia to Madrid* (2000), *Global Electronic Database of Multilateral Marine Treaties and Agreements* (1999, with S. McCann, E. Chia, and K. Jackson). and *Asia in Antarctica* (1994, with B. W. Davis). E-mail: R.A.Herr@utas.edu.au.

Andrew Jordan lectures in environmental politics in the School of Environmental Sciences at the University of East Anglia. He has published extensively on the long-term impact of the European Union on the traditional style, structures, and procedures of British environmental policy. He co-edits two academic journals, *Environment and Planning (Government and Policy)* and *Global Environmental Change*, and was a contributing author to the Intergovernmental Panel on Climate Change's (IPCC) third assessment report. Among his latest books are*Environmental Policy in the EU* (2002) and *The Europeanization of British Environmental Policy* (2002).
E-mail: A.Jordan@uea.ac.uk.

Benito Müller is a Senior Research Fellow at the Oxford Institute for Energy Studies, which he joined in February 1996, and an Associate Fellow of the University's Environmental Change Institute, the Royal Institute of International Affairs (London), and the Stockholm Environment Institute (Oxford). He has also recently been elected to the Executive Committee of *Climate Strategies.* He received his PhD from the University of Oxford, where he is a member of the Philosophy Faculty, specializing in philosophy of language and of science, and was formerly a Research Fellow at Wolfson College and a Lecturer in Logic at the Queen's College, Oxford. He has a diploma in mathematics from the Eidgenössische Technische Hochschule (ETH) in Zürich, Switzerland. His work in the field of climate change has focused on socio-economic and political issues, in particular issues of equity in allocating emission targets and in impact burden sharing. He was co-author of a major study on the impacts of the climate change regime on global fossil-fuel markets, *Fossil Fuels in a Changing Climate* (2000, with U. Bartsch) and has written several analytic pieces on US climate policy.
E-mail: benito.mueller@philosophy.oxford.ac.uk.

Gill Seyfang is a Senior Research Associate with the Centre for Social and Economic Research on the Global Environment (CSERGE) at the University of East Anglia, Norwich, UK. Her research focuses on alternative strategies for sustainable development and consumption, at both local and global levels, and developing innovative methods to evaluate their social, environmental, and economic impacts. Her doctoral study of a community-based initiative (LETS, a local currency) as a tool for sustainable local development led to further work with time-based local currencies (time banks) and subsequent research has covered micro-credit, ethical trade, and sustainable consumption. She recently edited the book *Corporate Responsibility and Labour Rights: Codes of Conduct in the Global Economy* (2002, with R. Jenkins and R. Pearson).
E-mail: G.Seyfang@uea.ac.uk.

Keith Suter is a social commentator, strategic planner, conference speaker, author, and broadcaster. He is the Director of Studies of the Australian branch of the International Law Association and was elected to the Club of Rome in 1993. Suter has written on the law and politics of Antarctica for almost three decades. His first doctorate was on the international law of guerrilla warfare and his second was on the economic and social consequences of the arms race. From 1991 to1998 he was President of the Centre for Peace and Conflict Studies at the University of Sydney. He also lectures at the University of New South Wales on the politics of foreign aid. In 1986, the International Year of Peace, he was awarded the Australian Government's Peace Medal, and in 1994 he was voted

'Australian Communicator of the Year'. Recent books include *In Defence of Globalisation* (2001), *Legal Studies 1* (2000, with K. Keeley, J. McCarthy, and R. Watt) and *Global Agenda: Economics, the Environment and the Nation-State* (1995). E-mail: Keith.Suter@wesleymission.org.au.

Davor Vidas is a Senior Research Fellow at the Fridtjof Nansen Institute. He gained a doctorate in law from the University of Zagreb, where he taught international law (1984–92). After joining the FNI in 1992, he led several international research projects on Antarctic law and politics, the polar oceans, the law of the sea, and environmental protection, and served as Director of the Institute's Polar Programme (1995–2000). He is also co-director of the international postgraduate course on 'The Law of the Sea' at the Inter-University Centre Dubrovnik, Croatia. He has been an adviser to the Norwegian delegation to Antarctic Treaty meetings since 1992. Among his recent publications are the edited volumes *Protecting the Polar Marine Environment* (2000), *Implementing the Environmental Protection Regime for the Antarctic* (2000), and *Order for the Oceans at the Turn of the Century* (1999, with W. Østreng). E-mail: davor.vidas@fni.no.

Introduction

Olav Schram Stokke and Øystein B. Thommessen

It is only appropriate that the tenth edition of this *Yearbook*, which was first launched at the Rio Conference on Environment and Development in 1992, is published to coincide with the 'Rio plus 10' World Summit on Sustainable Development in Johannesburg. From the outset, the aim of this *Yearbook* has been to provide independent analysis and carefully researched documentation of (1) how far the international community has come in addressing the main challenges in a wide range of environment and development issues, (2) the obstacles to achieving adequate responses, and, not least, (3) what needs to be done to overcome those obstacles. To this end, its four sections are designed with a view to enabling readers to assess whether the frequently bold objectives that are stated in international treaties or at global conferences are followed up by equally bold practices.

The first, *analytical*, section of the *Yearbook* provides concise articles that evaluate the achievements as well as the limitations of international or transnational efforts to manage specific environmental problems. These analyses are made by independent experts who are instructed to identify what they consider to be the main impediments to effective governance in the pertinent areas and to pinpoint policy options that may be conducive for dealing with those impediments, as well as the conditions for such policies to be effective.

In the same vein, the three subsequent *descriptive* sections of the *Yearbook* provide systematic, detailed, and updated information about the substantive regulations, decision-making procedures, and institutional capacities of the major global and regional conventions, international organizations, and civil society groups that address environment and development issues. Particular attention is given to features that are usually required for the effective implementation of such rules—such as financial resources, adequate review procedures, reporting and inspection arrangements, and systems for dispute settlement.

The Johannesburg Summit forms a point of reference for several contributors to the edition's Current Issues and Key Themes section. Gill Seyfang and Andrew Jordan analyse the contributions of such environmental mega-conferences to international and global governance. In their view, the 1972 Stockholm Conference and the Rio Conference were events which shaped much of the present landscape of international environmental organizations, principles, and overarching policy objectives. But while these large conferences have been significant in setting new agendas, endorsing new principles, and creating new and more inclusive international institutions, they have also been plagued by political overstretch and an inability to narrow their focus onto those particular issues that can be dealt with adequately only at the global level. The very broad agenda of the Johannesburg Summit suggests that this conference will be no exception in that regard. A crucial effectiveness criterion for mega-conferences on environment and development is whether they generate processes which produce substantial financial transfers, or, more generally, resources for *capacity enhancement* relevant for meeting environmental challenges in developing countries. The authors note that none of the conferences to date have had a high score on that criterion.

This attention to the capacity-building aspect of international governance marks several of the other contributions to this edition as well. Under the Ramsar Convention on Wetlands, for instance, incentives for listing a site in the Montreux Record, which indicates that the area in question is undergoing detrimental changes in its ecological character, are provided by the expert assistance that can be obtained under the Ramsar Advisory Mission and the financial resources disbursed from the Small Grants Fund. Other means for sharing of resources, expertise, and information under this convention are such innovative practices as 'twinning' or 'networking' of sites in different countries that are either similar in character or linked by bird migration routes.

Similar observations are made by Richard Herr on the South Pacific Regional Environmental Programme (SPREP), which has contributed to national implementation of environmental policies primarily by means of capacity building, consciousness raising, and technical aid transfers. These functions are also important, as Herr demonstrates, for the ability of SPREP to support Pacific island states in their efforts to develop and articulate a common regional platform in broader international forums such as the Johannesburg Summit.

In the combat against global warming, capacity enhancement is as relevant for emissions mitigation, which has dominated the climate debate so far, as it is for adaptation to climate impacts, which will receive growing attention in the years ahead. Benito Müller places this issue squarely in the context of global equity. According to Müller, the success of the global climate regime hinges less on its ability to achieve 'meaningful participation' in the form of emissions-mitigation commitments by developing countries than on the preparedness of wealthier countries to shoulder a substantial part of the climate *impact costs* that are bound to strike developing countries with particular force.

To emphasize programmatic functions and capacity enhancement is not to argue that further *regulatory advances* are not called for in some of the most salient environmental policy areas. As noted by Davor Vidas, the 1991 Environmental Protocol to the Antarctic Treaty was an instant political success by silencing external critics, especially during the regular 'Question of Antarctica' debates in the UN General Assembly and within the green movement, which had threatened to undermine the legitimacy of the Antarctic Treaty System. At the same time, as Vidas demonstrates, a closer examination of Protocol provisions reveals problematic vagueness with regard to their spatial scope, the standard for triggering comprehensive environmental impact assessments, and the jurisdictional basis for dealing with third-party activities in the Antarctic. Moreover, while the Environmental Protocol had called upon parties to elaborate rules and procedures on liability for damage arising from activities undertaken in the region, highly relevant on account of growing tourism in the Antarctic, little or no progress has been made to date.

In the climate field, similarly, most would agree that, even if fully and conscientiously implemented, the emissions reduction and limitation commitments under the Kyoto Protocol are thoroughly inadequate to halt or even to slow down significantly the process of global warming. Its effectiveness therefore depends decisively on its dynamic nature—i.e. its ability to pave the way for broader and eventually more ambitious commitments. Müller highlights another aspect of dynamism, however: the ability of the regime to generate incentives to stimulate innovations in energy-efficient production, and North–South spillover of such technologies, that will permit a gradual delinkage of economic growth from the growth in consumption of fossil fuels.

Certain other developments in international environmental governance are also reflected in the assessments made in this edition. Greater *transparency* of decision making relevant to environment and development is spreading into realms traditionally characterized by restrictive access policies, including international living-resource management and global trade governance. Environmental civil society organizations, including Friends of the Earth International, whose policies and strategies are presented and assessed by Keith Suter in this edition, have contributed to this change. In some areas, the role of civil society groups goes beyond that of an observer to intergovernmental deliberations. In the Ramsar Convention on Wetlands, as shown by Michael Bowman, four environmental groups have been accorded the formal status of partner organizations and may designate representatives in the Convention's scientific and technical body. One of them, the IUCN, even provides secretariat services; and non-governmental organizations may (and do) initiate processes of identifying ecological deterioration in sites that are listed as Wetlands of International Importance. Both environmental groups and international secretariats have been skilful in using the Internet to make relevant information easily accessible and thus expand public participation.

We introduce one new agreement in the Agreements section of this *Yearbook*, namely the International Treaty on Plant Genetic Resources for Food and Agriculture (ITPRGFA), adopted in November 2001.

This section also contains major revisions of those entries covering the Convention on Access to Information, Public Participation in Decision Making and Access to Justice in Environmental Matters (Århus Convention), which entered into force in October 2001; the Convention on Long-Range Transboundary Air Pollution (LRTAP); the United Nations Framework Convention on Climate Change (UNFCCC), including the Bonn Agreements reached during the second part of the sixth Conference of the Parties (CoP) in Bonn in July 2001 and the measures adopted at the seventh CoP in Marrakech in October/November 2001; the Convention on the Prior Informed Consent Procedure for Certain Hazardous Chemicals and Pesticides in International Trade (Rotterdam Convention on PIC); the Stockholm Convention on Persistent Organic Pollutants (Stockholm Convention on POPs); the International Convention for the Prevention of Pollution from Ships, 1973, as modified by the Protocol of 1978 relating thereto (MARPOL 73/78); the International Convention on the Establishment of an International Fund for Compensation for Oil Pollution Damage 1992 (1992 Fund Convention), which replaces the International Convention on the Establishment of an International Fund for Compensation for Oil Pollution Damage 1971 (1971 Fund Convention); the United Nations Convention on the Law of the Sea (LOS Convention); the Convention on the Protection of the Black Sea against Pollution (Bucharest Convention); the Convention for the Protection of the Marine Environment and the Coastal Region of the Mediterranean (Barcelona Convention), including the new Protocol Concerning Co-operation in Preventing Pollution from Ships and, in Cases of Emergency, Combating Pollution of the Mediterranean Sea, adopted in January 2002; the Regional Convention for the Conservation of the Red Sea and Gulf of Aden Environment; the Convention for the Protection of the Marine Environment and Coastal Zone of the South-East Pacific; the Convention for the Regulation of Whaling (ICRW); the Convention on Biological Diversity (CBD), including the new guidelines and measures adopted at the sixth meeting of the Conference of the Parties in April 2002; the Convention on the Conservation of Migratory Species of Wild Animals (CMS), including the new Agreement on the Conservation of Albatross and Petrels (ACAP), adopted in June 2001; and the International Tropical Timber Agreement, 1994 (ITTA, 1994).

Extensive revisions since the previous edition have also been made on entries in the Intergovernmental Organizations section, for example the European Union (EU): Environment; the International Oil Pollution Compensation Funds (IOPC

Funds); the United Nations Children's Fund (UNICEF); the United Nations Development Programme (UNDP); the United Nations Industrial Organization (UNIDO); the World Health Organization (WHO); the World Trade Organization (WTO); and the World Bank.

In the Other NGO Networks, Instruments, and Resources subsection, we present new short descriptions of the Genetic Resources Action International (GRAIN); the International Institute for Sustainable Development (IISD); and the Stakeholder Forum for Our Common Future. Since, apart from those for some major organizations, the NGO entries are more condensed than the IGO entries, we recommend that readers who are interested in membership illustrations of the former should visit our website at <http://www.greenyearbook.org>.

In the process of updating information in these sections, completed in June 2002, all organizations and secretariats listed have had an opportunity to review a draft description of their activities. The responsibility for the selection of entries and the organization of information is, however, ours. As previously, we welcome comments from readers who disagree with our presentation or have other suggestions. Please use our feedback form, available at our website at <http://www.greenyearbook.org>. You may also contact us by mail: The Editors, *Yearbook of International Co-operation on Environment and Development*, The Fridtjof Nansen Institute (FNI), PO Box 326, N-1326 Lysaker, Norway; by telefax: +47 67 111 910; or by e-mail: <green.yearbook@fni.no>.

Polhøgda, Lysaker, Norway
July 2002

Current Issues and Key Themes

The Johannesburg Summit and Sustainable Development: How Effective Are Environmental Mega-Conferences?

Gill Seyfang and Andrew Jordan

The Long Road to Johannesburg

The Johannesburg Summit will be the fourth environmental mega-conference organized by the United Nations since 1972. Environmental mega-conferences are substantially different to the many environmental and sustainability conferences that have been convened around the world to establish new cross-national policies, monitor the implementation of existing ones, and promote long-term strategic thinking. Most of these smaller conferences[1] focus on a specific regional problem such as acid rain, a particular polluting substance or substances (e.g. those that are ozone depleting), or a specific 'sectoral' issue such as human health, food, or human population. Mega-conferences, on the other hand, try to take a synoptic overview of the relationship between human society and the natural world. Consequently, they tend to be held much less frequently than other conferences, the main argument being that a long time-frame is needed to encompass the breadth and complexity of the issues under consideration. So, rather than tackle a discrete environmental problem, they seek to provide an opportunity to consider the whole trajectory of human development, over much longer time-frames than national or even regional environmental policy is normally developed. Environmental mega-conferences are also 'big' in many other respects. They are self-consciously high-profile events, attracting world leaders and their deputies rather than just environment ministers and their specialist advisers. They excite global media interest, attract thousands of representatives of civil society, and are normally preceded by many years of careful planning and debate at the national and sub-national level.

The first environmental mega-conference was held in Stockholm in 1972, the second took place in Rio in 1992 (the 'Earth Summit'), the third in New York in 1997 ('Earth Summit II'), and the fourth in Johannesburg in 2002 (the World Summit on Sustainable Development (WSSD)—or 'Rio + 10'). Thirty years and two conferences after Stockholm, now is an appropriate time to assess the value of holding environmental mega-conferences. Are they the only way in which society can grapple meaningfully with the expansive agenda of sustainable development? Or are they as much a symptom of the problems of unsustainable development as an effective institutional mechanism for addressing them?

This chapter charts the history and evolution of the environmental mega-conferences since 1972—and examines their effectiveness in terms of setting the world onto a more sustainable path of development. After describing their history and organization, we identify a series of functions that, over the years, mega-conferences have sought to perform. We reflect upon their effectiveness at fulfilling these functions and their wider role in environmental governance. Are they, as critics would maintain, a convenient smokescreen which protects the more important drivers and forums of unsustainable development from serious critical scrutiny? Or are they an imperfect but nonetheless important mechanism for making slow but steady progress towards sustainable development at the global level? We conclude that, in spite of their very obvious flaws and the popular media image of them as expensive 'talking shops',[2] environmental mega-conferences *do* have an important part to play in steering and auditing the effectiveness of global environmental governance.

The United Nations Conference on the Human Environment (The Stockholm Conference): Stockholm, 1972

With a growing awareness among industrialized countries of environmental problems such as cross-boundary air and water pollution, pressure was growing for a global environmental summit as early as the mid-1960s. The hope was that a global environmental conference would tap the emerging global consciousness, which had been pricked by the first pictures taken of Earth from space. The political initiative appears to have come from the Swedish government, which at the time was under strong domestic political pressure to address the issue of acid rain in Western Europe. Scientists, too, played an important role: a Swedish representative apparently proposed the idea of an environmental mega-conference at the 1968 Economic and Social Council Biosphere meeting hosted by the UN. Other states agreed it was a good idea, and Sweden offered to be the host. Four years later, in 1972, Stockholm hosted the first global conference on a single issue—the United Nations Conference on the Human Environment (UNCHE).

Nowadays, not a week goes by without a large international conference taking place in some part of the world or other. But Stockholm was genuinely mould breaking. Nothing remotely like it had ever been attempted before. Since then, mega-conferences have been held on population, women, and human settlements, but Stockholm was the first co-ordinated attempt to discuss an international issue at the global level. The conference itself was headed by an industrious Canadian, Maurice Strong, and was attended by representatives from 113 states as well as from important international organizations such as the International Labour Organization and the World Bank.[3] Although political support for environmental protection was at an all-time high, the conference organizers soon discovered that many participants wanted to talk about issues other than 'the environment' (or, more specifically, cross-border pollution issues such as acid rain and marine and river pollution). Chief among these were issues of poverty and social justice. These and other human-development concerns, which centred on such thorny issues as the terms of international trade, development aid, and access to technology, were first raised by developing countries during the preparatory process. The Group of 77 (G77) developing countries, which was established in 1964, was adamant that environmental and human-development issues had to be discussed together, rather than in isolation. But, in the absence of a conceptual rationale for linking the two (e.g. sustainable development), the G77 struggled to push this point home.[4] Meanwhile, a coalition of industrial country representatives known as the Brussels group (which included the USA, the UK, France, Belgium, and Germany) worked hard on the margins to undermine the environmental outcomes of the conference, namely the proposed United Nations Environment Programme (UNEP), and to protect their existing trade and industry interests at the expense of developing countries.[5]

The Stockholm Conference eventually produced three major documents: a Declaration on the Human Environment; an Action Plan for the Human Environment; and a Resolution on Institutional and Financial Arrangements. This first environmental mega-conference successfully identified the terms of what is now a continuing global environmental debate. In so doing, it laid the foundations of the international system of environmental law and defined the terms of the global debate on the environment and development. For instance, the core principle that a nation state's sovereignty over the use of its own environmental resources should not impact negatively on other states was negotiated at Stockholm, as were many others.[6] Despite the efforts of the Brussels group, the Stockholm documents acknowledged that the priorities of developing countries were different from those of the industrialized nations. This required nothing less than a probing reassessment of the ultimate purpose of human development.

Stockholm also made a pioneering effort to incorporate the voice of what is now popularly known as 'global civil society'. For instance, parallel NGO conferences were held outside the main venue, including an Environmental Forum, as well as the more radical People's Forum and Dai Dong, which drafted alternative sets of principles and proposals. Finally, Stockholm set in motion a process of institution building at the national level. Through processes of consultation, discussion, and policy review, a lot of countries had prepared in advance of the conference proper. These networks of knowledge and political support were put to good effect by the many national environmental ministries that were established after Stockholm to implement the conference's bold agenda. These activities were given a strong push when, a few months after the conference, European political leaders met in Paris to give European political integration a 'more human face'. The summit successfully initiated a process of institution building, which bore many hundreds of items of EU environmental policy.[7] Regional inter-governmental conferences were also convened in the decade after Stockholm, and these generated a suite of conventions—for example, Bonn, 1976 (covering the Rhine); Paris, 1974 (covering marine pollution from land-based sources); Oslo, 1974 (sea dumping); and Geneva, 1979 (acid rain; the LRTAP). Many of these conventions were, in due course, given sharper teeth by EU legislation as part of a self-perpetuating dynamic of strengthening protection. Of course, Stockholm did not, of itself, generate these changes, but it encouraged them by emphasizing the commonality of national purpose.

However, Stockholm failed to resolve the difficult conceptual relationship between the environment and development. Although many countries took steps to live up to their pledges, the overall follow-up was weak. In 1982, UNEP held a ten-year follow-up meeting which concluded that, in spite of the widespread support for the Stockholm principles, there was little in the way of long-term, integrated environmental thinking and management planning. That meeting did, however, set in motion a process that created the World Commission on Environment and Development, chaired by Gro Harlem Brundtland.[8] The Brundtland Commission duly provided the first coherent justification for treating the environment and development as two intimately interlinked problems. Having received the commission's report, in 1989 the UN agreed to convene a global conference to implement sustainable development, which was held at Rio in 1992.[9]

The United Nations Conference on Environment and Development (The 'Earth Summit'): Rio, 1992

The 1992 conference in Rio was significantly bigger than the one in Stockholm. The agenda was broader and much more complex. Physically, Rio eclipsed Stockholm in terms of the number of participants involved. It also generated much more media attention and attracted many more senior politicians, especially world leaders. The framework conventions on biodiversity and climate change, which were signed but not negotiated at Rio, will always be associated with the Earth Summit. But, strictly speaking, the main outputs of this, the second mega-conference, were threefold: Agenda 21; a statement of forest principles; and the Rio Declaration. These were designed to build upon the work done at Stockholm. Thus the Rio Declaration recast the Stockholm Declaration in the new language of sustainable development, while Agenda 21 was intended to be the UN's blueprint for implementing sustainable development. A new piece of UN machinery, the Commission on Sustainable Development,[10] was created to maintain peer pressure on states to fulfil their Rio commitments.[11]

However, in spite of these impressive achievements, Rio failed to secure long-term agreement on the need for the more equitable world order that Brundtland and others had called for. As was the case with Stockholm, Rio conspicuously failed to reconcile the conflicting demands of industrialized and industrializing countries. If anything, it helped to clarify the limits of environmental mega-diplomacy at a time when many assumed that the world's ills could be solved by holding a big environmental conference. This point was cogently expressed by Michael Grubb and his co-writers, who argued that Rio simply provided a new arena in which many very old grievances about human consumption (in the North) and population growth (in the South) could be articulated with much greater clarity and volume.[12] In effect, existing positions were polarized at Rio by the experience of meeting together under the media spotlight, not reconciled. Of course, after Rio, unsustainable development continued apace, and little of the 'new and additional' money mentioned in Agenda 21 for sustainable development in developing countries ever materialized.[13] But, as with Stockholm, Rio did create new institutional processes of change that subsequently unfolded at national and sub-national tiers of governance. The Local Agenda 21 (LA21) process is one prominent example;[14] another is the UNCSD's benchmarking exercise, which has succeeded in encouraging states to provide a more comprehensive account of their own national sustainable development strategies.[15]

The UN General Assembly Special Session on Sustainable Development ('Earth Summit II'): New York, 1997

Soon after Rio, the UN General Assembly requested a formal review of the implementation of Agenda 21. The UN General Assembly Special Session on Sustainable Development (UNGASS) was held in New York five years after Rio. Although its formal task was to review Agenda 21, UNGASS (or 'Earth Summit II', as it became known) was inevitably portrayed as a litmus test of government's support for, and record of, implementing sustainable development. The meeting produced two main outcomes: a six-paragraph 'statement of commitment' and a 'Programme of Action for the Further Implementation of Agenda 21'. The organizers had hoped to keep the conference agenda narrow and focused, but as soon as the meeting opened the agenda began to broaden, as different groupings pushed their own pet concerns. In the end, the meeting struggled even to agree upon a statement on common concerns such as forests, climate change, trade, and globalization.[16] The UNGASS did, however, agree upon a new programme of work for the UNCSD, blessed the LA 21 process, and paved the way for the ten-year review of Rio I in 2002.

The World Summit for Sustainable Development: Johannesburg, 2002

Dubbed 'Rio +10', the World Summit for Sustainable Development (WSSD) is the main follow-up to the 1992 Earth Summit. It is expected to be as high profile and significant as Rio, and will provide the opportunity for concrete steps to be taken towards implementing the principles agreed at earlier mega-conferences. The preparations for the WSSD began in May 2001, with the first of a series of four global preparatory conferences and a number of regional and national consultation exercises to set the agenda and propose solutions. It will be the first major environment and development conference to have a formally structured official input from a wide range of 'major groups' of stakeholders identified at Rio (e.g. youth, farmers, businesses, women) rather than relying upon the unofficial 'side events' to provide a proxy input from global civil society. It will also provide an opportunity for world leaders to recover some of the ground they lost in 1997, by ratifying a number of global agreements (e.g. the Kyoto Protocol and the conventions on biodiversity and desertification).

Environmental Mega-Conferences: An Evaluation

Each mega-conference was very much a product of the time in which it was held. Each one reflected policies, political priorities, and institutional practices which were considered appropriate at the time, but which now appear somewhat outdated. Simply put, Stockholm placed the 'environment' on political agendas both internationally and in nation states. But it was a somewhat narrow, technocratic definition, which centred on particular polluting activities without really addressing human needs and wants. Rio tried to respond to Brundtland's challenge to link human development and the environment, but failed to achieve a lasting reconciliation or deliver much new finance for sustainable development.

What lessons can be drawn from the 30-year experience of trying to solve global environmental problems by holding regular mega-conferences? Advocates of mega-diplomacy claim that the conferences have to be mega-sized in order to adequately capture the complexity of the issues under discussion and the myriad competing viewpoints. But critics feel their size makes them ill-suited to dealing with the detailed, nitty-gritty problems associated with actually implementing sustainable development in specific localities or sectors. One of their main drawbacks is that such conferences simply encourage politicians to make grandiose promises that they have no real intention of ever implementing. One Zairean participant at the 1997 'Earth Summit II' articulated this view when he described them as an 'Earth Summit circus'[17] which allows everyone periodically to pledge themselves publicly to implementing sustainable development and then return home to resume 'development as usual'. The truth probably lies between these two extremes. Because of their power and size, mega-conferences are undeniably good at doing some things. But their size also makes them institutionally 'clumsy' and thus ill-suited to tackling certain items on the sustainable-development agenda.

How, then, should we evaluate the effectiveness of mega-conferences? Like Peter Haas,[18] we believe that it is incredibly difficult to measure their direct contribution to environmental problem solving. That said, it is possible to evaluate them according to some of the intermediate functions that they have individually or collectively sought to perform. Six functions in particular stand out as having dominated the work of the mega-conferences: setting global agendas; facilitating 'joined-up' thinking; endorsing common principles; exercising leadership by defining new objectives; building institutional capacity; and making global governance more legitimate in the eyes of governments, business, and civil society by promoting social inclusiveness.[19] In the remainder of this chapter, we try to assess how effective the mega-conferences have been at performing these functions. In so doing, we look for evidence of institutional learning—that is, have the organizers of mega-conferences learned lessons and made improvements on the journey from Stockholm to Johannesburg, or do the same old problems resurface time after time?

Setting Global Agendas

Anthony Downs believed that environmental concern is normally created by the build-up of unforeseen crises.[20] However, once they have made the political agenda, environmental issues have to be kept there, which is one of the functions of big conferences. There is no doubt that mega-conferences are immensely successful at raising public attention on issues of global concern. There are very few other occasions when environmental issues have received such intense media attention as they did in the run up to the 1992 Earth Summit. Environmental pressure groups usually criticize politicians for not doing enough when they arrive at mega-conferences, but they have their own reasons for attending and being seen to confront political leaders and industry representatives. As well as maintaining public attention, mega-conferences also focus the debate around several, otherwise disconnected, issues such as poverty, health, and environmental quality. The Stockholm Conference, for instance, brought to a head the simmering conflict between the environment and development. Subsequent conferences have continued to work on that relationship, and the agenda is growing in a way that does justice to the interconnected and multi-dimensional philosophy of sustainable development.

In a fragmented world made up of over 200 sovereign states, the UN is probably the *only* effective forum in which the global dimensions of common problems such as sustainable development can be adequately resolved. Advocates of big conferences claim that they are the only politically realistic means of discussing big issues which have a genuinely 'global' reach. Mega-conferences provide a relatively open forum in which states, international organizations, and NGOs can meet to plan the future trajectory of human development. In fact, it is debatable whether environmental conferences would attract as much interest (at least from senior politicians) if they weren't so big. By commanding the front pages of national newspapers, the mega-conferences introduce debates about the environment and development to homes and businesses all over the world. Consequently, the general level of awareness about global problems is raised many times over. 'Sustainable development' becomes a more popular term in public discourse; individuals learn about their part in global processes; and citizens are empowered to ask their leaders awkward questions about human development and demand appropriate action. Of course, in practice, the principle of sustainable development is still not a matter of sustained media attention at the national level. On balance, though, environmental mega-conferences are probably getting better at raising awareness, although steps must be taken to ensure that they do not simply 'recycle' decisions that have already been taken in (or avoided by) different forums.

'Joining up' Problems

World-wide problems such as poverty, inequality, environmental protection, and development priorities are wide-ranging and long-term, requiring solutions and new thinking outside the scope of most daily political realities. More often than not, they are dealt with in a disconnected and *ad hoc* way. Mega-conferences are a means to promote joined-up thinking around joined-up concepts. So, although the term 'sustainable development' was not formally coined by the Stockholm Conference, Stockholm played an important part in its creation and dissemination. Mega-conferences make it possible to hold a global dialogue about global issues. While there are often problems with implementation and follow up, mega-conferences also have huge symbolic importance. They force politicians to raise their horizons and consider strategic, longer-term questions that might otherwise be sidelined by day-to-day economic and political exigencies.

Yet this ability to set global agendas, and discuss big, integrated questions, is held within a constraining framework of political and economic pre-commitments, which are often not open to debate in the conferences. To put it another way, not all aspects of sustainable development are actually opened up for discussion; some things are firmly off the agenda. Some are discussed in other, more specialized venues such as the World Bank and the IMF (e.g. financial flows) or the World Trade Organization (WTO) (e.g. trade flows). More often than not, these economic, social, and political agendas are kept quite separate. Even in the environmental domain, important but more specific issues are considered in separate institutional venues such as the Kyoto Protocol process or that governing biotechnology and biodiversity.[21] In effect, mega-conferences are simply too big and cumbersome to unpick the most intractable disputes arising from the implementation of sustainable development. These have to be resolved in smaller, less politicized venues. The difficulty lies in preventing these different sectors from pursuing conflicting agendas, as in the case of climate change and trade,[22] or ozone depletion and climate change,[23] to name just two. Somehow, future environmental mega-conferences have to become sustainability mega-conferences which maintain the necessary breadth of vision while at the same time addressing some of the more specific, long-standing contradictions between international trade, the environment, and finance policy.

On balance, environmental mega-conferences are getting better at taking a joined-up view of human problems. The agendas at Rio and Johannesburg are considerably more wide ranging than the one at Stockholm. The problem is that, in the quest for comprehensiveness (or joined-uppedness), mega-conferences are finding it harder and harder to get anything fully into focus. New ways must be found in preparatory processes to identify meaningful priorities for effective negotiation and transparently audited implementation. Johannesburg in particular must secure agreement across a considerably broader sweep of issues than were discussed at Stockholm, and then turn that consensus into a committed and steady process of change: not easy.

Endorsing Common Principles

The agreements and principles signed at environmental mega-conferences are rarely binding. They tend to be guidelines and recommendations, standards, and resolutions. An oft-heard criticism of mega-conferences is that they are little more than high-profile (and hugely expensive) talking shops which give the illusion that the world is changing when it is not.[24] Politicians arrive, make their pre-prepared speeches, and haggle over the wording of a formal communiqué, before emerging bleary-eyed just before dawn breaks. They may offer token amounts of new finance or sign a new environmental agreement, but most politicians use mega-conferences to make only very marginal changes to the status quo. The conferences have produced so little concrete change because the declarations and agreements made there are voluntary, monitoring is difficult, and compliance is not generally followed up. It is indicative that some of the largest environmental pressure groups such as Greenpeace and WWF have turned their attention increasingly towards working directly in collaboration with industry, rather than through the formal apparatus of the state and international systems of diplomacy.[25]

Nevertheless, environmental mega-conferences have provided an important and authoritative source of 'soft law'—that is, a halfway stage in the development of more binding legal frameworks. States will always interpret soft laws in a variety of ways—as justification for action that would not otherwise be countenanced, or as a vaguely stated and therefore acceptable obligation. However, there is strong expectation that soft laws will be generally adhered to over both short and long term, and that what is now 'soft' will gradually become 'harder', more precise, and more legally binding.[26] It is striking how many of the principles contained in the Stockholm Declaration now form the basis of national, regional, and EU laws. With hindsight, Stockholm and Rio were important sources of soft law, but future conferences are likely to be less important, as politicians move on from defining common principles to agreeing more detailed objectives and programmes of action.

Providing Leadership

Mega-conferences have become more effective at exercising world leadership by defining fresh objectives for action at lower tiers of governance. This occurred for the first time at Rio, with the adoption of Agenda 21 as a blueprint for action at lower levels of governance. However, it is becoming increasingly clear that a system of review and monitoring, coupled with comprehensive preparatory processes for each mega-conference, would encourage a more successful implementation. Important lessons were learned at the 1997 UNGASS. Although 'Earth Summit II' was never intended to be a repeat of Rio, there was a widespread feeling afterwards that it had been poorly prepared and had failed to move the debate along.[27] Upon reflection, some of the participants felt that UNGASS had underestimated the importance of having a lengthy preparatory process, culminating in a concrete agenda.[28] There was no figure such as Maurice Strong raising political and media awareness in national capitals beforehand, and there was insufficient preparation in New York. Consequently, too many participants arrived, gave their pre-prepared statements, and then left, without ever engaging in the type of meaningful debate that mega-conferences are supposed to facilitate. The WSSD has tried hard to overcome some of these problems by hosting several global preparatory conferences, which have been underway since 2001, alongside national and regional preparations.

The underlying problem, which is far from being satisfactorily addressed, is how to ensure that mega-conferences concentrate on the problems that cannot adequately be addressed at lower levels of governance. Here, one needs to ask how well mega-conferences are abiding by the federal principle of subsidiarity (the idea that problems should be tackled at the lowest effective level of governance). Many elements of the sustainability agenda, such as the transfer of pollutants across borders or the operation of world markets, can be effectively resolved only at an international level. For instance, some transboundary pollution problems (e.g. acid rain) are almost certainly better addressed at a regional level. Over the years mega-conferences have powerfully revealed the extent to which not all 'global' environmental problems are actually global. The G77 first made this point in Stockholm, when it sought to draw attention to the local causes of environmental degradation in developing countries. At Rio, this argument was linked to an equally powerful condemnation of consumption in industrialized countries. In effect, the G77 said that, although the symptoms of poverty and (over)consumption may be global, the causes are very often much more local.

In summary, there are very real limits to what can be resolved by world leaders meeting in mega-summits and signing global agreements. The underlying problem is that most sustainability problems do not come in neat packages. Disentangling 'global' from 'local' issues is (and will remain) extremely difficult because participants in mega-conferences have very different conceptions of what is or is not global. The signs are that the organizers of mega-conferences have still not struck the right balance because, in Johannesburg, negotiators will grapple with a slew of problems ranging from toxic pollution in the North to contraception in the South.

Capacity Building

Mega-conferences create new environmental institutions in the UN, such as UNEP, the CSD, and the less well-known UN Department for Policy Co-ordination and Sustainable Development (DPSCD).[29] Mega-conferences have also given periodic shots in the arm to environmental ministries, agencies, and departments the world over through the creation of national sustainability plans and LA21s. This is presumably why advocates of mega-conferences such as Maurice Strong firmly believe that they should be judged as one contribution to a much larger process of societal and institutional change, rather than isolated, one-off events.[30] This is what Strong means when he says 'the *process* is the policy'.[31] Thus, while politicians' promises may not be immediately fulfilled, mega-conferences provide important yardsticks which domestic pressure groups can use to maintain influence. Over time, conference after conference produces a cycle of ever-increasing domestic commitment. We may describe this process as a one-way ratchet which tightens slowly but very securely; despite the slow pace and continual frustrations, there is inexorable forward movement. To give an example, Stockholm created UNEP, which worked hard to prepare the way for the Rio Summit, which established the UNCSD. The creation of the UNCSD is evidence that learning does occur; policy makers realized that, without such a body, it would be all too easy to recycle promises made at previous mega-conferences.

However, critics claim that these new institutional innovations are weak. The UNEP and UNDP have no secure funding, and so cannot plan for the long term. Neither organization has much legislative power or the ability to enforce agreements or protocols. The UNCSD, being dependent on what states voluntarily submit, has struggled to move issues forward successfully during its annual review sessions. These institutions need to be vested with far greater legal and administrative powers in order to function better as engines of sustainability.[32]

Mega-conferences also indirectly build new institutional capacity by creating domestic political opportunity structures. They do this by providing an opportunity for policy makers to embrace values and make promises which they would not normally consider within their own domestic sphere. National environment ministries have probably gained the most from mega-conferences. Indeed, many owe their existence to the Stockholm Conference, and many more benefit at home because of the opportunities created by mega-conferences. For instance, they secure new mandates and powers through their own activities in international forums, or the pledges made by their prime ministers, which they use to obtain leverage over cognate departments at home. Mega-conferences therefore allow environment ministries to play what political scientists term 'two-level games'.[33]

Fostering Inclusiveness and Legitimacy

A common complaint about mega-conferences is that they are, by their very nature, remote and elitist in comparison with more local environmental management systems, in which people can more directly participate. Big conferences may be ideally suited to providing international organizations and states with a comfortable setting in which to discuss new priorities and monitor old ones, but they struggle to capture grassroots debate about sustainable development. Mega-conferences are a magnet for the large and better-resourced interest groups, but these cannot be said to represent the full array of public opinion on any given issue. What has normally happened (see above) is that parallel conferences grow up alongside the intergovernmental ones to meet this need. Statements and 'visions' are adopted there by non-governmental organizations, but they remain outside the formal negotiation process. Legitimacy remains a serious concern for the planners of mega-conferences. After all, it is not beyond the bounds of possibility that future conferences might be invaded by the same street protesters that now follow the G8 and WTO summiteers around the world.

However, over time the mega-conferences have taken steps to make themselves more inclusive. Although 113 states participated in the Stockholm Conference, only two sent heads of state. More than 170 states participated at Rio, 108 of which sent their heads of state. Official participation was much lower in the 1997 meeting, although this was never planned to be as big as the one at Rio.[34] The participation of civil society has also increased significantly over time, especially in the recent past. NGOs in particular have grown in numbers: at Stockholm there were 134 NGOs in attendance, of which about a tenth were from developing countries; at Rio there were more than 1400 accredited NGOs, a third of which were from developing countries.[35] Outside the conferences themselves, host countries and NGOs have worked hard to produce informal venues for discussion and debate. About 17,000 people attended the parallel NGO Forum at Rio[36]. The Johannesburg Summit is expected to match these numbers.

Stakeholder groups also have a structured input into the UNCSD, for example (more than 1000 are officially accredited). This was a major step forward for NGOs, as they now have direct access to the agenda-setting process, although critics maintain that it simply has a 'decoy effect' of drawing attention (and debate) from more important forums.[37] Finally, the Internet is being used to find new ways to expand public participation. For instance, individuals may participate in the preparations for Johannesburg 2002 through websites and conferences, such as the UK government's Sustainable Development website (<http://www.sustainable-development.gov.uk>) and UNED-UK's preparatory conference on sustainable consumption and production. Another participatory initiative is the 'Earth Summit for All' educational web portal to help people to learn about and take part in the first mega-conference of the Internet era (<http://earthsummit.open.ac.uk/>). This website provides an opportunity for World Summit delegates and ordinary people to hold on-line discussions and collaborate in advance around a number of key topics. It provides a tool for developing the all-important practical projects needed to solve the major environmental and social problems that the Johannesburg Summit will be tackling, such as co-operative community networks and fair trade.

Conclusion

Environmental mega-conferences are an established part of the landscape of modern international environmental governance. That in itself is a good measure of their success. In fact, the conferences at Stockholm and Rio did much to create that landscape of international environmental organizations, legal principles, and policy objectives. By providing a global forum for the discussion of matters of universal concern, they have also played an important part in entrenching the language and practice of sustainable development into national policies, business operations, and public discourse.

In terms of the six functions outlined above, their record is actually not so impressive. Mega-conferences have successfully set new agendas, endorsed new principles of common action, and built new institutional capacity. They are more joined up than they used to be, and active steps are being taken to improve their legitimacy by engaging with civil society. However, a difficult balance still needs to be found between achieving a global perspective on joined-up problems and identifying topics that can genuinely be debated and resolved by leaders meeting at a global level. At best, they exercise real global leadership; at worst, they simply recycle old decisions that have not been properly implemented or legitimize the status quo. Crucially, the failure of successive conferences to finance appropriate development is seen as the most important weakness in the eyes of many developing countries. To conclude, environmental mega-conferences have their flaws, and only an exceptionally naive optimist would claim that they—and they alone—will carry society in the direction of sustainable development. However, environmental mega-conferences do serve an important function in contemporary environmental governance, even though they are not the panaceas that some had hoped they might be.

Notes and References

The authors are extremely grateful to an anonymous reviewer, Tim O'Riordan, and the editor, Olav Schram Stokke, for their perceptive comments on an earlier draft of this chapter, the funding for which was provided by the UK ESRC under its Programme on Environmental Decision-Making (PEDM). The PEDM, which runs from 2001 to 2006, is co-ordinated by the School of Environmental Sciences at the University of East Anglia in Norwich. For further details see: <http://www.uea.ac.uk/env/cserge>.

1. For a comprehensive list, see Peter Haas (2002), 'UN Conferences and Constructivist Governance of the Environment', *Global Governance*, 8, 82–3.
2. See, for example Jacques Fomerand (1996), 'UN Conferences: Media Events or Genuine Diplomacy?', *Global Governance*, 2: 3, 361–75.
3. UNEP, 'Stockholm 1972'. <http://www.unep.org/Documents/Default.asp?DocumentID=97>.
4. Marc Williams (1997), 'The G77 and Global Environmental Politics', *Global Environmental Change*, 7: 3, 295–98.
5. Mick Hamer (2002), 'Plot to Undermine Global Pollution Controls Revealed', *New Scientist* (2 January 2002).
6. Peter Haas, Marc Levy, and Edward Parson (1992), 'Appraising the Earth Summit: How Should We Judge UNCED's Success?', *Environment*, 34: 8, 6–11, 26–33; UNEP, 'Stockholm 1972'.
7. Andrew Jordan (ed.) (2002), *Environmental Policy in the European Union* (London: Earthscan Publications).
8. World Commission on Environment and Development (WCED) (1987), *Our Common Future* (Oxford: Oxford University Press).
9. Michael Grubb, Matthias Koch, Kay Thomson, Abby Munson, and Francis Sullivan (1993), *The 'Earth Summit' Agreements: A Guide and Assessment* (London: Earthscan Publications).
10. Tom Bigg and Felix Dodds (1997), 'The UN Commission on Sustainable Development', in Felix Dodds (ed.), *The Way Forward: Beyond Agenda 21* (London: Earthscan Publications), 15–36.
11. Andrew Jordan (1993), 'The International Organisational Machinery for Sustainable Development', *The Environmentalist*, 14: 1, 23–33.
12. Grubb, Koch, Thomson, Munson, and Sullivan (1993), *The 'Earth Summit' Agreements*, 57.
13. UNEP (1999), *Global Environmental Outlook* (London: Earthscan Publications); United Nations (2001), *Implementing Agenda 21: Report of the Secretary-General*, ECOSOC, E/CN.17/2002/PC.2/7 (New York: United Nations).
14. William Lafferty and Katarina Eckerberg (eds.) (1998), *From the Earth Summit to LA21* (London: Earthscan); Tim O'Riordan and Heather Voisey (eds.) (1998), *The Transition to Sustainability* (London: Earthscan Publications).
15. Farhana Yamin (1999), 'The CSD Reporting Process: A Quiet Step Forward for Sustainable Development', in Helge Ole Bergesen *et.al* (eds.), *Yearbook of International Co-operation on Environment and Development* (London: Earthscan Publications).
16. Andrew Jordan and Heather Voisey (1998), 'The "Rio Process": The Politics and Substantive Outcomes of "Earth Summit II"', *Global Environmental Change*, 8: 1, 93–7.
17. Ibid., 94.
18. Peter Haas (2002), 'UN Conferences and Constructivist Governance of the Environment', *Global Governance*, 8, 80–81.
19. Compare with Haas (2002), 'UN Conferences and Constructivist Governance of the Environment', 81–7.
20. See the discussion in Andrew Jordan and Tim O'Riordan (2000), 'Environmental Politics and Policy Processes', in O'Riordan (ed.), *Environmental Science for Environmental Management* (Harlow: Prentice Hall), 63–5.
21. Peter Newell and Ruth Mackenzie (2000), 'The 200 Cartagena Protocol on Biosafety', *Global Environmental Change*, 10: 4, 313–17.
22. A. Kim (2001), 'Institutions in Conflict: The Climate Change Flexibility Mechanisms and the Multinational Trading System', *Global Environmental Change*, 11: 3, 251–5.
23. Joanna Depledge (2001), 'New Challenges for the Ozone Regime', *Global Environmental Change*, 11: 4, 343–7.
24. Fomerand (1996), 'UN Conferences: Media Events or Genuine Diplomacy?', 361–75; Neil Middleton, Phil O'Keefe, and Sam Moyo (1993), *Tears of the Crocodile: From Rio to Reality in the Developing World* (London: Pluto).
25. Chris Rose (1996), 'The Future of Environmental Campaigning', *RSA Journal*, 144: 5467, 49–55; Peter Rawcliffe (1998), *Environmental Pressure Groups in Transition* (Manchester: Manchester University Press), 88–92.
26. Patricia Birnie and Alan Boyle (1992), *International Law and the Environment* (Oxford: Clarendon Press).
27. Jordan and Voisey (1998), 'The "Rio Process"'.
28. Derek Osborn and Tom Bigg (1998), *Earth Summit II: Outcomes and Analysis* (London: Earthscan Publications).
29. Lowell Flanders (1997), 'The UN Department for Policy Coordination and Sustainable Development (DPCSD)', *Global Environmental Change*, 7: 4, 391–4.
30. Jordan and Voisey (1998), 'The "Rio Process"', 93 (see note 12).
31. Quoted in Haas (2002), 'UN Conferences and Constructivist Governance of the Environment', 86.
32. Jürgen Tritten, Uschi Eid, Sascha Müller-Kraenner, and Nika Greger (2001), *From Rio to Johannesburg: Contributions to the Globalization of Sustainability* (Berlin: Heinrich Böll Foundation); Bigg and Dodds (1997), 'The UN Commission on Sustainable Development'.
33. Robert Putnam (1988), 'Diplomacy and Domestic Politics', *International Organisation*, 42, 427–61.
34. International Institute for Sustainable Development (IISD) (1997), *Earth Negotiations Bulletin*, 5: 8, (30 June 1997) <http://www.iisd.ca/linkages/csd/enb0588e.html>.
35. UNCED Secretariat (1992), *Facts and Figures on UNCED RIOCENTRO*, UNCED/DPI/RIOCENTRO LSF/ICD (press release, 12 June 1992), and UN (1972), title unknown, A/CONF.48/INF.6/Rev.1, (10 November 1972), both cited in Haas, Levy, and Parson (1992), 'Appraising the Earth Summit'.
36. UN (1997), 'UN Conference on Environment and Development (1992)', <http://www.un.org/geninfo/bp/enviro.html>.
37. Royal Institute of Environmental Affairs (2000), *Global Environmental Institutions: Analysis and Options for Change* (London: Royal Institute of Environmental Affairs), 24.

The Global Climate Change Regime: Taking Stock and Looking Ahead

Benito Müller

Introduction

Climate change may well be the biggest and most complex environment-related problem for international co-operation this century and beyond. In the last ten years, the issue has been the focus of intense and, given its complexity, remarkably successful global negotiations under the United Nations Framework Convention on Climate Change (UNFCCC).[1] These negotiations have concentrated on establishing a multilateral emission-mitigation regime. This 'mitigation agenda' found its culmination in the recently finalized Kyoto Protocol, which is likely to come into force by the time of the World Summit on Sustainable Development in Johannesburg in 2002, the tenth anniversary of the Framework Convention. This article argues that—notwithstanding some widespread Northern misconceptions—the UNFCCC regime is unlikely to succeed unless the key Southern (equity) concern of (sharing) human-impact burdens is put firmly on its agenda for the coming years. It also suggests that the forthcoming eighth Conference of the UNFCCC Parties, hosted by the Indian government in New Delhi, presents a unique opportunity to set such a process in motion.

The Phenomenon

Global climatic changes are nothing new. The last 500 millennia, for example, have seen regular cycles in the Earth's climate, alternating between ice ages and interglacial periods (see Fig. 1). Indeed, everything else being equal, evidence suggests that we are at the peak of one of these main interglacial periods, which accounts for the worry in the late 1970s about the onset of another ice age.[2] Yet these worries were not particularly acute. After all, the main cycle—with a temperature variation of 12°C—has a cooling period of over 80,000 years. '*Après nous le déluge*' becomes less problematic at these time-scales, both as a statement and as an attitude.

This situation, however, has since changed dramatically, as witnessed in the recent *Third Assessment Report* of the Intergovernmental Panel on Climate Change (IPCC).[3] The global average surface temperature—having increased by about 0.6°C over the twentieth century—is projected to increase between 1.4 and 5.8°C over this century, at a rate 'very likely [³90 per cent] to be without precedent during at least the last 10,000 years'. The threat of an impending iceage has given way to concerns about much more immediate climatic changes in the 'opposite direction'. The reason is that, in the course of the last century, mankind has unintentionally become a force to be reckoned with in influencing the Earth's climatic system. It graduated—or blundered—from 'climate taker' to 'climate maker'.

Fundamental Distinctions

The most general distinction between the causes of the current climatic changes is thus between 'natural', on the one hand, and 'anthropogenic' ('human-induced', 'man-made'), on the other. A paradigm of natural climate variations are the ice-age cycles of geological time-scales, some of which prove to be closely correlated with anomalies in the terrestrial orbit.[4] Yet there are other natural causes which can lead to changes in regional and global climates.

Take the phenomenon of 'volcanic winters'. The sulphur-dioxide emissions of the volcanic eruption on the Aegean island of Thera (Santorini) in 1628 BC,[5] for example, have been used to explain the average global cooling of 1.5°C over the following one hundred years,[6] which, in turn, has been suggested as one of the key factors in the downfall of the Minoan civilization during the first half of the sixteenth century BC.[7] Other natural climate-change events have been identified as having had equal, if not worse, social impacts—the 3 to 5°C cooling following the Toba (Indonesia) eruption of about 73,000 years ago apparently almost spelled the end of humankind.[8]

Anthropogenic causes, in turn, are based largely in human energy use and agricultural practices relating to the emission of greenhouse gases. Rice cultivated under flooded conditions generates methane emissions into the atmosphere as a result of the decomposition of organic matter. Deforestation reduces the absorption of carbon dioxide (CO_2) through vegetation growth. However, the biggest anthropogenic cause of climate change by a long way is not these agricultural practices, but the use of fossil carbon—coal, oil, and gas—as combustion fuels in all economic sectors: transport, domestic heating, industrial production, electricity generation, and so on.

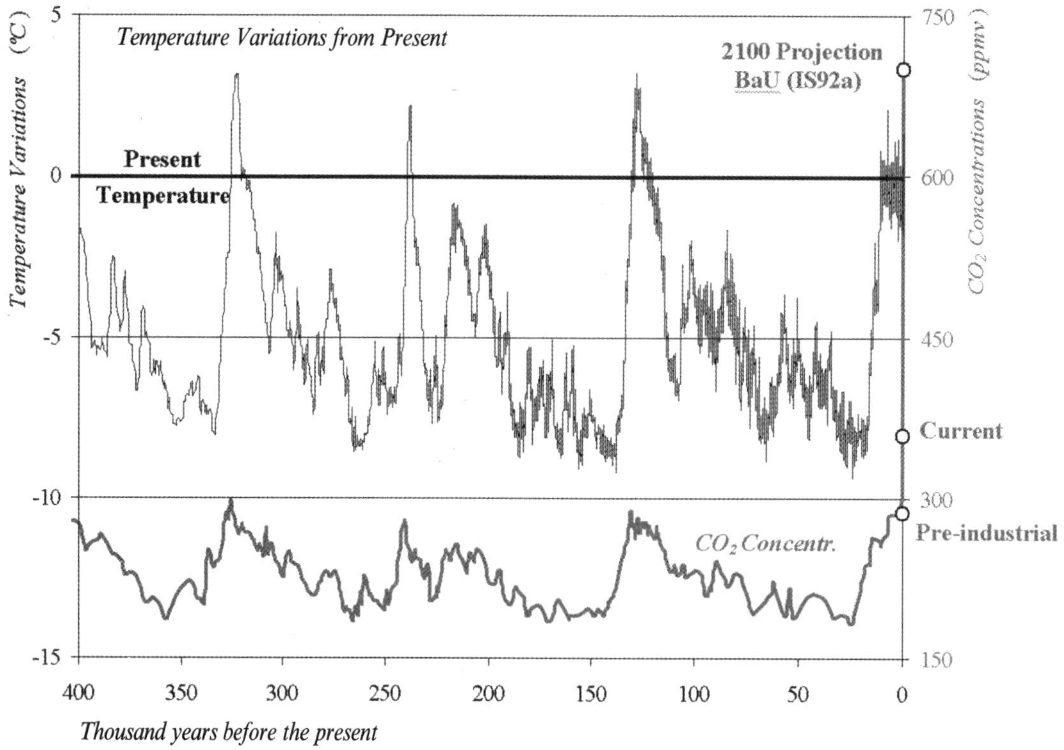

Figure 1. CO_2 Concentrations and Temperature Variations (from Present)

Sources: Pre-historic Temperature and CO_2 Concentrations: J. R. Petit, J. Jouzel, D. Raynaud, N. I. Barkov, J.-M. Barnola, I. Basile, M. Bender, J. Chappellaz, M. Davis, G. Delayque, M. Delmotte, V. M. Kotlyakov, M. Legrand, V. Y. Lipenkov, C. Lorius, L. Pepin, C. Ritz, E. Saltzman, and M. Stievenard (1999), 'Climate and Atmospheric History of the Past 420,000 Years from the Vostok Ice Core, Antarctica', *Nature*, 3: 429–36; CO_2 Concentrations: Pre-industrial (= 280 ppm), Current (1998 = 365 ppm), 2100 Projections (= 540–970 ppm, IS92a = 710 ppm), Intergovernmental Panel on Climate Change (IPCC) (2001), [TAR1] *Climate Change 2001*: *The Scientific Basis* (Cambridge: Cambridge University Press).

There will obviously be differences in the relative shares of CO_2 emissions for these sectors within a country, but arguably the most significant differences are not within but between countries. In 1998, for example, the CO_2 emissions per head of population ranged from the United States with 20,000 kg, at one end of the spectrum, to least developed countries such as Sierra Leone with 110 kg, at the other.[9] Given the importance of energy in economic growth and the historic world-wide reliance on fossil energy sources, it will not be surprising to find (see Fig. 2) that, over the last century, industrialized countries (the North = OECD and the economies in transition of the former Soviet Union and Eastern Europe) have collectively discharged five times the emissions of the developing world (the South),[10] a fact which gives some idea of the regional distribution of causal responsibilities for (potentially inevitable) anthropogenic climate-change impacts.[11]

The reason for drawing the distinction between anthropogenic and natural causes lies in the possibility of attacking a root cause of the problem: while it is well within our ability to reduce greenhouse-gas emissions, it is unlikely that our 'geo-engineering' skills will ever be able to control volcanic activity, let alone the terrestrial orbit around the Sun. However, humans must be singled out not only as causes but also as recipients of climate-change impacts. The fact of the matter is, climate change is only a problem because of adverse impacts on life-systems. And this is true regardless of whether the impacts are anthropogenic or not.

As it happens, climate-change impacts are divided not only with respect to their cause ('natural' versus 'anthropogenic'), but also relative to who or what they affect, namely 'social-' or 'human impacts' on human systems ('Society'), on the one hand, and 'ecological ones' on natural ecosystems ('Nature') on the other. One and the same cause can obviously give rise to a variety of impacts, both on different social systems—social groups, countries, or regions—and on different natural ecosystems—such as tropical rain forests or coral reefs. Many pollution problems give rise to both types of impact. What distinguishes climate change is the nature and potential seriousness of its human impacts, which transform the issue from a purely

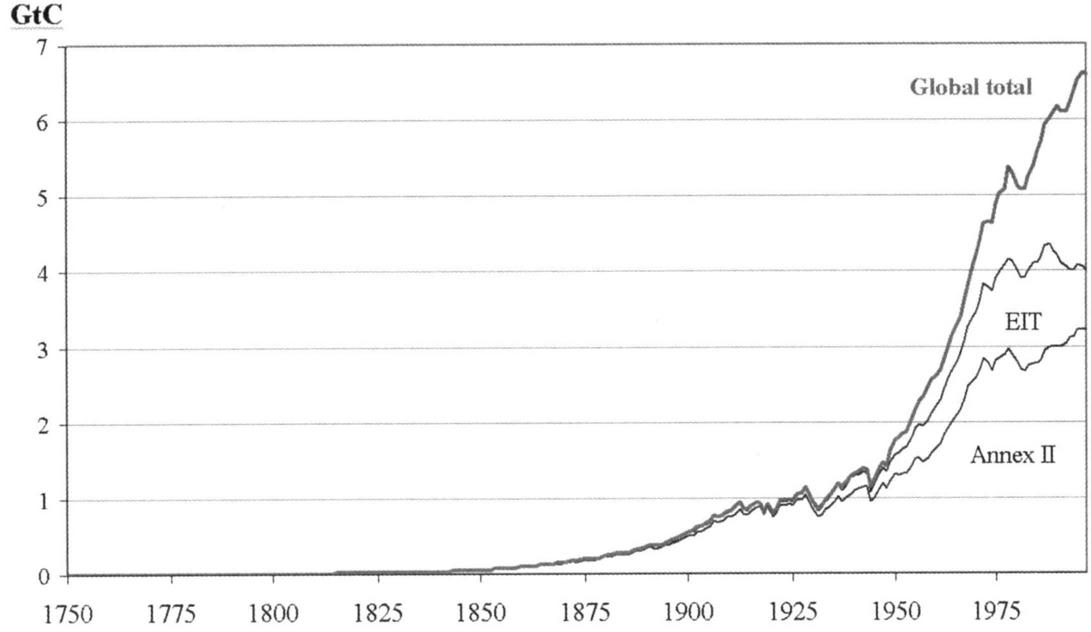

Figure 2. CO_2 Emissions: Fossil-Fuel Burning, Cement Manufacture, and Gas Flaring, 1751–1998

'Annex II' ≈ 1990 OECD, 'EIT' = Economies in Transition (FSU and Eastern Europe).
Source: G. Marland, T. A. Boden, and R. J. Andres (2001), 'Global, Regional, and National Annual CO_2 Emissions from Fossil-Fuel Burning, Cement Production, and Gas Flaring, 1751–1998 (revised July 2001)', <http://cdiac.ornl.gov/ftp/ndp030/region98.ems>.

environmental problem into an environment- and development-related one. Moreover, the anthropogenic components of climate change additionally introduce issues of interpersonal justice between those who have been causing the impacts and those who suffer them.

The Story to Date: An Environmental(ist) Pollution Agenda

The International Response: IPCC, UNFCCC, and the Kyoto Protocol[12]

Knowledge of 'greenhouse gases' and a 'greenhouse effect' is, again, nothing new:

> As early as 1827, the French scientist Fourier[13] suggested that the earth's atmosphere warms the surface by letting through high-energy solar radiation but trapping part of the longer-wave heat radiation coming back from the surface. ... At the end of the nineteenth century the Swedish scientist Arrhenius[14] postulated that the growing volume of carbon dioxide emitted by the factories of the Industrial Revolution was changing the composition of the atmosphere, increasing the proportion of greenhouse gases, and that this would cause the earth's surface temperature to rise.[15]

However, it took the international community until the late 1970s to become interested in the phenomenon, with the first World Climate Conference taking place in 1979 under the aegis of the World Meteorological Organization (WMO). Driven by further rising public concern in developed countries about *industrial pollution*—smog, acid rain, toxic rivers, and lakes, etc.—a series of international meetings led in 1988 to the formation of the Intergovernmental Panel on Climate Change (IPCC) 'to assess the scientific, technical, and socio-economic information relevant for the understanding of the risk of human-induced climate change'.[16] To date, the IPCC has published three Assessment Reports—the latest in 2001—which have been extremely influential in shaping the global climate-change agenda. After considerable debate about the findings of the 1990 *First Assessment Report*, the ministerial segment of the Second World Climate Conference (1990) called for the initiation of progress towards negotiating a UN climate-change regime.

The initial phase of regime formation culminated very speedily at the 1992 Rio Earth Summit in the UN Framework Convention on Climate Change (UNFCCC). In light of the excellent and detailed exposition of this Convention and its related legal instruments in the Agreements section of the *Yearbook*, there is no need to introduce its detail here except for three of its key 'architectural elements'.

- **Article 2** defines the ultimate objective of this Convention as: 'to achieve ... stabilization of greenhouse gas concentrations in the atmosphere at a level that would prevent dangerous anthropogenic interference with the climate system. Such a level should be achieved within a time-frame sufficient to allow ecosystems to adapt naturally to climate change, to ensure that food production is not threatened and to enable economic development to proceed in a sustainable manner.'

- **Article 3** (on Principles) stipulates in its first paragraph that: 'The Parties should protect the climate system for the benefit of present and future generations of humankind, on the basis of equity and in accordance with their common but differentiated responsibilities and respective capabilities. Accordingly, the developed country Parties should take the lead in combating climate change and the adverse effects thereof.'[17]

The equity-related differentiation principles regarding *responsibilities* and *capabilities* of Article 3 found their way into the architecture of the Convention primarily through the introduction of two lists of countries: *Annex I*, containing the industrialized countries with their significant historical emission records (Fig. 2), and *Annex II*, with the affluent industrialized countries. For example, the Parties included in Annex I commit themselves, in conformity with the degree of their responsibility in

- **Article 4.2,** to adopt policies and measures 'with the aim of returning individually or jointly to their 1990 levels these anthropogenic emissions of carbon dioxide and other greenhouse gases not controlled by the Montreal Protocol' by the end of the 1990s, thus demonstrating 'that developed countries are taking the lead in modifying longer-term trends in anthropogenic emissions consistent with the objective of the Convention.'

- **Article 4.4,** in turn, demands that Annex II Parties should 'assist the developing country Parties that are particularly vulnerable to the adverse effects of climate change in meeting costs of adaptation to those adverse effects.'

To be clear, the target of returning to 1990 levels by the year 2000 was stated as an aspiration without legally binding status. On 15 October 1992, the United States of America—preceded only by three small island states—was the first major country, North or South, to ratify the Convention, which came into force on 21 March 1994.

In April 1995, the first session of the Conference of the Parties (CoP1) in Berlin adopted what became known as the 'Berlin Mandate'.[18] In it, the Parties concluded that the Annex I commitments in Article 4 of the Convention were not adequate and agreed to begin a process 'to take appropriate action for the period beyond 2000'. This process was, *inter alia*, meant 'to set quantified limitation and reduction objectives within specified time-frames, such as 2005, 2010, and 2020' for Annex I Parties, and 'not introduce any new commitments for Parties not included in Annex I', thus reaffirming the need for Annex I leadership in conformity with the demands on equity by the existing differences in causal responsibility.

The ensuing negotiations—carried out under the aegis of the 'Ad Hoc Group on the Berlin Mandate' (AGBM)—found their culmination in the morning of 11 December 1997 at the third session of the CoP in Kyoto, when the chairman of the negotiations, Ambassador Estrada-Oyuela, declared the Kyoto Protocol to be unanimously agreed.[19] The Protocol's key response to the Berlin Mandate was set down in two Annexes—listing greenhouse gases (Annex A) and *legally binding* percentage reduction figures (Annex B)—and in **Article 3**:

3.1 The Parties included in Annex I shall, individually or jointly, ensure that their aggregate anthropogenic carbon dioxide equivalent emissions of the greenhouse gases listed in Annex A do not exceed their assigned amounts, calculated pursuant to their quantified emission limitation and reduction commitments inscribed in Annex B and in accordance with the provisions of this Article, with a view to reducing their overall emissions of such gases by at least 5 per cent below 1990 levels in the commitment period 2008 to 2012.

3.2 Each Party included in Annex I shall, by 2005, have made demonstrable progress in achieving its commitments under this Protocol.

In keeping with the Berlin Mandate, the Protocol did not introduce emission targets—or 'QELRCs' (Quantified Emission Limitation and Reduction Commitments)—for developing countries. And, while it fell short of providing Annex I targets for the year 2020 mentioned in the mandate, it did provide for additional, post-2012 commitment periods:[20]

3.9 Commitments for subsequent periods for Parties included in Annex I shall be established in amendments to Annex B to this Protocol, ... The Conference of the Parties ... shall initiate the consideration of such commitments at least seven years before the end of the first commitment period.

The *Yearbook* UNFCCC reference entry is witness to the fact that there is much more to the architecture of the emission mitigation regime introduced by the Protocol than just these targets and timetables enshrined in Article 3. And while it is not possible to characterize these features in more detail in the present context, some of the most recent achievements cannot be left completely unmentioned. Having achieved a political breakthrough at the extraordinary CoP6-bis session in Bonn in July 2001, the negotiators reconvened for the seventh regular CoP session in November at Marrakech, where they succeeded in specifying the operational details of the Protocol sufficiently for it to become technically ratifiable.

The negotiations at Bonn and Marrakech were dominated by four distinct yet related problem areas, three of which concern the 'flexibilities' built into the Kyoto mitigation regime. Their success became manifest, for example, in the adoption of eligibility criteria for the three 'Kyoto mechanisms'—emissions trading, joint implementation, and the clean development mechanism (CDM)(see the *Yearbook* UNFCCC entry)—and in the election of a CDM Executive Board to facilitate a prompt start of CDM transactions. A second flexibility issue dominating the debate was the nature and volume of permissible greenhouse-gas 'sinks' through land-use (change) and forestry activities. A compromise on how much of the carbon absorbed from the atmosphere could be counted against the Kyoto emission targets was reached with the intention of enabling the ratification of some key countries, such as Japan and Russia. The third mitigation issue which exercised people's minds during the negotiations was the Kyoto target compliance. The compliance regime proposed under the Kyoto Protocol is one of the strongest of any multilateral treaty, and its institutional structure was sufficiently clarified for the language to become ratifiable, not withstanding a postponement of a decision on its legal nature to after its entry into force.

The fourth key issue area raised during the negotiations at Bonn and Marrakech was capacity building, technology transfer, and adverse climate-change effects on developing countries as described, in particular, in Articles 4.8 and 4.9 of the UNFCCC. The CoP decided to establish a Climate Change Fund and a Least Developed Country Fund under the Convention to complement the Adaptation Fund established in Bonn under the Kyoto Protocol.

There are quite a number of detailed studies readily available of what has become known as the Marrakech Accord and its socio-economic and environmental implications.[21] For the purposes of this paper, the overall conclusion to be drawn is that the task of finalizing the operational details of the Protocol has been completed, which puts the question of 'adequacy of commitments' again at centre stage, particularly in the run up to the 'second commitment period' negotiations scheduled in Article 3.9 to start not later than 2005.

National Implementation

The issue of adequacy of commitments is not new and, while negotiators felt themselves bound by the remit of the Berlin Mandate, other stakeholders did not. In July 1997—five months before the Kyoto Conference—the US Senate, for example, passed the 'Byrd–Hagel' Resolution (S.R. 98) stipulating that the United States should not be a signatory to any UNFCCC protocol which would 'mandate new commitments to limit or reduce greenhouse gas emissions for the Annex I Parties, unless the protocol … also mandates new specific scheduled commitments to limit or reduce greenhouse gas emissions for Developing Country Parties *within the same compliance period*'.[22]

On 13 March 2001, US President Bush withdrew from the Kyoto process for precisely such adequacy of commitments reasons. Indeed, his specific opposition to the Protocol was 'because it exempts 80 percent of the world, including major population centers such as China and India, from compliance, and would cause serious harm to the U.S. economy. … there is a clear consensus that the Kyoto Protocol is an unfair and ineffective means of addressing global climate change concerns.'[23]

What is the current state of Parties' emissions relative to the objectives set in the Convention and the Kyoto Protocol? As it happens, collectively, developed countries have already met their (implied) Kyoto target of a 5 per cent reduction in 1990 greenhouse-gas emissions by 2008–

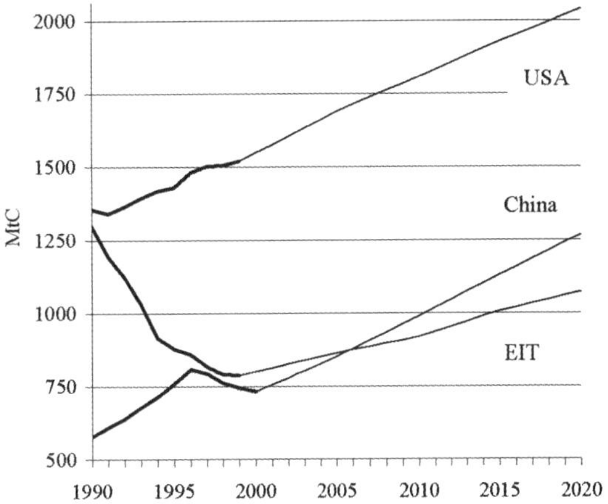

Figure 3. Carbon Dioxide Emissions, 1990–2020

Source: Benito Müller (2001), 'Fatally Flawed Inequity: Kyoto's Unfair Burden on the United States & the Chinese Challenge to American Emission Dominance', <www.wolfson.ox.ac.uk/~mueller>.

2012.[24] This may seem curious, in particular since the United States—the world's single largest greenhouse-gas emitter—has not made any particular headway in complying with the objective stated in Article 4.2 of the Framework Convention (let alone with its Kyoto commitment): far from having returned to their 1990 target level, US emissions at the end of the last decade overshot this level by around 12 per cent,[25] and the predicted trend (see Fig. 3) will hardly satisfy the Convention's stipulation that industrialized-country 'policies and measures will demonstrate that developed countries are taking the lead in modifying longer-term trends in anthropogenic emissions.'[26]

The reason why, collectively, Annex I still manages to be below the implied Kyoto mitigation requirement is the (unintentional) overachievement of the so-called economies in transition (EITs), i.e. the countries of Eastern Europe and the former Soviet Union. In industrialized countries, economic collapse is more often than not correlated with a reduction in greenhouse-gas emissions. Between 1990 and 1999, the Russian Federation, for example, experienced a drop in real GDP of 45 per cent,[27] with a concomitant reduction of CO_2 emissions of 36 per cent. The EITs collectively reduced their emissions over the same period by 39 per cent, from 1300 MtC to 790 MtC (Fig. 3),[28] at a 'cost' to the economies of $US420 billion—or, as it were, $US823/tC.[29]

In light of the overwhelming majority of studies predicting a traded carbon permit price of less than $US100/tC,[30] this has been a costly way to abate. By contrast, China, having turned around its emissions in 1996, thereafter mirrored the EIT reductions (Fig. 3) while continuing to enjoy an annual economic growth of between 7 and 9 per cent.[31] More precisely, unlike most Annex I countries, China managed (under no obligation) to reverse its emissions, leaving them by the end of the decade 9 per cent lower than their 1996 peak and 27 per cent up on the 1990 benchmark—less than half the previously predicted 67 per cent increase[32]—without prejudice to its remarkable economic growth.

The economic collapse of the EITs, obviously, was not due to a climate-change policy. And yet it is worth mentioning this 'carbon cost', if only to highlight that the resulting surplus permits—often referred to as 'hot air'—have not been some free windfall to the countries involved. Or, put differently, that this 'hot air' is not necessarily the sort of ill-gotten gain as is sometimes portrayed in arguments defending the environmental integrity of the regime.

Nonetheless, the collective return of Annex I emissions to 1990 levels can hardly be claimed to be the result of policies and measures demonstrating that developed countries are taking the lead in modifying longer-term trends in anthropogenic emissions, as demanded in Article 4.2 of the Convention. The conclusion thus has to be that the Convention's aspirational ('voluntary') target setting has not been a success.

As for the Kyoto Protocol, it is obviously too early to judge compliance with its legally binding targets. Moreover—due to its international flexibility mechanisms—the issue could not be discussed in terms of these simple domestic emissions. And yet since countries are not generally inclined to sign, let alone ratify, an international treaty without some confidence in their being able to comply with legally binding provisions, it seems that most of the Annex I Parties bar the United States consider compliance possible, given their declared intention to ratify by WSSD.

Equity: The Northern Perspective

Concerning equity, one issue has dominated the debate to date, namely quantified developing-country emission targets—the issue of 'meaningful developing country participation', as it has somewhat euphemistically become known in the US context. Developing countries have had some success in demanding, on grounds of differentiated responsibilities, that industrialized countries take the lead in adopting legally binding emission targets. However, this has by no means been universally accepted. As a matter of fact, a rejection on grounds of (1) unfair cost distribution and (2) environmental ineffectiveness has—as mentioned above—led to arguably the greatest set-back to the global climate-change effort to date: the US administration's withdrawal from the Kyoto regime.

Ad (1) above: The (perceived) 'enormity' of any cost is inevitably in the eye of the beholder. In the case of the United States, a study supported by the American Petroleum Institute, which had a considerable impact on American perceptions of the Kyoto Protocol,[33] predicted what has become accepted as a 'worst-case' estimate for US mitigation costs under the Kyoto Protocol, namely a 2 per cent reduction of gross domestic product from 'Business as Usual' (BaU). Whether such a change in the way of life is bearable or not is one thing, but it is and remains a matter of life-*style*. And it is difficult to see how even this sort of maximum life-style impact could turn the absence of developing-country targets into an unfair competitive disadvantage, given the projected increase in the North–South welfare gap for the period (see Fig. 4).

Ad (2) above: It is thus not surprising that the Bush administration's rejection of the Kyoto Protocol on grounds of imposing these 'unfair costs' has not found a great deal of empathy in the rest of the world. The environmental integrity point, however, has had more of a following. Indeed, the fact that the Kyoto Protocol is unable to deliver the objective of the Convention is universally accepted. Yet most people involved in the debate also realize that it was never meant to be more than a first, albeit important, step in this direction.

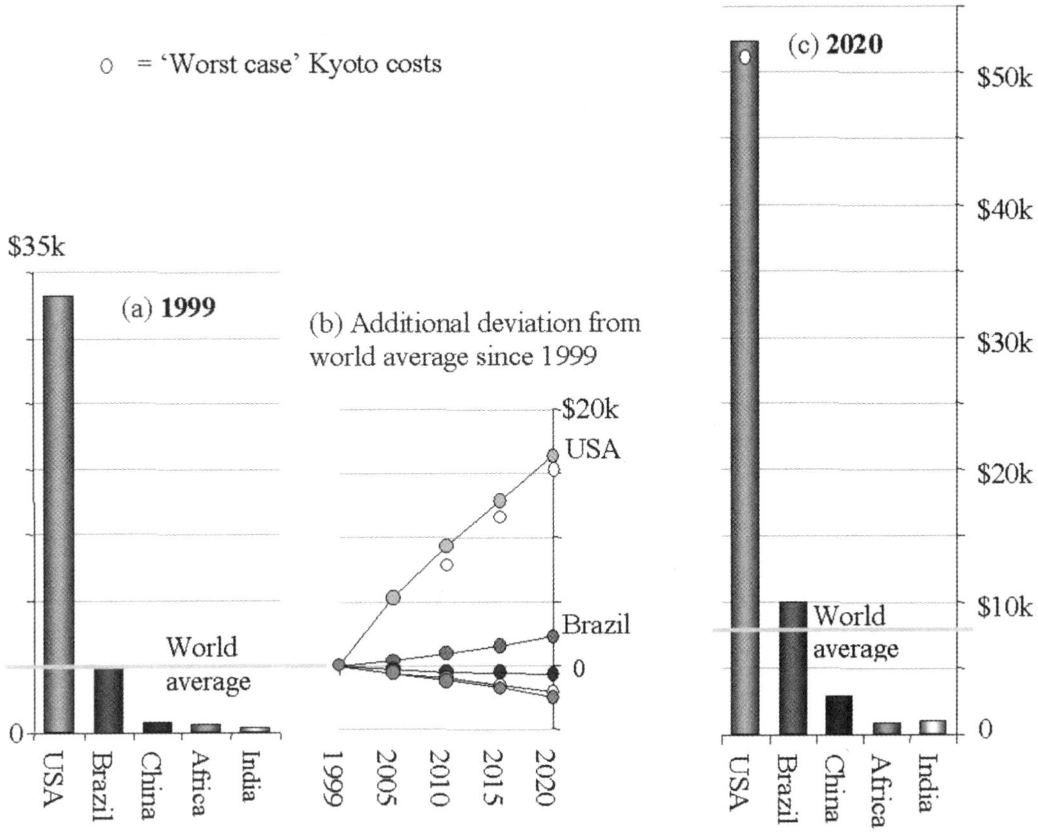

Figure 4. Per Capita GDP Projections: BaU and Kyoto Costs, 1999–2020 ('000 US 1997 $)

Source: Benito Müller, Axel Michaelowa, and Christiaan Vrolijk (2001), *Rejecting Kyoto: A Study of Proposed Alternatives to the Kyoto Protocol* (London: Climate Strategies), 4; <http://www.climate-strategies.org/rejectingkyoto2.pdf>.

Outside the Bush administration, concern about the environmental integrity of the multilateral regime has led to a focus on designing the mitigation regime of the envisaged second commitment period (2013–17) and beyond. In particular—seemingly unaware of recent developments in China[34] and the possibility that, with sufficient momentum, the decarbonization of industrialized country economies is likely to spill over to the rest of the world (whether they want it or not, with or without targets)[35]—many environmentally concerned protagonists have exercised their minds about including *developing* countries in a second commitment period target system in order to ensure the environmental integrity of the regime.

There is a large number of proposals as to how this might be achieved, many of which deal explicitly with the issue of distributive justice (often forcefully raised by developing-country stakeholders). Some of them are based on *ex ante* allocations of country quotas ('assigned amounts'), such as the 'grandfathering'[36] and 'per capita'[37] proposals, and their mixtures of both diachronic (e.g. 'contraction and convergence'[38]) and synchronic (e.g. 'preference score'[39]) varieties. Others involve more 'flexible' targets based, for example, on 'emission intensities'[40] or 'price caps'.[41] Studies and publications on the merits and shortcomings of these and many other proposals for introducing developing-country mitigation targets are too numerous to be presented, let alone properly discussed, within the confines of this article. However, information is readily available,[42] which is why we shall now turn to an issue which appears to be less appreciated but arguably as important, namely the question why emission *mitigation* has managed to dominate the multilateral climate-change debate to this date.

Environmental Protection and the Concept of 'Sustainable Development'

The dominance of emission mitigation in the international climate-change debate is reflected in the proportion of text afforded to this issue in the language of the international treaties. While there are some articles in both the Convention and the Protocol which are concerned with other matters, the majority deal with mitigation issues, such as international transfers of emission quotas ('flexibility mechanisms'), land use and land-use change ('sinks'), the regime for complying with the quantified emission targets, and the compilation of national emission data ('National Communications'), to name just some of the issues which have exercised many a mind in the past couple of years.

The agenda to date has been about the emission-mitigation burdens for a variety of reasons, some more pragmatic, others more philosophical. At the pragmatic end of the spectrum is the fact that greenhouse-gas emissions can readily be fitted into an existing paradigm in the industrialized North: air and atmospheric pollution. This has been recognized as a problem (smog, acid rain, etc.) by governments in industrialized countries for many decades, and most of them have introduced elaborate institutional structures (environment protection agencies, etc.) to deal with it. While it is not altogether clear whether the problem of mitigating greenhouse-gas emissions is best served by a subsumption under the air-pollution paradigm, the fact remains that in most countries—particularly in the North—climate change has been handed over to institutions dealing primarily with the protection of the natural environment.

Another pragmatic reason—with 'philosophical undertones', as it were—lies in the possibility of attacking the problem (anthropogenic climate change) at its root cause. While there have been voices suggesting that it might be better to spend the effort and money on improving adaptive capacities rather than reducing emissions,[43] the majority view by far is that, since it is possible to attack the root cause of the problem, it is better to do so than to deal solely with the effects—particularly if the cause is people, who, after all, can be held responsible for their actions.

Yet, arguably the most fundamental reason for the focus on mitigation in the current regime is to be found at the philosophical end of the spectrum: the perceptions of the very nature of climate change, the views of 'what it is really all about'. More specifically, the focus on mitigation is the result of a dominant Northern perception of things. To understand the nature of this perception and the way it arose, it may be useful to turn briefly to the nature and history of the closely related concepts of 'sustainability' and 'sustainable development'.

It is rare that the creation of a concept is precisely dated. 'Sustainable development', according to Ashok Khosla,[44] was launched on 5 March 1980 in the *World Conservation Strategy*, prepared jointly by IUCN - The World Conservation Union, WWF (formerly the World Wildlife Fund), and the UN Environment Programme (UNEP). Two things are worth highlighting in the present context. For one there is the notion's impeccable ecological parentage, exemplified in the IUCN's declared mission: 'to influence, encourage and assist societies throughout the world to conserve the integrity and diversity of nature and to ensure that any use of natural resources is equitable and ecologically sustainable.'[45]

And then there is the date itself: predating the Rio Earth Summit (1992) as well as the Brundtland Commission's report on *Our Common Future* (1987), it marked the end of a decade of intense public concern about industrial pollution. Almost by definition, the public concerned was that of the industrialized North. Significantly, the decade began with the Conference on the Human Environment (UNCHE, Stockholm, 1972), the first UN forum concerned with global environment and development needs. Although UNCHE 'indicated that "industrialised" environmental problems, such as habitat degradation, toxicity, and acid rain, were not necessarily relevant issues for all countries. ... it was the pending environmental problems that dominated the meeting and led to wider public environmental awareness.'[46] It thus seems safe to say that in the 1980s 'sustainable development' was about environmental or ecological sustainability. It was about living (consuming) 'within one's ecological means'. Or, to use a health metaphor, it was appropriate to obesity clinics, but not to famine relief.

Returning to the climate-change concerns of the developed North, it stands to reason that their emergence in the late 1970s and early 1980s at the height of popular concerns about industrial pollution of the local environment is responsible for the 'ecological view' of the problem. As a typical example of this (still prevailing) view, take the most recent edition of *Social Trends*, a flagship survey of the UK Office for National Statistics. Climate change is

Table 1. Environmental Concerns, England and Wales, 2001 (percentage of 'personally very worried')

Disposal of hazardous waste	66%
Effects of livestock methods	59%
Pollution in rivers and seas	55%
Pollution in bathing waters and on beaches	52%
Traffic exhaust fumes and urban smog	52%
Loss of plants and animals in the UK	50%
Ozone-layer depletion	49%
Tropical forest destruction	48%
Climate change/global warming	46%

Source: Table 11.1 in Jill Matheson and Penny Babb (eds.), (2002), 'National Statistics', *Social Trends*, 32 (London: The Stationary Office), p. 180.

given some prominence, namely under the *Air and Atmospheric Pollution* (*sic!*) section of Chapter 11 on *The Environment*. Table 1 shows the population's degree of 'worriedness' about the issue, but, more importantly in the present context, it clearly demonstrates with its juxtapositions what sort of problem climate change is perceived to be. Indeed, according to this official survey, 'climate change is recognised as one of the greatest threats to our environment.'[47]

The most recent *Annual Report* of the US Council of Economic Advisers—just to give a non-Eurocentric example—characterizes climate change as a 'potential problem [which] spans both generations and countries, implicating simultaneously the environment, on the one hand, and the world's fundamental economic reliance on fossil fuels ... on the other.'[48]

Climate change in the industrial world is thus perceived mainly as a problem of polluting the environment, of degrading ecosystems. As such, its essence is seen to be that of a wrongful act against 'Nature'. Accordingly, environmental effectiveness—the capacity to 'make good' the human-inflicted harm on Nature— becomes a key criterion in assessments of climate-change measures. The chief victim from this perspective is Nature; mankind's role is primarily that of culprit. And while climate impacts on human welfare are regarded as potentially life-style-threatening, they are taken to be self-inflicted and hence largely 'deserved'. Environmental integrity ('to do justice to Nature') is the overriding moral objective.

To be sure, these views are by no means inappropriate—to the *Northern* context. Industrialized countries still have to learn how to live sustainably, in the original environmental meaning of the term. And this lesson must include a drastic reduction of greenhouse-gas emissions as the uppermost objective. Yet, this real need for emission mitigation in the industrial context should not blind one to the possibility that, for others, the 'climate change reality' may be fundamentally different.

Looking Ahead: A Human(ist) Impact Agenda?

Equity: A North-South Divide

While there has been some technological progress since the Minoan late bronze age—with a concomitant increase in adaptive capacity—the fact that a mere 1.5°C change may have been sufficient to precipitate the collapse of one of the most advanced civilizations of the time might provide food for thought, given the range of 1.4 to 5.8°C projected for this century. The Summary for Policy Makers of the IPCC's recent *Synthesis Report* reinforces such unease, not only about impacts but also about their distribution.

The reality of climate change for the South (see Box 1: *Southern Realities*) is quite different from the one experienced in the North (see above). For many, if not most, developing countries the phenomenon of climate change—like volcanic eruptions, floods, and earthquakes—is *not* really a problem of sustainable development (in the technical sense of learning 'to live within one's environmental means'); it is primarily a matter of natural-disaster management. The only difference between climate-change impacts and other natural disasters is the possibility of anthropogenic attribution, the issue of human causal responsibility. As such, the phenomenon—unlike, say, earthquakes—comes arguably within the remit of corrective interpersonal justice regarding damages and restitution.

Box 1. The Third Assessment Report: Synthesis Summary for Policy Makers

Southern Realities

Recent regional changes in climate, particularly increases in temperature, have already affected hydrological systems and terrestrial and marine ecosystems in many parts of the world. ... Preliminary indications suggest that some social and economic systems have been affected by recent increases in floods and droughts, with increases in economic losses for catastrophic weather events. [Question 2]

Reductions of greenhouse gas emissions, even stabilization of their concentrations in the atmosphere at a low level, will neither altogether prevent climate change or sea-level rise nor altogether prevent their impacts. [Question 6]

When considered by region, adverse effects are projected to predominate for much of the world, particularly in the tropics and subtropics. [Question 3]

A Question of Equity

The impacts of climate change will fall disproportionately upon developing countries and the poor persons within all countries, and thereby exacerbate inequities in health status and access to adequate food, clean water, and other resources. Populations in developing countries are generally exposed to relatively high risks of adverse impacts from climate change. In addition, poverty and other factors create conditions of low adaptive capacity in most developing countries. [Question 3]

The impact of climate change is projected to have different effects within and between countries. The challenge of addressing climate change raises an important issue of equity. [Question 6]

A Question of Responsibility?

Mitigation and adaptation actions can, if appropriately designed, advance sustainable development and equity both within and across countries and between generations. Reducing the projected increase in climate extremes is expected to benefit all countries, particularly developing countries, which are considered to be more vulnerable to climate change than developed countries. Mitigating climate change would also lessen the risks to future generations from the actions of the present generation. [Question 6]

[T]he development of planned adaptation strategies to address risks and utilize opportunities can complement mitigation actions to lessen climate change impacts. However, adaptation would entail costs and cannot prevent all damages. The costs of adaptation can be lessened by mitigation actions that will reduce and slow the climate changes to which systems would otherwise be exposed.[Question 6]

Source: Intergovernmental Panel on Climate Change (IPCC) (2002), *Climate Change 2001: Synthesis Report – Summary for Policy Makers*, Question 2, <http://www.ipcc.ch/pub/tar/syr/index.htm>.

Given its governmental approval,[49] it is significant that the *Synthesis Report* Summary for Policy Makers does mention disproportionate impacts on developing countries (Box 1: *A Question of Equity*). However, it is equally telling of the Summary to stop short of referring to the problem in terms of 'responsibilities', and focus instead on the fact that additional mitigation may reduce the severity of impacts (Box 1: *A Question of Responsibility?*). There can be no doubt that the need to adapt must be minimized—at the very least for those parties who are largely innocent—and that the effort required to do so must be carried by those who are, if not guilty, then at least largely causally responsible. And yet, as we are beyond the point of being able to prevent impacts altogether, one question can no longer be avoided: who is going to bear the burden of the residual, unavoided impacts?

Given the expected distribution of these impact burdens and its discrepancy with causal responsibilities, it should not be surprising that a recent study[50] found this to be the one key equity concern of developing-country governments. In contrast to the perception in the North, climate change in the South has come to be seen primarily as a problem of harm to human beings, harm which is largely *other*-inflicted, and not life-*style*-, but *life*-threatening, in character.

What may be more of a surprise is the finding that, in the Northern hemisphere—where discussions on equity have been spearheaded largely by non-government stakeholders (academic, NGO)—the main equity problem is regarded to be the issue of allocating emission-mitigation targets. Moreover, this is often taken to be a problem mainly because it is seen to be a *sine qua non* for an expansion of the mitigation regime to developing countries, itself viewed as necessary to guarantee the environmental integrity of the regime.

For the South, the issue of sharing their impact burdens equitably is much closer to home than injuries to coral reefs or other non-human life systems: it is an issue of interpersonal justice, an issue of human perpetrators and human victims. The Southern view has been succinctly summarized by Sokona, Najam, and Huq:

> The third assessment report of the Intergovernmental Panel on Climate Change has made it abundantly clear that even if the Kyoto Protocol is implemented in full, the impacts of global climate change will start being felt within the next few decades and that the most vulnerable communities and countries are those which are already the poorest and least able to adapt to these changes. The threat is especially pressing for the least developed countries and the small island developing countries, where any economic development they may be able to achieve in the next few decades is in real danger of literally being swept away due to human induced climate change. In the past, climatic disasters such as floods, cyclones, and droughts may have been attributable to nature alone; in the future they will definitely have a component that is human induced. More importantly, it is also clear that the contribution of these countries to the climate change problem is minuscule. The result is that those who have been least responsible for creating the crisis are most at risk from its ravages.[51]

If the Northern protagonists are prepared to 'do justice to Nature', then they should also be prepared to do the same for their fellow human beings in the South. In other words, the environmentalist agenda which has so far dominated the international climate-change regime has to be complemented by a humanist[52] agenda, addressing the very real concerns of climate-change impacts on human beings. What we need is a regime with not just environmental integrity but also *human integrity*.

A New Delhi Mandate

Even though the dominant Northern environmentalist agenda has left its mark at the very heart of the multilateral framework,[53] there are some articles of the Framework Convention which would seem to permit redressing the balance:

> UNFCCC Article 3 (Principles).2. The specific needs and special circumstances of developing country Parties, especially those that are particularly vulnerable to the adverse effects of climate change ... should be given full consideration.
>
> UNFCCC Article 4 (Commitments).4. The developed country Parties and other developed Parties included in Annex II shall also assist the developing country Parties that are particularly vulnerable to the adverse effects of climate change in meeting costs of adaptation to those adverse effects.[54]

To be perfectly clear, the need to redress the balance regarding human impacts does not supplant the need for further emission reductions in the second commitment period and beyond! And while the bulk of these will have to remain in the industrialized world, the view that developing-country emissions need to be addressed cannot be ignored. However, there are other ways of addressing these emissions in the first decades of this century than a simplistic transferral of the Northern model by asking developing countries to take on quantified emission limitation and reduction commitments.

For one, as mentioned earlier, sufficiently strong Annex I commitments could have technology spillover effects which could deal with the issue of developing country emissions without the need for quantified constraints. Even if industrialized countries should feel worried about their capacity to generate such spillovers, there are ways of introducing quantified developing-country targets which do not impose disproportionate obligations on them. For example, the North could accept a quantity of 'Certified Emission Reduction Obligations' (CEROs)—to be undertaken in developing countries under the existing Clean Development Mechanism, one of the Kyoto flexibilities (see UNFCCC *Yearbook* entry)—as part of *Annex I commitments.* For the sake of economic efficiency and North–North equity, these CEROs could be tradable and grandfathered. Indeed, to avoid South–South inequities, a number of tradable 'CER permits' (CERPs)—permits to generate CERs—greater or equal to the total of CEROs for the commitment period could be distributed among developing countries on a per capita basis. While it is not certain whether such a scheme would be acceptable, the fact remains that there are ways of addressing developing-country emissions without imposing obligations disproportionate with their responsibilities.

During the high-level segment at CoP7 in Marrakech, Thiru T. R. Baalu, India's Minister for Environment and Forests, left no doubt about his government's view on these matters:

> The efforts so far have been focussed on mitigation. In the coming decades, adaptation needs to be given much greater attention. The next decade, Mr. President, therefore should see concrete implementation of existing mitigation commitments and active consideration and action on adaptation to the adverse impacts of climate change.

Given India's offer to host CoP8 in New Delhi following the WSSD, and the focus on the role of developing countries which this CoP will inevitably attract (in particular if the Kyoto Protocol should come into force by the WSSD, as planned), there seems to be an unique chance for India to take the lead and have her capital associated with a mandate which could catalyze the formation of a proper human-impacts regime in the same way in which the mandate associated with the German capital managed to catalyze the formation of the emissions-mitigation regime.

It may be questionable whether the feat of the Ad Hoc Group on the Berlin Mandate in finishing negotiations in less than three years could be emulated in this context, so as to conclude an 'Impacts Protocol' by 2005, when negotiations on the second commitment period are officially meant to begin. But there can be little doubt that substantive progress on such a protocol would facilitate these Kyoto successor negotiations. Whether India will wish to grab this opportunity and take such a lead, and whether the rest of the world would be willing to follow, remains to be seen. The fact remains that the international climate-change regime under the Framework Convention can hope to achieve its objective only if it addresses these humanist concerns by being as much about innocent humans as it is about healthy ecosystems.

Notes and References

The author is grateful to Brian Buck, Joanna Depledge, Sebastian Oberthür, and Olav Schram Stokke for their help and critical review.

1. See Agreements section in this *Yearbook.*
2. See, for example, Fred Hoyle (1981), *Ice* (London: Hutchinson).
3. See, for example, Joanna Depledge (2002), *The Third Assessment Report of the IPCC,* Royal Institute of International Affairs Briefing Paper (London: Royal Institute of International Affairs).
4. See, for example, John Imbrie and Katherine Palmer Imbrie (1997), *Ice Ages: Solving the Mystery* (Cambridge, MA: Harvard University Press); or Richard B. Alley (2000), *The Two-Mile Time Machine: Ice Cores, Abrupt Climate Change and our Future* (Princeton, NJ: Princeton University Press).
5. Sturt W. Manning (1999), *A Test of Time: The Volcano of Thera and the Chronology and History of the Aegean and East Mediterranean in the Mid Second Millennium BC* (Oxford: Oxbow Books); <www.rdg.ac.uk/~lasmanng/testoftime.html>.
6. 1647 BC: +0.65°C, 1559 BC: –0.9°C, relative to present. J. R. Petit, J. Jouzel, D. Raynaud, N. I. Barkov, J.-M. Barnola, I. Basile, M. Bender, J. Chappellaz, M. Davis, G. Delayque, M. Delmotte, V. M. Kotlyakov, M. Legrand, V. Y. Lipenkov, C. Lorius, L. Pepin, C. Ritz, E. Saltzman, and M. Stievenard (1999), 'Climate and Atmospheric History of the Past 420,000 Years from the Vostok Ice Core, Antarctica', *Nature,* 3, 429–36; Data Source: 'Historical Isotopic Temperature Record from the Vostok Ice Core', <http://cdiac.esd.ornl.gov/ftp/ trends/temp/ vostok/vostok.1999.temp.dat>.
7. '... the eruption on Thera could have lowered annual average temperatures by 1 to 2 degrees across Europe, Asia and North America. ... the summer temperatures would have dropped more—suggesting years of cold, wet summers and ruined harvests': Jessica Cecil (2001), 'Ancient Apocalypse: The Fall of the Minoan Civilisation', <http://www.bbc.co.uk/history/ancient/ apocalypse_minoan1.shtml >. For more details on the eruption, see Chapter 5 of Floyd W. McCoy and Grant Heiken (2000), *Volcanic Hazards and Disasters in Human Antiquity,* Special Paper 345 (Boulder, CO: Geological Society of America).
8. Michael R. Rampino and Stanley H. Ambrose (2000), 'Volcanic Winter in the Garden of Eden: The Toba Supereruption and the Late Pleistocene Human Population Crash', in McCoy and

Heiken, *Volcanic Hazards and Disasters in Human Antiquity*, 71–82, at 71.

9. Gregg Marland, Thomas A. Boden, and Robert J. Andres (2002), 'Global, Regional, and National Fossil Fuel CO_2 Emissions', Carbon Dioxide Information Analysis Center, Oak Ridge National Laboratory, <http://cdiac.esd.ornl.gov/trends/emis/em_cont.htm>.
10. Source: World Resources Institute (WRI), 'Contributions to Global Warming Map', <http://www.wri.org/ climate/contributions_map.html>.
11. However, caution should be taken when interpreting such figures. If, for example, like the author, one is of the opinion that these responsibilities need to be compared in terms of average yearly per capita emissions, the Northern responsibility increases to fifteen times that of the South.
12. For more details on the institutional structure and the procedural rules, see, for example, Joanna Depledge (2002), *A Guide to the Climate Change Process* (Bonn: Climate Change Secretariat).
13. Baron Jean-Baptiste Joseph Fourier (1768–1830), French mathematician, physicist, and Egyptologist.
14. Svante August Arrhenius (1859–1927), Swedish physical chemist.
15. Michael Grubb with Christiaan Vrolijk and Duncan Brack (1999), *The Kyoto Protocol: A Guide and Assessment* (London: Royal Institute of International Affairs), 4.
16. Intergovernmental Panel on Climate Change, 'About IPCC', <http://www.ipcc.ch/about/about.htm>.
17. 'Adverse effects of climate change' means changes in the physical environment or biota resulting from climate change which have significant deleterious effects on the composition, resilience, or productivity of natural and managed ecosystems or on the operation of socio-economic systems or on human health and welfare (UNFCCC, Article 1, Definitions).
18. United Nations Framework Convention on Climate Change (UNFCCC) (1995), *The Berlin Mandate: Decision 1/CP.1*; <unfccc.int/resource/docs/cop1/07a01.htm>.
19. Grubb (1999), *The Kyoto Protocol*, 111.
20. Indeed, according to Article 9, a review of the Kyoto Protocol 'in the light of the best available scientific information and assessments on climate change and its impacts, as well as relevant technical, social and economic information' might have to be undertaken as early as 2003, assuming entry into force by WSSD.
21. Suraje Dessai (2001), *The Climate Regime from The Hague to Marrakech: Saving or Sinking the Kyoto Protocol*, Working Paper 12 (Norwich: Tyndall), <http://www.tyndall.ac.uk/publications/working_papers/working_papers.shtml>; Thomas Legge and Christian Egenhofer (2001), *After Marrakech: the Regionalisation of the Kyoto Protocol*, CEPS Commentary (Brussels: Centre for European Policy Studies), <http://www.ceps.be/Commentary/Nov01/Marrakech,htm>; Asbjørn Torvanger (2001), *An Evaluation of Business Implications of the Kyoto Protocol*, Report 2001–05 (Oslo: Center for International Climate and Environmental Research–Oslo), <www.cicero.uio.no/publications/detail.asp?1690>; Odile Blanchard, Patrick Criqui, and Alban Kitous (2002), *After The Hague, Bonn and Marrakech: the Future International Market for Emissions Permits and the Issue of Hot Air* (Grenoble: Institut D'Economie et de Politique de L'Energi), <http://www.upmf-grenoble.fr/iepe/textes/Cahier27Angl.pdf>; Michel G. J. den Elzen and André P. G. de Moor (2002), *The Bonn Agreement and Marrakesh Accords: An Updated Analysis*, RIVM report 728001017/2001 (Bilthoven: National Institute of Public Health and the Environment (RIVM)), <http:/www.rivm.nl/ieweb/ieweb/Reports/rep728001017_marrakech.pdf>; Donald Goldberg and Katherine Silverthorne (2002), 'The Marrakech Accords', *ABA Newsletter* [American Bar Association], 5: 2, <http://www.abanet.org/environ/committees/climatechange/newsletter/jan02/goldberg.html>; Andreas Löschel and ZhongXiang Zhang (2002), 'The Economic and Environmental Implications of the US Repudiation of the Kyoto Protocol and the Subsequent Deals in Bonn and Marrakech', <http://papers.ssrn.com/abstract=299463>; Christiaan Vrolijk (2001), *The Marrakesh Accords*, RIIA Meeting Report (London: Royal Institute of International Affairs), <http://www.riia.org/Research/eep/cop7meeting.pdf>; Tata Energy Research Institute (2001), Review of CoP7, <http://www.teriin.org/climate/cop7.htm>; Christiaan Vrolijk (2002), *A New Interpretation of Kyoto: The Hague, Bonn and Marrakesh*, RIIA Briefing Paper (London: Royal Institute of International Affairs) forthcoming; Christiaan Vrolijk (2002), 'The Marrakesh Accords: A Brief Point by Point Description and Comments', Annex to Vrolijk (2002), *A New Interpretation of Kyoto*, forthcoming.
22. Emphasis added.
23. <http://www.whitehouse.gov/news/releases/2001/03/20010314.html>.
24. See, for example, Sebastian Oberthür and Hermann E. Ott, with Richard G. Tarasofsky (1999), *The Kyoto Protocol: International Climate Policy for the 21st Century* (Berlin: Springer), 273.
25. 1990: 1355 MtC; 1999: 1520 MtC.
26. UNFCCC, Article 4.2 (a).
27. Measured in local currency units. Source: International Monetary Fund (IMF) (2001), *World Economic Outlook 2001*, Real Gross Domestic Product, local currency (LCU bn), <http://www.imf.org/external/pubs/ft/weo/2001/01/data/index.htm>.
28. MtC = Million ('Mega') tonnes of Carbon. 1 unit C = 3.67 units CO_2. Data Source: Energy Information Administration (EIA), World Carbon Dioxide Emissions from the Consumption and Flaring of Fossil Fuels, 1980–1999, <http://www.eia.doe.gov/emeu/international/environm.html#IntlCarbon>.
29. 1997 $US. Source: Energy Information Administration (EIA) (2001), International Energy Outlook 2001, <http://www.eia.doe.gov/oiaf/ieo/appendixes.html#appen>. Table A3. World Gross Domestic Product (GDP) by Region, Reference Case, 1990–2020 (billion 1997 dollars).
30. See, for example, Chapter 16 in Ulrich Bartsch and Benito Müller (2000), *Fossil Fuels in a Changing Climate: Impacts of the Kyoto Protocol and Developing Country Participation* (Oxford: Oxford University Press).
31. International Monetary Fund (2001), *World Economic Outlook 2001*, Real Gross Domestic Product, Constant Prices (billions of local currency units).
32. International Energy Agency (2000), *World Energy Outlook*.
33. Benito Müller (2000), 'Congressional Climate Change Hearings: Comedy or Tragedy?', <http://www.wolfson. ox.ac.uk/~mueller>.
34. David G. Streets, Kejun Jiang, Xiulian Hu, Jonathan E. Sinton, Xiao-Quan Zhang, Deying Xu, Mark Z. Jacobson, and James E. Hansen (2001), 'Recent Reductions in China's Greenhouse Gas Emissions', *Science*, 294, 1835–7.
35. Michael Grubb, Chris Hope, and Roger Fouquet (2002), 'The Climatic Implications of the Kyoto Protocol: The Contribution of International Spillover', *Climatic Change* (forthcoming).
36. Allocation in proportion to baseline (benchmark) emission figures.
37. Allocation in proportion to baseline (benchmark) population figures.
38. See, for example, Aubrey Meyer (2000), *Contraction & Convergence: The Global Solution to Climate Change* (Dartington: Green Books); or Anil Agarwal and Sunita Narain (2000), 'Addressing the Challenge of Climate Change: Equity, Sustainability and Economic Effectiveness', in Mohan Munasinghe and Rob Swart (eds.), *Climate Change and its Linkage with Development, Equity, and Sustainability* (Geneva: Intergovernmental Panel on Climate Change).

39. Benito Müller (1999), *Justice in Global Warming Negotiations: How to Obtain a Procedurally Fair Compromise* (Oxford: Oxford Institute for Energy Studies).
40. See, for example, Kevin A. Baumert, Ruchi Bhandari, and Nancy Kete (1999), 'What Might a Developing Country Climate Commitment Look Like?', *Climate Notes* (Washington, DC: World Resources Institute).
41. See, for example, William Pizer (1999), 'Choosing Price or Quantity Controls for Greenhouse Gases', *Climate Issues Brief 17* (Washington, DC: Resources for the Future).
42. See, for example, Intergovernmental Panel on Climate Change (IPCC) (2001), [TAR3] *Climate Change 2001: Mitigation* (Cambridge: Cambridge University Press); Munasinghe and Swart (eds.) (2000), *Climate Change and its Linkage with Development, Equity, and Sustainability*; Benito Müller, Axel Michaelowa, and Christiaan Vrolijk (2001), *Rejecting Kyoto: A Study of Proposed Alternatives to the Kyoto Protocol* (London: Climate Strategies), <http://www.climate-strategies.org/rejectingkyoto2.pdf>; Jos Sijm, Jaap Jansen, and Asbjørn Torvanger (2001), 'Differentiation of Mitigation Commitments: The Multi-Sector Convergence Approach', *Climate Policy*, 1, 481–97; Lasse Ringius, Asbjørn Torvanger, and Bjart Holtsmark (1998), 'Can Multi-Criteria Rules Fairly Distribute Climate Burdens? OECD Results from Three Burden Sharing Rules', *Energy Policy*, 26, 777–93; or Cédric Philibert and Jonathan Pershing (2001), 'Considering the Options: Climate Targets for All Countries', *Climate Policy*, 1, 211–27.
43. Thomas C. Schelling (1997), 'The Cost of Combating Global Warming', *Foreign Affairs* (November/ December).
44. Ashok Khosla (2001), 'The Road from Rio to Johannesburg', *Millennium Papers*, 4 (London: UNED Forum).
45. World Conservation Union (IUCN) (2000), 'About IUCN', <http://www.iucn.org/2000/about/content/index.html>.
46. Rosalie Gardiner (2001), 'Earth Summit 2002 Explained', *Earth Summit 2002 Briefing Paper* (London: UNED Forum), 1; <http:// www.earthsummit2002.org/Es2002.PDF>.
47. Jill Matheson and Penny Babb (eds.) (2002), 'National Statistics', *Social Trends*, 32 (London: HM Stationery Office), 183. To be sure, not all of the concerns listed in Table 1 are merely about natural ecosystems, and it would be simplistic to expect them to be, given the complex interactions involved. Nevertheless, the issues listed are overall significantly closer to the ecological paradigm than they are to the natural disaster one.
48. Council of Economic Advisers (2002), *Annual Report* (Washington, DC: US Government Printing Office), 244; <http://w3.access.gpo.gov/eop/index.html>.
49. 'This summary, approved in detail at IPCC Plenary XVIII (Wembley, United Kingdom, 24–29 September 2001), represents the formally agreed statement of the IPCC concerning key findings and uncertainties contained in the Working Group contributions to the Third Assessment Report.' Intergovernmental Panel on Climate Change (IPCC) (2002), [TAR-SRa] *Climate Change 2001: Synthesis Report – Summary for Policy Makers*, <http://www.ipcc.ch/pub/tar/syr/index.htm>.
50. Benito Müller (forthcoming August 2002), *Equity in Climate Change: The Great Divide* (Oxford: Oxford Institute for Energy Studies).
51. Youba Sokona, Adil Najam, and Saleemul Huq (2002), *Climate Change and Sustainable Development: Views from the South* (London: International Institute for Environment and Development), 2.
52. Apart from designating a philosophical and literary movement which originated in northern Italy in the second half of the fourteenth century, the term 'humanism' is used to describe 'any philosophy which recognizes the value or dignity of man'. Paul Edwards (ed.) (1967), *The Encyclopedia of Philosophy*, 4 (London: Collier Macmillan Publishers), 69–70.
53. For example, while both human and ecological impacts are mentioned in the central passages from the Convention mentioned earlier, there seems to be an (unconscious) ranking which puts the latter before the former.
54. Article 4.4, interestingly, is a commitment not on Annex I (large emitters) but on Annex II (affluent) Parties, which arguably means that it is based on the principle of the ability to pay ('solidarity'), thus not dependent on the ability to separate anthropogenic from natural impacts.

Environmental Protection in the South Pacific: The Effectiveness of SPREP and its Conventions

Richard Herr

Introduction

The peoples of the South Pacific region have long been concerned with protecting the varied, fragile, and vulnerable environments that surround their myriad and far-flung islands. Yet the 22 Pacific island countries (PICs) that make up this region are comprised entirely of developing states and territories with all the needs and limitations that third- or fourth-world status implies.[1] Thus a certain tension between environmental protection and sustainable development is both inevitable and pervasive across the South Pacific. This tension began to be felt virtually from the beginning. Independence swept through the region in the 1960s and 1970s, focusing attention on the new microstates' development needs as an immediate priority. Largely as a result of these needs a substantial degree of productive regional co-operation emerged to meet the challenges posed. Indeed, over time the South Pacific region has become replete with international regimes and specialist intergovernmental organizations (IGOs) to assist with meeting its multifaceted developmental needs.[2] Environmental concerns were slower to make their way onto the regional stage. Nevertheless, a regime to address the region's environmental protection needs has been well supported since these were accepted as significant in the mid-1970s. Today, the core of this regime, the South Pacific Regional Environment Programme (SPREP), has become an essential element in the area's system of environmental protection as well as a central actor well able to hold its own in regional affairs.

The contemporary SPREP operates as a regional IGO from its headquarters in Apia, Samoa, with a staff of nearly 70 serving the organization's 26 members. SPREP's mandate spans a wide but not comprehensive range of regional environmental concerns. Its mission is defined as 'to promote co-operation in the South Pacific region and to provide assistance in order to protect and improve its environment and ensure sustainable development for present and future generations.'[3] As such, the organization's ambit of direct operations is narrower than its membership, being confined to the South Pacific region even though it has members from beyond that region. SPREP's current work programme reflects the timing of its entry into the regional system and the evolution of the South Pacific's environmental agenda. The former consideration has been a constraining factor from its beginning, as SPREP has had to find its way within a pre-existing regional system where initially it played only a subordinate role. The latter is influenced not only by internal developments but also by the global state of play, so that world priorities must be included in SPREP planning.

Perhaps significantly, as the first step towards becoming an IGO, SPREP moved to a separate headquarters in 1992, the same year that the United Nations Conference on the Environment and Development met in Rio de Janeiro. Thus, as the global community prepares to meet in Johannesburg in late August 2002 at the World Summit on Sustainable Development (WSSD) to assess its progress over the last decade, the South Pacific will have occasion to reflect on the effectiveness of its own regional regime. An increasingly vital part of the SPREP regime has been its institutionalization over the decade—an influence that is likely to be evident in Johannesburg. SPREP was unable to play a large part in preparing PIC participants in Rio due to its status in the early 1990s, but it is playing a central role in the lead up to 'Rio+10'. The weight the region will carry at the World Summit may depend, in real measure, on how well its own environmental protection regime has performed over these years. The effectiveness of the SPREP within its region, however, hangs on how capably it has carried out its mission within the constraints imposed on it by the nature of the region it serves. This has been a difficult balancing act and one that is still very much in evolution. Yet the past decade of experience and the years before, during its formation, suggest the SPREP regime has substantially advanced the cause of environmental protection in the South Pacific.

The Problem of Regional Environmental Protection in the South Pacific

The challenge of environmental protection in the South Pacific is as varied and complex as the tens of thousands of islands, islets, atolls, motu, reefs, rocks, skerries, and sandbanks that make up the terrestrial portion of this vast

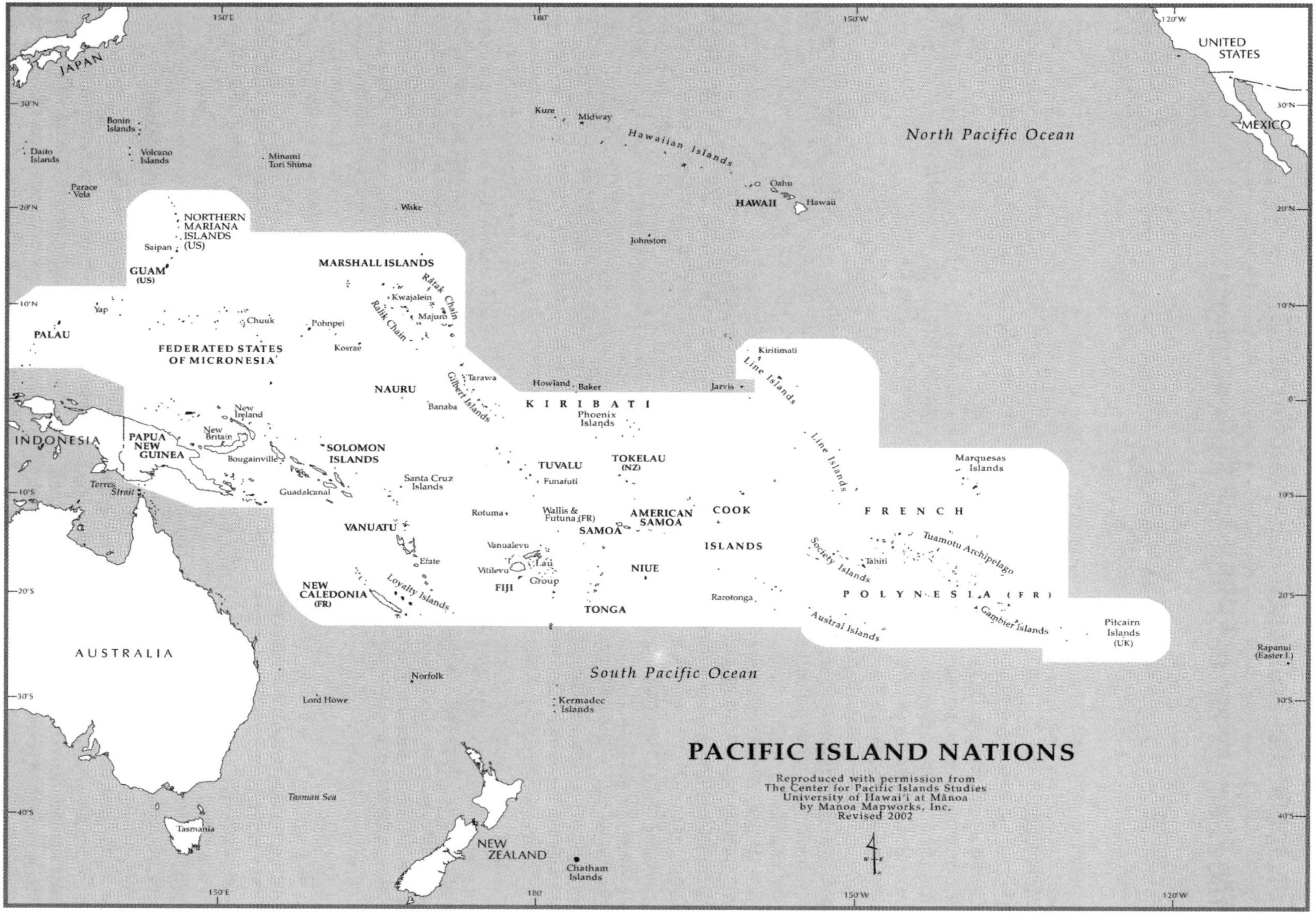
PACIFIC ISLAND NATIONS
Reproduced with permission from
The Center for Pacific Islands Studies
University of Hawai'i at Mānoa
by Manoa Mapworks, Inc,
Revised 2002
North Pacific Ocean
South Pacific Ocean
Tasman Sea
JAPAN
UNITED STATES
MEXICO
INDONESIA
AUSTRALIA
Tasmania
NEW ZEALAND
Chatham Islands
PALAU
GUAM (US)
Saipan
NORTHERN MARIANA ISLANDS (US)
FEDERATED STATES OF MICRONESIA
Yap
Chuuk
Pohnpei
Kosrae
MARSHALL ISLANDS
Kwajalein
Majuro
Ratak Chain
Ralik Chain
NAURU
Banaba
Tarawa
Gilbert Islands
KIRIBATI
Phoenix Islands
Howland
Baker
Jarvis
Kiritimati
Line Islands
PAPUA NEW GUINEA
New Ireland
New Britain
Bougainville
Torres Strait
SOLOMON ISLANDS
Guadalcanal
Santa Cruz Islands
VANUATU
Efate
NEW CALEDONIA (FR)
Loyalty Islands
TUVALU
Funafuti
TOKELAU (NZ)
Rotuma
Wallis & Futuna (FR)
SAMOA
AMERICAN SAMOA
Vanualevu
Vitilevu
Lau Group
FIJI
NIUE
TONGA
COOK ISLANDS
Rarotonga
FRENCH POLYNESIA (FR)
Marquesas Islands
Tuamotu Archipelago
Society Islands
Tahiti
Austral Islands
Gambier Islands
Pitcairn Islands (UK)
Rapanui (Easter I.)
HAWAII
Hawaii
Oahu
Hawaiian Islands
Kure
Midway
Johnston
Wake
Minami Tori Shima
Bonin Islands
Volcano Islands
Daito Islands
Parace Vela
Norfolk
Lord Howe
Kermadec Islands
150°E
180°
150°W
120°W
30°N
20°N
10°N
0°
10°S
20°S
30°S
40°S

region. Its landforms range from Papua New Guinea's 'continental' geography, with ice-capped mountains, through coral atolls, to jack-in-the-box volcanic cinder cones in Tonga that routinely rise and fall below sea level.[4] Its aquatic areas are vast in scope but also diverse. They include the world's deepest ocean trenches and the largest expanses of marine waters enclosed as lagoons. Given the small size of the land masses, rivers and lakes are a rarity in the region outside the larger islands of Melanesia, but then, outside this sub-region, fresh water itself can be a rarity. The human dimension is no less complex. The region's population of nearly six million is divided among 22 island polities, ranging in size from Papua New Guinea (more than 4.5 million) to Pitcairn (fewer than 50).[5] Their political status varies from the nine fully independent states,[6] through five self-governing states in free association with a larger state,[7] to eight territories in a range of dependent relationships.[8] These physical and political factors have ensured that, like other issues in the South Pacific, the task of problem solving offers no economies of scale but rather the reverse— confronting serious and intractable diseconomies of scale.

The severity of the environmental protection problem is dependent, in large part, on the impositions made both on the region's environment and on the resources available to meet these demands. Here the South Pacific is caught in the same bind that besets the developing world elsewhere. Economic development is a high priority across the region. Among the independent Pacific island countries, the per capita domestic product ranges from a low of AUD$756 for Kiribati to a high of AUD$3118 for Fiji.[9] Thus the development pressure on the environment is immense both at sea and ashore. To name but a few of the locally generated environmental problems facing the region: beaches are mined for concrete sand; forests are felled for timber and firewood; vital water lens are polluted or compromised by over-use or sea-water intrusion; microhabitats are destroyed by population pressures; lagoons and reefs are degraded by improper waste disposal; and fishery resources are stretched beyond breaking point by a swelling population. These problems would be bad enough, but the South Pacific's environment is also a victim of significant problems sourced from outside the region.

Undoubtedly the gravest 'imported' problem is sea-level rise due to global warming. The region has contributed very little to the greenhouse gases causing the problem, but its consequences could be catastrophic for the South Pacific. With the exception of the inhabitants of the Melanesian islands, the region's people are all coastal dwellers. They are obliged to be. There is no hinterland in Polynesia or Micronesia. Indeed, the vast majority of the islands in these two ethno-geographic areas are low-lying atolls with only a few metres' clearance above sea level. Any sea-level rise will have profound effects for the entire region, but for the atoll states, such as Kiribati and Tuvalu, even a modest rise could be a nation-ending event. The likelihood of such consequences has been closely monitored in the region since the mid-1980s. SPREP researchers have recently challenged the predictions of the Intergovernmental Panel on Climate Change with their findings of sea-level rise more than ten times that expected. Rises of up to 25 cm per year may be in train.[10] Although they are disputed by other data, were these extremes to be realized over a single generation, the most vulnerable PICs would become non-viable for human habitation if not disappear altogether.

As disastrous as global warming may prove to be, it is not the only 'foreign' environmental misery confronting the region. The South Pacific's remoteness, relatively small populations, and, until recently, dependent status made it a desirable nuclear-testing ground. France ended its testing programme as late as 1996. The region has inherited the toxic legacy of these activities. Moreover, the vast and deep expanses of the Pacific Ocean appealed to the nuclear powers as a tempting and accessible dumping ground for their home-grown wastes. And what was possible for nuclear wastes might be practical for other toxic wastes, especially in the high-seas areas beyond national jurisdictions. From the 1970s, extensive but under-exploited stocks of tuna attracted distant-water fishing nations to the region and so gave rise to another externally imposed environmental protection problem. Small but valuable stands of tropical hardwoods in Melanesia similarly drew extra-regional interests into the South Pacific in the 1980s and 1990s, with environmentally damaging consequences.

Whether local in origin or externally generated, all of these concerns have fallen largely on policy makers from a small number of developing microstates with limited capacity to meet the burgeoning challenges confronting their countries. In a very real sense, the problem of environmental protection in the South Pacific was not so much that it was a necessary and increasingly salient issue for the PIC policy makers. Rather, it was how any solution could be afforded within the constraints facing these developing polities. Providentially, as the awareness of the extent of the environmental problems facing the newly independent states has grown, so too has the international support system for addressing such issues multilaterally within the region. This is not to suggest the two have been evenly matched. It would be impossible to manage all the diverse types of environmental problems in the Pacific islands collectively even if the political will existed to pursue this course of action. Nevertheless, a regional response to some of the environmental protection issues has added real capacity to the over-extended PICs.

The Origins of the South Pacific's Environmental Protection Regime

SPREP was the first line of the international response to the issue of protecting the South Pacific environment. However, it has developed, evolved, and reacted to the changing international conditions. It is helpful, therefore, to put the objectives and scope of SPREP into some historical context in order to assess how well it is addressing the environmental problems of the South Pacific. SPREP itself traces its origins back to a regional symposium in 1969 that recommended the appointment of an ecological adviser to the South Pacific Commission (SPC), which at the time was the only IGO in the region.[11] In a more formal sense, however, the creation in the mid-1970s of the United Nations Environment Programme (UNEP) and its Regional Seas project gave a focus to a broader regional environmental protection programme. In 1976 a Convention on Conservation of Nature in the South Pacific (the Apia Convention) committed a limited number of SPC members to wildlife and habitat protection in the South Pacific.[12] When a more substantive developmental commitment was wanted, however, institutional demarcation reared its head. The rivalry that characterized relations between the SPC and the politically active South Pacific Forum[13] ensured that the idea could not be captured wholly by either body. Instead, what came to be called the South Pacific Regional Environment Programme proceeded as a shared activity from its establishment in 1980. It was lodged in Noumea with the SPC, which also provided secretariat services, while the forum's economic arm, the South Pacific Bureau for Economic Co-operation (SPEC) provided the chair for the annual co-ordinating meeting of the four agencies involved in the programme––the SPC, SPEC, and two United Nations agencies. From 1982, when its first Action Plan for Managing the Natural Resources of the South Pacific Region was drafted, SPREP enjoyed increased autonomy within the SPC framework.[14] This Action Plan, which has been revised four times in the years since, has provided the basic direction for SPREP and its work programme.

Increasing enthusiasm for the potential of a regional approach to environmental protection led in 1986 to the drafting of the Convention for the Protection of the Natural Resources and Environment of the South Pacific Region (the SPREP Convention).[15] The Convention was intended to commit its parties to protecting the natural land and marine resources of the South Pacific, particularly through its protocols on waste dumping and pollution emergencies. Again, the effect of formulating an instrument for co-operation tended to stimulate a desire for greater institutional autonomy. The Convention did not, however, create SPREP as an IGO. This did not occur until the early 1990s. The programme's supporters were especially active among the members of the South Pacific Forum (now the Pacific Islands Forum) because the political aspects of environmental protection were becoming increasingly significant globally. They wished to participate in these debates with the assistance of SPREP as well as to get out from under the SPC charter's ban on political activities.[16] By 1990, this sentiment was sufficiently solidified to lead this group within SPREP to seek full legal autonomy. A ministerial-level meeting of SPREP participants in 1991 formally proposed IGO status for SPREP and accepted Samoa's offer to host the headquarters. While the programme moved to Apia in 1992, the Agreement Establishing the South Pacific Regional Environment Programme (the Agreement Establishing SPREP) was not opened for signature until the following year.[17] It entered into force on 31 August 1995, when Niue became the tenth country to ratify the agreement. Its origins in the SPC continued to be a significant influence on the new IGO, however. SPREP's membership remained nearly identical to that of the SPC rather than mirroring the politically more restrictive membership of the South Pacific Forum.[18]

The breadth of membership has been a mixed blessing for SPREP. It has allowed retention of the geographic comprehensiveness of the SPC but at the cost of some of the political authority of the forum. Also, at times SPREP is compelled by its funding arrangements to distinguish between those activities open to all its PIC members and those available only to the forum's PIC members, as some donors exclude dependencies from using their assistance. The balance between cost and benefit in SPREP's compromise over its membership might be debated, but it does seem to have worked surprisingly well in practice. Even those PICs lacking the international legal personality to sign the SPREP agreement have been able to become members in their own right and participate generally in the organization's activities. However, at times SPREP is unable to transcend an advisory role to act on behalf of its membership. It is scarcely as politically constrained as is the SPC, but the political diversity of its membership imposes practical limitations on how far it can go with an issue and how fully it can count on the support of its members. Nevertheless, SPREP has become a robust and active agency for environmental protection well supported by its members. The extent of this support may be seen both in SPREP's growth as an institution and in its expanding work programme.

SPREP's first annual report records a staff of 53 and a global budget of $US7,327,289, but with only $US563,245 (8 per cent) coming from members for what were described as 'primary functions'.[19] Its last published report gives figures of 71 staff and $US7,768,633, with core funding from members largely unchanged.[20] While the growth may appear modest, the absolute sums raised are substantial in their own right and provide a significant base for the South Pacific's co-operation in environmental protection. Secondly, it is noteworthy that these come largely from outside the region from sources that would not be able to contribute to a regional environmental programme without a vehicle such as SPREP.[21] It should be recalled that, whatever growth has occurred, it has taken place in an era of general contraction of support for the regional IGOs.[22] In addition, this growth included a substantial commitment in the form of a new headquarters opened in 2000 just outside Apia, near the former home of Robert Louis Stevenson at Vailima. The work programme of SPREP has grown over the past six years as well. AusAID, the Australian aid agency, reviewed SPREP in 2000 and found that the organization had provided annually between 120 and 150 acts of assistance or projects to its PIC members in recent years.[23] These activities ranged over five major programme areas under the 1997–2000 Action Plan:

1. biodiversity and natural resource conservation;
2. climate change and integrated coastal management;
3. waste management, pollution prevention, and emergencies;
4. environmental management, planning, and institutional strengthening; and
5. environmental education, information, and training.[24]

Projects under each of these areas were divided between 'international/regional activities' and 'in-country activities', with SPREP taking the lead in the former. 'In-country activities' have tended to be in the form of assistance to individual members in meeting their identified environmental needs.

This thematic approach has been maintained in the 2001–2004 Action Plan, which has regrouped the 1997–2000 Action Plan programme areas under four headings or 'key result areas':

1. nature conservation;
2. pollution prevention;
3. climate change and variability; and
4. economic development.[25]

The first three of these areas continued many of the programmes and projects of the earlier Action Plan, but the fourth—economic development—has made a bold play for a role long dominated by other regional agencies. 'Nature conservation' as a rubric covers such activities as the conservation area approach to promoting biodiversity; extended training in ecosystems management; and the promotion of public awareness of biosafety. Although 'pollution prevention' has displayed many elements of continuity from the earlier plan, it seeks to develop new projects in the areas of hazardous-waste pollution control; marine pollution; and waste minimization. The area of 'climate change' clearly addresses the Pacific islands' long-standing anxieties with regard to sea-level rise. However, the projects listed under this heading demonstrate the constraints on the PICs in responding constructively. Projects here focus on promoting understanding the issue and enhancing the regional monitoring capacity as well as offering policy advice on responding to the issue.

It would be unfair to suggest that the area of 'economic development' has been added specifically to claim priority within the Pacific islands for SPREP at Johannesburg on sustainable development. Nevertheless, it has reinforced the role SPREP will play at the WSSD. The projects that SPREP will pursue in this issue area do not seek to challenge the development activities of other regional agencies so as to claim a leading role in interpreting and advising on the economic consequences of environmental protection. This applies particularly to projects aimed at improving the linkages between national planning and environmental strategies; assessing the environmental impact of tourism; and considering aspects of urbanization. Just how well SPREP will manage this entrepreneurial role within the regional system will depend on how aggressively it is pursued and how the other agencies react to this 'economic' elaboration of the SPREP mandate over the next few years.

The International Response to the Region's Environmental Protection Needs

The process of institutionalizing SPREP as a regional IGO contributed both to the form and to the content of the current environmental protection regime in the South Pacific. And these origins demonstrated most powerfully the international dimension to environmental protection in the region. International co-operation necessarily stands at the centre of the SPREP regime, but it appears in many guises. Naturally, the routine operation of SPREP's governance mechanisms (annual officials' meetings, regular workshops, occasional ministerial meetings, and four-yearly regional conservation conferences) serves as a key mechanism in promoting international co-operation. Its annual officials' meeting brings together 26 countries to consider the region's environmental protection needs and to devise programmes and projects to address those needs. Its institutionality brings together resources from members and donors to pay for these activities. SPREP's work programme and the opportunity to use its organizational strengths to advance the environmental objectives of other nations and agencies in the South Pacific has added substantially to its international impact. Indeed, as noted above in the discussion of the sources of the SPREP budget, one of the more significant contributions that SPREP makes to environmental protection in the South Pacific is that its existence makes available an institutional vehicle for raising and distributing large amounts of extra-regional aid for use in the region.

The development of an institutional platform greatly assisted the quality of international co-operation, but it was not the sum of international co-operation in support of an environmental protection regime in the South Pacific during the 1980s and 1990s. The very process of giving SPREP legal corporeality proved to be a significant factor in its own right. Some of the more important international conventions promoting environmental protection in the South Pacific were drafted through, or associated with, SPREP before it became an IGO. The more important developments within the SPREP process included conventions to bind members of the regime to new areas of co-operation or to prevent extra-regional activity from threatening regional environmental values. The first of these was the 1986 Convention for the Protection of the Natural Resources and Environment of the South Pacific Region (SPREP Convention).[26] This Convention added in the same year a specific Protocol for the Prevention of Pollution of the South Pacific Region by Dumping.[27] Even the treaty that established SPREP as an autonomous IGO did more than address the needs of institutionality. Its ambit of operations set out specific obligations for promoting environmental protection that went well beyond the 1986 SPREP Convention and entrenched fundamental elements of its Action Plans, such as monitoring the environment, promoting public awareness, and transferring knowledge through training.

As important as the SPREP-related treaties are, parallel actions outside the regime itself have added real value to environmental protection in the South Pacific. The most symbolically important of these was the South Pacific Nuclear Free Zone Treaty (SPNFZ), given the impact that nuclear testing has had on the course of regionalism in the South Pacific.[28] This 1985 treaty was negotiated under the auspices of the South Pacific Forum, and it is unlikely, even had it enjoyed institutional autonomy at the time, that SPREP could have been the lead agency for it. French and American membership in SPREP would have proved an impossible obstacle. This capacity by the region to pursue its environmental objectives through various channels has proved a benefit rather than a sign of weakness in the SPREP regime itself. Indeed, the forum has proved especially productive in politically contentious areas. The Convention to Ban the Importation into Forum Island Countries of Hazardous and Radioactive Wastes and to Control the Transboundary Movement and Management of Hazardous Wastes within the South Pacific Region (the Waigani Convention) is just such a measure. SPREP may not have been able to provide leadership for this treaty but the forum could.[29] This agreement, which adds a regional dimension to the 1989 Basel Convention, helps to reinforce the pollution-control measures introduced through the 1986 SPREP Convention and its subsequent protocol on ocean dumping. SPREP was nominated to provide secretariat services for the Waigani Convention, however. The central position that SPREP has come to occupy within the region in assisting its members with major multilateral environmental treaties has not come without a price. According to an Australian aid agency review, SPREP may be neglecting the Apia and SPREP conventions—its basic charter obligations—while promoting the aims of other treaties.[30]

While SPREP has inherited a great deal from its origins within the SPC and historical ties to the South Pacific Forum, the broader regime has enjoyed support from other regional organizations in the South Pacific. The most celebrated of these legal instruments is the 1989 Convention for the Prohibition of Fishing with Long Driftnets in the South Pacific (the Wellington Driftnet Convention).[31] This environmental measure to curtail both wasteful fishing and destructive by-catch methods was sponsored by the Forum Fisheries Agency (FFA). While it did not directly involve SPREP, the Wellington Driftnet Convention was influenced by data on fishing collected and maintained by the SPC, which then housed SPREP, and where interaction among programmes was common. SPREP's marine living resources interests continue to keep it involved with the SPC and the FFA—a relationship that has been cemented through a recent Global Environment Facility (GEF) project. The Strategic Action Programme for International Waters of the Pacific Small Island Developing States is an ambitious five-year project to assist participating countries in developing management and conservation arrangements for their oceanic fisheries resources. An integrated coastal watershed component of this activity will focus, *inter alia*, on freshwater supplies, marine protected areas, and sustainable coastal fisheries. Climate change research similarly has developed closer relations with another regional agency—the South Pacific Applied Geoscience Commission (SOPAC).

National Implementation

There are several important aspects to the influence of the SPREP regime on the national implementation of environmental protection. First and perhaps foremost has been the consciousness-raising role the regime has played across the region. When the SPREP regime began in the mid-1970s, very few Pacific island countries had governmental divisions or departments dealing with the environment, while today virtually all do.[32] Secondly, the regime has played a capacity augmentation role for individual PIC members by offering outside assistance in cases where these small island states would be unable to address matters solely from their own resources. Generally this tends to be viewed from the perspective of aid or expertise, but the value of information sharing about broader issues and diplomatic support to enable national positions in international fora should not be underestimated. Many of SPREP's PIC members could not meet the demands made of them by the international community or be able to participate in relevant international conventions if their national efforts were not augmented by SPREP resources. Thirdly, through the agency of the SPREP organization, direct aid transfers and programmes are offered to assist members to meet their own internal national environmental objectives.

From early in the 1990s, SPREP has assisted its Pacific islands membership with the development of National Environment Management Strategies (NEMS). These assessments of national environmental protection needs have served subsequently as benchmarks for progress not only by SPREP's developing members but also for SPREP itself.[33] Because the NEMS were located very firmly in the development role of SPREP, it is scarcely surprising that nearly half (49 per cent) of the NEMS priorities revolved around meeting the constraints on underdeveloped countries facing environmental challenges. The needs identified in the NEMS focused on capacity building, training assistance, institutional strengthening, and the like.[34] Indeed, the AusAID review of SPREP found that about 86 per cent of one set of NEMS proposals were for 'preparatory and supportive activities rather than for actual implementation of resource management action'.[35] While this review was relatively accepting of SPREP's efforts to meet the needs recorded in the NEMS, it expressed concern at the failure of member PICs to follow up on their obligations and to allocate resources for national implementation.[36] The report does not specify the grounds for this finding, although SPREP's director, Tamari'i Tutangata, indicated recently that SPREP's PIC members were unable to implement fully its programmes due to 'funding and equipment problems'.[37] However much such an explanation might be expected in a developing nations context, if valid, it does suggest a continuing imbalance between SPREP's programme goals and its members' capacity.

Just how highly national implementation should be ranked in evaluating SPREP may be a moot point. As noted above, SPREP's mandate is defined in terms of promoting co-operation in the South Pacific region and providing assistance to the region's developing members to achieve its environmental goals. Clearly its primary role is to assist its members to co-operate in meeting their international objectives and to aid them in protecting their national environmental assets. It is not a prescriptive regime that seeks national compliance with independently established regime standards. Thus SPREP has not been heavily or directly engaged with the irresponsible logging practices in Melanesia or with land-sourced marine pollution from mining. Both of these might be addressed under conventions that fall within the broader SPREP regime, but the remedies have generally been left to bilateral mechanisms or more political avenues within the regional system. The SPREP contribution to national implementation of environmental protection in the South Pacific has tended to be limited to capacity building, consciousness raising, and technical aid transfers.

Impact of the SPREP Regime

There can be little doubt that the SPREP regime has had a significant and positive impact on the problem of environmental protection in the South Pacific. This may be seen in the two levels at which the regime operates. Internationally, SPREP is both a product of international co-operation and a vehicle for promoting multilateral co-operation. The access that its PIC members have had to international environmental issues is striking, as is their capacity to articulate a common regional perspective on important international issues. SPREP has also had a profound effect at the domestic level, particularly through aid transfers and capacity building. A substantial factor in the regime's impact is the organization at the heart of the regime. Without SPREP, it is doubtful that so many small and impoverished countries could have acted in concert across so many issues or have achieved such an international impact. This impression of success is not just one from the perspective of the PICs.

According to the AusAID review, SPREP has been an effective organization, albeit not without some difficulties. It raised nearly $US30 million in the five years from 1995 to 2000 for environmental projects, represented the region and its PIC members well in international environmental fora, and amassed a substantial database on the region's environment.[38] However, an assessment of a sample of 16 SPREP projects led the review team to conclude that, although its projects were reasonably effective, more could be done to improve their long-term impact. It found that too many projects were 'good' or 'best practice' in reaching their planned outcomes but were less successful in contributing to SPREP's longer-range goals. The review noted that the funding structure of the organization placed too much emphasis on individual projects rather than on pursuing an integrated programme of activities. This appeared an inevitable consequence not just because the aid execution aspect of SPREP's work programme tends to compel a project orientation, but also as a practical effect of accountability in meeting the requirements of individual project donors.

The major elements of the international impact of SPREP as an effective regional agent for environmental protection have been canvassed above. However, there can be little better illustration of the growing value of this impact than in the role that SPREP has played in preparing the region and its members for the Johannesburg World Summit. SPREP's secretariat has co-chaired the regional working group established within the South Pacific's inter-agency co-ordination mechanism—the Council of Regional Organizations in the Pacific (CROP). SPREP researchers and officials have contributed both to the process of regional consultation and to major elements of the regional submission, including participation in the Asia-Pacific preparatory meeting (November 2001) and the Small Island Developing States preparatory meeting (January 2002). There has been a profound change from the situation that existed before the 1992 Earth Summit.

Barriers to Progress

Several outstanding issues suggest that, as successful as the SPREP regime has been over the past decade, there are legitimate grounds for some doubt about the future. The potential impediments range from the scale of the challenges facing the region, through the difficulties of holding its diverse membership together, to the organizational issues confronting SPREP. Naturally, there is a mismatch between the PICs and planetary problems such as global warming, but this asymmetry exists virtually across the board for all issues, especially for the 20 SPREP members smaller than Fiji. As noted above, despite the importance of the South Pacific Forum members in securing the autonomy of SPREP, the organization's formal membership is larger and more politically diverse. As the demands of effective environmental protection escalate, the difficulties in maintaining consensus also increase. Not surprisingly, this obstacle looms largest where the greatest national interests are involved. The most public of these areas of internal conflict is Australia's position on the Kyoto Protocol. Climate change is simply too serious a threat for the low-lying islands at risk to take lightly.[39] While this dispute does not undermine the other work of SPREP, it does demonstrate the constraints imposed on the organization with the diversity of membership it maintains.

Over the past decade, the SPREP regime has come to revolve more tightly around its organizational core, and thus SPREP's institutional health must figure very prominently in any speculation about its future. The critical issue for SPREP as an IGO is the evolving international system. It is significant that, when SPREP was moved from its ambiguous programme status under the SPC, its name was not changed. This was a deliberate ploy by supporters of the change in the organization's status. The timing of the change in status was somewhat unfortunate as SPREP was established as an IGO amid the collapse of the Cold War. Although there were already straws in the wind indicating that post-Cold War support for regional organizations in the South Pacific was declining,[40] members of the South Pacific Forum, especially New Zealand, wanted to give SPREP's activities a higher level of institutional support than appeared to be available through the SPC. Hence they resolved to secure an autonomous existence for SPREP. The forum members, nevertheless, were aware that highlighting the IGO status of SPREP would attract questions about the additional cost-sharing burden that its institutionalization would require. These issues had to be addressed to complete the process, but, by dealing with them after the decision was made to establish SPREP as an autonomous body, the first decision to pursue autonomy was less fraught. An important legacy of this process was an uncertain subscription formula for members that treats the annual assessments as 'voluntary'.

The difficulty of this historical baggage for SPREP as it faces the challenges of the twenty-first century arises from the impact of diminishing institutional support from external donors in the region. The PIC members of SPREP have only limited capacity to pay for the costs of the operation of the organization. Indeed, donors pay for at least 90 per cent of SPREP's activities. Moreover, the four non-PIC members pay the bulk of the remaining 10 per cent that comes from members and that goes to paying for the organization's core costs.[41] This makes for a number of institutional difficulties that loom large on the horizon. The members' contributions have not increased, thus widening the gap between the organization's administrative budget and its donor-funded activities budget. Perhaps the most serious consequence of this is the greater leverage given to donors over the work programme of SPREP. Certainly it has contributed significantly to the problem of integrating its projects and activities more cogently into a disciplined regional programme. It also raises issues of 'ownership' of these activities and imposes more burdens on SPREP's governance processes. These organizational challenges are intractable, but they must be managed if the regime is to become more robust and effective. Perhaps the most encouraging sign for the future is the evidence that the problems are being recognized and addressed. And, in contrast with other areas of regionalism in the South Pacific, SPREP's experience does show real signs of coping with these difficulties in large measure because it has earned the strong support of its members. If the SPREP regime is to remain vital in the twenty-first century, such support will need to increase commensurate with the diversifying environmental challenges.

Notes and References

The author gratefully acknowledges the comments of Robert Hall, Richard Kenchington, Eve Richards, and Olav Schram Stokke on an earlier draft of this paper.

1. The South Pacific region stretches from Palau to Pitcairn and from the Northern Marianas to New Caledonia.
2. For an overview of the region's system of IGOs, see Richard A. Herr (1998), 'Restructuring Foreign and Defence Policy: the Pacific Islands', in Anthony McGrew and Christopher Brook (eds.), *Asia-Pacific in the New World Order* (London: Routledge/ Open University).
3. Found at website, <http://www.sprep.org.ws/>.
4. For a general treatment of this diversity, see Christopher S. Lobban and Maria Schefter (1997), *Tropical Pacific Island Environments* (Mangilao: University of Guam Press).
5. Secretariat of the the Pacific Community (2000), *Pocket Statistical Summary 2000* (Noumea: Pacific Community).
6. Fiji, Kiribati, Nauru, Papua New Guinea, Samoa, Solomon Islands, Tonga, Tuvalu, and Vanuatu.
7. Cook Islands, Federated States of Micronesia, Marshall Islands, Niue, and Palau.
8. American Samoa, French Polynesia, New Caledonia, Northern Marianas, Pitcairn, Tokelau, and Wallis and Futuna.
9. Secretariat of the Pacific Community (2000), *Pocket Statistical Summary 2000*. Nauru's figures are not available, but this once wealthy microstate is in the throes of a serious economic readjustment in the wake of the depletion of its phosphate.
10. Anon. (1999), 'Smaller all the Time', *Environment*, 41: 10, 9.
11. SPREP (South Pacific Regional Environment Programme) (1995/6), *Annual Report*, Apia, 9. The SPC still uses this acronym but was renamed in 1998 as the Pacific Community.
12. *Australian Treaty Series* (1990), no. 41.
13. The South Pacific Forum has a political mandate and is comprised of the 14 independent and self-governing PICs plus Australia and New Zealand.
14. SPREP (1995/6), *Annual Report*, Apia, 9.
15. *Australian Treaty Series* (1990), no. 31.
16. The South Pacific Forum owed its creation in large part to this limitation. Being forced to keep its activities 'non-political', the PIC members of the SPC had been unable to use this arena to attack French nuclear testing in the region. In 1971, the independent and self-governing countries invited Australia and New Zealand to join them in a new arrangement that would have political competency—a heads-of-government meeting called the South Pacific Forum.
17. *Australian Treaty Series* (1995), no. 24.
18. It includes all the 22 PICs that are members of the SPC as well as four of the five 'metropolitan' states of the SPC—Australia, France, New Zealand, and the United States. Only one SPC member—the United Kingdom—has remained outside SPREP.
19. SPREP (1995/6), *Annual Report*, 35–6 and 40.
20. SPREP (2000), *Annual Report*, i. It should be noted that membership subscriptions have not increased in the years since 1995 and that these fees are 'non-compulsory' (personal communication).
21. The largest share of SPREP's work programme is paid for from 'extra-budgetary' funds (funding that is not derived from members' assessed subscriptions). While the percentage varies from year to year, SPREP *Annual Reports* suggest that the four non-PIC members—Australia, France, New Zealand, and the USA—contribute only about 40 per cent of these extra-budgetary funds. Thus other sources, such as various UN agencies and non-member countries, contribute the majority of the funding for SPREP activities.
22. 'Regional Programmes in Danger' (1998), *Pacific Islands Monthly* (December), 28.
23. AusAID (2000), *SPREP 2000: Review of the South Pacific Regional Environment Programme – Summary Report*, 12.
24. SPREP (1997), *Action Plan for Managing the Environment of the South Pacific Region: 1997–2000*, Apia.
25. SPREP (2000), *Action Plan for Managing the Environment of the Pacific Islands Region: 2001–2004*, Apia.
26. *Australian Treaty Series* (1990), no. 31. This treaty is also sometimes known as the Noumea Convention, perhaps to help distinguish it better from the SPREP Agreement that established SPREP as an IGO.
27. Australia Department of Foreign Affairs and Trade (1986), *Select Documents on International Affairs*, no. 34: 6, 176.
28. *Australian Treaty Series* (1986), no. 32.
29. This convention is not yet in force, but its details are available through the Australian Treaties Library website, <http://www.austlii.edu.au/au/other/dfat/>.
30. AusAID (2000), *SPREP 2000: Review of the South Pacific Regional Environment Programme – Summary Report*, 5.
31. *Australian Treaty Series* (1992), no. 30.
32. SPREP (2000), *Annual Report*, Apia, ii.
33. AusAID (2000), *SPREP 2000: Review of the South Pacific Regional Environment Programme – Summary Report*, 4.
34. Ibid.
35. Ibid.
36. Ibid.
37. Tamari'i Tutangata (2002), 'SPREP's Year Ahead', *Pacific Islands Monthly* (February), 48.
38. Ibid., 11–12.
39. Jemima Garrett (1998), 'Climate Debacle', *Pacific Islands Monthly* (January), 55.
40. 'Fisheries Aid: Patterns and Sources' (1990), in Richard A. Herr (ed.), *The Forum Fisheries Agency* (Suva: University of the South Pacific), 188.
41. SPREP (1995/6), *Annual Report*, Apia, 4.

The Protocol on Environmental Protection to the Antarctic Treaty: A Ten-Year Review

Davor Vidas

Introduction

Ten years have passed since the Protocol on Environmental Protection to the Antarctic Treaty (Protocol) was adopted.[1] What impact has the Protocol made since then? Has it proved a successful response to the problems for which it was negotiated? Has it been fully implemented? Such questions suggest the need to review and assess the Protocol's performance over the past decade.[2]

Although the Protocol is now legally in force, a review of it solely as an environmental law treaty would enable only a partial assessment of its impact over the past ten years. In the brief review that follows, the Protocol will be looked upon from several angles. As an international environmental law instrument, the Protocol was adopted to supplement the Antarctic Treaty and to minimize the environmental impact of human activities in the Antarctic. From a political perspective, however, its negotiation and adoption aimed primarily to solve a major crisis which enveloped the Antarctic Treaty system (ATS) at the end of 1980s.

The Protocol and Crisis Solving: A Political Perspective

The specific situation of the Antarctic in international affairs provides the context for any international instrument adopted as a component of the ATS, the main elements of which are rooted in an unresolved issue over sovereignty. In the first half of the twentieth century, seven states—Argentina, Australia, Chile, France, New Zealand, Norway, and the United Kingdom—put forward territorial claims to parts of the Antarctic. None of these claims has ever received general recognition. In 1959, all the seven claimant countries and the other five original signatories to the Antarctic Treaty (Belgium, Japan, South Africa, the Soviet Union, and the United States) agreed to put aside their competing positions on territorial claims in the Treaty area and achieved an 'agreement to disagree' on the sovereignty issue (Article IV), for the sake of establishing a unique form of international governance for the Antarctic.[3] This has developed into the 'Antarctic Treaty System', a regional network of international instruments and decision-making structures for Antarctic affairs.[4] The essential requirement in the development of the ATS was to build it through various co-operatively agreed ways in order not to prejudice the position of any country claiming sovereignty in the Antarctic or that of countries not recognizing the claims.[5] The annual Antarctic Treaty Consultative Meeting (ATCM) is the main policy-making body that regulates the entire spectrum of human activities in the Antarctic. The Antarctic Treaty Consultative Parties have decision-making capacity in this forum, the main mode of operation being the adoption of decisions by *consensus*.

In this manner, while the 1959 Antarctic Treaty did not contain any elaborated provisions concerning environmental protection,[6] the Consultative Parties have developed a long-standing record of issue-specific approaches to this question. These were introduced to the ATS first through a large number of recommendations adopted at the Consultative Meetings and later through international conventions.[7] The negotiation of the Convention on the Regulation of Antarctic Mineral Resource Activities (CRAMRA)[8] between 1982 and 1988 was a continuation of issue-specific and preventive approaches to Antarctic environmental protection.

Concurrently, several types of 'external pressure' were being exerted on the ATS. As of 1983, a debate on the 'Question of Antarctica' was initiated by several developing countries in the UN General Assembly. The ATS was criticized as an exclusive club of wealthy states that were negotiating matters with global implications among themselves—the Antarctic minerals issue being the prime example. Soon afterwards, various environmental NGOs picked up the critique of the ATS from the perspective of demanding higher environmental consciousness in decisions regarding Antarctic affairs. These demands concurred at a later stage with those of the domestic public in several Consultative Parties.

In June 1988 the Consultative Parties adopted CRAMRA, and the Convention was opened for signature in November of the same year. Shortly afterwards the

'CRAMRA crisis' shook the ATS: in the spring of 1989 Australia and France announced that they would not sign CRAMRA, and thereafter New Zealand, which had already signed the Convention, declined to ratify it. It thus became clear that CRAMRA had no prospects of entering into force.[9] Instead of proceeding with the signing or ratification of CRAMRA, several countries proposed the negotiation of a new instrument that would ban mineral-related activity and introduce a comprehensive environmental protection system in the Antarctic. Following a decision of the fifteenth ATCM, held in Paris in autumn 1989,[10] a Special Consultative Meeting was convened in 1990 to negotiate a new environmental protection instrument. The negotiations were conducted expeditiously, and in less than a year a new legal instrument—the Protocol on Environmental Protection to the Antarctic Treaty—was adopted.

The Consultative Parties' new start after the abandonment of CRAMRA in 1989 can *not* be attributed to CRAMRA's containing insufficient environmental safeguards. These were in fact very stringent.[11] The 'fault' of CRAMRA may rather have been the failure of the Parties to give it proper marketing as an environmental protection instrument, which should have begun already with the choice of title given to that convention. It was a complex combination of economic and political factors that led the Consultative Parties to abandon CRAMRA. Aside from the awareness that, for the foreseeable future, any mineral activities in the Antarctic would lack commercial significance, the major factors included the following: (1) fears that CRAMRA would disturb the sensitive balance on sovereignty positions in the Antarctic; (2) the political-ideological critique of the ATS from a group of developing countries in the UN General Assembly; (3) pressures from environmental NGOs; and (4) domestic policy considerations which related to some of the above factors.

Although the Consultative Parties may have appeared to be urgently negotiating and adopting the Protocol in their zeal to prevent and respond to threats to the Antarctic environment, they were primarily reacting to two sets of acute *political* problems. The first was the challenge to the Consultative Parties' legitimacy of governing the Antarctic from actors external to the ATS. The second and equally important problem was the struggle to maintain internal cohesion and balance within the ATS, especially with regard to the sovereignty issue. Although in themselves not always directly or exclusively related to environmental protection, these incentives were substantial and prompted the Parties to agree expeditiously on issues relating to human activities and environmental protection in the Antarctic.

Article 7 of the Protocol was crucial in this respect. This Article states unambiguously that 'any activity relating to mineral resources, other than scientific research, shall be prohibited'. This single provision is basically a response to the many criticisms voiced against CRAMRA. Firstly, the Article rendered the sovereignty issue redundant, insofar as a 'delimitation' in relation to mineral rights was no longer required. Secondly, it neutralized the criticism from a group of developing countries, which, since 1989, had been demanding in the UN General Assembly that a ban on mineral activities be introduced in the Antarctic. Thirdly, the provision allowed the Consultative Parties to present themselves as environmentally highly conscious, more so in the Antarctic than anywhere else on the globe. The provision thereby satisfied many of the demands for which environmental NGOs had campaigned. This latter point was instrumental for several of the Consultative Parties in dealing with domestic policy concerns.

In adopting the Protocol, the Consultative Parties endorsed a legally binding instrument, but the incentives for doing this so quickly were inspired primarily by political rather than environmental protection reasons. The Environmental Protocol was, in a political sense, effective immediately upon adoption, and as such it has continued to be a success. For instance, after consensus resolution was adopted at the 1994 General Assembly session that expressly acknowledged the merits of the ATS in the governance of Antarctic affairs,[12] this acknowledgement was reiterated and strengthened by the UN General Assembly resolutions on the 'Question of Antarctica' adopted at the 1996 and 1999 Assembly sessions.[13] The 'Question of Antarctica', once a serious challenge to the legitimacy of the ATS, now remains a triennial formality that repetitively confirms the merits of the ATS.

It is here that the lasting impact of the Protocol is apparent. Indeed, as explained above, the Protocol has in many ways been greatly instrumental in strengthening international co-operation within the ATS as well as in changing the broader international community's perception about the ATS. However, with the Protocol in force and the changed political context relating to Antarctic affairs, the impending challenge remains the implementation of the Protocol as an *environmental* protection treaty.

In the remainder of this article the Protocol will be briefly reviewed first from a legal perspective, then from an environmental management perspective, and finally from the perspective that there persists an unfinished agenda for the Protocol. It is not the purpose of this article to enter into any extensive analysis or description of the provisions of the Protocol; these are available elsewhere.[14] What will be provided here is a concise review of the basic proclaimed objective of the Protocol—'the comprehensive protection of the Antarctic environment and dependent and associated ecosystems'[15]—in a ten-year retrospective. The review will also highlight some aspects of the Protocol that, while perhaps of less interest at the time of its adoption, need to be more carefully considered in the current phase of implementation.

The Protocol on Paper: A Legal Perspective

The content of the Protocol's provisions, by and large, did not result from new writing. To a great extent, the Protocol and its Annexes evolved from a 'cut and paste' operation. Many provisions in the Annexes were extrapolated from earlier recommendations.[16] Even some of the Protocol's basic environmental principles were drawn from CRAMRA—the very instrument that the Protocol has superseded.[17]

While the Protocol brought little fresh regulation to the ATS, it did introduce several new elements. Firstly, the Protocol approached the protection of the Antarctic environment in a *comprehensive* rather than in the issue-specific manner that has characterised earlier ATS instruments. Secondly, the Protocol 'codified' the existing recommendations into a *legally binding* instrument. And thirdly, the Protocol provided for the establishment of a *new institution* within the ATS, the Committee for Environmental Protection (CEP).

The legal form used—a protocol to the Treaty rather than a free-standing convention—was innovative for the ATS. The choice of this form resulted in a framework document accompanied by more flexible annexes. The latter are subject to a fast-track amendment mechanism that can enable timely responses to changing environmental conditions and demands.

The legal position of the Protocol in the overall ATS has, in itself, also been an innovation. The Protocol *supplements* the Antarctic Treaty and neither modifies nor amends the Treaty (Article 4(1)). As to the Annexes, Article 9(1) states that 'Annexes to this Protocol shall form an integral part thereof'. Annexes I–IV, which were adopted in the 'Protocol package' in Madrid on 4 October 1991, became effective simultaneously with the entry into force of the Protocol. These four Annexes relate, respectively, to environmental impact assessment, conservation of Antarctic fauna and flora, waste disposal and waste management, and prevention of marine pollution. Annex V, on 'Area Protection and Area Management', however, was embodied in Recommendation XVI–10, adopted at the sixteenth ATCM in Bonn, only some weeks after the adoption of the Protocol, and thus required a separate procedure for becoming effective. After more than a decade since its adoption, Annex V has yet to become effective.[18]

The Protocol addressed environmental protection through two essentially different approaches: the blanket *prohibition* of mining—the one activity regulated under CRAMRA—and the detailed *regulation* of other activities in the Antarctic.[19] The Protocol may thus be seen as consisting of two main 'units', determined by the type of activity in the Antarctic. Mineral activities gave rise to one unit, which is contained in Articles 7 and 25(5): an indefinite prohibition of any such activities (except scientific research).[20] This may be regarded as an entirely new approach, the direct opposite of the approach taken under CRAMRA. However, it can also be argued that no substantial difference was introduced by the Protocol's mining ban. Under CRAMRA, a consensus of Parties was required to start a mining operation; the same would suffice to revise the Protocol's mining ban.

The second main 'unit' of the Protocol concerns the *regulation* of other human activities. This unit comprises all the remaining provisions of the Protocol and its Annexes and thus creates an environmental protection regime for the Antarctic. In this regard, Article 3(1) of the Protocol formulates environmental principles and, *inter alia*, states:

> The protection of the Antarctic environment and dependent and associated ecosystems and the intrinsic value of Antarctica, including its wilderness and aesthetic values and its value as an area for the conduct of scientific research, in particular research essential to understanding the global environment, shall be fundamental considerations in the planning and conduct of all activities in the Antarctic Treaty area.

For activities *not* prohibited in the Antarctic, with the exception of those undertaken pursuant to CCAMLR or the Seals Convention,[21] the Protocol requires an environmental impact assessment (EIA) at the planning stage; an EIA is required if the activity is determined to have at least a 'minor or transitory impact' on the Antarctic environment or on dependent and associated ecosystems.[22] We will return to those requirements when reviewing the Protocol in its practical operation as an environmental management tool.

Even the basic provisions of the Protocol have given rise to legal dilemmas. For example, it is unclear which *activities* are covered by the Protocol, since it variously refers to 'all activities' and, in many places, just to 'activities', while in Articles 3(4), 8(2) and 15(1)(a) the Protocol defines which activities it addresses more specifically by relating to activities pursuant to Article VII(5) of the Antarctic Treaty. Domestic implementing legislation reveals different understandings by the Parties with regard to the scope of activities covered by the Protocol.

The legal status of the Protocol as a 'supplement to the Antarctic Treaty' (Article 4), on the one hand, and its proclaimed role as an instrument for the 'comprehensive protection of the Antarctic environment and dependent and associated ecosystems' (Article 2), on the other, give rise to some inherent fundamental contradictions. An unambiguous determination of the *area of application* of the Protocol as an environmental protection instrument is hampered by the fact that the Protocol lacks any specific provision as to its territorial scope. On the one hand, this apparent omission would seem to be attributed to the fact that the Protocol is meant to be a supplement to the Antarctic Treaty. Thus, in the absence of any provision to the contrary, its area of application should be understood as identical to that of the Antarctic Treaty, i.e., south of 60°S.[23] Moreover, the essence of the Protocol lies in Article 3, which encompasses 'activities in the *Antarctic Treaty area*'[24]. The Protocol uses the formulation 'Antarctic Treaty area' throughout the text of its provisions. Indeed, since the adoption of the Protocol, the Consultative Parties have declared at several of their gatherings (both formal and informal) that they agree that the area of application of the Protocol is the same as that of the Antarctic Treaty.

On the other hand, confining the Protocol to a geographic limit that seems inadequate in the context of its environmental protection provisions may be seen as contrary to the main (proclaimed) purpose of the instrument.[25] Article 3 demonstrates the contradiction of the Protocol in being limited to 'activities in the Antarctic Treaty area', but at the same time this Article relies on the concept of the 'protection of the Antarctic environment and dependent and associated ecosystems'. The ecosystems being referred to are assumed to be linked to the biological (not the political) boundaries of the Antarctic. However, discussions among the Parties, especially relating to the liability regime, have failed to show any common understanding of the meaning of this term.

Moreover, it has been questioned whether all the provisions of the Protocol should be understood to apply to the *entire* area south of 60°S. The difference between the two main aspects of the Protocol—one prohibitory (Article 7) and the other regulatory—becomes apparent here. For example, does the mining ban contained in Article 7 apply to the portion of the 'seabed beyond the limits of national jurisdiction', which under the letter of the 1982 UN Convention on the Law of the Sea could be regarded as the international seabed area and, as such, would fall under the competence of the International Seabed Authority? Views expressed by several Consultative Parties thus far, as well as their domestic legislation for implementing the Protocol, provide different responses to this question.[26] A further question is whether the Protocol applies to the continental shelf off Antarctica but south of 60°S, or whether it applies to the Antarctic continental shelf that extends even north of 60°S.[27] These considerations may have important implications for possible mineral activities on the continental shelf.[28]

As the above discussion shows, legal dilemmas and some major contradictions encumber the Protocol.[29] However, in spite of this the Protocol has strengthened the *legal* regime for protecting the Antarctic environment by providing a comprehensive instead of an issue-specific approach. Not only is this comprehensive approach contained in a legally binding instrument, but it is also equipped with a new advisory institution, the CEP. The question now is whether this overall legal strengthening, in conjunction with the individual provisions of the Protocol, has made an impact on the improved environmental protection and management practices in, and regarding, the Antarctic.

The Protocol in Practice: An Environmental Management Perspective

The Environmental Protocol is indeed one of the most stringent international agreements to date. It was, however, only shortly before entry into force of the Protocol that the Consultative Parties began enquiring as to the actual state of the environment that the Protocol was intended to protect. Postponements rather than haste characterized the process of producing a 'State of the Antarctic Environment' assessment, the need for which was not expressed before the 1996 ATCM.[30] Incidentally, the time used for discussions alone on how to structure a future 'State of the Antarctic Environment' assessment far exceeded the time used to negotiate and adopt the Protocol itself.

Overall, however, no 'State of the Antarctic Environment' assessment is needed for a general conclusion that, by any normal standard, the Antarctic environment is remarkably clean. The perception of the Antarctic as being in imminent environmental danger prior to the negotiation of the Protocol was misleading. This has been confirmed by a recent regional report for the Ross Sea region.[31] Human activities in the Antarctic, though gradually increasing, remain very limited in number and scope, and those to which the Protocol applies in reality are restricted mainly to scientific research, to related logistics for maintenance of scientific bases and transport, and to the relatively small amount of Antarctic tourism.[32] This is not to deny possible local environmental impacts from activities in the Antarctic.[33] However, activities to which the Protocol does apply present far less of a threat to the Antarctic environment than those originating outside the region—to which the Protocol does not apply and which require action at either global or national level, or both.

When an accident occurs in the Antarctic, it is likely to attract considerable publicity, far more than an accident of similar magnitude in most other places in the world. A significant aspect of the Antarctic in environmental debate is as a *symbol* of one of the last surviving wilderness areas on the planet.[34] Because of this symbolic role, as observed earlier, 'human activities in the Antarctic are evaluated not only by the actual pressure exerted on the environment but also by the attitude demonstrated.'[35] An important feature of Antarctic environmental protection is the recognition by those involved that this unique and special environment must be preserved.

Thus, the real test for assessing the impact of the Protocol as an international regime lies not necessarily in the direct evaluation of the change in the state of the Antarctic environment, but rather in an evaluation of the *behaviour* that can contribute to the main proclaimed objective of the Protocol. Has the Protocol led to any change in this respect? At the outset, the answer is affirmative—despite the Protocol having been negotiated in haste and with an imminent political agenda, and thus being hampered by some important contradictions. Several aspects of the Protocol, and the political will of the Parties to implement them, are directly responsible for the practical impact on improved environmental management in the Antarctic.

Increased Domestic Awareness

The legally binding nature of the Protocol requires that each Party 'take appropriate measures within its competence, including the adoption of laws and regulations, administrative actions and enforcement measures, to insure compliance'.[36] Even before the entry into force of the Protocol, the Consultative Parties began elaborating and adopting their domestic implementing legislation. Already at the adoption of the Protocol, the Parties agreed that, pending its entry into force, it was desirable to apply Annexes I–IV, 'in accordance with their legal systems and to the extent practicable'.[37] This indication of political will to implement elements of the Protocol voluntarily has been followed up through an information exchange at a series of ATCMs, commencing with the Venice Meeting in 1992. All this has resulted in the increased awareness, from both domestic agencies and operators, of environmental considerations when planning Antarctic operations. Moreover, the codification into national laws of considerations that were earlier scattered in a number of recommendations and other instruments has provided more clearly defined requirements and legal obligations for the conduct of Antarctic operations.

The CEP and Increased Transparency

The establishment of a new institution under the Protocol, the Committee for Environmental Protection, has been instrumental in increasing transparency at the ATS level of what are otherwise discretionary national implementation practices. The CEP, to which each Protocol party is a member, is established as a technical body with the purpose of providing advice and formulating recommendations to the Parties in matters relating to the implementation of the Protocol; the advice is then further considered by the decision-making body, the ATCM.[38] The Parties have the obligation of reporting annually on the steps taken to implement the Protocol (Article 17); these reports are circulated to all the other Parties, presented at the CEP, considered at the ATCM, and then made publicly available. The CEP plays the key role in annually cross-checking domestic implementation.[39]

Strictly legally, this annual reporting had to await the entry into force of the Protocol and the establishment of the CEP. But the political will of the Parties to implement aspects of the Protocol ahead of its entry into force should also be noted here. As early as the 1992 ATCM, an initiative was given to set up an informal discussion group to review the implementation of the Protocol.[40] At the next meeting, in 1994, the Parties agreed that a Transitional Environmental Working Group (TEWG) be established that would be operative from the ATCM in Seoul in 1995. The TEWG would deal with items which, following the entry into force of the Protocol, would be handled by the CEP.[41] The TEWG operated through the 1997 ATCM.

Following the establishment of the CEP in 1998, the record of annual reporting over the past four meetings has gradually improved. The format of the reports has also been under scrutiny, hence a proposal at the 1999 ATCM to develop a standard for annual reports.

Inspection of Environmental Practices

The Protocol contributed to inspections under Article VII of the Antarctic Treaty, placing more emphasis on environmental practices than before. Under the Protocol, an element of those inspections is now directly related to the promotion of environmental protection in the Antarctic (Article 14(1)). This increases mutual control among the Parties with regard to their environmental management practices in conducting operations in the Antarctic. Inspection reports are first sent to the inspected Parties, who are given the opportunity to comment; the reports are then circulated (with any comments made on them by the inspected Parties), following a procedure similar to that for the annual reports by Parties under Article 17.

Interpreting 'minor or transitory impact'

The Protocol requires an EIA for any proposed activity in the Antarctic before that activity may proceed, unless it is determined that the activity will have *less than* a 'minor or transitory impact' on the Antarctic environment.[42]

An EIA can be initial (IEE) or comprehensive (CEE), the latter if a proposed activity is likely to have *more than* a minor or transitory impact. Whether or not an EIA is required and which type of EIA is needed for any proposed activity is determined under the 'appropriate national procedures'.[43] The evaluation of whether an activity may have a 'less than', 'equal to', or 'more than' a 'minor or transitory' impact is left to the Parties. The contents of this evaluative standard would be, it has been stated, developed through practice.[44] The Protocol stopped short of entitling an independent or collective body to evaluate EIA requirements for proposed activities. Only draft CEEs are scrutinized by both the CEP and ATCM, yet these bodies have no power of veto which could prevent any such activity from proceeding. As to IEEs, Parties need to make them 'available on request'; only an annual list of completed IEEs is to be circulated to other Parties, forwarded to the CEP, and made publicly available. Devoid of a common frame of reference, the practice of various Parties inevitably varies. The 'Guidelines for EIA in Antarctica', adopted by the Consultative Parties at the Lima Meeting in 1999, confirmed in respect of the notion of 'minor or transitory impact' that 'no agreement on this term has so far been reached', and that its interpretation will therefore need to be made on a 'case by case site specific basis'.[45] From the information circulated among the Parties thus far, it is apparent that approximately 300 IEEs have been prepared, while at the same time no more than ten CEEs have been made. This could be the result of different interpretations as to when a CEE is required, but could equally, especially in border-line cases, be attributed to a tendency to avoid the technically complex preparation and time-consuming review of a draft CEE. Therefore the unclear notion of 'minor or transitory impact', combined with different procedural requirements for IEEs and CEEs, may result in quite undesirable side effects for the practical implementation of the Protocol.

As shown above, the Protocol, despite some vagueness, has greatly influenced behaviour related to minimizing the environmental impacts of activities in the Antarctic. It is, however, difficult and probably premature to conclude on this basis alone that the practical implementation of the Protocol has been a major success. Findings of recent Antarctic inspections have confirmed the reality that the implementation record of the Parties remains uneven, and it is certainly not possible to assess implementation by viewing the Parties as a homogeneous group.[46] Moreover, whereas an individual Party may have developed adequate practices in implementing some aspects of the Protocol, it may have employed inadequate procedures in respect to others.

The Unfinished Agenda

There remain several major sets of issue areas on which the Parties will have to focus more closely in order to enhance the implementation of the Protocol. The basic reason for this is the specific political and legal situation of the Antarctic, where the need to maintain a balance on sovereignty positions has led to various open questions. These have become even more apparent in the current phase of the implementation of the Protocol.

Issues of Jurisdiction, Control, and Enforcement

Ensuring a comprehensive implementation of the Protocol requires the introduction of innovative mechanisms to enable control and enforcement in the Antarctic. Related to this is the need to establish an effective jurisdiction over activities in the Antarctic Treaty area. The Antarctic Treaty regulates jurisdiction in quite a limited manner[47] and fails to resolve the question of jurisdiction over nationals of Treaty parties who are not observers or exchanged scientists; nor does the Treaty address the question of jurisdiction over nationals of third states. This lack of a comprehensive jurisdictional regime was not of particular concern in the decades immediately following the adoption of the Antarctic Treaty.

Nowadays, particularly with the growth in Antarctic *tourism*, the question of jurisdiction needs to be readdressed. Otherwise it will become increasingly difficult to ensure compliance with the Protocol in a situation where close to half of the vessels visiting Antarctica on tourist cruises fly flags of third states, often various 'flags of convenience'. At present, Parties rely to a degree on informal regulations by IAATO (the International Association of Antarctic Tour Operators) to ensure compliance by tour operators with the Protocol, which is a pragmatic solution, yet one without any legal guarantee.[48]

The problem occurs when an offence by a third party breaches legislation for implementing environmental regulations, such as regulations under the Protocol. In cases when flag state enforcement fails (as it often does), the need arises for a complementary means. At ATCMs in 1996 and 1997, the Parties initiated discussion on the need for introducing such complementary means in the Antarctic context.[49] Since all the regularly used gateway ports to the Antarctic are subject to the jurisdiction of the Protocol parties (Argentina, Australia, Chile, New Zealand, South Africa, and the United Kingdom), a concept such as 'departure state jurisdiction' was proposed by the United Kingdom.[50] Moreover, this concept was not confined to the obvious departure ports but rather to all the Parties equally, regardless of whether or not vessels departed from their territories directly to the Antarctic. This would in practice mean solving the question of jurisdiction *in* the

Antarctic waters by dealing with it *outside* of the Antarctic Treaty area. However, although there is a general understanding among the Parties regarding the need for improved mechanisms to ensure the effective implementation of the Protocol, opposition remains to far-reaching proposals such as 'departure state jurisdiction'. How can issues of jurisdiction be adequately solved to enhance implementation of the Protocol but not disturb the balance on sovereignty positions as preserved in Article IV of the Antarctic Treaty? This question remains a major item on an unfinished agenda.

Liability Regime for Environmental Damage

In Article 16 of the Protocol, the Parties undertook 'to elaborate rules and procedures relating to liability for damage arising from activities undertaken in the Antarctic Treaty area and covered by this Protocol. Those rules and procedures shall be included in one or more Annexes.'

In the aftermath of the adoption of the Protocol, the Consultative Parties established at the 1992 ATCM the Group of Legal Experts on Liability, which first met in 1993. Although the Group initially showed steady progress, signs gradually emerged of an approaching stalemate on several crucial issues. The Group was then requested to report to the Tromsø ATCM in 1998, which it did by listing key pending issues for an Antarctic liability regime.[51] Thereupon, the Group was actually dissolved. In other words, as stated in official documents, the Consultative Parties decided that the 'Group of Legal Experts on Liability, by submitting its report, has fulfilled its task and its work is now completed; [and that] the further negotiation of an annex or annexes on liability be undertaken in Working Group I of the ATCM.'[52] The sense of urgency and the main change in the course that was agreed upon at the 1998 ATCM were prompted by the entry into force of the Protocol a few months before that meeting. Viewed retrospectively, the task of the Group of Legal Experts resembled a 'mission impossible': equipped with no real policy guidance, with no risk assessments available of actual activities in the Antarctic,[53] and mainly devoid of natural science and technical expertise, this Group was left to discuss various legal (and often rather theoretical) options in a vacuum.[54]

Deliberations over liability, now in a policy rather than a legal forum, have continued since the 1999 ATCM. A renewed listing of key issues has been made, and the major policy dilemmas, including the choice between a piecemeal or an overall approach in creating a liability regime under the Protocol, have been revisited. A 'step-by-step' approach has been reverted to. This was originally triggered by a US proposal tabled in 1996, which then indicated that the Group of Legal Experts was approaching a dead-end. The Parties have now agreed to elaborate a draft for an annex on 'the liability aspects of environmental emergencies, as a step in the establishment of a liability regime in accordance with Article 16 of the Protocol.'[55] The question remains of course whether the choosing of this more pragmatic approach will eventually fulfil the requirements of Article 16—i.e., how many 'steps' will be needed.

Improving the Annexes

A closer analysis of various provisions of the Annexes to the Protocol reveals regulatory gaps and vague language. These shortcomings were partly unintended by-products of the hasty negotiation of the Protocol and partly the deliberate results of adopting the texts by consensus, thereby agreeing on the lowest commonly acceptable standards. The need for improvements in the individual Annexes has increasingly been recognized.

At CEP IV in St Petersburg, in July 2001, the Committee decided to begin conducting a *rolling review* of the Annexes. The review is due to begin with Annex II, 'Conservation of Antarctic Fauna and Flora', at the next meeting of the CEP, to be held in Warsaw in September 2002.[56] The ATCM endorsed this proposal.[57] Inherent in the original design of the Protocol as a framework instrument with various annexes is the enhanced flexibility of the latter to be updated to reflect changing environmental challenges, acquired knowledge, and new practices. While an amendment of the Protocol has to undergo a complex procedure analogous to that of the Antarctic Treaty itself,[58] the Annexes can be modified under a simplified procedure by a measure adopted at the ATCM, which is then, if after one year's time without explicit opposition, deemed to have been approved and becomes effective.[59]

However well conceived this revision system may seem, it faces practical obstacles. The domestic implementation legislation of several Parties simply incorporates provisions from both the Protocol and the Annexes, without making distinctions regarding the revision procedures for these. Thus, for some countries, an ongoing review process of Annexes at the ATS level might result in the challenge of revising respective provisions in domestic laws, whose revision procedure is not necessarily as flexible as that for the Annexes themselves. This, in turn, may result in resistance towards modification of the Annexes at the ATCMs. Perhaps a combination of a rolling review at the annual CEP and periodic, yet less frequent, revision meetings for the Annexes could both satisfy the demands for responsiveness of the Annexes and placate the concerns of domestic legislators in some countries.

Antarctic Treaty Secretariat

In contrast to most contemporary multilateral environmental treaties, the Protocol contains no provision for the establishment of a secretariat. The lack of permanent institutions must be seen in a wider ATS context, where a careful preservation of balance on sovereignty positions coupled with a low level of activities in the Antarctic has, for many years, prevented institutionalization of Antarctic affairs. Even the main decision-making forum of the ATS—the Consultative Meeting—has no institutional legal personality of its own; it is rather a periodic intergovernmental diplomatic conference of participating states.

With the advent of the Protocol, and with significant new requirements for information exchange and reporting introduced in the ATS (which, from the original 12, now also numbers 45 states), the need for permanent technical support has been recognized by the Consultative Parties. Although discussed by the Parties earlier, it was not until after the Protocol's adoption that the need to establish a permanent secretariat was first formally recognized and agreed to, at the 1992 ATCM.[60] Since that meeting, however, the question of the location of the secretariat has postponed its establishment. The 1992 candidacy of Argentina as a prospective host country for the secretariat was met with reservation from the United Kingdom, and the stalemate on this issue endured for nearly a decade. However, improved relationships between these two countries in recent years, combined with the Argentine commitment to comprehensive reorganization of the structure of its Antarctic programme,[61] resulted at the latest ATCM in 2001 in the UK joining the consensus on Buenos Aires as the seat of the secretariat.[62]

Although efforts towards the establishment of the secretariat have gained momentum by the recent consensus regarding its seat,[63] additional time will certainly be needed to reach agreement on legal and, especially, funding arrangements—and not least to secure the approval of these in the domestic forums of all the Parties.[64] Meanwhile, the CEP operated for its first four years and performed its initial tasks well, also thanks to the efficiency and enthusiasm of its chair and the logistical support furnished by his home institution, the Norwegian Polar Institute. While this temporary arrangement may have functioned well in the initial years, the increasing complexity and scope of tasks required from the CEP clearly demand a permanent secretariat if the implementation of the Protocol is not to be hampered by the lack of support needed for technical follow up.[65]

Ten Years After: What Has Been Achieved?

From the above brief review, the impact that the Protocol has had since its adoption can be summarized as follows:

Firstly, politically, the Protocol exerted a significant impact immediately upon its adoption. However, it then responded to various external and internal challenges to the governance of Antarctic affairs by the Consultative Parties. As such, the Protocol has significantly contributed both to strengthening international co-operation within the ATS and to changing the perception about the ATS in the broader international community. This impact appears to be a lasting one.

Secondly, the legal effect of the Protocol has accurately been summarized as a 'positive but limited contribution'.[66] This contribution has been made in three main ways: by introducing a comprehensive instead of an issue-specific approach in Antarctic environmental protection; by doing this in a legally binding instrument; and by establishing a new institution, the CEP, with an advisory role in the implementation of the Protocol. Despite these positive contributions, however, the Protocol has introduced some legal dilemmas. These can be attributed partly, on the one hand, to the Protocol's being stretched between its status as a supplement to the Antarctic Treaty and, on the other, to its proclaimed role as an instrument for the comprehensive protection of the Antarctic environment and dependent and associated ecosystems.

Thirdly, as to Antarctic environmental management, the Protocol has enabled a change in behaviour relating to minimizing environmental impacts of activities in the Antarctic in three major ways: by increasing awareness of domestic agencies, by increasing the transparency of domestic implementation, and by increasing mutual control of environmental practices in the Antarctic. The full effect of these changes, however, remains hampered by the wide interpretation possibilities of some core requirements under the Protocol, such as the standard for conducting EIAs and, especially, the trigger for CEEs, which remain in a 'grey zone'.

Finally, an unfinished agenda persists for the Protocol to apply comprehensively to activities in the Antarctic. The main items on that agenda include: the unresolved issues of jurisdiction, control, and enforcement in the Antarctic, especially regarding activities by third parties, such as tourism; the adoption of a liability regime for environmental damage; the improvement of Annexes through rolling review; and the establishment of the secretariat. The question remains whether it is possible for the Parties to respond fully to all these agenda items, or whether in some instances it is better to seek out pragmatic solutions.

Notes and References

I am indebted to Chris Joyner, Mike Richardson, and Olav Schram Stokke for comments on a draft of this article. I also wish to acknowledge the support provided to the FNI's research projects on Antarctic affairs by the Tinker Foundation, New York, within which part of the research for this article has been carried out. The views and opinions in this article are my own, and do not necessarily reflect the views of any agency or institution.

1. The Protocol was adopted on 4 October 1991 and entered into force on 14 January 1998. For a reference to the source text of this and any other international instrument cited in this article, see the agreements section in the present *Yearbook*. While the Protocol is open for accession by any state party to the Antarctic Treaty, the current state of participation, as of 28 February 2002, comprises all the 27 Antarctic Treaty Consultative Parties, yet only two among 18 non-Consultative Parties (Greece and Ukraine). For a list of state parties to the Antarctic Treaty, see the agreements section in the present *Yearbook*.
2. Ten years ago, following the adoption of the Protocol, this *Yearbook* published a review of environmental protection in the Antarctic; see Olav Schram Stokke (1992), 'Protecting the Frozen South', *Green Globe Yearbook*, 1, 133–40.
3. For comprehensive studies, see Sir Arthur Watts (1992), *International Law and the Antarctic Treaty System* (Cambridge: Grotius Publications); and Peter J. Beck (1986), *The International Politics of Antarctica* (London: Croom Helm).
4. On the notion and components of the ATS, see Davor Vidas (1996), 'The Antarctic Treaty System in the International Community: An Overview', in Olav Schram Stokke and Davor Vidas (eds.), *Governing the Antarctic: The Effectiveness and Legitimacy of the Antarctic Treaty System* (Cambridge: Cambridge University Press), 35–48. See also the agreements section in the present *Yearbook*.
5. Note here the interplay between various provisions of the Antarctic Treaty, especially Arts. IV and IX.
6. See Art. IX(1) of the Antarctic Treaty.
7. Note here especially the 1964 Recommendation III–8 ('Agreed Measures for the Conservation of Antarctic Fauna and Flora'), the 1972 Convention for the Conservation of Antarctic Seals (Seals Convention) and the 1980 Convention on the Conservation of Antarctic Marine Living Resources (CCAMLR).
8. For an overview, see Christopher C. Joyner (1996), 'The Effectiveness of CRAMRA', in Stokke and Vidas (eds.), *Governing the Antarctic*, 152–62. See also Francisco Orrego Vicuña (1988), *Antarctic Mineral Exploitation: The Emerging Legal Framework* (Cambridge: Cambridge University Press); and Rüdiger Wolfrum (1991), *The Convention on the Regulation of Antarctic Mineral Resource Activities: An Attempt to Break New Ground* (Berlin: Springer–Verlag).
9. Ratification by *all* the claimant countries was in effect a prerequisite for entry into force; see Art. 62(1) of CRAMRA in conjunction with provisions on the establishment of and membership in the institutions under the Convention.
10. See Recommendation XV–1 (1989); text reprinted in John A. Heap (ed.) (1994), *Handbook of the Antarctic Treaty System*, 8th edn (Washington, DC: US Department of State), 2005–7.
11. See William M. Bush (1992), 'The 1988 Wellington Convention: How Much Environmental Protection?', in Joe Verhoeven, Philippe Sands, and Maxwell Bruce (eds.), *The Antarctic Environment and International Law* (London: Graham & Trotman), 69–83; Francisco Orrego Vicuña (1996), 'The Effectiveness of the Protocol on Environmental Protection to the Antarctic Treaty', in Stokke and Vidas (eds.), *Governing the Antarctic*, 197–8; Watts (1992), *International Law and the Antarctic Treaty System*, 276; and Wolfrum (1991), *The Convention on the Regulation of Antarctic Mineral Resource Activities*.
12. UNGA resolution 49/80.
13. UNGA resolutions 51/56 and 54/45, respectively.
14. Among many analyses of the Protocol available to date, see especially Orrego (1996), 'Effectiveness of the Protocol', 174–202; Francisco Orrego Vicuña (1996), 'The Legitimacy of the Protocol on Environmental Protection to the Antarctic Treaty', in Stokke and Vidas (eds.), *Governing the Antarctic*, 268–93; and Francesco Francioni (1993), 'The Madrid Protocol on the Protection of the Antarctic Environment', *Texas International Law Journal*, 28, 47–72.
15. Art. 2 of the Protocol.
16. See Orrego (1996), 'Effectiveness of the Protocol', 190–202.
17. See Christopher C. Joyner (1996), 'The Legitimacy of CRAMRA', in Stokke and Vidas (eds.), *Governing the Antarctic*, 255–67.
18. As of 28 February 2002, only one Consultative Party—India—has yet to approve Recommendation XVI–10, thereby alone blocking Annex V from becoming legally effective.
19. See, however, para. 7 of the Final Act of the Eleventh Special Antarctic Treaty Consultative Meeting, regarding the activities already regulated under CCAMLR, the Seals Convention, and the International Convention for the Regulation of Whaling; text reprinted in Heap (ed.) (1994), *Handbook of the Antarctic Treaty System*, 2016–18.
20. The Protocol does contain certain other prohibitions, such as the prohibition on introducing dogs onto land or ice shelves in Antarctica (Annex II, Art. 4(2)), but it is the mining ban that has been the outstanding prohibitory feature of the Protocol.
21. See para. 8 of the Final Act of the Eleventh Special ATCM.
22. Art. 8 and Annex I to the Protocol.
23. Art. 4 of the Protocol, in conjunction with Art. VI of the Antarctic Treaty (of course, with the derogation clause contained in the latter article, explicitly preserving the high-seas rights in the Antarctic Treaty area). See comment by William M. Bush (1992–), *Antarctica and International Law: A Collection of Inter-State and National Documents* (Dobbs Ferry, NY: Oceana Publications), Booklet AT91C, 2; at another place Bush comments, 'the area south of 60 degrees south latitude ... is the same as the area of operation of the protocol'; ibid., Booklet AT91D, 11.
24. Art. 3(1) of the Protocol (emphasis added). See also comment by Bush (1992–), *Antarctica and International Law*, Booklet AT91C, 2.
25. Similarly, Bush, in ibid., 2–3.
26. For a detailed examination of this issue, see Davor Vidas (1999), 'Southern Ocean Seabed: Arena for Conflicting Regimes?', in Davor Vidas and Willy Østreng (eds.), *Order for the Oceans at the Turn of the Century* (The Hague: Kluwer Law International), 291–314.
27. On the Chilean interpretative declaration in this connection, first made on the occasion of signing and reaffirmed when ratifying the Protocol, see Maria Luisa Carvallo and Paulina Julio (2000), 'Implementation of the Antarctic Environmental Protocol by Chile: History, Legislation and Practice', in Davor Vidas (ed.), *Implementing the Environmental Protection Regime for the Antarctic* (Dordrecht: Kluwer Academic Publishers), 342–3.
28. See, further, Davor Vidas (2000), 'The Antarctic Continental Shelf Beyond 200 Miles: A Juridical Rubik's Cube', in Vidas (ed.), *Implementing the Environmental Protection Regime for the Antarctic*, 261–72.
29. See, especially, Orrego (1996), 'Effectiveness of the Protocol'.
30. See para. 163 of the *Final Report of the Twentieth Antarctic Treaty Consultative Meeting, Utrecht, 29 April – 10 May 1996* (1997) (The Hague: Netherlands Ministry of Foreign Affairs). At the latest (fourth) meeting of the Committee for Environmental Protection (CEP IV), held in St Petersburg, 9–13 July 2001, 'SCAR apologised that it had been unable to provide the Scoping

Study for a State of the Antarctic Environment Report. It will be provided by SCAR to CEP V'; see para. 94 of the 'Report of the Committee for Environmental Protection', in *Final Report of the Twenty-Fourth Antarctic Treaty Consultative Meeting, St. Petersburg, Russian Federation, 9–20 July 2001* (2002) (Moscow: Ministry of Foreign Affairs of the Russian Federation).

31. *Ross Sea Region: A State of the Environment Report for the Ross Sea Region of Antarctica* (2001) (Christchurch: New Zealand Antarctic Institute).
32. The one human activity in the Antarctic region that today presents a real threat to the Antarctic ecosystem—the illegal, unreported, and unregulated (IUU) fishing in the Southern Ocean—is beyond the scope of the Protocol.
33. See, for instance, *Ross Sea Region* (2001), 3.20–3.21.
34. Stokke (1992), 'Protecting the Frozen South', 133.
35. Olav Schram Stokke and Davor Vidas (1996), 'Introduction', in Stokke and Vidas (eds.), *Governing the Antarctic*, 5–6.
36. Protocol, Art. 13(1). For a review of domestic implementation of the Protocol, see Kees Bastmeijer (2000), 'Implementing the Environmental Protocol Domestically: An Overview', in Vidas (ed.), *Implementing the Environmental Protection Regime for the Antarctic*, 287–307.
37. Para. 14 of the Final Act of the Eleventh Special ATCM.
38. See Arts. 11 and 12 of the Protocol. On CEP, see Olav Orheim (2000), 'The Committee for Environmental Protection: Its Establishment, Operation and Role within the Antarctic Treaty System', in Vidas (ed.), *Implementing the Environmental Protection Regime for the Antarctic*, 107–24.
39. Note, however, that annual reports are not discussed at the CEP unless a specific question is raised; see para. 6 of the 'Report of the Committee for Environmental Protection', in *Final Report of the Twelfth Antarctic Treaty Special Consultative Meeting, The Hague, 11–15 September 2000* (2001) (The Hague: Netherlands Ministry of Foreign Affairs), Annex D.
40. See also Bastmeijer (2000), 'Implementing the Environmental Protocol Domestically', 289.
41. See *Final Report of the Eighteenth Antarctic Treaty Consultative Meeting, Kyoto, Japan, 11–22 April 1994* (1994) (Tokyo: Japanese Ministry of Foreign Affairs), paras. 39–43.
42. Protocol, Art. 8 and Annex I.
43. Protocol, Annex I, Art. 1(1).
44. See para. 30 of the 'Report of the Meeting of the Committee for Environmental Protection, Tromsø, 25–29 May 1998' (1998), in *Final Report of the Twenty-Second Antarctic Treaty Consultative Meeting, Tromsø, Norway, 25 May – 5 June 1998* (Oslo: Norwegian Ministry of Foreign Affairs), Annex E.
45. Guidelines are appended to Resolution 1 (1999), in *Final Report of the Twenty-Third Antarctic Treaty Consultative Meeting, Lima, Peru, 24 May – 4 June 1999* (Lima: Peruvian Ministry of Foreign Affairs), Annex C.
46. See reports from a joint inspection by United Kingdom and German observers in January 1999 (doc. XXIII ATCM/WP 23, 1999), by Belgium and France in September 1999 (doc. XXIV ATCM/INFO 9, 2001), by Norway in January 2001 (doc. XXIV ATCM/WP 25, 2001), and by the United States in February 2001 (doc. XXIV ATCM/INFO 17, 2001). Inspection reports presented at XXIV ATCM are available at <www.24atcm.mid.ru>.
47. Art. VIII of the Antarctic Treaty.
48. On the current issues of Antarctic tourism, see Mike G. Richardson (2000), 'Regulating Tourism in the Antarctic: Issues of Environment and Jurisdiction', in Vidas (ed.), *Implementing the Environmental Protection Regime for the Antarctic*, 71–90.
49. See, especially, the United Kingdom (1997), 'Enhancing Compliance with the Protocol: Departure State Jurisdiction', doc. XXI ATCM/WP 22.
50. Ibid.
51. See 'Liability – Report of the Group of Legal Experts' (1998), doc. XXII ATCM/WP 1.
52. See paras. 1 and 2 of Decision 3 (1998), 'Liability'; and paras. 61–84 of *Final Report of the XXII ATCM*. For an analysis of the result of the work of the Group, see René Lefeber (2000), 'The Prospects for an Antarctic Environmental Liability Regime', in Vidas (ed.), *Implementing the Environmental Protection Regime for the Antarctic*, 199–217.
53. The first such risk assessment appeared only in 1999: COMNAP (1999), 'An Assessment of Environmental Emergencies Arising from Activities in Antarctica', doc. XXIII ATCM/WP 16.
54. See a review by Mari Skåre (2000), 'Liability Annex or Annexes to the Environmental Protocol: A Review of the Process within the Antarctic Treaty System', in Vidas (ed.), *Implementing the Environmental Protection Regime for the Antarctic*, 163–80.
55. See Decision 3 (2001) in *Final Report of the XXIV ATCM*, Annex B.
56. See para. 6 of the 'Report from CEP IV, July 9–13, 2001, St. Petersburg, Russia' (2002), in *Final Report of the XXIV ATCM*.
57. *Final Report of the XXIV ATCM* (2002), para. 41.
58. Compare Art. 25 of the Protocol with Art. XII of the Antarctic Treaty.
59. For further details and safeguards incorporated in that procedure, see the standard amendment/modification clause of the Annexes.
60. See *Final Report of the Seventeenth Antarctic Treaty Consultative Meeting, Venice, Italy, 11–20 November 1992* (1993) (Rome: Italian Ministry of Foreign Affairs), para. 43.
61. See *Final Report of the XXIV ATCM* (2002), paras. 21–3 and Appendix 3, 'Statement by the Minister of Defense of Argentina, Dr Horacio Jaunarena (Buenos Aires, 6 July 2001)'.
62. See ibid., para. 20 and Appendix 3, 'UK Response to Argentine Defence Minister's Statement of 6 July 2001'.
63. See also ibid., Decision 1 (2001).
64. For a review of some major issues involved, see Francesco Francioni (2000), 'Establishment of an Antarctic Treaty Secretariat: Pending Legal Issues', in Vidas (ed.), *Implementing the Environmental Protection Regime for the Antarctic*, 125–40.
65. On functions of the CEP and their practical implementation, see Orheim (2000), 'Committee for Environmental Protection', 113–24.
66. See Orrego (1996), 'Effectiveness of the Protocol', 201–2.

The Ramsar Convention on Wetlands: Has it Made a Difference?

Michael Bowman

Introduction

We left her standing upon the thin peninsula of firm, peaty soil which tapered out into the widespread bog. From the end of it a small wand planted here and there showed where the path zigzagged from tuft to tuft of rushes among those green-scummed pits and foul quagmires which barred the way to the stranger. Rank reeds and lush, slimy water-plants sent an odour of decay and a heavy miasmatic vapour into our faces, while a false step plunged us more than once thigh-deep into the dark quivering mire, which shook for yards in soft undulations around our feet. Its tenacious grip plucked at our heels as we walked, and when we sank into it it was as if some malignant hand was tugging us down into those obscene depths, so grim and purposeful was the clutch in which it held us.

Afficionados of tales of criminal detection will doubtless recognize this passage as an extract from Sir Arthur Conan Doyle's famous story *The Hound of the Baskervilles*,[1] where Sherlock Holmes and his stalwart companion Dr Watson pursue their quarry across the grim reaches of the Grimpen Mire. The Mire (which elsewhere in the book is variously described, along with the moors which surround it, as wild, desolate, lifeless, treacherous, mean, melancholy, God-forsaken, dismal, gloomy, and ill-omened) serves both as a suitably menacing backcloth to the chilling tale of the ghostly hound which haunts the Baskerville family and as a metaphor for the mystery in which the two heroes find themselves floundering, albeit temporarily.

In fact this thoroughly negative image of swamps, marshes, fens, mires, bogs, and other wetlands is one that has persisted in human consciousness throughout time. Holdgate has reminded us that Grendel, 'the monster in Beowulf, the earliest epic in the English language, "held the moors, the fen and the fastness" and ravaged Seeland from his swampy home',[2] while similar ideas have been encapsulated in folk songs and stories over the centuries.[3] These unfavourable perceptions have been strongly reinforced by the realization that wetlands form the breeding grounds of *Anopheles* mosquitoes, which are the carriers of the potentially fatal disease malaria. Given their profound lack of appeal in human estimations, the most favourable treatment that wetlands have traditionally been able to expect has involved malign neglect, while in many cases they have come under direct and deliberate attack. Commonly this has taken the form of destruction of their natural characteristics through drainage, either for the creation of agricultural or residential land or simply in order to combat the insect foe. Although the traditions of 'aquatic' civilizations, which adapted themselves to the rigours and perturbations of natural water cycles, have persisted in some parts of the world, many regions have seen the adoption of a 'hydraulic' culture, which has sought to regulate and control water flow through the construction of dams, dikes, and similar devices. As a consequence, over half of the wetlands that are thought formerly to have existed in the United States, for example, have now disappeared. Some experts believe this rate of loss to be in line with that experienced globally. In the case of particular wetland types, such as peatlands, the extent of loss may be much greater. In general, moreover, this transformation has been viewed either as a small price to pay for the resulting benefits, or as a desirable end in itself.[4]

In view of this long tradition of human antipathy, it is perhaps surprising to note that February of each year now witnesses the commemoration around the globe of World Wetland Day, intended in large part as a celebration of the virtues and values of wetland ecosystems. The year 2002 marks the sixth such occasion, the event having been inaugurated in 1997 as a result of a decision taken the previous year at the sixth (Brisbane) meeting of the Conference of the Parties (CoP) to the Convention on Wetlands of International Importance.[5] The CoP in fact called for the designation of a week of commemoration centred around the date of 2 February, the day upon which the convention had itself been adopted at Ramsar, in Iran, some 25 years previously.

This seemingly dramatic turnabout in human attitudes towards wetlands has been occasioned by the growing realization of the many vital functions performed by wetland ecosystems. As one eminent authority has put it:[6]

> Wetlands perform a wide range of functions that are essential for supporting plant and animal life and for maintaining the quality of the environment. These functions include: flood control; shoreline stabilization; sediment, nutrient and toxicant retention; and food chain support.

On the final point specifically he notes that 'two-thirds of the fish we eat depend on wetlands at some stage in their life cycle' and that, 'in the Gulf of Mexico alone, 90 percent of the fish harvested are wetland-dependent species'.[7] For many people, particularly perhaps in the developed world, it is the importance of wetlands as waterfowl habitat which has provided the major stimulus for reappraisal of the need for their conservation. Habitat destruction is the most significant of all the threats to bird species, and the loss of wetland areas is commonly cited as being particularly damaging in that regard.[8]

It is undoubtedly mistaken, however, to regard this change in sentiment as a sudden and dramatic volte-face, or to attribute it exclusively to the influence of the Ramsar Convention, since there has, of course, always been some level of human appreciation of wetland values to set against the general sense of antipathy. Indeed, Conan Doyle himself was sufficiently perceptive to allow, through the musings of Dr Watson, that, when seen in the right light, wetlands might possess a distinct aesthetic appeal of their own.[9] He was also sufficiently erudite to recognize, via the activities of his fictional naturalist Stapleton (who, in a regrettable piece of casting, turns out ultimately to be the villain of the piece!) that wetlands play host to a great variety of fauna and flora, including many rare or endangered species.[10] Furthermore, the Ramsar Convention itself could scarcely have been adopted in the absence of a significant groundswell of concern over the loss of wetland ecosystems, prompted by growing recognition of their vital ecological role. What does seem to have occurred is that the principal proponents of the Convention, an *ad hoc* consortium of states and non-governmental organizations dismayed at the degradation and disappearance of wildfowl habitat, took the opportunity to harness their own particular preoccupations to the upsurge of general environmental concern that developed throughout the 1960s.[11] The Convention has subsequently been used as a vehicle for carrying the message regarding wetland values to an ever wider audience, in the hope of transforming previously negative attitudes and policies into a more environmentally sensitive programme of sustainable utilization. It will be apparent from the following discussion, however, that there is still a very long way to go.

The Ramsar Convention on Wetlands

As indicated in its preamble, the Ramsar Convention's principal objective is 'to stem the progressive encroachment on and loss of wetlands now and in the future'. It is beyond the scope of this short article to conduct an in-depth analysis of the Convention,[12] but a brief account of its principal provisions is appropriate in order to set an appraisal of its achievements into context. A key feature is the very wide definition of wetlands which the Convention, in Article 1, saw fit to adopt, namely:

> areas of marsh, fen, peatland or water, whether natural or artificial, permanent or temporary, with water that is static or flowing, fresh, brackish or salt, including areas of marine water the depth of which at low tide does not exceed six metres.

It is important to note the enormous variety of habitat types which this definition embraces, including not only those falling within traditional conceptions of wetlands (such as mangrove swamps, peat bogs, tidal flats, and water meadows), but also many other natural features (among them coastal beaches and waters, freshwater lakes and rivers, and even underground karst systems) and man-made sites (such as rice paddies, reservoirs, and flooded gravel pits). The unifying feature of this diverse array of geographical features, at least as originally perceived and reflected in the full title of the Convention, was their importance as waterfowl habitat, and it was indeed ornithological organizations that made most of the running as regards the adoption of Ramsar in the first place. Nevertheless, the intention was never to exclude or deny other wetland values, and more recently there has been a concerted attempt to de-emphasize the avian aspect to some extent, not least in order to attract the participation of developing countries, for whom the protection of waterfowl is unlikely to be considered the highest priority.

Central to the whole schema of the Convention is the creation under Article 2 of the List of Wetlands of International Importance, for which each party is obliged to designate at least one example upon signature, ratification, or accession. The boundaries of such sites are to be precisely described and delimited on a map, and may incorporate adjacent riparian and coastal zones, as well as islands and bodies of marine water deeper than 6 metres at low tide lying within the wetlands. The inclusion of a wetland in the list does not in any way prejudice the sovereign rights of the state in whose territory it is situated. States may add further sites, or extend existing ones, at any time but may also, on account of 'urgent national interests', restrict the boundaries of listed sites or delete them entirely. Wetlands are to be selected for the list on account of their international significance in terms of 'ecology, botany, zoology, limnology, or hydrology', though those of importance to waterfowl are singled out for priority attention. These rather vague principles have been the subject of clarification through the elaboration of more detailed criteria to govern the question of eligibility for listing.[13]

The substantive obligations relating to wetlands are set out in Articles 3 and 4. Under the former, the parties are to formulate and implement their planning so as to promote the conservation of listed sites and, as far as possible, the wise use of all wetlands in their territory. Once again, these vague and weakly drafted provisions have been the subject of considerable amplification through the establishment over time of a network of principles and criteria which now provide a reasonably sophisticated policy framework for the conservation and wise use of wetlands generally.[14] In addition, Article 3(2) provides that the parties must arrange to be informed at the earliest possible time of actual or likely changes in the ecological character of listed sites and transmit this information without delay to the Ramsar Bureau. The purpose of this provision is plainly to establish some form of international monitoring of the ecological condition of internationally important sites, and the Conference of the Parties is empowered under Article 6 to consider such information and to make appropriate recommendations to the parties.

Under Article 4, the parties are to promote the conservation of wetlands and waterfowl by establishing nature reserves on wetlands, whether included in the list or not, and to provide adequately for their wardening. In particular, where they delete or restrict the boundaries of listed sites, they are as far as possible to compensate for this through the creation of additional nature reserves. Supporting obligations relate to the encouragement of research and the exchange of information regarding wetlands, the training of personnel for wetland research, management, and wardening, and the attempt to increase waterfowl populations in such habitat.

The institutional arrangements under the Convention were initially rather rudimentary, with provision for only two organs, namely the Ramsar Bureau and a Conference of the Contracting Parties. As to the former, secretariat services are provided by IUCN – The World Conservation Union, which constitutes a most interesting example of a non-governmental organization providing formal services to sovereign states for the purposes of a particular treaty regime. This arrangement was originally intended to be only provisional, but has in fact endured to the present, with the bureau's role having been significantly consolidated during the late 1980s through the establishment of proper budgetary arrangements. As to the latter, the text of the Convention itself referred only to occasional, *ad hoc* conferences on the conservation of wetlands and waterfowl, but these have been transformed by the 1987 amendments into regular triennial meetings of a Conference of the Parties, with enhanced provision for decision making and financial matters. The most recent CoP was held at San José, Costa Rica, in 1999 and the next is scheduled for Valencia, Spain, in November 2002. These organs have subsequently been supplemented by a Standing Committee and a Scientific and Technical Review Panel (STRP), to deal with administrative and technical issues respectively. In addition, *ad hoc* committees and working groups have been extensively employed to handle particular tasks. The STRP is of particular interest in that, although its composition is determined on a regional basis, its members act in an individual capacity and not as representatives of their country of origin. Each contracting party is, however, encouraged to nominate its own qualified expert to act as a focal point for liaison with the STRP, which also maintains formal links with the scientific organs of other conservation conventions and with a range of technical organizations.[15]

A notable feature has been the very substantial involvement of NGOs in all aspects of Ramsar's programme of work. Indeed, it is plausible to claim that they have been more successfully integrated into the mainstream of activities under this Convention than under any other. Four such groups—IUCN itself, Birdlife International, Wetlands International, and the World Wide Fund for Nature—have been accorded the formal status of partner organizations for the purposes of the Convention.[16] Further confirmation of the importance of their role lies in the invitation to each of them to designate a representative 'to participate as a member of the STRP and to liaise with their relevant expert networks or specialist groups to provide the necessary expertise and advice' to the panel in undertaking its work plan.[17]

After a relatively slow start, Ramsar has been reasonably successful in attracting parties, of which there are now more than 130. The process of designating wetlands for the List of Wetlands of International Importance has also progressed quite steadily, and there are currently over 1100 sites occupying a total area in excess of 96 million hectares. They range from tiny sites of no more than 1 hectare, such as Ile Alcatraz in Guinea and Hosnie's Spring on Christmas Island, to the vast expanses of Canada's Queen Maud Gulf and the Okavango Delta in Botswana, each of which covers some 6–7 million hectares. Plainly, many states have gone far beyond the minimum obligation of designating one site, with the UK having listed more than150, though most of these are of relatively small size.

Implementation of Ramsar Obligations

In common with most international treaties, the prospects for the achievement of Ramsar's aims lie in achieving a successful blend and balance between action at the national and international levels. An interesting illustration of this approach may be found in the process of enhancing awareness of wetland values and functions. This has been confirmed as a key objective of the Ramsar system and is pursued through its Outreach Programme, embracing activity at a variety of levels.[18] This includes the development at the national level of educational programmes concerning wetlands, both through formal academic instruction and, more generally, through provision of information to the public at zoos, museums, and dedicated wetland centres; the organization at the regional level of conferences and workshops devoted to wetland issues; and, globally, the dissemination of information by the Ramsar Bureau itself. The development of an impressive website, together with the preparation of a regular newsletter and numerous specialist publications,[19] demonstrate that the bureau has been particularly active in this regard. Nevertheless, when it comes to the implementation of substantive commitments to sustainable development, experience of conservation treaties generally suggests that the practical limitations of international institutions in terms of powers, finance, and resources, reinforced by the still strong attachment to the concept of national sovereignty, tend to result in the primary emphasis being placed upon national activities and agencies. The role of international agencies lies principally in the realms of monitoring. An effective system of reporting by states upon national measures adopted in implementation of their obligations provides the necessary link between these two aspects.

Implementation at the National Level [20]

Site Designation

An important first step in this regard is the designation of sites for the List of Wetlands of International Importance. The current *Strategic Framework and Guidelines for the Future Development of the List*, adopted at CoP 7 in 1999,[21] sets an ambitious target of 2000 sites to be designated by 2005, which represented an increase of over 100 per cent on the number of sites listed at that time. The CoP has continually encouraged parties to go beyond the minimum obligation of listing one site, and several have added repeatedly to their original list of designations, with Australia, Italy, and the UK especially prominent in that regard. Nevertheless, it was noted at CoP 7 that around 550 of all designated sites were located in just 13 countries, while 69 parties had fewer than five sites and 35 had not gone beyond the minimum of one designated wetland. Naturally, much depends on geographical circumstances—island/peninsular states located on bird migration flyways (such as Italy and the UK) are likely to include numerous important coastal wetlands, while, by contrast, Azraq Oasis in Jordan is reckoned to be that country's only wetland of significance to waterfowl—but there is plainly considerable scope for further expansion of the list. It is not simply a matter of mere numbers, however, and CoP resolutions have frequently drawn attention to the need to secure the designation of particular wetland types which are under-represented in the list and/or subject to particular risk of degradation, such as peatlands and inter-tidal wetlands.[22]

It is clear in this context that much depends upon states themselves possessing full and reliable information regarding their own wetland resources, and the parties have been urged to undertake a full inventory in accordance with agreed criteria and standards.[23] At San José, some 67 parties reported that there was in existence for their country or region a directory of potential Ramsar sites, while 46 indicated that they had undertaken a national inventory of wetlands in their territory and a further 41 that they intended to do so in the near future. However, a report by Wetlands International tended to confirm suspicions that many of these inventories covered only the more important sites or merely part of the national territory, and a relatively modest target was therefore set of 50 parties having completed a full inventory by the time of the next CoP in 2002.

National Wetland Policies and Institutions

A significant proportion of the activities undertaken within the Ramsar system has been directed towards the establishment of a clear policy framework for the conservation and wise use of wetlands, and a crucial indicator of the success achieved by the Convention concerns the extent to which such principles have been embraced at the national level. The adoption and implementation of a national wetland policy has emerged as one of the highest Ramsar priorities, and recently approved guidelines are intended to assist in that regard.[24] While in 1993 only two parties (Canada and Uganda) had formally adopted such policies, by 1999 the number had expanded to 22. A further 31 indicated that such policies were currently under development, while 24 others advised that such instruments were planned for the near future. A goal of 100 parties with national wetland policies or similar strategies integrated within broader environmental/water policies was set for CoP 8.

The review of national laws and institutions in order to ensure their compatibility with the Ramsar obligations of conservation and wise use is also an important priority.[25] At San José it was reported that some 45 parties had completed such reviews and that in 36 cases this had resulted in the adoption of appropriate revisions or amendments. It remained unclear, however, to what precise extent these reviews had been effective in promoting Ramsar objectives. Once again, a target was set of 100 parties having undertaken such reviews by CoP 8. One specific institutional development which is considered desirable is the establishment of a national wetland committee to provide a focus for domestic implementation of the Convention,[26] and 52 parties indicated at San José that they had established such a group (which in most cases incorporated some non-governmental representation), while 87 in total had introduced at least some kind of mechanism for securing co-operation between agencies responsible for wetland-related activities. Since only 21 national committees had been in existence just four years earlier, this was counted reasonable progress. A goal was set for 2002 of establishing co-ordinating mechanisms in *all* contracting parties and formal national committees in 100 of those. A similar process of identifying progress, priorities, and targets with respect to other Ramsar objectives, including the integration of the conservation and wise-use principle into domestic planning and decision-making processes, the conduct of environmental impact assessments, and the training of appropriate personnel, was also undertaken.

The relatively 'soft' nature of most Ramsar obligations suggests that this strategy of coaxing governments towards the progressive adoption of appropriate mechanisms and policies for wetland conservation is generally sound and sensible, though there is a risk that the emphasis upon simple quantitative indicators may operate to the detriment of qualitative aspects. The record reveals that the Ramsar institutions are alive to this risk, though measurement of the *actual effectiveness* of wetland policies is, of course, a much more complex and problematic business than simply the head-counting processes referred to above.

Site Management

One obvious indicator of the extent to which contracting parties have successfully implemented their Ramsar obligations concerns the ongoing ecological condition of sites on the list, the preservation of which represents one of the principal objectives of the Ramsar system.[27] The achievement of this goal clearly depends upon effective management at site level, and the identification and implementation of conservation and management priorities for each site consequently constitutes an important aspect of the wise-use concept. At CoP 7, management plans were reported to be in place for 416 listed sites, which then represented some 44 per cent of the total. The aim was to increase this proportion by CoP 8 to 75 per cent of the sites in each contracting party, as well as to ensure the effective implementation of such plans.

Where effective management is lacking, there is an obvious risk that environmental quality will deteriorate, and it is in these circumstances that the duty to report adverse changes may come into play. At San José, some 35 parties reported such changes in well over 100 listed sites, with two indicating that *all* their designated wetlands were at risk. Of course, it is extremely difficult to judge the extent to which this represents an accurate reflection of the ecological condition of listed sites generally, since there is a significant chance that adverse changes may go unreported. Indeed, discussions at the 26th meeting of the Standing Committee in December 2001[28] emphasized the extent to which NGOs, rather than governments themselves, had been responsible for initiating the process of identifying ecological deterioration. On the one hand, this provides welcome confirmation of the vital role to be played by the non-governmental sector, but, on the other, it offers little reassurance regarding the existence of genuine political will or technical capacity on the part of governments to give effect to the environmental commitments they have undertaken.

In circumstances where wetland habitat has been seriously degraded or lost entirely, there is an obvious need to retard or reverse such processes, and consideration has accordingly been given to the question of wetland restoration.[29] At CoP 7, no fewer than 76 parties reported that some restoration or rehabilitation work had been undertaken, though it was conceded that most of this was on a relatively minor scale. A target was set of all parties having identified priority sites for restoration by 2002, with projects actively under way in 100 of those.

Reports on Implementation

The ability to monitor progress in the fashion outlined above plainly depends on the appropriate information being forthcoming from the parties through submission of their national reports upon implementation. In fact the text of Ramsar establishes no obligation in that regard, but the majority of parties did comply with a request to present national reports at the first meeting of the CoP, and this has become an established feature of the system. Response rates have fluctuated somewhat over the years, and attempts have been made to ensure that the format of reports is kept under review so as to avoid the creation of excessive burdens. At San José, satisfaction was expressed that reports had been provided by 107 of the then 113 parties,[30] which represents a reasonably impressive return by the standards of environmental treaties generally.

Implementation at the International Level

As with so many other aspects of the Convention, the arrangements established in the actual text regarding implementation of the substantive obligations it imposed were extremely sketchy, and it has subsequently proved necessary to expand upon these through the evolving practice of the parties.

The Role of the Conference of the Parties

Under Article 6(2)(a), the CoP is given a general power to discuss the implementation of the Convention and, as indicated above, this is supplemented by further, more specific powers, including the discussion of changes to the List of Wetlands of International Importance, the consideration of information regarding ecological change at listed sites, the making of general or specific recommendations regarding the conservation, management, and wise use of wetlands and their flora and fauna, and the acquisition of data and statistics on wetland issues. At each meeting of the CoP, resolutions or recommendations are adopted relating to particular sites. At San José, for example, proposals to establish extensive waterway links between various countries in Central and Eastern Europe were noted with concern, and the parties were urged to undertake full environmental impact assessments. On the positive side, the CoP acknowledged the significant efforts made by the Spanish authorities to address the impacts of the escape of toxic mining waste upstream of the Donana site and urged the continuation of all possible measures to maintain its ecological character. Following repeated expressions of concern, the CoP acknowledged the efforts of the Greek government to improve the condition of its Ramsar sites through the adoption of management plans and legislative measures, with significant progress recorded at Lake Miki Prespa, Lake Kirkini, and the Evros Delta.[31]

The Montreux Record and Related Developments

Over the course of time, the Ramsar Conference of the Parties has considerably developed these basic arrangements, although it remains the case that the system is heavily oriented towards the facilitation of compliance, rather than the imposition of enforcement measures. One important step was the establishment at the 1987 meeting of the CoP of the so-called Montreux Record of sites which are undergoing changes in their ecological character, which broadly parallels the List of World Heritage in Danger provided for in Article 11(4) of the World Heritage Convention. Wetlands currently so recorded include Lac Tonga (Algeria), Donau-March-Auen (Austria), Srebarna (Bulgaria), Laguna del Tigre (Guatemala), Keolodeo National Park (India), Azraq Oasis (Jordan), Ichkeul (Tunisia), the Ouse Washes (UK), and the Everglades (USA). Iran and Greece each have a number of sites on the record. Parties are required to report upon measures which have been taken to safeguard such sites, with a view to their ultimate removal from the record. At San José, it was reported that several sites could be so removed, among them Ringkobing Fjord in Denmark, Tendrivska and Yagorlytska Bays in Ukraine, and three sites in Greece. The procedure for operation of the record has been modified over the years and, although the possibility of its initiation by non-state entities has been retained, the recent modifications suggest a determination on the part of states not to lose control of the process.[32] Significantly, both the decisions to incorporate sites in and remove them from the record is ultimately that of the state in whose territory they are located, and it is plain that there are substantially fewer sites on the record (59 by late 2001) than those in respect of which adverse changes have been reported. It may well be argued that the existing system is unduly deferential to considerations of national sovereignty.

It is important to understand that the Montreux Record itself is not intended primarily as a finger-pointing exercise, and that various forms of assistance may be available to states with sites in danger. Chief among these is the procedure currently known as the Ramsar Advisory Mission (originally the Monitoring Procedure), which generally involves a site visit by a multi-disciplinary team of wetland experts who produce a detailed analysis of the situation and recommendations for remedial action. Around 50 of these missions have now been organized, with recent instances involving sites in the Czech Republic, Germany, Bulgaria, Argentina, and the UK. In several cases there have been joint missions with other agencies, such as IUCN and the World Heritage Committee.

A further important development was the establishment in 1990 of a fund, now known as the Ramsar Small Grants Fund (SGF), designed to provide assistance to developing countries and economies in transition with various aspects of wetland conservation and management. It was reported at CoP 7 that the SGF had provided funding for 113 small projects in such countries to a total amount of SFr3,815,821. These have been devoted to such purposes as the study and improvement of individual listed sites, the development of management plans at both site and national level, the training and equipping of staff, the support of regional meetings and workshops, and the conduct of studies preparatory to states joining the Convention. The resources available to the fund are modest, however, and it was noted at San José that the projects funded represented fewer than half of those submitted by eligible countries. The stated aim was to increase the fund's resources to $US1 million per annum.[33] By March 2002, total contributions to the Fund from its inception amounted to almost SFr 5 million. During the year 2001 a further 14 projects were supported, to a total of SFr 556,304. The provision of funding also operates at the regional level through the Wetlands for the Future Fund, administered jointly by the Ramsar Bureau and the US authorities, which in recent years has contributed some $US250,000 per annum towards capacity building in Latin American countries.[34] In addition, it should not be overlooked that substantial funding for wetland-related projects may be available from external sources, including the GEF, and that if such applications relate to Ramsar activities or listed sites it may well boost their prospects of success.

Direct Co-operation among the Parties

These activities may also be seen within the wider context of Article 5 of the Ramsar Convention, which requires the parties to consult with each other about implementing obligations arising from the Convention, especially with regard to transboundary wetlands and shared water systems. Furthermore, they are to 'endeavour to co-ordinate and support present and future policies and regulations concerning the conservation of wetlands and their flora and fauna'. The collaborative effort envisaged by this provision may operate at a variety of levels. As regards transboundary wetlands there are already a number of co-operative arrangements in existence, the best known of which is perhaps the tripartite mechanism established by Denmark, Germany, and the Netherlands regarding the Wadden Sea.[35] Other examples relate to Lake Victoria and the Lake Chad Basin. In 1999, at CoP 7, detailed guidelines were established to regulate the question of international co-operation,[36] and the following year saw a joint mission to the Djoudj/Diawling sites in Senegal and Mauritania. As regards shared water systems, a recent report prepared by the World Conservation Monitoring Centre revealed that, of around 1000 Ramsar sites surveyed, some 28 per cent fell within international river basins, and guidelines were also established to deal with this particular aspect of Article 5.[37] Fortunately this is an area in which co-operation is now relatively well established, and it was noted that there were already in existence more than 200 such agreements at the international or regional levels. Finally, a number of co-operative arrangements have now been established for the conservation and management of wetland flora and fauna, especially migratory waterbirds, among them the North American Waterfowl Management Plan, the Western Hemisphere Shorebird Reserve Network, and the Asia-Pacific Migratory Waterbird Conservation Strategy.

In addition, there are various other means by which states may benefit from each other's experience and resources. One interesting possibility concerns the 'twinning' or 'networking' of sites in different countries, an idea which has been adopted by France and Romania regarding their Camargue and Danube Delta sites and, trilaterally, by Papua New Guinea, Australia, and Indonesia with respect to the Tonda Wildlife Management Area, Kakadu National Park, and Wasur National Park. Such arrangements are designed to encourage the sharing of information, expertise, and resources in relation to the management of similar sites or those linked by migration routes. They may accordingly provide a framework for the provision of development assistance of a targeted kind or the exchange of personnel for training purposes. It was noted at CoP 7 that this was an idea which had been under-exploited, however, with only 25 parties reporting the adoption of such arrangements. A target was set of 100 twinning arrangements in place by CoP 8. More generally, there are considerable opportunities for affluent countries to provide assistance to the less developed members of the international community, as exemplified by the joint project between Mauritania and the Netherlands regarding the sustainable utilization of the Banc d'Arguin. Finally, there is now substantial evidence of co-operative activities, particularly seminars and workshops, at the regional level, prompted in large part by the emergence of a committee structure based upon regional representation.[38]

Conclusions

The above survey demonstrates the considerable progress which has been made in the realms of wetland conservation over the thirty years since the Ramsar Convention was concluded, not least in the rehabilitation of the image of wetland features in human consciousness. Although the provisions of the Convention as originally drafted were deficient in various respects, a great deal of time and effort has been devoted to their clarification, amplification, and development, primarily through CoP resolutions, and this has undoubtedly enhanced the potential of Ramsar to advance the cause of wetland conservation.[39] The general strategy of coaxing the parties gradually towards the adoption of progressive and sustainable policies of wetland management is undoubtedly the correct one, though care must be taken to ensure that the current emphasis upon simple, quantitative indicators is not allowed to mask underlying problems of a more substantive nature. Furthermore, it must not be overlooked that Ramsar activities are occurring against a background of constantly increasing demands for economic development, and that there are still few signs that nature conservation has yet been translated to its proper place at the heart of the political decision-making process. In that context the symbolic significance of Ramsar listing may occasionally yield ostensibly more dramatic benefits in the struggle to forestall environmentally damaging development projects, such as the decision by South Africa, as reported at CoP 6, to abandon a scheme for mining at the St Lucia site or the announcement by Trinidad and Tobago at a recent Standing Committee meeting that a proposal for development at Nariva Swamp had been withdrawn following a complaint by a tourist!

The pertinent question, to conclude, is not so much whether the Ramsar Convention has made a difference, but whether that difference will prove sufficient in the long term. For, unlike the fictional exploits of celebrated detectives, the story of wetland conservation is by no means one where eventual success can be taken for granted from the outset. Rather, as with the Grimpen Mire, it presents the risk that, unless a safe and true path is plotted through the morass, even renowned experts may ultimately flounder.

Notes and References

1. Originally serialized in the *Strand* magazine in 1901–2 and published as a book in 1902; see Sir Arthur Conan Doyle (1981 edn), *The Hound of the Baskervilles* (London/New York/ Ringwood/Toronto/Auckland: Penguin Books).
2. In Patrick J. Dugan (ed.) (1993), *Wetlands in Danger* (London: Mitchell Beasley), Foreword.
3. See, e.g., the Ballad of Long Lankin, a modern rendition of which may be found on the 1975 Steeleye Span album *Commoners Crown* (Chrysalis Records): 'Beware the moss, beware the moor, beware of Long Lankin. Be sure the doors are bolted well, lest Lankin should creep in.'
4. See generally Dugan, *Wetlands in Danger*, 44–7.
5. 1971 Convention on Wetlands of International Importance especially as Waterfowl Habitat, 996 UNTS 245. For the decision in question, see Action 3.1.5., Strategic Plan 1997–2002, Brisbane Proceedings, Vol.5/12.
6. Edward Maltby (1991), 'Wetlands and their Values', in Max Finlayson and Michael Moser (eds.), *Wetlands* (Oxford/New York: Facts on File), 8.
7. *Ibid.*
8. See generally Michael J. Bowman (1999), 'International Treaties and the Global Protection of Birds: Part I', *Journal of Environmental Law* 11, 87, 88–9, and authorities there cited.
9. 'Outside the sun was sinking low and the west was blazing with scarlet and gold. Its reflection was shot back in ruddy patches by the distant pools which lay among the Great Grimpen Mire.... All was sweet and mellow and peaceful in the golden evening light.' Conan Doyle (1981), *The Hound of the Baskervilles*.
10. For discussion of these aspects of the story, see the Sherlock Holmes Exhibition Catalogue, Part V—Some Scientific Problems, <http://www.westminsteronline.org/holmes 1951/ catalogue/p30.htm>.
(i) At p. 74 Watson and Stapleton discuss the possibility that the ghostly sound they have just heard was the booming of a bittern, 'a very rare bird—practically extinct—in England now'. The bittern is indeed a bird of wetland habitat, very occasionally found in the south-west of England, the booming cry of which is audible from up to 5 km. It became extinct in England around 1850 following the drainage of large areas of its habitat, but began to reappear around the turn of the century (when the story was written); resumption of breeding was confirmed in 1911. The British population peaked around 1950 and then declined again. However, 2001 was reported to be an excellent year for bitterns in the UK, with 30 breeding males (see *Reader's Digest* (2nd edn, 1974), *Book of British Birds*, 162; J. T. R. Sharrock (1976), *Atlas of Breeding Birds in Britain and Ireland* (Calton: T. & A. D. Poyser), 56–7; *Birds*, Royal Society for the Protection of Birds (spring 2002), 61. (ii) At p. 75 Stapleton breaks off their conversation to pursue what Watson describes as 'a small fly or moth', declaring that it 'is surely Cyclopides'. This name may be unfamiliar to modern enthusiasts but was apparently in use in the nineteenth century in relation to five species, one of which was found in Britain—the Chequered Skipper (*Carterocephalus Palaemon*). It is generally classified as a butterfly, though skippers are similar in appearance to moths and sometimes classified as a third sub-order of *Lepidoptera*, rendering Watson's description understandable. The Chequered Skipper is not found on Dartmoor, however, and the fictional specimen could plausibly only have been some other species of skipper. Since Stapleton was supposed to have been an entomological expert recognized by the British Museum, his error may seem less reasonable! (iii) At p. 76 Beryl Stapleton refers to the moor being rich in orchids and requests Watson to retrieve one growing 'among the mare's tails yonder'. Again, various species of orchid are found on Dartmoor and there has been speculation as to the one to which the author intended to refer.
11. On the background to the adoption of the Convention, see Geoffrey W. T. Matthews (1993), *The Ramsar Convention on Wetlands: Its History and Development* (Gland: Ramsar Bureau). Particularly prominent among the states which undertook preparatory work were the Netherlands and the Soviet Union, while the principal non-governmental contributions were made by the World Conservation Union (IUCN), the International Council for Bird Protection (ICBP), and the International Waterfowl Research Bureau (IWRB). See also note 16.
12. For more comprehensive analyses, see Simon Lyster (1985), *International Wildlife Law* (Cambridge: Grotius), ch.10; Michael J. Bowman (1995), 'The Ramsar Convention Comes of Age', *Netherlands International Law Review*, 42, 1 (also published in 2001 on the website of the Ramsar Convention, <http:// www.ramsar.org>).
13. For the current criteria, see Ramsar Resolution VII.11, Annex.
14. See REC. C.4.10 and RES. C.5.6.
15. See generally Resolution VII.2.
16. See Resolution VII.3. Birdlife International was formerly the International Council for Bird Preservation (ICBP); Wetlands International was recently formed through the amalgamation of the International Waterfowl and Wetlands Research Bureau (IWRB), which played a leading role in the drafting and elaboration of the Convention, the Asian Wetlands Bureau, and Wetlands for the Americas.
17. Resolution VII.2, para.8(c).
18. For the current Programme, see Resolution VII.9.
19. As to which, see the reference section in this *Yearbook*.
20. Details of many of the issues referred to may be found in the Ramsar Convention Work Plan, 2000–2002, Resolution VII.27, Annex.
21. Resolution VII.11.
22. As to which, see Recommendation 7.1 and Resolution VII.21.
23. Resolution VII.20.
24. Resolution VII.6.
25. Resolution VII.7.
26. REC. C.5.7.
27. Work Plan, General Objective 5.
28. A report of the meeting may be found on the Ramsar website, <http://www.ramsar.org>.
29. Resolution VII.17.
30. See Resolution VII.27, para.2. The remainder were urged to do so as soon as possible.
31. See generally Resolution VII.12.
32. Cf. the procedure as described in Resolutions C.5.4, Annex, and VI.1, Annex.
33. See generally Resolution VII.5.
34. See generally Recommendation 7.4.
35. See Jens A. Enemark (1993), 'Wise Use of the Wadden Sea', in T. J. Davis (ed.), *Towards the Wise Use of Wetlands* (Gland: Ramsar Convention Bureau).
36. Resolution VII.19.
37. Resolution VII.18.
38. On this point, see Resolution VII.1.
39. On this point particularly, see Bowman (1995), 'The Ramsar Convention Comes of Age'.

Friends of the Earth International

Keith Suter

A Movement within the Movement

This article examines Friends of the Earth International (FoEI). Given its diversity, FoEI is perhaps a 'movement' within the environmental movement. Its federal style of governance is very different from (say) the more centralized Greenpeace. While FoEI is the set of initials for the international headquarters (based at Amsterdam in the Netherlands—<www.foei.org>), it can also be seen as the totality of the Friends of the Earth groups around the world. To get a more accurate assessment of Friends of the Earth, the second, broader approach is the one used in this article: 'FoEI' is used to describe the entire movement, and 'Friends of the Earth' refers to a particular grouping within that movement.

The article begins with an overview of FoEI as an organization and a summary of its history. It then looks at the list of FoEI campaigns and makes some assessments of the organization. It concludes with some challenges confronting FoEI. In essence, the entire environment movement in 2002 has progressed since 1972; although the threats to the environment remain clear, just what should be done about them is not so apparent.

Organization

FoEI is an environmental non-governmental organization (NGO), with observer status at several intergovernmental organizations (such as FAO, IMO, UNEP, and the International Whaling Commission). Its objectives are: to protect the Earth against deterioration and to repair damage inflicted upon the environment as a result of human activity and negligence; to preserve the Earth's ecological, cultural, and ethnic diversity; to increase public participation and democratic decision making in the protection of the environment and the management of natural resources; to achieve social, economic, and political justice and equal access to resources and opportunities on a local, national, and international level; and to promote environmental sustainable development on a local, national, and global level.

FoEI membership is based on national member groups and affiliated NGOs. Each national member group is an autonomous body with its own budget (which also makes contributions to the FoEI Secretariat). There is a total of 66 national groups in 64 countries and one territory. Within the national groups there are about one million members world-wide, thereby making FoEI one of the world's largest environment NGOs. There are also 12 affiliated NGOs.

The FoEI International Secretariat has nine professional staff and four volunteers. The Secretariat handles a budget of around EUR 1,167,000 (2002), which comes from national member groups and philanthropic bodies in Europe and the USA. The FoEI Secretariat co-ordinates the movement's activities at the international level. The agenda is very broad, with campaigns and projects running on energy/climate change, mining, wetlands, international financial institutions, genetically modified organisms, forests, ecological debt, desertification, Rio+10, transnational corporations, and environmentally sustainable trade. FoEI has also maintained its interests in such long-standing subjects as Antarctica and maritime issues. This range of issues would permit the organization to claim to have one of the most ambitious agendas of any environment NGO.

FoEI has a wide range of activities and techniques. It is engaged in rallies and demonstrations; it lobbies governments, political parties, corporations, and unions; it uses the Internet, the media, and community education programmes to convey information. One of the reasons why people get attracted to the organization is the wide variety of forms of participation it offers.

History

FoEI was created by the late David Brower (1912–2000), an American environmental activist.[1] Brower was a determined, passionate, abrasive, single-minded defender of the environment who was nominated for the Nobel Peace Prize three times (1978, 1979, and 1989). In 1952 Brower (a former World War II combat soldier) became the Sierra Club's first executive director, at a time when the club was a group of about 2000 wealthy Californians interested in hiking, photography, and picnics. He transformed the organization into one that campaigned to save the environment. In Brower's time the membership went up to 80,000 members nation-wide with assets of over $US3 million. The increase in funding and members was attributed to Brower's innovative use of unorthodox advertising campaigns showing the ravages of economic exploitation on animals and the environment. Although these were then novel approaches, they are now standard techniques. Brower opposed the creation of two additional dams in the USA's Grand Canyon. The Sierra Club won the argument and so beat the government agencies in favour of the dams. The government retaliated by removing the club's tax-exempt status, in order to damage its financial basis. Under US law, organizations that receive such status can devote only a limited part of their time and resources to influencing government policy. Brower continued his campaigns by taking on nuclear power and the big energy utilities. This means that he was also an early opponent of nuclear power (something which is now commonplace among the environment movement, not least FoEI).[2] In May 1969 Brower was removed by the Sierra Club board because he was seen as too controversial and he was offending potential donors (such as those in the nuclear power industry).

Fired with zeal to do even more to protect the environment, Brower that same year immediately formed Friends of the Earth. Ultimately, his passionate style became too much for that organization as well, and so he was driven out of it in 1984. There were complaints about his chaotic style of working and his interfering in the day to day operation of the organization. (Brower then formed a third organization—Earth Island Institute—and continued campaigning on environmental matters right up until his death.)

Friends of the Earth was created as a new type of environmental NGO: aggressive, skilled in using the media, politically active, and drawn from a cross-section of the community. The new organization had a broad political aim: protecting the environment in its widest possible sense. It also had the capacity to become an international organization concerned with the bigger issues of the environment. While it began in the USA, it soon developed separate local branches around the world. By January 1971 FoEI had acquired its international status through the participation of delegates from European countries. This internationalization enabled it to be accepted onto the roster of NGOs recognized by the UN Economic and Social Council (ECOSOC), thereby permitting FoEI to have 'observers' at UN conferences (with the right to watch proceedings but not to vote and with no automatic right to speak).[3]

The organization's popularity was due to the nature of the cause. There was a genuine concern about the state of the world, and many people were worried about the direction in which current trends were heading. The first Earth Day (in which the organization was heavily involved) took place on 22 April 1970, and 20 million Americans took part in demonstrations and seminars. Another indicator of the increasing concern about the environment was the popularity of such books as the Club of Rome's *Limits to Growth*, published in early 1972.[4]

In June 1972 the United Nations held the Stockholm Conference on the Human Environment. Peter Stone was then a UN official helping to organize the conference. His resulting book[5] recalled the assistance that the new organization gave to the conference with its publications. These included the free daily magazine issued during the conference called *Eco*—the first of many such editions of this lively, *ad hoc*, irreverent publication. FoEI was one of the most active of the approximately 300 NGOs that attended. It had made its mark among a crowded field of NGOs.

FoEI Campaigns

As at April 2002, FoEI had 12 broad campaign areas, grouped under three headings. The first six are on 'safeguarding Earth'. On climate change, FoEI is committed to the substantial reduction of global greenhouse-gas emissions and to increasing the use of alternative energy to combat the dangerous consequences of global warming. It believes that only through an equitable distribution of the Earth's finite resources, based on renewable energy, energy efficiency, and sustainable consumption patterns, can we avoid disastrous changes in climate and provide a better quality of life for all people.

On genetically modified organisms (GMOs), FoEI is allied to the sceptics, who doubt that GMOs will be as safe from contamination as predicted by GMO corporations. FoEI questions both the need for GMOs (when there are other, less capital-intensive farming methods available) and the wisdom of relying so heavily on corporations supplying the organisms.

On forests, FoEI is committed to the conservation of all remaining forest ecosystems and to the restoration of forest ecosystems. FoEI emphasizes the important—if neglected—role that forests play in maintaining the health of the planet: from keeping the water clean, to combating global warming, to maintaining the rich biodiversity of the planet.

On desertification, FoEI has publicized the dangers arising from the conversion of productive rangeland or cropland into desert through intensive land use (such as overgrazing) and the role that climate change is playing in eroding the quality of cropland. It has called for more sustainable and equitable approaches to land use.

On Antarctica, FoEI was one of the founder members in 1978 of the Antarctic and Southern Oceans Coalition (ASOC). ASOC now includes 240 NGOs in 50 countries and has observer status at intergovernmental conferences on Antarctica. It continues to campaign to protect the continent's biological diversity and pristine wilderness, including the surrounding oceans and marine life.

Finally, on maritime affairs, FoEI is particularly concerned about pollution at sea and the avoidance of over-exploitation of marine resources. It is an observer at the International Maritime Organization in London.

The second group of campaign areas are described as 'resisting economic globalization'. On international financial institutions (IFIs), FoEI has targeted the International Monetary Fund, the World Bank, and regional development banks (such as the Asian Development Bank). FoEI had three broadly defined objectives: IFIs should stop lending money for fossil fuel (oil and gas) and mining projects; there should be greater civil society control over IFIs (which tend to be run by international bureaucrats, hardly accountable to politicians in their member countries, let alone the general public); and there should be a break-up of the 'Washington Consensus' (an economic philosophy based on reducing government intervention in the economy, with more scope for the market system of economics and transnational corporations to operate).

On transnational corporations, FoEI sees their thirst for profits as a major cause of many environmental and social problems and so has urged that they should have greater social accountability. FoEI was one of the first environmental NGOs to recognize that saving the planet would require more attention to controlling transnational corporations. Unlike Greenpeace, which is entering into some dialogue with some transnational corporations, FoEI remains hostile to them and is insisting on far greater corporate accountability.

Finally, on mining, FoEI has argued for a radical reduction in the production of raw materials and a shift in worldwide consumption patterns. Mining and drilling have caused a range of social and environmental problems.

The third group is labelled 'finding solutions'. On trade, environment, and sustainability, FoEI has said that it is possible for trade to be harnessed as a positive force in the development of sustainable societies. However, this requires equity among countries, peoples, and generations, a reduction in resource use and consumption, and increased trade with local communities and regions, with guarantees that trade rules will not weaken environmental protection. There should also be greater public participation in decision making.

In its ecological debt campaign, FoEI has called for the recognition and payment of this debt. This is somewhat different from the international NGO Jubilee 2000 campaign for the relief of debt that is owed to northern banks by developing countries. FoEI has argued that the production and consumption patterns that drive northern economies cause environmental deterioration all over the world, and it has said that it is unjust that the richest 20 per cent of the world's population should consume 80 per cent of the planet's natural wealth. The extraction of this natural wealth for industrialized countries has also caused social and environmental damage in the South. FoEI wants rich northern governments to recognize that poor southern countries are owed an ecological debt and that the debt has to be repaid. In particular, it is necessary to restore areas in southern countries affected by the extraction of natural resources and export monocultures so that local and national communities are able to recover their capacity for self-sufficiency. There should also be the repatriation of cultural and natural heritage and the elimination of all weapons of mass destruction and toxic substances that threaten the life of the planet.

Finally, FoEI has said that it is producing a 'radical and comprehensive' document to go to the World Summit on Sustainable Development in September 2002. Its early assessment of the conference's preparations was hostile, with documents on its website suggesting that the conference would not achieve much.

To conclude, here are three observations about FoEI's campaigns. First, this is an impressive range of issues. But how deep do they go? In other words, the campaigns contain many aspirational points, but it is not clear under each one just how effective FoEI actually is. On Antarctica, for example, there is little happening because there is little to happen: mining has been stopped but the exploitation of living resources proceeds. Meanwhile, media and governments are no longer so concerned about the continent.

Second, the list provides an infrastructure; even if there is little happening at this very moment, it is there for when it is needed. Taking the example of Antarctica, there may be an increase in government and media interest if the current rate of global warming continues and there is a consequent melting of the ice sheet. The media and concerned individuals will know where to go because FoEI has maintained the issue on its list of campaigns.

Finally, the highly devolved nature of FoEI's organization may be seen in the way that almost every campaign has a different website contact person in each country. FoEI is not a highly centralized organization with a large international secretariat; rather, it relies on its colleagues in national sections.

Assessing FoEI

What, therefore, can be said about FoEI overall? First, it has survived. Environmental issues go in cycles, and some NGOs fold during the downturn in the cycles. But FoEI has kept going for over three decades, during which time many other environmental NGOs have collapsed. Its organizational culture of youthful energy and creative demonstrating has helped draw and maintain supporters, not least when the public's attention has been diverted to other matters (such as the need to fight economic downturns).

All political issues move in cycles. There are times when environmental issues have a particular 'salience' in the media. 'Salience' refers to 'the sense of urgency attached to doing something about a particular matter or issue'.[6] For example, the US political scientist M. J. Peterson has applied the term to the rise and fall of public concern about environmental issues, in particular Antarctica (a matter in which FoEI has been involved for much of the organization's life, notably as 'observers' at governmental conferences).[7] Environmental issues have risen and fallen. The concern over Antarctica is a good example of what was a major issue in the 1980s and is far less of one in 2002. But FoEI is probably as strong now as it has ever been in terms of global membership numbers and finances. It has been able to tailor its campaigns to fit the emerging issues (or even to help create those emerging issues).

This continued existence is all the more amazing given FoEI's diverse campaign agenda. Professional marketing companies would advise an organization to concentrate on just a few key topics. But FoEI has opted for a very broad-based approach—and it has still managed to survive. It has not fragmented over disagreements between members over what should be covered, and it has not disappeared because it has spread itself too thinly trying to cover a lot of issues.

Second, FoEI has expanded the geographical spread of its membership. It is not an obviously US organization—it has a truly global, multicultural style. The Sierra Club, by contrast, remains very much an American NGO, based in the USA, with US members and mostly US interests. There is no problem with this form of national identity, of course, but FoEI's global image shows that it has been able to maintain Brower's original vision for it.

Besides having national sections in the USA and Western Europe, the organization has set up some national sections in developing countries and, in the past decade or so, in Eastern Europe. There is also Friends of the Earth Middle East (FoEME), whose projects include transboundary ecosystems, such as the Dead Sea basin, the Gulf of Aqaba, and the Eastern Mediterranean. FoEI has shown that it can find a home in a variety of political cultures.

It is interesting to note the speed with which FoEI took advantage of the end of the Cold War in 1990–91. The Sustainable Europe Campaign (SEC) network, organized by Friends of the Earth Europe, links 30 countries across greater Europe, from Ireland to Russia and Georgia, and from Scandinavia to Malta, in action research and campaigning to promote sustainable production and consumption. SEC, which began in 1992, is assessing what sustainable development means in practical terms and how this can be achieved. It is based on three principles (which in themselves show a broad definition of 'environment'): the need for (1) measurable progress towards sustainable production and consumption, that is, the Earth's carrying capacity; (2) balanced opportunities for development among all countries, including equal access to the world's resources; and (3) total quality of life rather than just materialism as a guiding force in public policy and values. The intention is to take the campaign's outcomes to other consumer societies, such as those in the USA and Japan.[7]

Also worth noting is the advantage that so many NGOs in developed countries (and to an increasing extent in developing countries) have received from the Internet and e-mail.[8] These technologies have considerably enhanced the ability to communicate at great speed across national boundaries, in particular in sharing information and preparing for co-ordinated campaigns.

Third, FoEI has maintained the vision of an active, broad-based membership. There is no one standard FoE activist or member. Members are recruited for what they can contribute to the work. For some, it could be financial donations, while others may have more time but less money available and so serve as a volunteer. FoEI's flexibility enables people to do what they can.

Similarly FoEI's campaigns are characterized by flexibility and agility. The organization knows how to get media coverage. Indeed, Peter Stoett, in his study of the international politics of whaling, notes the ability of FoEI to attract media coverage to whatever cause is underway. For example, at a particularly tense time at the International Whaling Commission in 1979, FoEI held a demonstration that attracted 12,000 people in London and received more than 300 mentions in the media in a month. It was equally skilled in publicizing the dangers of the UK's nuclear energy policy, and to publicize the lack of progress on recycling there was a mailing of empty beverage cans to the British prime minister. Stoett writes admiringly that this 'type of media blitz has occurred with similar success rarely'.[9]

Fourth, FoEI has been good at 'global', 'national', and 'local' campaign themes. Indeed, it has been able to make good use of 'thinking globally and acting locally'. Another FoEI campaign has been that of saving the rainforests of

Sarawak, Malaysia, and working with the indigenous peoples there, the Penan. Al Gore, later US vice- president, recalled the time when he was a senator that the Penan sent a delegation to the USA, with the help of FoEI. The delegation alerted Gore to their plight—which he compared with the plight of peoples persecuted by the World War II Axis countries (Germany and Italy).[10] The US environmental lawyer Bruce Rich has been very critical of the World Bank and the exploitation of tropical rainforests. He has identified Friends of the Earth Malaysia as a good supporter of the Penan and a harsh critic of the World Bank's development projects in Sarawak.[11] Meanwhile, as an example of a local campaign, there is the publication by John Button for FoE-UK and FoE-Australia on the very basic issues of 'how to be green' in the home, in the garden, in eating, in looking after one's health and children, at work, and in transport.[12]

Finally, FoEI has taken a very broad definition of what are 'environmental' issues. As the preceding survey has shown, the organization has been involved in a variety of campaigns. Ramachandra Guha and Juan Martinez-Alier, writing from the point of view of developing countries, have been critical of the set of environmental values that underpin the campaigns of NGOs from developed countries, which they believe do not give enough attention to social justice issues, especially poverty. Thus, in the North there is the saying 'no humanity without nature', while in the South the phrase is 'no nature without social justice'.[13] FoEI endeavours to blend both. Indeed, with some of its national sections in the South, the movement is well aware of perspectives other than the northern ones.

Thus FoEI was part of the anti-MAI coalition and opposed some of the policies of the World Trade Organization (WTO). The Multilateral Agreement on Investment (MAI) was drafted in secrecy by the club of developed countries in the Organization for Economic Co-operation and Development (OECD) as a basic treaty to facilitate international investment. The intention was to create a 'level playing field' so that foreign corporations could invest as easily in a national project as the local companies; there could be no governmental reserving of projects for domestic companies. FoEI was among the network of NGOs that obtained drafts of the document and throughout 1998 and 1999 stimulated a public debate over the MAI's implications. The NGOs created the controversy and alerted the media to the secret agreement. Eventually the OECD governments withdrew the document. It was a great success for the NGOs.

Where to for FoEI?

This review ends with four speculations on the future of FoEI. The speculations apply generally to the environment movement, but FoEI is particularly vulnerable because it has defined 'environment' so broadly.

First, is there a risk that the environment movement is winning battles but losing the war? FoEI is just over thirty years old, and its lifetime encompasses much of the lifetime of the modern environment movement. A great deal has been achieved in those three decades. There are now national ministries of the environment, international environmental treaties, the UN Environment Programme, international conferences, and local, national, and international 'plans of environmental action', and citizens and the mass media are far more aware of environmental issues than ever before. FoEI was in at the beginning of this process—it predates almost all the items listed in the previous sentence—and it can claim some credit for the progress that has been made.

But we are still talking about an 'environmental crisis', and there is scientific speculation that the planet will encounter some major environmental problems (such as climate change). What has gone wrong? Individual battles have been won but overall the war is still being lost. There has not been, for example, a fundamental shift in the behaviour of people around the globe. Indeed, the signs are pointing the other way: there continues to be a consumerist society and there are rising expectations in all countries (no politician has yet become a head of government on an environment-protecting ticket, and all politicians promise continued economic growth). There is popular American support for President Bush's opposition to the Kyoto Protocol, China has ambitious programmes for its economic development (very much on the Western industrial model, with the inevitable problems of pollution, etc.), and there are similar economic programmes in India.

Somehow people are aware that there are environmental problems, but they are fatalistically resigned to carrying on with life almost as usual. The risk to FoEI—and all other environmental NGOs—is that public support will drift away as people become reconciled to living with environmental problems rather than taking the drastic actions necessary to prevent them.

To take an example from another field: alcoholism. Various national and local NGOs have been created during the past century or so to combat this problem. More people still die from alcohol in most societies than from narcotic drugs, and alcohol has decimated many indigenous peoples. But public opinion has become reconciled to living with the problems it causes rather than taking drastic steps to curb them. Those of us involved in anti-alcohol NGOs are now seen as quixotic participants in a lost cause. Could FoEI go the same way as people learn to live with environmental destruction?

Second, there is still—after three decades—no specific environmentalist ideology. FoEI has been very active in particular campaigns. It probably regards itself as more active in campaigns than any other environmental NGO. But while the activities are there, there is no basic, uniting belief system that underpins them. This may become more of a problem as FoEI increases its geographic spread and takes on an increasingly diverse range of national/local sections. What will hold all the national sections/local branches together? Diversity can be a great strength—but it can also be a great weakness.

Third, given FoEI's lack of an agreed political ideology, there is the problem of assessing where the organization falls in terms of the distinctions made by Andrew Dobson of the UK's University of Keele between 'environmentalism' and 'ecologism': 'environmentalism' argues for a managerial approach to environmental problems, secure in the belief that they can be solved without fundamental changes in present values or patterns of production and consumption, whereas 'ecologism' holds that a sustainable and fulfilling existence presupposes radical changes in our relationship with the non-human natural world, and in our mode of social and political life.[14] Dobson notes that the queen of England does not suddenly become a 'political ecologist' simply by having her fleet of limousines converted to lead-free petrol.

According to these definitions, FoEI would presumably see itself as a believer in ecologism. But it has not been effective in conveying that ideology—or in achieving major breakthroughs. Indeed, FoE-UK is one of the groups examined by Dobson as an example of how difficult it is to follow through with the latter ideology. He notes the problem FoE-UK had in the 1980s in its campaign to remove CFCs from aerosols. Although this was successful, the green political activists said that FoE-UK should have campaigned against all aerosols. By campaigning for CFC-free aerosols, FoE-UK was still condoning self-indulgence, vanity, and wholly unsustainable patterns of consumption.[15] In other words, FoE-UK was seen as too moderate by the greens. Ironically, Jonathan Porritt, one of the UK's best-known environmental campaigners, was both director of FoE-UK and a spokesperson for the Ecology Party. Indeed, Porritt is quoted as saying that, having written two general election manifestos for the UK Ecology Party, he 'would be hard put even now to say what our ideology is'.[16]

Works unite and teachings divide. People can be drawn together to focus on a common task (such as cleaning up from an oil spill) because there is a major job to be done. However, if, after the oil spill has been cleaned up, people are invited to explain why they were willing to assist in the work, there would be divisions of opinion and possibly an end to the friendly atmosphere. Some may have environmental reasons, others financial motives, and others religious grounds, etc. As long as the attention is on the common task, then there is co-operation. It is therefore easier for FoEI—and all other environmental NGOs—to keep the focus on the task rather than on the motivations. Thus avoiding matters of ideology enables the organization to keep going. If some members really thought through what would be required to deal with environmental problems (such as having no aerosols at all), then they might decide to learn to live with those problems. But if there is no clear vision, how do you know if you are winning (or losing)?

Finally, of which 'Earth' is FoEI a friend? Arne Naess of Norway has popularized the distinction between the 'shallow' and 'deep' ecology movements.[17] This has stimulated a debate over what 'Earth' environmentalists are setting out to save: the interests of humankind or, more generally, all life on the planet? I suggest that most people who support the environment movement are out to save themselves first; saving other species is incidental to that main task. Thus some people are active in saving whales but are willing to eat fish or meat. This is a variation of the 'environmentalism'–'ecologism' tension examined above. If FoEI is too radical, it could lose some of its members. But if it is not radical enough, it may not save the Earth.

To sum up, FoEI has been one of the world's most active environmental NGOs. It has achieved a great deal. But it has some large challenges ahead of it. The challenges are not unique for FoEI and apply in general terms to most of the other parts of the environment movement. FoEI's special vulnerability derives from its policy of defining the environment so broadly and trying to deal with so many issues.

Notes and References

1. Brower's death brought forth various tributes on the Internet. This section has drawn upon: 'The Arch-Druid Passes', *CounterPunch* (7 November 2000), <www.counterpunch.org/brower.html>; Daniel Coyle, 'The High Cost of Being David Brower', *Outside Mag* (December 1995), <www.outsidemag.com/magazine/1295/12f_high.html>; 'David Brower Dies', *Friends of the Earth – US News Release* (6 November 2000), <www.foe.org/act/browerrelease.html>; 'A Tribute in Quotes', *Earth Island Journal*, 16:1 (2001), <www.earthisland.org/eijournal>; and Clara Y. Milt, 'David Brower', *Internet Obituary Network*, <http://obits.com/browerdavid.html>.
2. See Michael Flood, Robin Grove-White, and Keith Suter (1977), *Uranium, the Law and You: A Comment on the Individual, the State and Nuclear Power* (Sydney: FOE Australia and British FOE).
3. See Sally Morphet (1996), 'NGOs and the Environment', in Peter Willetts (ed.), *The Conscience of the World: The Influence of Non-*

Governmental Organizations in the UN System (London: Hurst), 116–46.
4. Donella H. Meadows, Dennis L. Meadows, Jorgen Randers, and William W. Behrens (1972), *Limits to Growth: Report to the Club of Rome* (London: Pan).
5. Peter Stone (1975), *Did We Save the Earth at Stockholm? The People and Politics in the Conference on the Human Environment* (London: Earth Island), 52, 55, 133, 135–8.
6. M. J. Peterson (1988), *Managing the Frozen South: The Creation and Evolution of the Antarctic Treaty System* (Berkeley: University of California Press), 10.
7. Michael Carley and Ian Christie (2000), *Managing Sustainable Development* (London: Earthscan Publication), 281–5.
8. For example, see Jenny Pickerill (2001), 'Environmental Internet Activism in Britain', *Peace Review* [London] (September), 365–70.
9. Peter Stoett (1997), *The International Politics of Whaling* (Vancouver: University of British Columbia Press), 16, 95–6, 191.
10. Al Gore (1992), *Earth in the Balance: Forging a New Common Purpose* (London: Earthscan Publication), 284–5.
11. Bruce Rich (1994), *Mortgaging the Earth: The World Bank Environmental Impoverishment and the Crisis of Development* (London: Earthscan Publication), 133–4, 162.
12. John Button (1989), *How to be Green* (Sydney: Random House).
13. Ramachandra Guha and Juan Martinez-Alier (1997), *Varieties of Environmentalism: Essays North and South* (London: Earthscan Publication), 21.
14. Andrew Dobson (2000), *Green Political Thought* (London: Routledge), 2.
15. Ibid., 205.
16. Ibid., 13.
17. Arne Naess (1989), *Ecology, Community and Lifestyle* (Cambridge: Cambridge University Press).

Agreements on Environment and Development

Note to this section regarding adoption and status of participation of agreements

The terms used in this section, denoting various stages in the status of participation related to international agreements, are legal-technical ones, based on the Law of Treaties as contained in the 1969 Vienna Convention on the Law of Treaties and in the 1986 Vienna Convention on the Law of Treaties between States and International Organizations or between International Organizations, as well as in customary international law. To provide easier reference for readers who are not lawyers, some basic explanations of terms used in the treaty-making process are here provided.

Upon the negotiation of a treaty, there are often several stages required before it enters into force:

- *Adoption* is the formal act by which the form and content of a proposed treaty text are established. As a general rule, the adoption of the text of a treaty takes place through the expression of the consent of the states participating in the treaty-making process. As a rule, however, adoption does not yet mean a consent of a state to be bound by a treaty.
- *Signature* may sometimes be definitive, meaning that it establishes the consent of the state to be bound by the treaty. This is usual in most bilateral treaties. For multilateral treaties, however, the signature is as a rule not definitive, meaning that the treaty is subject to ratification, acceptance, or approval in order to enter into force. Although in those cases the signature does not establish the consent to be bound, it is a means of authentication and expresses the willingness of the signatory state to continue the treaty-making process (i.e. to proceed to ratification, acceptance, or approval). It also creates an obligation to refrain, in good faith, from acts that would defeat the object and the purpose of the treaty.
- *Ratification* defines an international act whereby a state indicates its consent to be bound to a treaty if the parties intended to show their consent by such an act. In the case of multilateral treaties the usual procedure is for the state to notify the depositary of its ratification; the depositary keeps all parties informed of the situation regarding ratifications. The institution of ratification grants states the necessary time-frame to seek the required approval for the treaty on the domestic level and to enact the necessary legislation to give domestic effect to that treaty.
- *Acceptance* or *approval* have the same legal effect as ratification and consequently express the consent of a state to be bound by a treaty. In the practice of certain states, acceptance and approval have been used instead of ratification when, at a national level, constitutional law does not require the treaty to be ratified by the head of state.
- *Act of formal confirmation* is used as an equivalent for the term 'ratification' when an international organization expresses its consent to be bound to a treaty.
- *Entry into force* of an international treaty does not necessarily coincide with its ratification (acceptance, approval) by individual states. It is common for multilateral treaties to provide for a fixed number of states to express their consent for entry into force. Some treaties provide for additional conditions to be satisfied, e.g. by specifying that a certain category of states must be among the consenters. The treaty may also provide for an additional time period to elapse after the required number of countries have expressed their consent or the conditions have been satisfied. A treaty enters into force for those states which gave the required consent. A treaty may also provide that, upon certain conditions having been met, it shall come into force provisionally.
- *Accession* is the act whereby a state accepts the offer or the opportunity to become a party to a treaty already negotiated and signed by other states. It has the same legal effect as ratification. Accession usually occurs after the treaty has entered into force. The conditions under which accession may occur and the procedure involved depend on the provisions of the treaty; a treaty might provide for the accession of all other states or for a limited and defined number of states.

Convention on Access to Information, Public Participation in Decision Making and Access to Justice in Environmental Matters (Århus Convention)

Objectives
To guarantee the rights of access to information, public participation in decision making, and access to justice in environmental matters in order to contribute to the protection of the right of every person of present and future generations to live in an environment adequate to his or her health and well-being.

Scope
Legal scope
Open to member countries of the UN Economic Commission for Europe (UNECE), regional economic integration organizations constituted by sovereign States members of the UNECE (e.g. the European Union), other states having consultative status with the UNECE, and any other States members of the UN.

Geographic scope
Regional. UNECE region (Europe and North America). Potentially global.

Time and place of adoption
25 June 1998, Århus.

Entry into force
30 October 2001.

Status of participation
20 ratifications, approvals, acceptances, or accessions by 10 June 2002. 25 Signatories, including the European Community, without ratification, acceptance, or approval.

The Secretary-General of the UN acts as depositary.

Affiliated instruments and organizations
The Convention also contains two *annexes* which form an integral part of the Convention.

The Executive Secretary of the UNECE carries out the secretariat functions.

Co-ordination with related instruments
No formal co-ordination yet, but mechanisms for co-ordination are expected to be developed with other UNECE environmental conventions having provisions on public participation, in particular the Convention on Environmental Impact Assessment in a Transboundary Context, the Convention on the Protection and Use of Transboundary Watercourses and International Lakes, and the Convention on the Transboundary Effects of Industrial Accidents (see this section).

Secretariat
UN Economic Commission for Europe (UNECE),
Environment and Human Settlements Division (ENHS),
Bureau 332,
Palais des Nations,
CH-1211 Geneva 10,
Switzerland
Telephone: +41-22-9172384
Telefax: +41-22-9070107/9170634
E-mail: public.participation@unece.org

Secretary to the Convention
Mr Jeremy Wates.

Finance
To be decided by the first Meeting of the Parties.

Rules and standards
The Convention requires Parties to ensure that the public has access to environmental information, can participate in environmental decision making, and have access to a review procedure before a court of law or an independent and impartial body in environmental matters.

The general provisions of the Convention cover aspects important for the implementation of the Convention, such as compatibility among its elements, guidance to the public in taking advantage of it, environmental education and awareness building, and support to groups promoting environmental protection. The general provisions make it clear that the Convention is a floor, not a ceiling. Parties may introduce measures for broader access to information, more extensive public participation in decision making, and wider access to justice in environmental matters than required by the Convention. The Convention also makes it clear that existing rights and protection beyond those of the Convention may be preserved and that the public shall benefit from these rights without discrimination as to citizenship, nationality, or domicile.

The Convention stands on three 'pillars': access to information, public participation, and access to justice. Access to information, the first pillar, concerns the right of the public to seek information from public authorities and the obligation of public authorities to provide information in response to a request; it also concerns the right of the public to receive information and the obligation of authorities to collect and disseminate information of public interest without the need for a specific request.

The second pillar of the Convention, concerning public participation, relies upon the other two pillars for its effectiveness—the information pillar to ensure that the public can participate in an informed fashion, and the access-to-justice pillar to ensure that participation happens in reality and not just on paper. The public-participation pillar is divided into three parts. The first part lays down quite detailed rules concerning the participation by the public that may be affected by or is otherwise interested in decision making on a specific activity; the activities are listed in Annex I to the Convention. The second and third parts concern in less detail the participation of the public in the development of plans, programmes, and policies relating to the environment and of laws, rules, and legally binding norms.

The third pillar of the Convention, concerning access to justice, enforces both the information and the participation pillars in domestic legal systems, and strengthens enforcement of domestic environmental law.

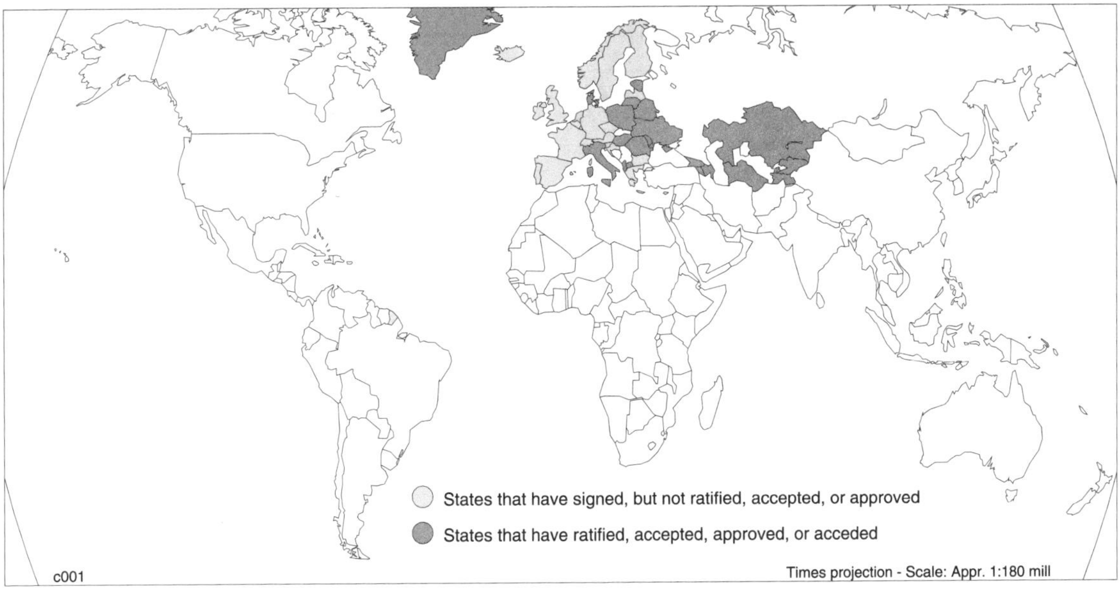

Specific provisions enforce the provisions of the Convention that convey rights onto members of the public, articles 4 and 6. The access-to-justice pillar also provides a mechanism for the public to enforce environmental law directly.

Monitoring/implementation

Review procedure

The Parties to the Convention shall keep under continuous review the implementation of the Convention and, with this purpose in mind:

• review the policies for and legal and methodological approaches to access to information, public participation in decision making, and access to justice in environmental matters, with a view to further improving them;

• exchange information regarding experience gained in concluding and implementing bilateral and multilateral agreements or other arrangements having relevance to the purposes of the Convention and to which one or more of the Parties are a party;

• seek, where appropriate, the services of competent international bodies and scientific committees in methodological and technical aspects.

The Meeting of the Parties shall establish, on a consensus basis, optional arrangements of a non-confrontational, non-judicial, and consultative nature for reviewing compliance with the provisions of the Convention. These arrangements shall allow for appropriate public involvement.

Decision-making bodies

Political

The Meeting of the Parties is the supreme authority. The first meeting of the Parties will be held in Lucca, Italy, from 21 to 23 October 2002. Thereafter, ordinary meetings of the Parties shall be held at least once every two years. A Working Group to prepare for the first meeting of the Parties held its first session in Geneva from 28 to 30 November 2001 and its second session in Geneva from 21 to 24 May 2002; a third session is scheduled to be held in Pula, Croatia from 8 to 10 July 2002

Pending the entry into force, the Meeting of the Signatories operating under the UNECE Committee on Environmental Policy was the body to discuss and make recommendations concerning the future of the Convention. Two meetings of Signatories were held, in 1999 and 2000.

The Meeting of the Parties shall by consensus agree upon and adopt at its first meeting rules of procedure. It may consider, as necessary, establishing on a consensus basis financial arrangements.

The Meeting of the Parties shall keep under continuous review the implementation of the Convention (see Monitoring/implementation, above), harmonize policies with other ECE bodies and other competent international bodies, establish subsidiary bodies, prepare protocols and amendments to the Convention, and undertake additional actions.

National and international agencies and qualified NGOs may attend the Meetings of the Parties as observers and contribute to its work.

Scientific/technical

The second meeting of the Signatories established three intergovernmental working groups dealing with compliance and rules of procedure, pollutant release and transfer registers (PRTR), and genetically modified organisms (GMOs) respectively. Draft rules of procedure and a draft compliance mechanism have been elaborated, so the first working group has completed its mandate. The second working group is aiming to present a draft protocol on pollutant release and transfer registers to the fifth Ministerial Conference, 'Environment for Europe', in Kiev in May 2003. The third working group—mandated to further the application of the Convention with respect to GMOs—is pursuing a legally binding as well as a recommendatory track to fulfil its mandate. The second meeting of Signatories also set up task forces on access to justice and electronic tools.

Publications

Up-to-date information is available from the Secretariat.

Sources on the Internet

<http://www.unece.org/env/pp>

Convention on Environmental Impact Assessment in a Transboundary Context (Espoo Convention)

Objectives

• to enhance international co-operation in assessing environmental impacts, in particular in a transboundary context;
• to promote environmentally sound and sustainable development;
• to support the development of anticipatory policies and of measures preventing, mitigating, and monitoring significant adverse environmental impacts in general and more specifically in a transboundary context;
• to promote measures taken at an early planning stage of proposed activities aimed at preventing potentially harmful environmental impacts, in particular those with a transboundary dimension, and to strive towards convergence of relevant national policies and practices;
• to provide for notification and consultation among states concerned on all major projects under consideration that are likely to cause significant adverse environmental impact across boundaries;
• to promote public information and public participation in relevant decision-making processes.

Scope

Legal scope
Open to member countries of the UN Economic Commission for Europe (UNECE), regional economic integration organizations constituted by sovereign States members of the UNECE, and other European States having consultative status with the UNECE.

The second Meeting of the Parties adopted an Amendment which will allow other member States of the UN to become Party to the Convention upon approval by the Meeting of the Parties. This amendment has not yet entered into force.

Geographic scope
Regional. UNECE region (Europe and North America).

Time and place of adoption

25 February 1991, Espoo.

Entry into force

10 September 1997.

Status of participation

38 Parties, including the European Union, by 10 June 2002. Six Signatories without ratification, acceptance, or approval.

Affiliated instruments and organizations

Amendment to the Convention on Environmental Impact Assessment in a Transboundary Context, Sofia, 27 February 2001. (Not yet in force.)

The Convention also contains seven *appendices* (see Rules and standards below) which form an integral part of the Convention.

Secretariat

UNECE, Environment and Human Settlements Division (ENHS),
Palais des Nations,
CH-1211 Geneva 10, Switzerland
Telephone: +41-22-9172448
Telefax: +41-22-9170-107/634
E-mail: wiecher.schrage@unece.org

Information contact
Mr Wiecher Schrage.

Finance

Costs of meetings, documentation, and secretariat services are covered by the regular budget of UNECE. Lead countries for activities in the work plan are responsible for related costs.

The first meeting of the Parties in May 1998 adopted Decision I/8 on the budget and financial arrangements for the period until the second Meeting of the Parties. The second meeting of the Parties in February 2001 adopted a corresponding Decision II/13 for the period until the third meeting of the Parties. According to the Decisions, the Parties would contribute to the budget of the Convention on a voluntary basis.

Budget
In accordance with Decisions I/8 and II/13, the budget for the Secretariat was fixed at $US52,150 for the period May 1998 to February 2001 and $52,150 between February 2001 and the third meeting of the Parties in 2004.

Rules and standards

The Convention stipulates measures and procedures to prevent, control, or reduce any significant adverse effect on the environment, particularly any transboundary effect on human health and safety, flora, fauna, soil, water, climate, landscape, and historical monuments, which is likely to be caused by a proposed economic activity or any major change to an existing economic activity listed in *Appendix 1*.

Appendix 1 covers 17 groups of activities, such as nuclear and thermal power stations, road and railway construction, chemical installations, waste-disposal facilities, oil refineries, oil and gas pipelines, mining, steel production, pulp and paper manufacturing, and the construction of dams and reservoirs.

Concerned Parties may apply the provisions of the Convention also to other activities (general guidance is included in *Appendix III* for this purpose), and enter into bilateral or multilateral agreements.

Parties will have to establish an environmental impact assessment (EIA) procedure involving public participation and the preparation of EIA documentation described in *Appendix II*. An EIA has to be carried out before the decision is taken to authorize or undertake a proposed activity listed in *Appendix I*.

Parties will also endeavour to ensure that the EIA principles are applied to policies, plans, and programmes. A country under the jurisdiction of which a proposed activity is envisaged will have to notify accordingly any country likely to be affected by it as early as possible and no later than when informing its own public about the proposed activity. The country of origin has to transmit to the affected country or countries the relevant EIA documentation for comments on the proposed activity and its possible transboundary effects.

Arrangements will have to be made in order to ensure that the public, including the public of the affected country or countries, is given the opportunity to submit

comments on or objections to the proposed activity.

Consultations may be held between the countries concerned in respect of possible alternatives to the proposed activity, including the no-action alternative and possible measures to mitigate adverse effects. Affected countries will be informed about the final decision on the proposed activity and the reasons and considerations on which it is based. Post-project analysis may be undertaken in order to monitor compliance with the conditions set out in the authorization of the activity and the effectiveness of mitigation measures.

Monitoring/implementation

Review procedure

The Parties to the Convention shall keep under continuous review the implementation of the Convention and, with this purpose in mind:

• review the policies and methodological approaches to EIA by the Parties with a view to improving EIA procedures further in a transboundary context;

• exchange information regarding experience gained in concluding and implementing bilateral and multilateral agreements;

• seek, where appropriate, the services of competent international bodies and scientific committees in methodological and technical aspects.

When a country considers that it may be affected by a significant adverse transboundary impact of a proposed activity, and when no notification has taken place, the concerned countries shall, at the request of the affected country, exchange sufficient information to enable discussions to take place on whether there is likely to be a significant adverse transboundary impact.

If those countries agree that there is likely to be a significant adverse transboundary impact, the provisions of the Convention will apply accordingly. If those countries cannot agree whether there is likely to be a significant adverse transboundary impact, any such country may submit that question to a commission of inquiry in accordance with *Annex IV* to the Convention to advise on its likelihood, unless they agree on another method of settling this question.

The second meeting of the Parties in its decision II/4 established the Implementation Committee for the review of compliance by the Parties with their obligations under the Convention. The Committee will report to the third meeting of the Parties.

Data and information systems programmes

The Database on Environmental Impact Assessment in the Transboundary Context (EnImpAs) is collecting information concerning project proposals encompassed by the Convention and is designed to facilitate implementation of the Convention to the largest possible extent. It is hosted by the Ministry of the Environment in Poland and available on their website at: <http://www.mos.gov.pl/enimpas>.

Decision-making bodies

Political

The Meeting of the Parties will take place once every two years in order to review national policies and strategies promoting EIA, to consider relevant technical aspects, and to exchange information regarding experience gained in concluding and implementing relevant bilateral and multilateral agreements. The first meeting of the Parties was held in Oslo in May 1998 and the second in Sofia from 26 to 27 February 2001. The third meeting of the Parties is expected to be held Croatia in spring 2004.

Where appropriate, the Meeting will consider and, where necessary, adopt proposals for amendments to the Convention. Agreement on the proposed amendment should be reached by consensus. If no agreement is reached, the amendment shall, as a last resort, be adopted by a three-quarter majority vote of the Parties present and voting at the Meeting.

Scientific/technical

To be decided by the Meeting of the Parties.

Publications

• ECE Environmental Series;

• *Environmental Conventions Elaborated under the Auspices of the UN/ECE*, 1992.

Sources on the Internet

<http://www.unece.org/env/eia>

Annex 16, vol. II (Environmental Protection: Aircraft Engine Emissions) to the 1944 Chicago Convention on International Civil Aviation

Objectives

• to provide international standardization, through certification procedures, of limitations on aircraft engine emissions;
• to ensure that newly designed engines employ the best available emissions-reduction technology.

Scope

Legal scope
Membership is restricted to International Civil Aviation Organization (ICAO) members. A convention providing for the establishment of ICAO was signed at Chicago on 7 December 1944. The organization came into existence on 4 April 1947, after 26 states had ratified the Chicago Convention.

Geographic scope
Global.

Time and place of adoption

30 June 1981, Montreal.

Entry into force

18 February 1982. Entry into force of ICAO annexes is facilitated by a 'tacit consent' procedure, enabling dissenting countries to notify their differences within a specified time-limit, after which the annexes become generally applicable.

Status of participation

187 member States by 4 April 2002. All ICAO member States are potentially involved, although in practice only those ICAO member States manufacturing aircraft and engines are directly involved.

Affiliated instruments and organizations

Annex 16 was originally drafted by a committee of experts nominated by member States plus observers from international organizations. Annexes to the Chicago Convention on International Civil Aviation are adopted and revised by the ICAO Council upon recommendation by the expert committee (see below).

The most recent amendment was adopted by the Council on 26 February 1999 and entered into force on 4 November 1999. This amendment is a significant change in that it represents a further reduction by an average of about 16 per cent in the stringency of the nitrogen oxide emissions standards for future production engines and will be applicable to new engine designs after 2003.

The Committee on Aviation Environmental Protection (CAEP), at their fifth meeting in January 2001, considered potential measures for emissions reduction based on operational practices and market-based instruments, which were amalgamated in the CAEP action plan on emissions, a route map for the Committee's work in this area. The Committee also approved a work programme. Among the tasks envisaged in this programme, CAEP called for the further development of the elements necessary for an emissions trading programme. Such a programme would be consistent with the Kyoto Protocol to the United Nations Framework Convention on Climate Change (UNFCCC) (see this section), which recognizes ICAO as the global instrument through which industrialized countries can pursue the limitation or reduction of greenhouse gas emissions from international aviation.

All member States have the opportunity to comment on the provisions before adoption or to disapprove them and file differences (Article 38 of the Convention).

Policy directions for the reduction of aircraft engine emissions are contained in Appendices H and I of ICAO Assembly Resolution A33-7: Consolidated Statements of Continuing ICAO Policies and Practices Related to Environmental Protection, adopted by the 33rd Session of the ICAO Assembly on 5 October 2001.

ICAO places equal emphasis on environmental issues relating to aircraft noise, provisions for which are contained in the related instrument, Annex 16, vol. I (Environmental Protection: Aircraft Noise) (see below). Amendment to this volume entered into force on 21 March 2002.

Administrative functions under the Chicago convention are performed by the ICAO secretariat in Montreal.

Co-ordination with related instruments
ICAO has been liaising with the Conference of the Parties to the UNFCCC, the Intergovernmental panel on Climate Change (IPCC), the Montreal Protocol on Substances that deplete the Ozone Layer (see this section), and the UN Economic Commission for Europe (UN/ECE) regarding its Convention on Long-Range Transboundary Air Pollution (LRTAP) (see this section).

Secretariat

International Civil Aviation Organization (ICAO),
999 University Street, Montreal,
Quebec H3C 5H7,
Canada
Telephone: +1-514-9548219
Telefax: +1-514-9546077
E-mail: icaohq@icao.int

Secretary-General (ICAO)
Mr Renato Cláudio Costa Pereira
(1 August 1997–31 July 2003).

Number of staff
323 professionals and 474 support staff (March 2002).

Finance

Budget
The Annex does not provide for regular meetings and programme activities. Costs of meetings, documentation, and secretariat services are covered by the regular ICAO budget.

Special funds
None.

Rules and standards

Member States are not required to report compliance, only non-compliance.

Monitoring/implementation

Review procedure

The objectives are considered to have been met in that all newly designed aircraft engines comply with the requirements of Annex 16, although a number of countries have filed notifications under Article 38 of the Convention regarding different national standards.

Notifications of national differences in standards are recorded and regularly communicated to all members by way of supplements to Annexes. With regard to Annex 16, vol. II, seven member States had notified national differences and 26 had reported conformity. The remaining members are presumed to be tacitly conforming. The following States notified ICAO of differences by 30 March 1999: France, the Netherlands, New Zealand, Qatar, the Russian Federation, Saudi Arabia, and Vanuatu.

With regard to Annex 16, vol. I, on aircraft noise (see above), nine member States had notified national differences in standards and 18 had reported conformity. The remaining members are presumed to be tacitly conforming. The following States had notified ICAO of differences by 30 March 1999: Canada, Germany, Japan, the Netherlands, New Zealand, the Russian Federation, Switzerland, the United Kingdom, and the USA.

These notifications are made public.

Potential factors affecting compliance include technical difficulties in meeting the requirements, disagreement with the need for specific aspects of the requirement, and the cost of compliance testing. A problem of major concern to developing countries is the potential for unilateral or regional operating restrictions on older aircraft not conforming to Annex 16.

Continuous review of Annex 16 by the expert committee and the ICAO Council takes into account inputs from manufacturers, operators, airport management, etc. The flexible ICAO procedure for amendment of technical annexes allows timely adjustment.

Dispute-settlement mechanisms

Disputes are normally considered by the ICAO Council, with possible recourse to international arbitration or adjudication.

Decision-making bodies

Political

The Assembly, composed of delegates from all the Contracting States, meets every three years. The Council, the executive organ, is composed of 33 representatives of Contracting States elected by the Assembly; it is in session almost continuously. The Council elects its own president.

Scientific/technical

ICAO's technical work in the environmental field is undertaken by the Council's Committee on Aviation Environmental Protection (CAEP). The Committee was established in 1983 to supersede the Committee on Aircraft Noise (CAN-1972) and the Committee on Aircraft Engine Emissions (CAEE-1977). CAEP's main objective is to discuss and recommend measures to control or minimize the environmental impact of aircraft noise and aircraft engine emissions. It is responsible for proposing the noise and emissions standards for aircraft certification contained respectively in Annex 16, vols. I and II, and all relevant guidance material. The expert committee, composed of 19 member States and 12 observers (Greece, Norway, and ten international organizations), reviews, refines, and updates the provisions as necessary. The fifth meeting of CAEP was held between 8 and 17 January 2001 in Montreal. The meeting was attended by 18 Committee members and 11 observers (one observer nominated by a state and ten observers nominated by international organizations).

Publications

The ICAO secretariat publishes current activities in *ICAO Journal* as well as a wide range of information materials for government and public distribution.

Sources on the Internet

<http://www.icao.int>

Convention on Long-Range Transboundary Air Pollution (LRTAP)

Convention on Long-Range Transboundary Air Pollution (LRTAP)

Objectives

• to protect human beings and their environment against air pollution;
• to limit and, as far as possible, gradually to reduce and prevent air pollution, including long-range transboundary air pollution.

Scope

Legal scope
Open to member States of the UN Economic Commission for Europe (UNECE), the European Community, and other states having consultative status with the UNECE.

Geographic scope
Regional. UNECE region (Europe, Central Asia, and North America).

Time and place of adoption

13 November 1979, Geneva.

Entry into force

16 March 1983.

Status of participation

48 Parties, including the European Community, by 11 June 2002. Two Signatories without ratification, accession, acceptance, or approval.

The Secretary-General of the UN acts as depositary.

Affiliated instruments and organizations

Protocol to the Convention on Long-Range Transboundary Air Pollution on Long-Term Financing of the Co-operative Programme for Monitoring and Evaluation of the Long-Range Transmission of Air Pollutants in Europe (EMEP), Geneva, 28 September 1984. Entered into force on 28 January 1988. 39 Parties, including the European Community, by 11 June 2002. No Signatories without ratification, approval, or acceptance.

The basic objective of the Protocol is:
• to share the costs of a monitoring and evaluation programme which forms the backbone for review and assessment of relevant air pollution in Europe in the light of agreements on emission reduction. The main objective of EMEP is to provide governments with information on the deposition and concentration of air pollutants as well as on the quantity and significance of long-range transmission of pollutants and of fluxes across boundaries. EMEP has four main components: (*a*) collection of emission data for sulphur dioxide (SO_2), nitrogen oxides (NO_X), volatile organic compounds (VOCs), ground-level ozone, and, more recently, persistent organic pollutants (POPs) and heavy metals and other air pollutants; (*b*) measurement of air and precipitation quality; (*c*) modelling of the movement of air pollutants; and (*d*) integrated assessment modelling.

Protocol to the Convention on Long-Range Transboundary Air Pollution on Further Reduction of Sulphur Emissions (1994 Sulphur Protocol), Oslo, 14 June 1994. Entered into force on 5 August 1998. 25 Parties, including the European Community, by 11 June 2002. Four Signatories without ratification, accession, acceptance, or approval.

The Protocol follows the former Sulphur Protocol adopted in Helsinki on 8 July 1985, which entered into force on 2 September 1987. The basic objective of the first Protocol was to reduce the annual sulphur emissions or the transboundary fluxes by at least 30 per cent as soon as possible and at the latest by 1993, using 1980 levels as the basis for calculation of reductions.

The basic objective of the 1994 Sulphur Protocol is:
• to reduce sulphur emissions to ensure, as far as possible, without entailing excessive cost, that in the long run 'critical loads'—the rates of sulphur deposition which ecosystems and other receptors can tolerate in the long term without suffering damage—are no longer exceeded.

1994 Sulphur Protocol

Protocol to the Convention on Long-Range Transboundary Air Pollution concerning the Control of Emissions of Nitrogen Oxides or their Transboundary Fluxes (1988 NO_X Protocol), Sofia, 31 October 1988. Entered into force on 14 February 1991. 28 Parties, including the European Community, by 11 June 2002. One Signatory without ratification, accession, acceptance, or approval.

The basic objective of the Protocol is:

• to take effective measures to control and/or reduce the Parties' national annual emissions of nitrogen oxides or their transboundary fluxes so that these, at the latest by 31 December 1994, do not exceed their national annual emissions of such substances for 1987 or any previous year to be specified upon signature of, or accession to, the Protocol.

Protocol to the Convention on Long-Range Transboundary Air Pollution concerning the Control of Emissions of Volatile Organic Compounds or their Transboundary Fluxes (1991 VOC Protocol), Geneva, 18 November 1991. Entered into force on 29 September 1997. 21 Parties by 11 June 2002. Six Signatories, including the European Community, without ratification, accession, acceptance, or approval.

The basic objective of the Protocol is:

• to control and reduce the emissions of VOCs in order to lessen the transboundary fluxes and the fluxes of the resulting secondary photochemical oxidant products so as to protect human health and the environment from adverse effects.

This Protocol offers flexibility to the Parties, which is a completely new feature of this type of international agreement. There are options not only to select the base year, but also, for large countries, to designate particular areas within a country in which the reduction obligation applies, and, for low-emitting countries, to freeze rather than reduce emissions.

Protocol to the 1979 Convention on Long-Range Transboundary Air Pollution on Heavy Metals (1998 Heavy Metals Protocol), Århus, 24 June 1998. (Not yet in force.) Nine States and the European Community had ratified by 11 June 2002. 27 Signatories without ratification, accession, acceptance, or approval. Enters into force on the ninetieth day after the deposit of the sixteenth instrument of ratification, acceptance, approval, or accession.

The Protocol concentrates at first on cadmium, mercury, and lead. It includes provisions for adding other metals in future if international action is needed. The basic objectives of the Protocol are:

• to reduce emissions for these three metals below their levels in 1990 (or an alternative year between 1985 and 1995);

• to reduce emissions from industrial sources (iron and steel industry, non-ferrous metal industry), combustion processes (power generation, road transport), and waste inceneration. It lays down stringent limit values for emissions from stationary sources and suggests best available techniques (BAT) for these sources, such as special filters or scrubbers for combustion sources or mercury-free processes;

• to phase out leaded petrol;

• to lower heavy metal emissions from other products, such as mercury in batteries, and to propose the introduction of management measures for other mercury-containing products, such as electrical components (thermostats, switches), measuring devices (thermometers, manometers, barometers), fluorescent lamps, dental amalgam, pesticides, and paint.

Protocol to the 1979 Convention on Long-Range Transboundary Air Pollution on Persistent Organic Pollutants (1998 POPs Protocol), Århus, 24 June 1998. (Not yet in force.) Nine States had ratified by 11 June 2002. 27 Signatories, including the European Community, without ratification, accession, acceptance, or approval. Enters into force on the ninetieth day after the deposit of the sixteenth instrument of ratification, acceptance, approval, or accession.

The Protocol focuses on a list of 16 substances that have been singled out according to agreed risk criteria. The substances comprise eleven pesticides, two industrial chemicals, and three by-products/contaminants. The basic objective of the Protocol is:

• to control, reduce, or eliminate discharges, emissions, and losses of POPs to the environment. The Protocol bans the

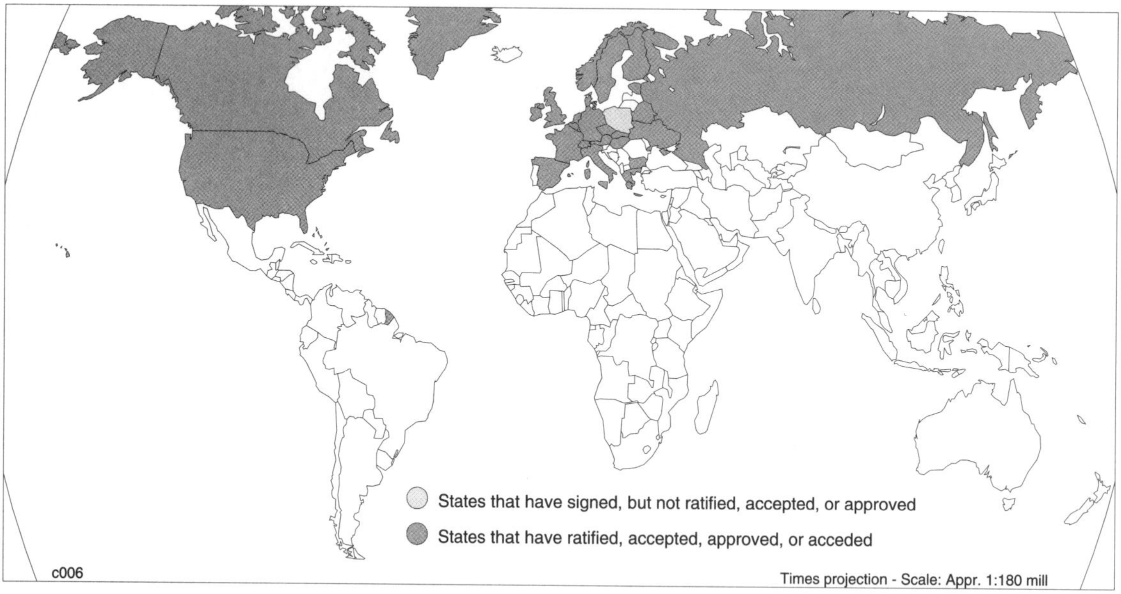

1988 NO_x Protocol

production and use of some products outright (aldrin, chlordane, chlordecone, dieldrin, endrin, hexabromobiphenyl, mirex, and toxaphene). Others are scheduled for elimination at a later stage (DDT, heptachlor, hexachlorobenzene (HCB), and polychlorinated biphenyls (PCBs)). Finally, the Protocol severely restricts the use of DDT, HCH (including lindane), and PCBs.

The Protocol includes provisions for dealing with the wastes of products that will be banned. It also obliges Parties to reduce their emissions of dioxins, furans, polycyclic aromatic hydrocarbons (PAHs), and HCB below their levels in 1990 (or an alternative year between 1985 and 1995). For the incineration of municipal, hazardous, and medical waste, it lays down specific limit values.

The Protocol has the same goal as the Stockholm Convention on Persistent Organic Pollutants (see this section). It seeks to eliminate or reduce the same 12 substances as those included in Annex A, B, and C of the Stockholm Convention. However, this Protocol also targets chlordecone and HCB (both pesticides); hexabromobiphenyl (an industrial chemical); and PAHs (which, like dioxins and furans, can be created inadvertently by combustion).

Protocol to the 1979 Convention on Long-Range Transboundary Air Pollution to Abate Acidification, Eutrophication and Ground-level Ozone (1999 Multi-Effects Protocol), Gothenburg, 30 November 1999. (Not yet in force.) Four States had ratified by 11 June 2002. 27 Signatories without ratification, accession, acceptance, or approval. Enters into force on the ninetieth day after the deposit of the sixteenth instrument of ratification, acceptance, approval, or accession.

The basic objective of the Protocol is:

- to control and reduce emissions of sulphur, NO_x , VOCs, and ammonia that are produced by anthropogenic activities and are likely to cause adverse effects on human health, natural ecosystems, materials, and crops, due to acidification, eutrophication, or ground-level ozone as a result of long-range transboundary atmospheric transport.

The Protocol sets emission ceilings for 2010 for sulphur, NO_x, VOCs, and ammonia. These ceilings were negotiated on the basis of scientific assessments of pollution effects and abatement options. Parties whose emissions have a more severe environmental or health impact and whose emissions are relatively cheap to reduce will have to make the biggest cuts. Once the Protocol is fully implemented, Europe's sulphur emissions should be cut by at least 63 per cent, its NO_x emissions by 41 per cent, its VOC emissions by 40 per cent, and its ammonia emissions by 17 per cent compared to 1990.

The Protocol also sets tight limit values for specific emission sources (e.g. combustion plant, electricity production, dry cleaning, cars, and lorries) and requires best available techniques to be used to keep emissions down. VOC emissions from such products as paints or aerosols will also have to be cut. Finally, farmers will have to take specific measures to control ammonia emissions. Guidance documents adopted together with the Protocol provide a wide range of abatement techniques and economic instruments for the reduction of emissions in the relevant sectors, including transport.

The UN Economic Commission for Europe (UNECE), through the Air Pollution Section of the UNECE Environment and Human Settlements Division, plays a central role as secretariat for the elaboration of the Convention and its protocols and for follow-up action to implement them.

Co-ordination with related instruments

Work on drafting revised or new protocols is co-ordinated through the ECE secretariat, with other competent bodies, especially as regards airborne pollution of adjacent regional sea areas, e.g. the Baltic Sea, through the Helsinki Commission (see this section), and the North Sea, through the OSPAR Commission (see this section).

Secretariat

UNECE, Environment and Human Settlements Division (ENHS),
Palais des Nations,
CH-1211 Geneva 10,
Switzerland

1991 VOC Protocol

Telephone: +41-22-91723-70/54
Telefax: +41-22-9170621
E-mail: air.env@unece.org

Director (ENHS Division)
Mr Kaj Bärlund.

Chief, Air Pollution Section (ENHS Division)
Mr Keith Bull.

Number of staff
Four professionals and two support staff in the Air Pollution Section (May 2002).

Finance

Costs of meetings, documentation, and secretariat services are covered by the regular budget of UNECE. International co-ordination costs for the EMEP programme are financed by mandatory contributions from the Parties to a UN-administered trust fund. Costs of other co-operative programmes are covered by voluntary contributions of participating Parties.

Budget
The actual budget for the EMEP programme was $1,932,978 in 2000 and $2,040,495 in 2001 and is expected to remain at that level in 2002 and 2003.

The co-ordination costs for financing the core activities of the Convention and its Protocols, other that those covered by the EMEP Protocol, were US$1,705,000 in 2001, and are $1,817,950 for 2002; they are expected to remain at that level in 2003 and 2004.

	Year		
	2000	2005	2010
Austria	80		
Belarus	38	46	50
Belgium	70	72	74
Bulgaria	33	40	45
Canada	30		
Croatia	11	17	22
Czech Republic	50	60	72
Denmark	80		
Finland	80		
France	74	77	78
Germany	83	87	
Greece	0	3	4
Hungary	45	50	60
Ireland	30		
Italy	65	73	
Liechtenstein	75		
Luxembourg	58		
Monaco*	12	37	50
Netherlands	77		
Norway	76		
Poland	37	47	66
Portugal	0	3	
Russian Federation	38	40	40
Slovakia	60	65	72
Slovenia	45	60	70
Spain	35		
Sweden	80		
Switzerland	52		
Ukraine	40		
United Kingdom	50	70	80
European Community	62		

* = Amendment adopted at nineteenth session of the Executive Body in 2001.

Rules and standards

Parties are committed to:

• develop by means of exchanges of information, consultation, research, and monitoring, and without undue delay, policies and strategies which shall serve as a means of combating the discharge of air pollutants;

• exchange information on and review their policies, scientific activities, and technical measures aimed at combating, as far as possible, the discharge of air pollutants which may have adverse effects, thereby contributing to the reduction of air pollution, including long-range transboundary air pollution;

• develop the best policies and strategies, including air-quality management systems, and, as part of them, control measures compatible with balanced development, in particular by using the best available technology (BAT) that is economically feasible and low- or non-waste technology.

The sulphur emission reductions in the schedule presented on this page give the emission ceilings referred to in the *1994 Sulphur Protocol* (percentage of sulphur emissions reductions, taking 1980 as the base year and the year 2000 for Greece and Portugal).

The *1991 VOC Protocol* specifies three options for emission reduction targets that

1998 Protocol on Heavy Metals

have to be chosen upon signature:
(*a*) a 30 per cent reduction in emissions of VOCs by 1999, using either 1988 or any other year between 1984 and 1990 as the base year. This option was chosen by Austria, Belgium, Finland, France, Germany, the Netherlands, Portugal, Spain, Sweden, and the United Kingdom with 1988 as the base year, by Denmark with 1985 as the base year, by the Czech Republic, Italy, and Luxembourg with 1990 as the base year, and by Liechtenstein, Switzerland, and the USA with 1984 as the base year;
(*b*) the same reduction as for (*a*) within a Tropospheric Ozone Management Area (TOMA) specified in Annex I to the Protocol and ensuring that by 1999 total national emissions do not exceed 1988 levels. (Annex I specifies TOMAs in Norway (base year 1989) and Canada (base year 1988));
(*c*) finally, where emissions in 1988 did not exceed certain specified levels, Parties may opt for a stabilization at that level of emission by 1999 (this was been chosen by Bulgaria, Greece, and Hungary).

Monitoring/implementation

Review procedure

An Implementation Committee was established by the Executive Body in December 1997. The primary functions of the Implementation Committee are to review compliance by the Parties with the reporting requirements of the protocols, and to report on compliance with or implementation of specified obligations in an individual protocol. It is also able to receive submissions from Parties relating to compliance. Two-year reviews are conducted based on detailed questionnaires. At the same time, monitoring data on actual depositions of air pollution are collected and analysed under the EMEP programme and submitted yearly to the Executive Body.

35 Parties (79.5 per cent of the Parties) submitted national reports as requested by the major review in 1998. Parties were requested to update the 1998 major review in 2000. 37 Parties replied to the request for updated information, though only 13 Parties had submitted reports by April 2000 (the due date). Five Parties (France, Greece, Liechtenstein, Luxembourg, and the European Community) had repeatedly been identified as being in non-compliance with their reporting obligations under the Protocols, either in respect of reporting on their emission data or on their strategies and policies, or both. These Parties were urged by the Executive Body to comply with their reporting obligations as soon as possible, but no later than 31 January 2001. Liechtenstein, Luxembourg, and the European Community had, despite two reminder letters, not met the Executive Body's request and were still in non-compliance with their reporting obligations in September 2001. The Executive Body in December 2001 expressed its serious concern over this situation and urged the three Parties to comply with their reporting obligations and provide as soon as possible, but no later than 31 January 2002, all the missing information on their national emissions and, if they could not comply fully within this timeframe, to draw up a precise timetable in agreement with the Secretariat before 31 January 2002 for the provision of that information. The next major review was started in January 2002 and will be reported to the Executive Body in December 2002.

The national emission data and other information required from Parties to the protocols currently in force were further specified in the work plan for implementation of the Convention in December 2001. The Implementation Committee noted in their report to the Executive Body in October 2001 that the annual data reported by Parties to the 1988 NO_x, 1991 VOC, and 1994 Sulphur Protocols were generally more complete in comparison to those of the previous years. It was noted that some Parties had improved their record significantly. On the whole the coverage of emission data reporting had improved since the Implementation Committee started examining the completeness of reported data. Nevertheless, the Executive Body in December 2001, based on the report from the Committee, expressed its concern that the Russian Federation and Spain continued to be in non-compliance with the emission data reporting obligations and that they should provide all the missing information on their national emissions by 31 January 2002.

Periodic published reviews of national

1998 Protocol on Persistent Organic Pollutants (POPs)

reports on their strategies and policies and the data collected through EMEP and other co-operative programmes under the Convention have served as a mechanism to encourage compliance. The reviews are published after de-restriction by the Executive Body for the Convention. The publicity resulting from NGO participation in the annual meetings of the Executive Body may also encourage compliance.

Implementation of protocols

• *The 1985 Sulphur Protocol*: The first Sulphur Protocol contains two requirements of Parties which remain of particular relevance. The first is to make a 30 per cent cut in sulphur emissions or their transboundary fluxes as soon as possible (the Protocol specified at the latest by 1993, compared to levels in 1980). At the seventh session of the Executive Body in December 1989 the then Parties to the Protocol expressed a common understanding about the interpretation of this provision that it 'means that reductions to that extent should be reached in that time-frame and the levels maintained or further reduced after being reached'. The second requirement is to report emissions of sulphur annually to the Executive Body.

All 21 Parties to the Protocol met the required reductions in 1993. Many Parties significantly exceeded the reductions required, with Austria, Finland, and Sweden reducing emissions by more than 80 per cent. While achieving the required reduction in 1993, Bulgaria narrowly failed to achieve the target in 1994 and 1995, but met it in the years 1996 to 1998; future projections indicate the likelihood of its continuing to achieve the target in future years. For Estonia, the Protocol entered into force on 5 June 2000, but available data suggests its full compliance with the 30 per cent sulphur emission reduction.

• *The 1988 NO_X Protocol*: Arguably the principal obligation on Parties to the NO_X Protocol is to control and/or reduce their total annual emissions of nitrogen oxides or their transboundary fluxes. It was proposed that these, at the latest by 31 December 1994, should not exceed such emissions for 1987. At its fourteenth session in December 1996, the Executive Body confirmed its understanding that the obligation 'should be taken to mean that emission levels for the years after 1994 should not exceed those specified in that paragraph'. Official submissions suggest that the requirement was met in each of the years 1994–6 by 17 of the 26 Parties to the Protocol. Bulgaria, the Czech Republic, Germany, and Ukraine went significantly further, with at least one year in the 1994–6 period when emissions were more than 40 per cent lower than in 1987. France narrowly failed to achieve the target for each year in the period 1994–6, but provides no projections to indicate future trends. The USA exercised an option and specified a base year of 1978 when it signed the Protocol, so its target became to control and/or reduce its total annual emissions of nitrogen oxides or their transboundary fluxes so that these, at the latest by 31 December 1994, did not exceed such emissions for 1978, and to ensure that its national average annual transboundary fluxes or national average annual emissions for the period from 1 January 1987 to 1 January 1996 did not exceed those for the calendar year 1987. The USA failed to achieve the requirement for stabilization in 1994, but the target was achieved in 1995 and 1996; projections for future years indicate attainment of the target for the year 2000 and beyond. Additionally, the average of annual emissions in the period 1 January 1987 to 1 January 1996 was 21,813 kilotons, compared to emissions in 1987 of 20,689 kilotons, so this target was not achieved. Luxembourg submitted no emission data for the base year of 1987, but its emissions were more or less stable throughout the period 1980–96 in the years for which information is available. Greece ratified the Protocol in 1998 and provided emissions data for 1994–6, but not for the base year. The data provided shows a generally rising trend in emissions since 1985. Four Parties to the Protocol have not reported NO_X emissions for one or more of the years 1994–6, so it is not possible to state that they have met the Protocol's requirement. Of these four, Italy has not yet reported NOx emissions for 1996, though it attained the stabilization target in 1994 and 1995. Italy predicts a trend of declining emissions in the years to come. Liechtenstein attained the

1999 Multi-Effects Protocol

target in 1994 but has yet to submit data for 1995 and 1996, though it also predicts a trend of declining emissions. Spain's 1997 response explains that the apparently large rise in its emissions is the result of a methodological change in inventory compilation. When emissions are back-calculated to include off-road vehicles, its emissions rose 1 per cent in the period 1987–93, with a projection for the year 2000 indicating that the target will have been met at that time. The European Community has not reported NO_X emissions for any year, though it claimed in its questionnaire response to have achieved the stabilization target by 1994.

There is a requirement to make unleaded fuel sufficiently available to facilitate the circulation of vehicles fitted with catalytic converters, particularly along main international transit routes; 17 of the 26 Parties have either phased out leaded petrol completely or responded to the questionnaire in specific terms that they had met the terms of the requirement. The Czech Republic, Ireland, and Switzerland provided data which would imply that they had also met the requirement. It was not possible to determine from Bulgaria's response whether it had met the requirement, and the following countries either did not respond to the 2000 questionnaire or provided no information on this subject: France, Liechtenstein, Luxembourg, Spain, and Ukraine.

- *The 1991 VOC Protocol*: The first requirement is for the Parties to control and reduce VOC emissions. Taking the Parties as a whole, the emissions of VOC would appear to have reduced in the face of control measures, although the emissions data set is not complete. The provision in the Protocol which requires concrete reductions in national annual emissions of VOC lays out a number of options, one of which has to be chosen by the Party on signature. In all cases the target was to be achieved by the year 1999.

13 Parties (Austria, Belgium (since the Protocol entered into force for it in 2001, it had no obligations in 1999), Bulgaria, the Czech Republic, Denmark, Estonia, France, Germany, Hungary, the Netherlands, Slovakia, Switzerland, and the United Kingdom) have achieved the target levels of the Protocol. Due to their non-compliance with this reporting obligation, it is not possible to evaluate whether Liechtenstein and Spain have complied with their emission reduction obligations. Five Parties have not met their emission reduction obligations. Instead of reducing emissions by at least 30 per cent, Finland, Italy, and Sweden reduced emissions by only 24 per cent, Luxembourg by only 21 per cent. Instead of stabilizing, Norway's emissions increased by 41per cent, and instead of falling by 30 per cent, emissions in its Tropospheric Ozone Management Area (TOMA) increased by 6 per cent. For Liechtenstein and Spain, no data were submitted for 1999, and the most recent data submitted cast doubt on the ability of those Parties to comply with the emission reduction obligation. In conclusion, seven Parties (Finland, Liechtenstein, Luxembourg, Italy, Norway, Spain, and Sweden) were failing to comply with the VOC Protocol.

- *The 1994 Sulphur Protocol*: As regards the targets for 2000, 15 Parties attained the emission reductions required, while another four were on course to do so. The projection from Liechtenstein appears to show that its emissions in the year 2000 will have been 10 tons above its target. The European Community submitted no data on which its progress can be assessed. More stringent targets exist for the years 2005 and 2010 for some Parties (see previous table). An in-depth compliance review of the Protocol will be carried out by the Implementation Committee during 2002.

The three protocols that are likely to require review within the next few years are the 1998 Protocol on Heavy Metals, the 1998 Protocol on POPs, and the 1999 Multi-Effects Protocol. Each protocol will enter into force on the ninetieth day following the date on which the sixteenth instrument of ratification, acceptance, approval, or accession has been deposited. However, the timing of the review, as detailed in review clauses to each, is different for the three protocols: (a) the 1998 Protocol on POPs indicates that the first review should be complete no later than three years after entry into force; (b) the 1998 Protocol on

Heavy Metals specifies no time constraint on the review process, though it indicates that the procedures, methods, and timing are to be decided at a session of the Executive Body. Implicitly the review will take place after entry into force; (c) the 1999 Multi-Effects Protocol requires that the first review shall commence no later than one year after the date of its entry into force.

Observations or inspections
None by the Convention as such.

Environmental monitoring programmes
Monitoring data on effects of air pollution and their trends are collected and analysed by five of the six International Co-operative Programmes (ICPs) of the Convention's Working Group on Effects. Monitoring is focused on: forest ecosystems; chemistry and biology of surface waters; corrosion/deterioration of materials, including buildings and cultural heritage; natural vegetation and crops; and biological, chemical, and physical state of selected, well-defined ecosystems. National focal centres collect national data for submission to main programme co-ordination centres, one for each of the five programmes, which collate and analyse results (information is available on the Internet through the Convention's website, see Sources on the Internet, below).

Monitoring data on actual depositions and concentrations of air pollution are collected and analysed under EMEP (see above). The programme was originally established in 1977 by UNECE, the World Meteorological Organization (WMO), and the UN Environment Programme (UNEP). EMEP collects precipitation gas and aerosol chemistry data from some 100 ground-level monitoring stations in 35 UNECE countries. The data are collected daily and are analysed to establish the transportation patterns of essential pollutants. These data are analysed and results published by EMEP's Chemical Co-ordinating Centre (CCC) in Norway. Two meteorological synthesizing centres (MSCs) have been established by EMEP, in Norway and in the Russian Federation, to develop model calculations of long-range transport and deposition pollutants. (See Sources on the Internet, below.)

Data and information system programmes
The negotiations for the scheme for emission reductions of the 1994 Sulphur Protocol and the 1999 Multi-Effects Protocol are based on integrated assessment modelling such as the model known as the Regional Acidification Information and Simulation Model (RAINS), developed by the International Institute for Applied Systems Analysis (IIASA) in Austria. The Centre for Integrated Assessment Modelling (CIAM) has been established at IIASA to perform policy assessment to provide a basis for future negotiations of abatement measures.

Integrated assessment models use data from EMEP (emissions inventories and atmospheric transport models) and from the Working Group on Effects (critical loads and levels maps). The critical loads and levels data are provided by national focal centres to the Co-ordination Center for Effects and reported to the Working Group on Effects through an ICP on Mapping Critical Loads. Data on human health aspects are the responsibility of a joint task force between the Convention and the World Health Organization (WHO) (see IGOs).

Trade measures
No provisions on trade measures to penalize Parties for non-compliance.

Dispute-settlement mechanisms
If a dispute arises between two or more Parties as to the interpretation or application of the Convention, they shall seek a solution by negotiation or by any other method of dispute settlement acceptable to the parties to the dispute.

Decision-making bodies

Political
The Executive Body, formed of the Contracting Parties, meets at least annually. It reviews the implementation of the Convention and has established working groups to prepare appropriate studies, documentation, and recommendations to this end.

Scientific/technical
The Executive Body has established several standing subsidiary bodies to provide the necessary scientific expert advice for policy-making decisions. They are at present:

- Working Group on Effects (composed of government experts and others);
- Working Group on Strategies and Review (composed of government experts and others);
- EMEP Steering Body (composed of government experts and others).

In December 1997 the Executive Body established an Implementation Committee to review compliance by Parties with their obligations under the protocols to the Convention. The Committee is composed of nine legal experts and technical experts, nominated by Parties and elected by the Executive Body.

Publications

Up-to-date information on the operation of the Convention and its protocols is disseminated through documents for UNECE meetings, the UNECE Air Pollution Studies series, public-information brochures, etc.

Sources on the Internet

<http://www.unece.org/env/lrtap>

Scientific information on emissions from EMEP:
<http://www.emep.int>

United Nations Framework Convention on Climate Change (UNFCCC)

Objectives

• to stabilize greenhouse-gas concentrations in the atmosphere at a level that would prevent dangerous anthropogenic interference with the climate system, within a time-frame sufficient to allow ecosystems to adapt naturally to climate change;
• to ensure that food production is not threatened;
• to enable economic development to proceed in a sustainable manner.

Scope

Legal scope
Open to all member States of the UN, or of its specialized agencies, or that are Parties to the Statute of the International Court of Justice, and to regional economic integration organizations.

Geographic scope
Global.

Time and place of adoption

9 May 1992, New York.

Entry into force

21 March 1994.

Status of participation

186 Parties, including the European Economic Community by 1 July 2002. Two Signatories without ratification, acceptance, or approval.

The Secretary-General of the UN acts as depositary of both the Convention and the Kyoto Protocol.

Affiliated instruments and organizations

Annex I lists developed-country Parties that had to adopt measures aimed at returning their greenhouse-gas (GHG) emissions to 1990 levels by the year 2000. It includes the 24 original OECD members, 11 countries with economies in transition, and the European Union.

Annex II lists developed-country Parties which have a special obligation to help developing countries with financial and technological resources. It includes the 24 original OECD members and the European Union.

Berlin Mandate
The *Berlin Mandate* was adopted at the first Conference of the Parties (COP) on 7 April 1995. It acknowledges that the commitment of developed countries to take measures aimed at reducing their GHG emissions to 1990 levels by the year 2000 is not adequate to achieve the Convention's objective. The main objective of the Mandate was to strengthen the commitments for the developed-country Parties after the year 2000 without introducing any new commitments for developing countries, while reaffirming existing commitments of all Parties contained in Article 4.1 and continuing to advance their implementation. The *ad hoc* Group on the Berlin Mandate met for eight sessions before handing over the results of its work for completion to the third session of the COP in December 1997.

At the second COP, a large number of ministers agreed on the Geneva Ministerial Declaration, which provided political impetus to the Berlin Mandate process. They instructed their representatives to accelerate negotiations on the text of a legally binding protocol or another legal instrument, the outcome of which should encompass quantified legally binding objectives for emission limitations and significant overall reductions within specified time-frames.

By 1 June 1997 a draft text of an instrument was circulated in the six official languages of the UN and served as a basis for the negotiations leading up to the third COP. A number of other proposals on GHG emissions reductions were on the table during this period, including one by the Alliance of Small Island States for a 20 per cent reduction in carbon dioxide (CO_2) by the year 2005; one by the European Union for reductions of 7.5 per cent by 2005 and 15 per cent by 2010 in a 'basket' of gases including CO_2, methane (CH_4) and nitrous oxide (N_2O); one by Japan for a reduction of 5 per cent by 2008–12 (taken as an average over these years), although individual countries could opt for lower targets; one by the USA for returning all GHGs to 1990 levels by 2008–12; and one by the Russian Federation suggesting that each country reduce its emissions on the basis of its own proposed target, resulting in an overall reduction of some 3 per cent by 2010. The baseline for all proposed reductions would be the year 1990. After ten days of negotiations at the third COP, ministers and other high-level officials from 160 countries reached agreement on a protocol.

Kyoto Protocol to the United Nations Framework Convention on Climate Change (Kyoto Protocol), Kyoto, 11 December 1997. (Not yet in force.) Open for signature from 16 March 1998 to 15 March 1999 and open for accession from the day after the date on which it was closed for signature. 74 ratifications, acceptances, approvals, or accessions by 1 July 2002. 37 Signatories, including the European Economic Community, without ratification, acceptance, or approval. It enters into force on the 90th day after the date on which not fewer than 55 Parties to the Convention, incorporating Parties included in Annex I to the Convention which accounted in total for at least 55 per cent of the total CO_2 emissions for 1990 of the Parties included in Annex I, have deposited their instruments of ratification, acceptance, approval, or accession. *Annex A*, listing the GHGs and sectors/source categories lowered by quantified commitments in the Protocol, and *Annex B*, containing quantified emissions limitations or reduction commitments, form an integral part of the Protocol.

The Kyoto Protocol contains individual emission limitations and reductions commitments for Parties included in Annex I to the Convention covering the six main GHGs. These range from an 8 per cent reduction for countries to a 10 per cent increase by the period 2008–12, calculated as an average over these five years. Overall, these individual commitments will result in a reduction of 5.2 per cent in emissions of the six GHGs from 1990 levels of Annex I Parties. Reductions in the three most important gases, CO_2, CH_4, and N_2O, will be measured against a base year of 1990. Re-

United Nations Framework Convention on Climate Change (UNFCCC)

ductions in three long-lived industrial gases, hydrofluorocarbons (HFCs), perfluorocarbons (PFCs), and sulphur hexafluoride (SF_6), can be measured against either a 1990 or a 1995 baseline.

If compared to expected emissions levels for the year 2000, the total reductions required by the Protocol will actually be about 10 per cent; this is because many industrialized countries had not succeeded in meeting their earlier non-binding aim of returning their emissions to 1990 levels by the year 2000, and their emissions have in fact risen since 1990. Compared to the emissions levels that would be expected by 2010 without emissions-control measures, the Protocol target represents approximately a 30 per cent reduction. (See also Rules and standards, below.)

At the fourth COP during 2–14 November 1998, representatives of 170 governments adopted the two-year *Buenos Aires Plan of Action*. It contains six decisions (see Rules and standards, below) for future work under the Convention and the Kyoto Protocol. To strengthen the implementation of the Convention and prepare for the future entry into force of the Kyoto Protocol, it established deadlines for finalizing the outstanding details of the Kyoto Protocol.

At the fifth COP in Bonn from 25 October to 5 November 1999, ministers and officials from 166 governments agreed on a timetable for completing the outstanding details of the 1997 Kyoto Protocol by November 2000 in order to intensify the negotiating process on all issues before the sixth COP. The Conference also decided, *inter alia*, on how to improve the rigour of national reports from industrialized countries and strengthen the guidelines for measuring their GHG emissions. Action was also taken to address bottlenecks in the delivery and consideration of national communications by developing countries.

At the sixth COP in The Hague from 13 to 24 November 2000, ministers and other high-level officials from 178 governments made progress towards outlining a package of financial support and technology transfer to help developing countries contribute to global action on climate change. But the key political issues—including an international emissions trading system, a *Clean Development Mechanism (CDM)*, the rules for counting emissions reductions from carbon sinks such as forests, and a compliance regime—could not be resolved in the time available. These negotiations were suspended in late November 2000 but were continued at the resumed talks in Bonn from 16 to 27 July 2001. At this second part of the sixth COP, consensus was finally reached on the so-called *Bonn Agreements* (see Rules and standards, below), registering political consensus on key issues under the Buenos Aires Plan of Action. Work was also completed on a number of detailed decisions based on the Bonn Agreements, including on capacity building for developing countries and countries with economies in transition. However, decisions on several issues, notably the mechanisms, land use, land-use change, and forestry (LULUCF), and compliance, remained outstanding.

The seventh COP in Marrakech from 29 October to 9 November 2001 was attended by 4400 participants from 172 governments and 234 intergovernmental, non-governmental, and other observer organizations. The delegates intended to bring to a close three years of negotiations and complete tasks left unfinished at both parts of the sixth COP. The Parties agreed on a package deal, with key features including rules for ensuring compliance with commitments, consideration of LULUCF principles in reporting of such data, and limited banking of units generated by sinks under the Clean Development Mechanism (CDM) (the extent to which carbon dioxide absorbed by carbon sinks can be counted towards the Kyoto targets).

The meeting also adopted the *Marrakech Ministerial Declaration* as an input into the World Summit on Sustainable Development in Johannesburg. The Declaration emphasizes the contribution that action on climate change can make to sustainable development and calls for capacity building, technology innovation, and co-operation with the Convention on Biological Diversity and the Convention to Combat Desertification (see this section).

Kyoto Protocol mechanisms

The Protocol broke new ground with three innovative mechanisms aimed to maximize

Kyoto Protocol

the cost-effectiveness of climate change mitigation by allowing Parties to pursue opportunities to cut emissions, or enhance carbon sinks, more cheaply abroad than at home. To be eligible to participate in the mechanisms, Annex I Parties must have ratified the Kyoto Protocol and be in compliance with their methodological and reporting commitments under the Protocol.

The mechanisms consist of:

• *'joint implementation (JI)'*. The principle of 'activities implemented jointly' (AIJ) (Article 6) allows Annex I Parties to implement projects that reduce emissions, or increase removals by sinks, in the territories of other Annex I Parties. Emissions Reduction Units (ERUs) generated by such projects can then be used by investing Annex I Parties to help meet their emissions targets. To avoid double-counting, a corresponding subtraction is made from the host Party's assigned amount. However, under the AIJ pilot phase the investing country cannot claim credit for the reduced emissions. The second and fourth COP decided to continue the pilot phase. (See also Rules and standards, *Buenos Aires Plan of Action* and *Bonn Agreements*, below.) (The term 'joint implementation' does not appear in Article 6, but it has entered into common usage as convenient shorthand.);

• *clean development mechanism (CDM)*. CDM, defined in Article 12, allows Annex I Parties to implement projects that reduce GHG emissions in non-Annex I Parties and has the additional goal of assisting non-Annex I Parties in achieving sustainable development and contributing to the ultimate objective of the Convention. Under the CDM, Annex I Parties may use 'certified emission reductions' (CERs) generated by project activities in non-Annex I Parties to contribute to compliance with their emission commitments. The Protocol envisages a prompt start to the CDM, allowing CERs to accrue from projects from the year 2000 onwards. The election of the CDM executive board at the seventh COP, and the beginning of its work, has already effected this prompt start. The ten-member executive board supervises the CDM, operating under the authority of the Conference of the Parties serving as the Meeting of the Parties to the Kyoto Protocol (COP/MOP) (a role being performed by the COP until the COP/MOP meets). Key initial tasks of the executive board are to develop simplified procedures to encourage small-scale projects, notably for renewable energy and energy-efficiency activities, and to accredit independent organizations, known as operational entities, pending their formal designation by the COP or COP/MOP;

• *emissions trading*. Emissions trading, as set out in Article 17, permits Annex I Parties to acquire assigned amount units (AAUs) from other Annex I Parties that find it easier, relatively speaking, to meet their emissions targets. This enable Parties to utilize lower cost opportunities to curb emissions or increase removals, irrespective of where those opportunities exist, in order to reduce the overall cost of mitigating climate change. Similarly, Annex I Parties may also acquire CERs (from CDM projects), ERUs (from joint implementation projects), or RMUs (from sink activities) from other Annex I Parties. In order to address the concern that some Parties could 'over-sell' and then be unable to meet their own targets, each Annex I party is required to hold a minimum level of AAUs, CERs, ERUs, and/or RMUs. This is known as the commitment period reserve and cannot be traded. If an Annex I Party goes below its commitment period reserve, it is given 30 days to restore the reserve to its required level.

A computerized system or registries will keep track of transactions in AAUs, CERs, ERUs, and RMUs. There are three components to the registry system:

• Each Annex I Party must establish and maintain a national registry. Transactions between Parties or between account-holding legal entities will take place through these national registries.

• The executive board of the CDM will establish and maintain a CDM registry. This will contain CER accounts for non-Annex I Parties participating in the CDM.

• In addition, the Secretariat will establish and maintain a transaction log. This will verify transactions of AAUs, CERs, ERUs, and RMUs as they are proposed, including their issuance, transfers and acquisitions between registries, cancellation, and retirement.

Secretariat

Climate Change Secretariat (UNFCCC),
Haus Carstanjen,
Martin-Luther-King-Strasse 8,
D-53175 Bonn,
Germany

Mail address:
PO Box 260124,
D-53153 Bonn,
Germany

Telephone: +49-228-8151000
Telefax: +49-228-8151999
E-mail: secretariat@unfccc.int
or first initial last name@unfccc.int

Executive Secretary
Ms Joke Waller-Hunter.

Information Officer
Mr Kevin Grose.

Number of staff
63 professionals and 68 support staff (May 2002). Augmented by short-term staff and consultants as needed.

Information is also available through:
UNEP Information Unit for Conventions,
International Environment House
15 chemin des Anémones,
CH-1292 Châtelaine,
Switzerland
Telephone: +41-22-9799242
Telefax: +41-22-7973464
Contact: Mr Michael Williams
E-mail: mwilliams@unep.ch

Finance

The Convention defines a mechanism for providing financial resources for projects which address climate change. This financial mechanism is operated, on an interim basis and under the guidance of the COP, by the Global Environment Facility (GEF) (see IGOs). Projects supported by the GEF are implemented through three implementing agencies: the UN Development Programme (UNDP), the UN Environment Programme (UNEP), and the World Bank (see IGOs). The GEF provides resources for investment projects having global environmental benefits, including projects that reduce emissions of GHGs by increasing energy efficiency and the use of renewable energies. It also supports the building of capacity of developing countries to implement the Convention and prepare national communications to the COP. The GEF promotes bilateral and multilateral co-financing and the leveraging of private sector participation and resources.

The interim arrangements were reviewed by the first COP. It was agreed that the GEF would continue to serve as the interim financial mechanism. (See also Rules and standards, *Buenos Aires Plan of Action*, below.)

Budget
The approved core budget was $US11.6 million in 2000 and $11.3 million for 2001. A programme budget of $16.1 million for 2002 and $16.8 million for 2003 was approved by the seventh COP. It also approved a contingency budget for conference servicing of $5,661,800 for the years 2002–03.

Special funds
A Trust Fund for Participation in the UNFCCC Process is designed to receive voluntary contributions to support the participation in the COP and its subsidiary bodies of the representatives of developing-country Parties, in particular those that are least developed countries or small island developing States, and of other Parties with economies in transition. The resources needed for this Fund were estimated to be $3.7 million for the years 2000–01. Total income was $2.9 million and total expenditure $3.7 million for this period. The resources needed for the Fund are estimated to be $3.4 million for the years 2002–03.

A Trust Fund for Supplementary Activities serves as an important resource for the Secretariat in its attempts to respond to the emerging needs and requests of the COP and its subsidiary bodies. It is used for a variety of activities, including the convening of various workshops and seminars and the production of CD-ROMs, the publication *Who is Who in the UNFCCC Process: Directory of Participants at Meetings of the Convention Bodies*, the Secretariat's website, and website modules devoted to the intergovernmental meetings, as well as running the UNFCCC Fellowship Programme for professionals from developing countries. The voluntary resources needed for this Fund were estimated to be $6.2 million for the years 2000–01. Total income for this period was $5.9 million. Actual expenditure was $3.4 million in 2001–02. The voluntary resources needed for the Fund are estimated to be $7.3 million for the years 2002–03.

Around $6.8 million of additional contributions will also be needed during the years 2002–03 to support the prompt start of the CDM.

Rules and standards

The Parties of the Convention undertake:

- to develop, periodically update, publish, and make available to the COP national inventories of emissions from sources and removals by sinks of all GHGs not controlled by the Montreal Protocol (see this section), using comparable methodologies;
- to formulate, implement, publish, and regularly update national and, where appropriate, regional programmes containing measures to mitigate climate change by addressing emissions, sinks, and reservoirs of GHGs and to facilitate adequate adaptation to climate change;
- to promote and co-operate in the development, application, and diffusion of technologies, practices, and processes that control, reduce, or prevent GHG emissions;
- to promote sustainable management, and promote and co-operate in the conservation and enhancement, as appropriate, of all sinks and reservoirs of GHGs;
- to promote and co-operate in scientific, technical, socio-economic, and other research, systematic observation, and development of data archives related to the climate system.

The developed-country Parties (including countries with economies in transition) shall adopt national policies and take corresponding measures on the mitigation of climate change, by limiting their anthropogenic emissions of GHGs and protecting and enhancing their GHG sinks and reservoirs. These policies and measures will demonstrate that developed countries are taking the lead in modifying longer-term trends in anthropogenic emissions consistent with the objective of the Convention, recognizing that the return by the end of the present decade to earlier levels of anthropogenic emissions of GHGs not controlled by the Montreal Protocol would contribute to such modification.

These Parties may implement such policies and measures jointly with other Parties, and each of these Parties should communicate, within six months of the entry into force of the Convention and periodically thereafter, detailed information on its policies and measures, as well as on its resulting projected anthropogenic emissions by sources and removals by sinks of GHGs, with the aim of returning these emissions individually or jointly to their 1990 levels.

The developed-country Parties (*not* including countries with economies in transition) shall provide new and additional financial resources to meet full agreed costs incurred by developing-country Parties in complying with their obligations concerning communication of information.

The developed-country Parties shall also provide such resources, including those for transfer of technology, needed by the developing-country Parties to meet the agreed full incremental costs of implementing their commitments.

Each developing-country Party shall make its initial communication within three years of the entry into force of the Convention for that Party or of the availability of financial resources.

The extent to which developing-country Parties will effectively be able to implement their commitments under the Convention will depend on the effective implementation by developed-country Parties of their commitments under the Convention relating to financial resources and their willingness to transfer technology and take fully into account that economic and social development and poverty eradication are the first and overriding priorities of the developing-country Parties.

Parties that are least-developed countries may make their initial communication at their discretion.

Kyoto Protocol

The main provisions of the *Kyoto Protocol* imply, e.g.:

- Parties shall, individually or jointly, ensure that their aggregate anthropogenic carbon dioxide equivalent emissions of the GHGs listed in Annex A do not exceed their assigned amounts, calculated pursuant to their quantified emission limitation and reduction commitments inscribed in Annex B and the provisions of Article 3, with a view to reducing their overall emissions of such gases by at least 5 per cent below 1990 levels in the commitment period 2008–12.

The 5.2 per cent reduction in total developed-country emissions will be realized through national reductions as presented in the schedule.

- Each Party included in Annex I shall, by 2005, have made demonstrable progress in achieving its commitments.
- The net changes in GHG emissions by sources and removals by sinks resulting from direct human-induced land-use change and forestry activities, limited to afforestation, reforestation, and deforestation since 1990, measured as verifiable changes in carbon stocks in each commitment period, shall be used to meet the commitments of each Party included in Annex I. The GHG emissions by sources and removals by sinks associated with those activities shall be reported in a transparent and verifiable manner and reviewed in accordance with Articles 7 and 8.

The Protocol encourages governments to pursue emissions reductions by improving energy efficiency, reforming the energy and transportation sectors, protecting forests and other carbon 'sinks', promoting renewable forms of energy, phasing out inappropriate fiscal measures and market imperfections, and limiting methane emissions from waste management and energy systems. It creates new incentives for technological creativity and the adoption of 'no-regrets' solutions that make economic and environmental sense irrespective of climate change.

- Prior to the first session of the COP serving as the Meeting of the Parties to the Protocol, each Party included in Annex I shall provide, for consideration by the Subsidiary Body for Scientific and Technological Advice, data to establish its level of carbon stocks in 1990 and to enable an estimate to be made of its changes in carbon stocks in subsequent years;
- Any emission reduction units, or any part of an assigned amount, which a Party acquires from another Party in accordance with the provisions of Article 6 or of Article 17 shall be added to the assigned amount for the acquiring Party. Any emission reduction units, or any part of an assigned amount, which a Party transfers to another Party shall be subtracted from the assigned amount for the transferring Party. Any certified emission reductions which a Party acquires from another Party in accordance with the provisions of Article 12 shall be added to the assigned amount for the acquiring Party. At the third COP, Parties decided that the COP should consider issues related to the three mechanisms.
- If the emissions of a Party included in Annex I in a commitment period are less than its assigned amount, this difference shall, on request of that Party, be added to the assigned amount for that Party for subsequent commitment periods.
- Each Party included in Annex I shall strive to implement the commitments mentioned above in such a way as to minimize adverse social, environmental, and economic impacts on developing-country Parties. The Meeting of the Parties (MOP) to the Protocol shall, at its first session, consider what actions are necessary to minimize the adverse effects of climate change and/or the impacts of response measures on Parties. Among the issues to be considered shall be the establishment of funding, insurance, and transfer of technology.

GHG emission targets

Per cent change of GHG emissions by the commitment period 2008–12, taking 1990 as base year	
Australia	+8
Austria	–13
Belgium	–7.5
Bulgaria	–8
Canada	–6
Croatia	–5
Czech Republic	–8
Denmark	–21
Estonia	–8
Finland	0
France	0
Germany	–21
Greece	+25
Hungary	–6
Iceland	+10
Ireland	+13
Italy	–6.5
Japan	–6
Latvia	–8
Liechtenstein	–8
Lithuania	–8
Luxembourg	–28
Monaco	–8
Netherlands	–6
New Zealand	0
Norway	+1
Poland	–6
Portugal	+27
Romania	–8
Russian Federation	0
Slovakia	–8
Slovenia	–8
Spain	+15
Sweden	+4
Switzerland	–8
Ukraine	0
United Kingdom	–12.5
USA	–7
European Community	–8

Note: GHG emissions as listed in the Annex A. Some Parties with economies in transition use base years other than 1990: Bulgaria (1988), Hungary (average of 1985–7), Poland (1988), and Romania (1989).

The six decisions of the *Buenos Aires Plan of Action* are related to:

- the financial mechanism. The Parties agreed that the GEF should be the mechanism to enable developing-country Parties to meet, among other things, the agreed full costs of preparing national communications by maintaining and enhancing national capacity. The fourth COP also decided that the GEF should be an entity entrusted with the operation of the financial mechanism under the Convention and agreed to review its action every four years;

• the development and transfer of technology. This includes a decision on technology transfer under which the Subsidiary Body for Scientific and Technological Advice (SBSTA) (see Decision-making bodies, below) is requested to establish a consultative process to consider a preliminary list of issues and questions about technology transfer. The process is expected to result in recommendations on a 'framework for meaningful and effective actions' to implement Article 4.5 of the Convention. The decision also urges developed-country Parties to provide a list of publicly owned and environmentally sound technologies related to the adaptation and mitigation of climate change. It urges developing-country Parties to submit a list of their prioritized technology needs;

• implementation of Article 4.8 and 4.9 of the Convention (covering also Articles 2.3 and 3.14 of the Kyoto Protocol). This includes, *inter alia*, a decision to consider further issues related to identification of the adverse impacts of climate change and the impacts of implementing response measures under the Convention. The decision also calls for consideration of the actions needed to address these impacts, such as funding, insurance, and transfers of technology;

• activities implemented jointly (AIJ). The Parties agreed to continue the AIJ pilot phase so that developing-country Parties can build capacity and gain further experience;

• the work programme on mechanisms of the Kyoto Protocol. The programme was decided on with a view to taking decisions at the sixth COP in 2000 on the Protocol's flexibility mechanisms, including recommendations to the COP/MOP. Under the mechanisms, Parties can gain credit towards reaching their own reduction targets by helping other countries lower their emissions. An 'emissions trading' regime will allow industrialized-country Parties to buy and sell parts of their assigned amounts among themselves. The Clean Development Mechanism (CDM) and joint implementation (JI) program will provide credits for financing emissions-avoiding projects in developing countries and countries with economies in transition respectively that would not have occurred in the absence of such financing;

• preparations for the first MOP to the Kyoto Protocol. The fourth COP allocated the preparatory work needed for the first MOP. SBSTA will address, *inter alia*, guidelines for national communications, the Subsidiary Body for Implementation (SBI) will address guidelines for review of implementation by expert review teams, and SBI and SBSTA will jointly consider procedures and mechanisms related to compliance. Parties also selected tasks that should be accomplished by the first MOP, including actions related to policies and measures, carbon sinks other than forests, and guidelines for implementing JI.

The main decisions of the *Bonn Agreements* are related to:

• financial assistance—with agreement to establish three new funds: a special climate change fund and a least developed countries fund under the Convention, and an adaptation fund under the Kyoto Protocol, which will be managed by the GEF (see Finance, above);

• technology transfer—with agreement to set up a new Expert Group on Technology Transfer;

• adverse impacts of climate change and response measures on developing countries—including agreement on financial assistance to address adverse impacts and an obligation for Annex I Parties to report on their efforts to minimize these impacts;

• the Kyoto Protocol mechanisms—including agreement on: the eligibility of projects under joint implementation and the CDM; how to operationalize the Protocol's requirement that the use of the mechanisms be 'supplemental' to domestic action; provisions to prevent overselling through emissions trading; and the composition of the CDM executive board;

• land use, land-use change, and forestry—including agreement to expand the list of eligible 'sink' activities under the Protocol, subject to certain conditions and accounting rules;

• compliance—with consensus on the institutional structure of the compliance system under the Kyoto Protocol and the consequences that Parties will face if they fail to meet their emission commitments.

The *Marrakech Accord*, a set of detailed decisions giving effect to the Bonn Agreements, consist of five main elements:

• commitments. At the heart of the Protocol lie its *legally-binding emissions targets* for Annex I Parties. All Parties are also subject to a set of *general commitments*.

• implementation. To meet their targets, Annex I Parties must put in place *domestic policies and measures* that cut their GHG emissions. They may also offset their emissions by increasing the removal of GHGs by *carbon sinks*. Supplementary to domestic actions, Parties may also use the three mechanisms—*joint implementation*, the *clean development mechanism* and *emissions trading*—to gain credit for emissions reduced (or GHGs removed) at lower cost abroad than at home.

• minimizing impacts on developing countries. The Protocol and its rulebook include provisions to address the specific needs and concerns of developing countries, especially those most vulnerable to the adverse effects of climate change and to the economic impact of response measures. Among these is the establishment of a new *adaptation fund*.

• accounting, reporting, and review. Rigorous monitoring procedures are in place to safeguard the Kyoto Protocol's integrity, including an *accounting system*, regular *reporting* by Parties, and *in-depth review* of those reports by expert review teams.

• compliance. A *Compliance Committee*, consisting of a facilitative and an enforcement branch, will assess and deal with any cases of non-compliance.

Monitoring/implementation

Review procedure

The COP shall keep under regular review the implementation of the Convention and any related instruments that the Conference may adopt and shall make the decisions necessary to promote the effective implementation of the Convention. To this end it shall:

• periodically examine the obligations of the Parties;

• promote and facilitate the exchange of information on, and the co-ordination of, as appropriate, policies, strategies, and measures adopted by the Parties to address climate change and its effects;

• promote and guide the development and periodic refinements of comparable methodologies;

• assess the implementation of the Convention by the Parties, the overall effects of the measures taken pursuant to the Convention, in particular environmental, economic, and social effects, and the extent to which progress towards the objective of the Convention is being achieved;

• consider and adopt regular reports on the implementation of the Convention and ensure their publication;

• seek to mobilize financial resources.

National communications in accordance

with Article 4.2.*b* and 12 of the Convention should describe the Parties' efforts to implement the Convention and quantify present and projected emissions. The Secretariat completed reviews of the first national communications from Annex I Parties in 1997 with the publication of a compilation and synthesis report and reports on individual in-depth reviews. The full texts of the in-depth reviews and the reports and a compilation and synthesis are accessible on the Internet (see Sources on the Internet, below).

The second COP requested Annex I Parties to submit their second national communication by 15 April 1997. For those Parties which were due to submit the first communication in 1996, an update of this communication was to be submitted by the same date; second national communications by Parties with economies in transition should in principle have been submitted not later than 15 April 1998. In accordance with a decision at the third COP, Croatia, Liechtenstein, Monaco, and Slovenia were added to Annex I. The first national communications from these Parties were due by 13 February 1999. National inventory data on emissions by sources and removals by sinks are to be submitted on an annual basis by 15 April of each year.

Of the second national communications that were due by 15 April 1997, six were received on time, 17 were received late, and one had still not been submitted as of May 2002. Of the second communications that were due by 15 April 1998, three were received on time, six were received late, and two had still not been submitted as of May 2002. Of the first national communications that were due by 13 February 1999, one was received on time, two were received late, and one had still not been submitted as of May 2002.

In accordance with decision 11/CP.4 of the COP at its fourth session, the third national communications should have been submitted to the Secretariat by 30 November 2001. As of June 2002, the Secretariat had received national communications from 22 Annex I Parties, 13 of which were submitted on or before the due date. All the national communications received to date have been posted on the Secretariat's website.

The Secretariat co-ordinates in-depth reviews of the national communications, and the reports are published and posted on the website. The Secretariat began its in-depth reviews of third national communications in the first half of 2002. As of May 2002, three Parties had been visited by international teams of experts. A number of review visits are planned for the remaining half of the year.

Subsequent communications will be submitted on a regular basis at intervals of three to five years. Each national communication should be subject to in-depth review and include detailed information on national policies and measures to mitigate climate change.

Of the first communications from developing-country Parties (non-Annex I Parties), six were received in 1997; four were received in 1998; 12 were received in 1999; 27 were received in 2000; and 27 were received in 2001. Seven initial national communications had been received by June 2002.

The fourth COP decided that the communications by non-Annex I Parties should be considered in a facilitative, non-confrontational, and open and transparent manner to ensure that the needs of developing countries identified in their initial communications are brought to the attention of the GEF.

Of the national GHG inventories for the period 1990–99, 20 were received by the due date of 15 April 2001, ten were received late, and eight had still not been submitted by May 2002. Some Parties submitted information in draft or preliminary form, or in parts, or submitted subsequent revisions to their inventories.

The fifth COP adopted, by its decision 6/CP.5, the guidelines for the technical review of GHG inventories from Parties included in Annex I to the Convention for a trial period covering inventory submissions due in 2000 and 2001. Of the national GHG inventories submitted for 2000, 23 Annex I Parties provided information in the common reporting format (CRF) as part of their annual inventory submission in 2000. For the period 2001, 30 Annex I Parties submitted their inventory using the CRF.

Environmental monitoring programmes
The *Intergovernmental Panel on Climate Change (IPCC)* was established in 1988 by UNEP and the World Meteorological Organization (WMO) (see IGOs). The IPCC assesses scientific information related to the various components of the climate change issue, such as emission of major GHGs, and evaluates the environmental and socio-economic impacts of climate change.

The Parties shall support international and intergovernmental efforts to develop and strengthen the capacities and capabilities of the developing countries in these activities, and promote access to, and exchange of, data and analysis thereof obtained from areas beyond national jurisdiction.

Data and information system programmes
The Secretariat's information unit has developed a number of products aimed at facilitating the task of those participating in the UNFCCC process. This includes a searchable database containing all of the official documents of the COP and its subsidiary bodies (see Decision-making bodies, below), national communications received by the Secretariat, in-depth reviews and web-only documents. In addition, a number of guides to the negotiating process are available in paper and electronic form through the UNFCCC website. The contents of this website are made available on CD-ROM for the benefit of users without access to the Internet.

Trade measures
No provisions on trade measures to penalize Parties for non-compliance.

Dispute-settlement mechanisms
In the event of a dispute between Parties concerning the interpretation or application of the Convention, the Parties concerned shall seek a settlement through negotiation or any other peaceful means of their own choice.

Decision-making bodies

Political
The Conference of the Parties (COP) is the supreme body of the Convention, that is, its highest decision-making authority. It is an association of all the countries that are Parties to the Convention. The COP meets every year, unless the Parties decide otherwise. The seventh COP was held in Marrakech between 29 October and 9 November 2001 and the eighth COP will be held in New Delhi between 23 October and 1 November 2002.

Any Party may propose amendments to the Convention. The COP may adopt amendments, annexes, and protocols to the Convention in accordance with the procedure set forth in the Convention. The Parties shall make every effort to reach agreement on any proposed amendment or annex to the Convention by consensus. If all efforts at consensus have been exhausted, the amendment shall, as a last resort, be adopted by a three-quarters majority vote of the Parties present and voting at the meeting. The COP will serve as the Meeting of the Parties to the Kyoto Protocol when it enters into force. This body, the COP/MOP, will meet during the same period as the COP. Parties to the Convention that are not Parties to the Protocol will be able to participate in the COP/MOP as observers, but without the right to take decisions.

Any body or agency, whether national or international, governmental or non-governmental, which is qualified in matters covered by the Convention, or the Kyoto Protocol, and which has informed the Secretariat of its wish to be represented at a session of the COP as an observer, may be so admitted unless at least one-third of the Parties present object.

Scientific/technical

The Convention established two permanent subsidiary bodies: the Subsidiary Body for Scientific and Technological Advice (SBSTA) and the Subsidiary Body for Implementation (SBI). These bodies give advice to the COP and each has a specific mandate. They are both open to participation by any Party, and governments often send representatives who are experts in the fields of the respective bodies.

The task of the SBSTA, as its name suggests, is to provide the COP with advice on scientific, technological, and methodological matters. Two key areas of work in this regard are promoting the development and transfer of environmentally friendly technologies and conducting technical work to improve the guidelines for preparing national communications and emission inventories. The SBI gives advice to the COP on all matters concerning the implementation of the Convention. A particularly important task in this respect is to examine the information in the national communications and emission inventories submitted by Parties in order to assess the Convention's overall effectiveness. The SBI reviews the financial assistance given to non-Annex I Parties to help them implement their Convention commitments, and advises the COP on the financial mechanism (operated by the GEF). The SBI also advises the COP on budgetary and administrative matters.

The SBSTA and SBI work together on cross-cutting issues that touch on both their areas of expertise. These include capacity building, the vulnerability of developing countries to climate change and response measures, and the Kyoto Protocol mechanisms.

The COP may establish additional bodies as needed. Thus far, it has established two:

- the Ad hoc Group on the Berlin Mandate (AGBM), which was set up at the first COP to conduct the talks that led to the adoption of the Kyoto Protocol. It met eight times (plus a continuation of the eighth session on the eve of the third COP) under the chairmanship of Raúl Estrada-Oyuela (Argentina);
- the Ad hoc Group on Article 13 (AG13), which was also launched by the first COP, to explore how to implement Article 13 of the Convention. Article 13 calls for the establishment of a 'multilateral consultative process' to help governments overcome difficulties they may experience in meeting their commitments. The AG13 met six times, under the chairmanship of Patrick Széll (the United Kingdom), and made its final report to the fourth COP in 1998. Although it was able to agree on almost all elements of a multilateral consultative process, there is still no consensus over the composition of the committee that would run this process.

In addition, the fourth COP established a joint working group under the SBSTA and SBI to develop the compliance system outlined in the Protocol. The joint working group met in parallel with the SBSTA and SBI and reported to the COP through the subsidiary bodies. It was not, therefore, a subsidiary body itself. The joint working group held its final meeting at the sixth COP in 2000.

The Kyoto Protocol will make use of the same permanent subsidiary bodies as the Convention, but only Parties to the Protocol will have the right to take decisions on Protocol matters. The COP/MOP will also be able to establish its own subsidiary bodies, if needed.

Bureaux

The work of the COP and each subsidiary body is guided by a Bureau, elected by Parties to the Convention usually at the start of each session of the COP. To ensure continuity, the elected Bureaux serve not only at sessions of the COP and subsidiary bodies but during inter-sessional periods as well.

The COP Bureau consists of 11 members: two are nominated by each of the five UN regional groups and one place is reserved for a representative of small island developing states. The members consist of the COP President, seven Vice-Presidents, the Chairpersons of the two subsidiary bodies, and a Rapporteur. The Bureaux of the SBSTA and the SBI consist of a Chairperson, a Vice-Chairperson, and a Rapporteur, who perform similar functions to their counterparts on the COP Bureau and usually serve for two years.

The COP, SBSTA, and SBI Bureaux will also serve the Protocol, but only members representing Parties to the Protocol will be able to sit on the Bureaux when Protocol issues are being discussed.

Convention bodies

The COP has established the following convention bodies:

- a Consultative Group of Experts on National Communications from Non-Annex I Parties (CGE). It was set up by the fifth COP in 1999 to help improve the process of preparing national communications from non-Annex I Parties under the Convention. It meets twice a year, in conjunction with sessions of the subsidiary bodies, and also holds workshops to gather regional expertise. It is composed of five experts from each of the UN developing-country regions (Africa, Asia, and Latin America and the Caribbean), six experts from Annex I Parties, and three experts from organizations with relevant experience;
- a least developed country expert group. It was established as part of the Marrakech Accords. Its objective is to provide advice to least developed countries (LDCs) on the preparation and implementation of national adaptation programmes of action. It is composed of 12 experts: five from African LDC Parties, two from Asian LDC Parties, two from small island LDC Parties, and three from Annex II Parties. In order to ensure linkages between the LDC expert group and the CGE on adaptation issues, at least one member from an LDC and one from an Annex II Party are also members of the CGE. The LDC expert group meets twice a year. It reports to the SBI, and its work will be reviewed by the ninth COP;
- an expert group on technology transfer. The central task of the expert group, launched by the Marrakech Accords, is to provide scientific and technical advice to advance the development and transfer of environmentally friendly technologies under the Convention. The expert group comprises 20 experts: three developing-country members each from Africa, Asia and the

Pacific, and Latin America and the Caribbean, one member from the small island developing states, seven from Annex I Parties, and three from relevant international organizations. The expert group meets twice a year, in conjunction with the subsidiary bodies, and reports to the SBSTA. The work of the group will be reviewed by the twelfth COP in 2006.

Kyoto Protocol bodies
The following bodies have been or will be set up:

• a CDM executive board. The board supervises the CDM under the Kyoto Protocol and prepares decisions for the COP/MOP (the COP will assume the COP/MOP's functions until the Protocol's entry into force). It undertakes a variety of tasks relating to the day-to-day operation of the CDM, including the accreditation of operational entities, pending their formal designation by the COP/MOP.

The CDM executive board is made up of ten members: one from each of the five official UN regions, one from the small island developing states, and two members each from Annex I and non-Annex I Parties. When the Protocol enters into force, representatives from countries that have not become Parties to the Kyoto Protocol will be replaced. Each member of the executive board is accompanied by an alternate member, from the same constituency. The executive board was elected at the seventh COP, and held its first meeting after the close of the session on 11 November 2001;

• an Article 6 supervisory committee. The committee will be established by the first COP/MOP. It will oversee a verification procedure for ERUs generated by joint implementation projects in host countries that are not fully meeting eligibility requirements relating to methodological and reporting obligations. The supervisory committee is composed of ten members, each accompanied by an alternate member including three from the EITs, three from Annex I Parties that are not EITs, three from non-Annex I Parties, and one from the small island developing states;

• a Compliance Committee. The Committee will begin operation after the Protocol's entry into force. It will function through a plenary, a bureau, a facilitative branch, and an enforcement branch. The committee is made up of 20 members, with ten serving in the facilitative branch and ten in the enforcement branch, each with an alternate member. The composition of each branch is the same as the CDM executive board, that is, one member from each of the five official UN regions, one from the small island developing states, and two members each from Annex I and non-Annex I Parties.

The plenary consists of the members of the two branches, with the Chairperson and Vice-Chairperson of each branch making up the Bureau. The plenary reports on the activities of the Committee to the COP/MOP, submits proposals on administrative and budgetary matters, and applies general policy guidance received from the COP/MOP. The Committee will meet at least twice a year.

The procedural rules of the three Kyoto Protocol bodies—the CDM executive board, the Article 6 supervisory committee, and the Compliance Committee—are all similar. Members are elected for two years and may serve for up to two consecutive terms. The positions of Chairperson and Vice-Chairperson are held on annual rotation by an Annex I and a non-Annex I Party (in the case of the Compliance Committee, both groups will hold the position of Chair for one of the two branches). Decisions are taken by consensus, although a three-quarters majority vote may be taken if all efforts at achieving consensus have been exhausted; in the case of the enforcement branch, a double majority of both Annex I and non-Annex I Parties is also needed. Members of the CDM executive board and the Article 6 supervisory committee must not have any financial interest in CDM or joint implementation projects.

Publications

Up-to-date information on the Convention is available through the Secretariat, or through the UNEP Information Unit on the Conventions (see above).

Sources on the Internet

<http://unfccc.int>

Yearbook reference

See Benito Müller (2002), 'The Global Climate Change Regime: Taking Stock and Looking Ahead', *Yearbook of International Co-operation on Environment and Development 2002/03*, 27–39.

Vienna Convention for the Protection of the Ozone Layer, including the Montreal Protocol on Substances that Deplete the Ozone Layer

Vienna Convention for the Protection of the Ozone Layer

Objectives

- to protect human health and the environment against adverse effects resulting or likely to result from human activities which modify or are likely to modify the ozone layer;
- to adopt agreed measures to control human activities found to have adverse effects on the ozone layer;
- to co-operate in scientific research and systematic observations;
- to exchange information in the legal, scientific, and technical fields.

Scope

Legal scope
Open to all states and regional economic integration organizations.

Geographic scope
Global.

Time and place of adoption

22 March 1985, Vienna.

Entry into force

22 September 1988.

Status of participation

184 Parties, including the European Economic Community, by 11 June 2002. No signature without ratification after 21 March 1986.

The Secretary-General of the UN acts as depositary.

Affiliated instruments and organizations

Montreal Protocol on Substances that Deplete the Ozone Layer, Montreal, 16 September 1987. Entered into force on 1 January 1989. 183 Parties, including the European Community, by 11 June 2002. No Signatories without ratification.

The basic objective of the Protocol is to protect the ozone layer by taking measures leading to total elimination of global emissions of ozone-depleting substances (ODS) on the basis of developments in scientific knowledge, taking into account technical and economic considerations and the needs of developing countries.

Amendment to the Montreal Protocol on Substances that Deplete the Ozone Layer (London Amendment), London, 29 June 1990. Entered into force on 10 August 1992. 163 Parties, including the European Community, by 11 June 2002. The London Amendment added 12 new chemicals to the list of controlled substances and 34 new chemicals to the list of transitional substances with reporting requirements. It also added provisions relating to technology transfer and established a financial mechanism which included the establishment of an Interim Multilateral Fund to assist eligible Parties to comply with the control measures. The Fund, which became operational on 1 January 1991, is administered by an Executive Committee of the Parties. Contributions are made by the developed countries. Developing countries with an annual consumption of more than 0.3 kg per capita of chlorofluorocarbons (CFCs) and more than 0.2 kg per capita of halons also make contributions to the Multilateral Fund. By 29 April 2002, 138 of the 183 Parties to the Montreal Protocol were classified as developing countries. They are referred to as Article 5 countries.

Adjustments for strengthening the reduction schedules for the original controlled substances came into force automatically in March 1991. The third meeting of the Par-

Montreal Protocol on Substances that Deplete the Ozone Layer

ties added Annex D, a list of products containing substances from Annex A, to the Protocol. From 27 May 1993 Parties cannot import these products from non-Parties.

Amendment to the Montreal Protocol on Substances that Deplete the Ozone Layer (Copenhagen Amendment), Copenhagen, 25 November 1992. Entered into force on 14 June 1994. 141 Parties, including the European Community, by 11 June 2002. The Copenhagen Amendment speeded up the phase-out dates for many ODS, included hydrochlorofluorocarbons (HCFCs), hydrobromofluorcarbons (HBCFs), and methyl bromide on the list of controlled substances (see below), and confirmed financial arrangements for supporting the Multilateral Fund (see below).

Amendment to the Montreal Protocol on Substances that Deplete the Ozone Layer (Montreal Amendment), Montreal, 17 September 1997. Entered into force on 10 November 1999. 80 Parties, including the European Community, by 11 June 2002. The Amendment added, *inter alia*, a ban on the import of methyl bromide; an export ban on ODS when a country does not comply with the production controls of the Protocol; and the establishment of a world-wide licensing system, effective in 2000, to track the import and export of ODS and prevent smuggling and illegal traffic of ODS.

Amendment to the Montreal Protocol on Substances that Deplete the Ozone Layer (Beijing Amendment), Beijing, 3 December 1999. Entered into force on 25 February 2002. 34 Parties, including the European Community, by 11 June 2002. The Amendment included bromochloromethane for immediate phase-out; it also introduced production controls as well as control of trade with non-Parties for HCFCs.

Annex I of the Convention sets forth important issues for scientific research on and systematic observation of the ozone layer. *Annex II* of the Convention describes the kinds of information to be collected and shared under its terms.

The World Meteorological Organization (WMO) (see IGOs), together with the UN Environment Programme (UNEP) (see IGOs), plays a central role in harmonizing the policies and strategies on research.

Co-ordination with related instruments
Parties to both the Montreal Protocol and the UN Framework Convention on Climate Change (UNFCCC) (see this section) have noted the interlinkages between implementation of the Montreal Protocol and the Kyoto Protocol to the UNFCCC. The greenhouse gases included in Annex A of the Kyoto Protocol embrace hydrofluorocarbons (HFCs) and perfluorcarbons (PFCs) in view of their high global warming potential, while under the Montreal Protocol these substances are promoted as alternatives to ozone-depleting substances. The Meetings of the Parties of the two agreements have agreed to co-operate in developing information on these substances that will help the relevant bodies to determine the availability and potential ways and means of limiting emissions of HFCs and PFCs.

Secretariats

UNEP, Ozone Secretariat,
PO Box 30552,
Nairobi,
Kenya

Telephone:	+254-2-621234/623850
Telefax:	+254-2-623913/623601
Telex:	22068 UNEPKE
Cable:	UNITERRA, NAIROBI
E-mail:	ozoneinfo@unep.org

Executive Secretary
Vacant.

Deputy Executive Secretary
Mr Michael Graber.

Senior Legal Officer
Mr Gilbert M. Bankobeza.

Number of staff
Six professionals and nine support staff (April 2002).

Secretariat of the Multilateral Fund for the Implementation of the Montreal Protocol, Montreal Trust Building,

London Amendment

1800 McGill College Avenue, 27th Floor,
Montreal, Quebec H3A 3J6,
Canada
Telephone: +1-514-2821122
Telefax: +1-514-2820068
E-mail: secretariat@unmfs.org

Chief Officer
Dr Omar E. El-Arini.

Number of staff
Ten professionals and 11 support staff (April 2002).

Finance

Budget
The administrative budget for the Convention was $US370,590 in 2001 and is $1,207,991 for 2002. The proposed budget for 2003 is $370,590. The administrative budget for the Protocol was $4,099,385 in 2001 and is $3,907,646 for 2002. The proposed budget for 2003 is $3,763,034. Budgets are financed through a Trust Fund administered by UNEP to which Parties contribute according to an agreed assessment schedule.

The administrative budget of the Executive Committee and the Secretariat of the Multilateral Fund for the Implementation of the Montreal Protocol was $32 million for the period 1991–2002 (including staff contracts into 2003).

Main contributors
Main contributors by 31 December 2001 to the Multilateral Fund in the period 1991–2001 were the USA, Japan, Germany, France, the United Kingdom, Canada, Italy, and Spain (accounting for almost 83 per cent of the assessed contributions).

Special funds
The Vienna Convention Trust Fund and Montreal Protocol Trust Fund are intended to ensure adequate finance for the Ozone Secretariat, to service the meetings and to promote the participation of developing countries. The original Protocol, signed in 1987, established a ten-year grace period before developing countries were obligated to follow the agreed reduction schedule for controlled substances.

The Interim Multilateral Fund was established in 1990, with an initial three-year (1991–3) budget of up to $160 million, to meet agreed incremental costs to developing countries of implementing the control measures. The budget was subsequently increased to $240 million after China and India had ratified the Montreal Protocol. The UN Development Programme (UNDP), the UN Industrial Development Organization (UNIDO), the World Bank, and UNEP serve as implementing agencies of the Fund. UNEP also serves as the treasurer. After the entry into force of the London Amendment in 1992, the 'interim' Fund formally became the Multilateral Fund, from 1 January 1993.

At the fifth meeting of the Parties in November 1993, a replenishment of $455 million was approved for the period from 1994 to 1996. At the eighth meeting of the Parties held in November 1996, a replenishment of the Multilateral Fund at a level of $466 million was decided for the period from 1997 to 1999. The replenishment for the three-year period from 2000 to 2002 was fixed at $440 million at the eleventh meeting of the Parties held in December 1999 in Beijing.

Rules and standards

Parties of the Montreal Protocol are committed to:
(*a*) control measures to reduce production and consumption of specific substances;
(*b*) control of trade with non-Parties;
(*c*) regularly scheduled assessment and review of control measures;
(*d*) reporting of data;
(*e*) co-operation in research, development, public awareness, and exchange of information;
(*f*) establishment of a financial mechanism and transfer of technology to assist developing countries.

If a developing country considers itself unable to comply with control measures because of inadequate financial or technological assistance provided under the Protocol, it may notify the Ozone Secretariat, and the Parties can consider not invoking non-compliance procedures against the notifying Party. Decisions by the Meeting of the Parties are to be governed by a balanced voting procedure: a two-thirds majority of

Copenhagen Amendment

Parties, comprising separate simple majorities among the developing and industrialized nations.

As amended by the second meeting of the Parties, in London in 1990, commitments on measures relating to substances that deplete the ozone layer (paragraph (*a*) above) involve the phase-out of a specified list of CFCs and halons and of carbon tetrachloride by the year 2000, as well as the phase-out of methyl chloroform by 2005, with scheduled interim reductions for each of the above classes of chemicals.

The London Amendment stipulates the reduction of consumption and production of CFCs by 50 per cent in 1995, by 85 per cent in 1997, and by 100 per cent in 2000.

The 1992 fourth meeting of the Parties adopted the Copenhagen Amendment to bring forward the phase-out of CFCs and carbon tetrachloride and methyl chloroform by four or more years. For the first time the Parties agreed to bring methyl bromide, a substance used for fumigation of soil, cut flowers, fruits, storage, and structure under the Protocol. The new agreement also stipulates that industrialized countries should phase out:

- halons by January 1994 instead of January 2000;
- hydrochlorofluorocarbons (HCFCs), a less damaging transitional substitute for CFCs, by 2030.

Beginning in 1990, and at least every four years thereafter, the Parties will assess the control measures provided for in the Protocol on the basis of available scientific, environmental, technical, and economic information. Such assessments have so far been completed in 1989, 1991, 1994, and 1998.

In 1997 the Parties to the Montreal Protocol adopted the Montreal Amendment (see above), providing for a ban on the export and import of methyl bromide to and from non-Parties to the Protocol commencing one year after the date of entry into force of the Amendment. A new Article 4A was introduced in the Protocol providing for any Party still producing ozone-depleting substances after the phase-out date to ban the export of used, recycled, and reclaimed substances other than for destruction. Article 4B of the Amendment introduced a licensing system by providing that, effective on 1 January 2000, each Party shall establish and implement a system for licensing the import and export of new, used, recycled, and reclaimed substances.

Monitoring/implementation

Review procedure

Each Party to the Vienna Convention reports every two years to the Secretariat a summary of measures undertaken in the various categories of scientific research and co-operation. These are reviewed and discussed at the Conference of Parties (COP) every three years (every two years until 1993). The reports are public.

The COP to the Convention in 1993 decided that a Party would have fulfilled its reporting obligations under the Convention if it fulfilled its reporting obligations under the Montreal Protocol.

Compliance with obligations under the Montreal Protocol is measured through specific reporting requirements. Compliance in general is monitored through consultations with the Parties concerned, with the Implementation Committee under Non-compliance Procedure for the Montreal Protocol, and with the Secretariat, and through deliberations of the annual Meeting of the Parties.

Parties to the Protocol provide the Secretariat with annual statistical data on production and on imports and exports of controlled substances, including imports and exports to Parties and non-Parties. The Secretariat prepares a report to the annual Meeting of the Parties by aggregating data in such a way that data declared by Parties at the time of their reporting remains confidential. These reports are public. Review of data in national reports is undertaken by the Secretariat and by the Implementation Committee under the non-compliance procedure of the Montreal Protocol, elected by Meetings of the Parties.

The due date for reporting for each year is 30 September of the succeeding year. Of the 151 Parties due to report for 1995, 107 Parties (71 per cent) reported, of which 91 Parties (60 per cent) reported complete data. Of the 154 Parties due to report for 1996, 111 Parties (72 per cent) reported, of which

Montreal Amendment

101 Parties (66 per cent) reported complete data. Of the 166 Parties due to report for 1997, all Parties reported complete data. Of the 175 Parties due to report for 1998, all Parties reported complete data. Of the 171 Parties due to report for 1999, 159 Parties (93 per cent) reported by 24 April 2002, all of which reported complete data. 86 Parties (49 per cent) reported within the deadline of 30 September 2000. Of the 175 Parties due to report for 2000, 135 Parties (77 per cent) reported by 24 April 2002, all of which reported complete data. 96 Parties (55 per cent) reported within the deadline of 30 September 2001.

The reports are prepared in such a way that the information declared as confidential by the Parties at the time of their reporting is not revealed. The reports contain enough information for any reader to verify the compliance of the Parties with the Protocol. The Secretariat distributes publication lists of these reports.

Observations or inspections
None by the Convention as such.

Environmental monitoring programmes
None by the Convention as such. The Global Ozone Observing System, established by the WMO, is the only provider of ozone-related information to UNEP's Global Environmental Monitoring Systems (GEMS) (see IGOs). It has approximately 140 monitoring stations world-wide, which are complemented by remote sensing techniques. It is capable of providing data on both the horizontal and the vertical distribution of ozone and also the total atmospheric concentration.

Trade measures
Trade sanctions are embodied in the Montreal Protocol. The objective of such restrictions is to stimulate as many nations as possible to participate in the Protocol by preventing non-participating countries from gaining competitive advantages and by discouraging the movement of CFC production facilities to such countries.

Each Party shall ban the import of controlled substances from any State not party to the Protocol. As of 1 January 1993 no Party may export any controlled substance to any State not party to the Protocol. As of 27 May 1993 no Party may import products, specified in Annex D of the Protocol, containing substances of Annex A to the Protocol from any non-Party.

At the sixth meeting of the Parties to the Montreal Protocol, the Parties decided not to elaborate the list of products containing controlled substances in Annex B as specified in Article 4, paragraph 3 *bis*, of the Montreal Protocol. This decision was taken in view of the tightening of the phase-out schedule for Annex B substances from 1 January 2000 to 1 January 1996 and ratification of the Protocol by an overwhelming majority of countries. The elaboration of the list called for in Article 4, paragraph 3 *bis*, of the Protocol would be of little practical consequence, and the work entailed in drawing up and adopting such a list would be disproportionate to the benefits, if any, to the ozone layer.

At the eighth meeting of the Parties to the Montreal Protocol in 1996, the Parties decided not to elaborate lists of products containing controlled substances in Group II of Annex C of the Protocol in view of the fact that they could not identify any products containing hydrobromofluorocarbons (HBFCs).

Dispute-settlement mechanisms
When approving the Convention, a Party may declare in writing that, for a dispute not resolved by negotiation, or through the good offices or mediation of a third party, it will accept one or both of the following means of dispute settlement as compulsory: arbitration in accordance with procedures adopted by the COP or submission to the International Court of Justice. If Parties have not accepted either procedure, the dispute shall be submitted to a conciliation commission created by the Parties to the dispute, the recommendations of which 'the Parties shall consider in good faith'.

Decision-making bodies

Political
The basic administrative mechanism for the Vienna Convention is the COP held every three years (every two years until 1993). The Bureau of the COP to the Vienna Conven-

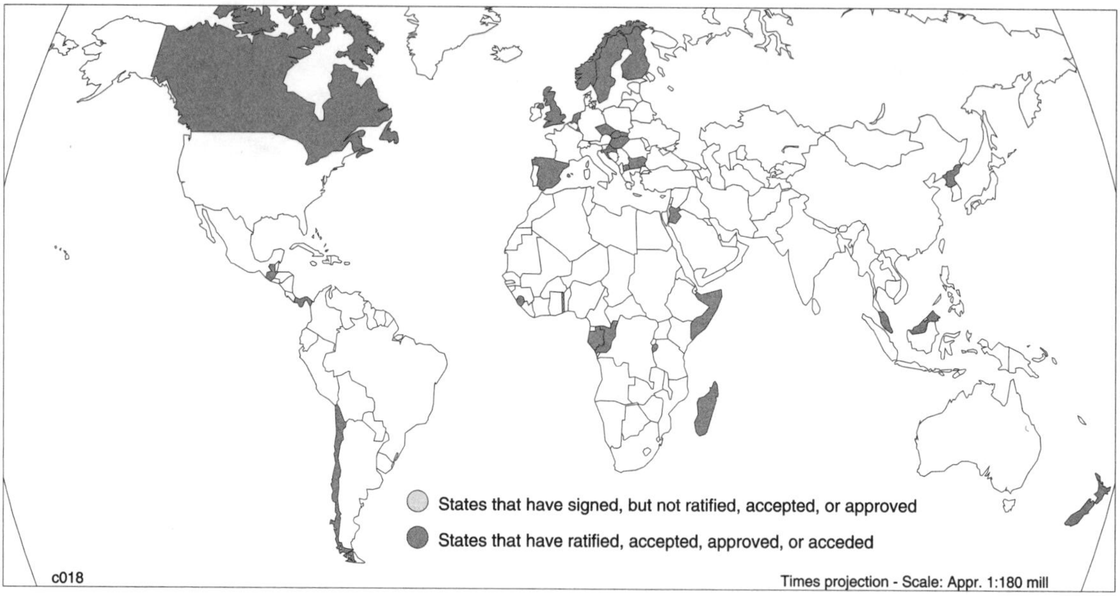

Beijing Amendment

tion meets intersessionally.

The COP is open to all governments, whether or not they are Parties to the Convention, as well as to observers from international agencies, industry, and non-governmental organizations. States that are not Parties and observers have no voting rights.

The basic administrative mechanism for the Montreal Protocol is the annual Meeting of the Parties. An Implementation Committee has been created, consisting of ten Parties, two each from five geographical groups (Africa, Asia, Eastern Europe, Latin America and the Caribbean, and Western Europe and others (Canada, USA, Australia, and New Zealand)). The Committee is charged with considering and reporting to the Meeting of the Parties any cases of non-compliance coming to its attention. The Meeting is ultimately responsible for deciding upon and calling for steps to bring about full compliance with the Protocol, including measures to assist a Party's compliance.

The Open-Ended Working Group of the Parties to the Montreal Protocol meets intersessionally to develop and negotiate recommendations for the Meeting of the Parties on protocol revisions and implementation issues.

The Meetings of the Parties and the Open-Ended Working Group of the Parties are open to all governments, whether or not they are Parties to the Protocol, as well as to observers from international agencies, industry, and non-governmental organizations.

The Executive Committee of the Multilateral Fund (see above) consists of 14 Parties made up of seven Article 5 and seven non-Article 5 countries. The Committee holds three meetings per year. The term of office of the Committee is one calendar year, and the Chair and Vice-Chair alternate each year between the two groups. The Committee is responsible for developing and monitoring the implementation of specific operational policies, guidelines, and administrative arrangements, including the disbursement of resources for the purpose of achieving the objectives of the Fund. It is assisted by a Secretariat located in Montreal.

The operations of the Executive Committee and the Fund Secretariat are financed by the Multilateral Fund. Through March 2002 the Executive Committee had held 36 meetings and taken decisions on policy issues and made disbursements amounting to over $1.3 billion, to support more than 4000 projects and activities in 132 Article 5 countries to be implemented through the four implementing agencies and by bilateral agencies. The implementation of these projects will result in the phase-out of the consumption of 158,855 ozone depleting potential (ODP) tonnes and the production of about 100,000 ODP tonnes of ODS. Of this total, about 81,000 ODP tonnes consumption and about 59,600 ODP tonnes production of ODS have been phased out. The Executive Committee has approved multi-year funding projects for the CFC production sector in China, India, and the Democratic People's Republic of Korea and for methyl bromide production in consumption phase-out in 18 countries. To facilitate the phase-out by Article 5 countries, the Committee has approved 116 country programmes (covering an estimated production of 129,000 ODP tonnes and consumption of more than 160,000 tonnes of ODS) and has funded the establishment and the operating costs of ozone offices in 122 countries.

Scientific/technical

The COP to the Vienna Convention has established a Meeting of Ozone Research Managers, composed of government experts on atmospheric research and on research related to health and environmental effects of ozone layer modification, which meets every three years (every two years until 1993). This group, working closely with the WMO, reviews ongoing national and international research and monitoring programmes to ensure proper co-ordination of these programmes and to identify gaps that need to be addressed. It produces a report to the COP with recommendations for future research and expanded co-operation between researchers in industrialized and developing countries.

At the 1989 meeting of Parties to the Montreal Protocol, an *ad hoc* Working

Group of Legal Experts on Non-Compliance Procedure was established. The Working Group, composed of government experts, was charged with elaborating further procedures on non-compliance. The non-compliance procedure established under Article 8 of the Montreal Protocol has been in operation since 1992 and was revised in 1998 to take into account new developments since 1992. The Implementation Committee, referred to above, is an integral part of this procedure.

The Montreal Protocol has established three Panels of Experts, to be convened at least one year before each assessment, which takes place once every four years:
(*a*) the Scientific Assessment Panel, composed of government experts and others, charged with undertaking the review of scientific knowledge in a timely manner as dictated by the needs of the Parties;
(*b*) the Technology and Economics Assessment Panel, which includes many industrial and non-governmental representatives. It analyses and evaluates technical options for limiting the use of ODS, estimates the quantity of controlled substances required by developing countries for their basic domestic needs and the likely availability of such supplies, and assesses the costs of technical solutions, the benefits of reduced use of controlled substances, and issues of technology transfer;
(*c*) the Environmental Effects Assessment Panel, which surveys the state of knowledge of impacts on health and the environment of altered ozone levels and the resultant increased ultraviolet radiation reaching the Earth's surface.

The Assessment Panels include experts from the non-governmental sector.

The project monitoring and evaluation system of the Multilateral Fund has been approved, along with the first work programme of evaluations.

To assist the work of the Executive Committee of the Multilateral Fund, two Subcommittees have been created from among the members of the Executive Committee. The Subcommittee on Project Review provides advice on project approval and related issues, while the Subcommittee on Monitoring, Evaluation, and Finance advises on project implementation and financial matters.

Publications

- *Montreal Protocol Handbook*;
- *Action on Ozone*;
- assessment reports;
- reports of the meetings of the Executive Committee of the Multilateral Fund;
- Country Programmes Summary Sheets (Multilateral Fund);
- Policies, Procedures, Guidelines and Criteria of the Multilateral Fund.

Sources on the Internet

<http://www.unep.org/ozone>
<http://www.unep.ch/ozone>
<http://www.unmfs.org>

Convention on the Ban of the Import into Africa and the Control of Transboundary Movements and Management of Hazardous Wastes within Africa (Bamako Convention)

Objectives

• to protect human health and the environment from dangers posed by hazardous wastes by reducing their generation to a minimum in terms of quantity and/or hazard potential;
• to adopt precautionary measures and ensure proper disposal of hazardous waste;
• to prevent 'dumping' of hazardous wastes in Africa.

Scope

Legal scope
Limited to member States of the Organization of African Unity (OAU).

Geographic scope
Regional.

Time and place of adoption

30 January 1991, Bamako.

Entry into force

22 April 1998.

Status of participation

18 Parties (ten ratifications and eight accessions) by 3 December 2001. 12 Signatories without ratification.

The OAU acts as depositary of the Convention.

Affiliated instruments and organizations

Annex I contains 48 categories of wastes which are subject to control under the Convention. The wastes are classified either as entirely hazardous, such as radionuclides, or as wastes having hazardous substances as part of their constituents, such as metal carbonyls or arsenic.

Annex II specifies the characteristics which identify waste as hazardous. There is, however, a catch-all provision which makes substances subject to regulation under the Convention if they have been declared hazardous and banned or if registration has been refused or cancelled by the country of manufacture or by the country of import and transit. An additional list of regulated substances may arise from the provisions which requires the Parties to inform the Secretariat of any substances not in Annex I which, under their national laws, are defined as hazardous. Similarly, radioactive wastes which are subject to international controls systems because of their characteristics are covered by the Convention.

Co-ordination with related instruments
Wastes from the operation of ships, the discharge of which is covered by other instruments, are specifically excluded from the applications of the Convention.

Secretariat

Information on the Convention is available from:
Organization of African Unity (OAU),
Attn Professor C. A. L. Johnson, Director a.i.,
Community Affairs Department,
PO Box 3243,
Addis Ababa,
Ethiopia
Telephone: +251-1-51-2456/7700 ext. 223 (direct)
Telefax: +251-1-51-7844/2622/3036
E-mail: johnson@telecom.net.et

Acting Director (Community Affairs Department)
Professor C. A. L. Johnson.

Head, Press and Information Division
Mr Desmond T. Orjiako (interim).

Number of staff
20 professionals and 14 support staff at the Community Affairs Department (December 2001).

Finance

The scale of contribution by the Parties to cover administrative expenses is to be decided at the first Conference of the Parties (COP)(see below).

Rules and standards

All Parties shall take appropriate legal, administrative, and other measures to prohibit the import of all hazardous wastes, when imported by third parties, from entering the territories of the Contracting Parties.

The Parties agree to ban the dumping of such wastes in the territorial sea, the continental shelf, and the exclusive economic zone.

On wastes generated within Africa, the Parties undertake to submit the details thereof to the Secretariat established by the Convention. Moreover, the Party within whose territory the wastes are generated is urged to ensure availability of disposal facilities; to minimize the output; and to impose strict liability on those generating the wastes. Such Parties are also required to ensure the adoption of precautionary measures to prevent release of such wastes and to enhance clean production methods. Every case of transfer of polluting technologies to Africa is to be kept under systematic review by the Secretariat, which is to make periodic reports to the COP.

Parties shall:
• prevent the export of hazardous wastes to the states which they know have prohibited the same;
• prevent the export of such wastes to a state which does not have the requisite disposal facilities.

In every case, the exported wastes must be handled in an environmentally sound manner.

To protect Antarctica, the Parties agree to prohibit any disposal within any area south of 60°S.

Each Party informs the Secretariat of the wastes banned under the Convention. The Secretariat, in turn, informs all other Par-

ties. It is thereafter the duty of every Party to prohibit the export of such wastes (see above), except for any Party which consents to the importation in writing. In every case, the Parties shall prohibit the export of such wastes to non-Parties which are developing countries.

Monitoring/implementation

Review procedure

Each Party undertakes to adopt national legislation to implement the Convention for the protection of human and environmental health. To that effect, they agree to adopt standards which are more stringent than those under the Convention or any other provision of international law.

The COP may adopt amendments and protocols to the Convention in accordance with the procedure set forth in the Convention.

When a Party has reason to believe that another Party is violating the provisions of the Convention, it shall inform the Secretariat and, concomitantly, convey the information to the Party against which the allegation is made. The Secretariat is required to take measures to verify the claim and to report to other Parties on its findings.

Observations or inspections

None by the Convention as such.

Trade measures

No provisions on trade measures to penalize Parties for non-compliance.

Dispute-settlement mechanisms

In the event of a dispute between Contracting Parties concerning interpretation or application of, or compliance with, the provision of the Convention, the Parties involved shall seek solution by negotiations or any other peaceful means of their own choice. Should this fail, the dispute shall be submitted either to an *ad hoc* organ set up by the COP for this purpose, or to the International Court of Justice.

Decision-making bodies

Political

The Conference of the Parties (COP), the supreme body of the Convention, consists of representatives of all the Contracting Parties. The first meeting of the COP will be convened by the Executive Director of OAU. As of December 2001 a date for the first meeting had not yet been decided. The COP determines the frequency of meetings.

Any body or agency, whether national or international, governmental or non-governmental, which is qualified in matters relating to hazardous wastes, and which has informed the Secretariat of its wish to be represented at a session of the COP as an observer, may be so admitted according to the rules of procedure of the Convention.

Scientific/technical

The COP establishes such subsidiary bodies as are deemed necessary for the implementation of the Convention.

Publications

Up-to-date information on the Convention is made available through OAU.

Convention on Civil Liability for Damage Caused during Carriage of Dangerous Goods by Road, Rail, and Inland Navigation Vessels (CRTD)

Objectives
To establish uniform rules ensuring adequate and speedy compensation for damage during inland carriage of dangerous goods by road, rail, and inland navigation vessels.

Scope
Legal scope
Open to all states. Regional integration organizations are not specified in the Convention.

Geographic scope
Global.

Time and place of adoption
10 October 1989, Geneva.

Entry into force
Not yet in force. The Convention requires five ratifications, acceptances, approvals, or accessions to enter into force.

Status of participation
No instrument of ratification, acceptance, or approval by 10 June 2002. Two Signatories in 1990 without ratification, acceptance, or approval.

The Secretary-General of the UN acts as depositary.

Affiliated instruments and organizations
The Inland Transport Committee of the UN Economic Commission for Europe (UNECE) fulfils the function of a standing forum for deliberations in matters concerning the Convention.

The corollary instrument addressing liability for damage from maritime transport of dangerous substances is the International Convention on Liability and Compensation for Damage in Connection with the Carriage of Hazardous and Noxious Substances by Sea (HNS Convention) adopted in 1996 (see this section).

Co-ordination with related instruments
An instrument addressing liability for dangerous activities is under consideration within the Council of Europe.

Secretariat
UNECE,
Transport Division,
Palais des Nations,
CH-1211 Geneva 10,
Switzerland
Telephone: +41-22-9172456
Telefax: +41-22-9170039
E-mail: olivier.kervella@unece.org

Director of Transport Division
Mr J. Capel Ferrer.

Chief, Dangerous Goods Section
Mr Olivier Kervella.

Number of staff
Four professionals and two support staff (May 2002) (for the overall work of the division on the transport of dangerous goods and perishable foodstuffs, which is not limited to CRTD matters).

Finance
Budget
The Convention does not provide for regular meetings and programme activities, or a secretariat. Therefore, under the Convention, regular administrative costs do not arise.

Special funds
None.

Rules and standards
The carrier, i.e. the registered owner or other person controlling a road vehicle or an inland navigation vessel, or the operator of a railway line, is liable for damage caused during the transport of dangerous goods.

Damage extends to loss of life or personal injury, loss of or damage to property, loss or damage by contamination to the environment, including reasonable measures for the reinstatement of the environment, and the costs of preventive measures.

The carrier's liability shall be covered by insurance or financial security, except that States or their constituent parts when acting as carriers do not require insurance cover.

The carrier may limit his liability per incident, in case of a road or rail carrier, to Special Drawing Rights (SDR) 18 million for claims concerning loss of life or personal injury, and to SDR12 million with respect to other claims; in the case of inland navigation vessels, these figures are SDR8 million and SDR7 million respectively.

No claim may be made beyond the regime jurisdiction against the carrier or any person engaged in the transport operation or in related salvage activities.

Action may be brought in the courts of Contracting Parties in which the incident occurred, or damage was sustained, or preventive measures were undertaken, or the carrier has his habitual residence. The carrier may establish a limitation fund in one of the courts where action has been brought. The court where the fund has been established will be responsible for deciding distribution of compensation.

Monitoring/implementation

Review procedure
The Convention does not require Parties to report implementation or supply data regularly and there are no mechanisms for a regular or periodic review of the regime. However, Parties having made reservations to the Convention shall notify to the depositary the contents of their national law.

The Convention also provides for simplified procedures for amendment of compensation figures. Requests for such amendments shall be supported by one-quarter, but at least three, of the Parties. Requests are considered by a Committee of the Parties, which adopts amendments of limitation figures by a two-thirds majority. An amendment shall be accepted if, within a period of 18 months, not at least one-quarter of the Parties have communicated their non-acceptance. Accepted amendments are binding on all Parties. In deciding, the Committee shall take into account past experience with incidents, changes in monetary value, and the anticipated impact of an amendment on insurance costs.

There are no procedures or mechanisms for the regular taking into account of scientific and technical information, except that dangerous goods are defined as those substances or articles which are either listed in the classes or covered by a collective heading of the classes of the European Agreement concerning the International Carriage of Dangerous Goods by Road (ADR) (see this section), or subject to the provisions of that Agreement. The regional ADR is regularly updated in the light of scientific and technical information.

Observations or inspections
None by the Convention as such.

Trade measures
No provisions on trade measures to penalize Parties for non-compliance.

Dispute-settlement mechanisms
No mention is made in the Convention of the settlement of disputes.

Decision-making bodies

Political
The Convention does not provide for the establishment of a separate institutional mechanism. The Inland Transport Committee of the UNECE fulfils the function of a standing forum for deliberations in matters concerning the Convention. Upon request of one-third, but at least three, of the Parties, the Inland Transport Committee shall convene a Conference of Parties for revising or amending the Convention. Moreover, the Inland Transport Committee shall convene, upon request of one-quarter, but at least three, of the Parties, a Committee constituted of one representative from each Contracting Party for amending compensation amounts according to simplified amendment procedures.

As yet here has been no meeting of the Committee of Contracting Parties or any Conference of Parties.

Scientific/technical
None.

Publications

- annual reports of the UNECE;
- *Explanatory Report* (ECE/TRANS/84);
- *Transport Information*, published annually by the UNECE.

Sources on the Internet

<http://www.unece.org/unece/trans/danger/danger.htm>

Convention on the Control of Transboundary Movements of Hazardous Wastes and their Disposal (Basel Convention)

Objectives
The goal of the Basel Convention is the environmentally sound management of hazardous wastes. To this end, the Convention pursues three key objectives:
- to reduce transboundary movements of hazardous wastes to a minimum;
- to dispose of these wastes as close as possible to where they are generated;
- to minimize their generation.

Scope
Legal scope
Open to all states and political and/or economic regional organizations.

Geographic scope
Global.

Time and place of adoption
22 March 1989, Basel.

Entry into force
5 May 1992.

Status of participation
151 Parties, including the European Economic Community, by 1 July 2002. Three Signatories without ratification, acceptance, or approval.

The Secretary-General of the UN acts as depositary of the Convention and its Protocol.

Affiliated instruments and organizations
Amendment to the Convention on the Control of Transboundary Movements of Hazardous Wastes and their Disposal (Ban Amendment), Geneva, 22 September 1995. (Not yet in force.) 29 states and the European Economic Community had ratified, accepted, or approved by 1 July 2002. In accordance with article 17 of the Convention, the Amendment has to be ratified by three-fourths of the Parties present at the time of the adoption of the Amendment (62 Parties) in order to enter into force.

The basic objective is to halt exports of hazardous wastes for final disposal, recovery, or recycling from developed countries (members of the Organization for Economic Co-operation and Development (OECD), European Community (EC), and Liechtenstein) to developing countries. The Amendment bans the export of hazardous wastes destined for final disposal with immediate effect. Export of wastes destined for recovery or recycling operations was phased out by 31 December 1997.

Basel Protocol on Liability and Compensation for Damage Resulting from Transboundary Movements of Hazardous Wastes and their Disposal (Basel Protocol), Basel, 10 December 1999. (Not yet in force.) 13 Signatories (Chile, Colombia, Costa Rica, Denmark, Finland, France, Hungary, Luxembourg, Monaco, Sweden, Switzerland, the Republic of Macedonia, and the United Kingdom) without ratification, acceptance, formal confirmation, approval, or accession by 1 July 2002. The Protocol is open to all states and regional economic integration organizations. It enters into force on the 90th day after the date of deposit of the 20th instrument of ratification, acceptance, formal confirmation, approval, or accession. The Protocol was adopted during the fifth meeting of the Conference of the Parties (COP-5), which was held in Basel between 6 and 10 December 1999.

The basic objective of the Protocol is to provide for a comprehensive regime for liability as well as adequate and prompt compensation for damage resulting from the transboundary movement of hazardous wastes and other wastes, including incidents occurring because of illegal traffic in those wastes.

The Protocol addresses who is financially responsible in the event of an incident. Each phase of a transboundary movement, from the point at which the wastes are loaded on the means of transport to their export, international transit, import, and final disposal, is considered. Delegates at COP-5 also adopted a decision for an interim arrangement to cover emergency situations until the Protocol enters into force.

The COP-5 adopted the *Basel Ministerial Declaration*. The Declaration, which will guide the activities of the Convention, outlines the main areas of focus during the next decade:
- prevention, minimization, recycling, recovery, and disposal of hazardous and other wastes subject to the Basel Convention;
- active promotion and use of cleaner technologies and production;
- further reduction of transboundary movements of hazardous and other wastes;
- prevention and monitoring of illegal traffic;
- improvement of institutional and technical capacity building, as well as development and transfer of environmentally sound technologies, especially for developing countries and countries with economies in transition;
- further development of regional and subregional centres for training and technology transfer;
- enhanced information exchange, education, and public awareness in all sectors of society;
- greater co-operation at all levels between countries, public authorities, international organizations, industry, NGOs, and academia;
- development of mechanisms for assuring implementation of the Convention (and amendments) and monitoring compliance.

The Basel Convention provides, in Article 14, regional centres for training and technology transfer. The Parties have emphasized the importance of the role of the Basel Convention Regional Centres (BCRCs), especially in enhancing the capacity of developing countries and countries with economies in transition in implementing the Convention. A total of 12 such centres have been established, in Latin America and the Caribbean: Argentina, El Salvador, and Trinidad and Tobago, with Uruguay as the co-ordinating centre; in Asia and the Pacific: China and Indonesia; in Africa: Egypt, South Africa, and Senegal, with Nigeria as the co-ordinating centre; and in Central and Eastern Europe: the Slovak Republic and the Russian Federation. More information

Convention on the Control of Transboundary Movements of Hazardous Wastes and their Disposal (Basel Convention)

is available at the website of the Secretariat (see Sources on the Internet, below).

The COP-5 established a very ambitious work programme for the Technical Working Group (TWG). The major task of TWG is to provide guidance to Parties in the fulfilment of environmentally sound management of the hazardous-wastes obligations under the Basel Convention. Currently, for this purpose, the TWG is preparing the following technical guidelines on environmentally sound management:

- used lead acid battery wastes;
- metal and metal compounds;
- plastic wastes and their disposal;
- dismantling of ships;
- environmentally sound management of POPs as waste. It is also continuing its scientific work on hazard characteristics.

Co-ordination with related instruments

The international organizations that are partners in the implementation of the Basel Convention are:

- Interpol, through co-operation on compliance and enforcement issues, including intelligence gathering, information exchange, guidance on codes of best practice, and training;
- the World Customs Organization (WCO), through harmonization of customs codes for wastes under the WCO Harmonized System and enforcement;
- the International Maritime Organization (IMO) (see IGOs), through co-operation in the area of prevention of dumping of wastes in the sea, ship wastes disposal, and recently on the disposal of wastes from the dismantling of ships and the transport of dangerous goods and wastes;
- the Organization for Economic Co-operation and Development (OECD) (see IGOs), through harmonization of legislation and procedures with regard to transboundary movements of wastes, including the classification of wastes and the development of the concept of environmentally sound management of wastes; and co-operation on the OECD/EUROSTAT (Statistical Office of the European Communities) questionnaire on the State of the Environment to ensure streamlining of data collection on hazardous wastes;
- the Organization for the Prohibition of Chemical Weapons (OPCW), through streamlining and exchange of information on the destruction/disposal of chemical weapons (some of which fall under the scope of the Basel Convention, as they may demonstrate or possess toxic properties under Annex III) and the decontamination of military sites;
- the UN Conference on the Transport of Dangerous Goods (UNCETDG), through formulation of procedures for and labelling of the transportation of dangerous goods, including chemicals and wastes;
- the World Health Organization (WHO) (see IGOs), on biomedical and health-care wastes;
- the International Labour Organization (ILO) (see IGOs), on occupational health;
- the Food and Agriculture Organization (FAO) (see IGOs), regarding issues of obsolete stocks of pesticides;
- the UN Industrial Organization (UNIDO) (see IGOs), on waste minimization in relation to the national cleaner production centres;
- the World Trade Organization (WTO) (see IGOs), on trade and environment;
- the UN Conference on Trade and Development (UNCTAD), on technical assistance;
- the International Atomic Energy Agency (IAEA), on issues related to disposal of radioactive wastes;
- UN regional commissions;
- the UN Commission on Human Rights;
- the Organization of African Unity (OAU), on the Bamako Convention and the follow-up action to the Rabat Declaration and Programme of Action on the Environmentally Sound Management of Unwanted Stockpiles of Hazardous Wastes and their Prevention;
- other regional organizations.

Secretariat

Secretariat of the Basel Convention (SBC),
International Environment House,
11–13 chemin des Anémones, Building D,
CH-1219 Châtelaine,
Switzerland

Ban Amendment

Telephone: +41-22-9178218
Telefax: +41-22-7973454
E-mail: sbc@unep.ch

Executive Secretary
Ms Sachiko Kuwabara-Yamamoto.

Number of staff
11 professionals and nine support staff (May 2002).

Finance

Implementation of the Convention and expenditures of the Secretariat are fully financed from contributions by the Parties to the two trust funds established under the Basel Convention. Parties pay their contributions on the basis of the UN scales of assessment to one of the trust funds, namely the Trust Fund for the Implementation of the Basel Convention. The Basel Convention Technical Co-operation Trust Fund consists of voluntary contributions made by Parties and non-Parties; the funding is for assistance to developing countries for the participation in the meetings of the Convention and for training.

Budget
The approved budget for the Trust Fund for the Implementation of the Basel Convention was $US4,201,854 in 2001 and is $4,201,854 in 2002. The budget for the years 2003–04 will be approved at COP-6 in December 2002.

The budget for the Basel Convention Technical Co-operation Trust Fund was $2,175,250 in 2001 and is $2,175,250 in 2002.

Special funds
An Interim Financial Mechanism to assist developing countries and countries with economies in transition to address emergency cases, compensation, and capacity building is being put in place.

Rules and standards

Parties shall:
• not allow the export of hazardous wastes or other wastes for disposal within the area south of 60°S, whether or not such wastes are subject to transboundary movement;
· prohibit or not permit the export of hazardous wastes and other wastes if the State of import does not consent in writing to the specific import, in the case where that State of import has not prohibited the import of such wastes;
• prohibit all persons under their national jurisdiction from transporting or disposing of hazardous wastes or other type of wastes unless such persons are authorized or allowed to perform such types of operations;
• designate or establish one or more competent authorities and one focal point.

States Parties of export shall not allow the generator of hazardous wastes or other wastes to commence the transboundary movement until it has received written confirmation that the notifier has received the written consent of the State of import.

In case of an accident occurring during transboundary movement of hazardous or other wastes or their disposal likely to present risks to human health and the environment in other States, those States must be immediately informed.

Parties shall adopt technical guidelines for the environmentally sound management of wastes subject to the Convention.

Waste exports are allowed only if the country of export does 'not have the technical capacity' or 'suitable disposal sites', and provided that the country of import has this capacity and facilities, in order to ensure environmentally sound disposal of the waste.

Monitoring/implementation

Review procedure
The Conference of the Parties (COP) shall keep under continuous review and evaluation the effective implementation of the Convention and shall undertake an evaluation of its effectiveness three years after the entry into force of the Convention, and at least every six years thereafter. Presently, the Legal Working Group is debating the issue of establishing a mechanism for monitoring and compliance which is to be adopted by COP-6.

Before the end of each calendar year, the Parties are required to transmit to the COP, through the Secretariat, a report on the previous calendar year, in accordance with articles 13 and 16 of the Convention.

National reporting is a tool for monitoring the implementation of the Convention by the Parties. It also serves to highlight the technical, legal, and other assistance required in Party countries for capacity building to implement the Convention successfully. The information provided by the Parties under national reporting on their country activities related to hazardous wastes and other wastes not only promotes improved information exchange between Parties but also make some of the crucial information related to the implementation of the Convention more visible.

The information/data reported by Parties in the completed questionnaires is reviewed, processed, organized, and repackaged by the Secretariat and is disseminated, as information products such as publications, statistical analysis, and graphical representation of the data, to Parties and others who are interested in the hazardous waste issues. The main publications are country fact sheets and compilation documents. These are available both in hard copy and in electronic form and are posted on the website of the Secretariat (see Sources on the Internet, below).

The country fact sheets (CFS) contain concise information on country activities related to hazardous wastes and other wastes. The Secretariat prepares individual CFS on an annual basis for each Party that reports for a given year.

The annual compilation document contains information/data provided by Parties in accordance with articles 13 and 16 of the Convention, in two parts. Part I of the document contains information on designation of focal points and competent authorities; national definitions of hazardous wastes; restrictions on transboundary movement of hazardous wastes and other wastes; reduction and/or elimination of the generation of hazardous wastes and other wastes; reduction of the amount of hazardous wastes and other wastes subject to the transboundary movement; effects on health and the environment; bilateral, multilateral, and regional agreements; disposal/recovery options available; and sources of technical and financial assistance.

Part II of the compilation document includes data on generation, export, and import of hazardous wastes and other wastes; disposal which did not proceed as intended; and accidents occurring during the transboundary movement and disposal of hazardous wastes and other wastes.

27 Parties had responded to the 1996 questionnaire by May 1999 and 65 Parties had responded to the 1997 questionnaire by 20 November 1999. 74 Parties had responded to the 1998 questionnaire by 15 October 2000, out of which there were 52 non-OECD reporting Parties. 89 Parties had responded to the 1999 questionnaire by 30 October 2001, out of which there were 67 non-OECD reporting Parties.

Decision-making bodies

Political

The Conference of the Parties (COP), the governing body of the Convention, shall keep under review and evaluate the effective implementation of the Convention, harmonize policies, establish subsidiary bodies, and undertake additional actions. The UN and its specialized agencies, as well as any states not party to the Convention, are invited to participate as observers at meetings of the COP. The COP can establish subsidiary bodies as deemed necessary for the implementation of the Convention. Any other body or agency, whether international or national, governmental or non-governmental, qualified in the matter of hazardous wastes or other wastes may participate as observers unless one-third of the Parties objects. Meetings are held every other year: COP-1 in December 1992, COP-2 in March 1994, COP-3 in September 1995, COP-4 in February 1998, and COP-5 in December 1999. COP-6 is scheduled to be held in Geneva from 9 to 13 December 2002.

The Extended Bureau, composed of actual Bureau members and previous Bureau members of the COP, is to provide general policy and general operational directions to the Secretariat between meetings of the COP and impart guidance and advice to the Secretariat on the preparation of agendas and other requirements of meetings and in any other matters brought to it by the Secretariat in the exercise of the functions, in particular regarding financial and institutional matters.

Scientific/technical

The COP has established:

- a Working Group for the Implementation of the Basel Convention (WGI), to facilitate the implementation of the Convention. It meets between the meetings of the COP. One of its main tasks is to prepare work for consideration of the COP;
- a Technical Working Group (TWG), to prepare technical guidelines for the environmentally sound management of hazardous wastes, to develop criteria on hazard characteristics of hazardous wastes, and to provide guidance on technical matters to the COP. Taking into account development with the Convention, the Group is actively involved in better clarifying what constitutes hazardous waste under the Convention;
- a Legal Working Group (LWG), to study the issues related to the establishment of a mechanism for monitoring the implementation of and compliance with the Convention, and to examine the issues related to the establishment of an emergency fund and the prevention and monitoring of illegal traffic in hazardous wastes.

The TWG and LWG also meet jointly to address common issues such as the Annex VII study and the legal and technical aspects of the dismantling of ships.

Publications

- Basel Convention Series;
- *Managing Hazardous Wastes* (bi-annual newsletter);
- *Status of Basel Convention Regional Centres* (annual).

Sources on the Internet

<http://www.basel.int>

Convention on the Prior Informed Consent Procedure for Certain Hazardous Chemicals and Pesticides in International Trade (Rotterdam Convention on PIC)

Objectives

• to promote shared responsibility and co-operative efforts among Parties in the international trade of certain hazardous chemicals in order to protect human health and the environment from potential harm;
• to contribute to their environmentally sound use, by facilitating information exchange about their characteristics, by providing for a national decision-making process on their import and export and by disseminating these decisions to Parties.

Scope

Legal scope
Open to all states and regional integration organizations.

Geographic scope
Global.

Time and place of adoption

11 September 1998, Rotterdam.

Entry into force

Not yet in force. Enters into force on the ninetieth day after the deposit of the fiftieth instrument of ratification, acceptance, approval, or accession.

Status of participation

22 ratifications, acceptances, approvals, or accessions by 10 June 2002. 60 Signatories, including the European Community, without ratification, acceptance, or approval.

The Secretary-General of the UN acts as depositary.

By April 2002, 172 countries had nominated 255 designated national authorities (DNAs) authorized to act on its behalf in the performance of the administrative functions required by the Convention.

Affiliated instruments and organizations

According to the Convention, export of a chemical can take place only with the prior informed consent (PIC) of the importing Party.

The PIC procedure is a means for formally obtaining and disseminating the decisions of importing countries as to whether they wish to receive future shipments of a certain chemical and for ensuring compliance with these decisions by exporting countries. The aim is to promote a shared responsibility between exporting and importing countries in protecting human health and the environment from the harmful effects of such chemicals.

The Convention covers pesticides and industrial chemicals that have been banned or severely restricted for health or environmental reasons by participating Parties, and which have been subject to notification by Parties for inclusion in the PIC procedure. Severely hazardous pesticide formulations that present a hazard under the conditions of use in developing-county Parties or Parties with economies in transition may also be nominated. The inclusion of chemicals in the PIC procedure is decided by the Conference of the Parties (COP). The Convention will initially cover at least 27 chemicals carried forward from the present voluntary PIC procedure, and hundreds more are likely to be added as the provisions of the Convention are implemented. Since the beginning of the interim period in September 1998, a further four pesticides have been added to the PIC procedure.

The PIC list includes the following 26 hazardous pesticides: 2,4,5-T, Aldrin, Binapacryl, Captafol, Chlordane, Chlordimeform, Chlorobenzilate, DDT, Dieldrin, 1,2-dibromoethane (EDB), Dinoseb and Dinoseb salts, Ethylene Dichloride, Ethylene Oxide, Fluoroacetamide, Heptachlor, Hexachlorocyclohexane (HCH) (mixed isomers), Hexachlorobenzene, Lindane, Mercury compounds, Methyl-parathion, Monocrotophos, Parathion, Pentachlorophenol, Phosphamidon, Toxaphene and certain formulations of Methamidophos, and Phosphamidon. The industrial chemicals are: Crocidolite, Polybrominated Biphenyls (PBBs), Polychlorinated Biphenyls (PCBs), Polychlorinated Terphenyls (PCTs), Toxaphene and Tris (2,3 dibromopropyl) Phosphate.

Certain specific groups of chemicals such as narcotic drugs and psychotropic substances, radioactive materials, wastes, chemical weapons, pharmaceuticals, and food and food additives are excluded from the scope of the Convention.

The Convention contains five *annexes* which form an integral part of the Convention:

- *Annex I* comprises information requirements for notifications made pursuant with Article 5 on procedures for banned or severely restricted chemicals;
- *Annex II* consists of criteria for listing banned or severely restricted chemicals in Annex III;
- *Annex III* lists chemicals subject to the PIC procedure (mentioned above);
- *Annex IV* contains information and criteria for listing severely hazardous pesticide formulations in Annex III;
- *Annex V* contains information requirements for export notification.

Co-ordination with related instruments

The original PIC procedure has been operated jointly by UNEP and FAO between 1989 and September 1998, based on the amended London Guidelines for the Exchange of Information on Chemicals in International Trade and the FAO International Code of Conduct on the Distribution and Use of Pesticides (see this section).

The new PIC procedure contained in the Convention is an improvement on the original procedure and is based largely on the experience gained during the implementation of the original.

Governments have agreed to continue to implement the interim PIC procedure, brought in line with the new procedures of the Convention until the Convention formally enters into force. This will avoid a break in the implementation of the PIC procedure.

There are a number of other international organizations whose activities are relevant to the implementation of the interim PIC procedures, and the Convention. For example, the assessment activities of the World Health Organization and the OECD (see IGOs), as well as the International Programme on Chemical Safety (IPCS), provide reference material for incorporation in Decision Guidance Documents (DGDs) and serve as information sources to importing countries on the hazards of PIC chemicals and alternatives.

There are also several other conventions which contain related provisions:

- The Basel Convention (see this section) also provides for export management and control regimes addressing highly toxic chemicals, although its scope is somewhat different, with the Rotterdam Convention focusing on chemicals in commerce and the Basel Convention focusing on wastes;
- The ILO (see IGOs) Convention concerning Safety in the Use of Chemicals at Work contains an export notification provision requiring member States, when exporting chemicals prohibited for reasons of safety and health at work, to communicate this fact and the reasons for the prohibition to the importing State;
- The Convention on Biological Diversity contains a provision related to informed consent somewhat similar in nature to the Rotterdam Convention;
- The Stockholm Convention on POPs (see this section) addresses many of the same chemicals as the Rotterdam Convention.

Secretariat

Establishment of a permanent Convention's secretariat, to be provided by UNEP and FAO, will be approved at the first COP. An Interim Secretariat is operative at the following addresses:

Interim Secretariat to the Rotterdam Convention,
Plant Protection Service,
Plant Production and Protection Division,
Food and Agriculture Organization (FAO),
Viale delle Terme di Caracalla,
I-00100 Rome,
Italy
Telephone: +39-06-57053441
Telefax: +39-06-57056347
E-mail: pic@fao.org

Executive Secretary
Dr Niek A. van der Graaf.

Interim Secretariat to the Rotterdam Convention,
UNEP Chemicals,
11–13 chemin des Anémones,
CH-1219 Châtelaine, Geneva,
Switzerland

Telephone:	+41-22-91781-75/84
Telefax:	+41-22-7973460
E-mail:	pic@unep.ch

Executive Secretary
Mr Jim Willis.

Finance

Budget
To be decided by the first COP.

Special funds
FAO and UNEP will maintain the level of contribution under the regular programme.

Rules and standards

The Convention provides for a process to add chemicals to the procedure. On taking domestic regulatory action to ban or severely restrict a chemical, participating countries are to submit a notification of this regulatory action to the Secretariat. Those notifications found to meet the information requirements of Annex 1 of the Convention are considered complete. When the Secretariat has received at least one notification from each of two PIC regions (see below) that are verified as complete, the chemical is reviewed by the interim Chemical Review Committee.

In the case of severely hazardous pesticide formulations a similar process is followed. A developing country or a country with an economy in transition can submit reports of pesticide poisoning incidents to the Secretariat. Where they are found to meet the information requirements of part 1 of Annex IV of the Convention, the Secretariat then collects the information listed in part 2 of Annex IV. The incident report and the information collected by the Secretariat are reviewed by the interim Chemical Review Committee

In both instances the Committee recommends to the Intergovernmental Negotiating Committee (INC) whether the chemical or formulation should be included in the interim PIC procedure. For each chemical the INC decides to include a decision guidance document (DGD) is circulated to DNAs. The DGD is intended to help governments assess the risks connected with the handling and use of the chemical and make more informed decisions about future import and use of the chemical, taking into account local conditions of use.

The seven PIC regions are Africa, Asia, Europe, Latin America and the Caribbean, the Near East, North America, and the Southwest Pacific.

The Convention contains provisions for the exchange of information among Parties about potentially hazardous chemicals that may be exported and imported and caters for a national decision-making process regarding import and compliance by exporters with these decisions.

The provisions regarding information exchange include:

• the requirement for a Party to inform other Parties of each ban or severe restriction on a chemical it implements nationally;
• the possibility for a developing-country Party or a Party with an economy in transition to inform other Parties that it is experiencing problems caused by a severely hazardous pesticide formulation under conditions of use in its territory;
• the requirement for a Party that plans to export a chemical that is banned or severely restricted for use within its territory to inform the importing Party that such export will take place, both before the first shipment and annually thereafter;
• the requirement that an exporting Party, when exporting chemicals that are to be used for occupational purposes, shall ensure that a safety data sheet that follows an internationally recognized format, setting out the most up-to-date information available, is sent to the importer;
• the requirement that exports of chemicals included in the PIC procedure and other chemicals that are banned or severely restricted domestically, when exported, are subject to labelling requirements that ensure adequate availability of information with regard to risks and/or hazards to human health or the environment.

Decisions taken by the importing Party must be trade neutral; that is, if the Party decides it does not consent to accepting imports of a specific chemical, it must also stop domestic production of the chemical for domestic use or imports from any non-party.

The Convention provides for technical assistance between Parties. Parties shall, taking into account in particular the needs of developing countries and countries with economies in transition, co-operate in promoting technical assistance for the development of the infrastructure and the capacity necessary to manage chemicals to enable implementation of the Convention. Parties with more advanced programmes for regulating chemicals should provide technical assistance, including training to other Parties in developing their infrastructure and capacity to manage chemicals throughout their life-cycle.

Each Party must nominateone or more designated national authorities (DNAs) authorized to act on its behalf in the performance of the administrative functions required by the Convention.

Monitoring/implementation

Review procedure
Each Party shall take such measures as may be necessary to establish and strengthen its national infrastructures and institutions for the effective implementation of this Convention. These measures may include, as required, the adoption or amendment of national legislative or administrative measures and may also cover:

• the establishment of national registers and databases including safety information for chemicals;
• the encouragement of initiatives by industry to promote chemical safety;
• the promotion of voluntary agreements, taking into consideration the provisions of Article 16 regarding technical assistance to developing countries and countries with economies in transition.

Each Party shall ensure, to the extent practicable, that the public has appropriate access to information on chemical handling and accident management and on alternatives that are safer for human health or the environment than the chemicals listed in Annex III.

The Parties agree to co-operate, directly or, where appropriate, through competent international organizations, in the implementation of this Convention at the subregional, regional, and global levels.

Nothing in this Convention shall be interpreted as restricting the right of the Parties to take action that is more stringently protective of human health and the environment than that called for in this Convention, provided that such action is consistent with the provisions of this Convention and is in accordance with international law.

The implementation of the Convention will be overseen by the COP. A Chemicals Review Committee (see Decision-making bodies, below) will regularly review notifications and nominations from Parties, and make recommendations to the COP on which chemicals should be included in PIC procedure. The Convention requires that the entire process be conducted in an open and transparent manner.

Observations or inspections
None by the Convention as such.

Trade measures
No provisions on trade measures to penalize Parties for non-compliance. However, according to Article 17, the COP shall develop procedures for dealing with non-compliance.

Dispute-settlement mechanisms
Parties shall settle any dispute between them concerning the interpretation or application of the Convention through negotiation or other peaceful means of their own choice.

A number of countries expressed the view that dispute settlement and the illicit trafficking of hazardous chemicals should be further discussed before the Convention enters into force.

Decision-making bodies

Political
During the interim period between signing and entry into force of the Convention, the Intergovernmental Negotiating Committee (INC) will continue to meet in order to oversee the implementation of the interim PIC procedure and to prepare for the first Conference of the Parties (COP). The eighth session of the INC was held in Rome from 8 to 12 October 2001 and the ninth session is scheduled to take place in Bonn from 30 September to 4 October 2002.

After the Convention enters into force, the COP will become the supreme authority. The first meeting of the COP shall be convened no later than one year after the entry into force of the Convention. Thereafter, ordinary meetings of the COP shall be held at regular intervals to be determined by the Conference.

The COP shall by consensus agree upon and adopt at its first meeting rules of procedure and financial rules for itself and any subsidiary bodies, as well as financial provisions governing the functioning of the Secretariat.

The COP shall keep under review and evaluate implementation of the Convention, harmonize policies, establish subsidiary bodies, and undertake additional actions.

National and international agencies and qualified NGOs may attend the COP's meetings as observers and contribute to its work.

Scientific/technical
An expert subsidiary body, the interim Chemical Review Committee (ICRC), is responsible for the procedure related to the inclusion of additional substances during the interim period. The ICRC reviews candidate chemicals and makes recommendations to the INC regarding their inclusion in the interim PIC procedure. The first session of the ICRC was held in Geneva from 21 to 25 February 2000, the second session was held in Rome from 19 to 23 March 2001, the third session was held in Geneva from 17 to 21 February 2002, and the fourth session is scheduled to take place in Rome in the first quarter of 2003.

The COP will, at its first meeting, establish a permanent subsidiary body, the Chemical Review Committee, for the purposes of performing the functions assigned to it by the Convention, such as reviewing information from the Parties and making recommendations to the COP. The members of the Committee shall be appointed by the COP and shall consist of a limited number of government-designated experts in chemicals management. The members shall be appointed on the basis of equitable geographical distribution, in particular ensuring a balance between developed and developing Parties. The Committee shall make every effort to make its recommendations by consensus.

Publications

Current information and reports of meetings and workshops are available from the Secretariat.

Sources on the Internet

<http://www.pic.int>

Convention on the Transboundary Effects of Industrial Accidents

Objectives

• to promote prevention of, preparedness for, and response to industrial accidents capable of causing transboundary effects, and international co-operation in these fields by mutual assistance, research, and development, as well as exchange of information and technology regarding industrial accidents in general, and to this end to strive towards convergence of relevant national policies and practices;
• to provide for notification among states concerned (*a*) on any proposed or existing hazardous activity capable of causing transboundary effects in the event of an industrial accident, and (*b*) on any industrial accident, or imminent threat thereof, which causes or is capable of causing transboundary effects;
• to provide for mutual assistance in the event of an industrial accident;
• to promote public information and participation in relevant decision-making processes concerning hazardous activities.

Scope

Legal scope
Open to member countries of the UN Economic Commission for Europe (UNECE), regional economic integration organizations constituted by sovereign States members of the ECE, and other European states having consultative status with the UNECE.

Geographic scope
Regional. UNECE region (Europe and North America).

Time and place of adoption

17 March 1992, Helsinki.

Entry into force

19 April 2000.

Status of participation

24 Parties, including the European Community, by 11 June 2002. Ten Signatories without ratification, acceptance, or approval.

The Secretary-General of the UN acts as depositary.

Affiliated instruments and organizations

The Convention contains also 13 *annexes* which form an integral part of the Convention.

The Executive Secretary of the UNECE carries out the secretariat functions.

Co-ordination with related instruments
Collaboration is taking place with other UNECE conventions, especially the Convention on the Protection and Use of Transboundary Watercourses and International Lakes (ECE Water Convention) (see this section).

Secretariat

UNECE, Environment and Human Settlements Division (ENHS),
Palais des Nations,
CH-1211 Geneva 10,
Switzerland
Telephone: +41-22-9173174
Telefax: +41-22-9170107
E-mail: sergiusz.ludwiczak@unece.org

Information contact
Mr Sergiusz Ludwiczak.

Finance

Costs of meetings, documentation, and secretariat services are covered by the regular budget of UNECE. A trust fund, based on voluntary contributions by Parties and other UNECE member countries, was established in order to contribute to the implementation of the work plan under the Convention.

Rules and standards

The Convention stipulates measures and procedures:
• to reduce the risk of industrial accidents and improve preventive, preparedness, and response measures, including restoration measures;
• to obtain and transmit identification of hazardous activities that are reasonably causing a transboundary effect;

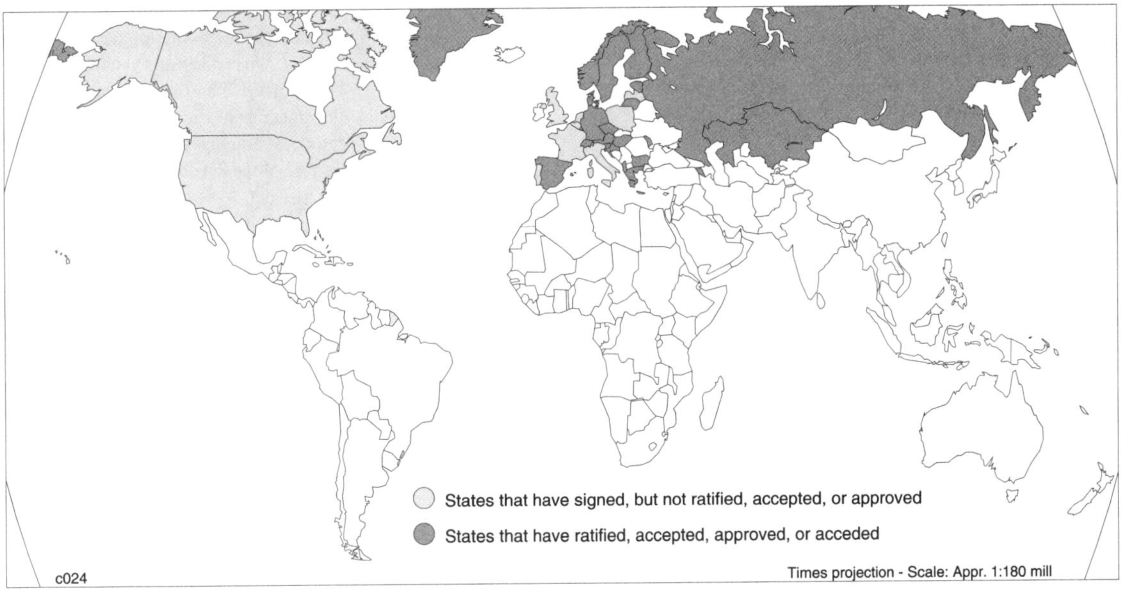

• to co-operate with other countries to develop off-site and on-site contingency plans, in particular joint contingency plans regarding industrial accidents, in order to respond properly and mitigate effects, including transboundary effects;
• to ensure that adequate information concerning hazardous activities is given to the public;
• to receive notification in the event of an industrial accident or imminent threat thereof;
• to request assistance from other countries in the event of an industrial accident in order to minimize its consequences, including its transboundary effect;
• to facilitate the exchange of safety technology and the provision of technical assistance;
• to benefit from international co-operation concerning prevention of, preparedness for, and response to industrial accidents, including exchange of information and experience gained from past industrial accidents and research and development in this field.

Monitoring/implementation

Review procedure

The Parties shall report periodically on the implementation of this Convention.

At its first meeting, the Conference of the Parties (COP) took a number of important decisions facilitating the implementation of the Convention and defining the priorities of work within its framework in the years ahead. One of the priority tasks is to enlarge the scope of the Convention's application to the entire UNECE region as soon as possible. The Parties agreed on guidelines to facilitate the identification of hazardous activities for the purpose of the Convention andon the format and procedures for reporting on the implementation of the Convention; they set up a Working Group on Implementation to monitor this process. The first Report on the Implementation of the Convention and the Conclusions and Recommendations for Strengthening the Implementation will be available at the second meeting of the COP. The Parties also agreed to continue work on the prevention of accidental water pollution.

The Parties to the Convention recognized the shortcomings of existing international civil liability instruments. In this context, they stressed the need for an appropriate regime, including a legally binding instrument, in the UNECE region on civil liability for damage caused by hazardous activities within the scope of this Convention and that on the Protection and Use of Transboundary Watercourses and International Lakes. A joint special session of the governing bodies of the two Conventions was held in Geneva from 2 to 3 July 2001. The joint special session decided that an intergovernmental negotiation process be entered into aimed at adopting a legally binding instrument on civil liability for transboundary damage caused by hazardous activities, within the scope of both Conventions. To this end, it established an intergovernmental Working Group on Civil Liability with a mandate to draw up the above mentioned legally binding instrument. Negotiations are well under way, and by May 2002 the Working Group had held three meetings; two more were planned for 2002.

To respond effectively and in a co-ordinated way to an industrial accident, Parties must be informed as soon as possible, since time is of the essence. The Convention consequently calls on Parties to set up special notification systems. The UNECE Industrial Accident Notification System has been developed with this in mind and accepted by the COP. It includes forms for giving early warning, providing information, and requesting assistance. This system will make it easier for a country where an industrial accident has taken place to notify all the others that could be affected and to give them the information they need to fight its possible effects.

Each Party must designate or set up competent authorities specifically responsible for the Convention's implementation. Other UNECE member countries have nominated focal points.

According to the Convention, Parties must also designate points of contact, to whom industrial accident notifications and requests for assistance must be addressed.

By April 2002, the network of points of contact comprised 36 countries and the European Community. The Secretariat regularly updates this list; however, access to it is restricted.

If there is a doubt whether an activity is likely to have a significant adverse transboundary impact and the Parties concerned do not agree on whether the activity is hazardous, in accordance with *Annex I*, the State which could be affected may submit the question to a commission of inquiry in accordance with *Annex II*. The requesting Party or Parties shall notify the secretariat that it is (they are) submitting questions to a commission of inquiry. The notification shall state the subject-matter of the inquiry, in accordance with *Annex III*, and all Parties will immediately be informed of it by the secretariat. The inquiry commission will consist of three members. Both the requesting Party and the other Party to the inquiry procedure shall appoint a scientific or technical expert, and the two experts so appointed shall designate by common agreement a third expert to be the president of the commission. The Parties to the inquiry procedure must facilitate the work of that commission by providing it with all relevant documents, facilities, and information and by enabling it to call witnesses or experts and receive their evidence. If one of the Parties to the inquiry procedure does not appear before the commission or fails to present its case, the other Party may request the commission to continue the proceedings and complete its work. The final opinion of the commission of inquiry shall reflect the view of the majority of its members and shall include any dissenting view.

Observations or inspections
None by the Convention as such.

Trade measures
No provisions on trade measures to penalize Parties for non-compliance.

Dispute-settlement mechanisms
If a dispute arises between two or more Parties over the interpretation or application of the Convention, they shall seek a solution by negotiation or by any other method of dispute settlement acceptable to the parties to the dispute.

Decision-making bodies

Political
The COP was constituted as the governing body at its first meeting in Brussels from 22 to 24 November 2000. The second meeting of the COP will be held in Chisinau (Republic of Moldova) from 6 to 8 November 2002. The COP will review the implementation of the Convention and fulfil such other functions as may be appropriate under the provisions of the Convention.

Where appropriate, the COP will consider and, where necessary, adopt proposals for amendments to the Convention. Agreement on the proposed amendment should be reached by consensus, with the exception of *Annex I*. When all efforts at consensus have been exhausted and no agreement reached, the amendment to *Annex I* shall, as a last resort, be adopted by a nine-tenths majority vote of the Parties present and voting at the meeting.

Scientific/technical
The COP will establish, as appropriate, working groups and other mechanisms to consider matters related to the implementation and development of the Convention.

At its first meeting, the COP set up a Working Group on Implementation and extended the mandate of the joint *ad hoc* expert group on water and industrial accidents to work on issues related to the prevention of accidental water pollution.

Publications

- UN Economic Commission for Europe (1994), *Convention on the Transboundary Effects of Industrial Accidents*, ECE/ENHS/NONE/2 (New York and Geneva: UN);
- *Industrial Accidents Manual* [available on the Convention's website].

In addition, up-to-date information is available from the secretariat.

Sources on the Internet

<http://www.unece.org/env/teia>

Convention to Ban the Importation into Forum Island Countries of Hazardous and Radioactive Wastes and to Control the Transboundary Movement and Management of Hazardous Wastes within the South Pacific Region (Waigani Convention)

Objectives

- to prohibit the importation of hazardous wastes and radioactive wastes into Pacific Islands developing Parties;
- to reduce the transboundary movement of hazardous wastes to a minimum consistent with their environmentally sound management;
- to treat and dispose of hazardous wastes as close as possible to their source of generation in an environmentally sound way;
- to minimize the generation of hazardous wastes (quantity-potential hazard).

Scope

Legal scope

Open to all members of the South Pacific Forum, other states not members of the South Pacific Forum that have territories in the Convention area, and other States that do not have territories in the Convention area pursuant to a decision of the Conference of the Parties (COP). Not open to economic regional organizations.

Geographic scope

Regional. The Convention area comprises:

- the land territory, internal waters, territorial sea, continental shelf, archipelagic waters, and exclusive economic zones established in accordance with the international law of countries and territories located within the South Pacific region;
- those areas of high seas which are enclosed from all sides by the exclusive economic zones referred to above;
- areas of the Pacific Ocean between the Tropic of Cancer and 60°S and between 130°E and 120°W to the Convention area.

Time and place of adoption

16 September 1995, Waigani.

Entry into force

21 October 2001.

Status of participation

Ten Parties by 15 February 2002. Five Signatories, without ratification, acceptance, or approval.

The Secretary-General of the South Pacific Forum Secretariat, Suva, Fiji, acts as depositary.

Affiliated instruments and organizations

Annexes contain detailed operational obligations on categories of wastes which are hazardous wastes, a list of hazardous characteristics, disposal operations, notification procedures, and arbitration.

Co-ordination with related instruments

Provisions are established to co-ordinate the Convention with:

- *Convention on the Control of Transboundary Movements of Hazardous Wastes and their Disposal (Basel Convention)* (see this section);
- *Convention on the Prevention of Marine Pollution by Dumping of Wastes and Other Matter (London Convention 1972)* (see this section);
- *International Convention for the Prevention of Pollution from Ships, 1973, as modified by the Protocol of 1978 relating thereto (MARPOL 73/78)* (see this section);
- *Convention for the Protection of the Natural Resources and Environment of the South Pacific Region (Noumea Convention)* (see Conventions within the UNEP Regional Seas Programme, this section);
- *Convention on the Prior Informed Consent Procedure for Certain Hazardous Chemicals and Pesticides in International Trade (Rotterdam Convention on PIC)* (see this section);
- *Stockholm Convention on Persistent Organic Pollutants (Stockholm Convention on POPs)* (see this section);
- *UN Convention on the Law of the Sea (LOS Convention)* (see this section);
- IAEA (see IGOs), regarding *Code of Practice on the International Transboundary Movement of Radioactive Wastes*;
- the South Pacific Nuclear Free Zone Treaty (see IGOs, IAEA).

A memorandum of understanding was passed with the Secretariat of the Basel Convention on 12 February 1996.

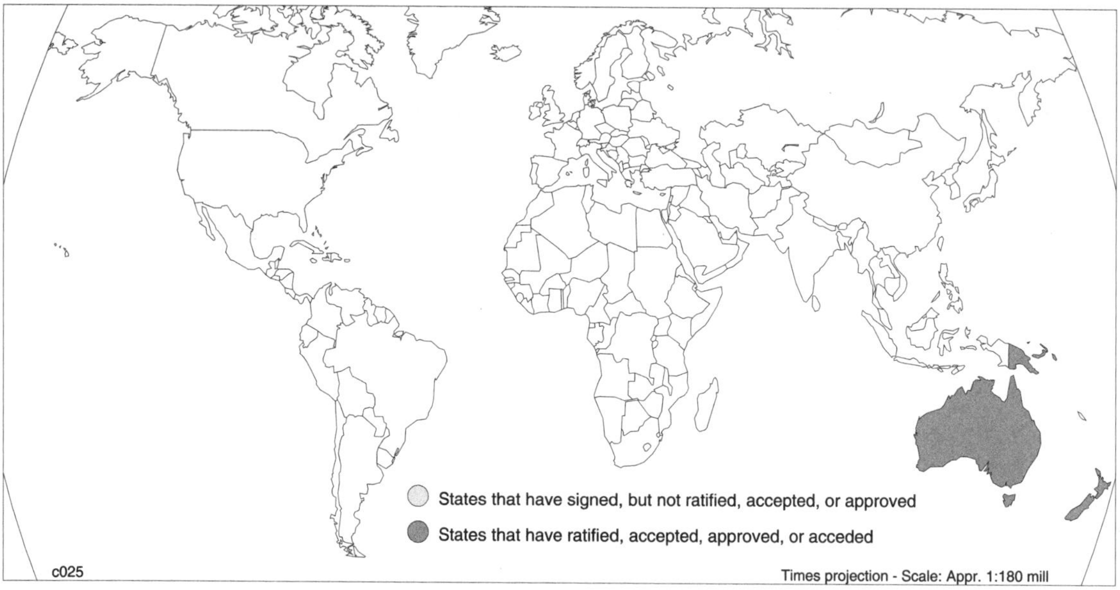

Secretariat

South Pacific Regional Environment Programme (SPREP),
PO Box 240, Vaitele,
Apia,
Western Samoa
Telephone: +685-21929
Telefax: +685-20231
E-mail: sprep@sprep.org.ws

Director
Mr Tamarii Pierre Tutangata.

Legal Officers
Mr Andrea Volentras and Dr Jacques Mougeot.

Finance

To be decided by the COP. External assistance is to be sought after.

Budget
Premature.

Special funds
The COP shall consider establishing a revolving fund to assist on an interim basis in case of emergency situations to minimize damage from disasters or accidents arising from transboundary movement or disposal of hazardous wastes within the Convention area.

Rules and standards

Each Pacific Island developing Party shall take appropriate legal, administrative, and other measures within the area under its jurisdiction to ban the import of all hazardous wastes and radioactive wastes from outside the Convention area. Such import shall be deemed an illegal and criminal act.

Each other Party shall take similar measures within the area under its jurisdiction to ban the export of all hazardous wastes and radioactive wastes to all Forum Island countries, or to territories located in the Convention area. Such export shall be deemed an illegal and criminal act.

To facilitate compliance with the above paragraphs, all Parties shall:

- forward in a timely manner all information relating to illegal hazardous wastes and radioactive import activity within the area under its jurisdiction to the Secretariat, which shall distribute the information as soon as possible to all Parties;
- co-operate to ensure that no illegal import of hazardous wastes and radioactive wastes from a non-Party enters areas under the jurisdiction of a Party to the Convention.

Each Party is recommended to become a Party to the London Convention 1972, the Noumea Convention and its Protocol for the Prevention of Pollution of the South Pacific Region by Dumping, and the Basel Convention. Each Party shall:

- ensure that, within the area of its jurisdiction, the generation of hazardous wastes is reduced at its sources to a minimum, taking into account social, technological, and economic needs;
- take all appropriate legal, administrative, and other measures to ensure that, within the area under its jurisdiction, all transboundary movements of hazardous wastes generated within the Convention area are carried out in accordance with the provisions of the Convention;
- designate or establish one competent authority and one focal point to facilitate the implementation of the Convention.

The exporting Party shall notify, or shall require the generator or exporter to notify, in writing, through its competent authority, the competent authority of the countries concerned of any proposed transboundary movement of hazardous wastes.

In case of an accident occurring during transboundary movement of hazardous wastes or their disposal likely to present risks to human health and the environment in other States and Parties, those States and Parties must be immediately informed.

Monitoring/implementation

Review procedure
The COP shall keep under continuous review and evaluation the effective implementation of the Convention. The first meeting of the COP shall consider the adoption of any additional measures in accordance with

the 'precautionary principle' relating to the implementation of the Convention.

The COP shall establish and/or designate such subsidiary bodies as are deemed necessary for the implementation of the Convention.

Each Party shall submit such reports as the COP requires regarding the hazardous waste generated in the area under its jurisdiction in order to enable the Secretariat to produce a regular hazardous wastes report.

Illegal traffic
Any transboundary movement of hazardous wastes taking place in contravention of the provisions of the Convention is considered as illegal traffic. Illegal traffic covers:
• movement without notification to all countries concerned;
• movement without the consent of a country concerned;
• movement where consent is obtained from countries though falsification, misinterpretation, or fraud;
• deliberate disposal of hazardous wastes in contravention with other relevant international instruments and general principles of international law;
• movement in contradiction with the import-export ban.

Co-ordination with the Secretariat of the Basel Convention is mandatory for the prevention and monitoring of illegal traffic in hazardous wastes.

Observations or inspections
None by the Convention as such.

Trade measures
No provisions on trade sanctions to penalize Parties for non-compliance.

Dispute-settlement mechanisms
Parties shall settle any dispute between them concerning the interpretation, application of, or compliance with the Convention, or any protocol thereto, through negotiation or other peaceful means of their own choice.

On becoming a member of the Convention, Parties may, by a written declaration, recognize as compulsory, in relation to any Party accepting the same obligation:
• arbitration in accordance with procedures adopted by the COP in Annex VII;
• submission of disputes to the International Court of Justice.

Decision-making bodies

Political
The COP shall keep under review and evaluate the implementation of the Convention, consider and adopt amendments or protocols, examine and approve the regular budget, harmonize policies, establish subsidiary bodies, and undertake additional actions.

The first meeting of the COP will be convened on the Marshall Islands on 22 July 2002. Thereafter, ordinary meetings shall be held at regular intervals to be determined by the COP at its first meeting. The quorum for meetings shall be two-thirds of the Parties.

Scientific/technical
To be established by the COP.

Publications

• Annual reports;
• SPREP Action Plans;
• *Management of Persistent Organic Pollutants in Pacific Island Countries* (2000).

Sources on the Internet

<http://www.sprep.org.ws>

Yearbook reference

See Richard Herr (2002), 'Environmental Protection in the South Pacific: The Effectiveness of SPREP and its Conventions', *Yearbook of International Co-operation on Environment and Development 2002/03*, 41–9.

European Agreement Concerning the International Carriage of Dangerous Goods by Inland Waterways (ADN)

Objectives

- to increase the safety of international carriage of dangerous goods by inland waterways;
- to contribute effectively to the protection of the environment by preventing any pollution resulting from accidents or incidents during such carriage;
- to facilitate transport operations and promote international trade.

Scope

Legal scope
Open to all member States of the UN Economic Commission for Europe (UNECE) whose territory contains inland waterways other than those forming a coastal route, which form part of the network of inland waterways of international importance as defined in the European Agreement on Main Inland Waterways of International Importance (AGN), 19 January 1996, Geneva. Not open to regional integration organizations.

Geographic scope
Regional (Europe, USA, and Canada).

Time and place of adoption

25 May 2000, Geneva.

Entry into force

The ADN enters into force one month after the date on which seven states mentioned in Article 10, paragraph 1, have either signed it without reservation as to ratification, acceptance, or approval or have deposited instruments of ratification, acceptance, approval, or accession.

Status of participation

No ratifications by 10 June 2002. Ten Signatories without ratification, acceptance, or approval.

The Secretary-General of the UN acts as depositary.

Affiliated instruments and organizations

The regulations annexed to this Agreement form an integral part of the Agreement. The regulations include:

- *Annex A*, which contains provisions concerning dangerous substances and articles;
- *Annex B.1*, which describes provisions concerning the carriage of dangerous goods in packages or in bulk;
- *Annex B.2*, which consists of provisions concerning the carriage of dangerous goods in tank vessels;
- *Annex C*, which sets forth requirements and procedures concerning inspections, the issue of certificates of approval, classification societies, derogations, special authorizations, checks, training, and examination of experts;
- *Annex D.1*, which contains general transitional provisions;
- *Annex D.2*, which includes supplementary transitional provisions applicable to specific inland waterways.

The Secretary-General of the UN (through the UNECE) and the Central Commission for the Navigation of the Rhine (CCNR) ensure the administration of the Agreement.

Co-ordination with related instruments
The UN Economic and Social Council (ECOSOC)'s Committee of Experts on Transport of Dangerous Goods and on the Globally Harmonized System of Classification and Labelling of Chemicals issues recommendations every two years. All international instruments dealing with the transport of dangerous goods, including this Agreement, the European Agreement Concerning the International Carriage of Dangerous Goods by Road (ADR) (see this section), the International Maritime Dangerous Goods Code (IMDG Code), and the International Civil Aviation Organization (ICAO)'s Technical Instructions for the Safe Transport of Dangerous Goods by Air, as well as national regulations, will be regularly revised and amended on the basis of these recommendations.

Secretariat

UNECE,
Transport Division,
Palais de Nations,
CH-1211 Geneva 10,
Switzerland
Telephone: +41-22-9172456
Telefax: +41-22-9170039
E-mail: olivier.kervella@unece.org

Director of Transport Division
Mr J. Capel Ferrer.

Chief, Dangerous Goods Section
Mr Olivier Kervella.

Number of staff
Four professionals and two support staff (May 2002) (for the overall work of the division on the transport of dangerous goods and transport of perishable foodstuffs).

Finance

Budget allocated by the UN.

Budget
No information available.

Special funds
None.

Rules and standards

The Agreement contains internationally agreed conditions for the international carriage of dangerous substances and articles in packages and in bulk on board inland navigation vessels and tank vessels, as well as uniform provisions concerning the construction and operation of such vessels. It also establishes international requirements and procedures for inspections, issue of certificates of approval, recognition of classification societies, monitoring, and training and examination of experts.

The Agreement will be regularly updated in the light of scientific and technical information.

Monitoring/implementation

Review procedure

Contracting Parties shall ensure that a representative proportion of consignments of dangerous goods carried by inland waterways is subject to monitoring in accordance with the provisions in Annex C, chapter 5. In order to carry out the checks provided for in this Agreement, the Parties shall use the checklist to be developed by the Administrative Committee (see Decision-making bodies, below). A copy of this checklist or a certificate showing the result of the check drawn up by the competent authority which carried it out shall be given to the master of the vessel and presented on request in order to simplify or avoid, where possible, subsequent checks.

The checks shall be random and shall as far as possible cover an extensive portion of the inland waterway network.

Without prejudice to other penalties which may be imposed, vessels in respect of which one or more infringements of the rules on the transport of dangerous goods are established may be detained at a place designated for this purpose by the authorities carrying out the check and required to be brought into conformity before continuing their journey, or may be subject to other appropriate measures, depending on the circumstances or the requirements of safety.

Checks may be carried out at the premises of undertakings, as a preventive measure or where infringements which jeopardize safety in the transport of dangerous goods have been recorded during the voyage. The purpose of such checks shall be to ensure that safety conditions for the transport of dangerous goods by inland waterways comply with the relevant laws.

Where appropriate and provided that this does not constitute a safety hazard, samples of the goods transported may be taken for examination by laboratories recognized by the competent authority.

Parties shall assist one another in order to give proper effect to these requirements. If the findings of a check on a foreign vessel give grounds for believing that serious or repeated infringements have been committed which, in the absence of the necessary data, cannot be detected in the course of that check, the competent authorities of the Parties concerned shall assist one another in order to clarify the situation.

Penalties for non-compliance are imposed in accordance with the national legislation of each Contracting Party.

Observations or inspections

Certificates of approval shall be issued by the competent authority of the Party where the vessel is registered or, in its absence, of the Party where it has its home port or, in its absence, of the Party where the owner is domiciled or, in its absence, by the competent authority selected by the owner or his representative. The other Parties shall recognize such certificates of approval. The period of validity, which shall not exceed five years, shall be entered on the certificate of approval.

If a vessel does not yet have a certificate of approval, or if the validity of the certificate of approval expired more than six months previously, the vessel shall undergo a first inspection.

If the vessel's hull or equipment has undergone alterations liable to diminish safety in respect to the carriage of dangerous goods, or has sustained damage affecting such safety, the vessel shall be presented without delay by the owner or his representative for further inspection.

To renew the certificate of approval, the owner of the vessel, or his representative, shall present the vessel for a periodic inspection. The owner of the vessel or his representative may request an inspection at any time. The competent authority shall establish the period of validity of the new certificate of approval on the basis of the results of the inspection.

If the competent authority of a Party has reason to assume that a vessel which is in its territory may constitute a danger in relation to the transport of dangerous goods for the persons on board, or for shipping or for the environment, it may order an inspection of the vessel. The competent authority shall supervise the inspection of the vessel. Under this procedure, the inspection may be performed by an inspection body designated by the Party or by a recognized classification society. The inspection body or the recognized classification society shall issue an inspection report certifying that the vessel conforms partially or completely with the provisions of the regulations set out in Annex B.1 and Annex B.2.

Trade measures
No provisions for trade measures to penalize Parties for non-compliance.

Dispute-settlement mechanisms
The Parties shall as far as possible settle disputes between them by negotiation. Any dispute which is not settled by negotiation shall be submitted to arbitration, and the arbitration shall be binding on the parties to the dispute.

Decision-making bodies

Political
After the Agreement enters into force, the Administrative Committee will be established to consider its implementation, any amendments proposed, and measures to secure uniformity in its interpretation and application. The Committee will consist of representatives of the Parties. The Executive Secretary of the UNECE shall convene the Committee annually, or at other intervals decided on by the Committee, and also at the request of at least five Parties.

The Committee may decide that other states which are not Parties, other member States of UNECE, the UN, or representatives of international NGOs may attend the sessions of the Committee as observers.

The Secretary-General of the UN and the Secretary-General of the Central Commission for the Navigation of the Rhine shall provide the Administrative Committee with secretariat services.

Scientific/technical
The Administrative Committee may set up such working groups as it may deem necessary to assist it in carrying out its duties.

A Safety Committee will be established to consider all proposals for the amendment of the Regulations annexed to the Agreement, particularly regarding safety of navigation in relation to the construction, equipment, and crews of vessels. The Safety Committee shall function within the framework of the activities of the bodies of the UNECE, of the Central Commission for the Navigation of the Rhine, and of the Danube Commission, which are competent in the transport of dangerous goods by inland waterways.

Publications

Regular publications from UNECE covering ADN activities are:

- annual reports of the UNECE;
- *Transport Information*, published by the UNECE;
- *UN Recommendations on the Transport of Dangerous Goods: Model Regulations* (2001) (ST/SG/AC.10/1/Rev.12);
- *UN Recommendations on the Transport of Dangerous Goods: Manual of Tests and Criteria* (1999) (ST/SG/AC.10/11/Rev. 3);
- *European Agreement Concerning the International Carriage of Dangerous Goods by Road (ADR)* (ECE/TRANS/140, vol. I and II);
- *European Agreement Concerning the International Carriage of Dangerous Goods by Inland Waterways (ADN)* (ECE/TRANS/150).

Sources on the Internet

<http://www.unece.org/unece/trans/danger/danger.htm>

European Agreement Concerning the International Carriage of Dangerous Goods by Road (ADR)

Objectives

- to increase the safety of international transport by road;
- to lay down provision concerning classification, packaging, labelling, and testing of dangerous goods, including wastes, in harmony with other requirements for other modes of transport, on the basis of the UN Recommendations on the Transport of Dangerous Goods;
- to lay down conditions for the construction, equipping, and operation of vehicles carrying dangerous goods by road.

Scope

Legal scope
Open to all member States of the UN, UN Economic Commission for Europe (UNECE), other European States, and other member States of the UN which may be invited to participate in the work of the UNECE for questions of specific interest to them, such as the transport of international dangerous goods. Not open to regional integration organizations.

Geographic scope
Regional (Europe, USA, and Canada), but, on account of its legal scope and the international nature of transport, it may extend globally.

Time and place of adoption

30 September 1957, Geneva.

Entry into force

29 January 1968.

Status of participation

38 Parties by 10 June 2002. No Signatories without ratification, acceptance, or approval.

The Secretary-General of the UN acts as depositary.

Affiliated instruments and organizations

Two Annexes are attached to the Agreement, concerning conditions of transport, transport equipment, and transport operations. One Protocol of signature is also attached, and a Protocol amending the Agreement entered into force on 19 April 1985.

The only amendment to the Agreement itself deals with the procedure for amendment of the Annexes. A new Protocol amending the Agreement itself (dealing with the definition of vehicles and again with the procedure for amendment of the Annexes) was adopted on 28 October 1993, but is not yet in force. The Annexes are regularly amended (usually every two years) in parallel with other agreements dealing with the transport of dangerous goods by other modes, such as the Regulations concerning the International Carriage of Dangerous Goods by Rail (RID), the International Maritime Dangerous Goods Code (IMDG Code), and the International Civil Aviation Organization (ICAO)'s Technical Instructions for the Safe Transport of Dangerous Goods by Air, on the basis of the regular updating of the UN Recommendations on the Transport of Dangerous Goods.

Past series of amendments to Annexes A and B of ADR entered into force on 1 July 2001.

Annexes A and B of ADR have now been annexed to Directive 94/55/EC of the Council of the European Union as amended in Directive 2001/7/EC by 29 January 2001, concerning the approximation of the laws of the member States of the European Union with regard to the transport of dangerous goods by road. This implies that the provisions of Annexes A and B of ADR apply not only to international transport but also to domestic traffic on the territory of member States of the European Union.

The Secretary-General of the UN ensures the administration of the Agreement through the UN Economic Commission for Europe (UNECE). The Inland Transport Committee of UNECE fulfils the function of a standing forum for deliberations in matters concerning the Agreement.

Co-ordination with related instruments
The UN Economic and Social Council (ECOSOC)'s Committee of Experts on Transport of Dangerous Goods and on the Globally Harmonized System of Classification and Labelling of Chemicals issues recommendations every two years. All international instruments dealing with the transport of dangerous goods, including this Agreement, RID, IMDG Code, and ICAO Technical Instructions, as well as national regulations, are regularly revised and amended on the basis of these recommendations. Annex III of the Basel Convention (see this section) is also based on the UN Recommendation of the Transport of Dangerous Goods. This mechanism ensures co-ordination and harmonization of provisions relating to classification, labelling, marking, packing, documentation, etc.

Secretariat

UNECE,
Transport Division,
Palais de Nations,
CH-1211 Geneva 10, Switzerland
Telephone: +41-22-9172456
Telefax: +41-22-9170039
E-mail: olivier.kervella@unece.org

Director of Transport Division
Mr J. Capel Ferrer.

Chief, Dangerous Goods Section
Mr Olivier Kervella.

Number of staff
Four professionals and two support staff (May 2002) (for the overall work of the division on the transport of dangerous goods and transport of perishable foodstuffs).

Finance

Budget allocated by the UN.

Budget
No information available.

Special funds
None.

Rules and standards

The Parties have agreed to ensure that certain dangerous goods are not accepted for international transport and that other goods be transported under conditions laid down in the Annexes. However, transport operations to which the Agreement applies shall remain subject to national or international regulations applicable in general to road traffic, international road transport, and international trade.

Annex A contains: general provisions;

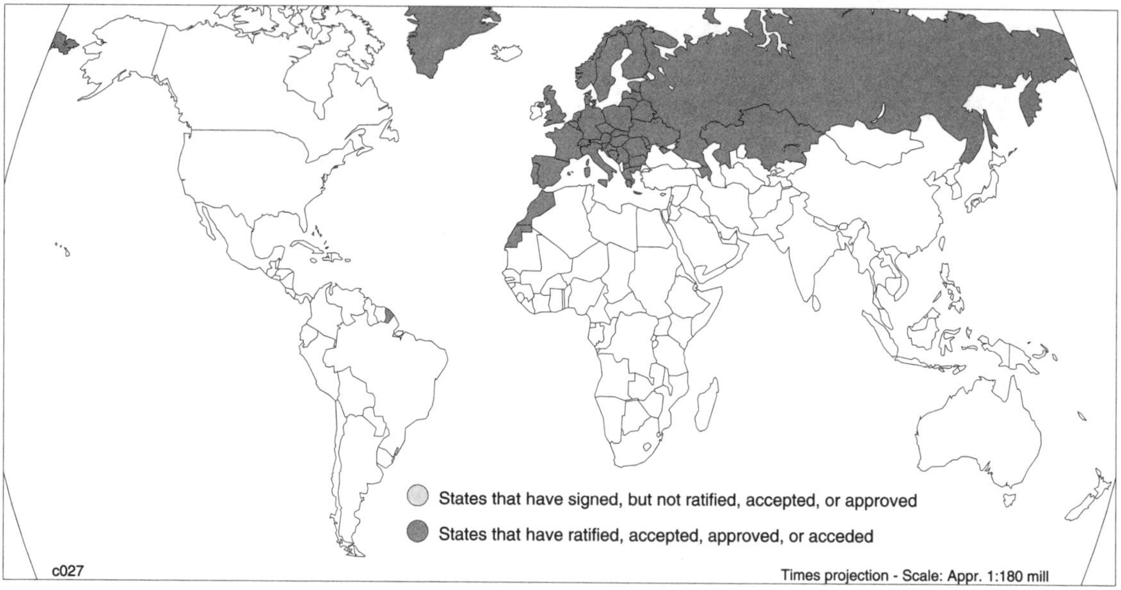

classification; a list of dangerous goods with special provisions and exemptions related to dangerous goods packed in limited quantities; packing and tank provisions; consignment procedures; requirements for the construction and testing of packagings, intermediate bulk container (IBCs), large packaging, and tanks; and provisions concerning the conditions of carriage, loading, unloading, and handling.

Annex B contains: requirements for vehicle crews, equipment, operation, and documentation; and requirements concerning the construction and approval of vehicles.

Monitoring/implementation

Review procedure

Distribution of documents of the Inland Transport Committee and its subsidiary bodies is limited to governments and specialized agencies, and to intergovernmental and non-governmental organizations which take part in the Committee and its subsidiary bodies.

There are no reporting requirements under the Agreement. Problems relating to the international transport of dangerous goods are regularly discussed by the UNECE Working Party on the Transport of Dangerous Goods (see below). Compliance with the ADR is controlled by the police or control authorities of each Contracting Party. Penalties for non-compliance are imposed in accordance with the national legislation of each Contracting Party.

The Agreement is regularly updated in the light of scientific and technical information. The latest revision includes new chapters on the safety obligations of the participants (ch. 1.4) and on checks and other support measures to ensure compliance with safety requirements (ch. 1.8).

Observations or inspections

None by the Agreement as such. Inspections are the responsibility of the competent authority of each Contracting Party.

Trade measures

No provisions on trade measures to penalize Parties for non-compliance.

Dispute-settlement mechanisms

The Parties shall as far as possible settle disputes between them by negotiation. Any dispute which is not settled by negotiation shall be submitted to arbitration, and the arbitration shall be binding on the parties to the dispute.

Decision-making bodies

Political

The Agreement does not provide for the establishment of a separate institutional mechanism. The Inland Transport Committee of the UNECE fulfils the function of a standing forum for deliberations in matters concerning the Agreement. Upon request of any Party, the Secretary-General of the UN shall convene a Conference of Parties for revising or amending the Agreement.

Scientific/technical

The UNECE Working Party on the Transport of Dangerous Goods meets twice a year and has 55 members of the UNECE, other interested international organizations, and non-governmental organizations. It discusses problems relating to the international transport of dangerous goods. There are joint meetings of the Working Party and of the RID Safety Committee.

Publications

A consolidated edition of ADR and its Annexes incorporating all amendments in force on 1 July 2001 was published under the symbol ECE/TRANS/140, vols. I and II. A CD-Rom is available.

Other regular publications from UNECE are:

- annual reports of the UNECE;
- *Transport Information*, published by the UNECE;
- *UN Recommendations on the Transport of Dangerous Goods: Model Regulations* (2001) (ST/SG/AC.10/1/Rev.12);
- *UN Recommendations on the Transport of Dangerous Goods: Manual of Tests and Criteria* (1999) (ST/SG/AC.10/11/Rev. 3);
- *European Agreement Concerning the International Carriage of Dangerous Goods by Inland Waterways (ADN)* (ECE/TRANS/150).

Sources on the Internet

<http://www.unece.org/unece/trans/danger/danger.htm>

FAO International Code of Conduct on the Distribution and Use of Pesticides

Objectives

The objectives of this Code are to set forth responsibilities and establish voluntary standards of conduct for all public and private entities engaged in or affecting the distribution and use of pesticides, particularly where there is no national law or only an inadequate law to regulate pesticides.

Specifically, the Code seeks:

- to promote practices which ensure efficient and safe use of pesticides while minimizing health and environmental concern;
- to establish responsible and generally accepted trade practices;
- to assist countries which have not established controls designed to regulate the quality and suitability of pesticide products needed in that country;
- to ensure that pesticides are used effectively for the improvement of agricultural production and of human, animal, and plant health;
- to implement, internationally, an 'information exchange and Prior Informed Consent (PIC) procedure' requiring that no international shipment of a pesticide which has been banned or severely restricted by a country in order to protect human health or the environment should proceed without the agreement of the importing country.

Scope

Legal scope

The Code was adopted unanimously by the Food and Agriculture Organization (FAO) Conference at its 1985 session. Membership of FAO is confined to nations; associate membership to territories or groups of territories. The European Union is given membership as a regional economic integration organization and can vote on behalf of its member States in certain matters.

Geographic scope

Global.

Time and place of adoption

19 November 1985, Rome.

Entry into force

Non-mandatory. However, at the request of FAO's member countries and in co-operation with the UN Environment Programme (UNEP), PIC has been converted into the legally binding Convention on the Prior Informed Consent Procedure for Certain Hazardous Chemicals and Pesticides in International Trade (Rotterdam Convention on PIC) (see this section).

Status of participation

Not applicable. FAO, which has adopted the Code, had 184 members, including the European Union, by May 2002.

A second revision of the Code of Conduct was initiated in 2000. In this respect, two sessions of the Panel of Experts have been held in December 2000 and June 2001 with the objective to draft a revised Code of Conduct. The revised Code of Conduct was circulated to governments and observers for comments. During the governmental Technical Consultation on the Code of Conduct, held in Rome in late May 2002, substantial progress was made in revising the Code.

Affiliated instruments and organizations

The Code is supported by a comprehensive set of technical guidelines on all aspects of pesticide management and control.

FAO, in close collaboration with other UN agencies such as UNEP, the World Health Organization (WHO), and the International Labour Organization (ILO) (see IGOs), assists governments to implement the Code. The Rotterdam Convention on PIC will come into force only after deposit of the 50th ratification. Given the need to implement the new procedure immediately, delegates adopted at the Diplomatic Conference in September 1998 an Interim Resolution which asks the Intergovernmental Negotiating Committee (INC) to oversee the implementation of the interim PIC procedure.

Co-ordination with related instruments

The FAO Conference authorized the Director-General to establish a programme jointly with UNEP for the implementation of PIC procedures. The voluntary PIC procedures have been transformed into the legally binding Rotterdam Convention on PIC.

Secretariat

Plant Protection Service,
Pesticide Management Unit,
Food and Agriculture Organization (FAO),
Viale delle Terme di Caracalla,
I-00100 Rome,
Italy

Telephone:	+39-06-57053441
Telefax:	+39-06-57056347
E-mail:	gerold.wyrwal@fao.org

Chief, Plant Protection Service
Dr Niek A. van der Graaff.

Pesticides Information Officer
Mr Gerold Wyrwal.

Finance

Budget

The administrative core budget, covered by FAO's regular budget, is approximately $US500,000 annually.

Special funds

Additional funds are available for technical assistance.

Rules and standards

Although the Code itself is voluntary in nature, it promotes the promulgation and enforcement of legislation governing the import, manufacture, sale, and use of pesticides. The Code takes into account the special circumstances of developing countries.

The supply of data for the registration and approval of pesticides for use in a country is based on harmonized pesticide registration requirements formulated by FAO. Such data, including toxicological information on the pesticide and its environmental effects, are provided by the pesticide industry for officials in the country to decide whether to approve or disapprove the use of the pesticide based on benefit–risk evaluation under conditions of use in the country.

The principle of PIC (see above) concerns the export and import of chemicals and pesticides that are banned or severely restricted

for health or environmental reasons. DNAs in participating countries have been invited to communicate their decisions on 26 pesticides and five industrial chemicals. Control actions taken for health or environmental reasons for the same chemical by two countries from two different PIC regions which is communicated to UNEP or FAO is sufficient to suggest a chemical become subject to the PIC procedure.

Monitoring/implementation

Review procedure

The current information on the operation and implementation of the Code is made through reports to the FAO Conference and reports of meetings and workshops which are published and sent to governments. The reports are public.

The provisions of the Code and progress in its implementation are reviewed regularly by panels of experts appointed to deal with specific topics on pesticides. These also include the joint FAO–UNEP panel, which specifically deals with PIC (see below).

In the implementation of PIC, FAO, jointly with UNEP, has published the *Guidance for Governments* document. In addition, FAO has published a decision guidance document (DGD) for each pesticide in the PIC procedure, while UNEP has published similar documents on the industrial and consumer chemicals.

Implementation required a preparatory phase, which included the appointment of DNAs by their respective governments and the development of a joint database on banned and severely restricted pesticides and other chemicals. The database now includes notifications of control actions, information sent to DNAs, responses from importing countries, notifications from exporting countries, addresses of DNAs, and the text of DGDs.

Monitoring of the implementation of the Code has made it possible to compile rather detailed 'national profiles' indicating the 'pre-Code' situation in 1986, as well as the status in 1993 concerning pesticide registration, use, management, and control, the enforcement of regulations, and the likely future technical assistance needs of member countries. This work relates directly to recommendations contained in chapter 19 of *Agenda 21* of the UN Conference on Environment and Development (UNCED) (Rio de Janeiro, 1992), and data in 'national profiles' are used routinely by FAO, among other things, in evaluating pertinent requests from developing countries for technical assistance.

Several countries have, consequent to the introduction of the Code, introduced laws in their countries for the effective control of pesticides. Certain countries have, of their own accord, incorporated the Code into their national pesticide legislation. Implementation is also carried out through regional and bilateral projects in individual countries. FAO holds regional workshops on the implementation of the PIC procedure.

Decision-making bodies

Political

The FAO Conference, which meets every two years, reviews the Code and makes recommendations to promote its implementation. The Conference is the major policy-making organ of FAO.

Scientific/technical

FAO and UNEP have established a Joint Expert Group on Prior Informed Consent. The Group is composed of independent experts, representing themselves and not their government, and selected by FAO, based on defined criteria. The function of the Group is to provide advice and guidance for the implementation of PIC, and to prepare and review DGDs and other technical matters. The first meeting of the Group was held in December 1989. Up to December 1996 the Group had met eight times. No further meetings were held.

Publications

Current information on the operation and implementation of the Code is available from FAO.

Sources on the Internet

<http://www.fao.org/AG/AGP/AGPP/Pesticid>

<http://www.fao.org/pic>

Stockholm Convention on Persistent Organic Pollutants (Stockholm Convention on POPs)

Objectives

To protect human health and the environment from persistent organic pollutants (POPs).

Scope

Legal scope
Open to all states and regional economic integration organizations.

Geographic scope
Global.

Time and place of adoption

23 May 2001, Stockholm.

Entry into force

Not yet in force. Enters into force on the 90th day after the deposit of the 50th instrument of ratification, acceptance, approval, or accession.

Status of participation

11 ratifications, acceptances, approvals, or accessions by 1 July 2002. 142 Signatories, including the European Community, without ratification, acceptance, or approval.

The Secretary-General of the UN acts as depositary.

Affiliated instruments and organizations

The Convention contains six *annexes* which form an integral part of the Convention:

• *Annex A* lists the following nine chemicals, produced or used, which are subject to *elimination* (with certain exemptions): aldrin, chlordane, dieldrin, endrin, heptachlor, hexachlorobenzene (HCB), polychlorinated biphenyls (PCBs), mirex, and toxaphene;
• *Annex B* includes the chemical DDT, produced or used, which is subject to *restriction* (with acceptable purposes or certain exemptions);
• *Annex C* lists the following four chemicals: dioxins, furans, HCB, and PCBs, which are produced and released *unintentionally* as the result of human activity—in particular via combustion such as hospital and municipal waste burning, and open burning of garbage;
• *Annex D* contains information requirements and criteria for screening substances that parties propose as additions to listed substances;
• *Annex E* includes information requirements for the risk profile;
• *Annex F* contains information on socio-economic considerations.

Co-ordination with related instruments
The Conference of the Parties (COP) shall co-operate closely with the bodies of the Basel Convention (see this section) on measures to reduce or eliminate releases from stockpiles and wastes, and in particular to prepare appropriate technical guidelines for the environmentally sound management of persistent organic pollutant wastes.

The secretariats of the Rotterdam Convention and Stockholm Convention will co-operate on matters relevant to chemicals covered by both instruments.

Secretariat

Establishment of a permanent Convention's secretariat will be approved at the first COP. An Interim UNEP Secretariat will be operative at the following address:

Interim Secretariat of the Stockholm Convention,
UNEP Chemicals,
11–13 chemin des Anémones,
CH-1219 Châtelaine, Geneva,
Switzerland
Telephone: +41-22-9178193
Telefax: +41-22-7973460
E-mail: pops@unep.ch

Director, UNEP Chemicals
Mr Jim Willis.

Co-ordinator
Mr David Ogden.

POPs Press Officer
Mr Michael Williams.
Michael.Williams@unep.ch

Finance

Budget
To be decided by the first COP.

Special funds
Parties are called upon to finance interim arrangements through the 'POPs Club' established by UNEP. The POPs Club is a creative financing mechanism for seeking to promote contributions to a trust fund from a broad range of donors, including governments, intergovernmental organizations, and NGOs.

Rules and standards

Parties are committed to reduce or eliminate releases of POPs from *intentional production and use* by:

• prohibiting and/or taking the legal and administrative measures necessary to eliminate the production, use, importation, and exportation of the nine POPs listed in Annex A;
• restricting the production and use of POPs listed in Annex B.

Parties are also committed to reduce or eliminate releases of POPs from *unintentional production* of each of the chemicals listed in Annex C.

The Convention provisions call for measures to reduce or eliminate releases of these POPs from stockpiles and wastes as well.

Parties to the Convention are required to promote best available techniques and practices for replacing existing POPs while preventing the development of new POPs. The Convention calls for substitution involving the use of safer chemicals and processes to prevent unintentionally produced POPs. The Convention also outlines the procedure for and criteria to be considered in identifying new POPs to be added to the Convention. Precaution is operationalized throughout the Convention, with specific references in the preamble, the objective, and the provision on the listing of new POPs.

The Convention provides for technical assistance between Parties. Parties shall, taking into account in particular the needs of developing countries and countries with economies in transition, co-operate in promoting technical assistance for the develop-

ment of the capacity necessary to manage chemicals to enable implementation of the Convention. Parties with more advanced programmes to provide financial and technical assistance for regulating chemicals should provide technical assistance, including training to other Parties in developing their infrastructure and capacity to reduce, with the aim of eliminating, where feasible, the uses and releases of POPs throughout their life-cycle.

Developed countries are required to provide new and additional financial resources, and a financial mechanism will help developing countries and countries with economies in transition meet their obligations under the Convention.

The Convention also includes provisions on, *inter alia*: information exchange; implementation plans; public information, awareness and education; and research, development and monitoring.

Monitoring/implementation

Review procedure

Each Party shall:

• develop and endeavour to implement a plan for the implementation of its obligations under this Convention;

• transmit its implementation plan to the COP within two years of the date on which this Convention enters into force for it;

• review and update, as appropriate, its implementation plan on a periodic basis and in a manner to be specified by a decision of the COP.

The Parties shall, where appropriate, cooperate directly or through global, regional, and subregional organizations, and consult their national stakeholders, including women's groups and groups involved in the health of children, in order to facilitate the development, implementation, and updating of their implementation plans.

The Parties shall endeavour to utilize and, where necessary, establish the means to integrate national implementation plans for POPs in their sustainable development strategies where appropriate.

Each Party shall report to the COP on the measures it has taken to implement the provisions of this Convention and on the effectiveness of such measures in meeting the objectives of the Convention. Each Party shall provide to the Secretariat:

• statistical data on its total quantities of production, import, and export of each of the chemicals listed in Annex A and Annex B or a reasonable estimate of such data;

· to the extent practicable, a list of the States from which it has imported each such substance and the States to which it has exported each such substance.

Such reporting shall be at periodic intervals and in a format to be decided by the COP at its first meeting.

Commencing four years after the date of entry into force of this Convention, and periodically thereafter at intervals to be decided by the COP, the Conference shall evaluate the effectiveness of this Convention.

In order to facilitate such evaluation, the COP shall, at its first meeting, initiate the establishment of arrangements to provide itself with comparable monitoring data on the presence of the chemicals listed in Annexes A, B, and C as well as their regional and global environmental transport. These arrangements:

• should be implemented by the Parties on a regional basis when appropriate, in accordance with their technical and financial capabilities, using existing monitoring programmes and mechanisms to the extent possible and promoting harmonization of approaches;

• may be supplemented where necessary, taking into account the differences between regions and their capabilities to implement monitoring activities;

• shall include reports to the COP on the results of the monitoring activities on a regional and global basis at intervals to be specified by the COP.

The evaluation described above shall be conducted on the basis of available scientific, environmental, technical, and economic information, including:

• reports and other monitoring information provided pursuant to Article 16, paragraph 2;

• national reports submitted pursuant to Article 15;

• non-compliance information provided pursuant to the procedures established under Article 17.

The COP shall, as soon as practicable, develop and approve procedures and institutional mechanisms for determining non-compliance and for the treatment of Parties found to be in non-compliance.

Observations or inspections
None by the Convention as such.

Trade measures
No provisions on trade measures to penalize Parties for non-compliance.

Dispute-settlement mechanisms
Parties shall settle any dispute between them concerning the interpretation or application of the Convention through negotiation or other peaceful means of their own choice.

Decision-making bodies

Political
After the Convention enters into force, the COP will become the supreme authority. The first meeting of the COP shall be convened no later than one year after the entry into force of the Convention. Thereafter, ordinary meetings of the COP shall be held at regular intervals to be determined by the Conference.

The COP shall keep under review and evaluate implementation of the Convention, harmonize policies, and establish subsidiary bodies as it considers necessary.

National and international agencies and qualified NGOs may attend the COP's meetings as observers and contribute to its work.

Scientific/technical
The COP will, at its first meeting, establish a subsidiary body, the Persistent Organic Pollutants Review Committee, for the purposes of performing the functions assigned to it by the Convention, such as reviewing information from the Parties and making recommendations to the COP. The members of the Committee shall consist of government-designated experts in chemicals assessment and management. The members shall be appointed on the basis of equitable geographical distribution, in particular ensuring a balance between developed and developing Parties. The Committee shall make every effort to make its recommendations by consensus.

Publications

Current information and reports of meetings and workshops are available from UNEP Chemicals (see Secretariat, above).

Sources on the Internet

<http://www.chem.unep.ch/pops>

Convention on the Prevention of Marine Pollution by Dumping of Wastes and Other Matter (London Convention 1972)

Objectives

To prevent indiscriminate disposal at sea of wastes liable to create hazards to human health, to harm living resources and marine life, to damage amenities, or to interfere with other legitimate uses of the sea. The fundamental principle of the Convention is the prohibition of dumping of certain wastes, the requirement of a specific permit prior to dumping of others, and the demand for a general permit for the rest. The first two categories are determined by Annexes.

Scope

Legal scope
Open for accession by 'any state'. Not open to regional integration organizations. Inter- and non-governmental organizations participate with observer status at the Consultative Meetings of the Contracting Parties of the Convention.

Geographic scope
In addition to the global seas, it includes the exclusive economic zones and territorial waters of the coastal states. The 1996 Protocol (not in force) broadens the scope to include the seabed and the subsoil thereof, but excludes internal waters of States.

Time and place of adoption

13 November 1972, London.

Entry into force

30 August 1975.

Status of participation

78 Parties by 31 May 2002. In addition, Hong Kong SAR of China has ratified as an associate member of IMO. Five Signatories without ratification, acceptance, or approval.

Affiliated instruments and organizations

• *Annex I* ('black list') includes radioactive wastes, industrial waste, incineration at sea, organohalogenic compounds, mercury and its compounds, and persistent plastics;
• *Annex II* ('grey list') includes products containing significant amounts of, among other things, lead, arsenic, copper, zinc, cyanides, fluorides, pesticides, and their by-products;
• *Annex III* concerns the criteria governing the issuing of permits and specifies the nature of the waste material, the characteristics of the dumping site, and the method of disposal.

1996 Protocol to the Convention on the Prevention of Marine Pollution by Dumping of Wastes and Other Matter, 1972 (1996 Protocol to the London Convention 1972), London, 7 November 1996. (Not yet in force.) 16 states had ratified by 31 May 2002. Nine Signatories subject to ratification or acceptance. Enters into force on the thirtieth day after the deposit of 26 instruments of ratification, acceptance, approval, or accession, of which at least 15 are Contracting Parties to the Convention. Expected to enter into force during 2003.

The basic objective of the Protocol adds to the existing provision that Parties shall where practicable eliminate pollution caused by dumping or incineration at sea of wastes or other matter. A fundamental principle of the Protocol is the prohibition of dumping of any wastes or other matter with the exception of these wastes or other matter listed in Annex 1, provided these wastes are assessed in accordance with the provisions set out in Annex 2 to the Protocol, before a permit for sea disposal can be issued.

According to *Annex 1 to the Protocol* the following wastes or other matter are those that may be considered for dumping: dredged material, sewage sludge, fish waste, vessels and platforms, inert, inorganic geological material, organic material of natural origin, and bulky items primarily comprising iron, steel, concrete, and similarly unharmful materials. It replaces the existing 'black' and 'grey' lists in Annex I and II of the Convention. *Annex 2 to the Protocol* replaces the existing Annex III of the Convention and constitutes a functional system for assessing the impact of dumping activities on the marine environment. *Annex 3 to the Protocol* deals with arbitral procedures.

IMO (see IGOs) is responsible for secretariat duties.

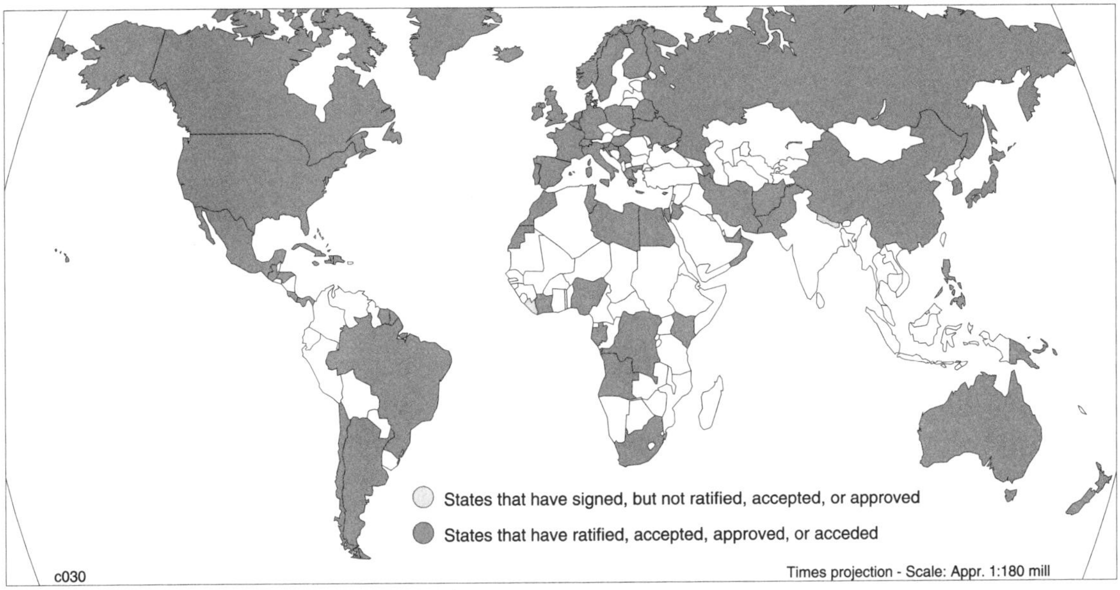

Convention on the Prevention of Marine Pollution by Dumping of Wastes and Other Matter (London Convention 1972)

Co-ordination with related instruments
Based on advice by IAEA (see IGOs), Contracting Parties in 1999 adopted guidelines for making judgements on whether materials eligible and planned to be dumped could be exempted from radiological control or whether a specific assessment was needed.

Secretariat

Office for the London Convention 1972,
c/o International Maritime Organization,
4 Albert Embankment,
London SE1 7SR,
United Kingdom
Telephone: +44-20-77357611
Telefax: +44-20-75873210

Finance

Contracting Parties contribute on a voluntary basis to projects promoting the implementation of the Convention and, after its entry into force, of the Protocol, to technical co-operation projects. Costs of administration of the Convention are covered by the regular IMO budget.

Rules and standards

The Parties are committed:

- individually and collectively, to promote effective control of all sources of pollution of the marine environment and to take all practicable steps to prevent pollution of the sea caused by the dumping of waste and other matter;
- to take effective measures individually and collectively to prevent marine pollution caused by dumping and to harmonize their policies;
- to prohibit the dumping of waste or other matter except as specified;
- to designate an appropriate authority to issue permits, keep records of dumping, monitor the condition of the seas, and report on these matters to IMO;
- to apply measures required to implement the Convention for all vessels and aircraft registered in its territory or flying its flag; loading in its territory or territorial sea any matter to be dumped; or believed to be engaged in dumping under its jurisdiction;
- to take measures to prevent and punish contravention of the Convention;
- to develop procedures for effective application on the high seas.

The Convention prohibits the dumping of wastes or other matter, including radioactive wastes under Annex I (the 'black list') of the Convention. Grey-listed wastes are categorized under Annex II and may be released only under a prior special permit based on conditions set by the Convention and its technical advisers. Dumping of all other matter is allowable only by a prior general permit.

The Amendment of Annexes I and II to extend the prohibition against dumping high-level radioactive waste into prohibition against dumping *all* radioactive wastes entered into force on 20 February 1994, following a moratorium on low-level radioactive wastes which was established in 1983 and extended in 1985. The IAEA (see IGOs) is the adviser to the Convention on radiological matters.

Similar amendments of Annexes I and II were approved to prohibit incineration of industrial waste and sewage sludge and to prohibit the dumping of industrial waste as from 1 January 1996. These legally binding decisions, which were preceded by earlier policy decisions to that effect, also entered into force on 20 February 1994.

Parties to the *1996 Protocol to the London Convention 1972* shall apply a *precautionary approach* to environmental protection from dumping of wastes or other matter, whereby appropriate preventative measures are taken when there is reason to believe that wastes or other matter introduced into the marine environment are likely to cause harm even when there is no conclusive evidence to prove a causal relation between inputs and their effects.

Taking into account the approach that the polluter should, in principle, bear the cost of pollution, each Party shall endeavour to promote practices whereby those it has authorized to engage in dumping or incineration at sea bear the cost of meeting the pollution prevention and control requirements for the authorized activities, having due regard to the public interest.

1996 Protocol to the London Convention 1972

Monitoring/implementation

Review procedure

Each Contracting Party shall take appropriate measures in its territory to prevent and punish conduct in contravention of the Convention. The Parties also undertake to issue instructions, assist one another, and work together in the development of co-operative procedures for the application of the Convention.

The Parties are required to notify IMO directly or through regional secretariats of the nature, quantity, location, time, and method of dumping of all permitted matter, of their monitoring of the condition of the sea, and of criteria, measures, and requirements adopted in issuing permits in the previous calendar year. The first deadline for reporting each year is 1 November of the succeeding year.

By 16 April 2002, 32 national reports (41 per cent of the Parties) had been submitted covering activities carried out in 1998. 24 national reports (31 per cent of the Parties) had been submitted covering activities carried out in 1999. 18 national reports (23 per cent of the Parties) had been submitted covering activities carried out in 2000. The latest final report with compilation of such data covers the permits issued in 1998.

Compliance is monitored and measured by the Consultative Meeting of the Contracting Parties and is given more attention in anticipation of the entry into force of the 1996 Protocol. The Consultative Meeting is able to exercise some control over compliance through notification of dumping activities and monitoring reports, but no formal non-compliance procedures, prior notification procedures, or multilateral consultation procedures have been established.

Notification procedures adopted by the Consultative Meeting also call for the Parties to report compliance monitoring and environmental impact assessments. Only 40 per cent of Contracting Parties have fulfilled their obligations under the Convention in this respect, and the Consultative Meeting has sought more effective implementation.

Compilation of data or information in national reports is made by the Secretariat. These reviews are public and the Secretariat distributes publication lists of such reviews. There is no independent verification of data or information.

The *1996 Protocol* provides that, no later than two years after the entry into force of the Protocol, the Meeting of Contracting Parties shall establish those procedures and mechanisms necessary to assess and promote compliance with the Protocol.

Decision-making bodies

Political

The Consultative Meeting of the Contracting Parties to the London Convention is the governing body and meets annually.

Scientific/technical

The Consultative Meeting requests advice from its subsidiary body the Scientific Group and, occasionally, from the Joint Group of Experts on Scientific Aspects of Marine Environmental Protection (GESAMP). The Scientific Group, composed of government experts, advises on scientific and technical co-operation and some compliance matters, reviews the provisions of the Annexes, and develops guidelines on monitoring programmes and issues concerning implementation of the Convention. GESAMP is composed of specialized experts nominated by the sponsoring agencies (IMO, FAO, UNESCO/IOC, WMO, WHO, IAEA, UN, and UNEP) (see IGOs). The Consultative Meeting has also established *ad hoc* groups to provide advice on specific issues such as reporting and compliance or the preparation of the review of the London Convention leading to the 1996 Protocol. These are composed of government experts.

Publications

IMO News (quarterly) and reports from IMO.

Sources on the Internet

<http://www.londonconvention.org>

International Convention for the Prevention of Pollution from Ships, 1973, as modified by the Protocol of 1978 relating thereto (MARPOL 73/78)

Objectives

• to eliminate pollution of the sea by oil, chemicals, and other harmful substances which might be discharged in the course of operations;
• to minimize the amount of oil which could be released accidentally in collisions or strandings by ships, including also fixed or floating platforms;
• to improve further the prevention and control of marine pollution from ships, particularly oil-tankers.

The Convention contains special provision for the control of pollution from more than 400 liquid noxious substances, as well as for sewage and garbage disposal, and the control of air pollution from ships' exhausts.

Scope

Legal scope

Open to all states. Not open to regional integration organizations. NGOs and IGOs participate with observer status at meetings of the International Maritime Organization (IMO) (see IGOs).

Geographic scope

The global seas.

The Convention designates the Antarctic, Mediterranean, Baltic, Red, and Black seas, the Gulf of Aden, the Persian Gulf area, and north-west European waters as special areas in which oil discharge is virtually prohibited and the wider Caribbean and the North Sea as special areas subject to more stringent requirements governing the disposal into the sea of ship-generated garbage. The Baltic Sea area is designated as a sulphur emission control area for air-pollution control.

Time and place of adoption

2 November 1973 and 17 February 1978 (Protocol), London.

Entry into force

2 October 1983.

Status of participation

121 Parties (96.41 per cent of world tonnage) by 31 May 2002. In addition, Hong Kong SAR of China has ratified as an associate member of IMO. 35 States have made exceptions for annexes III (18), IV (34), or V (13). No Signatories without ratification, acceptance, or approval.

IMO (see IGOs) acts as depositary.

Affiliated instruments and organizations

Protocol Relating to the International Convention for the Prevention of Pollution from Ships, London, 1978. The Protocol introduced stricter regulations for ships and stipulates that a ship may be cleared to operate only after surveys and the issuing of an International Oil Pollution Prevention (IOPP) Certificate. States which ratify the Protocol must also give effect to the provisions of the Convention; there is no need for a separate instrument of ratification for the latter. The Protocol and the Convention should therefore be read as one instrument.

The governing scheme of the technical *Annexes I–V* is regulation according to type of pollutant: oil, noxious liquid substances (such as chemicals), harmful substances in packaged form, sewage, and garbage. 121 Parties (96.41 per cent of world tonnage) of the Convention had accepted *Annexes I* and *II*, 103 Parties (82.63 per cent of world tonnage) had accepted *Annex III*, 87 Parties (47.29 per cent of world tonnage) had accepted *Annex IV*, and 108 Parties (88.73 per cent of world tonnage) had accepted *Annex V* by 31 May 2002. Of these, the only annex not yet in force is Annex IV. An additional annex, *Annex VI*, on air pollution from ships, was adopted on 26 September 1997. Five Parties (15.98 per cent of world tonnage) had accepted Annex VI by 31 May 2002. It enters into force 12 months after the acceptance by at least 15 Parties of the Convention with not less than 50 per cent of the gross tonnage of the world's merchant shipping fleet.

Several *amendments* have been adopted since 1984 and have come into force:

• *1992 amendments*, which came into force on 6 July 1995, are generally regarded as the most important changes made to the Convention since the adoption of the 1978 Protocol. In the past, MARPOL, the 1978 Protocol, and many amendments have been concerned mainly with minimizing operational pollution, and they have been concentrated principally on new ships. The 1992 amendments also introduced new regulations which are designed to reduce drastically pollution from accidents; they apply to existing as well as new tankers (see Rules and standards below);
• *1996 amendment* concerning reports of incidents involving oil or harmful substances entered into force under the Convention's tacit acceptance procedure on 1 January 1998;
• *1999 amendment*, which made certain-sized tankers carrying persistent oils (such as heavy fuel oil) as cargo subject to the same stringent requirements as crude-oil tankers;
• *2000 amendment*, adopted in 2000 (entered into force on 1 January 2002) to Annex III (*Prevention of Pollution by Harmful Substances Carried by Sea in Packaged Form*), which deletes tainting as a criterion for marine pollutants from the guidelines for the identification of harmful substances in packaged form. Tainting refers to the ability of a product to be taken up by an organism and thereby affect the taste or smell of seafood—making it unpalatable. A substance is defined as tainting when it has been found to taint seafood. The amendment means that products identified as being marine pollutants solely on the basis of their tainting properties will no longer be classified as marine pollutants;
• *2001 amendment*, adopted on 27 April 2001 (enters into force on 1 September 2002) to Annex I, which bring in a new global timetable for accelerating the phase-out of single-hull oil-tankers. The timetable will see most single-hull oil-tankers eliminated by 2015 or earlier. Double-hull tankers offer greater protection of the environment from pollution in certain types of accident. All new oil-tankers built since 1996 are required to have double hulls. The revised regulation identifies three categories of tankers, as follows:

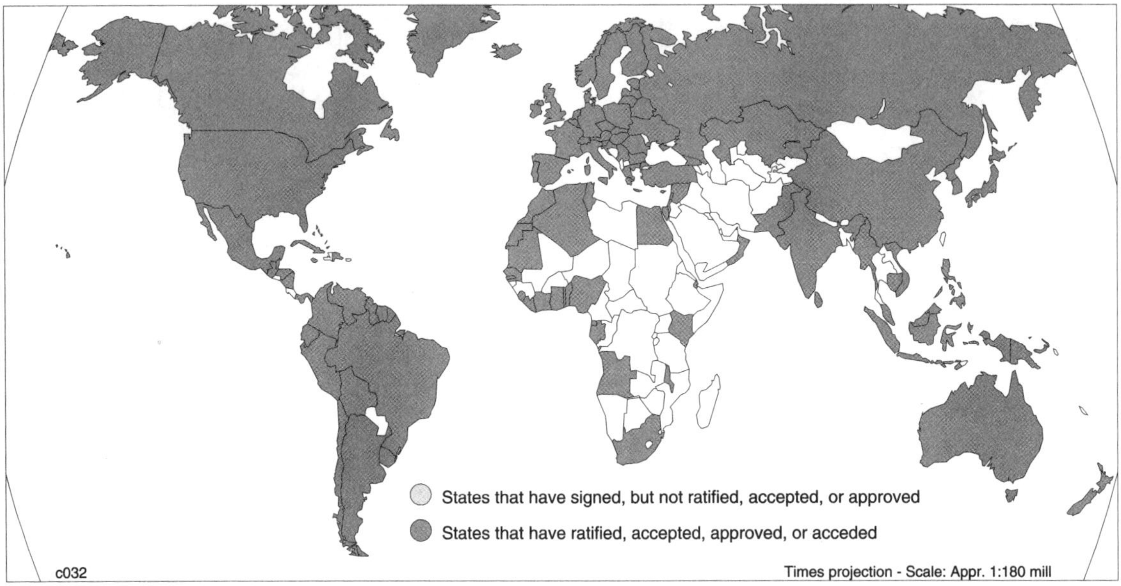

• *Category 1 oil-tanker* refers to oil-tankers of 20,000 tons deadweight and above carrying crude oil, fuel oil, heavy diesel oil, or lubricating oil as cargo, and of 30,000 tons deadweight and above carrying other oils, which do not comply with the requirements for protectively located segregated ballast tanks (commonly known as Pre-MARPOL tankers);
• *Category 2 oil-tanker* refers to oil-tankers of 20,000 tons deadweight and above carrying crude oil, fuel oil, heavy diesel oil, or lubricating oil as cargo, and of 30,000 tons deadweight and above carrying other oils, which do comply with the protectively located segregated ballast-tank requirements (MARPOL tankers);
• *Category 3 oil-tanker* refers to oil-tankers of 5000 tons deadweight and above but less than the tonnage specified for Category 1 and 2 tankers.

Although the new phase-out timetable sets 2015 as the principal cut-off date for all single-hull tankers, the flag state administration may allow for some newer single-hull ships registered in its country that conform to certain technical specifications to continue trading until the 25th anniversary of their delivery.

However, under the provisions of paragraph 8(b), any port State can deny entry of those single-hull tankers which are allowed to operate until their 25th anniversary to ports or offshore terminals. They must communicate their intention to do this to IMO.

As an additional precautionary measure, a Condition Assessment Scheme (CAS) will have to be applied to all Category 1 vessels continuing to trade after 2005 and all Category 2 vessels after 2010. A resolution adopting the CAS was passed at MEPC's 46th session in April 2001. Although the CAS does not specify structural standards in excess of the provisions of other IMO conventions, codes, and recommendations, its requirements stipulate more stringent and transparent verification of the reported structural condition of the ship and that documentary and survey procedures have been properly carried out and completed.

The scheme requires that compliance with the CAS is assessed during the Enhanced Survey Programme of Inspections concurrent with intermediate or renewal surveys at present required by resolution A.744(18), as amended.

IMO receives reports, carries out secretariat functions, and considers amendments to the Convention and its Annexes.

Co-ordination with related instruments
The Convention is a combination of two treaties adopted in 1973 and 1978 respectively.

The Marine Environment Protection Committee (MEPC), one of four main committees of IMO, is responsible for coordinating work with other IMO conventions and with UN Environment Programme (UNEP) conventions such as the 1989 Basel Convention (see this section).

Secretariat

MARPOL
c/o IMO (see IGOs).

Finance

Budget
Costs are covered by the regular IMO budget. No core budget available.

Special funds
None.

Rules and standards

The principal obligations of States Parties are:
• to give effect to the provisions of the Convention and Annexes in order to prevent pollution of the marine environment;
• to prohibit violations, establish sanctions thereto under the law of the administration of the ship concerned, and instigate proceedings if informed of a violation and satisfied that sufficient evidence is available;
• to prohibit violations, and establish sanctions for violations, within the jurisdiction of any Party, and either to cause proceedings to take place or to furnish information to the administration of the ship;
• to apply the provisions of the Convention as may be necessary to ensure that more favourable treatment is not given to ships of non-Parties;
• to co-operate in the detection of violations and in the enforcement of the Con-

vention.

The 1992 MARPOL Amendments include:

• an enhanced programme of inspections that apply to all oil-tankers aged five years and more;
• important new changes to the construction requirements for tankers of five years of age and above, including the mandatory fitting of double hulls or an equivalent design.

The amendments adopted in March 1992 have applied to all new tankers ordered after 6 July 1993. Tankers of 5000 d.w.t. and above must be fitted with double bottoms and double hulls extending the full length of the ship's side. The 'mid-deck' design is permitted as an alternative, and other designs may be allowed in due course, provided they ensure the same level of protection against pollution. A series of other amendments to specific regulations have been introduced since 1992.

Monitoring/implementation

Review procedure

Compliance with these commitments is monitored and measured primarily by circulating reports made to IMO by the Parties. Reports made by port States following inspections also enable some monitoring of compliance with their obligations by flag States.

Under the mandatory reporting system of MARPOL, Annex I, annual reports, covering the following matters, have to be submitted to the Convention secretariat for consideration:

(*a*) *Annual enforcement reports* by port and flag States. 18 reports (16 per cent of the Parties) were submitted on activities in 1998 within the deadline on 31 September 1999. 18 reports (16 per cent of the Parties) were submitted on activities in 1999 within the deadline on 31 September 2000.

(*b*) *Annual summary report* by the Party State's administration of incidents involving spillages of oil of more than 50 tons.

(*c*) *Annual assessment report*, including:

• a statistical report by the port State on the effectiveness of port State control (number of inspections and compliance rate);
• reports by the port State on MARPOL violations by ships resulting in detention or denial of entry into port;
• report on penalties imposed by the port State for violations of MARPOL.

18 assessment reports (16 per cent of the Parties) were submitted on activities in 1998 within the deadline on 31 September 1999. 18 assessment reports (16 per cent of the Parties) were submitted on activities in 1999 within the deadline on 31 September 2000.

However, only a small percentage of Parties have complied with the reporting requirements in the past few years. The reports, which are public, are regarded as useful to promote the effective implementation of the Convention, though some of them are not complete. There is no independent verification of data or information.

There are no formal provisions for a meeting of the Parties or for a non-compliance procedure.

The Maritime Safety Committee (MSC) and MEPC have reported a variety of causes which might contribute to the lack of effective implementation by flag States. These include the lack of trained and experienced technical personnel within the flag State administration; the inability to retain skilled personnel; the inappropriate delegation of inspection authority; or the use of insufficiently qualified and experienced surveyors. In addition, the record of port States in supplying reception facilities has been poor in some areas because of financial constraints. Provision of finance and technical assistance is an important factor in enabling some developing States to implement the Convention. The reports of the MSC and MEPC are public (see below).

Observations or inspections

None by the Convention as such, but it reaffirms the police powers of the port State where a ship is found.

Trade measures

No provisions on trade measures to penalize Parties for non-compliance.

Dispute-settlement mechanisms

Any dispute between two or more Parties shall, if settlement by negotiation has not been possible and if the Parties do not otherwise agree, be submitted, upon the request of any of them, to arbitration as set out in Protocol 2 to the Convention.

Decision-making bodies

Political

The MEPC is established as a main forum for activities relating to the Convention. It consists of all member States of IMO, and is empowered to consider any matter within the scope of IMO concerned with prevention and control of pollution from ships. In particular it is concerned with the adoption and amendment of conventions and other regulations and measures to ensure their enforcement. The MEPC was first established as a subsidiary body of the Assembly in 1973 and was raised to full constitutional status in 1985. NGOs which have granted consultative status with IMO and IGOs which have concluded agreements of co-operation with IMO are also represented at MEPC sessions.

Scientific/technical

The Sub-Committees on Bulk Liquids and Gases and Flag State Implementation are important subsidiary bodies of the MEPC as far as pollution aspects are concerned. The MEPC can also refer issues it considers appropriate to the other IMO sub-committees.

Publications

IMO News, and reports of the MEPC and MSC of IMO.

Sources on the Internet

<http://www.imo.org>

International Convention on Civil Liability for Bunker Oil Pollution Damage, 2001 (Bunkers Convention)

Objectives

To ensure that adequate, prompt, and effective compensation is available to persons who suffer damage caused by spills of oil, when the latter is carried as fuel in ships' bunkers.

Scope

Legal scope

Open to all states. Not open to regional integration organizations.

Geographic scope

The Convention applies to damage caused on the territory, including the territorial sea, and in exclusive economic zones of States Parties.

Time and place of adoption

23 March 2001, London.

Entry into force

Enters into force 12 months following the date on which 18 states, including five states each with ships whose combined gross tonnage is not less than 1 million gt, have either signed it without reservation as to ratification, acceptance, or approval or have deposited instruments of ratification, acceptance, approval, or accession.

Status of participation

This Convention is open for signature at the headquarters of IMO from 1 October 2001 until 30 September 2002 and thereafter remains open for accession.

The Secretary-General of the International Maritime Organization (IMO) (see IGOs) performs depositary functions.

Affiliated instruments and organizations

A diplomatic conference held from 19 to 23 March 2001 at IMO headquarters in London reached agreement on the details of the Convention. The Conference also adopted three resolutions associated with the Convention:

• *Resolution on limitation of liability.* The resolution urges all states that have not yet done so to ratify or accede to the Protocol of 1996 to amend the Convention on Limitation of Liability for Maritime Claims, 1976. The 1996 LLMC Protocol raises the limits of liability, and therefore amounts of compensation payable in the event of an incident, compared to the 1976 Convention. The LLMC Protocol had received four acceptances by 30 April 2001. It will enter into force 90 days after being accepted by ten states;

• *Resolution on promotion of technical co-operation.* The resolution urges all IMO member States, in co-operation with IMO, other interested states, competent international or regional organizations, and industry programmes, to promote and provide directly, or through IMO, support to states that request technical assistance for:

• the assessment of the implications of ratifying, accepting, approving, or acceding to and complying with the Convention;

• the development of national legislation to give effect to the Convention;

• the introduction of other measures for, and the training of personnel charged with, the effective implementation and enforcement of the Convention.

The resolution also urges all states to initiate action without awaiting the entry into force of the Convention;

• *Resolution on protection for persons taking measures to prevent or minimize the effects of oil pollution.* The resolution urges states, when implementing the Convention, to consider the need to introduce legal provision for protection for persons taking measures to prevent or minimize the effects of bunker oil pollution. It recommends that persons taking reasonable measures to prevent or minimize the effects of oil pollution be exempt from liability unless the liability in question resulted from their personal act or omission, committed with the intent to cause damage, or recklessly and with knowledge that such damage would probably result. It also recommends that states consider the relevant provisions of the International Convention on Liability and Compensation for Damage in Connection with the Carriage of Hazardous and Noxious Substances by Sea (HNS Convention) (see this section), as a model for their legislation.

Secretariat

c/o International Maritime Organization (IMO) (see IGOs).

Finance

Budget

Costs are covered by the regular IMO budget.

Rules and standards

The Convention provides a free-standing instrument covering pollution damage only. 'Pollution damage' means:

• loss or damage caused outside the ship by contamination resulting from the escape or discharge of bunker oil from the ship, wherever such escape or discharge may occur, provided that compensation for impairment of the environment other than loss of profit from such impairment shall be limited to costs of reasonable measures of reinstatement actually undertaken or to be undertaken;

• the costs of preventive measures and further loss or damage caused by preventive measures.

The Convention is modelled on the International Convention on Civil Liability for Oil Pollution Damage 1969 (1969 CLC) (see this section). As with that convention, a key requirement in the draft bunkers' convention is the need for the registered owner of a vessel to maintain compulsory insurance cover.

Another key provision is the requirement for direct action. This would allow a claim for compensation for pollution damage to be brought directly against an insurer.

Monitoring/implementation

Review procedure

The Convention requires ships over 1000 gross tonnage to maintain insurance or other financial security, such as the guarantee of a bank or similar financial institution, to cover the liability of the registered owner for pollution damage in an amount equal to the limits of liability under the applicable national or international limitation regime, but, in all cases, not exceeding an amount calculated in accordance with the Convention on Limitation of Liability for Maritime Claims, 1976, as amended.

Decision-making bodies

Political

The Bunkers Convention does not have its own institutional apparatus, such as a regular Conference of the Parties, and commitments are not regularly reviewed. Unlike the International Convention on Civil Liability for Oil Pollution Damage 1969 (1969 CLC) (see this section), the Convention does not have a fund which needs to be administered.

Scientific/technical

The Convention has no system or rules by which scientific and technical knowledge is incorporated into the decision-making process.

Publications

Up-to-date information on the Convention is available through *IMO News* (quarterly) and other reports from IMO.

Sources on the Internet

<http://www.imo.org>

International Convention on Civil Liability for Oil Pollution Damage 1969 (1969 CLC)

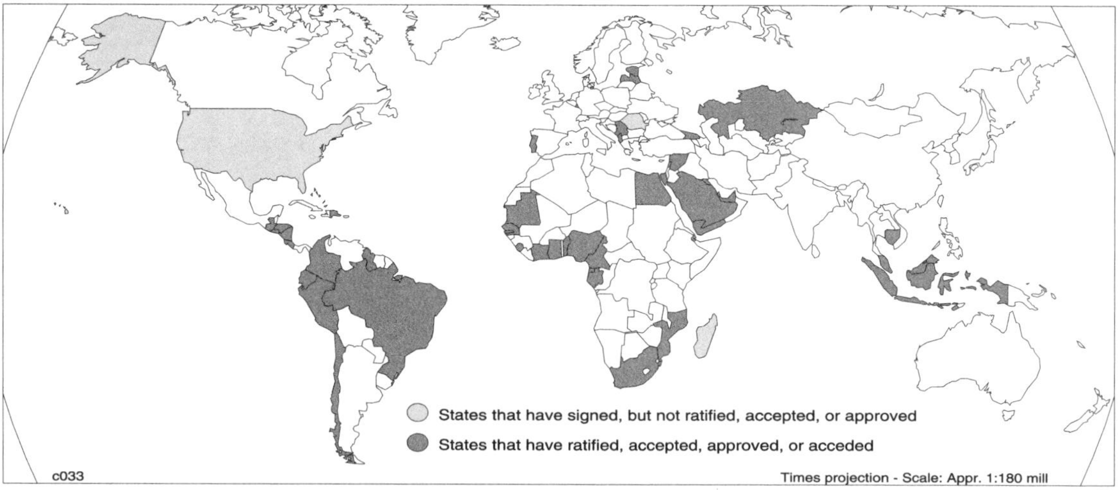

International Convention on Civil Liability for Oil Pollution Damage 1969 (1969 CLC)

Objectives

- to ensure that adequate compensation is available to persons who suffer pollution damage caused by spills of persistent oil from laden tankers;
- to harmonize international rules and procedures for determining questions of liability and for providing adequate compensation in such cases.

Scope

Legal scope

Open to states which are members of the UN, of any of the Specialized Agencies, of the International Atomic Energy Agency (IAEA) (see IGOs), or which are Parties to the Statute of the International Court of Justice. Not open to regional integration organizations.

Geographic scope

Pollution damage caused on the territory, including the territorial sea, of States Parties. The 1992 Protocol (see below) extended the scope to cover the exclusive economic zones (EEZ) of the States Parties.

Time and place of adoption

29 November 1969, Brussels.

Entry into force

19 June 1975.

Status of participation

51 remaining Parties by 1 March 2002. Three Signatories without ratification, approval, or acceptance. From 16 May 1998, Parties to the 1992 Protocol (see below) ceased to be Parties to the 1969 CLC due to a mechanism for compulsory denunciation of the 'old' regime established in the 1992 Protocol. However, for the time being the two regimes are co-existing, since there are a number of states which are Party to the 1969 CLC and have not yet ratified the 1992 regime (which is intended eventually to replace the 1969 CLC).

The Secretary-General of IMO (see IGOs) performs depositary functions.

Affiliated instruments and organizations

- *Protocol to the International Convention on Civil Liability for Oil Pollution Damage*, London, 1976. Entered into force on 8 April 1981. 55 Parties by 28 February 2002. No Signatories without ratification, acceptance, or approval.
- *Protocol to Amend the International Convention on Civil Liability for Oil Pollution Damage*, London, 1984. (Not in force.) Governments are urged not to ratify the 1984 Protocol but only the 1992 Protocol to avoid a situation in which two conflicting treaty regimes are operational. It is practically certain that this Protocol will never enter into force.
- *Protocol to Amend the International Convention on Civil Liability for Oil Pollution Damage*, London, 1992. Entered into force on 30 May 1996. 82 Parties by 1 March 2002. No Signatories without ratification, approval, or acceptance. The 1969 CLC as amended by the 1992 Protocol thereto is known as the *International Convention on Civil Liability for Oil Pollution Damage 1992*. (See also Status of participation, above.)

Co-ordination with related instruments

The necessary co-ordination with the operation of the 1992 Fund Convention is ensured by the International Oil Pollution Compensation Fund 1992 (IOPC Fund 1992).

Secretariat

None. Information is available from the IOPC Fund 1992 (see IGOs).

Finance

Budget

None.

Rules and standards

System of liability

The 1969 CLC covers pollution damage

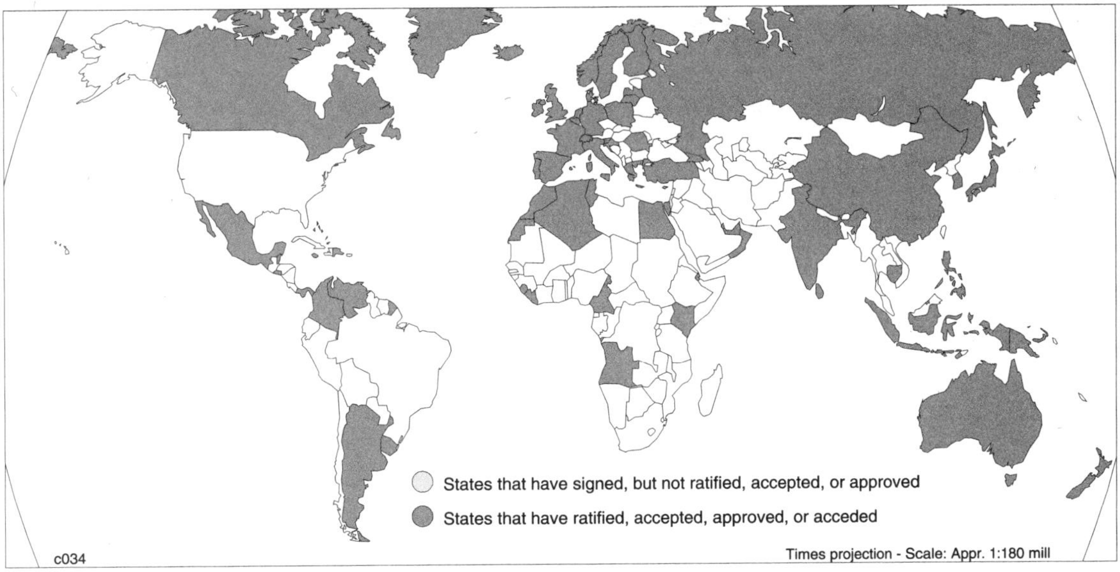

1992 Protocol to Amend the International Convention on Civil Liability for Oil Pollution Damage

suffered in the territory (including the territorial sea) of a State Party to the 1969 CLC. The flag of the tanker and the nationality of the shipowner are irrelevant.

The owner of a tanker has strict liability (i.e. he is liable also in the absence of fault) for pollution damage caused by persistent oil spilled from a laden tanker as a result of an incident. He is exempt from liability only in certain circumstances.

Under certain conditions the shipowner is entitled to limit his liability to 133 special drawing rights (SDR) of the International Monetary Fund (IMF) (see IGOs) per ton of the ship's tonnage or SDR14 million, whichever is the less.

Claims for pollution damage can be made only against the registered owner of the tanker concerned.

The owner of a tanker carrying more than 2000 tonnes of persistent oil as cargo is obliged to maintain insurance to cover his liability under the 1969 CLC. Tankers must carry a certificate on board attesting the insurance coverage. When entering or leaving a port or terminal installation of a State Party to the 1969 CLC, such a certificate shall also be carried by ships flying the flag of non-CLC States.

The 1969 CLC imposes on States Parties primarily the obligation to incorporate its provisions into domestic law.

The objective of the 1976 Protocol is to replace the original gold-based unit of account by special drawing rights (SDR) of the IMF.

Under the 1992 Protocol, compared with the original version of CLC, the shipowner's liability limit is substantially increased. A special limit of SDR3 million is introduced for small ships below 5000 units of gross tanker tonnage. The limit increases on a linear scale up to SDR59.7 million for ships over 140,000 units of gross tonnage. There is a simplified procedure for increasing the limits. By application of this procedure the limits will be increased by 50.37 per cent with effect from 1 November 2003.

The 1992 Protocol provides a wider scope of application on several points than the Conventions in their original versions. The geographical scope of the 1992 Protocol is extended to include the exclusive economic zone (EEZ) established under the United Nations Convention on the Law of the Sea (LOS Convention) (see this section). Pollution damage caused by spills of persistent oil from unladen tankers is covered under the 1992 Protocol in certain circumstances, and expenses incurred for preventive measures are recoverable even when no spill of oil occurs, provided that there was a grave and imminent threat of pollution damage. The Protocol includes a new definition of pollution damage which retains the basic wording of the present definition, but also adds a phrase to clarify that, for environmental damage, only costs incurred for reasonable measures to reinstate the contaminated environment are included in the concept of pollution damage.

Monitoring/implementation

Review procedure
None.

Observations or inspections
None.

Trade measures
None.

Dispute-settlement mechanisms
None.

Decision-making bodies

Political
The 1969 CLC does not have its own institutional apparatus, such as a regular Conference of the Parties. Commitments are not regularly reviewed. However, IMO (see IGOs), as depositary organization, shall convene a conference of States Parties if so requested by at least one-third of the Parties. Such conferences have been convened three times, i.e. for the adoption of the Protocols in 1976, 1984, and 1992.

Scientific/technical bodies
The CLC regime has no system or rules by which scientific and technical knowledge is incorporated into the decision-making process.

Publications

Up-to-date developments are reported in *IMO News*, published quarterly, and in the publications of the International Oil Pollution Compensation Fund 1992 (see IGOs).

International Convention on the Establishment of an International Fund for Compensation for Oil Pollution Damage 1992 (1992 Fund Convention)

Objectives

• to provide for a compensation system, supplementing that of the 1992 Protocol to Amend the International Convention on Civil Liability for Oil Pollution Damage 1969 (se this section), known as the International Convention on Civil Liability for Oil Pollution Damage 1992 (1992 CLC), in order to ensure full compensation to victims of oil pollution damage caused by persistent oil spilled from laden tankers;
• to distribute the economic burden between the shipping industry and oil cargo interests.

Scope

Legal scope
Open to States Parties to the International Convention on Civil Liability for Oil Pollution Damage 1992.

Geographic scope
Pollution damage caused in the territory, the territorial sea, or the exclusive economic zone (EEZ) of States Parties.

Time and place of adoption

27 November 1992, London.

Entry into force

30 May 1996. The Convention replaces the International Convention on the Establishment of an International Fund for Compensation for Oil Pollution Damage 1971 (1971 Fund Convention), adopted on 18 December 1971 in Brussels, which entered into force on 16 October 1978. The 1971 Fund Convention ceased to be in force on 24 May 2002.

Status of participation

76 Parties by 1 March 2002. One Signatory without ratification, approval, or acceptance.

The Secretary-General of IMO (see IGOs) performs depositary functions.

Affiliated instruments and organizations

The 1992 Fund Convention establishes a regime for compensating victims when the compensation under the 1992 CLC is inadequate. The International Oil Pollution Compensation Fund 1992 (IOPC Fund 1992) (see IGOs) was set up under the 1992 Fund Convention and was established for the purpose of administering the regime of compensation created by the 1992 Fund Convention. By becoming party to the 1992 Fund Convention, a state becomes a member of the IOPC Fund 1992.

Secretariat

International Oil Pollution Compensation Funds (IOPC Funds) (see IGOs),
23rd Floor,
Portland House,
Stag Place,
London SW1E 5PN,
United Kingdom
Telephone: +44-20-75927100
Telefax: +44-20-75927111
E-mail: info@iopcfund.org

Director
Mr Måns Jacobsson
(1 January 1985–31 December 2004).

Number of staff
14 professionals and 13 support staff (March 2002).

Finance

The system of compensation is financed by contributions of persons who receive more than 150,000 tonnes of crude or heavy oil after sea transport in a State Party during a calendar year. Contributions are determined in proportion to the quantity of oil received.

Budget
Annual joint secretariat costs amount to approximately £UK2.2 million.

Rules and standards

Compensation system
The 1992 Convention established the IOPC Fund 1992 (see IGOs) to administer the system of compensation set up under the Con-

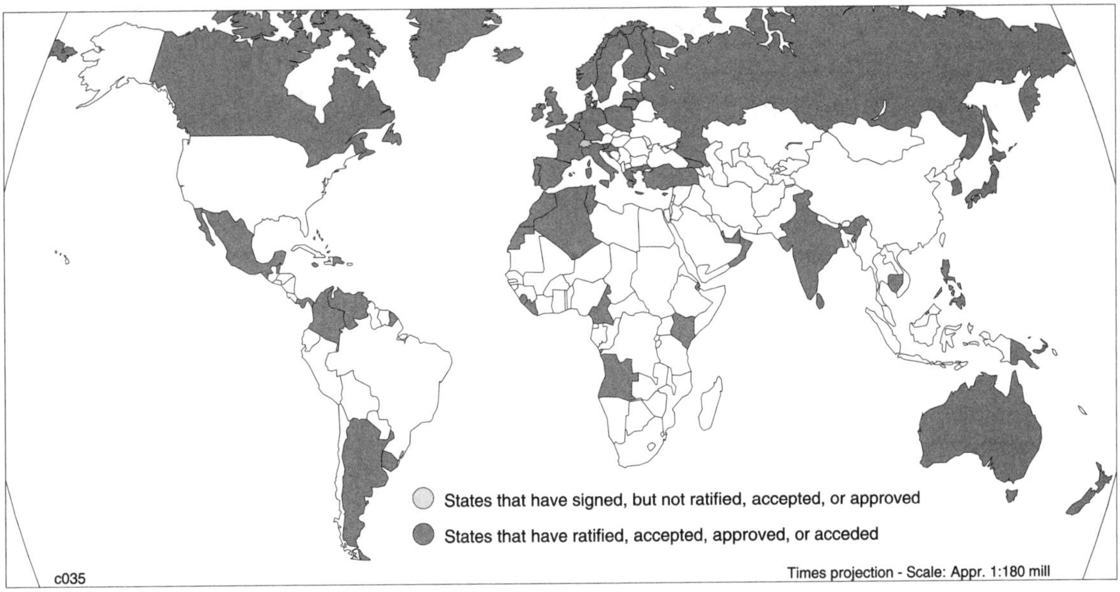

vention. The IOPC Fund 1992 pays compensation to those suffering oil pollution damage which are Parties to the 1992 Fund Convention who do not obtain full compensation under the 1992 Civil Liability Convention (1992 CLC) in the following cases:

• the shipowner is exempt from liability under the 1992 CLC because he can invoke one of the exemptions under that Convention;
• the shipowner is financially incapable of meeting his obligations under the 1992 CLC in full and his insurance is insufficient to satisfy the claims for compensation for pollution damage; or
• the damage exceeds the shipowner's liability under the 1992 CLC.

Compensation for a single incident was limited under the 1971 Fund Convention to 60 million special drawing rights (SDR) of the International Monetary Fund (see IGOs), including the amount actually paid by the shipowner and his insurer under the CLC.

Under the 1992 Fund Convention, the maximum amount of compensation payable by the IOPC Fund 1992 in respect of an incident is SDR135 million, including the amount actually paid by the shipowner and his insurer under the 1992 CLC. There is a simplified procedure under the 1992 Fund Convention for increasing the maximum amount payable by the IOPC Fund 1992. By application of that procedure the maximum amount will be increased to 203 million SDR with effect from 1 November 2003.

Pollution damage caused by spills of persistent oil from unladen tankers is covered under the 1992 Fund Convention in certain circumstances, and expenses incurred for preventive measures are recoverable even when no spill of oil occurs, provided that there was a grave and imminent threat of pollution damage. The Convention includes a new definition of pollution damage which adds a phrase to clarify that, for environmental damage, only costs incurred for reasonable measures to reinstate the contaminated environment are included in the concept of pollution damage.

Monitoring/implementation

Review procedure
Parties shall communicate annually a list of oil-receiving persons under their jurisdiction and the quantity of oil received by each person. These reports are confidential. The annual submission of lists of contributing persons is closely monitored by the IOPC Fund 1992 secretariat.

Observations or inspections
None by the Convention as such.

Trade measures
No provisions on trade measures to penalize Parties for non-compliance.

Dispute-settlement mechanisms
None.

Decision-making bodies

The IOPC Fund 1992 secretariat, led by the Director, is responsible for the conduct of business, including collection of contributions and settlements of claims under the 1992 Fund Convention.

Political
The 1992 Fund Convention has established two decision-making organs, the Assembly of all States Parties, which meets annually, and the Executive Committee, comprising 15 States Parties elected by the Assembly, which meets several times a year. The main function is to approve settlements of claims.

Scientific/technical
None.

Publications

Current developments are reported in the Fund's annual report. Also published periodically by the IOPC Fund 1992 secretariat are claims manuals.

Sources on the Internet

<http://www.iopcfund.org>

International Convention on Liability and Compensation for Damage in Connection with the Carriage of Hazardous and Noxious Substances by Sea (HNS Convention)

Objectives

To ensure that adequate, prompt, and effective compensation is available to persons who suffer damage caused by incidents in connection with the carriage by sea of hazardous and noxious substances (HNS).

Scope

Legal scope
Open to all states. Not open to regional economic integration organizations.

Geographic scope
The Convention applies to damage caused on the territory, including the territorial sea, and in exclusive economic zones of States Parties.

Time and place of adoption

3 May 1996, London.

Entry into force

Not yet in force. Enters into force 18 months after the date on which at least 12 states, including four states each with not fewer than 2 million units of gross tonnage, have expressed their consent to be bound by it, provided that persons in these states which will have to make payments into the general account have received at least 40 million tonnes of contributing HNS cargo in the preceding calendar year.

Status of participation

Two ratifications (1.80 per cent of world tonnage) by 31 May 2002. Eight Signatories without ratification, approval, or acceptance.

Affiliated instruments and organizations

Annex I consists of a certificate of insurance or other financial security in respect of liability for damage caused by hazardous and noxious substances.

Co-ordination with related instruments
The scope of the treaty is defined by reference to existing international lists of substances, enabling it to be modified as these are amended. The substances include oils and noxious liquid substances carried in bulk as defined in the MARPOL 73/78 (see this section) on marine oil pollution, dangerous, hazardous, or harmful substances, materials, and articles in packaged form covered by the International Maritime Dangerous Goods Code, and various other liquid substances, solid bulk materials, and liquefied gases, together with residues from the previous bulk carriage of substances covered by the above lists. At present, these lists apply to some 6000 substances.

The Convention shall not apply to pollution damage as defined in the International Convention on Civil Liability for Oil Pollution Damage 1969 (1969 CLC) (see this section).

The Marine Environment Protection Committee (MEPC), one of four main committees of IMO, is responsible for co-ordinating work with other IMO conventions.

Secretariat

A secretariat comprising a Director, and such staff as the administration of the HNS Fund may require, will be established following the entry into force of the Convention. Information is available from IMO (see IGOs).

Finance

Budget
Not yet applicable. The HNS Fund to be established under the Convention will prepare and submit financial statements and budget estimates for each calendar year to the Assembly (see Decision-making bodies, below).

Special funds
See HNS Fund, in Rules and standards, below.

Rules and standards

The Convention defines damage as including loss of life or personal injury; loss of or damage to property outside the ship; loss or damage by contamination of the environment; the costs of preventive measures; and further loss or damage caused by them.

The Convention introduces strict liability for the shipowner, higher limits than the present general limitation regimes, and a system of compulsory insurance and insurance certificates. States which are Parties can decide not to apply it to ships of 200 gross tonnage and below that carry HNS only in packaged form and are engaged on voyages between ports in the same State. Two neighbouring States can further agree to apply similar conditions to ships operating between ports in the two countries.

In order to ensure that shipowners engaged in the transport of HNS are able to meet their liabilities, the Convention makes insurance compulsory for them. A certificate of insurance must be carried on board and a copy retained by the authorities who keep record of the ship's registry.

It has generally been agreed that it would not be possible to provide sufficient cover by the shipowner liability alone for the damage that could be caused in connection with the carriage of HNS cargo. This liability, which creates a first tier of the Convention, is therefore supplemented by a second tier, the HNS Fund, financed by cargo interest.

The Fund will be involved in cases where:

- no liability for the damage arises for the shipowner. This could occur, for example, if the shipowner was not informed that a shipment contained HNS or if the accident resulted from an act of war;
- the owner is financially incapable of meeting the obligations under the Convention in full, and any financial security that may be provided under chapter II (on liability) does not cover or is insufficient to satisfy the claims for compensation for damage;
- the damage exceeds the owner's liability under the terms of chapter II.

Contributions to the second tier will be

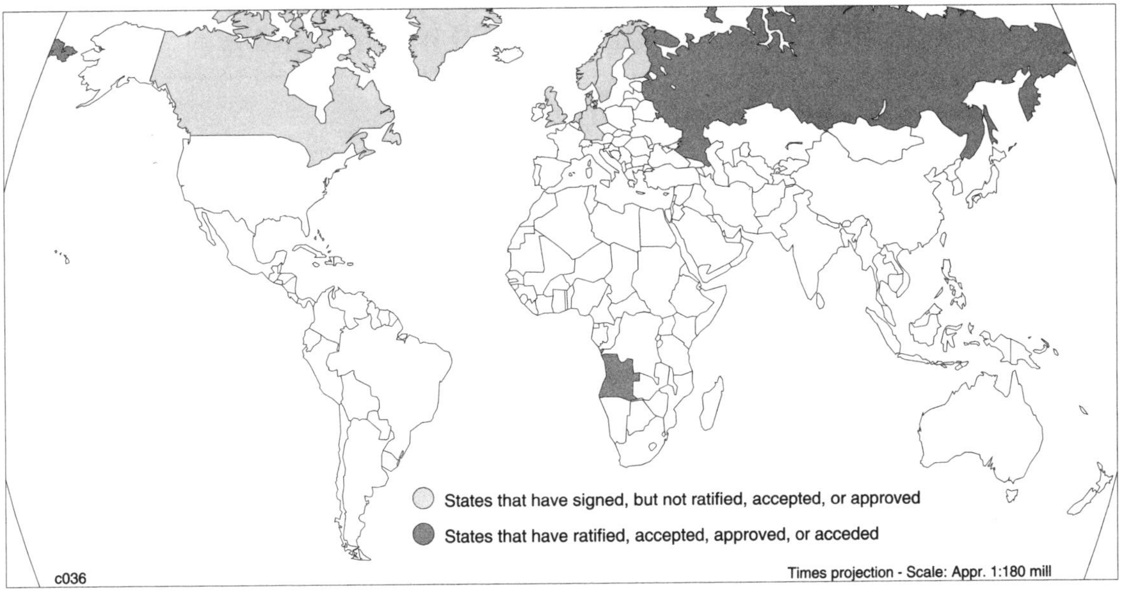

levied on persons in the Contracting Parties who receive a certain minimum quantity of HNS cargo during a calendar year. The tier will consist of one general account and three separate accounts for oil, liquefied natural gas (LNG), and liquefied petroleum gas (LPG). The system with separate accounts has been seen as a way to avoid cross-subsidization between different HNS substances.

The unit of account used in the Convention is the Special Drawing Right (SDR) of the International Monetary Fund (IMF) (see IGOs). At present SDR1 is roughly equivalent to £UK1. The liability limits contained in the first tier are based on the gross tonnage of the ship concerned and are as follows:

- for ships not exceeding 2000 gt, SDR10 million;
- for ships between 2001 and 50,000 gt, SDR1500 per ton, making a maximum of SDR82 million at 50,000 gt;
- for ships between 50,001 gt and 100,000 gt, SDR360 per ton, making a maximum of SDR100 million at 100,000 gt;
- for ships exceeding 100,000 gt, SDR100 million.

Once these limits are reached, compensation would be paid from the second tier, the HNS Fund, up to a maximum of SDR250 million (including compensation paid under the first tier). The Fund will be made up of contributions paid by the importers of HNS materials (primarily chemical companies).

Monitoring/implementation

Review procedure

Each State Party shall communicate to the Director the name and address of any person who in respect of the State is liable to pay contributions in accordance with the Convention, as well as data on the relevant quantities of contributing cargo for which such a person is liable to contribute in respect of the preceding calendar year.

Where a State Party does not fulfil its obligations to communicate to the Director the information referred to above, and this results in a financial loss for the HNS Fund, that State Party shall be liable to compensate the HNS Fund for such loss. The Assembly shall, on the recommendation of the Director, decide whether such compensation shall be payable by a State Party.

Where a person who is liable to pay contributions does not fulfil the obligations in respect of any such contribution or any part thereof and is in arrears, the Director shall take all appropriate action, including court action, against such a person on behalf of the HNS Fund with a view to the recovery of the amount due. However, where the defaulting contributor is manifestly insolvent or the circumstances otherwise so warrant, the Assembly may, upon recommendation of the Director, decide that no action shall be taken or continued against the contributor.

The Assembly shall review every five years the implementation of the Convention with particular reference to the performance of the system for the calculation of levies and the contribution mechanism for domestic trade; and to perform such other functions as are allocated to it under the Convention or are otherwise necessary for the proper operation of the HNS Fund.

Decision-making bodies

Political

The Fund will have an Assembly consisting of all States which are Parties and a Secretariat headed by a Director. The Assembly will normally meet once a year. The first session shall take place as soon as possible after the entry into force of the Convention.

Scientific/technical

The Assembly shall establish a Committee on Claims for Compensation, with at least seven and not more than 15 members, and any temporary or permanent subsidiary body it may consider to be necessary.

Publications

Up-to-date information on the Convention is available through *IMO News* (quarterly) and other reports from IMO.

Sources on the Internet

<http://www.imo.org>

International Convention on Oil Pollution Preparedness, Response, and Co-operation (OPRC)

Objectives

- to prevent marine pollution incidents by oil, in accordance with the precautionary principle, in particular by strict application of the International Convention for Safety of Life at Sea (SOLAS) and MARPOL 73/78 (see this section);
- to advance the adoption of adequate response measures in the event that an oil-pollution incident does occur;
- to provide for mutual assistance and co-operation between States for these aims.

Scope

Legal scope

Open to all states. Not open to regional integration organizations. An international conference comprised of 90 states drafted the final text and adopted the Convention.

Geographic scope

The global seas.

Time and place of adoption

30 November 1990, London.

Entry into force

13 May 1995.

Status of participation

66 Parties (53.76 per cent of world tonnage) by 31 May 2002. Nine Signatories without ratification, approval, acceptance, or accession.

The Secretary-General of the International Maritime Organization (IMO) (see IGOs) performs depositary functions.

Affiliated instruments and organizations

The *Annex* to the Convention provides general principles concerning reimbursements for the costs incurred by nations that assist in responding to spills. In the absence of an existing bilateral or multilateral arrangement, the requesting nation shall reimburse the assisting nation for the costs incurred. However, if an assisting nation acts on its own initiative, it will bear the costs. The costs are to be calculated according to the law and custom of the assisting nation.

Ten affiliated *Resolutions* were adopted by the Conference dealing with, for example, institutional matters, expansion of scope to hazardous substances, and technical co-operation and transfer of technology.

Protocol on Preparedness, Response and Co-operation to Pollution Incidents by Hazardous and Noxious Substances (OPRC-HNS Protocol), London, 15 March 2000. (Not yet in force.) One state (Ecuador) (0.05 per cent of world tonnage) had acceded by 31 May 2002. Seven Signatories without ratification, acceptance, or approval. Enters into force 12 months after ratification by no fewer than 15 States which are Party to the OPRC Convention.

The basic objective of the Protocol is that ships will be required to carry a shipboard pollution emergency plan to deal specifically with incidents involving hazardous and noxious substances (HNS). HNS are defined by reference to lists of substances included in various IMO Conventions and Codes. Among these are oils; other liquid substances defined as noxious or dangerous; liquefied gases; liquid substances with a flashpoint not exceeding 60°C; dangerous, hazardous, and harmful materials and substances carried in packaged form; and solid bulk materials defined as possessing chemical hazards.

The Protocol, when it comes into force, will ensure that ships carrying hazardous and noxious liquid substances are covered, or will be covered, by regimes similar to those already in existence for oil incidents.

IMO shall act as clearing-house for information submitted to it by the Parties and facilitate co-operation among the Parties in technical and educational matters.

Co-ordination with related instruments

As a follow-up to the Convention and, in particular, to the provision requiring all ships to carry oil-pollution emergency plans, the Marine Environment Protection Committee (MEPC), one of five main committees of IMO, adopted amendments to Annex 1 of MARPOL 73/78 (see this sec-

tion). Co-ordination with regional organizations or arrangements are recognized.

Secretariat

c/o IMO (see IGOs).

Finance

Budget
The Convention does not provide for regular meetings and programme activities or for a secretariat. Therefore regular administrative costs do not arise under the Convention.

Special funds
None.

Rules and standards

Parties must require ships, off-shore units, and seaports under their jurisdiction to have oil-pollution emergency plans. These are required for:

- oil-tankers of 150 gross tons and above, and other ships of 400 gross tons and above;
- any fixed or floating off-shore installation or structure engaged in gas or oil exploration, exploitation, production activities, or loading or unloading oil;
- any seaport and oil-handling facility that presents a risk of an oil-pollution incident.

The Convention has established a reporting procedure on oil-pollution incidents. Under this procedure, all persons having charge shall be required to report such incidents to the competent national authority, which must assess the incident and inform other States and/or IMO. Parties shall establish national and, as far as possible, regional systems for preparedness and response. They shall co-operate in pollution response, research, and technical matters.

Monitoring/implementation

Review procedure
Beyond the general obligations to co-operate in research and technical assistance, no provision for disclosure of data is made. Parties are required to ensure that current information is provided to IMO response and preparedness systems. Parties shall evaluate the effectiveness of the Convention together with IMO. No evaluation criteria or time-scales are given.

The MEPC has established the OPRC Working Group, which is open to representatives from all IMO members, UN organizations, and intergovernmental organizations in consultative status with IMO. The Working Group reports to the MEPC and meets in conjunction with MEPC meetings. According to the current work plan, the Working Group shall recommend ways and means to improve the involvement of industry (oil, shipping, oil-spill clean-up) in the implementation of the Convention.

Observations or inspections
None by the Convention as such.

Trade measures
No provisions on trade measures to penalize Parties for non-compliance.

Dispute-settlement mechanisms
None.

Decision-making bodies

The Convention does not establish a meeting of the Parties or similar institution. The MEPC is responsible for co-ordinating and administering the activities relating to the Convention. It consists of all member States of IMO. NGOs which have been granted consultative status with IMO are also represented at MEPC sessions, as are IGOs which have concluded agreements of co-operation.

Publications

IMO News and reports of the MEPC.

Sources on the Internet

<http://www.imo.org>

International Convention Relating to Intervention on the High Seas in Cases of Oil Pollution Casualties (Intervention Convention)

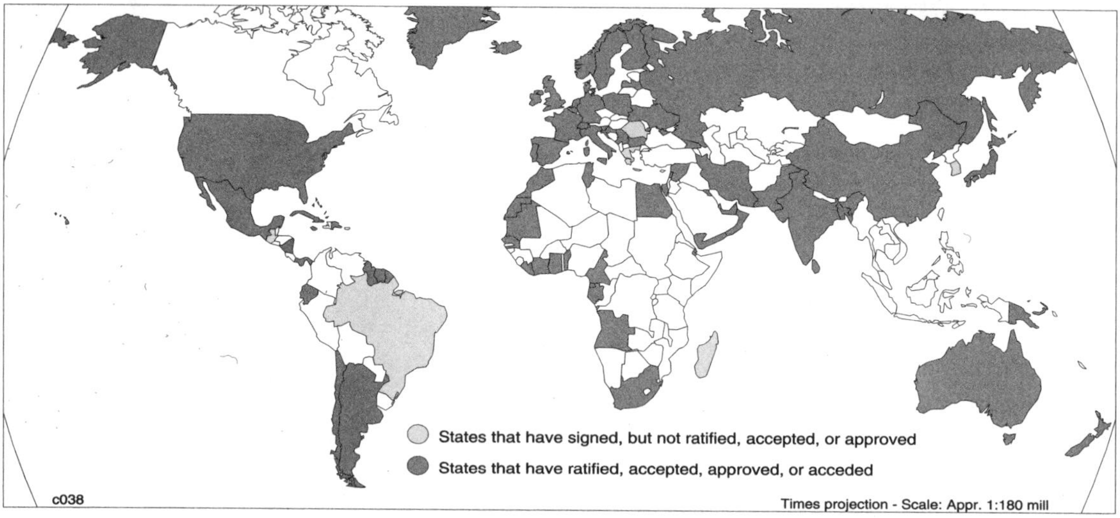

Objectives

- to protect the interest of peoples against the grave consequences of maritime casualties resulting in danger of oil pollution of the sea and coastline;
- to recognize that measures of an exceptional character to protect such interests might be necessary on the high seas, provided these do not affect the principle of freedom of the high seas.

Scope

Legal scope
Membership is open to member States of the UN, any specialized agency, or the International Atomic Energy Agency (IAEA) (see IGOs), or Parties to the Statute of the International Court of Justice.

Geographic scope
The global seas.

Time and place of adoption

29 November 1969, Brussels.

Entry into force

6 May 1975.

Status of participation

77 Parties (71.21 per cent of world tonnage) by 31 May 2002. Six Signatories without ratification or approval.

Affiliated instruments and organizations

Protocol Relating to Intervention on the High Seas in Cases of Marine Pollution by Substances Other than Oil, London, 2 November 1973. Entered into force on 30 March 1983. 44 Parties (44.59 per cent of world tonnage) by 31 May 2002. One Signatory without ratification or approval. The basic objective of the Protocol is to extend the 1969 Convention to apply also to substances other than oil, such as noxious substances, liquefied gases, and radioactive substances.

Secretariat

c/o International Maritime Organization (IMO) (see IGOs).

Finance

Budget
Costs are covered by the regular IMO budget.

Rules and standards

The following are imposed on Parties:

- to consult with other states affected before taking measures;
- to notify proposed measures to any person or company known to have interests which can reasonably be expected to be affected by those measures;
- to use best endeavours to avoid risk to human life and to afford assistance to persons in need;
- to notify without delay states and persons or companies concerned and the Secretary-General of IMO;
- to set up and maintain a list of independent experts;
- to ensure that measures taken are proportionate to the damage, actual or threatened, and necessary to protect the interest of the coastal state;
- to pay compensation for measures taken in excess of those reasonably necessary.

Monitoring/implementation

Review procedure
The Parties are required to report on measures taken under the Convention to IMO and to other states affected.

Decision-making bodies

IMO acts as reporting facility and maintains a list of independent experts.

Publications

Up-to-date information is made available through *IMO News* (quarterly).

Sources on the Internet

<http://www.imo.org>

United Nations Convention on the Law of the Sea (LOS Convention)

Objectives

- to establish a comprehensive legal order to promote peaceful uses of the oceans and seas, the equitable and efficient utilization of their resources, the conservation of their living resources, and the study and protection and preservation of the marine environment, as well as to facilitate international navigation;
- to integrate and balance the right to exploit natural resources with the duty to manage and conserve such resources and to protect and preserve the marine environment;
- to provide the comprehensive legal framework for the protection and preservation of the marine environment to be complemented and developed by further legal rules at the global or regional level and national measures. This is recognized in the UN Conference on Environment and Development (UNCED)'s Agenda 21, chapter 17, which states that the LOS Convention provides the international basis upon which to pursue the protection and sustainable development of the marine and coastal environment and its resources.

To encourage uniform application of the Convention, no reservations or exceptions may be made to the Convention.

Scope

Legal scope
Open to all states, certain self-governing associated states and territories, and international organizations to which their member states have transferred competence over matters governed by the Convention.

Geographic scope
Global.

Time and place of adoption

10 December 1982, Montego Bay, Jamaica.

Entry into force

16 November 1994.

Status of participation

138 Parties, including the European Community, by 11 June 2002. 32 Signatories have not yet ratified.

The Secretary-General of the UN acts as depositary for the Convention itself and both agreements listed below.

Affiliated instruments and organizations

Agreement relating to the Implementation of Part XI of the United Nations Convention on the Law of the Sea of 10 December 1982. Adopted on 28 July 1994 by the 48th session of the General Assembly of the UN. Entered into force on 28 July 1996. 105 Parties, including the European Community, by 11 June 2002. 13 Signatories have not expressed their consent to be bound.

With the entry into force of the LOS Convention, the ISA came into existence and the Agreement started to be provisionally applied pending its entry into force. The provisional application of the Agreement terminated at the date of its entry into force, on 28 July 1996. In addition to States Parties to the Convention, which are members of ISA *ipso facto*, States and entities which had been applying the Agreement provisionally, and for which it was not in force, were able to continue to be members of the Authority on a provisional basis, pending its entry into force for such States and entities. Such provisional membership terminated on 16 November 1998 in accordance with the relevant provisions of the Agreement. As at 9 May 2002, 34 of the Parties to the Convention had still to express their consent to be bound by the Agreement.

The Agreement consists of ten articles dealing mainly with procedural aspects such as signature, entry into force, and provisional application. Its Article 2 deals with the relationship between the Agreement and Part XI of the Convention, and it provides that the two shall be interpreted and applied together as a single instrument. In the event of an inconsistency between the Agreement and Part XI, however, the provisions of the Agreement shall prevail.

The Agreement was negotiated to facilitate universal participation in the Convention after a number of countries expressed difficulties with the sea-bed mining provisions contained in Part XI of the Convention. The Agreement addresses a number of those difficulties, particularly the request for a more market-oriented approach, and changes in the institutional arrangements and decision-making processes within the International Seabed Authority (ISA) (see Secretariats below). The Agreement deals with the various issues that were identified as problems during the informal consultations convened by the Secretary-General of the UN with a view to resolving certain outstanding issues regarding the deep sea-bed mining provisions of the Convention which impeded its universal acceptance. These include: costs to States Parties and institutional arrangements; decision-making mechanisms for the Authority; the Enterprise; transfer of technology; production policy; financial terms of contracts for deep sea-bed mining; and the review Conference.

Agreement for the Implementation of the Provisions of the United Nations Convention on the Law of the Sea of 10 December 1982 relating to the Conservation and Management of Straddling Fish Stocks and Highly Migratory Fish Stocks (1995 Fish Stocks Agreement). Adopted on 4 August 1995. Entered into force on 11 December 2001. 31 Parties by 11 June 2002. 38 Signatories, including the European Community, have not yet ratified.

The Agreement addresses the problems which have prevented the effective implementation of the relevant Convention provisions on the management and conservation of these resources and to facilitate and strengthen co-operation among States. It sets out principles for the conservation and management of straddling fish stocks and highly migratory fish stocks and establishes that such management must be based on the precautionary approach and the best available scientific information. The Agreement elaborates on the fundamental principle, established in the Convention, that States should co-operate to ensure conservation and promote the objective of the optimum utilization of fisheries resources both within and beyond the exclusive economic zone.

The Agreement attempts to achieve this objective by providing a framework for co-operation in the conservation and management of those resources. It promotes good order in the oceans through the effective management and conservation of high-seas resources by establishing, *inter alia*, detailed

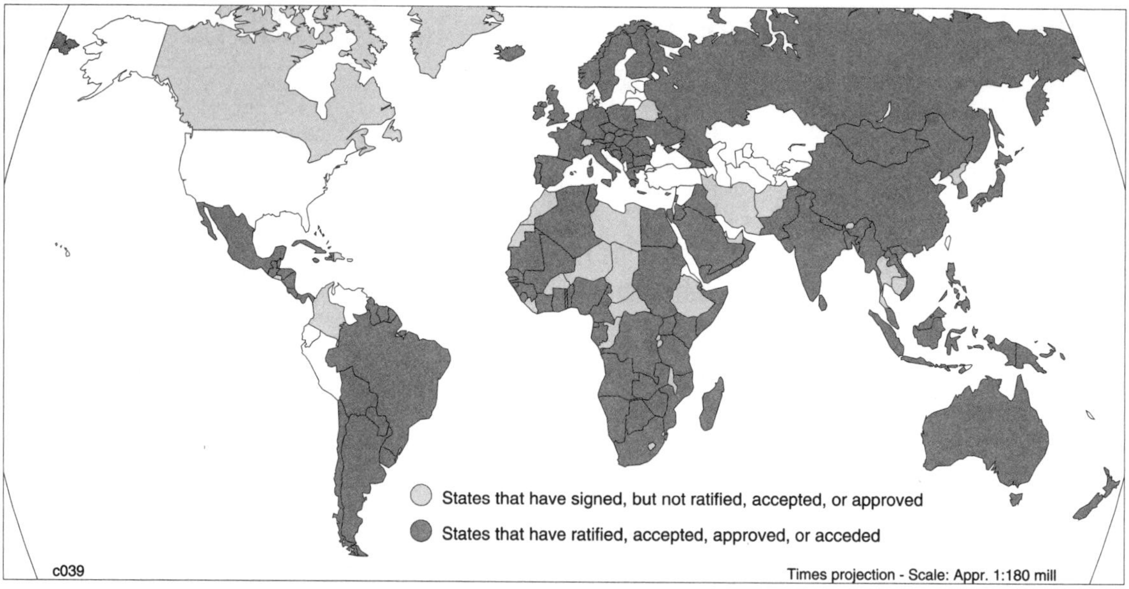

United Nations Convention on the Law of the Sea (LOS Convention)

minimum international standards for the conservation and management of straddling fish stocks and highly migratory fish stocks; ensuring that measures taken for the conservation and management of those stocks in areas under national jurisdiction and in the adjacent high seas are compatible and coherent; ensuring that there are effective mechanisms for compliance and enforcement of those measures on the high seas; ensuring an effective mechanism for settlements of disputes; and recognizing the special requirements of developing states in relation to conservation and management as well as the development, needs, and participation of these countries in the conservation and management of the two types of stocks mentioned above.

The Agreement gives prominence to subregional or regional fisheries management organizations or arrangements as the principal means for implementation of the measures designed to conserve and manage straddling fish stocks and highly migratory fish stocks.

Following the entry into force of the Convention, the *International Seabed Authority* was established in Kingston, Jamaica, and the *International Tribunal for the Law of the Sea* was established in Hamburg (see Secretariats, below). The members of the Tribunal were elected at the Meeting of the States Parties on 1 August 1996 and were sworn in by the Secretary-General of the UN at a ceremonial inauguration on 18 October 1996 in Hamburg. On 24 May 1999 the States Parties filled the seats of seven of the 21 judges whose terms of office expire on 1 October 1999. An election was convened on 16 May 2001 during the eleventh Meeting of the Parties to fill a vacancy left by the death of the Chinese judge.

On 19 April 2002, the Meeting of States Parties elected a judge to fill a vacancy that had arisen due to the demise of the judge from Belize. The Meeting also elected seven judges for a term of nine years, commencing from 1 October 2002.

The Convention provides for the establishment of the *Commission on the Limits of the Continental Shelf (CLCS)*, which is entrusted with making recommendations to coastal States on matters related to the establishment of the outer limits of their continental shelf where such limits extend beyond 200 nautical miles from the baselines (see also Decision-making bodies, below). Following the election of the 21 members of the CLCS on 13 March 1997 by the Meeting of States Parties, the CLCS commenced functioning in June 1997; it held its second session in September 1997, its third in May 1998, its fourth in August–September 1998, its fifth in May 1999, and its sixth in August–September 1999. Its seventh session in May 2000 was the first 'open-meeting' to be convened by the Commission. It was attended by policy makers and legal advisors from coastal states. Its eighth and ninth sessions were from August to September 2000 and in May 2001 respectively.

The tenth session of the Commission, held in March–April 2002, considered the first submission made on 20 December 2001 by the Russian Federation pursuant to article 76, paragraph 8, of the Convention. In the submission, the Russian Federation communicated to the Commission the proposed outer limits of its continental shelf beyond 200 nautical miles from the baselines.

The twelfth Meeting of States Parties to the Convention elected, on 23 April 2002, 21 members of the Commission for a term of five years, commencing from 16 June 2002. At its eleventh meeting in June 2002, the Commission was due to deliberate on the recommendations made by the sub-commission established to consider the submission made by the Russian Federation.

Co-ordination with related instruments

The provisions of the LOS Convention relating to the protection and preservation of the marine environment are further developed in a large number of global and regional instruments. A comprehensive list of such instruments has been compiled by the Division for Ocean Affairs and the Law of the Sea of the UN Office of Legal Affairs and was published in *Multilateral Treaties: A Reference Guide to Multilateral Treaties and Other International Instruments related to the United Nations Convention on the Law of the Sea* (revised and updated as of 31

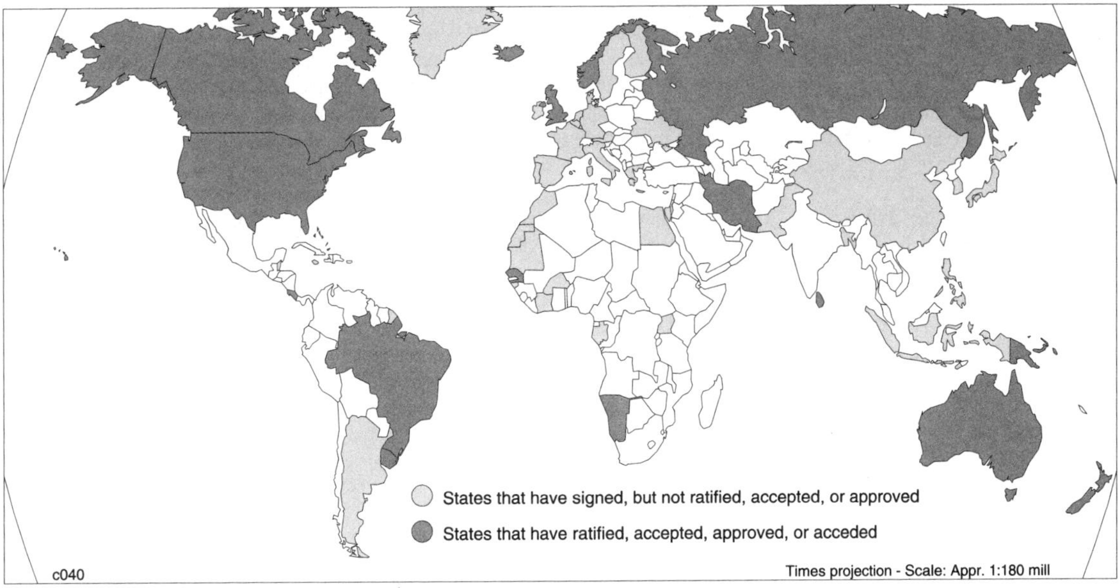

1995 Fish Stocks Agreement

December 1996).

Among the most relevant instruments at the global and regional level are:

- *International Convention for the Prevention of Pollution from Ships, 1973, as modified by the Protocol of 1978 relating thereto (MARPOL 73/78)* (see this section), and related International Maritime Organization (IMO) instruments on pollution from ships;
- *Convention on the Prevention of Marine Pollution by Dumping of Wastes and Other Matter (London Convention 1972)* and the *1996 Protocol to the London Convention 1972* (see this section);
- *Global Programme of Action for the Protection of the Marine Environment from Land-Based Activities*, Washington, DC, 1995;
- *Convention on Biological Diversity (CBD)*, 1992 (see this section);
- numerous regional instruments on protection of the marine environment, relating to different sources of marine pollution, co-operation on combating pollution incidents, and protection of marine areas and species (see this section).

Secretariats

Queries related to the Secretariat of the Convention itself and/or the Secretariat of the CLCS should be directed to:

Division for Ocean Affairs and the Law of the Sea,
Office of Legal Affairs,
DC2-0450,
United Nations,
New York, NY 10017,
USA
Telephone: +1-212-963-3962/3960
Telefax: +1-212-963-5847/2811
E-mail: doalos@un.org

Director
Madam Annick de Marffy.

Number of staff
For the years 2002–03, budgetary provisions have been made for 17 professionals and ten general service staff.

International Seabed Authority (ISA),
14-20 Port Royal Street,
Kingston,
Jamaica
Telephone: +809-9229105
Telefax: +809-9220195
E-mail: postmaster@isa.org.jm

Secretary-General
Mr Satya N. Nandan.

Number of staff
For 2001–02, budgetary provisions have been made for 19 professionals and 18 general service staff.

Registry of the International Tribunal for the Law of the Sea (ITLOS),
Am internationalen Seegerichtshof 1,
D-22609 Hamburg,
Germany
Telephone: +49-40-356070
Telefax: +49-40-35607275
E-mail: itlos@itlos.org

President
Mr P. Chandrasekhara Rao.

Vice-President
Mr L. Dolliver M. Nelson.

Registrar of the Tribunal
Mr Philippe Gautier (September 2001–September 2006).

Number of staff
For 2003, budgetary provisions have been made for 16 professionals and 21 support staff.

Finance

Budget
Annual costs at the Division for Ocean Affairs and the Law of the Sea were approximately $US2,866,200 for 2001, and are $3,113,500 for 2002 and $3,113,500 for 2003, paid from the regular UN budget. Occasionally expert groups are supported from extra-budgetary resources.

The budget for the ISA was approximately $5,275,200 in 2000. The budget of ISA is $10,506,400 for the years 2001–02. It is the first budget to cover a two-year financial period and was adopted by the ISA Assembly. It is paid by the members of ISA. Members agreed in 1998 to pay their contributions on the basis of the UN scale of assessment

The budget for the Tribunal was $8,090,900 in 2001, and is $7,807,500 in 2002 and $7,798,300 in 2003, paid by the Parties of the LOS Convention. Contributions of States Parties to the budget are to be based upon the scale of assessments of the regular budget of the UN for the preceding financial year, adjusted to take account of participation in the Convention.

Rules and standards

As regards the protection and preservation of the marine environment, States Parties must, *inter alia*:

- take all measures necessary to prevent, reduce, and control pollution of the marine environment from any source;
- assess the potential effects of planned activities on the marine environment and publish reports thereon;
- monitor the risks or effects of pollution and publish reports thereon;
- co-operate on a global or regional basis in formulating and elaborating international rules, standards, and recommended practices and procedures for the protection and preservation of the marine environment;
- give effect in national law to such adopted international rules, standards, practices, and procedures. For all sea-bed activities, i.e. pollution from sea-bed activities subject to national jurisdiction, pollution from activities in the area, pollution by dumping, and pollution from vessels, international rules and standards represent minimum standards. For all land-based activities, i.e. pollution from land-based sources and pollution from or through the atmosphere, national laws need take into account only international rules and standards;
- enforce national laws and regulations which give effect to applicable international rules and standards. While the flag State (State of vessel registry) bears the primary responsibility for enforcement, the Convention also gives the coastal State (in the maritime zones of which the vessel transits) and the port State (State whose ports, including offshore terminals, the vessel visits) enforcement rights;
- adopt measures for the conservation of living resources in maritime areas under their national jurisdiction, and co-operate with each other in taking such measures for high-seas fisheries;
- resort to the compulsory binding procedures provided for in the Convention for the peaceful settlement of their disputes.

The Convention's provisions on the protection and preservation of the marine environment do not apply to a warship, naval auxiliary, or other vessel or aircraft being used, for the time being, only on government non-commercial service. However, flag States are urged to apply these provisions so far as is reasonable and practicable.

Monitoring/implementation

Review procedure

The basic objectives of the Convention in the areas of environment and development have been incorporated into most global and regional instruments. National laws have been extensively amended and further developed, and new laws adopted, mostly in conformity with the Convention. Several international and regional organizations have also taken measures to adjust their mandate and activities to the provisions of the Convention.

It is left to the Parties to devise the ways and means of individually or jointly pursuing systematic and *ad hoc* monitoring programmes, taking into account similar programmes already established by other treaties and organizations.

Particularly in the field of the conservation of living resources and the protection and preservation of the marine environment, implementation of the Convention depends to a great extent on the legislative and other activities of 'competent international organizations' in various degrees. Scientific and technical groups are organized on an *ad hoc* basis to advise on specific issues.

States are regularly informed of national, bilateral, regional, and global legislative and policy developments by means of the *Annual Report of the Secretary-General on Oceans and the Law of the Sea* to the UN General Assembly, the *Law of the Sea Bulletin*, and the *Law of the Sea Information Circular*, as well as the website of the Division for Ocean Affairs and the Law of the Sea, Office of Legal Affairs, at <www.un.org/Depts/los>.

Consequent upon the entry into force of the Convention, and in recognition of the principle stated in the Convention that the problems of ocean space are closely interrelated and need to be considered as a whole, the UN General Assembly first explicitly confirmed in resolution 49/28 its role as the global forum competent to review and evaluate annually the implementation of the Convention and other developments relating to ocean affairs and the law of the sea. The General Assembly's consideration of all law of the sea and ocean affairs issues, including the marine environment and fisheries, under a single unified agenda item entitled 'Oceans and the Law of the Sea', as well as the monitoring of the implementation of the two Implementing Agreements, provides the opportunity for a comprehensive and integrated review of all developments and for recommending a co-ordinated approach to the implementation of the Convention and the Agreements, as well as for promoting compliance and follow-up on non-compliance in general terms.

In order to make the deliberations on oceans and the law of the sea in the General Assembly more effective, the seventh session of the Commission on Sustainable Development (see IGOs), held in New York from 19 to 30 April 1999, recommended the establishment of an open-ended informal consultative process under the aegis of the General Assembly. The consultative process would identify priority areas in ocean affairs, including the necessary actions to be taken. This goal would be achieved through a comprehensive, in-depth, and action-oriented discussion on ocean affairs held annually and open to all stake-holders such as states, UN programmes and agencies, and non-governmental organizations (NGOs).

Accordingly, the General Assembly, by its resolution 54/33 of 24 November 1999, decided to establish an open-ended informal consultative process in order to facilitate, in an effective and constructive manner, its own review of overall developments in ocean affairs.

Consistent with the legal framework provided by the LOS Convention and the goals of chapter 17 of Agenda 21, those involved in the Consultative Process discussed the annual report of the Secretary-General on oceans and the law of the sea and suggested particular issues to be considered by the General Assembly, with an emphasis on identifying areas where co-ordination and co-operation at the intergovernmental and inter-agency levels should be enhanced.

The President of the General Assembly appointed Ambassador Tuiloma Neroni Slade (Samoa) and Mr Alan Simcock (United Kingdom) as co-chairpersons of the first meeting of the Consultative Process in 2000, after consultations with member States, in accordance with paragraph 3 (e) of General Assembly resolution 54/33. Subsequently, in 2001 and 2002, both Ambassador Slade and Mr Simcock were reappointed as co-chairpersons for the second and third meetings, respectively, of the Consultative Process.

The meetings of the Consultative Process have adopted their own format and agenda by consensus. The format for each of the three meetings held thus far provided, among other things, the opportunity to receive input from major groups, as identified in Agenda 21, especially NGOs, and worked through plenary sessions and two discussions panels, having each a specific subject area of concentration. The areas of focus for each of the two discussion panels of the first, second and third meetings of the Consultative Process were, respectively: (i) responsible fisheries and illegal, unregulated, and unreported fisheries: moving from principles to implementation; (ii) economic and social impacts of marine pollution and degradation, especially in coastal areas: international aspects of combating them; (iii) marine science and the development and transfer of marine technology as mutually agreed, including capacity building in that regard; (iv) co-ordination and co-operation in combating piracy and armed robbery at sea; (v) the protection and preservation of the marine environment: integrated approach to the protection and preservation of the marine environment and to the conservation and management of its resources; (vi) international rules and standards and their enforcement: practical measures to underpin States' activities- monitoring and assessment, collective response to emergencies and regional considerations; (vii) capacity building: regional co-operation and integrated ocean management.

The third meeting of the Consultative Process again took up the subject of the protection and preservation of the marine environment in order to improve co-ordination of the work of the Consultative Process with the World Summit on Sustainable Development.

The reports of each of the three meetings of the Consultative Process have been composed of three parts: (i) issues to be suggested and elements to be proposed to the General Assembly; (ii) co-chairpersons' summary of discussions; and (iii) issues for consideration for possible inclusion in the agendas of future meetings.

The Consultative Process was established for an initial period of three years. The General Assembly will decide on the future handling of work on oceans and the law of the sea in the light of its review of the effectiveness and utility of the Consultative Process at its fifty-seventh session in 2002.

Dispute-settlement mechanisms

The Convention obliges parties to settle their disputes peacefully, and provides a selection of methods for doing so. The dispute settlement system under the Convention is, with limited exceptions, compulsory and binding. The Convention allows a choice of the International Tribunal for the Law of the Sea, the International Court of Justice, Arbitration, or Special Arbitration.

The International Tribunal for the Law of the Sea has jurisdiction over any dispute concerning the interpretation or application of the provisions of the Convention or of an international agreement related to the purposes of the Convention which is submitted to it in accordance with the Convention. Under the *1995 Fish Stocks Agreement* and the *1996 Protocol to the London Convention 1972*, the Parties to a dispute can, if they so agree, submit their dispute to the Tribunal, irrespective of whether they are also Parties to the Convention.

The Tribunal has exclusive jurisdiction, through its Sea-Bed Disputes Chamber, with respect to disputes relating to activities in the international sea-bed area. These matters include disputes between States Parties concerning the interpretation or application of the provisions of the Convention, along with those of the Agreement relating to the Implementation of Part XI of the Convention, concerning the deep sea-bed area; and disputes between States Parties or a contractor and the ISA. The Tribunal has established the Chamber of Summary Procedure, the Sea-Bed Disputes Chamber, and two standing special chambers: the Chamber on Fisheries Matters and the Chamber on the Marine Environment.

Decision-making bodies

Political

• *The UN General Assembly.* In 1994 the UN General Assembly confirmed that it was the global institution with the competence to undertake an annual consideration and review and evaluation of the implementation of the Convention and other developments relating to ocean affairs and the law of the sea. To facilitate a comprehensive and integrated review of all developments under the Convention and those taking place under other instruments and processes relating to the implementation and further development of the provisions of the Convention, and in order to promote a co-ordinated approach to implementation at the global, regional, and national level, the General Assembly has since 1994 consolidated all agenda items dealing with issues relating to oceans affairs and the law of the sea under a single item, 'Oceans and the Law of the Sea'. The Assembly adopts annually a resolution on oceans and the law of the sea, as well as one resolution on fisheries issues dealing, on alternate years, with the implementation of the 1995 fish stocks Agreement, as well as on other fisheries issues such as large-scale pelagic drift-net fishing, unauthorized fishing in zones of national jurisdiction and on the high seas, and fisheries' by-catch and discards. States are called upon in these resolutions to take certain action.

• *The Meeting of States Parties.* The Convention provides for the convening of meetings of States Parties by the Secretary-General when he considers it necessary. Such meetings can also be convened when a majority of the States Parties request it, provided that a meeting is not already scheduled to be held within six months of the request. Since the entry into force of the Convention, all meetings so far have been convened to deal primarily with organizational matters relating to the establishment of the Tribunal, the election of the members of the Tribunal, the consideration and adoption of the budget of the Tribunal, and the election of the members of the CLCS. The Meeting of States Parties is an independent forum with decision-making powers. Its future role in dealing with questions of implementation of the Convention, as well as its role in reviewing ocean and law of the sea issues, is currently under consideration. The twelfth Meeting of States Parties was held in New York from 16 to 26 April 2002 and the thirteenth Meeting of States Parties is scheduled to be held in New York from 9 to 13 June 2003.

• *The International Seabed Authority (ISA).* The ISA is the institution through which Parties to the Convention organize and control activities in an international sea-bed area beyond the limits of national jurisdiction, particularly with a view to administering the resources of that area. The functions, membership, and management of the Authority are affected by the Agreement on the Implementation of Part XI of the Convention (see Affiliated instruments and organizations, above). The Authority functions through three main organs: the Assembly, the supreme organ, which consists of all members of the Authority; the Council, the executive organ, with limited membership comprising 36 members; and the Legal and Technical Commission, comprising 21 members, which assists the Council by making recommendations. The Agreement has also established a Finance Committee of 15 members, to make recommendations to the Assembly and the Council on financial matters, including the budget of the Authority. In addition, the Authority has a Secretariat (see Secretariats, above), headed by a Secretary-General, which performs all functions entrusted to him by the organs of the Authority.

• *The International Tribunal for the Law of the Sea.* The Tribunal was established by the Convention for the peaceful settlement of disputes (see above). Through its Sea-Bed Disputes Chamber it also has jurisdiction to provide advisory opinions at the request of the Assembly or the Council of the ISA on legal questions arising within the scope of their activities. It is composed of 21 judges elected by States Parties to the Convention from among persons with recognized competence in the field of the law of the sea and representing the principal legal systems of the world. The first election was held in August 1996. The members of the Tribunal elect a President and a Vice-President, whose term of office shall be three years. The Tribunal also appoints its Registrar, for a term of five years, and other officers of the Registry as may be necessary. The President of the Tribunal, as well as the Registrar, reside at the seat of the Tribunal.

Scientific/technical

• *The Secretariat.* With a view to assisting the UN General Assembly in its annual consideration, review, and evaluation of developments pertaining to the implementation of the Convention, as well as other developments relating to ocean affairs and the law of the sea, the Secretary-General is called upon to report on such developments annually to the Assembly. In its resolution 49/28, the Assembly further clarified the nature and scope of the functions of the Secretary-General, including his responsibility of providing information, advice, and assistance to States and international organizations in the better understanding of the Convention, its wider acceptance, uniform and consistent application, and effective implementation.

The Convention also calls on the Secretary-General to perform various duties, among them that of depositary of the Convention and of charts or lists of geographical co-ordinates of baselines and outer limit lines of various maritime zones. The good offices of the Secretary-General were used to resolve the outstanding problems with provisions on the international sea-bed area which impeded universal acceptance of the Convention as a whole. The Division for Ocean Affairs and the Law of the Sea fulfils the responsibilities entrusted to the Secretary-General. It functions as the secretariat of the Convention and also services the meetings of States Parties and those of the CLCS, and the consultative process.

• *The Commission on the Limits of the Continental Shelf (CLCS).* The CLCS is composed of 21 members who are experts in the field of geology, geophysics, or hydrography, elected by States Parties to this Convention from among their nationals who serve in their personal capacities, having due regard to the need to ensure equitable geographical representation. The members are elected for five years and may be re-elected in accordance with Annex II, Article 2(4), of the Convention. The Division for Ocean Affairs and the Law of the Sea serves as the Secretariat of the CLCS (see Secretariats, above)

The CLCS shall consider the data and other material submitted by coastal States concerning the outer limits of the continental shelf in areas where those limits extend beyond 200 nautical miles, make recommendations, and provide scientific and technical advice.

Publications

• *Report of the Secretary-General on Oceans and the Law of the Sea*, submitted annually to the General Assembly under the item 'The Law of the Sea';

• *The Law of the Sea Bulletin* contains the texts of relevant national legislation and treaties, as well as other information on the law of the sea, as soon as they are available. Published three or four times a year;

• *Law of the Sea Information Circular* is circulated to members States of the UN and its objective is to communicate to all states and entities information on actions taken by States Parties in implementing the LOS Convention, in particular regarding the deposit obligation, as well as to report on activities undertaken by the Division in this respect.

Other Law of the Sea publications include collections and analyses of national legislation, legislative histories of Convention provisions, bibliographies, and expert advice on special issues such as baselines, maritime boundary delimitation, exclusive economic zones, high-seas fisheries, continental shelf, and marine scientific research.

Sources on the Internet

Related to the Convention itself, CLCS, and the Division:
<http://www.un.org/Depts/los>

Related to ISA:
<http://www.isa.org.jm>

Related to the Tribunal:
<http://www.itlos.org/>

Convention for the Protection of the Marine Environment of the North-East Atlantic (OSPAR Convention)

Objectives

• to safeguard human health and to conserve marine ecosystems and, when practicable, to restore marine areas which have been adversely affected;
• to take all possible steps to prevent and eliminate pollution and enact the measures necessary to protect the sea area against the adverse effects of human activities.

Scope

Legal scope

Open to coastal states bordering the maritime area (see below), any state located upstream on watercourses reaching the maritime area, or any regional economic integration organization having a member state to which the above paragraphs refer.

Geographic scope

Regional. The maritime area covers the North-East Atlantic (westwards to the east coast of Greenland and southwards to the Strait of Gibraltar), including the North Sea, and comprises the internal waters and the territorial sea of the Contracting Parties, the sea beyond and adjacent to the territorial sea under the jurisdiction of the coastal state to the extent recognized by international law, and the high seas, including the bed and subsoil thereof.

Time and place of adoption

22 September 1992, Paris.

Entry into force

25 March 1998. The Convention replaces the Convention for the Prevention of Marine Pollution by Dumping from Ships and Aircraft (Oslo Convention), adopted on 15 February 1972 in Oslo, which entered into force on 6 April 1974, and the Convention for the Prevention of Marine Pollution from Land-based Sources (Paris Convention), adopted on 4 June 1974 in Paris, which entered into force on 6 May 1978. Decisions, recommendations, and all other agreements adopted under the former Oslo and Paris Conventions will continue to be applicable, unaltered in their legal nature, unless they are terminated by new measures adopted under the OSPAR Convention.

Status of participation

16 Parties, including the European Community. No pending of ratification, acceptance, or approval by Signatories.

The French Government acts as depositary.

Affiliated instruments and organizations

The different sources of pollution are dealt with in separate annexes:
• *Annex I, On the Prevention and Elimination of Pollution from Land-based Sources*;
• *Annex II, On the Prevention and Elimination of Pollution by Dumping or Incineration.* This Annex , in conjunction with OSPAR Decision 98/2 on Dumping of Radioactive Wastes, which entered into force on 9 February 1999, prohibits the dumping of low and intermediate level radioactive waste;
• *Annex III, On the Prevention and Elimination of Pollution from Offshore Sources*;
• *Annex IV, On the Assessment of the Quality of the Marine Environment*;
• *Annex V, On the Protection and Conservation of the Ecosystems and Biological Diversity of the Maritime Area.* Adopted on 24 July 1998, entered into force on 30 August 2000. 12 Parties by 1 March 2002.

The Convention has also three appendices:
• *Appendix 1*: criteria for the definition of practices and techniques mentioned in paragraph 3(b)(i) of Article 2 of the Convention;
• *Appendix 2*: criteria mentioned in paragraph 2 of Article 1 of Annex I and in paragraph 2 of Article 2 of Annex III;
• *Appendix 3*: criteria for identifying human activities for the purpose of Annex V.

Co-ordination with related instruments

The OSPAR Commission (see Decision-making bodies, below) works with other regional seas conventions, such as the 1974 Helsinki Convention, the Barcelona Convention, the Convention on Long-Range Transboundary Air Pollution (see this section), and bodies such as IMO and ICES (see IGOs).

The declarations of the ministerial-level North Sea Conferences have laid down principles and targets for the reduction of marine pollution in the North Sea, including dumping. Some of these have been implemented within the framework of the former Oslo and Paris conventions.

Secretariat

OSPAR Secretariat,
New Court,
48 Carey Street,
London WC2A 2JQ,
United Kingdom
Telephone: +44-20-74305200
Telefax: +44-20-74305225
E-mail: secretariat@ospar.org

Executive Secretary
Mr Alan Simcock.

Number of staff
Five executive staff members and seven assistants (March 2002).

Finance

The annual budget of the OSPAR Commission is met by funds supplied by the Contracting Parties to the Convention.

Budget

The total budget was £UK877,512 in 2000 and £888,533 in 2001, and is £887,300 in 2002.

Rules and standards

The Contracting Parties shall apply:
• the *precautionary principle*: that is, that preventive measures are taken when there is reason to believe that substances or energy introduced, directly or indirectly, into the marine environment may create hazards to human health, harm living resources and marine ecosystems, damage amenities, or interfere with other legitimate uses of the sea even when there is no conclusive evidence of a causal relationship between inputs and their effects;
• the *polluter pays principle*: by virtue of which costs of pollution prevention, control, and reduction measures shall be borne by the polluter.

In implementing the Convention, Parties shall adopt programmes and measures containing, where appropriate, time-limits for their completion, which take full account of

the use of the best available techniques (BAT) and best environmental practice (BEP) designed to prevent and eliminate pollution to the fullest extent.

Contracting Parties shall take, individually and jointly, all possible steps to prevent and eliminate pollution:

- from land-based sources, in particular as provided for in Annex I;
- by dumping or incineration of wastes or other matter, in particular as provided for in Annex II;
- from offshore sources, in particular as provided for in Annex III.

Monitoring/implementation

Review procedure

The Parties shall report to the Commission at regular intervals on:

- the legal, regulatory, or other measures taken by them for the implementation of the provisions of the Convention and of decisions and recommendations adopted thereunder, including in particular measures taken to prevent and punish conduct in contravention of those provisions;
- the effectiveness of the measures referred to above;
- problems encountered in the implementation of the provisions referred to above.

The Commission shall:

- on the basis of the reports submitted by the Parties, assess their compliance with the Convention and the decisions and recommendations adopted thereafter;
- when appropriate, decide upon and call for steps to bring about full compliance with the Convention, and decisions adopted thereunder, and promote the implementation of recommendations, including measures to assist a Party to carry out its obligations.

The relevant specialist subsidiary body of the Commission, and subsequently the Commission itself, reviews data or information in the national reports. NGOs accredited to OSPAR as observers participate in this process. These reviews are public and the Secretariat of the Commission distributes lists of such reviews.

The Commission has presented a series of quality status reports to cover the maritime area of the Convention. Five regional quality status reports (rQSRs) have been synthesized into one holistic quality status report, the QSR 2000. The quality status reports will be used as a basis for improving ocean management in pursuit of the main aims of the Convention. The QSRs were published in 2000 and are available for viewing and downloading on the Convention's website (see below).

Decision-making bodies

Political

The OSPAR Commission, with representatives of each of the Parties, is the governing body and meets at least annually, sometimes at ministerial level. The next ministerial meeting will be held in 2003. The quorum for meetings shall be three-quarters of the Parties.

The Commission may adopt amendments, annexes, and protocols to the Convention by unanimous vote of the Parties. Some annexes and amendments to annexes may be adopted by a three-quarters majority vote of the Parties.

The Commission may unanimously decide to admit any state which is not a Party to the Convention, any international governmental organization, or any non-governmental organization to be represented by observers at its meetings, or at meetings of its subsidiary bodies. Such observers may present to the Commission any information or reports relevant to the objectives of the Convention.

Scientific/technical

See bodies in the context of the strategies under Monitoring/implementation above.

Publications

Annual reports, quality status reports, and reports of meetings held in the framework of OSPAR in addition to decisions, recommendations, and other agreements adopted by OSPAR.

Sources on the Internet

<http://www.ospar.org>

Convention on the Protection of the Marine Environment of the Baltic Sea Area (1992 Helsinki Convention)

Objectives

To take all appropriate measures, individually or by means of regional co-operation, to prevent and eliminate pollution in order to promote the ecological restoration of the Baltic Sea area and the preservation of its ecological balance.

Scope

Legal scope

Restricted to the Baltic Sea states and the European Community which participated in the 1992 Helsinki Conference and have ratified the Convention. Others upon invitation by all the Contracting Parties.

Geographic scope

Regional. The Convention covers the Baltic Sea and the entrance to the Baltic Sea bounded by the parallel of the Skaw in the Skagerrak at 57° 44.43′N and the drainage area to these waters. Internal waters are included.

Time and place of adoption

9 April 1992, Helsinki.

Entry into force

17 January 2000. The Convention replaces the Convention on the Protection of the Marine Environment of the Baltic Sea Area (1974 Helsinki Convention), adopted 22 March 1974 in Helsinki, which entered into force on 3 May 1980.

Status of participation

Ten Parties, including the European Community, by 1 July 2002. No Signatories without ratification, acceptance, or approval.

Affiliated instruments and organizations

The following attached *Annexes* form an integral part of the Convention:

- *Annex I*, on harmful substances to be controlled;
- *Annex II*, on criteria for the use of best environmental practice (BEP) and best available technology (BAT);
- *Annex III*, on criteria and measures concerning the prevention of pollution from land-based sources;
- *Annex IV*, on prevention of pollution from ships;
- *Annex V*, on exemptions from the general prohibition of dumping of waste and other matter in the Baltic Sea area;
- *Annex VI*, on prevention of pollution from offshore activities;
- *Annex VII*, on response to pollution incidents.

The Baltic Marine Environment Protection Commission–Helsinki Commission (HELCOM)–is the Commission for the purpose of the Convention.

On 10 September 2001 the ministers responsible for maritime transport, the ministers responsible for the environment from all the Baltic Sea states, and a representative from the European Community adopted the HELCOM Copenhagen Declaration and HELCOM Recommendation 22E/5, *Amendments to Annex IV 'Prevention of pollution from ships' to the Helsinki Convention.*

The HELCOM Copenhagen Declaration contains a package of measures to ensure the safety of navigation as well as the adequacy of emergency capacity in the Baltic Sea area. In order to ensure the legally binding character of the measures the ministers at the same time adopted corresponding amendments to the Helsinki Convention.

The HELCOM Copenhagen Declaration and HELCOM Recommendation 22E/5 were adopted at an Extraordinary Ministerial Meeting of the Helsinki Commission. The meeting was arranged at the request of Denmark, endorsed by Germany, following the biggest oil spill in the Baltic Sea in 20 years. The oil spill was a result of a collision between the tanker *Baltic Carrier* and the bulk carrier *Tern* in the Kadetrenden between Denmark and Germany. As a result of the collision 2700 tonnes of heavy fuel oil flooded into the Baltic Sea. The collision put to the fore the risks associated with the increasing maritime traffic in the Baltic Sea area and the need to address this.

Co-ordination with related instruments

The provisions concerning the prevention of pollution from ships follow closely the International Convention for the Prevention of Pollution from Ships, 1973, as modified by the Protocol of 1978 relating thereto (MARPOL 73/78) (see this section), where the Baltic Sea area is designated as a ëspecial areaí whereby far-reaching prohibitions and restrictions on the discharge of ship-generated wastes and cargo residues apply.

Secretariat

Helsinki Commission (HELCOM),
Katajanokanlaituri 6 B,
FIN-00160 Helsinki,
Finland

Telephone:	+358-9-6220220
Telefax:	+358-9-62202239
E-mail:	helcom@helcom.fi

Executive Secretary

Mr Mieczyslaw Ostojski.

Information Secretary

Ms Ulrike Hassink.

Number of staff

Eight professionals and seven support staff (February 2002).

Finance

The total amount of the annual or biennial budget, including any supplementary budget adopted by the Commission, shall be contributed by the Parties, other than the European Community (which contributes 2.5 per cent of the administrative costs), in equal parts, unless unanimously decided otherwise by the Commission.

Budget

The administrative core budget of the Secretariat was FIM10.1 million in 2001 and is FIM10.5 in 2002.

Rules and standards

The Parties shall:

- apply the *precautionary principle*, i.e. take preventive measures when there is reason to assume that substances or energy introduced, directly or indirectly, may create hazards in the marine environment to human health, harm living resources and marine ecosystems, damage amenities, or interfere with other legitimate uses of the sea,

even when there is no conclusive evidence of a causal relationship between inputs and their alleged effects;

• promote the use of best environmental practice (BEP) and best available technology (BAT). If the reduction of inputs, resulting from the use of BEP and BAT, as described in Annex II, does not lead to environmentally acceptable results, additional measures shall be applied;

• apply the *polluter-pays principle*;

• ensure that measurements and calculations of emissions from point sources to water and air, and of inputs from diffuse sources to water and air, are carried out in a scientifically appropriate manner in order to assess the state of the marine environment of the Baltic Sea area and ascertain the implementation of the Convention;

• use their best endeavours to ensure that the implementation of the Convention does not cause transboundary pollution in areas outside the Baltic Sea area. Furthermore, the relevant measures shall not lead to unacceptable environmental strains either on air quality and the atmosphere or on waters, soil, and groundwater. Nor shall they lead to unacceptably harmful or increasing waste disposal or to increased risks to human health.

Monitoring/implementation

Review procedure

Parties shall report to the Commission at regular intervals on:

(*a*) the legal, regulatory, or other measures taken for the implementation of the provisions of the Convention, of its Annexes, and of recommendations adopted thereunder;
(*b*) the effectiveness of the measures taken to implement the provisions referred to in paragraph (*a*) above;
(*c*) problems encountered in the implementation of the provisions referred to in paragraph (*a*) above.

On the request of a Party or of the Commission, the Parties shall provide information on discharge permits, emission data, and data on environmental quality, as far as available.

The Commission shall:

• keep the implementation of the Convention under continuous observation;

• make recommendations on measures relating to the purposes of the Convention;

• keep under review the contents of the Convention, and its Annexes, and recommend amendments as may be required, including the lists of substances and materials as well as the adoption of new Annexes;

• define pollution control criteria, objectives for the reduction of pollution, and objectives concerning measures, particularly those described in Annex III;

• receive, process, summarize, and disseminate relevant scientific, technological, and statistical information from available sources;

• seek the services of competent regional and other international organizations to collaborate in scientific and technological research, as well as other relevant activities pertinent to the objectives of the Convention.

Observers

The governments of Belarus and Ukraine and 13 intergovernmental bodies are participating in the work of the Commission as observers. The intergovernmental bodies are: the International Atomic Energy Agency (IAEA), the International Council for the Exploration of the Sea (ICES), the International Maritime Organization (IMO), the UN Environment Programme (UNEP), the World Health Organization, the Regional Office for Europe (WHO/EURO), the World Meteorological Organization (WMO) (see IGOs for descriptions of these six organizations), the Agreement on the Conservation of Small Cetaceans in the Baltic and North Seas (ASCOBANS) (see Convention on the Conservation of Migratory Species of Wild Animals, this section), the Oslo and Paris Commissions (OSPAR) (see this section), Baltic 21óAn Agenda 21 for the Baltic Sea Region, the Intergovernmental Oceanographic Commission (IOC), the International Baltic Sea Fishery Commission (IBSFC), the UN Economic Commission for Europe (UNECE), and the Council of Europe Development Bank.

16 NGOs have also been granted observer status with the Commission: the Alliance of

Maritime Regional Interests in Europe (AMRIE), the Baltic and International Maritime Council (BIMCO), the Baltic Farmers' Forum on Environment, the Baltic Ports Organization (BPO), BirdLife International, Coalition Clean Baltic (CCB), the Conference of Peripheral Maritime Regions of Europe (CPMR)—Baltic Sea Commission, the European Chemical Industry Council (CEFIC), the European Chlor-Alkali Industry (EURO CHLOR), the European Fertilizer Manufacturersí Association (EFMA), the European Sea Ports Organization (ESPO), the European Union for Coastal Conservation (EUCC), the International Council for Local Environmental Governments (ICLEI), the International Association of Oil and Gas Producers (OPG), the Union of the Baltic Cities (UBC), and the World Wide Fund For Nature (WWF) (see NGOs).

Public information on the operation and implementation of the decisions by the Commission is made available to governments through reports of the subsidiary bodies, projects, and workshops, as well as reports from the annual Helsinki Commission meetings. These reports are accessible on the website of the Helsinki Commission (see Internet Sources, below).

Environmental monitoring programmes
The Parties have agreed upon two main monitoring and assessment programmes: the Co-operative Monitoring in the Baltic Marine Environment (COMBINE) for environmental monitoring and assessment of the environmental state of the Baltic Sea; and the Pollution Load Compilation (PLC) for monitoring of anthropogenic emissions, discharges, and losses in the catchment area and the riverine load to the Baltic Sea, as well as assessment of their effects. The collection of data is performed according to agreed guidelines, and information is submitted to Thematic Data Centres, which work on a consultancy basis for the Commission.

Data and information-system programmes
The *Baltic Marine Environment Bibliography* has been produced by the Helsinki Commission since the 1970s. An on-line version of this database, *BALTIC*, was established in 1987. It is available through the website of the Helsinki Commission (see Sources on the Internet, below). It contains all aspects of the Baltic Sea area, for example, ecology, fauna and flora, fisheries, hydrography, pollution, environmental impact, research planning, and administrative measures.

Decision-making bodies

Political
The Baltic Marine Environment Protection Commission–Helsinki Commission (HELCOM)–was established for the purposes of the Convention. The offices of chairman and vice-chairman of the Commission rotate between the Parties in English alphabetical order every two years. Meetings of the Commission shall be held at least once a year upon convocation by the chairman. Extraordinary meetings shall, upon the request of any Party endorsed by another Party, be convened by the chairman and held as soon as possible, and not later than 90 days after the submission of the request.

Unless otherwise provided under the Convention, the Commission shall take its decisions unanimously. Each Party shall have one vote in the Commission. Regarding matters within the competence of the European Economic Community, the Community may vote on behalf of its member States.

The Commission may assume such functions as it deems appropriate to further the purposes of the Convention. The Commission appoints an executive secretary and makes provisions for the appointment of such other personnel as may be necessary, and determines the duties, terms, and conditions of service of the executive secretary.

The executive secretary is the chief administrative official of the Commission and shall perform the functions that are necessary for the administration of the Convention.

Scientific/technical
The work of the Commission is carried out by five subsidiary bodies and a Programme Implementation Task Force and is complemented by different working groups and projects. The subsidiary bodies are:

- a Strategy Group, which works to elaborate a coherent HELCOM policy and strategies for the protection of the Baltic Sea based on the concept of sustainable development. Improving the involvement and support from the business communities and financial institutions in both the private and the public sector is another task of this Group. Further, it monitors and assesses the implementation by the Parties of the Convention and HELCOM Recommendations;
- a Monitoring and Assessment Group, which identifies and quantifies the anthropogenic discharges/activities and their effects on the marine environment;
- a Sea-based Pollution Group, which identifies current and emerging issues related to sea-based sources of pollution and proposes actions to limit emissions and discharges. The Group works to ensure a swift national and transnational response to marine pollution incidents;
- a Land-based Pollution Group, which identifies current and emerging issues related to point and diffuse sources of land-based pollution, proposes actions, and promotes investment activities in order to reduce emissions and discharges.
- a Nature Conservation and Coastal Zone Management Group, which works towards conservation of natural habitats, biological diversity, and protection of ecological processes. The Group promotes ecosystem approaches for the sustainable use and management of coastal and marine natural resources. It fosters the development of Coastal Zone Management Plans as instruments of resource management for environmentally sustainable development in coastal and marine areas;
- a Programme Implementation Task Force, which co-ordinates the implementation of the Baltic Sea Joint Comprehensive Environmental Action Programme approved in 1992 and updated in 1998. It focuses on investment activities for point and non-point pollution sources and on planning and investment activities related to management programmes for coastal lagoons and wetlands.

Members of the Task Force are the Contracting Parties to the Convention, Belarus, the Czech Republic, Norway, the Slovak Republic, Ukraine, the Council of Europe Development Bank (CEDB), the European Bank for Reconstruction and Development (EBRD), the European Investment Bank (EIB), the Nordic Environment Finance Corporation (NEFCO), the Nordic Investment Bank (NIB), the World Bank (see IGOs), and the International Baltic Sea Fishery Commission (ISBFC).

Publications

Baltic Sea Environmental Proceedings.

Sources on the Internet

<http://www.helcom.fi>

Conventions within the UNEP Regional Seas Programme

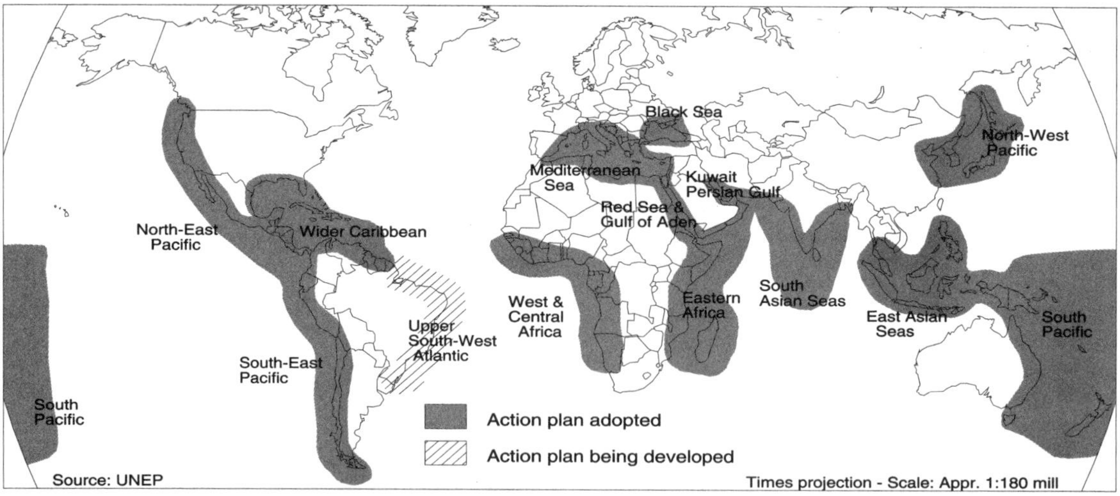

Areas covered by the UNEP Regional Seas Programme

Objectives

The Regional Seas Programme of the UN Environment Programme (UNEP) was established in 1974 to tie coastal nations together in a common commitment to mitigate and prevent degradation of the world's coastal areas, inshore waters, and open oceans.

Each programme is tailored to the specific needs of its coastal states, but is made of similar components:

• an Action Plan for co-operation on the management, protection, rehabilitation, development, monitoring, and research of coastal and marine resources;

• an intergovernmental agreement of a framework convention embodying general principles and obligations (although in some instances there are no legally binding agreements);

• detailed protocols dealing with particular environmental problems, such as oil spills, dumping, emergency co-operation, protected areas, and land-based activities.

Scope

Legal scope

Open to coastal states in the respective regions. In some cases, upon invitation, open to other states and intergovernmental integration organizations.

Geographic scope

Regional. The conventions address the needs of particular regions as perceived by the governments concerned. Together with the regional partner conventions covering areas such as the North-East Atlantic (see the OSPAR Convention, this section), the Baltic Sea area (see the 1992 Helsinki Convention, this section), and the Antarctic (see the Convention on the Conservation of Antarctic Marine Living Resources (CCAMLR), these conventions have a global scope.

There are so far ten regional conventions, covering:

• the Black Sea;
• the wider Caribbean;
• the East African seaboard;
• the Kuwait region;
• the Mediterranean;
• the Red Sea and the Gulf of Aden;
• the North-East Pacific
• the South Pacific;
• the South-East Pacific;
• the Atlantic coast of West and Central Africa.

The Convention for Co-operation in the Protection and Sustainable Development of the Marine and Coastal Environment of the North-East Pacific and its Plan of Action was adopted on 18 February 2002 in the city of Antigua, Guatemala. The Convention was signed by Costa Rica, El Salvador, Guatemala, Honduras, Nicaragua, and Panama at the official signing ceremony for the Convention. The Convention will be open for signature at Guatemala City from 19 February 2002 to 18 February 2003.

Action Plans have been established for the East Asian Seas, the North-West Pacific, and the South Asian Seas. An Action Plan for the Upper South-West Atlantic has been discussed since 1980.

Programme co-ordination

The programme is under the overall co-ordination of UNEP, but working with specialized agencies and co-operating intergovernmental organizations and centres dealing either with specific regions covered by the programme or with specific subjects common to most or all of the regions.

UNEP,
Division of Environmental Conventions,
PO Box 30552, Nairobi, Kenya
Telephone: +254-2-6240-11/33
Telefax: +254-2-624-300/618
E-mail: regional.seas@unep.org

Director
Mr Jorge Illueca.

Regional Seas Co-ordinator
Mr Ellik Adler.
Ellik.Adler@unep.org

Sources on the Internet

<http://www.unep.ch/seas>

A booklet, *Regional Seas: A Survival Strategy for Our Oceans and Coasts* (2000) is available at <http://www.unep.ch/conventions/info/infoindex.htm>

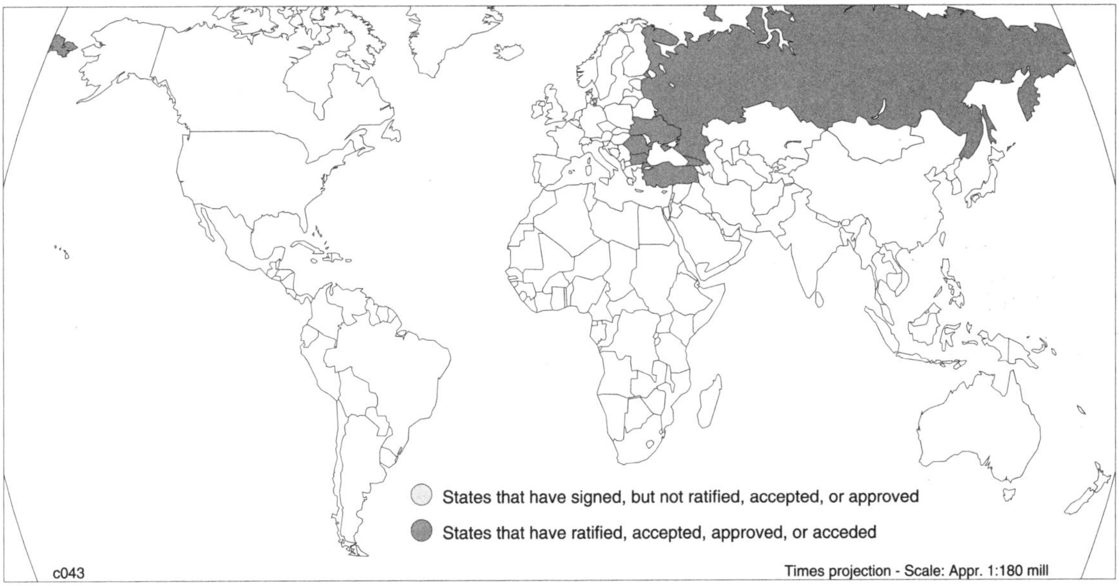

Convention on the Protection of the Black Sea against Pollution (Bucharest Convention)

Objectives
To undertake all necessary measures consistent with international law and in accordance with the provisions of this Convention to prevent, reduce, and control pollution thereof in order to protect and preserve the marine environment of the Black Sea.

Time and place of adoption
21 April 1992, Bucharest.

Entry into force
15 January 1994.

Status of participation
Six Parties by 1 April 2002. No Signatories without ratification, acceptance, or approval.

Affiliated instruments
- *Protocol on Protection of the Black Sea Marine Environment against Pollution from Land-Based Sources*, Bucharest, 21 April 1992. Entered into force on 15 January 1994. Same status of participation as the Convention;
- *Protocol on Co-operation in Combating Pollution of the Black Sea Marine Environment by Oil and Other Harmful Substances in Emergency Situations*, Bucharest, 21 April 1992. Entered into force on 15 January 1994. Same status of participation as the Convention;
- *Protocol on the Protection of the Black Sea Marine Environment against Pollution by Dumping*, Bucharest, 21 April 1992. Entered into force on 15 January 1994. Same status of participation as the Convention.

A *Strategic Action Plan for the Protection and Rehabilitation of the Black Sea (BSSAP)* was signed in Istanbul on 31 October 1996. The BSSAP is aimed at the pollution reduction, living resources management, and sustainable human development.

The *GEF Black Sea Pollution Recovery Project* supports the Black Sea regional aspects of the Black Sea Partnership for Nutrient Control. It will assist and strengthen the role of the Black Sea Commission (of the Bucharest Convention for the Protection of the Black Sea against Pollution) and ensure the provision of a suite of harmonized legal and policy instruments for tackling the problem of eutrophication, and release of certain hazardous substances, and to facilitate ecosystem recovery.

Secretariat
Commission on the Protection of the Black Sea Against Pollution,
Secretariat
Dolmbahce Sarayi II., Harakat Köskü,
80680 Besiktas,
Istanbul,
Turkey
Telephone: +90-212-258-9416/6716/6963/7750
Telefax: +90-212-2279933
E-mail: info@blacksea-environment.org

Executive Director
Mr Plamen Dzhadzhev.

Pollution Monitoring and Assessment
Dr Oksana Tarasova.

GEF Project Co-ordinator
Ms Sema Acar.

Sources on the Internet
<http://www.blacksea-environment.org>

Convention for the Protection and Development of the Marine Environment of the Wider Caribbean Region

Objectives
To achieve sustainable development of marine and coastal resources in the wider Caribbean region through effective integrated management that allows for increased economic growth.

Time and place of adoption
24 March 1983, Cartagena de Indias.

Entry into force
11 October 1986.

Status of participation
21 Parties by 14 May 2002. Three Signatories, including the European Community, without ratification, acceptance, or approval.

Affiliated instruments
• *Protocol Concerning Co-operation in Combating Oil Spills in the Wider Caribbean Region (Oil Spills Protocol),* Cartagena de Indias, 24 March 1983. Entered into force on 11 October 1986. 21 Parties by 14 May 2002. Two Signatories without ratification, acceptance, or approval;

• *Protocol Concerning Specially Protected Areas and Wildlife to the Convention for the Protection and Development of the Marine Environment of the Wider Caribbean Region (SPAW Protocol)*, Kingston, 18 January 1990. Entered into force on 18 June 2000. Ten Parties by 14 May 2002. Six Signatories without ratification, acceptance, or approval.

• *Protocol Concerning Pollution from Land-Based Sources and Activities in the Wider Caribbean Region (LBS Protocol),* Oranjestad, 6 October 1999. (Not yet in force.) No state had ratified by 14 May 2002. Six Signatories without ratification, acceptance, or approval. Nine ratifications or accessions are required to enter into force.

Secretariat
UNEP Regional Co-ordinating Unit for the Caribbean Environment Programme (CAR/RCU),
14–20 Port Royal Street,
Kingston,
Jamaica
Telephone: +1-876-922926-7/8/9
Telefax: +1-876-9229292
E-mail: uneprcuja@cwjamaica.com

Co-ordinator
Mr Nelson Andrade Colmenares.

Deputy Co-ordinator
Mr Timothy Kasten.

Sources on the Internet
<http://www.cep.unep.org>

Convention for the Protection, Management, and Development of the Marine and Coastal Environment of the Eastern African Region

Objectives
To protect and manage the marine environment and coastal areas of the Eastern African region.

Time and place of adoption
21 June 1985, Nairobi.

Entry into force
30 May 1996.

Status of participation
Six Parties by 26 November 2001. Two Signatories, including the European Community, without ratification, acceptance, or approval.

Affiliated instruments
- *Protocol Concerning Protected Areas and Wild Fauna and Flora in the Eastern African Region*, Nairobi, 21 June 1985. Entered into force on 30 May 1996. Same status of participation as the Convention;
- *Protocol Concerning Co-operation in Combating Marine Pollution in Cases of Emergency in the Eastern African Region*, Nairobi, 21 June 1985. Entered into force on 30 May 1996. Same status of participation as the Convention.

The first Conference of the Parties (COP) of the Convention in 1997 had established an *Ad Hoc* Committee of Legal and Technical Experts to review the Convention and the Protocol Concerning Protected Areas and Wild Fauna and Flora in the Eastern African Region. The Committee held its first review meeting in Mauritius from 15 to 18 December 1998. Its reports and recommendations were submitted and discussed at the second COP in August 1999. At the second COP, a joint bureau for the Nairobi and Abidjan (West and Central African region) Conventions met and agreed to set up a joint programming unit in Nairobi to further co-operation on regional projects and international issues. In May 2000, a twinning agreement was signed with the Baltic Marine Environment Protection Commission to promote the exchange of experience (see the Helsinki Convention, this section).

Secretariat
UNEP Regional Co-ordinating Unit for the Eastern African Action Plan (EAF/RCU),
Botanical Gardens,
PO Box 487, Victoria,
Mahé,
Seychelles

Telephone:	+248-324525/224644
Telefax:	+248-322945/224500
E-mail:	rolphap@seychelles.net

Interim Co-ordinator
Mr Rolph Antoine Payet.

Sources on the Internet
<http://www.unep.ch/seas/main/eaf/eaf.html>

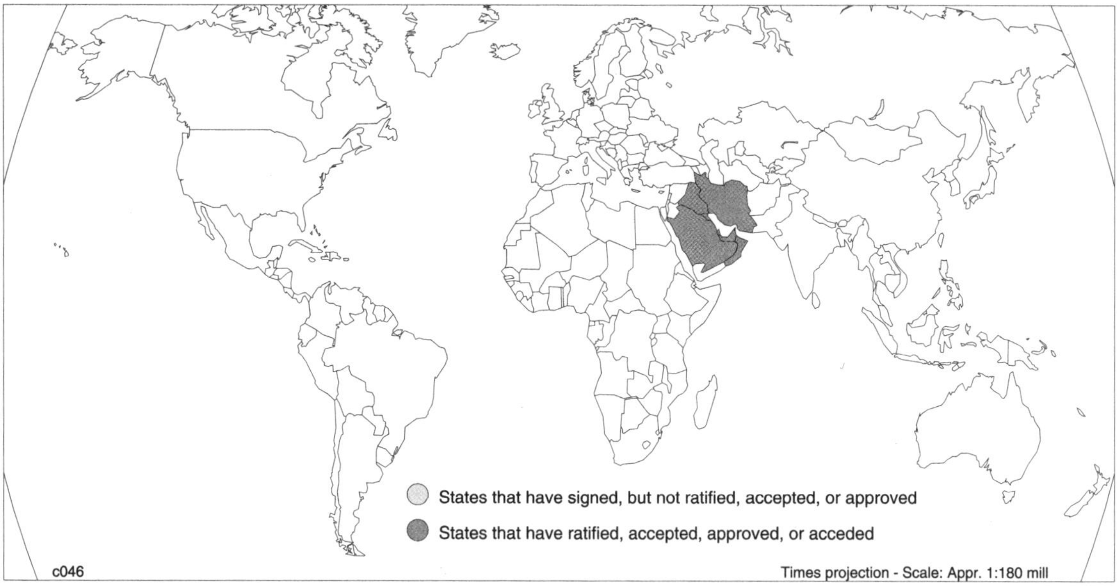

Kuwait Regional Convention for Co-operation on the Protection of the Marine Environment from Pollution

Objectives
To prevent, abate, and combat pollution of the marine environment in the region.

Time and place of adoption
24 April 1978, Kuwait.

Entry into force
1 July 1979.

Status of participation
Eight Parties by 28 November 2001. No Signatories without ratification, acceptance, or approval.

Affiliated instruments
- *Protocol concerning Regional Co-operation in Combating Pollution by Oil and other Harmful Substances in Cases of Emergency*, Kuwait, 24 April 1978. Entered into force on 1 July 1979. Same status of participation as the Convention;
- *Protocol concerning Marine Pollution resulting from Exploration and Exploitation of the Continental Shelf*, Kuwait 1989. Entered into force on 17 February 1990. Same status of participation as the Convention;
- *Protocol for the Protection of the Marine Environment against Pollution from Land-Based Sources*, Kuwait 1990. Entered into force on 2 January 1993. Six Parties by 28 November 2001. One Signatory without ratification, acceptance, or approval;
- *Protocol on the Control of Marine Transboundary Movements and Disposal of Hazardous Wastes and other Wastes*, Tehran, 17 March 1998. Five ratifications by 28 November 2001. Two Signatories without ratification, acceptance, or approval.

Drafts of the Protocol Concerning the Conservation of Biological Diversity and the Establishment of Protected and the Concept Paper on Biodiversity have been prepared. These documents will be reviewed in the Legal/Technical Experts Meeting of the Regional Organization for the Protection of the Marine Environment (ROPME) Contracting States in early 2002.

Secretariat
Regional Organization for the Protection of the Marine Environment (ROPME),
PO Box 26388,
13124 Safat,
Kuwait
Telephone: +965-531214-0/4
Telefax: +965-5324172
E-mail: ropme@kuwait.net
ropme@qualitynet.net

Executive Secretary
Dr Abdul Rahman Al-Awadi.

Acting Co-ordinator
Dr Hassan Mohammadi.

Marine Emergency Mutual Aid Centre (MEMAC),
PO Box 10112,
Manama,
Bahrain
Telephone: +973-274554
Telefax: +973-274551
E-mail: memac@batelco.com.bh

Director
Captain A. M. Al-Janahi.

Sources on the Internet
<http://www.unep.ch/seas/dumkap.html>
<http://www.computec.com.bh/memac>
<http://www.kuwait.net/~ropmek>

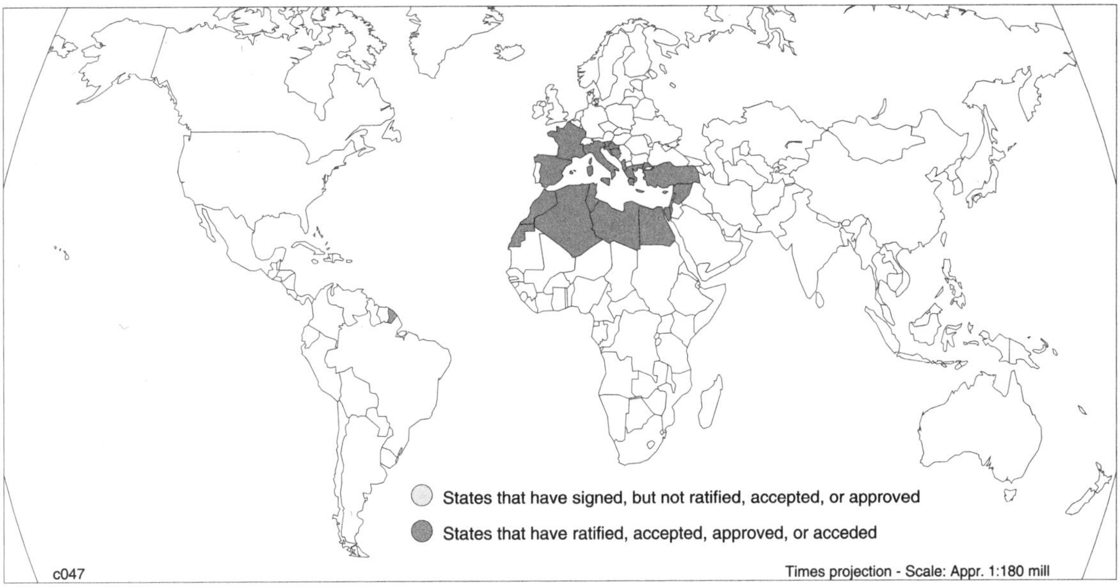

Convention for the Protection of the Marine Environment and the Coastal Region of the Mediterranean (Barcelona Convention)

Objectives

To achieve international co-operation for a co-ordinated and comprehensive approach to the protection and enhancement of the marine environment and the coastal region of the Mediterranean area.

Time and place of adoption

16 February 1976, Barcelona.

Entry into force

12 February 1978.

Status of participation

21 Parties, including the European Community, by 10 April 2002. No Signatories without ratification, acceptance, or approval.

Affiliated instruments

• *Protocol for the Prevention of Pollution of the Mediterranean Sea by Dumping from Ships and Aircraft or Incineration at Sea (Dumping Protocol)*, Barcelona, 16 February 1976. Entered into force on 12 February 1978. Same status of participation as the Convention. An amendment was adopted in Barcelona on 10 June 1995. (Not yet in force.) Ten acceptances, including the European Community, by 10 April 2002. 11 Parties to the Protocol had not yet accepted the amendment;

• *Protocol Concerning Co-operation in Combating Pollution of the Mediterranean Sea by Oil and Other Harmful Substances in Cases of Emergency (Emergency Protocol)*, Barcelona, 16 February 1976. Entered into force on 12 February 1978. Same status of participation as the Convention;

• *Protocol Concerning Co-operation in Preventing Pollution from Ships and, in Cases of Emergency, Combating Pollution of the Mediterranean Sea*, Valletta, 25 January 2002. (Not yet in force.) Enters into force on the thirtieth day following the deposit of the sixth instrument of ratification, acceptance, approval, or accession—and shall from that date replace the Emergency Protocol above in the relations between the Parties to both instruments. 15 Signatories without ratification, acceptance, or approval by 10 April 2002;

• *Protocol for the Protection of the Mediterranean Sea against Pollution from Land-Based Sources and Activities (LBS Protocol)*, Athens, 17 May 1980. Entered into force on 17 June 1983. Same status of participation as the Convention.

• *Protocol Concerning Mediterranean Specially Protected Areas (SPA Protocol)*, Geneva, 3 April 1982. Entered into force on 23 March 1986. Same status of participation as the Convention.

• *Protocol Concerning Specially Protected Areas and Biological Diversity in the Mediterranean (SPA and Biodiversity Protocol)*, Barcelona, 10 June 1995. Entered into force on 12 December 1999. Nine Parties, including the European Community, by 10 April 2002. Eight Signatories without ratification, acceptance, or approval;

• *Protocol for the Protection of the Mediterranean Sea against Pollution Resulting from Exploration and Exploitation of the Continental Shelf and the Seabed and its Subsoil (Offshore Protocol)*, Madrid, 14 October 1994. (Not yet in force.) Three ratifications by 10 April 2002. Nine Signatories without ratification, acceptance, or approval;

• *Protocol on the Prevention of Pollution of the Mediterranean Sea by Transboundary Movements of Hazardous Wastes and their Disposal (Hazardous Wastes Protocol)*, Izmir, 1 October 1996. (Not yet in force.) Three ratifications by 10 April 2002. Eight Signatories without ratification, acceptance, or approval.

Secretariat

UNEP Co-ordinating Unit for the Mediterranean Action Plan (MEDU),
48 Vassileos Konstantinou Avenue,
GR-11635 Athens, Greece
Telephone: +30-10-7273100
Telefax: +30-10-725319-6/7
E-mail: unepmedu@unepmap.gr

Sources on the Internet

<http://www.unepmap.org>

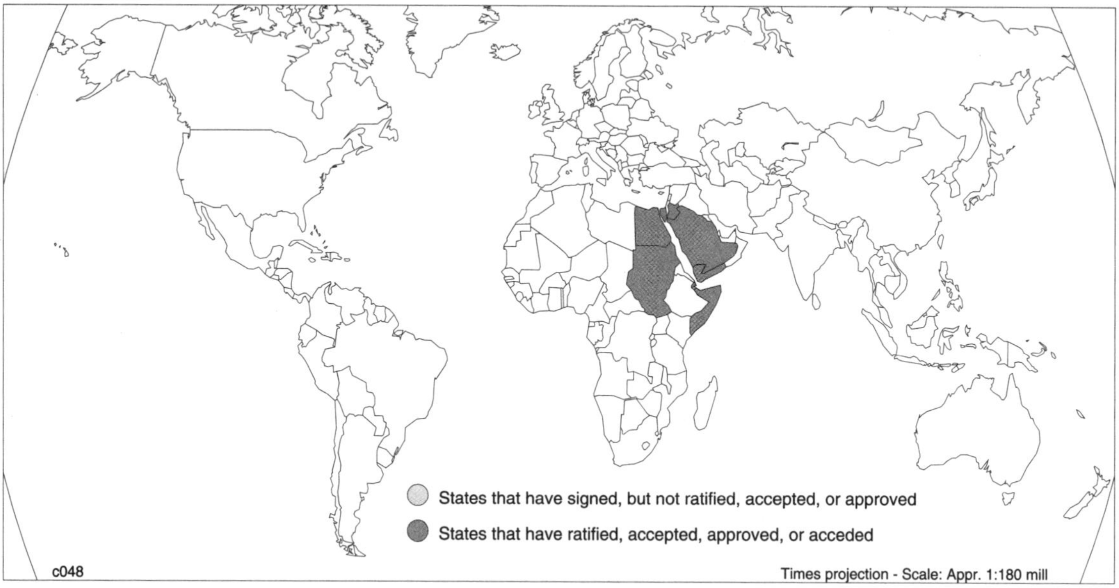

Regional Convention for the Conservation of the Red Sea and Gulf of Aden Environment

Objectives
To ensure conservation of the environment of the Red Sea and Gulf of Aden by the promotion, on a regional basis, of environmental protection and natural resources management in the marine and coastal areas of the region.

Time and place of adoption
14 February 1982, Jeddah.

Entry into force
20 August 1985.

Status of participation
Seven Parties (plus Palestine) by 1 December 2002. No Signatories without ratification, acceptance, or approval.

Affiliated instruments
Protocol Concerning Regional Co-operation in Combating Pollution by Oil and Other Harmful Substances in Cases of Emergency, Jeddah, 14 February 1982. Entered into force on 20 August 1985. Same status of participation as the Convention.

Monitoring/implementation
Consistent with Article XVI of the Convention, the Regional Organization for the Conservation of the Environment of the Red Sea and Gulf of Aden (PERSGA) was formally declared at the first Council Meeting in Cairo, Egypt, in September 1995.

In December 1998 the Secretary General of PERSGA and representatives of the three Global Environment Facility (GEF) (see IGOs) partners (UN Development Programme, UNEP and the World Bank), launched the Strategic Action Programme for the Red Sea and Gulf of Aden (SAP). This multidisciplinary undertaking focuses on eight components: capacity building for regional co-operation, reducing navigational risks and maritime pollution, sustainable use of living marine resources, conservation of habitats and biodiversity, development of a regional network of marine protected areas, support for integrated coastal-zone management, enhancement of public awareness and participation, and programme monitoring and evaluation.

Secretariat
Regional Organization for the Conservation of the Environment of the Red Sea and Gulf of Aden (PERSGA),
PO Box 53662,
Jeddah 21583,
Saudi Arabia
Telephone: +966-2-657322-4/8
Telefax: +966-2-6521901
E-mail: persga@persga.org

Secretary-General
Dr Nizar Ibrahim Tawfiq.

Sources on the Internet
<http://www.unep.ch/seas/main/persga/red.html>
<http://www.persga.org>

Convention for the Protection of the Natural Resources and Environment of the South Pacific Region (Noumea Convention)

Objectives
To protect and manage the natural resources and environment of the South Pacific region.

Time and place of adoption
24 November 1986, Noumea.

Entry into force
22 August 1990.

Status of participation
12 Parties by 15 February 2002. Three Signatories without ratification, acceptance, or approval.

Affiliated instruments
- *Protocol Concerning Co-operation in Combating Pollution Emergencies in the South Pacific Region*, Noumea, 1986. Entered into force on 22 August 1990. Same status of participation as the Convention;
- *Protocol for the Prevention of Pollution of the South Pacific Region by Dumping*, Noumea, 1986. Entered into force on 22 August 1990. 11 Parties by 16 June 1999. Four Signatories without ratification, acceptance, or approval.

Secretariat
South Pacific Regional Environment Programme (SPREP),
PO Box 240, Vaitele,
Apia,
Western Samoa

Telephone: +685-21929
Telefax: +685-20231
E-mail: sprep@sprep.org.ws

Director
Mr Tamarii Pierre Tutangata.

Legal Officers
Mr Andrea Volentras and Dr Jacques Mougeot.

Sources on the Internet
<http://www.sprep.org.ws>

Yearbook reference
See Richard Herr (2002), 'Environmental Protection in the South Pacific: The Effectiveness of SPREP and its Conventions', *Yearbook of International Co-operation on Environment and Development 2002/03*, 41–9.

Convention for the Protection of the Marine Environment and Coastal Zone of the South-East Pacific

Objectives
To protect the marine environment and coastal zones of the South-East Pacific.

Time and place of adoption
12 November 1981, Lima.

Entry into force
19 May 1986.

Status of participation
Five Parties by 1 May 2002. No Signatories without ratification, acceptance, or approval.

Complimentary instruments
• *Agreement on Regional Co-operation in Combating Pollution of the South-East Pacific by Hydrocarbons or Other Harmful Substances in Cases of Emergency*, Lima, 12 November 1981. Entered into force on 14 July 1986. Same status of participation as the Convention;
• *Supplementary Protocol to the Agreement on Regional Co-operation in Combating Pollution of the South-East Pacific by Hydrocarbons or Other Harmful Substances in Cases of Emergency*, Quito, 22 July 1983. Entered into force on 20 May 1987. Same status of participation as the Convention;
• *Protocol for the Protection of the South-East Pacific against Pollution from Land-Based Sources*, Quito, 22 July 1983. Entered into force on 21 September 1986. Same status of participation as the Convention;
• *Protocol for the Conservation and Management of the Protected Marine and Coastal Areas of the South-East Pacific*, Paipa, 21 September 1989. Entered into force on 17 October 1994. Same status of participation as the Convention;
• *Protocol for the Protection of the South-East Pacific against Radioactive Contamination*, Paipa, 21 September 1989. Entered into force on 25 January 1995. Five Parties by 1 May 2002. Same status of participation as the Convention.

Secretariat
Comisión Permanente del Pacífico Sur (CPPS),
Av. Carlos Julio Arosemena,
Km. 3.5 via a Daule,Guayaquil,
Ecuador
Telephone: +593-4-222120-2/3
Telefax: +593-4-2221201
E-mail: cpps@ecuanex.net.ec
sgeneral@cppsnet.org
cpps_pse@cppsnet.org

Secretary-General of CPPS
Ambassador Fernando Alzate Donoso.

Regional Co-ordinator, Plan of Action for the Protection of the Marine Environment and Coastal Areas of the South East Pacific
Dr Ulises Munaylla-Alarcón.

Sources on the Internet
<http://www.cpps-int.org>
<http://www.unep.ch/seas/dumsep.html>

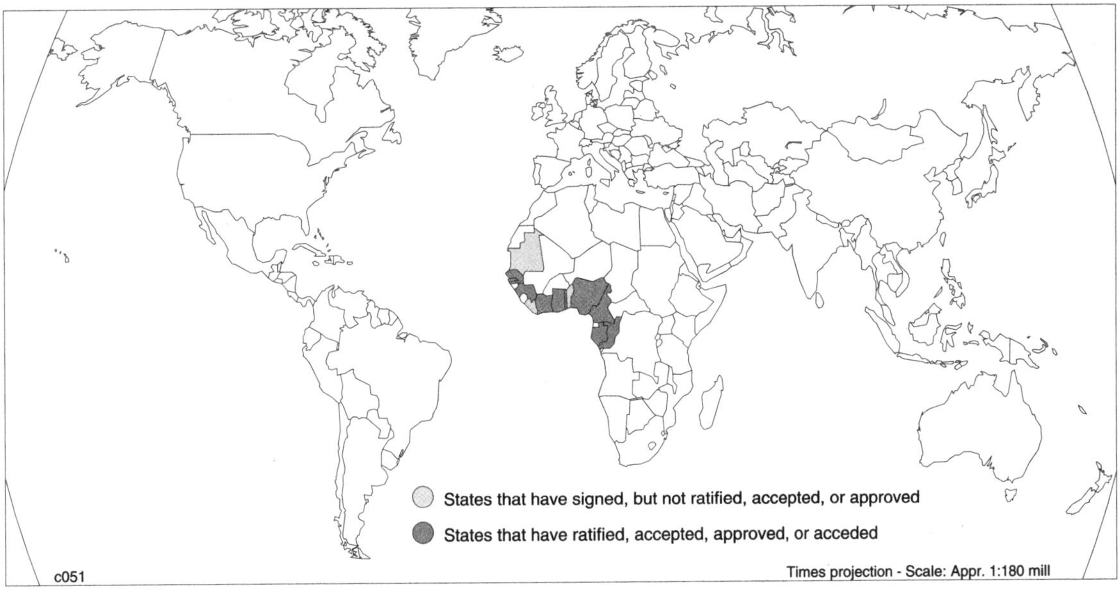

Convention for Co-operation in the Protection and Development of the Marine and Coastal Environment of the West and Central African Region

Objectives
To protect the marine environment, coastal zones, and related internal waters falling within the jurisdiction of the states of the West and Central African region.

Time and place of adoption
23 March 1981, Abidjan.

Entry into force
5 August 1984.

Status of participation
Ten Parties by 28 March 2002. Three Signatories without ratification, acceptance, or approval.

Affiliated instruments
Protocol Concerning Co-operation in Combating Pollution in Cases of Emergency, Abidjan, 23 March 1981. Entered into force on 5 August 1984. Same status of participation as the Convention.

Secretariat
UNEP Regional Co-ordinating Unit for the West and Central African Action Plan (WCAF/RCU),
c/o Ministère de l'Environnement et du Cadre de Vie,
20 BP 650,
Abidjan 20,
Côte d'Ivoire
Telephone: +225-20-211183
Telefax: +225-20-222050
E-mail: biodiv@africaonline.co.ci

Acting Co-ordinator
Ms Nasséré Kaba.

Sources on the Internet
<http://www.unep.ch/seas/dumwacaf.html>

Convention on the Conservation of Antarctic Marine Living Resources (CCAMLR)

Objectives
To conserve Antarctic marine living resources (the term 'conservation' includes rational use).

Scope
Legal scope
Open to all states and regional economic integration organizations.

Geographic scope
The Convention applies to the Antarctic marine living resources of the area south of 60ºS latitude and to the Antarctic marine living resources of the area between that latitude and the Antarctic Convergence which form part of the Antarctic marine ecosystem.

Time and place of adoption
20 May 1980, Canberra.

Entry into force
7 April 1982.

Status of participation
31 Parties, including the European Community, by 27 March 2002, of which 24 form part of the Commission. No Signatories without ratification, acceptance, or approval.

Instruments of accession to be deposited with the government of Australia.

Affiliated instruments and organizations
Conservation measures (see Rules and standards below).

Co-ordination with related instruments
The Convention is an additional component instrument of the Antarctic Treaty system (see this section).

Secretariat
CCAMLR,
PO Box 213,
North Hobart,
Tasmania, 7002,
Australia
Telephone: +61-3-62310366
Telefax: +61-3-62349965
E-mail: ccamlr@ccamlr.org

Executive Secretary
Dr Denzil Miller.

Number of staff
Four professionals and 19 support staff (March 2002).

Finance
The Commission adopts its budget and that of the Scientific Committee at each annual meeting. Each member contributes to the budget. Two criteria form the basis for allocating the budget: the amount harvested and equal sharing. The financial activities are conducted in accordance with financial regulations adopted by the Commission and subject to annual external audit.

Budget
The administrative core budget was $A2.122 million in 2000 and $2.470 million in 2001, and is $2.701 in 2002.

Special funds
Not applicable.

Rules and standards
The Commission for the CCAMLR is established with the following functions:
- to facilitate research into and comprehensive studies of Antarctic marine living resources and the Antarctic marine ecosystem (e.g. CCAMLR Ecosystem Monitoring Programme (CEMP) (see below));
- to compile data on the status of and changes in populations of Antarctic marine living resources;
- to ensure the acquisition of catch-and-effort statistics on harvested populations;
- to analyse, disseminate, and publish the information referred to above, and the reports of the Scientific Committee;
- to identify conservation needs and analyse the effectiveness of conservation measures;
- to formulate, adopt, and revise conservation measures on the basis of the best scientific evidence available;
- to implement a system of observation and inspection;

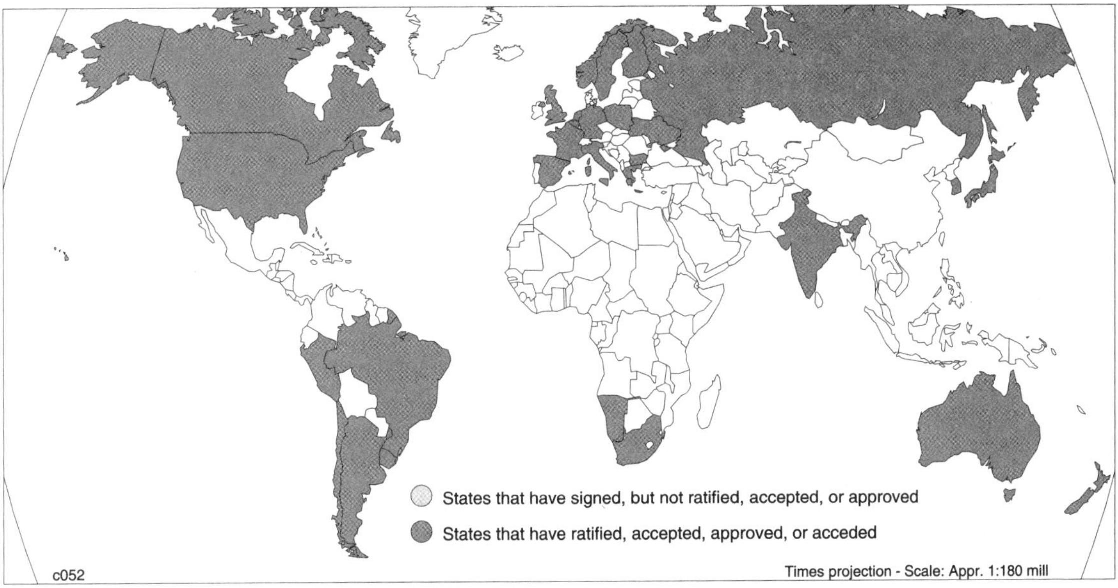

• to carry out such other activities as are necessary to fulfil the objective of the Convention;
• to publish and maintain a record of all conservation measures in force and notify them to all members.

Conservation measures shall become binding upon all members of the Commission 180 days after such notification. If a member, within 90 days, notifies the Commission that it cannot accept the conservation measure, in whole or in part, the measure shall not be binding upon that member.

Monitoring/implementation

Review procedure
Each Party is required to inform the Commission of any activities in violation of the Convention that come to its knowledge. The Commission calls the attention of any State which is not a party to the Convention to activities of its nationals or ships which are felt to be in contravention of the objectives of the Convention.

National reports are submitted in yearly, monthly, or five-day periods, depending on the nature of the report. Some reports are private, others public. There is no independent verification of data or information.

Observations or inspections
A system of inspection to verify compliance with measures adopted by the Commission was established in 1990. Inspection implies the monitoring for compliance with measures in force. Each Party nominates inspectors who are authorized to conduct inspections during the seasons. A scheme of international scientific observation was established in 1992. Observation implies the presence of scientific observers on board fishing and research vessels throughout the voyage.

Environmental monitoring programmes
The CCAMLR Ecosystem Monitoring Programme (CEMP) is intended to detect changes in the condition, abundance, and distribution of species which are not commercially harvested, but which provide some indication of the dynamics and well-being of particular ecosystems. Information obtained from monitoring 'indicator species' can be taken into account in the regulation of human activity to ensure conservation principles of the Convention are met.

Trade measures
An integrated set of political and legal measures was agreed in 1997 and 1998 in order to combat illegal, unregulated, and unreported fishing for Patagonian toothfish (*Dissostichus eleginoides*) in the Convention area. The effectiveness of these measures is being kept under review. Further measures are being considered which relate to Port State control, as well as trade-related measures.

Decision-making bodies

Political
Parties to the Convention give effect to its objectives and principles through the annual Meetings of the Commission. Adoption of measures, by consensus, is the exclusive function of the Commission.

Scientific/technical
The Scientific Committee, composed of experts representing governments, shall: provide a forum for consultation and co-operation concerning the collection, study, and exchange of information; establish criteria and methods; analyse data; and formulate proposals. It provides the essential input into the Commission's deliberations. Decisions in the Committee are reached by consensus.

A Standing Committee on Finance and Administration and a Standing Committee on Observations and Inspection meet each year.

Publications

The secretariat publishes, in addition to different manuals:
• *Report of the Annual Meeting of the Scientific Committee*;
• *Report of the Annual Meeting of the Commission*;
• *Conservation Measures in Force*;
• *Statistical Bulletin*;
• *CCAMLR Science*.

Sources on the Internet

<http://www.ccamlr.org>

International Convention for the Conservation of Atlantic Tunas (ICCAT)

Objectives
To co-operate in maintaining the population of tunas and tuna-like species found in the Atlantic Ocean and the adjacent seas at levels that will permit the maximum sustainable catch for food and other purposes.

Scope
Legal scope
Open to member States of the UN or any of its specialized agencies and to regional integration organizations.

Geographic scope
Regional. Applies to all waters of the Atlantic Ocean and adjacent seas, including the Mediterranean Sea. The longitude of 20°E is used, for scientific purposes, as the border between the Atlantic and the Indian Ocean.

Time and place of adoption
14 May 1966, Rio de Janeiro.

Entry into force
21 March 1969.

Status of participation
31 Parties, including the European Community, by 15 February 2002. One Signatory without ratification, acceptance, or approval.

The Director-General of FAO (see IGOs) acts as depositary.

Affiliated instruments and organizations
A Protocol enabling regional integration organizations to become Parties to the Convention was adopted in Paris on 10 July 1984 and entered into force on 19 January 1997.

A second Protocol was adopted in Madrid on 5 June 1992 to amend paragraph 2 of Article X of the Convention. (Not yet in force.) It enters into force after the deposit of instruments of ratification, acceptance, or approval of 75 per cent of those Contracting Parties which were Parties to the Convention at the time of the adoption of the Protocol, including all those classified as developed market-economy countries. 14 Contracting Parties to the Convention had ratified by 15 February 2002. 16 Contracting Parties to the Convention have not ratified, accepted, or approved. A special procedure was adopted for the entry into force of this Protocol which takes into account that the contributions of the countries with a developed market economy would increase, while those corresponding to developing countries would decrease.

Secretariat
International Commission for the Conservation of Atlantic Tunas (ICCAT),
Calle Corazón de Maria, 8 (6th floor),
E-28002 Madrid,
Spain
Telephone: +34-91-4165600
Telefax: +34-91-4152612
E-mail: info@iccat.es

Executive Secretary
Dr Adolfo Ribeiro Lima.

Assistant Executive Secretary (ad interim)
Dr Victor Restrepo.

Number of staff
Four professionals and 11 general service staff (February 2002).

Finance
Funding of the budget is by annual financial contributions made by the members of the Commission. Article X of the Convention defines the current procedures to calculate the country contributions to finance the Commission's budget.

Budget
The administrative core budget was ptas. 245,752,000 in 2000 and ptas. 252,943,060 in 2001, and is €EUR1,615,000 in 2002.

Rules and standards
The Commission (see below) shall be responsible for the study of populations of tunas and tuna-like fishes and such other species exploited in tuna fishing in the Convention area as are not under investigation by another international fishery organization.

Studies include:
• research on the abundance, biometry, and ecology of the fishes;
• the oceanography of their environment;
• the effects of natural and human factors upon their abundance.

If, based on scientific findings, the Commission considers it necessary, it recommends to the Parties regulatory measures to ensure maximum utilization of the populations of fish. Such regulatory measures may include a minimum and/or maximum size of fish which may be caught, restrictions on the amount of catch and/or effort, etc.

Monitoring/implementation
Review procedure
The Commission implements the Convention by co-ordinating research, collecting and disseminating statistics and other information on the biology and ecology of tunas and on oceanographic conditions, and by analysing all this information regarding the stock status of fish.

Observations or inspections
Observation and inspection is the responsibility of each Contracting Party government.

Environmental monitoring programmes
The Subcommittee on Environment of the Standing Committee on Research and Statistics reviews environmental conditions in relation to the fisheries. There is also a Subcommittee on By-Catch, which reviews the status of tuna fishery by-catch of non-target species.

Data and information system programmes
The ICCAT Secretariat maintains a database for tunas and related species which in-

cludes data on catches, fishing power, effort, biological information, and tagging releases and recoveries.

Trade measures
The Bluefin Tuna Statistical Document Programme implemented by the Commission requires all imports of bluefin tunas to Contracting Parties to be accompanied by a validated statistical document. The Commission passed a resolution to ensure the effectiveness of the ICCAT bluefin tunas conservation programmes, allowing the Commission to recommend the Contracting Parties to take non-discriminatory trade restrictive measures, consistent with their international obligations, on bluefin tuna products in any form, from any Party whose vessels have been fishing for Atlantic bluefin tunas in a manner which diminishes the effectiveness of the relevant conservation recommendations of the Commission on Atlantic bluefin tunas. Following this action plan, ICCAT recommended that Contracting Parties prohibit the import of any type of bluefin tuna product from Belize and Honduras (effective from August 1997) and from Panama (effective 1 January 1998).

In 1995 the Commission also adopted a resolution for an action plan to ensure the effectiveness of the conservation program for Atlantic swordfish, under which non-discriminatory trade restrictive measures may be taken with respect to Atlantic swordfish products from those non-contracting Parties whose vessels have been fishing for Atlantic swordfish in a manner which diminishes the effectiveness of the relevant conservation recommendations of the Commission. Under the provisions of the resolution, the Commission adopted, in 1999, a recommendation prohibiting the import of Atlantic swordfish from Belize and Honduras.

Dispute-settlement mechanisms
None.

Decision-making bodies

Political
The International Commission for the Conservation of Atlantic Tunas (ICCAT) is established as a governing body and meets annually, usually in November. The Commission, on the basis of scientific evidence, makes recommendations for the maintenance of the populations of tunas and tuna-like fish.

Scientific/technical
The Commission works through four standing committees, comprised of experts representing governments and others:
- Standing Committee on Research and Statistics (SCRS);
- Standing Committee on Finances and Administration (STACFAD);
- Compliance Committee;
- Permanent Working Group for the Improvement of ICCAT Statistics and Conservation Measures (PWG). This was established in 1992 to review compliance, by non-contracting Parties, of the regulatory measures recommended by the Commission.

Four panels have also been established to consider and, if necessary, initiate regulatory measures on species covered by the Convention:
- Panel 1: Tropical tunas;
- Panel 2: Temperate tunas (North);
- Panel 3: Temperate tunas (South);
- Panel 4: Other species.

Publications

The Commission publishes reports of findings, and up-to-date information is available through:
- *Biennial Report* (annually);
- *Statistical Bulletin* (annually);
- *Data Record* (annually);
- *Collective Volume of Scientific Papers* (previously 3–4 volumes per year; since 2000 published on a single volume on compact disc).

Sources on the Internet

<http://www.iccat.es>

International Convention for the Regulation of Whaling (ICRW)

Objectives
To establish regulations for purposes of conservation and utilization of whale resources, and to serve as an agency for the collection, analysis, and publication of scientific information related to whales and whaling.

Scope
Legal scope
Open to all States. Not open to regional integration organizations.

Geographic scope
Global.

Time and place of adoption
2 December 1946, Washington.

Entry into force
10 November 1948.

Status of participation
48 Parties by 10 June 2002. No Signatories without ratification, approval, or acceptance.

As in 2001, the issue of Iceland's adherence to the ICRW with a reservation to Paragraph 10(e) concerning the moratorium on commercial whaling was discussed at the 54th annual meeting in May 2002. There was again a difference of views as to whether the Commission should accept Iceland's reservation. A vote to uphold last year's decision that Iceland should 'assist in the meeting as an observer' was agreed by 25 votes to 20 votes.

Instruments of accession and withdrawal are to be deposited with the government of the USA.

Affiliated instruments and organizations
The *Schedule to the Convention*, adopted annually since 1949 at meetings of the International Whaling Commission (IWC) (see below), is an integral part of the Convention, and contains measures that govern the conduct of whaling by Parties to the Convention.

Co-ordination with related instruments
Although there are no formal mechanisms, Parties will be aware of related treaties and conventions, particularly the UN Convention on the Law of the Sea (LOS Convention) (see this section).

The Commission contributed to the elaboration of the 1984 UNEP–FAO Global Plan of Action for the Conservation, Management, and Utilization of Marine Mammals and has part of the responsibility for its implementation.

In July 2000, a memorandum of understanding was signed by the Secretariats of IWC and the Convention on the Conservation of Migratory Species of Wild Animals (CMS) (see this section). The purpose of the memorandum is to establish a framework of information and consultation between the two conventions in conserving migratory species.

Secretariat
International Whaling Commission (IWC),
The Red House,
135 Station Road,
Impington,
Cambridge CB4 9NP,
United Kingdom
Telephone: +44-1223-233971
Telefax: +44-1223-232876
E-mail: secretariat@iwcoffice.org

Secretary
Dr Nicola Grandy.

Number of staff
Four professionals and 12 support staff (June 2002).

Finance
The budget is financed mainly by contributions from Parties. Until the 54th annual meeting in 2002, there had been no special provisions relating to the economic standing of governments, the formula for contributions being based largely on the degree of involvement, and including shares for membership, whaling activity, and size of delegation to the annual meetings. However, since the 52nd annual meeting a Commission-appointed Task Force has been working to develop a more equitable scheme that would, among other things, take account of capacity to pay. The Task Force has not yet completed its work, but at its 54th annual meeting the Commission adopted an interim scheme that gives a substantial amount of relief to a number of member governments.

Budget
The annual actual budget was approximately £UK1,526,690 in 2000 and £1,291,521 in 2001, and is £1,348,690 in 2002. The administrative core budget was £1,060,342 in 2000 and £1,104,300 in 2001, and is £1,218,700 in 2002.

Special funds
The Commission allots part of its budget to a research fund for projects related to whales. The most important project has been the Comprehensive Assessment of Whale Stocks.

Rules and standards
The main duty of the Commission is to keep under review and revise as necessary the measures laid down in the Schedule to the Convention governing the conduct of whaling. These may include measures:

- to provide for the complete protection of certain species of whales;
- to designate specified ocean areas as whale sanctuaries;
- to set the maximum catches of whales which may be taken in one season;
- to prescribe open and closed seasons and areas for whaling;
- to fix size limits above and below which certain species of whales may not be killed;
- to prohibit the capture of suckling calves and female whales accompanied by calves;
- to require the compilation of catch reports and other statistical and biological records.

The Convention requires that amendments to the provisions of the Schedule with respect to the conservation and utilization of whale resources are based on scientific findings.

While the Commission generally acts by simple majority, amendment of the Schedule requires a three-quarter majority vote of those casting an affirmative or a negative vote.

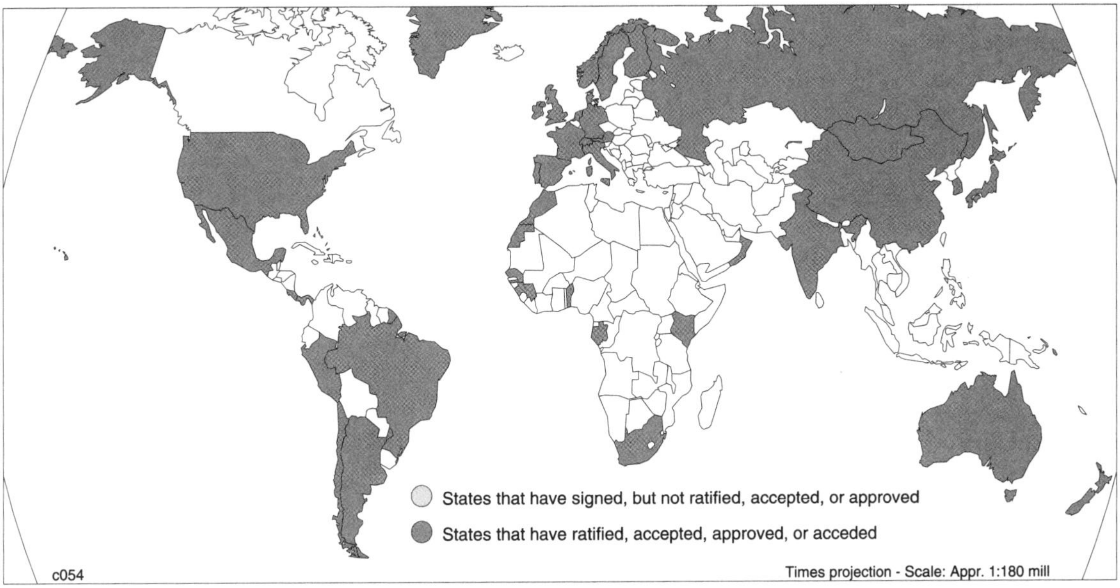

The Convention also establishes certain criteria for amendments to the Schedule and provides for a system of notification which allows Parties 90 days after notification of amendments to register an objection. Under an objection, the relevant passages are not enforceable against the country in question.

The Commission agreed in 1982 to set a zero quota on all commercially exploited stocks for the 1986 coastal and 1985–6 pelagic seasons, and thereafter a so-called moratorium, which is still in force, and initiated a comprehensive assessment of the effect of the decision on whale stocks that should have been finished by 1990. In addition, the Scientific Committee spent several years developing a Revised Management Procedure (RMP) for commercial whaling of baleen whales.

At the 1992 annual meeting the Commission adopted the specification developed by the Scientific Committee for the calculation of catch limits for baleen whales. In 1994, the Commission accepted and endorsed the RMP for commercial whaling and associated guidelines for surveys and collection of data. However, it noted that work on a number of issues, including specification of an inspection and observer system, remained to be completed before the Commission would consider establishing catch limits other than zero. A comparable management scheme for aboriginal subsistence whaling is now being developed by the Scientific Committee.

In 1979, the Commission established the Indian Ocean north of 55°S as a whale 'sanctuary' (i.e. an area where commercial whaling is prohibited). This provision was reviewed by the Commission at its annual meeting in 2002 with the result that the Indian Ocean sanctuary remains in place.

After detailed consideration of the legal, political, ecological, management, financial, and environmental issues, the Commission adopted the Southern Ocean sanctuary at the 1994 annual meeting. The purpose of the proposal was stated to be to contribute to the rehabilitation of the Antarctic marine ecosystem and the protection of all southern hemisphere species and populations of baleen and sperm whales on their feeding grounds. This would also link up with the Indian Ocean sanctuary to provide a large area within which whales would be free from commercial catching. The Southern Ocean sanctuary will be reviewed at the annual meeting in 2004.

A recent development is the Commission's consideration of whale-watching as a sustainable use of cetacean resources since 1993. The Commission has encouraged scientific consideration of this topic, and in 1996 adopted objectives and principles for whale-watching, developed by the Scientific Committee.

With increasing awareness that whales should not be considered apart from the marine environment which they inhabit, and that detrimental changes may threaten whale stocks, the Commission decided that the Scientific Committee should give some priority to research on the effects of environmental changes on cetaceans. The Scientific Committee examined this issue in the context of the RMP and agreed that the RMP adequately addressed such concerns. However, it went on to state that the species most vulnerable to such threats might well be those reduced to levels at which the RMP, even if applied, would result in zero catches. The Committee held two workshops, one in 1995 in Norway on the effects of chemical pollutants, and one in 1996 in the USA on the effects of climate change and ozone depletion. The Commission has endorsed the Scientific Committee's work on these issues and agreed to fund work to carry forward the recommendations specifically to design multidisciplinary and multinational research programmes in co-operation with other relevant organizations.

Aboriginal whaling for subsistence purposes is carried out by native peoples of Greenland, Bequia, Siberia, and Alaska, and the Commission and Scientific Committee are developing a Management Procedure specifically for such non-commercial operation. Catches for scientific purposes are taken by Japan. Norway has resumed commercial whaling under the objection procedure provided by the Convention and is setting its own national catch limits.

Monitoring/implementation

Review procedure

Parties are required to implement the regulations through internal legislation (copies of which are forwarded to the secretariat) and submit reports, as appropriate, on any infraction to the Commission. These reports are made public after submission to the Commission.

An International Observer Scheme was established in 1972 to encourage full and accurate reporting of commercial catches. The Convention requires reports on and penalties imposed for infractions. These reports are reviewed by the Infractions Subcommittee (see below) each year and are also made public after submission to the Commission.

In addition, the Aboriginal Subsistence Whaling Subcommittee and the Scientific Committee monitor and report on relevant matters. Any countries catching whales are required to submit whaling and other associated data to the Commission. There are no international observers currently monitoring whaling, although discussions on a new verification system are underway.

Observations or inspections

Compliance with the commercial whaling regulations was monitored by national inspectors and international observers, and their reports and the data submitted were reviewed by the Infractions and Scientific Committee as appropriate (see above).

Trade measures

No provisions on trade measures to penalize Parties for non-compliance, although these have sometimes occurred on a bilateral basis.

Dispute-settlement mechanisms

None.

Decision-making bodies

Political

The International Whaling Commission is established as a governing body and meets annually. It is composed of one member (Commissioner) from each Contracting Party, who may be accompanied by experts or advisers. The delegates may include industry and other non-governmental representatives as well as scientific advisers. Non-member governments, intergovernmental organizations, and international non-governmental organizations may also attend meetings by invitation in an observer capacity.

Scientific/technical

The Commission works through three standing committees:

- Scientific Committee, composed of government experts and others;
- Technical Committee, composed of experts representing governments;
- Finance and Administration Committee, composed of experts representing governments.

The Scientific Committee reviews scientific information related to the conservation and management of whales, the scientific programmes of the Parties, and scientific permit proposals and catches.

In addition, several subcommittees of the Commission are established, such as the Infractions Subcommittee and Aboriginal Subsistence Whaling Subcommittee.

Publications

The Commission publishes annual reports, a new *Journal of Cetacean Research and Management*, and special issues on whale science. It also holds and publishes catch and related data on whaling operations.

Sources on the Internet

<http://www.iwcoffice.org>

The Antarctic Treaty

Objectives

• to ensure that Antarctica is used for peaceful purposes only;
• to ensure the continuance of freedom of scientific investigation and international co-operation in scientific investigation in Antarctica;
• to set aside disputes over territorial sovereignty.

Scope

Legal scope

The Antarctic Treaty was ratified by 12 Signatory States. In addition it is open for accession by any state which is a member of the UN, or by any other state which may be invited to accede to the Treaty with the consent of all the Contracting Parties whose representatives are entitled to participate in the meetings provided for under Article IX of the Antarctic Treaty (hereinafter: Consultative Parties and Consultative Meetings).

The Consultative Parties are currently made up of the 12 original Signatories, which retain the consultative status unconditionally, and of the 15 acceding states which have been acknowledged to the consultative status conditionally, during such times as they demonstrate their interest in Antarctica by conducting substantial research activity there, such as the establishment of a scientific station or the dispatch of a scientific expedition. There are also 18 non-Consultative Parties, i.e. states which acceded to the Treaty without acquiring consultative status.

Geographic scope

The Antarctic Treaty applies to the area south of 60ºS.

Time and place of adoption

1 December 1959, Washington, DC.

Entry into force

23 June 1961.

Status of participation

45 Contracting Parties by 16 May 2002 (consisting of 27 Consultative Parties and 18 non-Consultative Parties).

Affiliated international instruments

The Antarctic Treaty system (ATS) provides the umbrella for a complex system of international instruments of importance for the environment. These include:

• the *Antarctic Treaty* itself (text in United Nations Treaty Series, vol. 402, 71);
• other treaties adopted on the basis of the Antarctic Treaty:

(*a*) *Convention for the Conservation of Antarctic Seals*, adopted at London on 1 June 1972, entered into force on 11 March 1978. 16 Parties by 16 May 2002. One Signatory (New Zealand) without ratification or acceptance. (Text in United Nations Treaty Series, vol. 1080, 175; reprinted in *International Legal Materials*, 11 (1972), 251.);

(*b*) *Convention on the Conservation of Antarctic Marine Living Resources (CCAMLR)*, adopted at Canberra on 20 May 1980, entered into force on 7 April 1982. 31 Parties by 27 March 2002. (Text reprinted in *International Legal Materials*, 19 (1980), 837.) (See also this section.);

(*c*) *Protocol on Environmental Protection to the Antarctic Treaty (Environmental Protocol)*, with four Annexes (Annex I, *Environmental Impact Assessment*; Annex II, *Conservation of Antarctic Fauna and Flora*; Annex III, *Waste Disposal and Waste Management*; and Annex IV, *Prevention of Marine Pollution*), adopted at Madrid on 4 October 1991. (Text reprinted in *International Legal Materials*, 30 (1991), 1461.) The Protocol with Annexes I–IV entered into force on 14 January 1998 after the deposit of instruments of ratification, acceptance, approval, or accession by all 26 States which were Antarctic Treaty Consultative Parties at the date of the adoption of the Protocol. As of 16 May 2002 there were 29 Parties (27 Consultative Parties and two non-Consultative Parties (Greece and Ukraine)). Ten Signatories without ratification, acceptance, or approval. The Protocol supplements the Antarctic Treaty. The annexes form an integral part of the Protocol. Annexes additional to Annexes I–IV may be adopted; thus Annex V, *Area Protection and Management*, was adopted as an annex to Recommendation XVI–10 at the Sixteenth Consultative Meeting, held in Bonn, 7–18 October 1991. 26 out of in total 27 Consultative Parties had accepted or approved Annex V by 16 May 2002. One additional Consultative Party (India) must accept or approve Recommendation XVI–10 containing Annex V before it can enter into force;

• other international instruments which may be adopted on the basis of the Antarctic Treaty, and under separate treaties associated with the Antarctic Treaty:

(*a*) 'measures in furtherance of the principles and objectives of the Antarctic Treaty', earlier known as *recommendations* of the Antarctic Treaty Consultative Meetings (ATCMs), of which over 250 have been adopted to date. This category of instruments split into three by a decision of the nineteenth ATCM (Seoul, May 1995): measures, decisions, and resolutions;

(*b*) measures adopted and in effect under separate treaties associated with the Antarctic Treaty (especially measures of the CCAMLR Commission);

(*c*) various *other instruments*, such as the decisions of Special Consultative Meetings, the results of Meetings of Experts, etc.

Co-ordination with related instruments

ATS has developed through the negotiation of additional component instruments (see above) rather than by a revision of the Antarctic Treaty itself. Part of this process has reference to regulations embodied in other international treaties such as the International Convention for the Prevention of Pollution from Ships, 1973, as modified by the Protocol of 1978 relating thereto (MARPOL 73/78) (see this section), relating to control of marine pollution in the Antarctic Treaty area.

Secretariat

ATS has no permanent secretariat to date, but the Consultative Parties reached a consensus in July 2001 on the location of a future ATS secretariat in Buenos Aires (Decision 1(2001)). The ATS still operates primarily through annual ATCMs hosted in rotation by Consultative Parties. So far, 24 ATCMs have been held in the past 40 years. The twenty-fourth ATCM was held

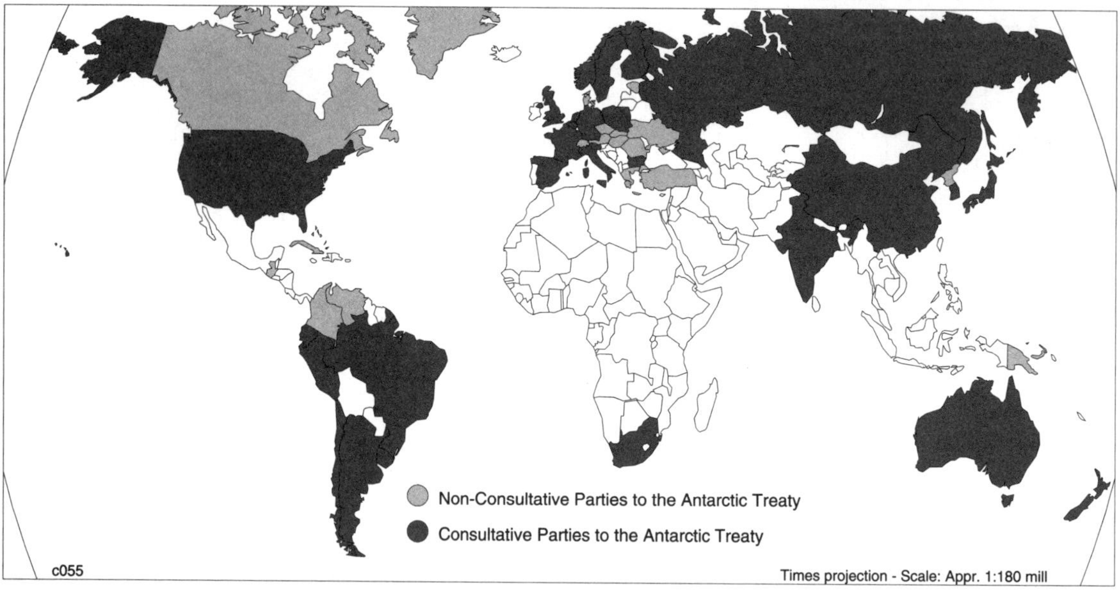

The Antarctic Treaty

in St Petersburg, Russia, from 9 to 20 July 2001 and the twenty-fifth ATCM will be held in Warsaw, Poland, from 10 to 20 September 2002. CCAMLR (see this section) has a permanent secretariat.

Information on ATS is available nationally from the relevant government department of the Contracting Parties. A list of national contact points for all Treaty Parties was published in US Department of State, *Handbook of the Antarctic Treaty System*, 8th edn (Washington, DC, April 1994), 291–5. Pursuant to a resolution adopted at the 1998 ATCM, a host country of the Meeting is encouraged to establish a homepage on the Internet and to maintain it three months after the conclusion of a Meeting. Thus far, Norway, Peru, Russia, and Poland, as host countries of the 1998, 1999, 2001, and 2002 ATCMs respectively, have maintained such homepages, making the official documentation of the Meetings publicly available upon their conclusion. A decision has also been adopted at the 1999 ATCM for the establishment of the Committee for Environmental Protection (CEP) homepage. (See Sources on the Internet, below.) In addition, information is available from the depositary government to the Antarctic Treaty:

Office of Oceans Affairs OES/OA,
Room 5805,
Bureau of Oceans and International Environmental and Scientific Affairs,
United States Department of State,
Washington, DC 20520-7818,
USA
Telephone: +1-202-6473262
Telefax: +1-202-6471106

International Affairs Officer
Mr Harlan K. Cohen.

Rules and standards

The Treaty imposes a wide range of obligations on Parties. These include prohibition of all military activities, nuclear explosions, and disposal of radioactive waste in Antarctica, as well as requirements to exchange and make freely available information resulting from scientific research activities.

The Environmental Protocol commits the Parties to comprehensive protection of the Antarctic environment and its dependent and associated ecosystems and defines the Antarctic as a natural reserve devoted to peace and science. Building on the existing body of ATS instruments, the Protocol elaborates detailed, mandatory rules to ensure that activities in the Antarctic do not result in adverse environmental effects.

All human activities are subject to detailed rules relating to: environmental impact assessment; conservation of Antarctic fauna and flora, including prohibitions on introduction of alien species; waste disposal and waste management; and prevention of marine pollution. In addition, an extensive system of protected areas has been established.

Related provisions call for environmental monitoring (see Monitoring and implementation, below).

Monitoring and implementation

Review procedure
The various elements of the ATS make provision for the exchange of information of the activity of Parties in the Antarctic Treaty area. The Protocol calls for annual exchange of information by each Party on what steps have been taken to implement the Protocol. There are also specific requirements under the individual components of the ATS, such as catch data and exploitation effort (see CCAMLR, this section).

Observations or inspections
The Antarctic Treaty accords to Consultative Parties rights of inspection of each other's stations, installations, and equipment in the area, to promote compliance. Observers may be appointed by each Consultative Party. Both the CCAMLR and the Environmental Protocol build on these provisions.

Trade measures
No provisions on trade measures to penalize Parties for non-compliance, except for the measures agreed within the CCAMLR (see this section).

Dispute-settlement mechanisms
Both the Antarctic Treaty and the CCAMLR provide for a variety of peaceful means of dispute settlement, including

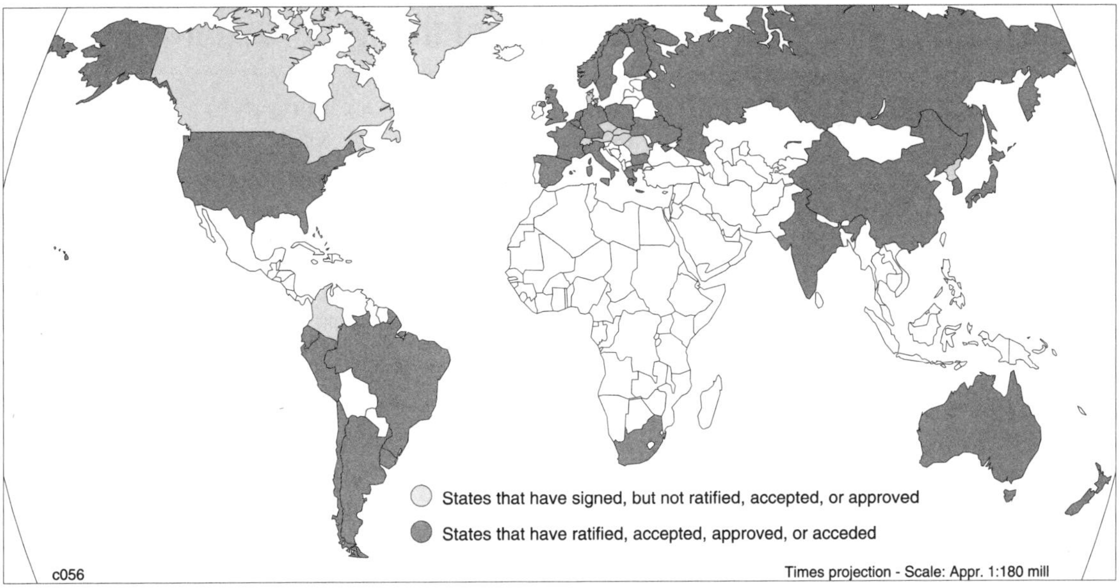

Protocol on Environmental Protection to the Antarctic Treaty (Environmental Protocol)

a referral of disputes to the International Court of Justice.

The Environmental Protocol introduces compulsory procedures (at the request of any party to a dispute) for its dispute settlement, based on a choice of forum approach (either the International Court of Justice or the special arbitration tribunal, to be instituted in accordance with a schedule to the Protocol).

Decision-making bodies

Political

The Antarctic Treaty Consultative Meeting is the principal decision-making forum of the Antarctic Treaty. Meetings are held annually (every two years up to 1991), hosted in rotation by Consultative Parties. The ATCM adopts measures to regulate the activity in the area. Since 1983 non-Consultative Parties have been invited to attend ATCMs, though only Consultative Parties may take part in decision making.

Meetings are also attended regularly by the representatives of the Commission for the Conservation of Antarctic Marine Living Resources (CCAMLR), the Scientific Committee on Antarctic Research (SCAR), and the Council of Managers of National Antarctic Programmes (COMNAP), as observers. In addition, by invitation of the Consultative Parties, other inter- and non-governmental organizations, currently including the Antarctic and Southern Ocean Coalition (ASOC), the Intergovernmental Oceanographic Commission (IOC), the International Association of Antarctica Tour Operators (IAATO), the International Hydrographic Organization (IHO), the International Maritime Organization (IMO) (see IGOs), the UN Environment Programme (UNEP) (see IGOs), the World Meteorological Organization (WMO) (see IGOs), the IUCN – The World Conservation Union (see NGOs), and the World Tourism Organization (WTO), may designate experts to attend the ATCMs.

According to Article XII, the Antarctic Treaty opens the possibility for a special conference to review the operation of the Treaty. Such a conference may be convened at the request of any Consultative Party once the Treaty has been in force for 30 years (that is, after 23 June 1991). All Parties, not just Consultative Parties, have the right to participate in this conference.

Scientific/technical

Based on the Environmental Protocol, the Committee for Environmental Protection (CEP) was established at the 1998 ATCM, as an advisory body to the ATCM.

The Treaty and its various component instruments contain requirements that activities in the region be based on scientific advice. The work of SCAR, a committee of the non-governmental International Council for Science (ICSU), forms an integral part of the input to decisions taken by the ATCMs. The Environmental Protocol also requires that environmental policies drawn up and adopted by the ATCM shall draw upon 'the best scientific and technical advice available'. The role of SCAR and COMNAP is crucial in this respect.

Publications

Treaty publications are available nationally from the relevant government department of the Parties. Extensive documentation is published by CCAMLR (see this section). In addition, SCAR produces scientific reports related to Antarctic research.

The latest (eighth) edition of the *Handbook of the Antarctic Treaty System* was published by the US Department of State in 1994. *SCAR Bulletin*, a quarterly publication of SCAR within *Polar Record*, the journal of Polar Publications at the Scott Polar Research Institute (see above), also publishes material from ATCMs.

Sources on the Internet

Related to ATCM:
<http://www.25atcm.gov.pl>

Related to CEP:
<http://cep.npolar.no>

Yearbook reference

See Davor Vidas (2002), 'The Protocol on Environmental Protection to the Antarctic Treaty: A Ten-Year Review', *Yearbook of International Co-operation on Environment and Development 2002/03*, 51–60.

Convention Concerning the Protection of the World Cultural and Natural Heritage (World Heritage Convention)

Objectives

- to establish an effective system of collective identification, protection, and preservation of cultural and natural heritage around the world considered to be of outstanding universal value to humanity;
- to provide both emergency and long-term protection for monuments, groups of buildings, and sites with historical, aesthetic, archaeological, scientific, ethnological, or anthropological value, as well as outstanding physical, biological, and geological formations, habitats of threatened species of animals and plants, and areas with scientific, conservation, or aesthetic value.

Scope

Legal scope
Open to all states and members of UNESCO (see IGOs), and to other states upon invitation of the UNESCO General Conference. Not open to regional integration organizations.

Geographic scope
Global.

Time and place of adoption

16 November 1972, Paris.

Entry into force

17 December 1975.

Status of participation

170 Parties by 24 April 2002. The Director-General of UNESCO acts as depositary.

Affiliated instruments and organizations

The *World Heritage List*, where 721 sites had been inscribed (554 cultural, 144 natural, and 23 with both cultural and natural attributes), in 124 countries which are Parties to the Convention, by June 2001. The list will be updated following the next meeting of the Committee in late June 2002.

Co-ordination with related instruments
The World Heritage Centre meets regularly with the secretariats of other international conventions, such as the Ramsar Convention, the Convention on Biological Diversity (CBD), the Convention on International Trade in Endangered Species of Wild Fauna and Flora (CITES), the Convention to Combat Desertification (CCD), and the Convention on the Conservation of Migratory Species of Wild Animals (CMS) (see this section), to exchange information and to co-ordinate action. A joint website is established at <http://www.biodiv.org/convention/partners-websites.asp>.

Secretariat

World Heritage Centre,
UNESCO,
7 place de Fontenoy,
F-75352 Paris 07 SP, France
Telephone: +33-1-45681-571/876
Telefax: +33-1-45685570
E-mail: wh-info@unesco.org

Director of the World Heritage Centre
Mr Francesco Bandarin.

Number of staff
22 professionals and ten general service staff under its Regular Programme budget (April 2002).

Finance

Budget
The administrative core budget, provided by UNESCO's Regular Programme, was $US4, 926,600 for the years 2000–01. This figure consists of $3,857,700 for staff and $1,068,900 for direct and indirect programme costs.

Special funds
Through the World Heritage Fund, established in 1978, any individual, nation, or institution may voluntarily contribute (in accordance with their GNP) to the protection of the heritage in countries where national resources are insufficient. The Fund can be used for preparatory assistance (preparation on World Heritage nominations), technical co-operation (directly for projects at World Heritage properties), training, and emergency assistance. The Fund's total annual budget was $4,348,000 in 2001 and is $4,105,000 for 2002 and $3,995,000 for 2003, with contributions from the Parties to the Convention. The main recipients are Parties from the developing countries. In addition there is a World Heritage Emergency Reserve Fund, created in 1994, with a total of $600,000 for 2002 and $600,000 for 2003.

Rules and standards

Each Party shall:

- recognize that the duty of identification, protection, conservation, and transmission to future generations of the cultural and natural heritage belongs primarily to that State;
- integrate the protection of their heritage into comprehensive planning programmes, set up services for the protection of their heritage, develop scientific and technical studies, and take necessary legal, scientific, administrative, and financial steps to protect their heritage;
- assist each other in the protection of the cultural and natural heritage.

Parties are called upon to draw up an inventory of property belonging to their cultural and natural heritage. A World Heritage List of sites of outstanding universal value has been established by the World Heritage Committee, to be updated every year. A second inventory, the List of World Heritage in Danger, includes those monuments, buildings, and sites for which major conservation operations are urgently needed.

Any Party may request assistance for property forming part of its listed heritage, and such assistance may be granted by the World Heritage Fund in the form of studies, provision of experts, training of staff, and supply of equipment, loans, or subsidies.

Monitoring/implementation

Review procedure
Parties report to the UNESCO General Conference in their general reports. A complete report from the World Heritage Committee is submitted to the UNESCO General Conference every two years.

Measurement of the compliance of Parties to commitments are undertaken through the procedures for monitoring of the condition and conservation status of World Heritage properties. This task is undertaken for natural properties by the IUCN – The World Conservation Union (see NGOs), which prepares regular reports for the World Heritage Committee, and for cultural sites by the UNESCO Secretariat, in consultation with the International Council for Monuments and Sites (ICOMOS), the International Centre for the Study of the Preservation and Restoration of Cultural Property (ICCROM), and the countries concerned.

Monitoring is the responsibility of the Parties concerned and commitment to provide periodic reports on the state of conservation of the site is consistent with the principles set out in the Convention. Monitoring, as part of the site management process, remains the responsibility of the Parties where the site is located.

A consensus was reached in 1997 that Parties would provide, in accordance with Article 29 of the Convention, periodic reports on the application of the Convention and the state of conservation of World Heritage properties. The World Heritage Committee, at its twenty-second session held in December 1998, adopted a number of decisions with regard to the submission of periodic reports. The Committee agreed on the periodicity of the reporting, the contents of the reports, and the manner in which it will handle the Parties' reports.

The Committee has chosen a regional approach to periodic reporting as a means to promote regional collaboration and to be able to respond to the specific characteristics of each region. For each of them, periodic reporting strategies will be developed to ensure full participation of Parties, competent institutions, and regional expertise. The World Heritage Centre will synthesize the national reports by regions. In doing so, full use will be made of the available expertise of the advisory bodies (see above), Parties, and competent institutions available within the regions.

The final result of each regional strategy will be a Regional State of the World Heritage Report. The Committee will examine these reports according to a pre-established schedule. This schedule is based on a six-year cycle, and the ongoing examination will take place during the period 2000–06. The Committee responds to the Regional State of the World Heritage Report by formulating recommendations to Parties and drawing conclusions for its own policy and decision making. The response is included in its report to the UNESCO General Conference.

Decision-making bodies

Political

The General Assembly of States Parties meets during the UNESCO General Conference every two years. The Assembly elects the World Heritage Committee for a period of six years. The Committee, which meets once a year, consists of representatives from 21 of the States Parties to the Convention and makes the decisions relating to the implementation of the Convention, including the allocation of funds. It has established a World Heritage Bureau, which performs a number of functions on behalf of the Committee. This consists of seven members and meets twice a year.

Scientific/technical

Technical and scientific advice is provided by NGOs such as IUCN (see NGOs) for the natural heritage and by ICOMOS and ICCROM for the cultural heritage (see above).

Publications

The World Heritage Centre publishes *World Heritage Newsletter* (six times a year) and *World Heritage Review* (six times a year).

UNESCO publishes regularly an up-to-date *World Heritage List* and *List of States Parties*. A map of sites is available from the Secretariat.

Sources on the Internet

<http://whc.unesco.org>

Convention on Biological Diversity (CBD)

Objectives

The objectives of this Convention are:

- the conservation of biological diversity;
- the sustainable use of its components;
- the fair and equitable sharing of the benefits arising out of the utilization of genetic resources, including by appropriate access to genetic resources and by appropriate transfer of relevant technologies (taking into account all rights over those resources and to technologies), as well as by appropriate funding.

Scope

Legal scope
Open to all states and regional economic integration organizations.

Geographic scope
Global.

Time and place of adoption

The agreed text of the Convention was adopted on 22 May 1992 at Nairobi. It was opened for signature in Rio de Janeiro on 5 June 1992.

Entry into force

29 December 1993.

Status of participation

183 Parties, including the European Community, by 1 July 2002. Five Signatories, without ratification, acceptance, or approval.

The Secretary-General of the UN acts as depositary.

Affiliated instruments and organizations

Cartagena Protocol on Biosafety to the Convention on Biological Diversity (Cartagena Protocol on Biosafety), Montreal, 29 January 2000. (Not yet in force.) 21 ratifications by 1 July 2002. 89 Signatories, including the European Community, without ratification, acceptance, or approval. It enters into force on the 90th day after the date of deposit of the 50th instrument of ratification, acceptance, approval, or accession by States or regional economic integration organizations that are Parties to the Convention.

The basic objective of the Protocol is to contribute to ensuring an adequate level of protection in the field of the safe transfer, handling, and use of living modified organisms (LMOs) resulting from modern biotechnology that may have adverse effects on the conservation and sustainable use of biological diversity, taking also into account risks to human health, and specifically focusing on transboundary movements. It establishes an advanced informed agreement (AIA) procedure prior to the first intentional transboundary movement of LMOs for intentional introduction into the environment of the Party of import.

The Conference of the Parties (COP) to the Convention has established an open-ended *ad hoc* Intergovernmental Committee for the Cartagena Protocol on Biosafety (ICCP) with a mandate to undertake, with the support of the Executive Secretary, the preparations necessary for the first meeting of the Parties to the Protocol, at which time the Committee will cease to exist. The first meeting of the ICCP was held in Montpellier, France, from 11 to 15 December 2000, the second meeting was held in Nairobi, Kenya, from 1 to 5 October 2001, and the third meeting of the ICCP was held in The Hague, Netherlands, from 22 to 26 April 2002. Issues discussed at these meetings included decision making; information sharing; capacity building; handling, transport, packaging, and identification of LMOs; compliance; liability and redress for damage resulting from transboundary movements of LMOs; monitoring and reporting; Secretariat; guidance to the financial mechanism; rules of procedure for the meeting of the Parties; and consideration of other issues necessary for the effective implementation of the Protocol.

The Global Environment Facility (GEF) (see IGOs), following its restructuring in 1994, has been designated by the COP as the institutional structure to operate the financial mechanism. The GEF projects have been implemented through the World Bank, the UN Development Programme (UNDP), and the UN Environment Programme (UNEP) (see IGOs), but regional development banks, the UN Industrial Development Organization (UNIDO), and the UN Food and Agriculture Organization (FAO) can also access GEF funds under expanded opportunities. The relationship between the GEF and the Convention has been guided by the Memorandum of Understanding between the COP to the Convention and the Council of the GEF, which was agreed in 1996. The GEF has allocated over $US1.3 billion to biodiversity activities on a grant basis since its establishment.

Co-ordination with related instruments
At its sixth meeting, the COP envisaged that the Convention will fulfil its leadership role in international biodiversity issues, and thus requested the Executive Secretary to collaborate closely with all relevant international instruments and processes to enhance policy coherence, including biodiversity-related conventions (CITES, Wetlands (Ramsar), CMS, and World Heritage conventions (see this section)), the UN Framework Convention on Climate Change (UNFCCC) and the Convention to Combat Desertification (CCD) (see this section), and intergovernmental organizations, such as the Food and Agriculture Organization (FAO), UNESCO (see IGOs), the Intergovernmental Oceanographic Commission (IOC), and others. In many cases, memoranda of co-operation have been signed between respective secretariats.

The secretariats of the biodiversity-related conventions have a joint website at <http://www.biodiv.org/convention/partners-websites.asp> and are collaborating on methodologies for harmonizing national reporting; see <http://www.unep-wcmc.org/conventions/harmonization.htm>. The CBD and the Ramsar Convention on Wetlands are implementing a joint work plan, including the River Basin Initiative. The secretariats of the CBD and the CCD are developing a joint work programme.

The COP called for greater co-operation with the UNFCCC on issues such as drylands, forest biodiversity, coral reefs, and incentive measures. The Intergovernmental Panel on Climate Change (IPCC) has agreed to examine linkages between climate change and biodiversity as a contribution to work under the CBD to prepare scientific advice to the COP on the integration of biodiversity considerations into implementation of the UNFCCC and its Kyoto Protocol.

Convention on Biological Diversity (CBD)

The Secretariat is collaborating with UNESCO on the development of a global initiative on biodiversity education, training, and public awareness.

The COP has repeatedly emphasized the importance of developing a common understanding of the relationship between the CBD and the World Trade Organization (WTO) agreements, including the Agreement on Trade-Related Aspects of Intellectual Property Rights (TRIPs). It has emphasized that further work is required with respect to the relationship between intellectual property rights (IPRs), relevant provisions of TRIPs, and the CBD, in particular those on technology transfer and on traditional knowledge and biological diversity. The COP has invited the WTO to explore the interrelationship between the CBD and the TRIPs Agreement. The WTO has not yet responded to the COP's request, reiterated at the fifth COP, that the Executive Secretary be granted observer status on the TRIPs Council.

The COP has also sought to initiate co-operation with the World Intellectual Property Organization (WIPO) on the issue of IPRs arising from the implementation of the Convention, such as those in access and benefit sharing and Article 8(j) and related provisions.

Secretariat

Secretariat of the Convention on Biological Diversity,
World Trade Centre,
393 rue St Jacques, office 300,
Montréal, Québec H2Y 1N9,
Canada

Telephone:	+1-514-2882220
Telefax:	+1-514-2886588
E-mail:	secretariat@biodiv.org

Executive Secretary
Mr Hamdallah Zedan.

Chief, Division for Implementation and Outreach
Mr Arthur Nogueira.

Number of staff
The COP approved 36 professionals and 26 support staff for the years 2003–04.

Finance

The Secretariat for the CBD is financed from contributions made by Parties and non-Parties to the following three Trust Funds established by the COP: the General Trust Fund for the Convention on Biological Diversity (BY Trust Fund), which is funded from the assessed contributions of Parties to the CBD, based on the UN scales of assessment; the Special Voluntary Trust Fund (BE Trust Fund), for additional voluntary contributions in support of approved activities of the CBD; and the Special Voluntary Trust Fund (BZ Trust Fund), for facilitating participation of Parties in the Convention process. The BE and BZ Trust Funds are voluntary trust funds through which countries and organizations can support important work not provided for within the regular budget.

Budget and trust funds
The core budget for the BY Trust Fund was $US8,594,000 for 2001 and is $10,049,900 for 2002. The COP approved a core budget for the BY Trust Fund of $10,742,500 for 2003 and $11,214,300 for 2004.

The Special Trust Fund for additional voluntary contributions in support of approved activities was set at $2,547,500 for 2001, and is established at $2,128,900 for 2002, $4,186,800 for 2003, and $2,391,100 for 2004.

The Special Voluntary Trust Fund for facilitating participation of developing-country Parties in the Convention process was set at $2,011,600 for 2001, and is established at $2,988,700 for 2002, $3,148,200 for 2003, and $2,391,100 for 2004.

Status of contributions to the Trust Fund for the Convention
All States Parties are required to contribute to the trust funds of the Convention. States not Party to the Convention, as well as governmental, intergovernmental, and non-governmental organizations and other sources, are also urged to contribute to the trust funds.

As of May 2002, unpaid pledges prior to 2002 for the core budget (BY Trust Fund) were $882,063. Canada paid additional con-

Cartagena Protocol on Biosafety

tributions of $US600,000 to the core budget prior to 2002, and pledged additional contributions of $1,000,000 for the year 2002. The USA also pledged contributions of $175,000 to the core budget for the year 2002.

Countries that pledged to make additional voluntary contributions for the years 2001–02 were Australia, Canada, the Central African Republic, Denmark, the European Commission, France, Germany, Japan, New Zealand, Norway, Spain, Sweden, Switzerland, the Netherlands, the United Kingdom, and the USA. FAO also pledged towards the secondment of a Programme Officer to the Secretariat of the CBD in 1999.

Rules and standards

Each Contracting Party shall:

- develop national strategies, plans, or programmes for the conservation and sustainable use of biological diversity or adapt for this purpose existing strategies, plans, and programmes which shall reflect, *inter alia*, the measures set out in the Convention relevant to the Party concerned;
- integrate, as far as possible and as appropriate, the conservation and sustainable use of biological diversity into the relevant sectoral and cross-sectoral plans, programmes, and policies;
- identify components of biological diversity important for its conservation and sustainable use;
- monitor the components of biological diversity through sampling and other techniques;
- identify processes and categories of activities which have or are likely to have significant adverse impacts on the conservation and sustainable use of biological diversity;
- establish a system of protected areas or areas where special measures need to be taken to conserve biological diversity (*in situ* conservation);
- adopt measures for the *ex situ* conservation of components of biological diversity, preferably in the country of origin of such components;
- integrate consideration of the conservation and sustainable use of biological resources into national decision making;
- adopt economically and socially sound measures that act as incentives for the conservation and sustainable use of biological diversity;
- establish and maintain programmes for scientific and technical education and training in measures for the identification, conservation, and sustainable use of biological diversity and its components and provide support for such education and training for the specific needs of developing countries;
- introduce appropriate procedures requiring environmental impact assessment of its proposed projects that are likely to have significant adverse effects on biological diversity with a view to avoiding or minimizing such effects;
- create conditions to facilitate access to genetic resources for environmentally sound uses by other Contracting Parties;
- take legislative, administrative, or policy measures with the aim of sharing in a fair and equitable way the results of research and development and the benefits arising from the commercial and other utilization of genetic resources with the Contracting Party providing such resources;
- take legislative, administrative, or policy measures with the aim that Parties which provide genetic resources are provided access to and transfer of technology which makes use of those resources, on mutually agreed terms, including technology protected by patents and other intellectual property rights;
- promote technical and scientific co-operation with other Parties in implementing the Convention through the development and implementation of national policies;
- take legislative, administrative, or policy measures, as appropriate, to provide for the effective participation in biotechnological research activities by those Parties, especially developing countries, which provide the genetic resources for such research, and where feasible in such Parties;
- take all practical measures to promote and advance priority access on a fair and equitable basis by Parties, especially developing countries, to the results and benefits arising from biotechnologies based upon genetic resources provided by those Contracting Parties. Such access shall be on

mutually agreed terms.

The developed-country Parties shall:

- provide new and additional financial resources to enable developing-country Parties to meet the agreed full incremental costs to them of implementing measures which fulfil the obligations of the Convention.

Monitoring/implementation

Review procedure

The Parties shall present reports of measures they have taken for the implementation of the provisions of the Convention and their effectiveness in meeting the objectives of the Convention. The first reports were due to be submitted by 31 December 1997, and the second by 15 May 2001. As of May 2002, the Secretariat had received 130 first reports and 74 second reports from Parties and States.

At its fifth meeting, the COP invited countries to prepare detailed thematic reports on items scheduled for in-depth consideration at forthcoming meetings of the COP. For the sixth meeting (2002) these were alien species, benefit sharing, and forest ecosystems. As of May 2002, the Secretariat had received 53 thematic reports on alien invasive species, 13 thematic reports on access and benefit sharing, and 40 thematic reports on forest ecosystems. Parties are invited to submit thematic reports on mountain ecosystems, protected areas or areas where special measures need to be taken to conserve biological diversity, and transfer of technology and technology cooperation for consideration by the seventh meeting of the COP.

Based on the reports received, the Secretariat has been requested by the COP to prepare synthesis and analysis of the state of implementation of the Convention.

Decision-making bodies

Political

The COP, the governing body of the Convention, consists of representatives of Parties to the Convention. The COP initially met every year but decided, at its fifth meeting, that ordinary meetings shall be held every two years.

The COP considers and undertakes any action required for the achievement of the purpose of the Convention. This includes:

- reviewing scientific, technical, and technological advice;
- considering reports by Parties on their implementation of the Convention;
- considering and adopting protocols, amendments, or annexes;
- establishing such subsidiary bodies as may be necessary for the implementation of the Convention.

Decision on matters of procedure are taken by a majority vote of Parties present and voting. However, the Parties have not been able to reach agreement on voting procedures for all matters of substance. The effect of this is to make all substantive matters subject to agreement by consensus.

Observers may participate without the right to vote unless one-third of the Parties present object. Observers may include states not being Parties, or any body or agency, whether governmental or non-governmental, which is qualified in fields relating to conservation or sustainable use of biological diversity and which has informed the Secretariat of its wish to be represented.

The COP has met six times so far, respectively in Nassau (November–December 1994), Jakarta (November 1995), Buenos Aires (November 1996), Bratislava (May 1998), Nairobi (May 2000), and The Hague (April 2002). The seventh meeting will be held in Kuala Lumpur in the first quarter of 2004.

Scientific/technical

The Subsidiary Body on Scientific, Technical, and Technological Advice (SBSTTA), composed of experts representing governments, was established to provide the COP and, as appropriate, its other subsidiary bodies with timely advice relating to the implementation of the Convention. This body comprises government representatives competent in the relevant field of expertise. It has met seven times, in Paris (September 1995) and in Montreal (September 1996, September 1997, June 1999, February 2000, March 2001, and November 2001). The next meeting will be held in Montreal in March 2003.

The *Ad Hoc* Working Group on Article 8 (j) and related provisions was established by the COP at its fourth meeting to address implementation of the CBD's provisions on traditional knowledge and biological diversity. The Working Group held its first meeting in Seville, Spain, in March 2000 and its second meeting in Montreal in February 2002. On the basis of the Working Group's recommendations, the COP adopted a programme of work on traditional knowledge and the recommendations for the conduct of cultural, environmental, and social impact assessments regarding developments proposed to take place on, or which are likely to impact on, sacred sites and on lands and waters traditionally occupied or used by indigenous and local communities. The COP also decided to prepare a composite report on the status and trends regarding the knowledge, innovations, and practices of indigenous and local communities relevant to the conservation and sustainable use of biodiversity. The Working Group's next meeting is scheduled for January 2004.

The *Ad Hoc* Open-ended Working Group on access and benefit sharing was established by the COP at its fifth meeting, with the mandate to develop guidelines and other approaches. Building on the work of the Panel of Experts, the Working Group held its first meeting in Bonn, Germany, from 22 to 26 October 2001, and prepared the Bonn Guidelines on access to genetic resources and fair and equitable sharing of the benefits arising out of their utilization and an action plan for capacity building for access to genetic resources and benefit sharing, which were both adopted by the COP at its sixth meeting. The Working Group will meet again in December 2003.

In addition, a number of *ad hoc* technical expert groups on thematic areas have been established under the auspices of SBSTTA. These currently include expert groups on marine and coastal protected areas, mariculture, dryland biodiversity, and forest biodiversity.

Publications

- *Convention on Biological Diversity Handbook* (2001);
- *Global Biodiversity Outlook* (2001), a periodical report on the state of biodiversity world-wide and the implementation of the Convention.

Sources on the Internet

<http://www.biodiv.org>

Convention on the Conservation of Migratory Species of Wild Animals (CMS)

Objectives

To conserve those species of wild animals that migrate across or outside national boundaries by developing and implementing co-operative agreements, prohibiting the taking of endangered species, conserving habitat, and controlling other adverse factors.

Scope

Legal scope

Open to all states and regional economic integration organizations. Membership of subsidiary 'Agreements' under the Convention is open to all Range States (and the relevant regional integration organizations) for the species covered, including States that are not Parties to the parent Convention.

Geographic scope

Global.

Time and place of adoption

23 June 1979, Bonn.

Entry into force

1 November 1983.

Status of participation

79 Parties, including the European Community, by 1 February 2002. Four Signatories without ratification, acceptance, or approval.

Instruments of accession to be deposited with the government of Germany.

Affiliated instruments and organizations

• *Agreement on the Conservation of Seals in the Wadden Sea*, Bonn, 16 October 1990. Entered into force on 1 October 1991. Three Parties (Denmark, Germany, and the Netherlands) by 1 March 2002. No Signatories without ratification, acceptance, or accession;

• *Agreement on the Conservation of Bats in Europe (EUROBATS)*, London, 4 December 1991. Entered into force on 16 January 1994. 25 Parties (Albania, Bulgaria, Croatia, the Czech Republic, Denmark, Finland, France, Germany, Hungary, Ireland, Lithuania, Luxembourg, the Republic of Macedonia, Malta, Moldova, Monaco, the Netherlands, Norway, Poland, Portugal, Romania, Slovakia, Sweden, Ukraine, and the United Kingdom) by 1 January 2002. One Signatory to the Agreement (Belgium) without ratification, acceptance, or accession. Additional information is available at the EUROBATS Secretariat's website at <http://www.eurobats.org>;

• *Agreement on the Conservation of Small Cetaceans in the Baltic and North Seas (ASCOBANS)*, New York, 13 September 1991. Entered into force on 29 March 1994. Eight Parties (Belgium, Denmark, Finland, Germany, the Netherlands, Poland, Sweden, and the United Kingdom) by 1 March 2002. One Signatory (the European Community) without ratification, acceptance, or accession. Additional information is available at the ASCOBANS Secretariat's website at <http://www.ascobans.org>;

• *Agreement on the Conservation of African-Eurasian Migratory Waterbirds (AEWA)*, The Hague, 16 June 1995. Entered into force on 1 November 1999. 32 Parties (Benin, Bulgaria, the Republic of Congo, Croatia, Denmark, Egypt, Finland, Gambia, Georgia, Germany, Guinea, Jordan, Kenya, the Republic of Macedonia, Mali, Mauritius, Moldova, Monaco, the Netherlands, Niger, Romania, Senegal, Slovakia, South Africa, Spain, Sudan, Sweden, Switzerland, Tanzania, Togo, Uganda, and the United Kingdom) by 1 March 2002. (Mauritius and Sudan are neither Parties nor Signatories to the CMS.) Eight Signatories to the Agreement (Belgium, the European Community, France, Greece, Ireland, Luxembourg, Morocco, and Ukraine) without ratification, acceptance, or accession. There were 54 Signatories to the Final Act, including the European Community. Additional information is available at the AEWA Secretariat's website at <http://www.unep-wcmc.org/AEWA>;

• *Agreement on the Conservation of Cetaceans of the Black Sea, Mediterranean Sea, and Contiguous Atlantic Area (ACCOBAMS)*, Monaco, 24 November 1996. Entered into force on 1 June 2001. Ten Parties (Albania, Bulgaria, Croatia, Georgia, Malta, Monaco, Morocco, Romania, Spain, and Tunisia) by 1 February 2002. Five Signatories (Cyprus, France, Greece, Italy, and Portugal) without ratification, acceptance, or accession. There were 16 Signatories to the Final Act, including the European Community. Additional information is available at the ACCOBAMS Interim Secretariat's website at <http://www.accobams.mc>;

• *Agreement on the Conservation of Albatross and Petrels (ACAP)*, Canberra, 19 June 2001. (Not yet in force.) Two states (Australia and New Zealand) had ratified by 1 April 2002. Five Signatories (Brazil, Chile, France, Peru, and the United Kingdom) without ratification, acceptance, or accession. Expected to enter into force during 2002. Additional information is available at the ACAP Interim Secretariat's website at <http://www.ea.gov.au/biodiversity/international/albatross/index.html>.

Memoranda of understanding have also been concluded with a view to promoting the conservation of the western- and central-Asian populations of the Siberian crane (1 July 1993), the slender-billed curlew (10 September 1994), the marine turtles of the Atlantic coast of Africa (May 1999), the marine turtles and their habitats of the Indian Ocean and South-East Asia (July 2000), and the middle-European populations of the great bustard (November 2000).

Appendix I covers endangered migratory species, which benefit from strict protection.

Appendix II covers migratory species which have an unfavourable conservation status and which require international agreements for their conservation and management.

UNEP (see IGOs) provides the Secretariat and administers the trust fund for the Convention. Institutional arrangements for Agreements vary, being undertaken by various international organizations or governments.

Co-ordination with related instruments
Agreements between Range States should take account of related instruments such as the Ramsar Convention (see this section). A joint website, covering CITES, Ramsar, World Heritage, CBD (see this section), and CMS Conventions, is established at <http://www.biodiv.org/convention/partners-websites.asp>.

Secretariat

UNEP/CMS Secretariat,
United Nations Premises in Bonn,
Martin-Luther-King-Straße 8,
D-53175 Bonn,
Germany
Telephone: +49-228-815240-1/2
Telefax: +49-228-8152449
E-mail: cms@cms.unep.de

Executive Secretary
Mr Arnulf Müller-Helmbrecht.

Deputy Executive Secretary
Mr Douglas Hykle.

Number of staff
Five professionals and six support staff (April 2002).

Finance

The Convention is financed entirely by the Parties, on the basis of the UN scale, with a maximum of 25 per cent by any one Party. The Agreements are also to be financed by the Parties to them, but the basis varies.

Budget
The Conference of the Parties (COP), at its sixth meeting in November 1999, adopted a core budget of US$1,454,595 for 2001 and $1,770,430 for 2002. It also agreed to withdraw an additional $100,000 from the Trust Fund in order to finance consultancies during the biennium.

Special funds
The core budget includes funds to assist developing-country participants to attend meetings of experts and of the Standing Committee (see below). Further, some funding support for representatives of developing-country Parties for attendance at meetings of the COP and of the Scientific Council has been made available by a few European governments.

The size of the Trust Fund is variable (depending on contributions from member States).

Rules and standards

With respect to endangered migratory species listed in Appendix I, Parties that are Range States are to prohibit the taking of animals belonging to such species, with a few exceptions. Range States are to endeavour to conserve and, where possible, restore the habitats of these species; eliminate, prevent, or minimize impediments to their migration; and prevent, reduce, or control factors endangering them.

'Agreements' to benefit species listed in Appendix II are generally regional, sometimes on a north–south gradient, but taken together should have a global effect. These Agreements, within the framework of the 'umbrella' Convention, can stipulate precise conservation measures and implementation mechanisms.

The Convention provides for reservations on joining and with regard to species listed in the Appendices when they are amended. The Agreement on the Conservation of Seals in the Wadden Sea allows no reservations, whereas the Agreements on Bats in Europe, Small Cetaceans in the Baltic and North Seas, and African-Eurasian Migratory Waterbirds allow for reservations on species covered.

Monitoring/implementation

Review procedure
Parties to the Convention should inform the COP every three years of measures they are taking to implement the Convention for species listed in the Appendices. Provision of information has improved steadily. 44 per cent of the Parties submitted reports to the 1999 meeting. These reports are of varying comprehensiveness. Over the years CMS and its various agreements have developed approaches to reporting and information management that, although similar, are not integrated. The CMS Secretariat is now

leading efforts to synthesize and integrate the information contained in the national reports provided to the secretariats, and is developing a more integrated approach to reporting on migratory species. The reports, which are made public, are reviewed by the Secretariat and by the COP. No reviews are made by independent bodies.

Parties must also inform the Secretariat of exceptions made to the prohibition on the taking of Appendix I species, but, although the Secretariat is aware informally of some cases of such taking, it has never been informed by Parties officially.

Parties are required to inform the Secretariat of those species in the Appendices of which they consider themselves to be Range States. The Secretariat circulates Range State lists to Parties and experts for comments.

Observations or inspections
CMS starts investigations in cases of alleged non-compliance, thus preparing for possible recommendation by the COP in accordance with Article III (6) of CMS.

Trade measures
No provisions on trade sanctions to penalize Parties for non-compliance.

Dispute-settlement mechanisms
The Convention provides dispute-settlement procedures, that is, bilateral negotiation, followed by referral to the permanent Court of Arbitration. So far such disputes are not known to have arisen.

Decision-making bodies

Political
The COP is the decision-making organ and can amend the instruments under the Convention and adopt resolutions to improve its implementation. It meets every three years. The Standing Committee, consisting of regional representatives and the depositary government, provides general policy direction and carries out activities on behalf of the Conference between the triennial meetings. The seventh meeting of the COP will be held in Bonn from 18 to 24 September 2002.

Amendments to the Convention may be adopted by the COP by a two-thirds majority of members present and voting. They enter into force in regard to all Parties 90 days after the meeting, except for those Parties which file a written reservation within the 90-day period.

Scientific/technical
A Scientific Council is established to provide advice on scientific matters to the COP, to the Secretariat, and, when instructed, to any Party. It can recommend research, provide advice on migratory species listed in Appendices I and II, and advocate specific conservation and management measures to be included in agreements. The Council consists of experts (presently 70) appointed by individual Parties and by the Conference, and may include experts from non-governmental organizations in its working groups.

Agreements may provide for advisory bodies or advice from the Convention's Scientific Council.

Publications

The Secretariat publishes a list of Range States of all migratory species included in the two Appendices, a regular *CMS Bulletin*, and a brochure explaining the aims and operation of the Convention.

Sources on the Internet

<http://www.wcmc.org.uk/cms>

Convention on International Trade in Endangered Species of Wild Fauna and Flora (CITES)

Objectives

• to ensure, through international co-operation, that the international trade in species of wild fauna and flora does not threaten survival in the wild of the species concerned;
• to protect endangered species from over-exploitation by means of a system of import–export permits issued by a management authority under the control of a scientific authority.

Scope

Legal scope
Open to all states recognized by the UN. Not yet open to regional integration organizations.

Geographic scope
Global.

Time and place of adoption

3 March 1973, Washington, DC.

Entry into force

1 July 1975.

Status of participation

158 Parties by 1 May 2002. Two Signatories without ratification, acceptance, or approval.

Instruments of accession to be deposited with the government of Switzerland.

Affiliated instruments and organizations

• *Amendment Protocol*, Bonn 1979. Entered into force on 13 April 1987. Related to financial provisions;
• *Amendment Protocol*, Gaborone 1983. (Not yet in force.) 40 of the States that were Parties on 30 April 1983 had accepted this Amendment by 1 May 2002. 54 instruments of ratification, acceptance, approval, or accession are required for it to enter into force. Related to accession to the Convention by regional economic integration organizations;
• *Appendix I* offers the highest protection, and prohibits (with limited exemptions) the commercial international trade in wild-caught specimens of species threatened with extinction;
• *Appendix II* assigns the responsibility to exporting States to control, through a permit system, such trade in species which could become threatened with extinction if there were no such restriction;
• *Appendix III* requires Parties to control trade in specimens of species which have been protected in certain States and listed by those States;
• *Appendix IV* contains a model export permit. This is no longer used, and a new permit model is included in Resolution Conf. 10.2 (Rev.).

A principal decision of the ninth Conference of the Parties (CoP) at Fort Lauderdale in November 1994 approved new criteria for the inclusion of species in Appendices I and II.

Co-ordination with related instruments
The most important co-ordination is with the International Criminal Police Organization (ICPO-Interpol), the World Customs Organization (WCO), and the Convention on Biological Diversity (CBD) (see this section). A joint website, covering CMS, Ramsar, World Heritage, CBD (see this section), and CITES Conventions, is established at <http://www.biodiv.org/convention/partners-websites.as>.

TRAFFIC (Trade Records Analysis of Flora and Fauna in Commerce), UN Environment Programme-World Conservation Monitoring Centre (UNEP-WCMC), and IUCN – The World Conservation Union (see NGOs) are a few of the organizations which provide technical and scientific support to the Secretariat, the Parties, and the various CITES Committees to ensure that the Convention is implemented successfully.

Secretariat

UNEP/CITES Secretariat,
International Environment House,
15 chemin des Anémones,
CH-1219 Châtelaine, Geneva,
Switzerland

Telephone: +41-22-91781-39/40
Telefax: +41-22-7973417
E-mail: cites@unep.ch

Secretary-General
Mr Willem Wijnstekers.

Legal and Trade Policy Officer
Mr Juan Carlos Vasquez.

Number of staff
27 in total, of which more than one half are professionals (May 2002).

Finance

The budget is covered entirely by contributions of the Parties to a Trust Fund (established in 1984) administered by UNEP. Contributions from Parties are assessed in accordance with the UN scale of contributions.

Budget
The administrative core budget was SFr.10,017,244 in 2000 and Fr.7,594,800 in 2001, and is Fr.8,921,350 in 2002.

Counterpart contributions
The purpose of these contributions is to provide for specific projects not necessarily covered by the budget approved by the Parties. Generally, these projects involve surveys of species or improving enforcement of the Convention. Unlike contributions to the Trust Fund, money for the projects can come from Parties, but also from private industry, NGOs, and any individual who wishes to donate funds, but these have to be approved by the Standing Committee. The top five contributors are Japan, the European Commission, the United States Fish and Wildlife Service, the United Kingdom, and the Netherlands.

Rules and standards

Permits are required for species listed in Appendices I and II stating that export–import will not be detrimental to the survival of the species. Trade in species listed in Appendix III is regulated through the issuing of export permits where trade is from

the State that listed the species, or otherwise through the issuance of certificates of origin (see below).

If a country does not accept the placing of a species in a certain Appendix, it may enter a reservation (within a specified period of time).

Each Party is required to maintain records of trade in species covering:

- names and addresses of exporters and importers;
- numbers and types of permits and certificates granted;
- states with which trade has occurred;
- numbers or quantities and types of specimens and names of species traded.

Monitoring/implementation

Review procedure

The Parties have an obligation to provide an annual report on all trade in species of flora and fauna listed in the Appendices to the Convention and to provide a biennial report on legislative, regulatory, and administrative measures taken.

Not all Parties meet the reporting requirements; and even those which do submit annual reports often submit them long after the agreed deadlines. Moreover, many of the reports submitted are incomplete.

The annual statistical reports are a vital tool for monitoring both the levels of trade in the listed species and the implementation of the Convention. A comparison of the reports of each Party with those of the other Parties often reveals information on trade of which it was unaware, and can help to identify violations. 84 national reports (58 per cent of the Parties) for 1999 were submitted within the deadline on 31 October 2000. By 1999, a total of 17 Parties had never submitted an annual report, three of whom—Afghanistan, Djibouti, and Guinea-Bissau—have been Parties for more than five years. A further seven Parties, six of whom were Parties prior to 1995, have submitted 25 per cent or fewer of the required reports. 97 national reports (65 per cent of the Parties) for 2000 were submitted within the deadline on 31 October 2001. The annual reports are public.

The trade data or other information in national reports are reviewed by the Secretariat, the Animals and Plants Committees, and the CoP, as well as by independent non-governmental organizations such as WWF, IUCN (see NGOs), and TRAFFIC under contract with the Secretariat. The reviews are public after they have been distributed to the Parties.

Each Party is required to establish one or more *Management Authority* to certify that the species has been obtained within the State's protection laws and that shipment will not be harmful to the living specimen concerned. In addition, each Party is required to designate one or more *Scientific Authority* which provides, for example in matters related to the issuance of permits or certificates, advice to its Management Authority on whether the import or export will be detrimental to the survival of the species involved.

If the Secretariat considers that the provisions are not being correctly implemented, it is obliged to inform the Management Authority of the Party concerned, which should reply with the necessary information within one month.

Data and information-system programmes

The Wildlife Trade Monitoring Unit is a data management unit of the UNEP World Conservation Monitoring Centre (WCMC), the world biodiversity information and assessment centre of UNEP. A website is established at <http://www.unep-wcmc.org>. It maintains and updates a database containing all the information from the annual reports.

Trade measures

Although the Convention does not include any provisions to penalize Parties for non-compliance, the Parties have preferred to avoid being cited in the alleged infractions report. Moreover, in the most serious cases of non-compliance, the CoP and/or the Standing Committee, advised by the Secretariat, has gone so far as to recommend to the Parties not to accept or issue permits for trade from or to a particular country, pending the correction of the implementation problems that have been identified.

Decision-making bodies

Political

The CoP to CITES meets about every two years to examine progress in the restoration and conservation of protected species and to revise the Appendices as appropriate. Amendments to Appendices enter into force automatically in accordance with a procedure not requiring ratification. The majority of decisions (including changes in the Appendices) require a two-thirds majority, with each Party having one vote. The eleventh CoP was held from 10 to 20 April 2000 in Nairobi. The twelfth CoP should be held in Santiago, Chile, from 3 to 15 November 2002.

The CITES Standing Committee (SC), which meets annually, is elected at the CoP and is composed of representatives from the major geographic regions of CITES (the number of representatives from each region depends on the number of Parties in that region); one representative from the Depositary Government; one from the past host Party; and one from the next host Party. By April 2001 it had 16 members.

The SC provides policy guidelines to the Secretariat; proposes meetings and agendas; oversees the Secretariat's budget and fund-raising activities; appoints working groups; co-ordinates working groups and committees as required; drafts resolutions; acts as the Bureau of the meetings of the CoP; and reports to the CoP on SC activities.

Scientific/technical

The Animals Committee and Plants Committee meet annually and are composed of persons elected by the regions. A Nomenclature Committee is composed of persons chosen by the Parties. All committees have a chairman and vice-chair elected by the CoP.

Publications

CITES World (newsletter) (bi-annually). Other CITES publications, reports on surveys, Identification Manual, etc., are available through:

IUCN Publications Services Unit,
219c Huntington Road,
Cambridge CB3 0DL,
United Kingdom

Telephone: +44-1223-277894
Telefax: +44-1223-277175
E-mail: info@books.iucn.org
Internet: <http://www.iucn.org/bookstore>

Sources on the Internet

<http://www.cites.org>

Convention on Wetlands of International Importance especially as Waterfowl Habitat (Ramsar Convention)

Objectives
The Convention's mission is the conservation and wise use of wetlands by national action and international co-operation as a means to achieving sustainable development throughout the world.

Scope
Legal scope
Membership open to all member States of the UN or members of the specialized agencies and the International Atomic Energy Agency (IAEA) (see IGOs). Not open to regional integration organizations.

Geographic scope
Global.

Time and place of adoption
2 February 1971, Ramsar.

Entry into force
21 December 1975.

Status of participation
131 Parties by 8 April 2002. No Signatories without ratification, acceptance, or approval.

The Director-General of UNESCO (see IGOs) acts as depositary.

Affiliated instruments and organizations
• *Protocol to Amend the Convention on Wetlands of International Importance especially as Waterfowl Habitat, Paris, 1982.* Entered into force on 1 October 1986. The main objective of the Protocol is to establish a procedure for amending the Convention;
• *Amendments to Arts. 6 and 7 of the Convention, Regina, 1987.* Entered into force on 1 May 1994;
• *List of Wetlands of International Importance (Ramsar List).* The Ramsar List included 1148 wetland sites, totalling more than 96 million hectares, by 8 April 2002. The Ramsar Bureau collaborates closely with the IUCN, WWF International (see NGOs), Wetlands International, and Birdlife International.

Co-ordination with related instruments
The Ramsar Convention Bureau meets regularly and has bilateral memoranda of co-operation with the secretariats of other international conventions on nature conservation, such as the Convention on Biological Diversity (CBD), the Convention on International Trade in Endangered Species of Wild Fauna and Flora (CITES), the World Heritage Convention, the Convention to Combat Desertification (CCD), and the Convention on the Conservation of Migratory Species of Wild Animals (CMS) (see this section), to exchange information and to co-ordinate action. A joint website for biodiversity-related conventions is established at <http://www.biodiv.org/convention/partners-websites.as>. The Bureau also co-operates with the UNESCO Man and the Biosphere Programme.

Secretariat
Ramsar Convention Bureau,
Rue Mauverney 28,
CH-1196 Gland,
Switzerland
Telephone: +41-22-9990170
Telefax: +41-22-9990169
E-mail: ramsar@ramsar.org

Secretary-General
Mr Delmar Blasco.

Information Officer
Dr Dwight Peck.

Part of the Ramsar Secretariat is located at:
Mediterranean Wetlands Initiative (MedWet) Co-ordination Unit,
Villa Kazouli,
Lambraki & Kifissias,
GR-14561 Kifissia,
Greece
Telephone: +30-10-80809270
Telefax: +30-10-80809274
E-mail: kouvelis@medwet.org

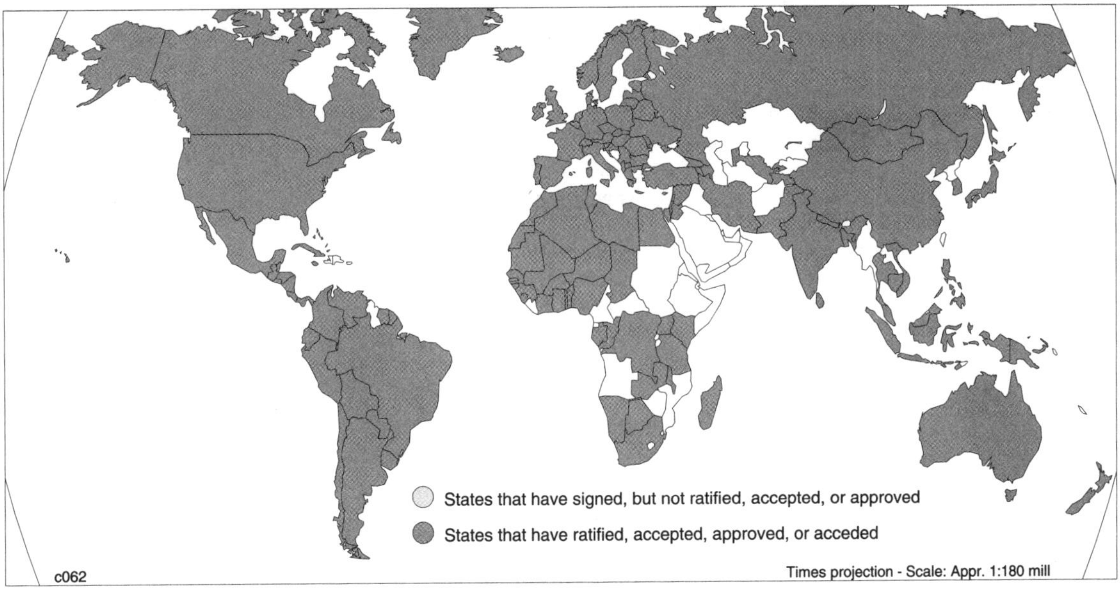

Number of staff
Eight professionals, eight support staff, and four interns at the Bureau (April 2002). The Bureau has two additional professionals on a non-permanent basis seconded by outside agencies, and there are two professionals and two support staff at the MedWet Co-ordination Unit (April 2002).

Finance

Income derives from the Contracting Parties according to the UN scale of assessments for the core funding. Specific projects of a similar magnitude are also undertaken outside the core budget.

Budget
The core budget was SFr. 3,045,000 in 2000 and Fr.3,106,000 in 2001, and is Fr.3,168,000 in 2002.

Special funds
The Wetland Conservation Fund, later renamed the Ramsar Convention's Small Grants Fund (SGF), was launched by the Convention in 1990 to assist developing countries by offering financial benefits as well as expert services in the implementation of the Convention. During its first year of existence (1991) contributions amounting to SFr.271,246 were received, and by March 2002 the contributions totalled Fr.4,926,092. Disbursements were Fr.556,304 in 2001. The strongest contributors over the period 1991–2001 were: Austria, Denmark, France, Germany, Iceland, Japan, the Netherlands, Norway, Sweden, Switzerland, the United Kingdom, and the USA, in addition to WWF International, Wetlands International, and the Netherlands Directorate General for International Co-operation.

14 projects were approved in 2001. Others were partially funded or referred to other agencies for further study or funding. Recipients in 2001 were Algeria, Belarus, Bulgaria, El Salvador, Guatemala, Lithuania, Mongolia, Morocco, Papua New Guinea, the Russian Federation, the Slovak Republic, Syria, Tanzania, and Yugoslavia.

A Wetlands for the Future Fund, a capacity-building programme for Latin America, is administered by the Bureau jointly with the US State Department and the US Fish and Wildlife Service, which are contributing to the Fund. Disbursements were $US750,000 in its first three-year phase. The Fund began its second three-year phase in 1999 and still disburses $250,000 per year.

Rules and standards

Parties shall:

• designate at least one national wetland for inclusion in a *List of Wetlands of International Importance*;

• formulate and implement their planning so as to promote the conservation of the wetlands included in the List, and as far as possible the wise use of wetlands in their territory;

• establish wetland nature reserves, co-operate in the exchange of information, and train personnel for wetlands management;

• co-operate with other countries concerning shared wetlands and shared wetland species.

Monitoring/implementation

Review procedure
Parties report to each Conference of the Contracting Parties (COP) according to an agreed format. Reports are also required when the ecological character of a listed site is changing or is likely to change so that international consultations may be held on the problem. The reports are due before each triennial meeting of the COP. In 1992, 51 national reports (67 per cent of the Parties) on implementation were submitted by the Parties as required under the Convention for the 1993 meeting. 90 national reports were received from the 92 Parties in advance of the COP in March 1996. Of 113 Parties at the time of the seventh COP in May 1999, 107 submitted national reports, three did not submit national reports, and three, having only just joined the Convention, were exempted from submitting a report. 18 reports were received within the deadline on 1 September 1998. The deadline for the submission of national reports for the eighth COP, covering activities carried out in 1999–2001, was 28 February

2002. 25 reports were received within the deadline. 128 Parties were due to report in advance of the eighth COP. The reports are available on the website (see below). Reviews of data or information in national reports by the secretariat and the Conference are not public, but the Bureau's analyses and the Conference's discussions of national reports are published in proceedings.

A Ramsar Advisory Mission, formally adopted by Recommendation 4.7 of the 1990 COP, is a technical mechanism to provide assistance to member States in the management and conservation of listed sites whose ecological character is threatened. The Ramsar Advisory Mission mechanism was formerly known as the Monitoring Procedure and the Management Guidance Procedure.

In 1990, at Montreux, the COP called for the maintenance of a Record of Ramsar sites where changes in ecological character have occurred, are occurring, or are likely to occur.

The Ramsar Advisory Mission was applied during 2000 to one Ramsar site in Tunisia and one in Senegal (joint missions with IUCN and the the World Heritage Centre) and to one site in Spain (purely Ramsar mission) and during 2001 to one Ramsar site in the Czech Republic, one in Togo, one in Germany, one in Bulgaria (joint mission with IUCN and the World Heritage Centre), one in Argentina, one in the United Kingdom, and one in India.

Observations or inspections
None by the Convention as such.

Environmental monitoring programmes
A Ramsar database has been elaborated with an agreed classification and data system for all listed wetland sites.

Trade measures
No provisions on trade sanctions to penalize Parties for non-compliance.

Dispute-settlement mechanisms
No provisions on dispute settlement. Disputes are resolved by discussions at the COP, followed by Conference recommendations.

Decision-making bodies

Political
The Conference of the Contracting Parties (COP) is the governing body and meets every three years. The implementation of the Convention is reviewed at these meetings. The seventh meeting of the COP was held in San José, Costa Rica, 10–18 May 1999, and the eighth meeting will be held in Valencia, Spain, 18–26 November 2002. Secretariat functions are performed by the Ramsar Convention Bureau, responsible to a Standing Committee of the Contracting Parties.

Scientific/technical
An expert group, the Scientific and Technical Review Panel, composed of independent scientific experts chosen to represent each of the six Ramsar regions of the world, has been established to guide policy decisions by the COP. It normally meets once a year.

Participation by non-governmental observers is encouraged both in meetings of the Contracting Parties and in the Panel. Partner NGOs are now full members of the Panel, but observers at the COP and in the Standing Committee.

Publications

In addition to annual reports and conference proceedings, the Ramsar Bureau publishes:

- *Ramsar Newsletter* (twice a year);
- *Directory of Wetlands of International Importance* (triennial);
- *Towards the Wise Use of Wetlands*, a collection of guidelines and case-studies;
- *The Legal Development of the Ramsar Convention* (1995);
- *The Economic Valuation of Wetlands* (1997);
- *Wetlands, Biodiversity, and the Ramsar Convention* (1997);
- *Ramsar Toolkit: Handbooks for the Wise Use of Wetlands* (2000).

Sources on the Internet

<http://www.ramsar.org>

Yearbook reference

See Michael Bowman (2002), 'The Ramsar Convention on Wetlands: Has It Made a Difference?', *Yearbook of International Co-operation on Environment and Development 2002/03*, 61–8.

Convention to Combat Desertification (CCD)

Objectives

To combat desertification and mitigate the effects of drought in countries experiencing serious drought and/or desertification, particularly in Africa, through effective actions at all levels, supported by international co-operation and partnership arrangements, in the framework of an integrated approach which is consistent with Agenda 21, with a view to contributing to the achievements of sustainable development in affected areas.

Scope

Legal scope
Open to all member States of the UN or any of its specialized agencies, Parties to the Statute of the International Court of Justice, and regional economic integration organizations.

Geographic scope
Global.

Time and place of adoption

17 June 1994, Paris.

Entry into force

26 December 1996.

Status of participation

179 Parties, including the European Community, by 10 June 2002. No Signatories without ratification, accession, acceptance, or approval.

The Secretary-General of the UN acts as depositary of the Convention.

Affiliated instruments and organizations

The full title of the Convention is the United Nations Convention to Combat Desertification in those Countries Experiencing Serious Drought and/or Desertification, Particularly in Africa.

The Convention contains five regional implementation annexes, for Africa, Asia, Latin America and the Caribbean, the northern Mediterranean, and Central and Eastern Europe. The annex covering Central and Eastern Europe constitutes the latest addition to the text of the Convention and was adopted at the fourth Conference of the Parties (COP). The African Annex is the most elaborate, both in form and content, of all the annexes. It comprises 19 articles and addresses a broad range of issues, including commitments and obligations of both African and developed-country Parties. Explicit reference is made with regard to technical assistance and co-operation to ensure that preference is given to the utilization of less costly local experts. Emphasis is placed on the need for increased co-ordination among the key players involved in desertification activities, including donors, national governments, NGOs, and local populations. The annex also contains provisions for financial mechanisms and resources, and co-ordination, partnership, and follow-up arrangements.

The other annexes are shorter, and reflect the different priorities of the regions. The Asian Annex is relatively general in scope, particularly concerning finances. The Latin American and Caribbean Annex mentions the important links between desertification and loss of biological diversity, as well as debt issues, unfavourable international economic trade practices, and other socio-economic factors. It also emphasizes traditional knowledge, know-how, and practices. The Northern Mediterranean Annex is more scientifically oriented. It stresses urbanization and agricultural practices as economic causes of desertification, and provides for collaboration with other regions in the preparation and implementation of action programmes. It is also unique in that it clearly disqualifies the region from eligibility for funds raised through the main Convention. The fourth COP decided to adopt as Annex V to the Convention a regional implementation annex for Central and Eastern Europe. It entered into force on 6 September 2001. It addresses particularly the crisis in agriculture as a result of soil depletion in arable lands. It also points to deforestation due to pollution stress and frequent wildfires as a serious problem and proposes co-ordination among Parties of the region.

The third COP started consultation on the 'Recife Initiative' to enhance the implementation of the obligations of the UNCCD. It was adopted at COP-4 as a declaration on the commitments to enhance the implementation of the obligations of the Convention.

A Global Mechanism, located at the International Fund for Agricultural Development (IFAD) (see IGOs) in Rome, undertakes actions to mobilize and maximize adequate and substantial financial resources to finance activities defined under action programmes. The COP endorsed collaborative institutional arrangements between IFAD, the UN Development Programme (UNDP), and the World Bank (see IGOs) in support of the Mechanism.

Co-ordination with related instruments
Co-ordinated activities take place with other relevant international agreements, particularly the UN Framework Convention on Climate Change (UNFCCC), the Ramsar Convention, and the Convention on Biological Diversity (CBD) (see this section).

Secretariat

Secretariat of the Convention to Combat Desertification,
Haus Carstanjen,
Martin-Luther-King-Straße 8,
D-53175 Bonn,
Germany

Postal address
PO Box 260129,
Haus Carstanjen,
D-53153 Bonn,
Germany
Telephone: +49-228-8152800
Telefax: +49-228-815289-8/9
E-mail: secretariat@unccd.int

UNCCD Executive Secretary
Mr Hama Arba Diallo.

Co-ordinator External Relations and Public Information
Mr Rajeb Boulharouf.

Number of staff
73 in total (professionals, support staff, and temporary staff) (April 2002).

Global Mechanism to the CCD,
c/o International Fund for Agricultural Development (IFAD) (see IGOs).

Managing Director
Mr Per Ryden.

Finance

The core budget is covered by all the Parties through the General Trust Fund for the Core Budget. Financial contributions were $US2.0 million by 15 April 2002 (13 per cent of expected contributions). There are three additional trust funds (see below).

Budget

The approved core budget was $14 million for the years 2000–01 and is $15.3 million for 2002–03.

Trust funds

A Special Trust Fund for Participation in the CCD process is established to fund participation of delegates from affected developing-country Parties to the sessions of the COP. In 2001 an amount of $1,354,000 was utilized under this Trust Fund to support the participation.

A Trust Fund for Supplementary Activities of CCD is established to support the participation of NGOs from affected developing countries and other purposes appropriate to the Convention. Contributions for the years 2000–01 were $6.8 million by 31 December 2001.

A Trust Fund for the Supplementary Contribution to the Convention Activities by the Host Government (Bonn Fund) is also established. The amount available for the years 2000–01 was $900,577.

Rules and standards

Affected-country Parties undertake:

- to give due priority to combating desertification and mitigating the effects of drought, and allocating adequate resources in accordance with their conditions and capabilities;
- to establish strategies and priorities, within the framework of sustainable development plans and/or policies, to combat desertification and mitigate the effects of drought;
- to address the underlying causes of desertification and pay special attention to the socio-economic factors contributing to desertification processes;
- to promote awareness and facilitate participation of local populations, particularly women and youth, with the support of non-governmental organizations;
- to provide an enabling environment by strengthening relevant existing legislation or by enacting new laws and establishing long-term policies and action programmes.

Developed-country Parties undertake:

- actively to support, as agreed, individually or jointly, the efforts of affected developing-country Parties, particularly those in Africa and the least-developed countries, to combat desertification and mitigate the effects of drought;
- to provide substantial financial resources and other forms of support to assist developing-country Parties, particularly those in Africa, effectively to develop and implement their own long-term plans and strategies to combat desertification and mitigate the effects of drought;
- to promote the mobilization of new and additional funding through the Global Environment Facility (GEF) (see IGOs);
- to encourage the mobilization of funding from the private sector and other non-governmental sources;
- to promote and facilitate access by affected-country Parties, particularly affected developing-country Parties, to appropriate technology, knowledge, and know-how.

Furthermore, Article 9 of the Convention states that, in carrying out their obligations, affected developing-country Parties and any other affected-country Party shall prepare, make public, and implement National Action Programmes.

National Action Programmes shall:

- incorporate long-term strategies to combat desertification and mitigate the effects of drought;
- give particular attention to the implementation of preventive measures;
- enhance national climatological and hydrological capabilities;
- promote policies and strengthen institutional frameworks;
- provide for effective popular participation;
- require regular review of implementation.

Elements of the National Action Programmes may include provisions relating to:

- improvements of national economic environments with a view to strengthening

programmes aimed at the eradication of poverty and at ensuring food security;
• sustainable management of natural resources;
• sustainable agriculture practices;
• development and efficient use of various energy sources;
• strengthening of capabilities for assessment and monitoring;
• capacity building, education, and public awareness.

Subject to their respective national legislation and policies, Parties shall exchange information on local and traditional knowledge, ensuring adequate protection for it and providing appropriate return from the benefits derived from it, on an equitable basis and on mutually agreed terms, to the local populations concerned.

Monitoring/implementation

Review procedure

Each Party is requested to communicate to the COP, for consideration at its ordinary sessions, reports on the measures which it has taken for the implementation of the Convention. While affected-country Parties describe the strategies and measures taken to combat desertification in their territories, developed countries report on the support provided to affected developing countries in the implementation of their National Action Programmes. The COP determines the timetable for submission and the format of such reports, and regularly reviews the implementation of the Convention and the functioning of its institutional arrangements in the light of the experience gained at the national, subregional, regional, and international levels and on the basis of the evolution of scientific and technological knowledge.

At its third session, the COP focused on national reports from the African region. COP-4 received the reports from countries of other regions and decided to improve the effectiveness of institutional mechanisms to review the implementation of the Convention.

Accordingly, an *ad hoc* working group was established to assist the COP in its in-depth review of reports submitted to its third and fourth sessions. The working group began operations at COP-4, and was convened again during the inter-session (19 March–6 April 2001) in order to conclude the revision of all the reports. COP-5 decided to establish a permanent subsidiary body to the COP—the Committee to Review the Implementation of the Convention (CRIC)—on the basis of proposals submitted from country Parties. CRIC will review updates to reports already available and/or new reports from all regions, to be submitted by 22 April 2002. COP-6 will receive and consider the reports from country Parties of all regions.

In 1999, 43 reports were submitted by African countries, 13 by developed countries, nine by UN agencies and bodies, and eight by other IGOs. 85 per cent of the Parties submitted reports as required. In 2000, 78 reports were submitted by Asian, Latin American and Caribbean, and northern Mediterranean countries, 13 by developed countries, eight by UN agencies and bodies, and two by other IGOs. 84 per cent of the Parties submitted reports as required. In 2001, one report was submitted by Asia.

The overall quality of the data submitted has so far been complete. The reports are made public by the Secretariat, which also distributes publication lists of such reviews.

Dispute-settlement mechanisms

Parties shall settle any dispute between them concerning the interpretation or application of the Convention through negotiation or other peaceful means of their own choice.

Concerning the interpretation or application of the Convention, Parties may, by a written declaration, recognize as compulsory, in relation to any Party accepting the following mutual obligations:
• arbitration in an annex in accordance with procedures adopted by the COP;
• submission of the dispute to the International Court of Justice.

At COP-2, in 1997, it was decided to include on the agenda consideration procedures and institutional mechanisms for the resolution of questions that may arise with regard to implementation and annexes containing arbitration and conciliation procedures. These outstanding items are still pending and will be placed on the agenda of COP-6.

Decision-making bodies

Political

The COP, the supreme body of the Convention, comprises representatives of all Parties to the Convention. It met once a year for its first five sessions and keeps under review and evaluates implementation of the Convention, harmonizes policies, establishes subsidiary bodies, and undertakes additional actions. National and international agencies and qualified NGOs may attend the COP's sessions as observers and contribute to its work.

COP-5, held in Geneva, Switzerland, from 1 to 12 October 2001, decided that COP-6 should be held in Bonn from 19 to 31 October 2003, in the event that no Party makes an offer to host that session.

Scientific/technical

The Committee on Science and Technology (CST) provides the COP with information and advice on scientific and technological matters relating to combating desertification and the effects of drought. The COP may, as necessary, appoint *ad hoc* panels to provide information and advice through the Committee on specific issues regarding science and technology. At the request of the COP the CST has carried out various activities, some of them through an *ad hoc* panel, which has been established to address specific issues such as traditional knowledge, benchmarks and indicators, early-warning systems, and survey and evaluation. COP-4 requested the Secretariat to guide the Parties so as better to reflect the technical and scientific activities in their national reports. It also requested the CST further to develop activities on early-warning systems and survey and evaluation in the Southern African region.

The Committee to Review the Implementation of the Convention (CRIC) is established to assist the COP in regularly reviewing the implementation of the Convention, and shall facilitate the exchange of information on measures adopted by the Parties, in order to draw conclusions and to propose to the COP concrete recommendations on further steps in the implementation of the Convention. The first session of the CRIC will be held in November 2002.

Publications

• CCD Convention kit comprising full text of the Convention, an explanatory booklet, *Down to Earth*, an explanatory leaflet, fact sheets, and a folder;
• *Down to Earth* (bi-annual newsletter);
• comics catalogue;
• *Lupo Alberto* (comics booklet);
• Teacher's Kit (map, a teacher's guide, and a series of case studies).

Sources on the Internet

<http://www.unccd.int>

FAO International Undertaking on Plant Genetic Resources

Objectives

To ensure that the diversity of plant genetic resources (PGR) of economic and/or social interest, particularly for food and agriculture, will be conserved, explored, evaluated, and made available for plant breeding and scientific purposes.

Scope

Legal scope

Open to all member States of the UN Food and Agriculture Organization (FAO) (see IGOs), non-member States which are members of the UN, and regional integration organizations.

Geographic scope

Global.

Time and place of adoption

23 November 1983, Rome.

Entry into force

1 January 1984.

Status of participation

113 countries had adhered to the Undertaking by October 2001.

Affiliated instruments and organizations

The Undertaking is overseen by the FAO Commission on Genetic Resources for Food and Agriculture (CGRFA), where governments have recently negotiated its revision in harmony with the Convention on Biological Diversity (CBD) (see this section). This process, launched by the 1993 FAO Conference, covered, *inter alia*, the issues of access on mutually agreed terms to PGR, including *ex situ* collections not addressed by the CBD, and the realization of 'Farmers' Rights'. The second session of the Conference of the Parties (COP) to the CBD recognized the special nature of agricultural biodiversity and its distinctive features and problems needing distinctive solutions, and declared its support for this process. The International Treaty on Plant Genetic Resources for Food and Agriculture (see this section) was adopted by the thirty-first session of the FAO Conference on 3 November 2001. It will enter into force 90 days after ratification by 40 countries.

The Commission covers all components of biodiversity of relevance to food and agriculture. In the field of PGR, the Commission has developed a number of negotiated elements which form the *FAO Global System on Plant Genetic Resources*. These include:

- *International Code of Conduct for Plant Germplasm Collecting and Transfer*, an important tool in regulating the collection and transfer of PGR, with the aim of facilitating equitable access to these resources and promoting their utilization and development. It was adopted by the FAO Conference in November 1993 and became operative in January 1994;
- *Draft Code of Conduct for Biotechnology*, as it affects the conservation and use of genetic resources for food and agriculture;
- *International Network of* Ex Situ *Collections, under the Auspices and/or Jurisdiction of FAO*. On 26 October 1994, 12 International Agricultural Research Centres of the Consultative Group on International Agricultural Research (CGIAR) signed agreements with FAO to bring their *ex situ* collections into the Network under its auspices. By September 1996, 40 countries had offered to put national *ex situ* collections under the auspices of FAO and/or to store international collections in their gene bank. During 1998 and 1999, agreements were signed with the governments of India, Papua New Guinea, Indonesia, and IPGRI, bringing regional collections of the International Coconut Genetic Resources Network (COGENT) held by the last named on behalf of COGENT under FAO auspices;
- *Network of* In Situ *Conservation Areas*, with special emphasis on wild relatives of cultivated plants, as well as on the promotion of 'on-farm' conservation and utilization of land races;
- *Crop related Networks*, a co-ordinated approach to identifying, evaluating, and conserving the genetic variability of selected crop species, with the aim of improving cultivars and their adaption to farmers' needs;
- *World Information and Early Warning System on Plant Genetic Resources (WIEWS)*, which collects and disseminates data and facilitates the exchange of information on PGR and related technologies and draws rapid attention to hazards threatening the operation of gene banks and the loss of genetic diversity throughout the world;
- *Report on the State of the World's Plant Genetic Resources*, a periodical report on the conservation and utilization of PGR, to assist the Commission in its monitoring function;
- *Global Plan of Action on Plant Genetic Resources*, a rolling plan aimed at rationalizing and co-ordinating efforts in this area to assist the Commission in its co-ordination function.

The first Report on the State of the World's PGR and Global Plan of Action were developed for the Fourth International Technical Conference on PGR (Leipzig, 17–23 June 1996). The Global Plan of Action was formally adopted by 150 countries at Leipzig. In adopting the World Food Summit Plan of Action in November 1996, countries committed themselves to implementing the Plan. The third COP to the CBD in Buenos Aires (4–15 November 1996) endorsed the Plan's policies and priorities and encouraged Parties actively to implement the Plan. The CGRFA monitors and oversees the implementation of the GPA. The new International Treaty on Plant Genetic Resources for Food and Agriculture recognizes that the Contracting Parties should promote its effective implementation to provide a coherent framework, *inter alia*, for capacity-building, technology transfer, and exchange of information;

- *International Fund for Plant Genetic Resources* (see Special funds, below).

Co-ordination with related instruments

The Commission facilitates co-operation with other conventions and IGOs, such as the Convention on Biological Diversity (CBD) (see this section) and the Commission on Sustainable Development (CSD) (see IGOs).

Secretariat

The Secretariat of the FAO Intergovernmental Commission on Genetic Resources

for Food and Agriculture acts as secretariat of the Undertaking.

Secretariat of the CGRFA,
c/o Food and Agricultural Organization (FAO),
Viale delle Terme di Caracalla,
I-00100 Rome,
Italy
Telephone: +39-06-57054986
Telefax: +39-06-57053057
E-mail: cgrfa@fao.org

Secretary
Dr José T. Esquinas-Alcázar.

Number of staff
Two professionals and three support staff supported by a number of professional staff from the FAO divisions concerned (May 2002).

Finance

International administration costs of the CGRFA are covered by the regular budget of FAO.

Budget
The administrative core budget was $US750,000 in 2001 and is $850,000 in 2002 and $850,000 in 2003.

Special funds
In November 1991 the FAO Conference approved an annex to the Undertaking which established that 'Farmers' Rights' should be implemented through an international fund on PGR to support plant genetic conservation and utilization programmes, particularly in the developing countries. The fund was not established.

The New International Treaty on Plant Genetic Resources for Food and Agriculture includes a funding strategy, as well as arrangements for the equitable sharing of benefits arising from the use, including commercial, of plant genetic resources for food and agriculture.

Rules and standards

In its current form, the Undertaking covers both *ex situ* and *in situ* conservation as well as sustainable utilization of PGR.

The Parties shall:

- provide access to the materials which have been collected or conserved in pursuance of its terms, and the export of such material for scientific or plant-breeding purposes is to take place unrestrictedly on the basis of mutual exchange or on mutually agreed terms;
- give early warning when there is reason to believe that the effective conservation of material held in a collection centre might be prejudiced, with a view to prompt international action to safeguard it;
- mount exploration missions to identify PGR which are in danger of extinction, as well as those that may be useful for development. They agree to put in place legislation to protect plants and their habitats and to take steps to collect genetic material;
- pledge themselves to build up institutional and technical capabilities in developing countries, intensifying plant-breeding and germplasm maintenance activities on the international level, establishing gene banks, setting up an internationally coordinated network of collections, putting in place an international data system, and providing an early warning system to alert the international community of threats to the continued security of any centre at which plant genetic material is collected.

The Undertaking is voluntary and, as such, does not impose legally binding obligations on the Parties. The new International Treaty on Plant Genetic Resources for Food and Agriculture, when it enters into force, will be legally binding.

Monitoring/implementation

Review procedure
States are required to provide the Director-General of FAO with annual reports of the steps which have been taken by them in pursuance of the terms of the Undertaking.

Observations or inspections
None by the Agreement as such.

Data and information-system programmes
See World Information and Early Warning System on PGR (WIEWS) under Affiliated instruments and organizations, above.

In preparation for the Fourth International Technical Conference on PGR (see above), more than 150 countries prepared detailed national reports. This information was captured in the WIEWS and formed the basis of the Report on the State of the World's PGR. This Report will be periodically updated under the guidance of the Commission. It underpins the rolling Global Plan of Action, which will also be periodically updated. The Commission oversees and monitors the implementation of the Plan.

For a full list of WIEWS databases, see the website at: <http://apps3.fao.org/wiews>.

The operation of the Undertaking is reviewed at regular meetings of the Commission.

Trade measures
No provisions on trade measures to penalize Parties for non-compliance.

Dispute-settlement mechanisms
The Undertaking makes no reference to dispute settlement. Matters of controversy between the Parties are usually resolved by negotiation and the agreed result endorsed, in appropriate cases, by the Commission or the FAO Conference.

Decision-making bodies

Political
The Commission on Genetic Resources for Food and Agriculture (CGRFA) (previously the Commission on Plant Genetic Resources (CPGR)), with 160 member countries and the European Community by May 2001, including donors and users of germplasm, funds, and technologies, monitors the implementation of the Undertaking and discusses, on an equal footing, matters related to PGR. It meets in regular sessions every two years. The Eighth Regular Session was held in Rome from 19 to 23 April 1999 and the Sixth Extraordinary Session, to finalize the revision of the Undertaking was held in Rome from 24 to 30 June 2001. The Commission can establish subsidiary intergovernmental working groups to assist it. Currently, there are working groups on animal and on plant genetic resources for food and agriculture.

Scientific/technical
None, but draws on the resources of FAO, as well as IPGRI (see above), which is part of the Consultative Group on International Agricultural Research (CGIAR).

Publications

- *The State of the World's Plant Genetic Resources for Food and Agriculture*;
- *Global Plan of Action on Plant Genetic Resources*;
- *Sovereign and Property Rights over Plant Genetic Resources*;
- *Identifying Genetic Resources and their Origin: The Capabilities and Limitations of Modern Biochemical and Legal Systems*;
- *Contribution to the Estimation of Countries' Interdependence in the Area of Plant Genetic Resources*;
- *Access to Plant Genetic Resources and Intellectual Property Rights*;
- *Recent Developments in Biotechnology as they Relate to Plant Genetic Resources for Food and Agriculture*;
- *Recent Developments in Biotechnology as they Relate to Animal Genetic Resources for Food and Agriculture*;
- *Transaction costs of Germplasm Exchange under Bilateral Arrangements.*

Sources on the Internet

<http://www.fao.org/ag/cgrfa>

International Treaty on Plant Genetic Resources for Food and Agriculture (ITPGRFA)

Objectives

To ensure the conservation and sustainable use of plant genetic resources (PGR) for food and agriculture and the fair and equitable sharing of the benefits arising out of their use, in harmony with the Convention on Biological Diversity, for sustainable agriculture and food security.

Scope

Legal scope
Open to all members of the UN Food and Agriculture Organization (FAO) (see IGOs), and non-member States which are members of the UN, or any of its specialized agencies, or of the International Atomic Energy Agency.

Geographic scope
Global.

Time and place of adoption

3 November 2001, Rome.

Entry into force

Not yet in force. Enters into force on the 90th day after the deposit of the 40th instrument of ratification, acceptance, approval or accession, provided that at least 20 instruments of ratification, acceptance, approval, or accession have been deposited by members of the FAO.

Status of participation

Seven ratifications, acceptances, approvals, or accessions by 13 June 2002. 50 Signatories, including the European Community, without ratification, acceptance, or approval. The Treaty is open for signature followed by ratification, acceptance, or approval at the FAO from 3 November 2001 to 4 November 2002, and for accession from 5 November 2002.

The Director-General of the FAO acts as depositary.

Affiliated instruments and organizations

The Treaty was adopted by the 31st session of the FAO Conference and was approved with 116 favourable votes and two abstentions. There were no votes against. The Treaty revises the International Undertaking on Plant Genetic Resources (see this section).

The FAO Commission on Genetic Resources for Food and Agriculture (CGRFA) acts as the Interim Committee for the Treaty (see description of the CGRFA under the International Undertaking on Plant Genetic Resources entry in this section). The Treaty also covers following four supporting components:

• *Global Plan of Action on Plant Genetic Resources*, a rolling plan aimed at rationalizing and co-ordinating efforts in this area. The first Report on the State of the World's PGR and Global Plan of Action (GPA) was formally adopted by 150 countries at the Fourth International Technical Conference on PGR in Leipzig from 17 to 23 June 1996. The Commission monitors and oversees the implementation of the GPA. The Treaty recognizes that Contracting Parties should promote its effective implementation to provide a coherent framework, *inter alia*, for capacity-building, technology transfer, and exchange of information;

• Ex Situ *Collections of PGR for Food and Agriculture*, held by the International Agricultural Research Centres (IARCs) of the Consultative Group on International Agricultural Research (CGIAR) and other International Institutions. On 26 October 1994, 12 IARCs of the CGIAR signed agreements with the FAO to bring their *ex situ* collections into the Network under its auspices. The Treaty recognizes the importance of these collections and call upon the IARCs and other international institutions holding *ex situ* collections to sign agreements with the Governing Body of the Treaty (see Decision-making bodies, below) with regard to such collections. This will provide a secure long-term legal framework for these important collections;

• *International Plant Genetic Resources Networks*. Co-operation in international PGR for food and agriculture networks will be encouraged or developed on the basis of existing arrangements and consistent with the terms of the Treaty, so as to achieve as complete coverage as possible of PGR for food and agriculture. The Parties will encourage, as appropriate, all relevant institutions, including governmental, private, non-governmental, research, breeding, and other institutions, to participate in the international networks;

• *Global Information System on Plant Genetic Resources for Food and Agriculture*. The Parties shall co-operate to develop and strengthen a Global Information System to facilitate the exchange of information, based on existing information systems, on scientific, technical, and environmental matters related to PGR for food and agriculture, with the expectation that such exchange of information will contribute to the sharing of benefits by making information on PGR for food and agriculture available to all Parties. In developing such a Global Information System, co-operation will be sought with the Clearing House Mechanism of the Convention on Biological Diversity (see this section).

Based on notification by the Parties, early warning should be provided about hazards that threaten the efficient maintenance of PGR for food and agriculture, with a view to safeguarding the material. The Parties shall also co-operate with the Commission in its periodic reassessment of the state of the world's PGR for food and agriculture in order to facilitate the updating of the rolling Global Plan of Action (see above).

The Treaty contains two *annexes*, which form an integral part of the Treaty. *Annex I* consists of a list of crops covered under the multilateral system (see Rules and Standards, below). *Annex II* consists of dispute-settlement procedures.

Co-ordination with related instruments
The Treaty is in harmony with the Convention on Biological Diversity (CBD). The Commission facilitates co-operation with other conventions and IGOs, such as the CBD and the Commission on Sustainable Development (CSD) (see IGOs).

By decision VI/6, the Conference of the Parties to the CBD 'appeals to Parties and other governments to give priority consideration to the signature and ratification of the International Treaty on Plant Genetic Resources for Food and Agriculture, so that it may enter expeditiously into force'.

Secretariat

The Secretary of the Governing Body shall be appointed by the Director-General of the FAO, with the approval of the Governing Body. The Secretariat of the Commission acts as the Secretariat for the Interim Committee of the Treaty.

Secretariat of the CGRFA,
c/o Food and Agricultural Organization (FAO),
viale delle Terme di Caracalla,
I-00100 Rome, Italy
Telephone: +39-06-57054986
Telefax: +39-06-57053057
E-mail: cgrfa@fao.org

Secretary
Dr José T. Esquinas-Alcázar.
Jose.Esquinas@fao.org

Number of staff
Two professionals and three support staff, aided by a number of professional staff from the FAO divisions concerned (May 2002).

Finance

The Treaty provides for Parties to implement a funding strategy. In order to mobilize funding for priority activities, plans, and programmes, in particular in developing countries and countries with economies in transition, and taking the Global Plan of Action into account, the Governing Body shall periodically establish a target for such funding. The Parties shall take the necessary and appropriate measures within the Governing Bodies of relevant international mechanisms, funds, and bodies to ensure that priority and attention to the effective allocation of predictable and agreed resources for the implementation of plans and programmes under the Treaty. The share of the monetary benefits arising from commercialization will also be part of the funding strategy.

Financial rules are to be decided by the first session of the Treaty's Governing Body. The Interim Committee will prepare draft financial rules for the consideration by the Governing Body.

Budget
To be adopted by the Governing Body. The administrative core budget of the Commission is $US850,000 in 2002 and $850,000 in 2003, covered by the regular budget of the FAO.

Special funds
None as yet. The Governing Body shall establish, as needed, an appropriate mechanism, a trust account, for receiving and utilizing financial resources that will accrue to it for purposes of implementing the Treaty.

Rules and standards

Scope
The scope of the Treaty is all plant genetic resources (PGR) for food and agriculture.

General provisions
The Contracting Parties shall:
• promote an integrated approach to the exploration, conservation, and sustainable use of PGR for food and agriculture;
• take steps to minimize or, if possible, eliminate threats to PGR for food and agriculture;
• develop and maintain appropriate policy and legal measures that promote the sustainable use of PGR for food and agriculture;
• integrate into its agriculture and rural development policies and programmes, activities referred to above, and co-operate with other Parties, directly or through the FAO and other relevant international organizations, in the conservation and sustainable use of PGR for food and agriculture;
• promote the provision of technical assistance to Parties, especially those that are developing countries or countries with economies in transition, either bilaterally or through the appropriate international organizations, with the objective of facilitating the implementation of the Treaty.

Farmers' rights
In Article 9, the Treaty recognizes the enormous contribution that the local and indigenous communities and farmers of all regions of the world, particularly those in the centres of origin and crop diversity, have made and will continue to make for the conservation and development of PGR which

constitute the basis of food and agriculture production throughout the world.

The Parties agree that the responsibility for realizing 'farmers' rights', as they relate to PGR for food and agriculture, rests with national governments. In accordance with their needs and priorities, each Party should, as appropriate, and subject to its national legislation, take measures to protect and promote Farmers' Rights.

Nothing in Article 9 shall be interpreted to limit any rights that farmers have to save, use, exchange, and sell farm-saved seed/propagating material, subject to national law and as appropriate.

Multilateral system of access and benefit-sharing
In their relationships with other States, the Parties recognize the sovereign rights of States over their own PGR for food and agriculture, including that the authority to determine access to those resources rests with national governments and is subject to national legislation.

In the exercise of their sovereign rights, the Parties agree to establish a multilateral system, which is efficient, effective, and transparent, both to facilitate access to PGR for food and agriculture, and to share, in a fair and equitable way, the benefits arising from the utilization of these resources, on a complementary and mutually reinforcing basis.

The multilateral system shall cover the PGR for food and agriculture listed in Annex I, established according to criteria of food security and interdependence. It shall include all PGR for food and agriculture listed in Annex I that are under the management and control of the Parties and in the public domain and also PGR held in the *ex situ* collections of the International Agricultural Research Centres of the Consultative Group on International Agricultural Research (CGIAR).

Facilitated access to plant genetic resources for food and agriculture within the multilateral system
The Parties agree that facilitated access to PGR for food and agriculture under the multilateral system shall be in accordance with the provisions of this Treaty and to take the necessary legal or other appropriate measures to provide such access to other Parties through the system.

Access shall be provided through standard material transfer agreements, to be adopted by the Governing Body.

In emergency disaster situations, the Parties agree to provide facilitated access to appropriate PGR for food and agriculture in the system for the purpose of contributing to the re-establishment of agricultural systems, in co-operation with disaster relief co-ordinators.

Benefit-sharing in the multilateral system
The Parties recognize that facilitated access to PGR for food and agriculture which are included in the multilateral system constitutes itself a major benefit of the system and agree that benefits arising from the use, including commercial, of PGR for food and agriculture under the system shall be shared fairly and equitably through the following mechanisms: the exchange of information, access to and transfer of technology, capacity-building, and the sharing of the benefits arising from commercialization, taking into account the priority activity areas in the rolling Global Plan of Action, under the guidance of the Governing Body. The sharing of the monetary benefits of commercialization shall include a requirement that a recipient who commercializes a product that is a PGR for food and agriculture and that incorporates material accessed from the multilateral system, shall pay an equitable share of the benefits arising, except when the product is available without restriction to others for further research and breeding.

The Parties agree that benefits arising from the use of PGR for food and agriculture that are shared under the system should flow primarily, directly and indirectly, to farmers in all countries, especially in developing countries, and countries with economies in transition, who conserve and sustainably utilize PGR for food and agriculture.

Monitoring/implementation

Review procedure
The Governing Body shall, at its first meeting, consider and approve co-operative and effective procedures and operational mechanisms to promote compliance with the provisions of this Treaty and to address issues of non-compliance. These procedures and mechanisms shall include monitoring, and offering advice or assistance, specifically legal advice or legal assistance, when needed, in particular to developing countries and countries with economies in transition.

Observations or inspections
None by the Agreement as such.

Trade measures
No provisions on trade measures to penalize Parties for non-compliance.

Dispute-settlement mechanisms
Parties shall settle any dispute between them concerning the interpretation or application of the Convention through negotiation. If the Parties concerned cannot reach agreement by negotiation, they may jointly seek the good offices of, or request mediation by, a third party.

Decision-making bodies

Political
After the Treaty enters into force, the Governing Body will become the supreme authority. Following the entry into force of the Treaty, ordinary sessions shall be held at least once every two years. These sessions should, as far as possible, be held back-to-back with the regular sessions of the CGRFA.

The Governing Body shall keep under review and evaluate implementation of the Treaty; co-operate with other relevant bodies (including in particular the Conference of the Parties to the CBD); harmonize policies; consider and adopt amendments; and establish subsidiary bodies as it considers necessary.

National and international agencies and qualified NGOs may attend sessions of the Governing Body as observers.

All decisions of the Governing Body shall be taken by consensus unless—by consensus—another method of arriving at a decision on certain measures is reached.

Scientific/technical
To be established.

Publications

For a list of main publications on PGR, see the FAO International Undertaking on Plant Genetic Resources entry. For publications that are not available online, please contact the CGRFA Secretariat.

Sources on the Internet

<http://www.fao.org/ag/cgrfa>

International Tropical Timber Agreement, 1994 (ITTA, 1994)

Objectives

• to provide an effective framework for consultation, international co-operation, and policy development among all members with regard to all relevant aspects of the world timber economy;
• to provide a forum for consultation to promote non-discriminatory timber trade practices;
• to contribute to the process of sustainable development;
• to enhance the capacity of members to implement a strategy for achieving exports of tropical timber and timber products from sustainable managed sources by the year 2000;
• to promote the expansion and diversification of international trade in tropical timber from sustainable sources by improving the structural conditions in international markets;
• to promote and support research and development with a view to improving forest management and efficiency of wood utilization as well as increasing the capacity to conserve and enhance other forest values in timber-producing tropical forests;
• to develop and contribute towards mechanisms for the provision of new and additional financial resources and expertise needed to enhance the capacity of producing members to attain the objectives of this Agreement;
• to improve market intelligence with a view to ensuring greater transparency in the international tropical timber market;
• to promote increased and further processing of tropical timber from sustainable sources in producing member countries with a view to promoting their industrialization and thereby increasing their employment opportunities and export earnings;
• to encourage members to support and develop industrial tropical timber reforestation and forest management activities as well as rehabilitation of degraded forest land, with due regard for the interest of local communities dependent on forest resources;
• to improve marketing and distribution of tropical timber exports from sustainable managed sources;
• to encourage members to develop national policies aimed at sustainable utilization and conservation of timber-producing forests and their genetic resources and at maintaining the ecological balance in the regions concerned, in the context of tropical timber trade;
• to promote the access to, and transfer of, technologies and technical co-operation to implement the objectives of this Agreement;
• to encourage information sharing on the international timber market.

Scope

Legal scope

Open to any state that produces or consumes tropical timber, and to intergovernmental organizations having responsibilities in respect of the negotiation, conclusion, and application of international agreements.

Geographic scope

Global.

Time and place of adoption

26 January 1994, Geneva. The 1994 Agreement is the successor agreement to the ITTA, 1983, which was adopted on 18 November 1983 in Geneva.

Entry into force

1 January 1997 for an initial period of four years. Extended for a period of three years with effect from 1 January 2001 until 31 December 2003. (The ITTA, 1983, entered into force on 1 April 1985.)

Status of participation

57 members (Belgium and Luxembourg occupying a joint membership), comprising 31 producing and 26 consuming members, including the European Community, by 1 May 2002. The members represent 90 per cent of world trade in tropical timber and over 75 per cent of the world's tropical forests. No Signatories without ratification, acceptance, approval, definitive signature, or provisional application.

The Secretary-General of the UN acts as depositary.

Affiliated instruments and organizations

The International Tropical Timber Organization (ITTO), established by the ITTA, 1983, administers the provisions and supervises the operation of this Agreement. It has the following mission statement: 'The ITTO facilitates discussion, consultation and international co-operation on issues relating to the international trade and utilization of tropical timber and the sustainable management of its resource base.'

ITTO Yokohama Action Plan 2002–2006

ITTO charted its course for the next five years under the new 'Yokohama Action Plan', approved by the Council (see Decision-making bodies, below) in 2001. The Plan, which is operational from 2002 to 2006, was developed after wide consultation between member governments, environmental NGOs, the timber trade and industry, and other international organizations. Its aim is to accelerate progress towards achieving exports of tropical timber and timber products from sustainably managed sources, and it sets six major goals:
• to improve the transparency of the international timber market;
• to promote tropical timber from sustainably managed sources;
• to support activities to secure the tropical forest estate;
• to promote the sustainable management of tropical forests;
• to promote the increased and further processing of tropical timber from sustainable sources;
• to improve the industry's efficiency of processing and utilization of tropical timber from sustainable sources.

ITTO initiatives on forest law and enforcement

In November 2001 the Council launched a range of new activities on forest law enforcement and to combat the illegal trade of timber. Failures in forest law enforcement and problems of illegal trade in forest products had been the subject of intense debate within the Council. In reaching its decision, the Council recognized that all countries and the ITTO had a role to play in combating activities that undermine sustainable

forest management. Resources are now being provided to assist countries to address unsustainable timber harvesting, forest law enforcement, and illegal trade in tropical timber.

Co-ordination with related instruments
ITTO is active in post-UNCED initiatives and is currently a member of the Collaborative Partnership on Forests (CPF), which has been established to support the work of the UN Forum on Forests (UNFF). In commodities and trade, ITTO is recognized as an International Commodity Body (ICB) by the Common Fund for Commodities, which has co-financed six ITTO projects. Liaison with UNCTAD and attendance at the Trade and Environment Committee of the World Trade Organization (WTO) (see IGOs) is complemented by links with trade and environmental NGOs for the promotion of sustainable forest management and trade in tropical timber. ITTO serves in the Timber Working Group of the Convention on International Trade in Endangered Species (CITES) (see this section), and associates with the Center for International Forestry Research (CIFOR), part of the Consultative Group for International Agricultural Research (CGIAR) network. Its work on guidelines, criteria, and indicators for sustainable forest management was the first in the field, and the Organization actively participates in regional initiatives along these lines, such as the Pan European, Montreal, and Tarapoto processes.

ITTO and the African Timber Organization (ATO) signed an agreement to co-operate on the implementation of principles, criteria, and indicators for the sustainable management of African forests. The agreement outlined the setting up of an ITTO–ATO co-operation mechanism to promote sustainable forest management in Africa, and a mechanism to enhance co-operation on the implementation of the ATO/ITTO principles, criteria, and indicators.

Secretariat

International Tropical Timber Organization (ITTO),
International Organizations Center, 5th Floor,
Pacifico-Yokohama,
1-1-1, Minato-Mirai,
Nishi-ku,
Yokohama,
220-0012 Japan
Telephone: +81-45-2231110
Telefax: +81-45-2231111
E-mail: itto@itto.or.jp

Executive Director
Dr Manoel Sobral Filho.

Information Officer
Mr E. Collins Ahadome.

Number of staff
17 professionals and 18 support staff (March 2002).

Finance

The administrative budget is financed by annually assessed contributions from all member countries in proportion to their votes in the International Tropical Timber Council (ITTC) (see below). In hosting ITTO, the government of Japan and the City of Yokohama provide office accommodation, contribute three support staff, and cover the administrative costs of the biannual Council sessions.

Budget
The administrative budget was $US4.5 million in 2000 and $4.6 million in 2001, and is $4.5 million in 2002.

Main contributors
All the members contributed to the administrative budget in 2001 except for the European Union *per se*, whose constituent states contribute.

83.0 per cent fulfilled their financial obligations as required by the Agreement in 1999, 85.0 per cent fulfilled their obligations in 2000, and 86.1 per cent fulfilled their obligations in 2001.

Special funds
Project activities are funded from voluntary contributions of members, trade associations, service groups, the private sector, and the *Common Fund for Commodities*. Generally, contributions earmarked for specific projects are pledged by donors at each Council session, i.e. twice a year. Project proposals originate from members and are technically appraised by an independent Panel of Experts before being examined by the relevant committee. ITTO funding is a grant, not a loan. $US227 million had been donated for the implementation of projects and pre-project and other activities by December 2001; accumulated disbursements at this date were $214 million.

Main contributors in 2001 were Japan, Switzerland, the USA, Australia, Finland, the Republic of Korea, the Netherlands, Sweden, and the private sector (Ito-Yokado Corporation and York Mart of Japan).

Recipients are producer member countries and consumer countries with developing economies.

The *Bali Partnership Fund* is a fund established under the ITTA, 1994, to assist members to make the necessary investments to achieve the Year 2000 Objective (see below).

Rules and standards

Members are required:

- to pay their annual assessed contributions to the administrative account;
- to the fullest extent possible not inconsistent with their national legislation, to furnish, within a reasonable time, statistics and information on timber, its trade, and the activities aimed at achieving sustainable management of timber-producing forests, as well as other relevant information as requested by the Council. The Council shall decide on the type of information to be provided under this paragraph and on the format in which it is to be presented;
- to review and assess annually: (a) the international timber situation; (b) other factors, issues, and developments considered relevant to achieve the objectives of the Agreement;
- to exchange views among member countries regarding: (a) the status of sustainable management of timber-producing forests and related matters in member countries; (b) resource flows and requirements in relation to objectives, criteria, and guidelines set by the Organization.

Members are committed to the Objective 2000 under which the Organization aims to enhance the capacity of members to implement a strategy for achieving exports of tropical timber and timber products from sustainably managed sources. Members are invited to submit reports to the Council annually on their progress towards achieving the objective.

In May 2000 the Council conducted a full review of progress towards achieving Objective 2000 and recognized that much progress had been made by Members, especially in the area of policy reforms and legislation, but progress towards meeting the overall objective had not been sufficient. The Council reaffirmed the full commitment of Members to move as rapidly as possible towards achieving exports of tropical timber and timber products from sustainably managed sources under Objective 2000.

Measures to Promote and Support Sustainable Trade
The ITTO 2001 market discussion was held on 30 May 2001 at a joint session of the committees during the thirtieth Session of the Council in Yaoundé, Cameroon. The theme of the discussion was 'Regulations for a Sustainable Timber Trade – Relevant Issues'. The 2001 discussion was organized by the Trade Advisory Group to the International Tropical Timber Council (ITTC). Some 300 participants gathered to discuss a wide range of issues related to the sustainable management and conservation of tropical forests and the promotion of a sustainable tropical timber industry and trade.

Following up on recommendations made by the annual market discussion, the ITTC approved several major initiatives to promote trade and trade co-operation, including the implementation of a study to identify measures to bring increased transparency to the tropical hardwood plywood trade and analyse the causes of market fluctuations and price instability; an assessment of the feasibility of and the support for a tropical timber promotion campaign; a study on international markets for wooden furniture; and an assessment of the multiple benefits of downstream processing in producer countries.

ITTO Guidelines and Manuals
The ITCC has adopted guidelines for the sustainable management of natural tropical forests, for the establishment and sustainable management of planted tropical forests, and for the conservation of biological diversity in tropical production forests, as well as criteria for the measurement of sustainable tropical forest management. The Organization also prepared guidelines for the protection of tropical forests against fire and for the management of secondary tropical forests, tropical forest restoration, and the rehabilitation of degraded forest lands. The ITTO Manual for Project Formulation contains guidelines for ensuring local community participation in the project cycle and to take account of the environmental impacts of projects.

All these commitments and guidelines have been adopted by the ITTC (see below) after due consultation in the ITTO forum, where, apart from members, non-governmental conservation organizations and timber trade associations also take part. Legal implementation and enforcement of practical measures are left to member countries themselves.

The operational activities of the Committees are:

- recommendations to the Council on project and pre-project proposals and on the policy work programme, including the ITTO Action Plan;
- effective appraisal, monitoring, evaluation, and follow-up of projects and pre-projects and the development of policy ideas;
- specific technical tasks allotted to each committee under the ITTA, 1994.

Criteria and Indicators and Forest Auditing
Following Council agreement on standard formats for reporting on sustainable forest management progress using the ITTO criteria and indicators, the Organization made financial provisions to undertake a major training programme to train officials, forest managers, forest concessionaires, and others directly involved in sustainable forest management in the effective use of the ITTO reporting formats at both national and forest management levels. Ten national-level training workshops will be conducted in major producer countries, building up on the four regional training workshops convened in 2000–01. More than 500 professionals, mostly from the private sector and forest communities, are expected to benefit and increase capability in the use of criteria and indicators to assess progress and monitor trends in sustainable forest management.

Monitoring/implementation

Review procedure

Members are expected to submit data annually on their national production, trade, supply, stocks, consumption, and prices of tropical timber for the *Annual Review and Assessment of the World Tropical Timber Situation*. Members are required to supply other statistical data and specific indicators as requested by the Council.

Members are also required to report annually on activities aimed at achieving sustainable forest management and on progress towards ITTO's Year 2000 Objective. Ten members submitted such reports during 1999, 27 members submitted such reports during 2000, and seven members submitted such reports during 2001.

48 statistical reports (88.9 per cent of members) were submitted in 1999, 49 reports (87.5 per cent of members) in 2000, and 49 reports (82.4 per cent of members) in 2001. A summary of these reports is public.

The assessment of compliance by members to ITTA principles is the responsibility of the Council and the Permanent Committees (see Decision-making bodies below). Emphasis is placed on the monitoring and review of ITTO projects and the programme set up by the Action Plan. An expert panel has been established for the technical assessment of project proposals. There is no independent verification of data or information, but non-governmental organizations (NGOs) may address report issues in the Council (see below). They are accorded observer status and are given the chance to speak. These reviews are public and the secretariat distributes a publications list and Council reports.

Observations or inspections

None by the Agreement as such.

Environmental monitoring programmes

ITTO supports several projects, pre-projects, and activities that include various environmental monitoring components.

Trade measures

Nothing in the ITTA, 1994, authorizes the use of measures to restrict or ban international trade in timber and timber imports, particularly measures concerning imports and utilization.

Dispute-settlement mechanisms

Any complaint that a member has failed to fulfil its obligations under the Agreement and any dispute concerning the interpretation or application of the Agreement shall be referred to the Council for decision. Decisions of the Council shall be final and binding.

Decision-making bodies

Political

The ITTA, 1994, has established the International Tropical Timber Organization (ITTO), which functions through its supreme governing body, the International Tropical Timber Council (ITTC). The Council meets twice a year and consists of all members of the Organization.

Voting, very rarely used, is based on simple majorities in each of the producer and consumer caucuses. Only financial members may vote, and the 1000 votes allotted to each caucus are shared out among these members according to the rules set out in the ITTA, 1994.

The Council's work consists in formulating overall policies, approving the programme of work for the Organization, allocating funds for its implementation, recommending amendments to the Agreement, and undertaking an annual review and assessment of the tropical timber market and economy. Non-member governments and organizations may attend upon invitation from the Council as observers of the meetings of the Council.

Scientific/technical

The Permanent Committees, which are open to all members, are:

- Committee on Economic Information and Market Intelligence;
- Committee on Reforestation and Forest Management;
- Committee on Forest Industry;
- Committee on Finance and Administration.

All committees are composed of government experts and experts from trade organizations and conservation NGOs.

Publications

Annual reports, *Annual Review of the World Tropical Timber Situation*, Council reports, technical series, policy development series, information papers, pre-project and project reports, and reports of seminars and workshops are published regularly. ITTO also has two serial publications: *Tropical Forest Update* (quarterly newsletter) and *Market Information Report* (bi-monthly newsletter).

Sources on the Internet

<http://www.itto.or.jp>

Convention on Assistance in the Case of a Nuclear Accident or Radiological Emergency (Assistance Convention)

Objectives

• to set out an international framework aimed at facilitating the prompt provision of assistance in the event of a nuclear accident or radiological emergency, directly between States Parties, through or from the International Atomic Energy Agency (IAEA) (see IGOs), and from other international organizations;
• to minimize consequences and to protect life, property, and the environment from effects of radioactive releases.

Scope

Legal scope
Open to all states, international organizations, and regional integration organizations.

Geographic scope
Global.

Time and place of adoption

26 September 1986, Vienna.

Entry into force

26 February 1987.

Status of participation

80 states and three intergovernmental organizations (the Food and Agriculture Organization (FAO), the World Health Organization (WHO), and the World Meteorological Organization (WMO) (see IGOs) were Parties by 23 November 2001. 20 Signatories without ratification, acceptance, or approval.

The IAEA acts as depositary.

Affiliated instruments and organizations

No amendments have been proposed.

The IAEA is in charge of administering the Convention.

Co-ordination with related instruments
The IAEA Board of Governors has established an Expert Working Group to consider additional measures to improve co-operation in the field of nuclear safety.

Secretariat

IAEA (see IGOs).

Finance

Budget
Costs are covered by the regular IAEA budget.

Special funds
Not applicable.

Rules and standards

Parties shall co-operate between themselves and with the IAEA to facilitate prompt assistance in the event of a nuclear accident or radiological emergency.

Parties shall request the Agency to use its best endeavours in accordance with the provisions of this Convention to promote, facilitate, and support the co-operation between the Parties provided for in this Convention.

If a Party needs assistance in the event of a nuclear accident or radiological emergency, whether or not such an accident or emergency originates within its territory, jurisdiction, or control, it may call for such assistance from any other Party, from the Agency, or from other IGOs.

A Party to which a request for such assistance is directed shall promptly decide and notify the requesting Party, directly or through the Agency, whether it is in a position to render the assistance requested, and the scope and terms of the assistance.

A Party may request assistance relating to medical or temporary relocation into the territory of another Party of people involved in a nuclear accident or radiological emergency.

A Party requesting assistance shall provide the assisting State with such information as may be necessary for that Party to determine the extent to which it is able to meet the request.

Parties shall notify the IAEA of experts,

equipment, and materials which could be made available in case of a nuclear accident or radiological emergency.

Monitoring/implementation

Review procedure

There are no reporting obligations under the Convention unless a nuclear accident or radiological emergency occurs, which has not been the case since 1986. The IAEA has, however, been asked for assistance 19 times in the framework of this Convention: in the case of the radiological accidents or incidents at Goiânia, Brazil, in September 1987, in Nicaragua in August 1987, in Uganda in November 1988, in El Salvador in February 1989, in Tunisia in December 1990, in Viet Nam in January 1993, in Costa Rica in May 1993, in Estonia in November 1994, in Chile and Peru in August 1996, in Russia and Venezuela in June 1997, in Bangladesh in July 1997, in Georgia in October 1997, in Russia (Chechenia) in January 1998, in Georgia in August 1998 and in October 1998, in Turkey in January 1999, and in Peru in March 1999.

No compliance controls are provided.

All information on implementation of the Convention is made available directly to governments and the competent authorities designated. In addition, the IAEA issues a wide range of public information materials relating to the Convention. There is no independent verification of data or information.

At national level, designated national authorities are responsible for issuing and receiving notifications and information.

Observations or inspections

None by the Convention as such.

Trade measures

No provisions on trade measures to penalize Parties for non-compliance.

Dispute-settlement mechanisms

In the event of a dispute between the Parties, or between a Party and the IAEA, concerning the interpretation and application of the Convention, the Parties shall consult with a view to settling the dispute by negotiation or by any other peaceful means.

However, if the dispute cannot be settled within one year from the request for consultation, the dispute shall be submitted to arbitration or referred to the International Court of Justice for decision.

A Party may declare that it does not consider itself bound by either or both of these dispute-settlement procedures when signing, ratifying, approving, or acceding to the Convention.

Decision-making bodies

Political

The only organ referred to in the Convention is the IAEA. No meeting of Parties has taken place so far.

Scientific/technical

Technical assistance is provided by the IAEA. No long-term scientific advisory functions or participation from NGOs and industry are foreseen.

Publications

Up-to-date information is available through *IAEA Bulletin* (quarterly) and the IAEA's annual reports.

Sources on the Internet

<http://www.iaea.org/worldatom/Documents/Legal/cacnare.shtml>

Convention on Early Notification of a Nuclear Accident (Notification Convention)

Objectives

To provide relevant information about nuclear accidents with possible international transboundary consequences as early as possible in order to minimize environmental, health, and economic consequences.

Scope

Legal scope
Open to all states, international organizations, and regional integration organizations.

Geographic scope
Global.

Time and place of adoption

26 September 1986, Vienna.

Entry into force

27 October 1986.

Status of participation

84 states and three intergovernmental organizations (the Food and Agriculture Organization (FAO), the World Health Organization (WHO), and the World Meteorological Organization (WMO) (see IGOs) were Parties by 23 November 2001. 17 Signatories without ratification, acceptance, or approval.

The International Atomic Energy Agency (IAEA) (see IGOs) acts as depositary.

Affiliated instruments and organizations

No amendments have been proposed.

The IAEA Secretariat is in charge of administering the Convention.

Co-ordination with related instruments
The IAEA Board of Governors has established an Expert Working Group to consider additional measures to improve co-operation in the field of nuclear safety.

Secretariat

IAEA (see IGOs).

Finance

Budget
Costs are covered by the regular IAEA budget.

Special funds
Not applicable.

Rules and standards

In the event of any nuclear accident with actual or potential transboundary effects involving its facilities or activities from which a release of radioactive material occurs or is likely to occur, the Party shall notify other states which may be physically affected, directly or through the IAEA, and the IAEA itself, of the nature of the accident, its location, and the time of its occurrence.

The State Party is also required to provide other states and the IAEA promptly with specified information relevant to minimizing the radiological consequences in those states.

Parties are further required to respond to a request by an affected State for additional information or consultation.

In addition, each Party shall make known its competent authorities or point of contact responsible for issuing and receiving the notification and information referred to above.

States may voluntarily notify accidents related to military nuclear activities, with a view to minimizing the radiological consequences of the nuclear accident. All five nuclear-weapon states have declared their intention to make such notifications.

The information to be provided in case of a nuclear accident shall comprise the following data:
(*a*) the time, the exact location where appropriate, and the nature of the accident;
(*b*) the facility or activity involved;
(*c*) the assumed or established cause and the foreseen development of the nuclear accident relevant to the transboundary release of the radioactive material;
(*d*) the general characteristics of the radio-

active release, including, as far as practicable and appropriate, the nature, probable physical and chemical form, quantity, composition, and effective height of the radioactive release;
(*e*) information on current and predicted meteorological and hydrological conditions necessary to forecasting the transboundary release of the radioactive materials;
(*f*) the results of environmental monitoring relevant to the transboundary release of the radioactive materials;
(*g*) the off-site protective measures taken or planned;
(*h*) the predicted behaviour over time of the radioactive release.

Monitoring/implementation

Review procedure
The information above shall be supplemented by further relevant information on the development of the emergency situation with the inclusion of its foreseeable and actual termination. Information may be used without restriction except when such information is provided in confidence by the notifying Party.

All information on implementation of the Convention is made available directly to governments and the competent authorities designated. In addition, the IAEA issues a wide range of public information materials relating to the Convention. There is no independent verification of data or information.

At national level, designated national authorities are responsible for issuing and receiving notifications and information.

Observations or inspections
None by the Convention as such.

Trade measures
No provisions on trade measures to penalize Parties for non-compliance.

Dispute-settlement mechanisms
In the event of a dispute between the Parties, or between a Party and the IAEA, concerning the interpretation and application of the Convention, the Parties shall consult with a view to settling the dispute by negotiation or by any other peaceful means.

However, if the dispute cannot be settled within one year from the request for consultation, the dispute shall be submitted to arbitration or referred to the International Court of Justice for decision.

A Party may declare that it does not consider itself bound by either or both of these dispute-settlement procedures when signing, ratifying, approving, or acceding to the Convention.

Decision-making bodies

Political
The only organ referred to in the Convention is the IAEA. No meetings of Parties have taken place so far.

Scientific/technical
Technical assistance is provided by the IAEA. No long-term scientific advisory functions or participation from NGOs and industry are foreseen.

Publications

Up-to-date information is available through *IAEA Bulletin* (quarterly) and the IAEA's annual reports.

Sources on the Internet

<http://www.iaea.org/worldatom/Documents/Legal/cenna.shtml>

Convention on Nuclear Safety

Objectives

• to achieve and maintain a high level of nuclear safety world-wide through the enhancement of national measures and international co-operation, including, where appropriate, safety-related technical co-operation;
• to establish and maintain effective defences in nuclear installations against potential radiological hazards in order to protect individuals, society, and the environment from harmful effects of ionizing radiation from such installations;
• to prevent accidents with radiological consequences and to mitigate such consequences should they occur.

Scope

Legal scope
Open to all states and regional organizations of an integration or other nature.

Geographic Scope
Global.

Time and place of adoption

17 June 1994, Vienna. Open for signature on 20 September 1994.

Entry into force

24 October 1996.

Status of participation

53 states and one intergovernmental organization (European Atomic Energy Community (EURATOM)) were Parties by 12 April 2002. 18 Signatories without ratification, acceptance, or approval.

The International Atomic Energy Agency (IAEA) (see IGOs) acts as depositary.

Affiliated instruments and organizations

No amendments have yet been proposed. Any Contracting Party may propose amendments. Proposed amendments shall be considered at a meeting of the Contracting Parties (see Decision-making bodies, below).

The IAEA Secretariat is in charge of administering the Convention.

Co-ordination with related instruments
None.

Secretariat

IAEA (see IGOs).

Finance

Budget
Costs are covered by the regular IAEA budget.

Special funds
Not applicable.

Rules and standards

The specific safety obligations in the Convention are based on what are termed fundamental safety provisions rather than on very detailed standards; guidance on the more detailed internationally agreed safety standards are already available and these are also continually updated.

The fundamental safety obligations of the Convention begin with a requirement for each State to maintain a legislative and regulatory framework; that is, to have:
• specific national safety requirements;
• a licensing procedure;
• inspection, assessment, and enforcement policies.

There is also a requirement that the body which implements the regulatory function be separate from other bodies concerned with the promotion and utilization of nuclear energy. The Convention underscores that the prime responsibility for safety rests with the State where a nuclear installation is located, and more specifically the holder of the operating licence, that is, the utility or operating organization.

There is a series of general safety obligations which emphasizes the need:
• to take steps to assure that all organizations involved with nuclear installations give priority to safety;
• to provide adequate financial and human resources;
• to give attention to human factor and quality assurance.

There is also a series of more detailed obligations related to siting, design, construction, and operation requirements. These speak to the need:
• to evaluate all site-related factors, such as those pertaining to seismology and flooding;
• to use proven technologies;
• to have approved operating procedures;
• to report promptly on accidents;
• to collect and analyse operating experience;
• to minimize nuclear waste;
• to prepare and test emergency plans.

In addition, the obligations contain some requirements for interactions with neighbouring countries:
• States should, upon request, provide information to a neighbouring state in the vicinity of a proposed nuclear installation (if they are likely to be affected) to enable them to assess the probable safety impact on their territory;
• States should also ensure that their own population and the competent authorities of states in the vicinity of a nuclear installation are provided with appropriate information for emergency planning and response;
• States which do not have a nuclear installation but could be affected by a neighbouring country's installation should have emergency plans which are tested.

The Convention has 16 specific articles defining obligations of the Convention, and it provides for a forum to discuss nuclear safety conditions in each State. The forum will be the mechanism to identify problems, concerns, and uncertainties or omissions. The Convention also provides a mechanism to make the public aware of the issues.

Monitoring/implementation

Review procedure
Each Contracting Party shall, prior to meetings of the Contracting Parties, submit a report on the measures it has taken to implement each of the obligations of the Convention—as these meetings are held for the purpose of reviewing the reports submitted. Subgroups comprised of representatives of the Parties may be established and may function during the review meetings as deemed necessary for the purpose of reviewing subjects contained in the reports. Each Party shall have a reasonable opportunity to discuss the reports submitted by other Parties and to seek clarification of such reports.

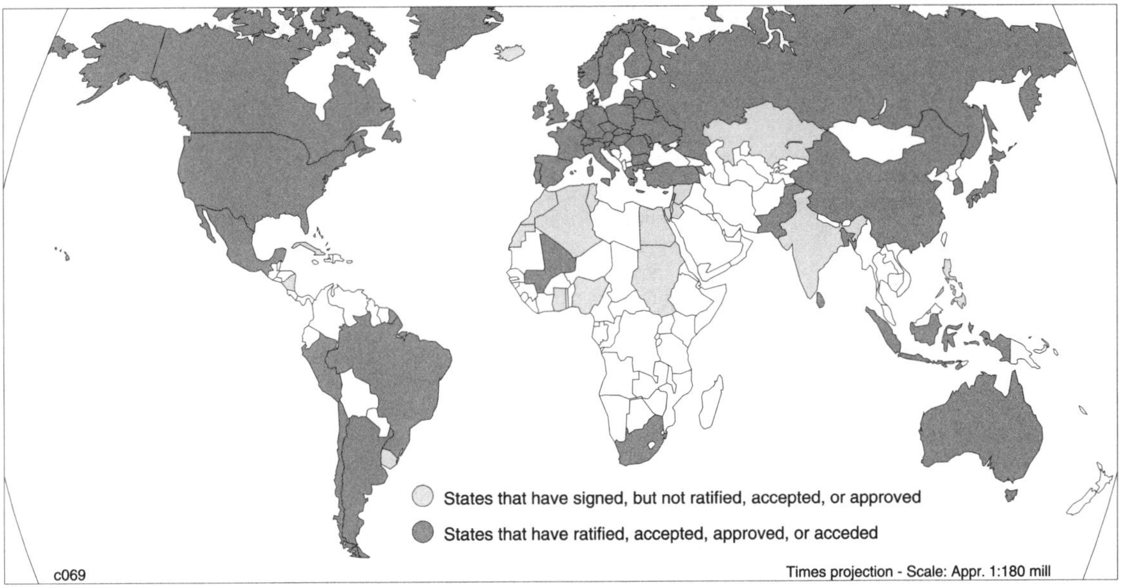

The first Review Meeting pursuant to Article 20 of the Convention was held at the Headquarters of IAEA, being the Secretariat under the Convention, in Vienna between 12 and 23 April 1999.

45 Contracting Parties participated, namely: Argentina, Armenia, Australia, Austria, Belarus, Belgium, Brazil, Bulgaria, Canada, Chile, China, Croatia, the Czech Republic, Denmark, Finland, France, Germany, Greece, Hungary, Ireland, Italy, Japan, the Republic of Korea, Latvia, Lebanon, Lithuania, Luxembourg, Mexico, the Netherlands, Norway, Pakistan, Peru, Poland, Portugal, Romania, the Russian Federation, Slovakia, Slovenia, South Africa, Spain, Sweden, Switzerland, Turkey, Ukraine, and the United Kingdom.

Six months before the Review Meeting, Contracting Parties submitted national reports on steps and measures taken to implement Convention obligations. In the following months the Parties reviewed each other's reports and exchanged written questions and comments. At the Review Meeting, Parties organized themselves into six country groups.

Pursuant to Article 25 of the Convention, the Parties adopted, by consensus, a document addressing issues discussed and conclusions reached, entitled *Summary Report of the Review Meeting of Contracting Parties to the Convention on Nuclear Safety*. It is available on the IAEA's website at: <http://www.iaea.org/worldatom/Documents/Legal/revmtg0199.shtml>.

Observations or inspections
None by the Convention as such.

Trade measures
No provisions on trade measures to penalize Parties for non-compliance.

Dispute-settlement mechanisms
In the event of a disagreement between two or more Parties concerning the interpretation and application of the Convention, the Parties shall consult within the framework of the meeting of the Parties with a view to resolving the disagreement.

Decision-making bodies

Political
The meeting of the Contracting Parties is the governing body of the Convention. Each Party shall be represented at such meetings by one delegate and by such alternates, experts, and advisers as it deems necessary. The meeting shall keep under review and evaluate implementation of the Convention. It shall also consider and adopt, by consensus, amendments to the Convention. In the absence of consensus, the meeting shall decide whether to submit proposed amendments to a diplomatic conference. A decision to submit a proposed amendment to a diplomatic conference shall require a two-thirds majority vote of the Contracting Parties present and voting at the meeting, providing that at least one-half of the Parties are present at the time of voting. The diplomatic conference shall make every effort to ensure amendments are adopted by consensus. Should this not be possible, amendments shall be adopted with a two-thirds majority of all Parties.

The Parties may invite, by consensus, any IGO which is competent in respect of matters governed by the Convention to attend, as an observer, any meeting, or specific sessions thereof. Observers shall be required to accept in writing, and in advance, confidentiality according with the provisions in the Convention.

The first meeting of the Parties was held at the IAEA from 22 to 25 April 1997.

Scientific/technical bodies
To be decided. Technical assistance may be provided by the IAEA if such services can be undertaken within its programmes and regular budget or from voluntary funding provided from another source. No long-term scientific advisory functions or participation from NGOs and industry are foreseen.

Publications

Up-to-date information is available through *IAEA Bulletin* (quarterly) and the IAEA's annual reports.

Sources on the Internet

<http://www.iaea.org/worldatom/Documents/Legal/nukesafety.shtml>

Vienna Convention on Civil Liability for Nuclear Damage

Objectives
To establish minimum standards to provide financial protection against damage resulting from peaceful uses of nuclear energy.

Scope
Legal scope
Open to all member States of the UN, or members of the UN specialized agencies or the International Atomic Energy Agency (IAEA) (see IGOs). Not open to regional integration organizations.

Geographic scope
Global.

Time and place of adoption
21 May 1963, Vienna.

Entry into force
12 November 1977.

Status of participation
33 Parties by 6 March 2002. Six Signatories without ratification, acceptance, or approval.

The IAEA acts as depositary.

Affiliated instruments and organizations
• *Optional Protocol Concerning the Compulsory Settlement of Disputes*, Vienna, 1963 (see below). Entered into force on 13 May 1999 upon the second ratification. Two Parties by 6 March 2002. Three Signatories without ratification, acceptance, or approval.
• *Joint Protocol Relating to the Application of the Vienna Convention and the Paris Convention*, Vienna, 21 September 1988. Entered into force on 27 April 1992. 24 Parties by 6 March 2002. 10 Signatories without ratification, acceptance, or approval. The Paris Convention on Third Party Liability in the Field of Nuclear Energy is regional in scope and administered by the OECD Nuclear Energy Agency (NEA). The address of the Agency is Le Seine-St Germain, 12 boulevard des Îles, F-92130 Issy-les-Moulineaux, France. Telephone: +33-1-45248200. Telefax: +33-1-45241110. Internet: <http://www.nea.fr>
• *Protocol to Amend the Vienna Convention on Civil Liability for Nuclear Damage*, Vienna, 12 September 1997. (Not yet in force.) Four ratifications by 6 March 2002. 11 Signatories without ratification, acceptance, or approval. Open for signature by all states until its entry into force. It enters into force three months after the date of deposit of the fifth instruments of ratification, acceptance, or approval. The main objective of the Protocol is to set the possible limit of the operator's liability at not less than 300 million Special Drawing Rights (SDRs).

The IAEA Secretariat is in charge of administering the Convention.

Co-ordination with related instruments
Since 1987 a review of all aspects of international law on liability for nuclear damage has been instituted by the Standing Committee on Liability for Nuclear Damage, within the framework of the IAEA. The first stage of this work led to the adoption of the Joint Protocol (see above). With respect to the revision of the Vienna Convention, the next stage led to the adoption of both the Protocol to Amend the Vienna Convention on Civil Liability for Nuclear Damage (see above) and a new convention in 1997.
• *Convention on Supplementary Compensation for Nuclear Damage*. Adopted in Vienna on 12 September 1997. (Not yet in force.) Three ratifications by 6 March 2002. 10 Signatories without ratification, acceptance, or approval. Enters into force on the ninetieth day following the date on which at least five states with a minimum of 400,000 units of installed nuclear capacity have deposited an instrument. The main objective of the Convention is to define additional amounts to be provided through contributions by States Parties on the basis of installed nuclear capacity and UN rate of assessment. It is an instrument to which all states may adhere regardless of whether they are parties to any existing nuclear liability conventions or have nuclear installations on their territories.

Secretariat
IAEA (see IGOs).

Finance
Budget
No costs of administration.

Special funds
None.

Rules and standards
The operator of a nuclear installation shall be liable for nuclear damage on provision of proof that such damage was caused by an incident within the installation, or involving nuclear material originating therefrom or being sent thereto.

The liability of the operator in such a case shall be absolute, but the courts may make a finding of contributory negligence on the part of the person suffering such damage; in any case the operator will not be liable if the nuclear incident was due directly to act of armed conflict, civil war, insurrection, or a grave natural disaster of an exceptional character.

The Convention has established limits of liability and limitation of action.

The operator is required to maintain insurance or financial security to cover liability.

Parties shall:
• ensure the payment of compensation in cases where they do not provide for insurance of the operator or beyond the yield of such insurance and up to the operator's liability;
• provide for necessary jurisdictional competences, and recognize final judgements entered by foreign courts in accordance with the Convention.

They shall not invoke immunities in legal proceedings under the Convention.

The principal benefit for all countries participating in the Convention is the right of their nationals to claim compensation in case of nuclear damage caused by installations situated in the territory of a Contracting Party. Currently, the minimum amount of compensation is subject to review and subsequent adoption; the benefit may be expected to increase substantially in the near future.

Monitoring/implementation

Review procedure
There is no mechanism for the promotion of implementation and follow-up on non-compliance. Parties do not regularly report about implementation and do not have to disclose or supply data.

Observations or inspections
None by the Convention as such.

Trade measures
No provisions on trade measures to penalize Parties for non-compliance.

Dispute-settlement mechanisms
The Convention has no rules concerning the settlement of disputes, but the International Conference on Civil Liability for Nuclear Damage of 1963 adopted an Optional Protocol Concerning Compulsory Settlement of Disputes (see above).

Decision-making bodies

Political
The Convention does not provide for institutional or administrative arrangements. No regular meetings or programme activities are envisaged. A Standing Committee on Civil Liability for Nuclear Damage was established within the framework of the IAEA. This Committee has met occasionally to discuss issues relevant to the Convention. The Committee was composed of 15 States. Limitations concerning participation were removed as the Committee was transformed into an open-ended negotiation forum and renamed a Standing Committee on Liability for Nuclear Damage. Currently, about 60 delegations from both developing and industrialized countries as well as NGOs attend its sessions, and the mandate of the Committee has been extended to include international liability matters.

Scientific/technical
There are no elaborated mechanisms for regular review of provisions or consideration of scientific and technical information. However, the Board of Governors of the IAEA may take decisions on minor technical issues. The Board may also provide legal assistance if requested in case of countries without nuclear programmes. Participation does not imply any financial obligations.

Publications

Up-to-date information is available through *IAEA Bulletin* (quarterly) and the IAEA's annual reports.

Sources on the Internet

<http://www.iaea.org/worldatom/Documents/Legal>

Convention on the Protection and Use of Transboundary Watercourses and International Lakes (ECE Water Convention)

Objectives

• to strengthen national and international actions aimed at the protection and ecologically sound management of transboundary waters, both surface waters and groundwaters, and related ecosystems, including the marine environment;
• to prevent, control, and reduce the releases of hazardous, acidifying, and eutrophying substances into the aquatic environment;
• to promote public information and public participation in relevant decision-making processes.

Scope

Legal scope
Open to member countries of the UN Economic Commission for Europe (UNECE), the European Union (EU), and other European states having consultative status with the UNECE.

Geographic scope
Regional. UNECE region (Europe and North America).

Time and place of adoption

17 March 1992, Helsinki.

Entry into force

6 October 1996.

Status of participation

33 Parties, including the European Union, by 10 June 2002. Two Signatories without ratification, acceptance, or approval.

Affiliated instruments and organizations

Protocol on Water and Health to the Convention on the Protection and Use of Transboundary Watercourses and International Lakes, London, 17 June 1999. (Not yet in force.) Seven states had ratified, approved, or acceded by 10 June 2002. 29 Signatories without ratification, acceptance, or approval. It enters into force on the ninetieth day after the date of deposit of the sixteenth instrument of ratification, acceptance, approval, or accession.

The basic objective of the Protocol is to promote, at all appropriate levels, the protection of human health and well-being, through improving water management, including the protection of water ecosystems, and through preventing, controlling, and reducing water-related disease.

The Convention also contains four *annexes* which form an integral part of the Convention.

Co-ordination with related instruments
Collaboration is taking place with other UNECE conventions, especially the Convention on the Transboundary Effects of Industrial Accidents (see this section).

Secretariat

UNECE, Environment and Human Settlements Division (ENHS),
Palais des Nations,
CH-1211 Geneva 10, Switzerland
Telephone: +41-22-917-2373/1499
Telefax: +41-22-907-0634/0107
E-mail: rainer.enderlein@unece.org

Secretary to the Meeting of the Parties
Mr Rainer E. Enderlein.

Finance

Not applicable.

Rules and standards

The Parties shall take all appropriate measures:
• to prevent, control, and reduce pollution of waters causing or likely to cause transboundary impact;
• to ensure that transboundary waters are used with the aim of ecologically sound and rational water management, conservation of water resources, and environmental protection;
• to ensure that transboundary waters are used in a reasonable and equitable way, taking into particular account their transboundary character, in the case of activities which cause or are likely to cause transboundary impact;
• to ensure conservation and, where necessary, restoration of ecosystems.

In taking these measures, the Parties shall be guided by the following principles:
• the *precautionary principle*, by virtue of which action to avoid the potential transboundary impact of the release of hazardous substances shall not be postponed on the ground that scientific research has not fully proved a causal link between those substances, on the one hand, and the potential transboundary impact, on the other hand;
• the *polluter-pays principle*, by virtue of which the costs of pollution prevention, control, and reduction measures shall be borne by the polluter;
• water resources shall be managed so that the needs of the present generation are met without compromising the ability of future generations to meet their own needs.

The Parties will have to set emission limits for discharges from point sources based on the best available technology; issue authorizations for the discharge of waste water and monitor compliance therewith; adopt water-quality criteria and define water-quality objectives; apply at least biological treatment or equivalent processes to municipal waste water; develop contingency plans; apply environmental impact assessment and the ecosystem approach in water management; and develop and implement appropriate measures and best environmental practices to reduce the input of nutrients and hazardous substances from diffuse sources, in particular from agriculture.

The riparian Parties shall co-operate on the basis of equality and reciprocity, in particular through bilateral and multilateral agreements, in order to develop harmonized policies, programmes, and strategies covering the relevant catchment areas, or parts thereof, aimed at the prevention, control, and reduction of transboundary impact, and at the protection of the environment of transboundary waters or the environment influenced by such waters, including the marine environment.

Monitoring/implementation

Review procedure
The Parties shall report periodically on the implementation of this Convention.

The Meeting of the Parties (see below)

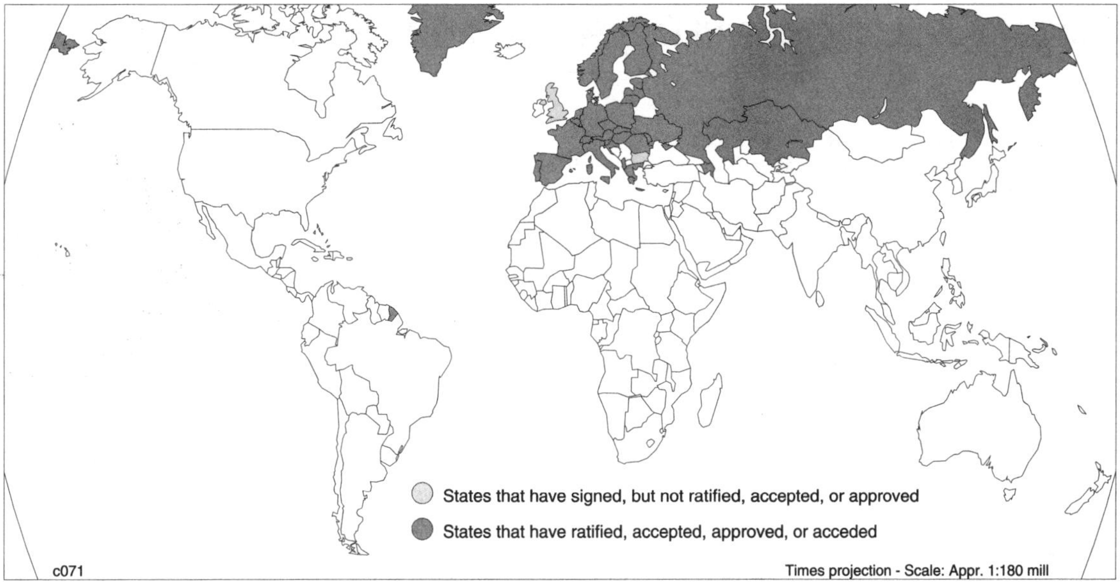

shall keep the Convention under continuous review and, with this purpose in mind:

- review the policies for and methodological approaches to the protection and use of transboundary waters of the Parties with a view to improving further the protection and use of transboundary waters;
- exchange information regarding experience gained in concluding and implementing bilateral and multilateral agreements or other arrangements regarding the protection and use of transboundary waters to which one or more of the Parties are party.

The programme of work (2000–03) covers four priority areas: implementation and compliance; integrated management of water and related ecosystems; monitoring and assessment; and water and human health.

A joint special session of the governing bodies of this Convention and that on the Transboundary Effects of Industrial Accidents was held in Geneva from 2 to 3 July 2001 with a view to considering entering into an intergovernmental negotiation process for an appropriate regime in the UNECE region on civil liability for damage caused by hazardous activities within the scope of both Conventions. It established an open-ended intergovernmental Working Group with a mandate to draw up the above-mentioned legally binding instrument. All UNECE member countries, as well as observers, in particular interested NGOs and representatives of the insurance sector, international organizations, and other stakeholders, were invited to participate in the business of the Working Group.

Environmental monitoring programmes
Parties bordering the same transboundary water shall establish and implement joint programmes for monitoring the conditions of transboundary waters, including floods and ice drifts, as well as transboundary impact; agree upon pollution parameters and pollutants whose concentrations in transboundary waters shall be regularly monitored; carry out joint or co-ordinated assessments of the condition of transboundary waters and the effectiveness of measures taken to prevent, control, and reduce transboundary impact; exchange reasonably available data on environmental conditions of transboundary waters, including monitoring data; inform each other about critical situations that may have transboundary impact; and make available to the public results of water and effluent sampling, together with the results of checking compliance with the water-quality objectives and the permit conditions.

Decision-making bodies

Political
The Meeting of the Parties is the supreme decision-making body. At their meetings, which shall be held at least every three years, the Parties shall keep under continuous review the implementation of the Convention and consider and adopt proposals for further development or amendments.

The first meeting was held in Helsinki from 2 to 4 July 1997, the second meeting was held in The Hague from 23 to 25 March 2000, and the third meeting will be held in Spain in autumn 2003. A joint special session of the governing bodies of this Convention and that on the Transboundary Effects of Industrial Accidents was held from 2 to 3 July 2001 (see Monitoring/implementation above).

The Bureau (a chairperson and two vice-chairpersons elected by the Meeting of the Parties and the Chairpersons of Working Groups), with the assistance of the Secretariat, shall carry out the tasks entrusted to it by the Meeting of the Parties.

The first meeting of the Signatories to the Protocol on Water and Health was held in Budapest from 2 to 3 November 2000.

Scientific/technical
The implementation of the programme of activities is supported by working groups on water management, legal and administrative aspects, monitoring and assessment, and water and health, as well as by an expert group on water and industrial accidents.

Publications

- UNECE Water Series.

Sources on the Internet

<http://www.unece.org/env/water>

Tables of Agreements and Degrees of Participation, by Country

Abbreviations

General Environmental Concerns

Convention on Access to Information, Public Participation in Decision-Making and Access to Justice in Environmental Matters: ***Århus Convention***

Convention on Environmental Impact Assessment in a Transboundary Context: ***Espoo Convention***

Atmosphere

Annex 16, vol. II (Environmental Protection: Aircraft Engine Emissions) to the 1944 Chicago Convention on International Civil Aviation: ***Aircraft Engine Emissions (ICAO)***

Convention on Long-Range Transboundary Air Pollution: ***Transb. Air Pollution (LRTAP)***

- ***1994 Sulphur Protocol***
- ***1998 NO_x Protocol***
- ***1991 VOC Protocol***
- ***1998 Heavy Metals Protocol***
- ***1998 POPs Protocol***
- ***1999 Multi-Effects Protocol***

United Nations Framework Convention on Climate Change: ***Climate Change (UNFCCC)***

- ***Kyoto Protocol***

Vienna Convention for the Protection of the Ozone Layer: ***Ozone Layer Convention***

- Montreal Protocol on Substances that Deplete the Ozone Layer: ***Montreal Protocol***
- ***London Amendment***
- ***Copenhagen Amendment***
- ***Montreal Amendment***
- ***Beijing Amendment***

Hazardous Substances

Convention on the Ban of the Import into Africa and the Control of Transboundary Movements and Management of Hazardous Wastes within Africa: ***Bamako Convention***

Convention on Civil Liability for Damage Caused during Carriage of Dangerous Goods by Road, Rail, and Inland Navigation Vessels: ***CRTD***

Convention on the Control of Transboundary Movements of Hazardous Wastes and their Disposal: ***Basel Convention***

- **Ban Amendment**

Convention on the Prior Informed Consent Procedure for Certain Hazardous Chemicals and Pesticides in International Trade: ***PIC Convention***

Convention to Ban the Importation into Forum Island Countries of Hazardous and Radioactive Wastes and to Control the Transboundary Movement and Management of Hazardous Wastes within the South Pacific Region: ***Waigani Convention***

Convention on the Transboundary Effects of Industrial Accidents: ***Transb. Effects of Indust. Accidents***

European Agreement Concerning the International Carriage of Dangerous Goods by Inland Waterways: ***Dangerous Goods by Waterways***

European Agreement Concerning the International Carriage of Dangerous Goods by Road: ***Dangerous Goods by Road (ADR)***

FAO International Code of Conduct on the Distribution and Use of Pesticides: ***Distrib. and Use of Pesticides***

Stockholm Convention on Persistent Organic Pollutants: ***POPs Convention***

Marine Environment

Global Conventions

Convention on the Prevention of Marine Pollution by Dumping of Wastes and Other Matter: ***London Convention 1972***

- ***1996 Protocol to LC 1972***

International Convention for the Prevention of Pollution from Ships, 1973, as modified by the Protocol of 1978 relating thereto: ***MARPOL 73/78***

International Convention on Civil Liability for Oil Pollution Damage 1969: ***1969 CLC***

- ***1992 CLC Protocol***

International Convention on the Establishment of an International Fund for Compensation for Oil Pollution Damage 1992:

- ***1992 Fund Convention***

International Convention on Liability and Compensation for Damage in Connection with the Carriage of Hazardous and Noxious Substances by Sea: ***HNS Convention***

International Convention on Oil Pollution Preparedness, Response, and Co-operation: ***OPRC***

International Convention Relating to Intervention on the High Seas in Cases of Oil Pollution Casualties: ***Intervention Convention***

United Nations Convention on the Law of the Sea: ***LOS Convention***
• ***1995 Fish Stocks Agreement***

Regional Conventions
Convention for the Protection of the Marine Environment of the North-East Atlantic: ***OSPAR Convention***
Convention on the Protection of the Marine Environment of the Baltic Sea Area: ***1992 Helsinki Convention***
Conventions within the UNEP Regional Seas Programme:
- Convention on the Protection of the Black Sea against Pollution: ***Black Sea***
- Convention for the Protection and Development of the Marine Environment of the Wider Caribbean Region: ***Wider Caribbean Region***
- Convention for the Protection, Management, and Development of the Marine and Coastal Environment of the Eastern African Region: ***Eastern African Region***
- Kuwait Regional Convention for Co-operation on the Protection of the Marine Environment from Pollution: ***Kuwait Region***
- Convention for the Protection of the Marine Environment and the Coastal Region of the Mediterranean: ***Mediterranean-Sea***
- Regional Convention for the Conservation of the Red Sea and Gulf of Aden Environment: ***Red Sea and Gulf of Aden***
- Convention for the Protection of the Natural Resources and Environment of the South Pacific Region: ***South Pacific Region***
- Convention for the Protection of the Marine Environment and Coastal Zone of the South-East Pacific: ***South-East Pacific***
- Convention for Co-operation in the Protection and Development of the Marine and Coastal Environment of the West and Central African Region: ***West and Centr. African Region***

Marine Living Resources
Convention on the Conservation of Antarctic Marine Living Resources: ***Antarc. Marine Living Res. (CCAMLR)***
International Convention for the Conservation of Atlantic Tunas: ***Atlantic Tunas (ICCAT)***
International Convention for the Regulation of Whaling: ***Regulation of Whaling (ICRW)***

Nature Conservation and Terrestrial Living Resources
Antarctic Treaty
• Protocol on Environmental Protection to the Antarctic Treaty: ***Environmental Protocol***
Convention Concerning the Protection of the World Cultural and Natural Heritage: ***World Heritage Convention***
Convention on Biological Diversity: ***Biological Diversity (CBD)***
• ***Biosafety Protocol***
Convention on the Conservation of Migratory Species of Wild Animals: ***Migr. Species of Wild Animals (CMS)***
Convention on International Trade in Endangered Species of Wild Fauna and Flora: ***CITES***
Convention on Wetlands of International Importance especially as Waterfowl Habitat: ***Ramsar Convention***
Convention to Combat Desertification: ***Conv. to Combat Desertification (CCD)***
FAO International Undertaking on Plant Genetic Resources: ***IU on Plant Genetic Resources***
International Treaty on Plant Genetic Resources for Food and Agriculture: ***Treaty on Plant Genetic Resources***
International Tropical Timber Agreement, 1994: ***Tropical Timber (ITTA, 1994)***

Nuclear Safety
Convention on Assistance in the Case of a Nuclear Accident or Radiological Emergency: ***Assistance Convention***
Convention on Early Notification of a Nuclear Accident: ***Notification Convention***
Convention on Nuclear Safety: ***Nuclear Safety***
Vienna Convention on Civil Liability for Nuclear Damage: ***Civil Liability for Nuclear Damage***

Freshwater Resources
Convention on the Protection and Use of Transboundary Watercourses and International Lakes: ***ECE Water Convention***

Key

General
States that have signed, but not ratified, accepted, or approved

States that have ratified, accepted, approved, or acceded

Antarctic Treaty
Non-Consultative Parties to the Antarctic Treaty

Consultative Parties to the Antarctic Treaty

Aircraft Engine Emissions (ICAO) and *Distrib. and Use of Pesticides*
Member States

IU on Plant Genetic Resources
States that have adhered to the Undertaking

Tropical Timber (ITTA, 1994)
Member States

	General Environmental Concerns		Atmosphere																Hazardous Substances											Marine Environment – Global Conventions						
	Århus Convention	Espoo Convention	Aircraft Engine Emissions (ICAO)	Transb. Air Pollution (LRTAP)	* 1994 Sulphur Protocol	* 1988 NOx Protocol	* 1991 VOC Protocol	* 1998 Heavy Metals Protocol	* 1998 POPs Protocol	* 1999 Multi-Effects Protocol	Climate Change (UNFCCC)	* Kyoto Protocol	Ozone Layer Convention	Montreal Protocol	* London Amendment	* Copenhagen Amendment	* Montreal Amendment	* Beijing Amendment	Bamako Convention	CRTD	Basel Convention	* Ban Amendment	PIC Convention	Transb. Effects of Indust. Accidents	Waigani Convention	Dangerous Goods by Waterways	Dangerous Goods by Road (ADR)	Distrib. and Use of Pesticides	POPs Convention	London Convention 1972	* 1996 Protocol to LC 1972	MARPOL 73/78	1969 CLC	* 1992 CLC Protocol	* 1992 Fund Convention	HNS Convention
Afghanistan			○								○										○							○		●						
Albania	●	●	○								●		●	●							●			●				○	○				●			
Algeria			○								●		●	●	●	●					●							○	○			●		●	●	
Andorra			○																		●	●														
Angola			○								●		●	●									○					○		●	●	●		●	●	●
Antigua & Barbuda			○								●	●	●	●	●	●	●				●							○	○	●		●		●	●	
Argentina			○								●	●	●	●	●	●	●				●		○					○	○	●	○	●		●	●	
Armenia	●	●	○	●				○	○	○	●		●	●							●		○	●				○	○							
Australia			○								●	○	●	●	●	●	●				●		○		●			○	○	●	●	●		●	●	
Austria	○	●	○	●	●	●	●	○	○	○	●	●	●	●	●	●	●				●	●	○	●			●	○	○			●				
Azerbaijan	●	●	○								●	●	●	●	●	●	●				●						●	○		●						
Bahamas			○								●	●	●	●	●	●					●							○	○			●		●	●	
Bahrain			○								●		●	●	●	●	●				●							○	○					●	●	
Bangladesh			○								●	●	●	●	●	●	●				●							○	○							
Barbados			○								●	●	●	●	●	●					●		○					○		●		●		●	●	
Belarus	●	○	○	●		●					●		●	●	●						●						●			●		●				
Belgium	○	●	○	●	●	●	●	○	○	○	●	●	●	●	●	●					●		○	○			●	○	○	●	○	●		●	●	
Belize			○								●		●	●	●	●					●							○	○			●		●	●	
Benin			○								●	●	●	●	●	●			●		●		○					○	○			●	●			
Bhutan			○								●																	○								
Bolivia			○								●	●	●	●	●	●	●				●							○	○			●				
Bosnia & Herzegovina			○	●							●		●	●							●						●	○	○							
Botswana			○								●		●	●	●	●					●							○								
Brazil			○								●	○	●	●	●	●					●		○					○	○	●	○	●	●			
Brunei Darussalam			○										●	●															○			●	●	●	●	
Bulgaria	○	●	○	●	○	●	●	○	●	○	●	○	●	●	●	●	●	●			●	●	●	●		○	●	○	○			●				
Burkina Faso			○								●		●	●	●	●			○		●		○					○	○							
Burundi			○								●	●	●	●	●	●	●	●	○		●							○	○							
Cambodia			○								●		●	●							●							○	○			●	●	●	●	
Cameroon			○								●		●	●	●	●			●		●		●					○					●	●	●	
Canada		●	○	●	●	●	○	●	●	○	●	○	●	●	●	●	●	●			●			○				○	●	●	●	●		●	●	○

Marine Environment: Global Conventions				Marine Environment: Regional Conventions											Marine Living Resources			Nature Conservation and Terrestrial Living Resources												Nuclear Safety				Freshwater Resources	
OPRC	Intervention Convention	LOS Convention	* Fish Stocks Agreement	OSPAR Convention	1992 Helsinki Convention	Black Sea	Wider Caribbean Region	Eastern African Region	Kuwait Region	Mediterranean Sea	Red Sea and Gulf of Aden	South Pacific Region	South-East Pacific	West and Centr. African Region	Antarc. Marine Living Res. (CCAMLR)	Atlantic Tunas (ICCAT)	Regulation of Whaling (ICRW)	Antarctic Treaty	* Environmental Protocol	World Heritage Convention	Biological Diversity	* Biosafety Protocol	Migr. Species of Wild Animals (CMS)	CITES	Ramsar Convention	Conv. to Combat Desertification (CCD)	IU on Plant Genetic Resources	Treaty on Plant Genetic Resources	Tropical Timber (ITTA, 1994)	Assistance Convention	Notification Convention	Nuclear Safety	Civil Liability for Nuclear Damage	ECE Water Convention	
		○																		●	○			●		●				○	○				Afghanistan
										●										●	●		●		●	●								●	Albania
		●								●						●				●	●	○		●	●	●	○			○	○	○			Algeria
																				●															Andorra
●	●	●														●				●	●					●	○								Angola
●		●					●										●			●	●	○		●		●	○								Antigua & Barbuda
●	●	●	○												●		●	◉	●	●	●	○	●	●	●	●	○	○		●	●	●	●		Argentina
																				●	●				●	●				●	●	●	●		Armenia
●	●	●	●									●			●		●	◉	●	●	●		●	●	●	●	○	○	●	●	●	●			Australia
		●	○														●	◍	○	●	●	○		●	●	●	○	○	●	●	●	●		●	Austria
																				●	●			●	●	●								●	Azerbaijan
●	●	●	●																		●	○		●	●	●	○								Bahamas
		●							●											●	●				●	●	○								Bahrain
	●	●	○																	●	●	○		●	●	●	○			●	●	●			Bangladesh
	●	●	●				●									●				●	●			●		●	○								Barbados
		○																		●	●			●	●	●				●	●	●	●		Belarus
	●	●	○	●											●			◉	●	●	●	○	●	●	●	●	○	○	●	●	●	●		●	Belgium
		●	○				●													●	●			●	●	●	○								Belize
	●	●												○			●			●	●	○	●	●	●	●	○								Benin
		○																			●							○							Bhutan
		●																		●	●	●		●	●	●	○		●				●		Bolivia
		●								●										●										●	●		●		Bosnia & Herzegovina
		●																		●	●	●		●	●	●									Botswana
●	○	●	●												●	●	●	◉	●	●	●			●	●	●		○	●	●	●	●	●		Brazil
		●																						●											Brunei Darussalam
●	●	●				●									●			◉	●	●	●	●	●	●	●	●	○			●	●	●	●	○	Bulgaria
		○	○																	●	●	○	●	●	●	●	○	○							Burkina Faso
		○																		●	●			●		●		○							Burundi
		○																		●	●			●	●	●		●	●						Cambodia
	●	●												●						●	●	○	●	●		●	○		●	○	○		●		Cameroon
●		○	●												●	●		◍	○	●	●	○		●	●	●		●	●	○	●	●			Canada

	General Environmental Concerns		Atmosphere																Hazardous Substances											Marine Environment – Global Conventions						
	Århus Convention	Espoo Convention	Aircraft Engine Emissions (ICAO)	Transb. Air Pollution (LRTAP)	* 1994 Sulphur Protocol	* 1988 NOx Protocol	* 1991 VOC Protocol	* 1998 Heavy Metals Protocol	* 1998 POPs Protocol	* 1999 Multi-Effects Protocol	Climate Change (UNFCCC)	* Kyoto Protocol	Ozone Layer Convention	* Montreal Protocol	* London Amendment	* Copenhagen Amendment	* Montreal Amendment	* Beijing Amendment	Bamako Convention	CRTD	Basel Convention	* Ban Amendment	PIC Convention	Transb. Effects of Indust. Accidents	Waigani Convention	Dangerous Goods by Waterways	Dangerous Goods by Road (ADR)	Distrib. and Use of Pesticides	POPs Convention	London Convention 1972	* 1996 Protocol to LC 1972	MARPOL 73/78	1969 CLC	* 1992 CLC Protocol	1992 Fund Convention	HNS Convention
Cape Verde			○								●		●	●	●	●	●				●							○		●						
Central African Rep.			○								●		●	●					○									○	○							
Chad			○								●		●	●	●	●	●		○				○					○	○							
Chile			○								●	○	●	●	●	●	●	●			●		○					○	○	●		●	●			
China			○								●	○	●	●	●						●	●	○					○	○	●	○	●		●		
Colombia			○								●	●	●	●	●	●					●		○					○	○			●	●	●	●	
Comoros			○								●		●	●	●						●							○	○			●		●	●	
Congo			○								●		●	●	●	●	●	●	●				○					○	○							
Congo (DR of)			○								●		●	●	●	●			●		●		○					○		●						
Cook Islands			○								●	●													●			○								
Costa Rica			○								●	○	●	●	●	●					●		○					○	○	●			●			
Côte d'Ivoire			○								●		●	●	●				●		●		○					○	○	●		●	●			
Croatia	○	●	○	●	●			○	○	○	●	○	●	●	●	●	●	●			●			●		○	●	○	○	●		●		●	●	
Cuba			○								●	●	●	●	●	●					●		○					○	○	●		●				
Cyprus	○	●	○	●				○	○		●	●	●	●	●						●	●	○					○		●		●		●	●	
Czech Republic	○	●	○	●	●	●	●	○	○	○	●	●	●	●	●	●	●	●			●	●	●	●		○	●	○	○			●				
Denmark	●	●	○	●	●	●	●	●	●	●	●	●	●	●	●	●					●	●	○	●			●	○	○	●	●	●		●	●	○
Djibouti			○								●	●	●	●	●	●	●		○		●							○	○			●	●	●	●	
Dominica											●		●	●	●						●							○				●		●	●	
Dominican Republic			○								●	●	●	●	●	●					●							○	○	●		●	●	●	●	
East Timor																																				
Ecuador			○								●	●	●	●	●	●					●	●	○					○	○			●	●			
Egypt			○								●	○	●	●	●	●	●		○		●							○	○	●		●	●	●		
El Salvador			○								●	●	●	●	●	●	●				●		●					○	○				●	●		
Equatorial Guinea			○								●	●	●															○				●	●			
Eritrea			○								●																	○								
Estonia	●	●	○	●		●	●				●	○	●	●	●	●					●	●		●			●	○				●	●			
Ethiopia			○								●		●	●							●							○	○							
Fiji			○								●	●	●	●	●	●									●			○	●					●	●	
Finland	○	●	○	●	●	●	●	●	○	○	●	●	●	●	●	●	●	●			●	●	○	●			●	○	○	●	○	●		●	●	○
France	○	●	○	●	●	●	●	○	○	○	●	●	●	●	●	●					●		○	○		○	●	○	○	●		●		●	●	

Marine Environment: *Global Conventions* (OPRC – * Fish Stocks Agreement); *Regional Conventions* (OSPAR Convention – West and Centr. African Region)

Marine Living Resources

Nature Conservation and Terrestrial Living Resources

Nuclear Safety

Freshwater Resources

Country	OPRC	Intervention Convention	LOS Convention	* Fish Stocks Agreement	OSPAR Convention	1992 Helsinki Convention	Black Sea	Wider Caribbean Region	Eastern African Region	Kuwait Region	Mediterranean Sea	Red Sea and Gulf of Aden	South Pacific Region	South-East Pacific	West and Centr. African Region	Antarc. Marine Living Res. (CCAMLR)	Atlantic Tunas (ICCAT)	Regulation of Whaling (ICRW)	Antarctic Treaty	* Environmental Protocol	World Heritage Convention	Biological Diversity	* Biosafety Protocol	Migr. Species of Wild Animals (CMS)	CITES	Ramsar Convention	Conv. to Combat Desertification (CCD)	IU on Plant Genetic Resources	Treaty on Plant Genetic Resources	Tropical Timber (ITTA, 1994)	Assistance Convention	Notification Convention	Nuclear Safety	Civil Liability for Nuclear Damage	ECE Water Convention
Cape Verde			●														●				●	●					●	○							
Central African Rep.			○																		●	●	○	○	●		●	○	○	●					
Chad			○																		●	●	○	●	●	●	●	○	○						
Chile	●	●	●											●		●		●	◉	●	●	●	○	●	●	●	●	○			○	○	●	●	
China	●	●	●	○													●	●	◉	●	●	●	○		●	●	●			●	●	●	●		
Colombia			○					●						●					◐	○	●	●	○		●	●	●	○		●				○	
Comoros	●		●						●												●	●			●	●	●	○							
Congo			○												●						●	●	○	●	●	●	●	○		●					
Congo (DR of)			●																		●	●		●	●	●	●			●	○	○			
Cook Islands			●	●									●									●	○				●								
Costa Rica			●	●				●										●			●	●	○		●	●	●	○	○		●	●			
Côte d'Ivoire	○	●	●	○											●		●				●	●		○	●	●	●	○	○	●	○	○			
Croatia	●	●	●								●						●				●	●	○	●	●	●	●				●	●	●	●	●
Cuba		●	●					●											◐		●	●	○		●	●	●	○			●	●	○	●	
Cyprus			●								●										●	●		●	●	●	●	○	○		●	●	●		
Czech Republic			●																◐	○	●	●	●	●	●	●	●	○			●	●	●	●	●
Denmark	●	●	○	○	●	●												●	◐	○	●	●	○	●	●	●	●	○	○	●	○	●	●		●
Djibouti	●	●	●									●										●	●		●		●								
Dominica	●		●					●										●			●	●			●		●	○							
Dominican Republic		●	○					●									○				●	●			●		●	○	○						
East Timor																																			
Ecuador	●	●												●					◉	●	●	●	○		●	●	●	○		●					
Egypt	●	●	●	○							●	●									●	●	○	●	●	●	●	○		●	●	●	○	●	
El Salvador	●		○																		●	●	○		●	●	●	○	○						
Equatorial Guinea		●	●														●					●			●		●	○							
Eritrea																					●	●			●		●		○						
Estonia						●													◐		●	●	○		●	●					●	●		●	●
Ethiopia			○																		●	●	○		●		●	○							
Fiji		●	●	●									●								●	●	●		●		●	○		●					
Finland	●	●	●	○	●	●										●		●	◉	●	●	●	○	●	●	●	●	○	○	●	●	●	●		●
France	●	●	●	○	●			●	●		●		●			●	●	●	◉	●	●	●	○	●	●	●	●	○	○	●	●	●	●		●

General Environmental Concerns | Atmosphere | Hazardous Substances | Marine Environment

Global Conventions

General Environmental Concerns / Atmosphere

	Arhus Convention	Espoo Convention	Aircraft Engine Emissions (ICAO)	Transb. Air Pollution (LRTAP)	* 1994 Sulphur Protocol	* 1988 NOx Protocol	* 1991 VOC Protocol	* 1998 Heavy Metals Protocol	* 1998 POPs Protocol	* 1999 Multi-Effects Protocol	Climate Change (UNFCCC)	* Kyoto Protocol	Ozone Layer Convention	Montreal Protocol	* London Amendment	* Copenhagen Amendment	* Montreal Amendment	* Beijing Amendment
Gabon			○								●		●	●	●	●	●	●
Gambia			○								●	●	●	●	●			
Georgia	●		○	●							●	●	●	●	●	●	●	
Germany	○	○	○	●	●	●	●	○	●	○	●	●	●	●	●	●	●	
Ghana			○								●		●	●	●	●		
Greece	○	●	○	●	●	●	○	○	○	○	●	●	●	●	●	●		
Grenada			○								●		●	●	●	●	●	
Guatemala			○								●	●	●	●	●	●	●	●
Guinea			○								●	●	●	●	●			
Guinea-Bissau			○								●							
Guyana			○								●		●	●	●	●	●	
Haiti			○								●		●	●	●	●	●	
Holy See (Vatican)				○														
Honduras			○								●	●	●	●	●	●		
Hungary	●	●	○	●	●	●	●	○	○	○	●		●	●	●	●	●	●
Iceland	○	○	○	●				○	○		●	●	●	●	●	●	●	
India			○								●		●	●	●			
Indonesia			○								●	○	●	●	●	●		
Iran (Islamic Rep. of)			○								●		●	●	●	●	●	
Iraq			○															
Ireland	○	○	○	●	●	●		○	○	○	●	●	●	●	●	●		
Israel			○								●	○	●	●	●	●		
Italy	●	●	○	●	●	●	●	○	○	○	●	●	●	●	●	●	●	
Jamaica			○								●	●	●	●	●	●		
Japan			○								●	●	●	●	●	●		
Jordan			○								●		●	●	●	●	●	●
Kazakhstan	●	●	○	●							●	○	●	●	●			
Kenya			○								●		●	●	●	●	●	
Kiribati			○								●	●	●	●				
Korea (DPR of)			○								●		●	●		●	●	●
Korea (Rep. of)			○								●	○	●	●	●	●	●	

Hazardous Substances

	Bamako Convention	CRTD	Basel Convention	* Ban Amendment	PIC Convention	Transb. Effects of Indust. Accidents	Waigani Convention	Dangerous Goods by Waterways	Dangerous Goods by Road (ADR)	Distrib. and Use of Pesticides	POPs Convention
Gabon										○	○
Gambia	●		●	●	●					○	○
Georgia			●							○	○
Germany		○	●	●	●	●		○	●	○	●
Ghana					○					○	○
Greece			●		○	●			●	○	○
Grenada										○	
Guatemala			●							○	○
Guinea	○		●		●					○	○
Guinea-Bissau	○				○					○	○
Guyana			●							○	
Haiti			○							○	○
Holy See (Vatican)											
Honduras			●							○	○
Hungary			●		●	●			●	○	○
Iceland			●							○	●
India			●							○	○
Indonesia			●		○					○	○
Iran (Islamic Rep. of)			●		○					○	○
Iraq										○	
Ireland			●							○	○
Israel			●		○					○	○
Italy			●		○	○		○	●	○	○
Jamaica										○	○
Japan			●		○					○	
Jordan			●							○	○
Kazakhstan						●			●	○	○
Kenya			●		○					○	○
Kiribati			●				●			○	○
Korea (DPR of)										○	
Korea (Rep. of)			●		○					○	○

Marine Environment – Global Conventions

	London Convention 1972	* 1996 Protocol to LC 1972	* MARPOL 73/78	1969 CLC	* 1992 CLC Protocol	1992 Fund Convention	HNS Convention
Gabon	●		●	●			
Gambia			●	●			
Georgia		●	●	●	●	●	
Germany	●	●	●		●	●	○
Ghana			●	●			
Greece	●		●		●	●	
Grenada					●	●	
Guatemala	●		●	●			
Guinea							
Guinea-Bissau							
Guyana			●	●			
Haiti	●						
Holy See (Vatican)							
Honduras	●		●	●			
Hungary	●		●				
Iceland	●	○	●		●	●	
India			●		●	●	
Indonesia			●	●	●		
Iran (Islamic Rep. of)	●						
Iraq							
Ireland	●	●	●		●	●	
Israel			●				
Italy	●		●		●	●	
Jamaica	●		●		●	●	
Japan	●		●		●	●	
Jordan	●						
Kazakhstan			●	●			
Kenya	●		●		●	●	
Kiribati	●						
Korea (DPR of)			●				
Korea (Rep. of)	●		●		●	●	

Marine Environment: Global Conventions				Marine Environment: Regional Conventions											Marine Living Resources			Nature Conservation and Terrestrial Living Resources												Nuclear Safety				Freshwater Resources	
OPRC	Intervention Convention	LOS Convention	* Fish Stocks Agreement	OSPAR Convention	1992 Helsinki Convention	Black Sea	Wider Caribbean Region	Eastern African Region	Kuwait Region	Mediterranean Sea	Red Sea and Gulf of Aden	South Pacific Region	South-East Pacific	West and Centr. African Region	Antarc. Marine Living Res. (CCAMLR)	Atlantic Tunas (ICCAT)	Regulation of Whaling (ICRW)	Antarctic Treaty	* Environmental Protocol	World Heritage Convention	Biological Diversity	* Biosafety Protocol	Migr. Species of Wild Animals (CMS)	CITES	Ramsar Convention	Conv. to Combat Desertification (CCD)	IU on Plant Genetic Resources	Treaty on Plant Genetic Resources	Tropical Timber (ITTA, 1994)	Assistance Convention	Notification Convention	Nuclear Safety	Civil Liability for Nuclear Damage	ECE Water Convention	
	●	●	○											●		●	●			●	●			●	●	●	○	○	●						Gabon
○		●												●						●	●	○	●	●	●	●									Gambia
●	●	●				●														●	●		●	●	●	●									Georgia
●	●	●	○	●	●										●		●	◉	●	●	●	○	●	●	●	●	○	○	●	●	●	●		●	Germany
○	●	●												●		●				●	●		●	●	●	●	○		●			○			Ghana
●	○	●	○							●					●			◎	●	●	●	○	●	●	●	●	○	○	●	●	●	●		●	Greece
		●					●										●			●	●	○		●		●	○								Grenada
	○	●					●											◎		●	●			●	●	●		○	●	●	●				Guatemala
○		●												●		●	●			●	●	○	●	●	●	●	○	●							Guinea
		●	○																		●		●	●	●	●									Guinea-Bissau
●	●	●																		●	●			●		●			●						Guyana
		●																		●	●	○				●	○	○							Haiti
																				●										○	○				Holy See (Vatican)
		●					○									●				●	●	○		●	●	●	○		●						Honduras
		●																◎	○	●	●	○	●	●	●	●	○			●	●	●	●	●	Hungary
●	●	●	●	●																●	●	○		●	●	●	○			○	●	○			Iceland
●	●	●													●		●	◉	●	●	●	○	●	●	●	●	○	●	●	●	●	○			India
		●	○																	●	●	○		●	●	●			●	●	●	●			Indonesia
●	●	○	●						●											●	●	○		●	●	●	○			●	●				Iran (Islamic Rep. of)
		●							●											●							○			●	●				Iraq
●	●	●	○	●													●			●	●	○	●	●	●	●	○	○	●	●	●	●			Ireland
●			○							●										●	●		●	●	●	●	○			●	●	○	○		Israel
●	●	●	○							●					●		●	◉	●	●	●	○	●	●	●	●	○	○	●	●	●	●		●	Italy
●	●	●	○				●													●	●	○	○	●	●	●	○								Jamaica
●	●	●	○												●	●	●	◉	●	●	●			●	●	●			●	●	●	●			Japan
		●									●									●	●	○	●	●	●	●		●		●	●	○			Jordan
																				●	●			●		●						○		●	Kazakhstan
●		●						●									●			●	●	●	●	●	●	●	○								Kenya
																				●	●	○				●									Kiribati
		○																◎	○	●	●	○					○			○	○				Korea (DPR of)
●	○	●	○												●	●	●	◉	●	●	●	○		●	●	●	○		●	●	●	●			Korea (Rep. of)

	General Environmental Concerns		Atmosphere															
	Aarhus Convention	Espoo Convention	Aircraft Engine Emissions (ICAO)	Transb. Air Pollution (LRTAP)	* 1994 Sulphur Protocol	* 1988 NOx Protocol	* 1991 VOC Protocol	* 1998 Heavy Metals Protocol	* 1998 POPs Protocol	* 1999 Multi-Effects Protocol	Climate Change (UNFCCC)	* Kyoto Protocol	Ozone Layer Convention	* Montreal Protocol	* London Amendment	* Copenhagen Amendment	* Montreal Amendment	* Beijing Amendment
Kuwait			○								●		●	●	●	●		
Kyrgyz Republic	●	●	○	●							●		●	●				
Laos			○								●		●	●				
Latvia	○	●	○	●				○	○	○	●	○	●	●	●	●		
Lebanon			○								●		●	●	●	●	●	
Lesotho			○								●	●	●	●				
Liberia			○								○		●	●	●	●		
Libyan Arab Jamah.			○								●		●	●	●			
Liechtenstein	○	●		●	●	●	●	○	○	○	●	○	●	●	●	●		
Lithuania	●	●	○	●				○	○		●	○	●	●	●	●		
Luxembourg	○	●	○	●	●	●	●	●	●	●	●	●	●	●	●	●	●	●
Macedonia (FYR of)	●	●	○	●							●		●	●	●	●	●	●
Madagascar			○								●		●	●	●	●	●	●
Malawi			○								●	●	●	●	●	●		
Malaysia			○								●	○	●	●	●	●	●	●
Maldives			○								●	●	●	●	●	●	●	
Mali			○								●	●	●	●	●			
Malta	●		○	●							●	●	●	●	●			
Marshall Islands			○								●	○	●	●	●	●		
Mauritania			○								●		●	●				
Mauritius			○								●	●	●	●	●	●		
Mexico			○								●	●	●	●	●	●		
Micronesia (FS of)			○								●	●	●	●	●	●	●	●
Moldova (Rep. of)	●	●	○	●				○	○	○	●		●	●	●	●		
Monaco	○		○	●	●		●				●	○	●	●	●	●	●	
Mongolia			○								●	●	●	●	●	●	●	
Morocco			○								●	●	●	●	●	●		
Mozambique			○								●		●	●	●	●		
Myanmar			○								●		●	●	●			
Namibia			○								●		●	●	●			
Nauru			○								●	●	●	●				

	Hazardous Substances											Marine Environment – Global Conventions						
	Bamako Convention	CRTD	Basel Convention	* Ban Amendment	PIC Convention	Transb. Effects of Indust. Accidents	Waigani Convention	Dangerous Goods by Waterways	Dangerous Goods by Road (ADR)	Distrib. and Use of Pesticides	POPs Convention	London Convention 1972	* 1996 Protocol to LC 1972	MARPOL 73/78	1969 CLC	* 1992 CLC Protocol	1992 Fund Convention	HNS Convention
Kuwait			●		○					○	○	○			●			
Kyrgyz Republic			●		●					○	○							
Laos										○	○							
Latvia			●			○			●	○	○			●	●	●	●	
Lebanon			●							○	○	○		●	●			
Lesotho	○		●							○	●							
Liberia										○	●	○		●		●	●	
Libyan Arab Jamah.	●		●							○		●						
Liechtenstein			●						●		○							
Lithuania			●			●			●	○	○			●		●	●	
Luxembourg			●	●	○	●		○	●	○	○	●		●	●			
Macedonia (FYR of)			●						●	○	○							
Madagascar			●		○					○	○				○			
Malawi			●							○	○			●				
Malaysia			●	●						○	○			●	●			
Maldives			●							○					●			
Mali	●		●		○					○	○							
Malta			●							○	○	●		●		●	●	
Marshall Islands										○				●		●	●	
Mauritania			●		○					○	○			●	●			
Mauritius	●		●							○	○			●		●	●	
Mexico			●							○	○	●		●		●	●	
Micronesia (FS of)			●				●				○							
Moldova (Rep. of)			●			●		○	●	○	○							
Monaco			●			●					○	●		●		●	●	
Mongolia			●		●					○	○							
Morocco		○	●						●	○	○	●	○	●		●	●	
Mozambique	●		●							○	○				●			
Myanmar										○				●				
Namibia			●		○					○								
Nauru			●				○				●	●						

Marine Environment — *Global Conventions* | *Regional Conventions*

Marine Living Resources

Nature Conservation and Terrestrial Living Resources

Nuclear Safety

Freshwater Resources

Country	OPRC	Intervention Convention	LOS Convention	* Fish Stocks Agreement	OSPAR Convention	1992 Helsinki Convention	Black Sea	Wider Caribbean Region	Eastern African Region	Kuwait Region	Mediterranean Sea	Red Sea and Gulf of Aden	South Pacific Region	South-East Pacific	West and Centr. African Region	Antarc. Marine Living Res. (CCAMLR)	Atlantic Tunas (ICCAT)	Regulation of Whaling (ICRW)	Antarctic Treaty	* Environmental Protocol	World Heritage Convention	Biological Diversity	* Biosafety Protocol	Migr. Species of Wild Animals (CMS)	CITES	Ramsar Convention	Conv. to Combat Desertification (CCD)	IU on Plant Genetic Resources	Treaty on Plant Genetic Resources	Tropical Timber (ITTA, 1994)	Assistance Convention	Notification Convention	Nuclear Safety	Civil Liability for Nuclear Damage	ECE Water Convention
Kuwait		●	●							●												○			○		●	○							
Kyrgyz Republic																					●	●					●								
Laos			●																		●	●					●								
Latvia	●	●				●															●	●		●	●	●					●	●	●	●	●
Lebanon	○	●	●								●										●	●				●	●	○			●	●	●	●	
Lesotho			○																			●	●		○		●								
Liberia	●	●	○												○						●	●	●		●		●	○		●					
Libyan Arab Jamah.			○								●						●				●	●				●	●	○			●				
Liechtenstein			○																			●		●	●	●	●	○			●	●			●
Lithuania						●															●	●	○	●	●	●					●	●	●	●	●
Luxembourg			●	○	●																●	●	○	●	●	●	●		○	●	●	●	●		●
Macedonia (FYR of)			●																		●	●	○	●	●	●	●		○		●	●		●	
Madagascar	●	○	●						○												●	●	○	○	●	●	●	○							
Malawi			○																		●	●	○		●	●	●	○	○						
Malaysia	●		●																		●	●	○		●	●	●			●	●	●			
Maldives			●	●																	●	●													
Mali			●																		●	●	○	●	●	●	●	○	○		○	○	●		
Malta	○		●	●							●										●	●		●	●	●	●		○						
Marshall Islands	●	●	●	○									●								●	●					●		○						
Mauritania	●	●	●	○											○						●	●		●	●	●	●	○							
Mauritius	●		●	●																	●	●	●		●	●	●	○			●	●			
Mexico	●	●	●					●										●			●	●	○		●	●	●	○	○		●	●	●	●	
Micronesia (FS of)			●	●									●									●					●								
Moldova (Rep. of)																						●	○	●	●	●	●				●	●	●	●	●
Monaco	●	●	●	●							●							●			●	●	○	●	●	●	●				●	●	○		
Mongolia			●															●			●	●	○	●	●	●	●				●	●			
Morocco	○	●	○	○							●						●	●			●	●		●	●	●	●	○	○		●	●	○	○	
Mozambique			●																		●	●	○		●		●	○							
Myanmar			●																		●	●	○		●		●			●		●			
Namibia			●	●												●	●				●	●	○		●	●	●		○						
Nauru			●	●									●									●	●				●								

	General Environmental Concerns		Atmosphere															
	Århus Convention	Espoo Convention	Aircraft Engine Emissions (ICAO)	Transb. Air Pollution (LRTAP)	* 1994 Sulphur Protocol	* 1988 NOx Protocol	* 1991 VOC Protocol	* 1998 Heavy Metals Protocol	* 1998 POPs Protocol	* 1999 Multi-Effects Protocol	Climate Change (UNFCCC)	* Kyoto Protocol	Ozone Layer Convention	* Montreal Protocol	* London Amendment	* Copenhagen Amendment	* Montreal Amendment	* Beijing Amendment
Nepal			○								●		●	●	●			
Netherlands	○	●	○	●	●	●	●	●	●	○	●	●	●	●	●	●	●	●
New Zealand			○								●	○	●	●	●	●	●	●
Nicaragua			○								●	●	●	●	●	●		
Niger			○								●	○	●	●	●	●	●	
Nigeria			○								●		●	●	●	●	●	
Niue											●	●						
Norway	○	●	○	●	●	●	●	●	●	●	●	●	●	●	●	●	●	●
Oman			○								●		●	●	●	●		
Pakistan			○								●		●	●	●	●		
Palau			○								●	●	●	●	●	●	●	●
Panama			○								●	●	●	●	●	●	●	●
Papua New Guinea			○								●	●	●	●	●			
Paraguay			○								●	●	●	●	●	●	●	
Peru			○								●	○	●	●	●	●		
Philippines			○								●	○	●	●	●	●		
Poland	●	●	○	●	○	○		○	○	○	●	○	●	●	●	●	●	
Portugal	○	●	○	●			○	○	○	○	●	●	●	●	●	●		
Qatar			○								●		●	●	●	●		
Romania	●	●	○	●				○	○	○	●	●	●	●	●	●	●	
Russian Federation		○	○	●	○	●					●	○	●	●	●			
Rwanda			○								●		●	●				
St Kitts & Nevis											●		●	●	●	●	●	
St Lucia			○								●	○	●	●	●	●	●	●
St Vinc. & Grenadines			○								●	○	●	●	●	●		
Samoa (Western)			○								●	●	●	●	●	●	●	●
San Marino			○	○							●							
São Tomé & Príncipe			○								●		●	●	●	●	●	●
Saudi Arabia			○								●		●	●	●	●		
Senegal			○								●	●	●	●	●	●	●	
Seychelles			○								●	○	●	●	●	●		

	Hazardous Substances											Marine Environment – *Global Conventions*						
	Bamako Convention	CRTD	Basel Convention	* Ban Amendment	PIC Convention	Transb. Effects of Indust. Accidents	Waigani Convention	Dangerous Goods by Waterways	Dangerous Goods by Road (ADR)	Distrib. and Use of Pesticides	POPs Convention	London Convention 1972	* 1996 Protocol to LC 1972	MARPOL 73/78	1969 CLC	* 1992 CLC Protocol	* 1992 Fund Convention	HNS Convention
Nepal			●							○	○	○						
Netherlands			●	●	●	○		○	●	○	●	●	○	●		●	●	○
New Zealand			●		○		●			○	○	●	●	●		●	●	
Nicaragua			●							○	○			●	●			
Niger	●		●							○	○							
Nigeria			●		●					○		●		●	●			
Niue							○				○							
Norway			●	●	●	●			●	○	○	●	●	●		●	●	○
Oman			●		●					○	○	●		●		●	●	
Pakistan			●		○					○	○	●		●				
Palau							○			○	○							
Panama			●	●	●					○	○	●		●		●	●	
Papua New Guinea			●				●			○	○	●		●		●	●	
Paraguay			●	●	○					○	○							
Peru			●		○					○	○			●	●			
Philippines			●		○					○	○	●		●		●	●	
Poland			●			○			●	○	○	●		●		●	●	
Portugal			●	●	○	○			●	○	○	●		●	●	●	●	
Qatar			●	●						○					●	●	●	
Romania			●						●	○	○			●	○	●		
Russian Federation			●			●			●		○	●		●		●	●	●
Rwanda	○									○	●							
St Kitts & Nevis			●							○				●	●			
St Lucia			●	●	○					○		●		●				
St Vinc. & Grenadines			●							○				●	●	●	●	
Samoa (Western)			●		●		●			○	●			●		●	●	
San Marino										○								
São Tomé & Príncipe										○	○			●	●			
Saudi Arabia			●		●					○	○				●			
Senegal	●		●		●					○	○			●	●			
Seychelles			●		○					○	○	●		●		●	●	

Marine Environment — *Global Conventions* | *Regional Conventions*; Marine Living Resources; Nature Conservation and Terrestrial Living Resources; Nuclear Safety; Freshwater Resources

OPRC	Intervention Convention	LOS Convention	* Fish Stocks Agreement	OSPAR Convention	1992 Helsinki Convention	Black Sea	Wider Caribbean Region	Eastern African Region	Kuwait Region	Mediterranean Sea	Red Sea and Gulf of Aden	South Pacific Region	South-East Pacific	West and Centr. African Region	Antarc. Marine Living Res. (CCAMLR)	Atlantic Tunas (ICCAT)	Regulation of Whaling (ICRW)	Antarctic Treaty	* Environmental Protocol	World Heritage Convention	Biological Diversity	* Biosafety Protocol	Migr. Species of Wild Animals (CMS)	CITES	Ramsar Convention	Conv. to Combat Desertification (CCD)	IU on Plant Genetic Resources	Treaty on Plant Genetic Resources	Tropical Timber (ITTA, 1994)	Assistance Convention	Notification Convention	Nuclear Safety	Civil Liability for Nuclear Damage	ECE Water Convention	
		●																		●	●	○		●	●	●	○		●						Nepal
●	●	●	○	●			●								●		●	◉	●	●	●	●	●	●	●	●	○	○	●	●	●	●		●	Netherlands
●	●	●	●									●			●		●	◉	●	●	●	○	●	●	●	●	○		●	●	●				New Zealand
	●	●					○													●	●	○		●	●	●	○			●	●	○			Nicaragua
		○																		●	●	○	●	●	●	●	○	○		○	○		●		Niger
●		●												●						●	●	○	●	●	●	●	○	○		●	●	○			Nigeria
		○	○																	●	●					●									Niue
●	●	●	●	●											●		●	◉	●	●	●	●	●	●	●	●	○	○	●	●	●	●		●	Norway
	●	●							●								●			●	●					●	○								Oman
●	●	●	○																	●	●	○	●	●	●	●				●	●	●			Pakistan
		●										○					●				●	○				●									Palau
	●	●					●						●			●	●			●	●	●	●	●	●	●	○		●	●	●				Panama
	●	●	●									●						◐		●	●			●	●	●	○		●						Papua New Guinea
		●																		●	●	○	●	●	●	●	○			○	○				Paraguay
●													●		●		●	◉	●	●	●	○	●	●	●	●	○		●	●	●	●	●		Peru
○		●	○																	●	●	○	●	●	●	●	○		●	●	●	○	●		Philippines
○	●	●			●										●			◉	●	●	●	○	●	●	●	●	○			●	●	●	●	●	Poland
	●	●	○	●													●			●	●	○	●	●	●	●	○	○	●	○	●	●		●	Portugal
	●	○							●											●	●			●		●									Qatar
●	○	●				●												◐	○	●	●	○	●	●	●	●	○			●	●	●	●	●	Romania
	●	●	●		●	●									●	●	●	◉	●	●	●			●	●		○			●	●	●	○	●	Russian Federation
		○																		●	●	○		●		●	○								Rwanda
		●															●			●	●	●		●		●									St Kitts & Nevis
		●	●				●										●			●	●			●	●	●									St Lucia
	●	●					●										●				●			●		●				●	●		●		St Vinc. & Grenadines
		●	●									●								●	●	●				●	○								Samoa (Western)
																	●			●	●					●									San Marino
		●														●					●		●	●		●									São Tomé & Príncipe
		●							●		●									●	●		●	●		●				●	●				Saudi Arabia
●	●	●	●											●			●			●	●	○	●	●	●	●	○	○		○	○				Senegal
●		●	●					●												●	●	○		●		●									Seychelles

	General Environmental Concerns		Atmosphere																Hazardous Substances											Marine Environment – *Global Conventions*						
	Arhus Convention	Espoo Convention	Aircraft Engine Emissions (ICAO)	Transb. Air Pollution (LRTAP)	* 1994 Sulphur Protocol	* 1988 NOx Protocol	* 1991 VOC Protocol	* 1998 Heavy Metals Protocol	* 1998 POPs Protocol	* 1999 Multi-Effects Protocol	Climate Change (UNFCCC)	* Kyoto Protocol	Ozone Layer Convention	* Montreal Protocol	* London Amendment	* Copenhagen Amendment	* Montreal Amendment	* Beijing Amendment	Bamako Convention	CRTD	Basel Convention	* Ban Amendment	PIC Convention	Transb. Effects of Indust. Accidents	Waigani Convention	Dangerous Goods by Waterways	Dangerous Goods by Road (ADR)	Distrib. and Use of Pesticides	POPs Convention	London Convention 1972	* 1996 Protocol to LC 1972	* MARPOL 73/78	1969 CLC	* 1992 CLC Protocol	1992 Fund Convention	HNS Convention
Sierra Leone			○								●		●	●	●	●	●	●										○				●	●	●	●	
Singapore			○								●		●	●	●	●	●				●								○			●		●	●	
Slovakia		●	○	●	●	●	●	○	○	○	●	●	●	●	●	●	●	●			●	●				○	●	○	○			●				
Slovenia	○	●	○	●	●			○	○	○	●	○	●	●	●	●	●				●		●	●			●	○	○	●		●		●	●	
Solomon Islands			○								●	○	●	●	●	●	●								●			○		●						
Somalia			○										●	●	●	●	●	●	○									○								
South Africa			○								●		●	●	●	●					●							○	○	●	●	●	●			
Spain	○	●	○	●	●	●	●	○	○	○	●	●	●	●	●	●	●	●			●	●	○	●			●	○	○	●	●	●		●	●	
Sri Lanka			○								●		●	●	●	●	●				●	●						○	○			●		●	●	
Sudan			○								●		●	●	●	●			●									○	○							
Suriname			○								●		●	●									●					○	○	●		●				
Swaziland			○								●		●	●					○									○								
Sweden	○	●	○	●	●	●	●	●	●	●	●	●	●	●	●	●	●	●			●	●	○	●			●	○	●	●	●	●		●	●	○
Switzerland	○	●	○	●	●	●	●	●	●	○	●	○	●	●	●	●					●		●	●			●	○	○	●	●	●		●	○	
Syrian Arab Rep.			○								●		●	●	●	●	●				●		○					○	○			●	●			
Taiwan																																				
Tajikistan	●		○								●		●	●	●								○					○	○							
Tanzania (UR of)			○								●		●	●	●				●		●		○					○	○							
Thailand			○								●	○	●	●	●	●					●		●					○	○							
Togo			○								●		●	●	●	●	●	●	●				○					○	○	○		●				
Tonga			○								●		●	●											○			○	○	●		●		●	●	
Trinidad & Tobago			○								●	●	●	●	●	●	●				●	●						○			●	●		●	●	
Tunisia			○								●		●	●	●	●	●		●		●	●	○					○	○	●		●		●	●	
Turkey			○	●									●	●	●	●					●		○					○	○			●		●	●	
Turkmenistan	●		○								●	●	●	●	●						●							○								
Tuvalu											●	●	●	●	●	●	●								●							●	●			
Uganda			○								●	●	●	●	●	●	●		●		●							○								
Ukraine	●	●	○	●	○	●	○	○	○		●	○	●	●	●	●					●						●		○	●		●				
United Arab Emirates			○								●		●	●							●							○	○	●			●	●	●	
United Kingdom	○	●	○	●	●	●	●	○	○	○	●	●	●	●	●	●	●	●			●	●	○	○			●	○	○	●	●	●		●	●	○
USA		○	○	●		●	○	●	○	○	●	○	●	●	●	●					○		○	○				○	○	●	○	●	○			

Marine Environment — Global Conventions: OPRC; Intervention Convention; LOS Convention; * Fish Stocks Agreement. Regional Conventions: OSPAR Convention; 1992 Helsinki Convention; Black Sea; Wider Caribbean Region; Eastern African Region; Kuwait Region; Mediterranean Sea; Red Sea and Gulf of Aden; South Pacific Region; South-East Pacific; West and Centr. African Region

Marine Living Resources: Antarc. Marine Living Res. (CCAMLR); Atlantic Tunas (ICCAT); Regulation of Whaling (ICRW)

Nature Conservation and Terrestrial Living Resources: Antarctic Treaty; * Environmental Protocol; World Heritage Convention; Biological Diversity; * Biosafety Protocol; Migr. Species of Wild Animals (CMS); CITES; Ramsar Convention; Conv. to Combat Desertification (CCD); IU on Plant Genetic Resources; Treaty on Plant Genetic Resources; Tropical Timber (ITTA, 1994)

Nuclear Safety: Assistance Convention; Notification Convention; Nuclear Safety; Civil Liability for Nuclear Damage

Freshwater Resources: ECE Water Convention

Country	OPRC	Intervention Convention	LOS Convention	* Fish Stocks Agreement	OSPAR Convention	1992 Helsinki Convention	Black Sea	Wider Caribbean Region	Eastern African Region	Kuwait Region	Mediterranean Sea	Red Sea and Gulf of Aden	South Pacific Region	South-East Pacific	West and Centr. African Region	Antarc. Marine Living Res. (CCAMLR)	Atlantic Tunas (ICCAT)	Regulation of Whaling (ICRW)	Antarctic Treaty	* Environmental Protocol	World Heritage Convention	Biological Diversity	* Biosafety Protocol	Migr. Species of Wild Animals (CMS)	CITES	Ramsar Convention	Conv. to Combat Desertification (CCD)	IU on Plant Genetic Resources	Treaty on Plant Genetic Resources	Tropical Timber (ITTA, 1994)	Assistance Convention	Notification Convention	Nuclear Safety	Civil Liability for Nuclear Damage	ECE Water Convention
Sierra Leone			●																			●			●	●	●	○			○	○			
Singapore	●		●																			●			●		●				●	●	●		
Slovakia			●																○	○	●	●	○	●	●	●	●				●	●	●	●	●
Slovenia	●	●	●								●										●	●	○	●	●	●	●				●	●	●	●	●
Solomon Islands			●	●									●					●			●	●					●	○							
Somalia			●						●			●												●	●										
South Africa		●	●													●	●	●	◉	●	●	●		●	●	●	●	○			●	●	●		
Spain	●	●	●	○	●						●					●		●	◉	●	●	●	●	●	●	●	●	○	○	●	●	●	●	○	●
Sri Lanka		●	●	●																	●	●	○	●	●	●	●	○			●	●	●		
Sudan			●									●									●	●			●		●	○	●		○	○	○		
Suriname		●	●																		●	●			●	●	●			●					
Swaziland			○																			●			●		●		○						
Sweden	●	●	●	○	●	●										●		●	◉	●	●	●	○	●	●	●	●	○	○	●	●	●	●		●
Switzerland	●	●	○		●													●	○	○	●	●	●	●	●	●	●	○		●	●	●	●		●
Syrian Arab Rep.		●									●										●	●				●	●	○	○		○	○	○		
Taiwan																																			
Tajikistan																					●	●		●		●	●								
Tanzania (UR of)			●						●												●	●		●	●	●	●	○							
Thailand	●		○																		●	○			●	●	●			●	●	●			
Togo			●												●						●	●	○	●	●	●	●	○		●					
Tonga	●	●	●	●																		●					●	○							
Trinidad & Tobago	●	●	●					●									●					●	●		●	●	●	○		●				●	
Tunisia	●	●	●								●						●				●	●	○	●	●	●	●	○	○		●	●	○		
Turkey							●				●								○		●	●	○		●	●	●	○			●	●	●		
Turkmenistan																					●	●					●								
Tuvalu			○										○									○					●								
Uganda			●	○																	●	●	●	●	●	●	●								
Ukraine		●	●	○			●									●			○	●	●	●		●	●	●					●	●	●	●	●
United Arab Emirates		●	○							●											●	●			●		●				●	●			
United Kingdom	●	●	●	●	●			●					○			●	●	●	◉	●	●	●	○	●	●	●	●	○	○	●	●	●	●	○	○
USA	●	●		●				●					●			●	●	●	◉	●	●	○			●	●	●			●	●	●	●		

General Environmental Concerns | Atmosphere | Hazardous Substances | Marine Environment

Global Conventions

	Århus Convention	Espoo Convention	Aircraft Engine Emissions (ICAO)	Transb. Air Pollution (LRTAP)	* 1994 Sulphur Protocol	* 1988 NOx Protocol	* 1991 VOC Protocol	* 1998 Heavy Metals Protocol	* 1998 POPs Protocol	* 1999 Multi-Effects Protocol	Climate Change (UNFCCC)	* Kyoto Protocol	Ozone Layer Convention	* Montreal Protocol	* London Amendment	* Copenhagen Amendment	* Montreal Amendment	* Beijing Amendment	Bamako Convention	CRTD	Basel Convention	* Ban Amendment	PIC Convention	Transb. Effects of Indust. Accidents	Waigani Convention	Dangerous Goods by Waterways	Dangerous Goods by Road (ADR)	Distrib. and Use of Pesticides	POPs Convention	London Convention 1972	* 1996 Protocol to LC 1972	MARPOL 73/78	1969 CLC	* 1992 CLC Protocol	1992 Fund Convention	HNS Convention
Uruguay			○								●	●	●	●	●	●	●				●	●	○					○	○			●		●	●	
Uzbekistan			○								●	●	●	●	●	●					●															
Vanuatu			○								●	●	●	●	●	●									○			○	○	●	●	●		●	●	
Vatican (see Holy See)																																				
Venezuela			○								●		●	●	●	●	●				●							○	○			●		●	●	
Viet Nam			○								●	○	●	●	●	●					●							○	○			●				
Yemen			○								●		●	●	●	●	●				●							○	○				●			
Yugoslavia			○	●							●		●	●							●						●	○	○	●		●	●			
Zambia			○								●	○	●	●	●						●							○	○							
Zimbabwe			○								●		●	●	●	●			●									○	○							
European Union	○	●		●	●	●	○	●	○		●	●	●	●	●	●	●	●			●	●	○	●				○	○							
Hong Kong SAR																●														●		●		●	●	

Marine Environment: Global Conventions (OPRC – Fish Stocks Agreement); Regional Conventions (OSPAR Convention – West and Centr. African Region)

Marine Living Resources (Antarc. Marine Living Res. – Regulation of Whaling)

Nature Conservation and Terrestrial Living Resources (Antarctic Treaty – Tropical Timber)

Nuclear Safety (Assistance Convention – Civil Liability for Nuclear Damage)

Freshwater Resources (ECE Water Convention)

Country	OPRC	Intervention Convention	LOS Convention	* Fish Stocks Agreement	OSPAR Convention	1992 Helsinki Convention	Black Sea	Wider Caribbean Region	Eastern African Region	Kuwait Region	Mediterranean Sea	Red Sea and Gulf of Aden	South Pacific Region	South-East Pacific	West and Centr. African Region	Antarc. Marine Living Res. (CCAMLR)	Atlantic Tunas (ICCAT)	Regulation of Whaling (ICRW)	Antarctic Treaty	* Environmental Protocol	World Heritage Convention	Biological Diversity	* Biosafety Protocol	Migr. Species of Wild Animals (CMS)	CITES	Ramsar Convention	Conv. to Combat Desertification (CCD)	IU on Plant Genetic Resources	Treaty on Plant Genetic Resources	Tropical Timber (ITTA, 1994)	Assistance Convention	Notification Convention	Nuclear Safety	Civil Liability for Nuclear Damage	ECE Water Convention
Uruguay	●		●	●												●	●		⬤	●	●	●	○	●	●	●	●		○		●	●	○	●	
Uzbekistan																					●	●		●	●	●	●								
Vanuatu	●	●	●	○												●						●			●		●			●					
Vatican (see Holy See)																																			
Venezuela	●							●									●		○		●	●	●		●	●	●		○	●					
Viet Nam			●																		●	●			●	●	●				●	●			
Yemen		●	●									●									●	●			●		●	○							
Yugoslavia		●	●																		●	●			●	●		○			●	●		●	
Zambia			●																		●	●			●	●	●	○							
Zimbabwe			●																		●	●	○		●		●	○			○	○			
European Union			●		●	●		○	○		●					●	●					●	○	●			●		○	●					●
Hong Kong SAR		●																						●											

Intergovernmental Organizations (IGOs)

including United Nations specialized agencies

Commission on Sustainable Development (CSD)

Objectives

• to monitor progress in the implementation of Agenda 21 and activities related to the integration of environmental and developmental goals throughout the UN system;
• to consider information provided by governments regarding the activities they undertake to implement Agenda 21;
• to review the progress in the implementation of the commitments set out in Agenda 21, including those related to the provision of financial resources and transfer of technology;
• to receive and analyse relevant input from competent non-governmental organizations (NGOs), including the scientific and the private sector;
• to enhance the dialogue, within the framework of the UN, with NGOs, and with the independent sector, as well as with other entities outside the UN system.

Organization

Type
Intergovernmental organ of the UN. Functional Commission of the UN Economic and Social Council (ECOSOC). Reports to the UN General Assembly through ECOSOC. Established as an institutional arrangement to the follow-up to the UN Conference on Environment and Development (UNCED) in Rio de Janeiro, June 1992.

Membership
The CSD is composed of representatives of 53 states, elected for a three-year period by ECOSOC. Other member States of the UN, non-member States, intergovernmental organizations (IGOs), including regional integration organizations, and accredited NGOs participate in the work of the CSD as observers.

Founded
16 February 1993.

Secretariat

CSD Secretariat,
Division for Sustainable Development,
UN Department of Economic and Social Affairs (DESA),
United Nations,
2 UN Plaza, Room DC2-2220,
New York, NY 10017,
USA
Telephone: +1-212-9633170
Telefax: +1-212-9634260
E-mail: dsd@un.org

Director
Ms JoAnne DiSano.

Information Officer
Ms Pragati Pascale (UN Department of Public Information).

Number of staff
Not applicable.

Activities

The first Multi-Year Thematic Programme of Work was agreed for 1994–6 with the following cross-sectoral clusters to be reviewed and monitored on a yearly basis:
• critical elements of sustainability (chs. 2–5 of Agenda 21);
• financial resources and mechanisms (ch. 33);
• education, science, transfer of environmentally sound technologies, co-operation, and capacity building (chs. 16 and 34–7);
• decision-making structures (chs. 8 and 38–40);
• roles of major groups (non-governmental sectors) (chs. 23–32).

The Programme also specified the sectoral clusters that would receive special attention between 1994 and 1996:
• 1994: health, human settlements, and fresh water (chs. 6, 7, 18, and 21); and toxic chemicals and hazardous wastes (chs. 19, 20, and 22);
• 1995: land, desertification, forests, and biodiversity (chs. 10–15);
• 1996: atmosphere, oceans, and all kinds of seas (chs. 9 and 17).

All cross-sectoral clusters were under review annually, with particular emphasis on selected chapters within a cluster. The purpose in combining sectoral themes with cross-sectoral chapters is to enable a more integrated view of how the cross-sectoral elements interact and contribute to the sectoral issues in the Agenda 21 implementation process.

According to a decision adopted at the Commission's first substantive meeting in June 1993, governments are encouraged to submit their national reports on the implementation of Agenda 21 not less than six months before the Commission's session. It is up to individual governments to decide on the degree of detail and regularity of their reporting to the CSD.

Reports are also requested from organizations of the UN system, including international financial institutions and the Global Environment Facility (GEF) (see this section), as well as international, regional, and subregional IGOs outside the UN system.

In carrying out its programme of work, the CSD took into account the results of major intergovernmental events and negotiating processes, with a view to integrating these activities in the review of the implementation of Agenda 21.

The 1997 session had an overall review and appraisal of Agenda 21 in preparation for that year's special session of the UN General Assembly (UNGA). The special session of the UNGA took place in New York on 23–7 June 1997.

The second Multi-Year Thematic Programme of Work for 1998–2002 was adopted by the UN General Assembly at its special session in June 1997. It follows the previous format but reduces the numbers of agenda items considered annually. The Programme specifies the following clusters that will receive special attention in the period:

- 1998: (*a*) freshwater management, (*b*) transfer of technology, capacity building, education, and science, and (*c*) industry;
- 1999: (*a*) oceans and seas, (*b*) consumption and production patterns, (*c*) tourism, and (*d*) review of Programme of Action for the Sustainable Development of Small Island Developing States (SIDS);
- 2000: (*a*) land resources, (*b*) financial resources, trade and investment, and economic growth, and (*c*) agriculture;
- 2001: (*a*) atmosphere and energy, (*b*) information for decision making and participation (*c*) international co-operation for an enabling environment, and (*d*) energy and transport as economic factors;
- 2002: comprehensive review of Agenda 21 implementation.

Poverty and consumption and production patterns are overriding issues for the sessions in this period. The elimination of annual examination of all cross-sectoral issues reduces the frequency of national reports dealing with these elements. The sixth CSD session took place from 20 April to 1 May 1998, the seventh session from 19 to 30 April 1999, the eighth session from 24 April to 5 May 2000, and the ninth session from 17 to 27 April 2001.

In 2000 the fifty-fifth session of the UN General Assembly decided that meetings of the tenth session of the CSD would be transformed into the Preparatory Committee for the World Summit on Sustainable Development (WSSD) (Johannesburg, from 26 August to 4 September 2002). The Summit is expected to undertake a critical review of progress achieved since the 1992 Rio Summit (UNCED), reinvigorate the global commitment to sustainable development, and decide on priorities for future work, taking into account new developments and challenges that have emerged since UNCED. CSD, acting as the preparatory committee for the Summit and being open for all States, has provided for active involvement of representatives of major groups from civil society, and has held four sessions. The first three sessions took place in New York from 30 April to 2 May 2001, from 28 January to 8 February 2002, and from 25 March to 5 April 2002. The fourth session took place in Indonesia (on ministerial level) from 27 May to 7 June 2002. For more information, see Sources on the Internet, below.

Decision-making bodies

The 53 members of the CSD are elected by the UN ECOSOC. The members serve for a three-year period and are encouraged to be represented at the ministerial level. Membership rotates among governments of the UN, drawn on the following geographical basis: Africa (13), Asia (11), Latin America and the Caribbean (10), and North America, Europe, and other (19). The CSD has its sessions annually for two or three weeks.

The members of the CSD elect the Chair and four Vice-Chairs for each session. These five members constitute the Bureau of the CSD.

The CSD establishes intersessional *ad hoc* expert groups to assist the Commission on issues related to the implementation of Agenda 21. In 1997 it created an Intergovernmental Forum on Forests.

The CSD receives substantive services from the Division for Sustainable Development (DSD) of the UN Department of Economic and Social Affairs (DESA).

Finance

CSD activities are financed through the regular UN budget and through voluntary extra-budgetary contribution.

Budget

Not applicable.

Publications

CSD Update (bi-monthly newsletter).

Sources on the Internet

<http://www.un.org/esa/sustdev/csd.htm>
<gopher://gopher.un.org:70/11/esc/cn17>

National implementations of the Agenda 21 commitments at:
<http://www.un.org/esa/agenda21/natlinfo>

Information on the World Summit on Sustainable Development (WSSD) in Johannesburg at:
<http://www.johannesburgsummit.org>.

European Union (EU): Environment

Objectives

Environment policy was built into the Treaty by the Single European Act of 1987 and its scope was extended by the Treaty on European Union of 1992. This allowed the use of majority voting on environmental legislation and introduced as a principle of Treaty law the concept of sustainable growth which respects the environment. While leaving plenty of scope for national action and allowing member States to take even tougher measures than those agreed at Union level, the Treaty says that Union policy should contribute to the pursuit of:

- preserving, protecting, and improving the quality of the environment;
- protecting human health;
- ensuring a prudent and rational utilization of natural resources;
- promoting measures at the international level to deal with regional or world-wide environmental problems.
- The Treaty requires Union policy to aim 'at a high level of protection' and at rectifying environmental damage at source, and to be based on taking preventive action and making the polluter pay.

The new Treaty of Amsterdam, when ratified, will further strengthen environmental objectives, particularly in terms of sustainable development and integration of environment into other policy areas.

Organization

Type

Intergovernmental organization (IGO). The institutions of the EU have a definite legal status and extensive powers of their own. The European Union, which incorporates the European Community (EC), comprises three juridically distinct entities: European Economic Community (EEC); Euratom; and European Coal and Steel Community (ECSC).

The EU consists of four main institutions, which all play an important role in EU environmental policy:

- the Council of Ministers;
- the European Commission;
- the European Court of Justice;
- the European Parliament.

Due to the central role of the European Commission in preparing, proposing, and verifying environmental legislation, we shall focus on this organization in the following.

Membership

Any European state can apply for membership. The terms of its admission will be agreed upon between the original member States and the applicant state. 15 member States (Austria, Belgium, Denmark, Finland, France, Germany, Greece, Ireland, Italy, Luxembourg, the Netherlands, Portugal, Spain, Sweden, and the United Kingdom) by June 2001.

Founded

The Treaty establishing the EEC was signed in Rome on 25 March 1957. (The European Community was founded on 8 April 1965. The European Union came into being on 1 November 1994.)

Secretariat

European Commission,
B-1049 Brussels,
Belgium
Telephone: +32-2-2991111
Telefax: Information is available from the switchboard operator.
E-mail: firstname.lastname@cec.eu.int

President
Mr Romano Prodi.

Commissioner for Environment
Ms Margot Wallström.

Environment Directorate-General (DG)
Postal address and telephone:
as above

Office locations:
Avenue de Bealieu 5,
Auderghem,
B-1160 Brussels,
Belgium

Centre Wagner,
Plateau de Kirchberg,
L-2929 Luxembourg

E-mail: envinfo@cec.eu.int

Head of Unit, Communications and the Civil Society
Ms Ylva Tiveus Kronlund.

European Environment Agency (EEA),
Kongens Nytorv 6,
DK-1050 Copenhagen K,
Denmark
Telephone: +45-33-36-7100
Telefax: +45-33-36-7199
E-mail: eea@eea.eu.int

Executive Director
Mr Domingo Jiménez-Beltrán.

Media Relations Manager
Mr Tony Carritt.

Number of staff
20,444 at the Commission (January 2002), 543 at the Environment DG (January 2002), and 80 at the EEA (December 2001).

Activities

The major environmental activities of the European Commission consist of:

- *Policy activities*, through developing EC Environmental Action Programmes (1973, 1977, 1983, 1987, 1992, and 2001). The Commission's proposal for a sixth Environmental Action Programme is under discussion in the Council and Parliament as of June 2001. On 7 June 2001, the Environment Council reached agreement on a common position on a far-reaching and ambitious legal text. This is likely to be formally adopted in the course of 2002. The programme takes a wide-ranging approach to the challenges ahead and gives a strategic direction to the Commission's environmental policy over the next decade, as the Community prepares to expand its boundaries. The new Programme identifies four priority areas:
- climate change;
- nature and biodiversity;
- environment, health, and quality of life;
- natural resources and waste.

To achieve improvements in these areas, the sixth Programme emphasizes the need to use legislation and a range of innovative instruments aimed at the market and informing the public, businesses, and public authorities. Effective implementation and more innovative solutions will be essential. The Commission recognizes that a wider constituency must be addressed, including business that can only gain from a successful environmental policy. A more effective use of legislation is sought, together with a more participatory approach to policy-making. Integration into other policy areas needs to be reinforced, and the objectives of the programme should be taken into account in the preparation of other policies.

The Programme provides a basis for the environmental dimension of the Community's strategy for sustainable development. It continues to pursue some of the targets from the fifth Environment Action Programme, which came to an end in 2000. But the sixth Programme goes further, adopting a more strategic approach. It calls for the active involvement and accountability of all sections of society in the search for innovative, workable, and sustainable solutions to environmental problems;

- *legal activities*, through providing environmental legislation in the form of regulations, directives, or decisions, and ensuring its correct implementation. Approximately 300 legal texts related to the environment currently exist;
- *research and technological development (RTD) activities*, through developing research and development programmes within the area of the environment. Since the early days of Community-supported research, sustainability has been a prominent feature in the Framework programmes. The Fifth Framework Programme (1998–2002) comprises four thematic programmes, and the environment features in two of them, i.e. in the quality of life and management of living resources (QoL); and in the energy, environment, and sustainable development (EESD):
  - Key Action 4 of the QoL Programme: Environment and Health, with the budget of €EUR160 million, finances projects tackling with health issues related to environmental hazards, such as air pollution, noise, chemicals, pesticides, radiation from electromagnetic fields, etc. Its aim is to determine how environmental factors contribute to health problems; to develop improved methods for risk assessment; to better inform the public on links between environment and health; and to provide a scientific basis for the development of adequate environmental and health policy measures;
  - Key Action 1 of the EESD Programme: Sustainable Management and Quality of Water, with a budget of €254 million, supports research actions on the sustainable use of water resources, the ecological quality of freshwater ecosystems and wetlands, the necessary treatment and purification technologies, pollution prevention and surveillance and communication systems. It aims at protecting and providing high quality water in sufficient quantity at affordable costs to society, while maintaining the various functional roles of ecosystems and better matching water demands with the availability of the resource;
  - Key Action 2 of the EESD Programme: Global Change, Climate, and Biodiversity (€301 million) aims at developing the scientific, technological, and socio-economic basis and tools necessary for the study and understanding of changes in the environment. It concentrates on global and regional environmental problems that have a potentially significant impact on Europe, such as climate change, ozone depletion, biodiversity loss, loss of habitats and fertile land, disruptions to ocean circulation, in the context of sustainable development. Priority is given to issues covered by international treaties or conventions where the European Community and/or its member States are signatories;
  - Key Action 3 of the EESD Programme: Sustainable Marine Ecosystems (€170 Million) aims at underpinning the emergence of new concepts for integrated management of European seas in the open ocean as well as in the coastal zone, including development of guidelines and tools, contributions to relevant conventions, and consideration of socio-economic driving forces and feedbacks, in order to achieve better forecasts of the environmental parameters, which have an impact on marine activities;
  - Key Action 4 of the EESD Programme: The City of Tomorrow and Cultural Heritage (€170 million) pursues the development of various visions for European cities, including their response to the influence of globalization. It aims to understand and resolve the complex and sometimes conflicting interrelationships between environmental conditions and objectives, economic vitality, social cohesion, and cultural identity. It pursues a mix of socio-economic, environmental, and technological approaches including the development, integration, and demonstration of technologies, tools, and methodologies to improve forecasting, monitoring, assessment, and benchmarking of emerging best practice. Furthermore, generic research activities in the fields of natural and technological hazards, Earth observation technologies and socio-economic aspects of environmental change in the perspective of sustainable development as well as the transnational use of research infrastructures is supported in the EESD Programme.

  The Sixth RTD Framework Programme (2002–2006) is currently under preparation and it is proposed to include environmental research in concentrating on sustainable development, global change and ecosystems, and on environmental aspects in genomics and biotechnology for health as well as in food quality and safety. However, the principle of sustainable development will be taken into account for all research priorities of the Framework Programme;
- *monitoring and implementation activities.* According to Article 211 of the EC Treaty, the Commission is responsible for ensuring that the EC environmental legislation is properly implemented in the member States. Wherever this is not the case, the Commission can apply Article 226 of the EC treaty (infringement proceedings) to ensure compliance. If a member State fails to comply, the Commission may bring the case before the European Court of Justice.

The Co-ordination of Information on the Environment (CORINE) Programme (1985–90) had as its principal aim to gather, co-ordinate, and ensure consistency of information on the state of the environment in the EU. The CORINE Programme wound up in 1990, the same year that the Council of Ministers adopted a regulation setting up the European Environment Agency (EEA) (Council Regulation (EEC) No. 1210/90 of 7 May 1990 on the establishment of the European Environment Agency and the European Environment Information and Observation Network).

The EEA is a legally independent EU body and began operations in Copenhagen in 1994. It is open to countries that share the objectives of the Agency and are able to participate in its activities. As of 1 January 2002 the Agency had 29 member countries. These are the 15 EU member States; Iceland, Norway, and Liechtenstein, which are members of the European Economic Area; and 11 of the 13 countries in Central and Eastern Europe and the Mediterranean area that are seeking accession to the EU—Bulgaria, Cyprus, the Czech Republic, Estonia, Hungary, Latvia, Lithuania, Malta, Romania, Slovenia, and the Slovak Republic. Their membership makes the EEA the first EU body to take in the candidate countries.

It is anticipated that the two remaining candidate countries, Poland and Turkey, will ratify their membership agreements during spring 2002. Negotiations with Switzerland on EEA membership began in 2001.

The EEA's core task is to provide objective, reliable, and comparable information to support the protection and improvement of the environment and the achievement of sustainable development. The Agency's primary target audience is policy makers, but its mandate also requires it to ensure the broad dissemination of environmental information to the public. The Agency constitutes the hub of a decentralized environmental information collection and distribution network, known as EIONET, which draws on some 600 existing environmental bodies and institutes across Europe.

The Agency is supported in its work by so-called European Topic Centres (ETCs), consortia of organizations contracted for their expertise to execute particular tasks set out in the Agency's multi-annual work programme. As of June 2002 the five ETCs and their leaders were as follows:

- Water: WRc plc, Medmenham, United Kingdom;
- Air and Climate Change: RIVM (National Institute for Public Health and Environment), Bilthoven, the Netherlands;
- Nature Protection and Biodiversity: Muséum National d'Histoire Naturelle, Paris, France;
- Terrestrial Environment: Autonomous University of Barcelona, Spain;
- Waste and Material Flows: Danish Environmental Protection Agency/City of Copenhagen, Denmark.

These ETCs, established during 2000 and 2001, are designed to build on the expertise and experience of the nine original ETCs while also introducing new experts and national partners, including several from Central and Eastern European countries.

Decision-making bodies

Decisions in environmental matters are normally taken by the European Parliament and the Council of Ministers, by way of co-decision (Article 175 (1) EC Treaty). In some cases, which are specifically enumerated in Article 175 (2), the Council decides by way of unanimity, after consultation of the European Parliament.

Environmental measures which concern the establishment or functioning of the internal market shall be based on Article 95 and adopted by co-decisions between the European Parliament and the Council.

Other measures—such as in agriculture, transport, and trade—follow the specific provisions which are laid down in the different provisions of the EC Treaty.

The co-decision procedure is described in Article 251 of the EC Treaty.

The EEA directs its work along the lines of a medium-term multi-annual work programme agreed upon by a Management Board consisting of one representative of each EEA member State, two representatives of the European Commission, and two scientific persons nominated by the European Parliament. They are assisted by a Scientific Committee whose members are appointed for a four-year term.

Finance

The budget is based on financial contributions from member States.

Budget

The total budget for the European Community was approximately €EUR93 billion in 2000 and €94 billion in 2001, and is €96 billion in 2002.

The budget for the Environment DG was approximately €63 million in 2000 and €230 million in 2001, and is €205 million in 2002.

The EEA's budget from European Commission funds was €18 million in 2000 and €19 million in 2001, and is €19.4 million in 2002. Further contributions to the EEA budget are made by member countries.

Special funds

The Financial Instrument for the Environment (LIFE) was established to assist the development and implementation of the EU's environmental policy. One of its components, LIFE Third Countries, may also provide financial support for capacity/institutional building activities in non-EU countries bordering the Mediterranean and the Baltic Sea,

The financing required for the first operational phase, from 1992 until 1994, was an estimated €400 million. For the second operational phase, from 1996 until 1999, €450 million was required. The third phase, from 2000 to 2004, was established by *Regulation (EC) No 1655/2000 of the European Parliament and of the Council of 17 July 2000 concerning the Financial Instrument for the Environment (LIFE)*. The financial framework is set at €640 million, 7 per cent of which is allocated to LIFE Third Countries.

Publications

The Environment DG produces a range of publications on environmental themes as well as three newsletters. Details can be found in the on-line publications catalogue on the Internet at:
<http://europa.eu.int/comm/environment/pubs_en.htm>

The EEA publishes:

- Five-yearly reports assessing the state of, and trends in, the pan-European environment:
  - *Europe's Environment: The Dobrís Assessment* (1995);
  - *Europe's Environment: The Second Assessment* (1998);
- Five-yearly reports assessing the state of, and trends in, the EU environment:
  - *Environment in the European Union* (November 1995);
  - *Environment in the European Union at the Turn of the Century* (1999);
- The *Environmental signals* series of annual indicator-based assessment reports:
  - *Environmental signals 2000*;
  - *Environmental signals 2001*;
- An annual indicator-based report on transport and environment (TERM):
  - *Are we moving in the right direction? TERM 2000*;
  - *TERM 2001: Indicators tracking transport and environment integration in the European Union*;
- The annual inventory of EU greenhouse gas emissions;
- Reports on specific environmental topics or themes, e.g.:
  - *Late lessons from early warnings: the precautionary principle 1896-2000*;
  - *Sustainable water use in Europe, parts 1, 2, and 3*;
  - *Down to earth: Soil degradation and sustainable development in Europe* (with UNEP);
  - *Environmental taxes: recent developments in tools for integration*;
  - *Nutrients in European ecosystems*;
  - *Dangerous substances in waste.*

All reports can be downloaded free of charge from the EEA's website (see below), which also carries regularly updated information about the Agency and its products.

Sources on the Internet

<http://europa.eu.int>
<http://europa.eu.int/comm/dgs/environment/index_en.htm>
<http://www.eea.eu.int>
<http://www.eionet.eu.int>

Food and Agriculture Organization (FAO)

Objectives

• to raise the levels of nutrition and standards of living of the populations of member countries;
• to secure improvements in the efficiency of production and distribution of all food and agricultural products;
• to improve the conditions of rural populations;
• to contribute towards an expanding world economy and towards ensuring freedom from hunger for humanity.

Organization

Type
Intergovernmental organization (IGO). A specialized agency of the UN. Linked to UN Economic and Social Council (ECOSOC).

Membership
Membership is confined to nations; associate membership to territories or groups of territories. The European Union (EU) is given membership as a regional integration organization and can vote on behalf of its member countries in certain matters. The total membership of FAO by 15 April 2002 was 183 countries and the EU.

Founded
16 October 1945.

Secretariat

FAO,
Viale delle Terme di Caracalla,
I-00100 Rome,
Italy
Telephone: +39-06-57051
Telefax: +39-06-57053152
E-mail: fao-hq@fao.org

Director-General
Dr Jacques Diouf.

Media Support
Mr Peter Lowrey.

Number of staff
939 professionals and 1187 support staff at headquarters, in addition to 581 professionals and 1138 support staff at field, regional, and country offices (July 2001).

Activities

In fulfilling its aims to combat poverty and malnutrition, FAO carries out four major functions: it collects, analyses, and disseminates information; advises governments on policies and programmes; provides technical assistance; and offers governments and experts a neutral forum in which to meet to discuss issues related to food and agriculture. The major areas of FAO activity are: crop production, livestock, natural resources, research and technology, rural development, nutrition, food and agricultural policy, fisheries, and forestry.

Main conventions on environment under the auspices of FAO
• *International Convention for the Conservation of Atlantic Tunas (ICCAT)*, Rio de Janeiro, 1966 (see Agreements);
• *FAO International Code of Conduct on the Distribution and Use of Pesticides*, Rome, 1985 (see Agreements);
• *FAO International Undertaking on Plant Genetic Resources*, Rome, 1983 (see Agreements);
• *Code of Conduct for Responsible Fisheries*, Rome, 1995;
• *Convention on the Prior Informed Consent Procedure for Certain Hazardous Chemicals and Pesticides in International Trade (PIC Convention)*, Rotterdam, 1998 (see Agreements). Operated jointly with the UN Environment Programme (UNEP);
• *International Plan of Action for the Management of Fishing Capacity*, Rome 1999;
• *Convention on the Conservation and Management of Fishery Resources in the South East Atlantic Ocean (SEAFO)*, Windhoek 2001;
• *International Treaty on Plant Genetic Resources for Food and Agriculture*, Rome, 2001 (see Agreements).

Environmental activities
FAO advises governments on policy planning and environmental protection in a wide range of sectors, including the management of soil and water resources, farming systems, genetic resources, irrigation systems, integrated pest management, integrated plant nutrition, and watershed management.

Decision-making bodies

The Conference, which meets every two years, is the major policy-making organ of FAO. All members are represented and each has one vote. The Conference is responsible for approving the FAO budget and Programme of Work, adopting procedural rules and financial regulations, admitting new members, formulating recommendations on food and agricultural questions, and reviewing the decisions of the FAO Council and subsidiary bodies. The thirty-second session of the Conference will be held in Rome from 29 November to 10 December 2003.

The FAO Council is composed of 49 members elected by the Conference for three-year terms. The Council is the executive organ of the Conference and exercises powers delegated to it by the Conference. The FAO Council is assisted by eight major committees covering agriculture; commodity problems; constitutional and legal matters; forestry; fisheries; world food security; finance; and FAO programmes.

Finance

Contributions from member countries for implementation of the Regular Programme of Work are based on per capita income. The Field Programme is financed by three major sources: government trust funds, the UN Development Programme (UNDP), and FAO's own Technical Co-operation Programme.

Budget
The budget was $US650 million for the years 2000–01 and is $651.8 million for 2002–03.

Special funds
The *Technical Co-operation Programme (TCP)* allows the Organization to respond to special needs of member countries. The total budget, financed by member countries through the regular budget, was $91.5 million for the years 2000–01 and is $95.1 million for 2002–03..

Publications

• *FAO Plant Protection Bulletin* (quarterly);
• *Food Outlook* (monthly).

Sources on the Internet

<http://www.fao.org>

Global Environment Facility (GEF)

Objectives

To serve as a mechanism for international co-operation for the purpose of providing new and additional grant and concessional funding to meet the agreed global environmental benefits in the following focal areas:

- biological diversity;
- climate change;
- international waters;
- ozone layer depletion.

Projects addressing land degradation, primarily desertification and deforestation, as they relate to the focal areas, are also eligible for funding.

The GEF shall ensure the cost-effectiveness of its activities in addressing the targeted global environmental issues, and shall fund programmes and projects which are country-driven and based on national priorities designed to support sustainable development.

Organization

Type

Intergovernmental organization (IGO). The GEF is implemented by the UN Development Programme (UNDP), the UN Environment Programme (UNEP), and the World Bank (see this section).

Membership

Any member State of the UN or any of its specialized agencies may become a Participant in the GEF. There were 171 Participants by 1 February 2002.

Founded

28 November 1991. The instrument establishing the new GEF entered into force on 1 July 1994.

Secretariat

GEF Secretariat,
1818 H Street NW,
Washington, DC 20433,
USA

Telephone: +1-202-4730508
Telefax: +1-202-522-3240/3245
E-mail: gef@gefweb.org
or secretariatofgef@worldbank.org
or [first initial last name]@worldbank.org

Chairman and Chief Executive Officer
Dr Mohamed T. El-Ashry.

External Relations Co-ordinator
Mr Hutton Archer.

Number of staff
30 professionals and ten administrative staff (January 2002).

Activities

The GEF was initially set up in 1991 as a three-year pilot programme, jointly implemented by UNDP, UNEP, and the World Bank. The aim was to provide grants and low-interest loans to developing countries to help them carry out programmes to relieve pressures on global ecosystems.

The restructured GEF is based on a set of principles agreed to by the Participants. The GEF operates the financial mechanism of both the Framework Convention on Climate Change (see Agreements) and the Convention on Biological Diversity (see Agreements). The Council approved an operational strategy for the GEF in October 1995.

There is agreement that the GEF should work with the regional development banks, the UN agencies, and bilateral agencies to involve them in GEF technical assistance and investment projects. The implementing agencies are working with the regional development banks and UN agencies on the modalities for such co-operation.

Decision-making bodies

The GEF has an Assembly, which consists of representatives of all participating countries. The Assembly meets every three years and had its first meeting in New Delhi in April 1998; its second meeting will be in Beijing in October 2002. The Assembly reviews the general policies and in addition evaluates the operation of the Facility on the basis of reports submitted by the Council. The Council is the main governing body responsible for developing, adopting, and evaluating the operational policies and programmes for GEF-financed activities. It consists of 32 members, with 16 members from developing countries (six each from Africa and Asia, and four seats for Latin America), 14 from developed countries, and two from the countries of Central and Eastern Europe and the former Soviet Union. The Council meets twice a year, or as frequently as necessary.

When consensus is not possible, a double-majority voting system is used, requiring a majority of participating countries and 60 per cent donor support. It is intended that the system should protect the interests of both donor and recipient countries.

The Scientific and Technical Advisory Panel (STAP) is an advisory body. UNEP serves as the secretariat for STAP.

Finance

Funding comes from the donors, which include both developing and developed countries. Contributions from developed countries are roughly in line with a formula based on their shares in the World Bank's International Development Association (see this section). 36 countries have announced pledges to the GEF, including ten developing countries. Total multilateral pledges and contributions to the Trust Fund were $US2 billion for 1994–7 and were estimated to be $2.38 billion for 1998–2001. Discussions for the third GEF Replenishment, which will provide funding for the period 2002–6, have begun. Multilateral pledges and contributions are estimated to be between $2.5 and $3.5 billion. GEF funding will be available for projects and other activities that address the Facility's objectives.

Budget

The total GEF corporate budget was $US39.2 million for the financial year 1998/99, $22.2 million for 1999/2000, $19.7 million for 2000/01, and $22.2 million for 2001/02. The core budget for the GEF Secretariat was $6.2 million for 1998/99, $6.6 million for 1999/2000, $6.9 million for 2000/01, and $8.02 million for 2001/02.

Main contributors

The main contributors are the USA, Japan, Germany, France, and the United Kingdom. These countries pledged 67.6 per cent of the Facility's funding for the 1998–2002 period.

Publications

GEF publishes annual reports, working-paper series, policy publications, and the *Operational Report*.

Sources on the Internet

<http://www.gefweb.org>

International Atomic Energy Agency (IAEA)

Objectives

• to encourage and assist research on and development and practical application of atomic energy for peaceful purposes throughout the world;
• to act as an intermediary in the supply of materials, services, equipment, and facilities;
• to foster the exchange of scientific and technical information;
• to encourage the exchange and training of scientists and experts;
• to establish standards and administer safeguards against the misuse of aid provided by or through the Agency;
• to carry out safeguards to verify compliance of non-nuclear weapon States party to the Non-Proliferation Treaty (NPT) and other treaties that they use fissionable material for peaceful purposes only.

Organization

Type
Intergovernmental organization (IGO). An independent IGO within the UN system.

Membership
Open to all states, whether UN members or not. 134 member States by June 2002. Not open to regional integration organizations.

Founded
29 July 1957.

Secretariat

International Atomic Energy Agency (IAEA),
Vienna International Centre,
Wagramerstrasse 5,
PO Box 100,
A-1400 Vienna,
Austria
Telephone: +43-1-26000
Telefax: +43-1-26007
E-mail: official.mail@iaea.org

Director-General
Dr Mohamed ElBaradei
(December 1997–December 2005).

Director, Division of Public Information
Mr David Kyd.

Number of staff
912 professionals and 1261 support staff (April 2001).

Activities

224 safeguard agreements were in force with 140 member States (and with Taiwan) involving 2467 safeguard inspections performed in 2000. There were 1094 nuclear installations under IAEA safeguards by the end of 2000. This represents approximately 95 per cent of the world's nuclear facilities and materials outside the five nuclear-weapon states. IAEA safeguards inspections in these facilities to verify that the fissionable material is used for peaceful purposes only.

Main conventions on environment under the auspices of IAEA
• *Vienna Convention on Civil Liability for Nuclear Damage*, Vienna, 21 May 1963 (see Agreements);
• *Joint Protocol Relating to the Application of the Vienna Convention and the Paris Convention on Third Party Liability in the Field of Nuclear Energy*, Vienna, 21 September 1988 (see Agreements, Vienna Convention on Civil Liability for Nuclear Damage);
• *Convention on the Physical Protection of Nuclear Material*, Vienna, 26 October 1979. Entered into force on 8 February 1987. 76 Parties (including the European Atomic Energy Community (EURATOM)) by 8 May 2002. Four Signatories without ratification, acceptance, or approval;
• *Convention on Assistance in the Case of a Nuclear Accident or Radiological Emergency (Assistance Convention)*, Vienna, 26 September 1986 (see Agreements);
• *Convention on Early Notification of a Nuclear Accident (Notification Convention)*, Vienna, 26 September 1986 (see Agreements);
• *Convention on Nuclear Safety*, Vienna, 17 June 1994 (see Agreements);
• *Joint Convention on the Safety of Spent Fuel Management and on the Safety of Radioactive Waste Management*, Vienna, 5 September 1997. Entered into force on 18

June 2001. 27 Parties by 6 March 2002. 15 Signatories without ratification, acceptance, or approval;

- *Convention on Supplementary Compensation for Nuclear Damage*, Vienna, 12 September 1997. (Not yet in force.) (See Agreements, Vienna Convention on Civil Liability for Nuclear Damage.)

International conventions which request member States to conclude agreements with the IAEA

- *Treaty for the Prohibition of Nuclear Weapons in Latin America (Treaty of Tlatelolco)*. Signed at Mexico, Distrito Federal, on 14 February 1967. Entered into force on 22 April 1968. 32 Parties by 1 January 2001. One Signatory without ratification, acceptance, or approval;
- *Treaty on the Non-Proliferation of Nuclear Weapons (NPT)*. Signed at London, Moscow, and Washington on 1 July 1968. Entered into force on 5 March 1970. 188 Parties by 20 June 2001. No Signatories without ratification, acceptance, or approval;
- *South Pacific Nuclear Free Zone Treaty (Treaty of Rarotonga)*. Signed at Rarotonga on 6 August 1985. Entered into force on 11 December 1986. 13 Parties by 1 January 2001. One Signatory without ratification, acceptance, or approval;
- *African Nuclear-Weapon-Free Zone Treaty (Treaty of Pelindaba)*. Signed at Cairo on 11 April 1996. (Not yet in force.) 15 ratifications by 9 January 2001. 35 Signatories without ratification, acceptance, or approval;
- *Treaty of the Southeast Asia Nuclear-Weapon-Free Zone (Treaty of Bangkok)*. Signed at Bangkok on 15 December 1995. Entered into force on 27 March 1997. Nine Parties by 1 January 2001. One Signatory without ratification, acceptance, or approval.

Environmental activities

Many of the IAEA programmes contribute directly or indirectly to the goals of sustainable development and protection of the environment as set out in *Agenda 21*, the outcome of the 1992 UN Conference on Environment and Development (UNCED). Of particular relevance in this context are the programmes on food and agriculture, isotope hydrology (work on both climate change and water resources), and waste management. The IAEA also takes an active role in inter-agency co-ordination of the implementation of Agenda 21.

Chapter 17 of the Agenda 21 agreement calls for 'new approaches to marine and coastal area management and development at the national, sub-regional, regional, and global levels' and the strengthening of inter-agency co-operation in this regard. Emphasis was also placed on building the capacities of national and regional institutions (especially in developing countries) for making environmental assessments and controlling marine pollution.

The IAEA Marine Environment Laboratory (MEL) in Monaco responds regularly to requests for technical assistance from many other UN agencies, international organizations, and governments. Within the UN, co-operative activities are formally established with the UN Environment Programme (UNEP) (see this section) and the Intergovernmental Oceanographic Commission (IOC) of UNESCO. There is also extensive collaboration with the World Meteorological Organization (WMO), the World Health Organization (WHO), and the Food and Agriculture Organization (FAO) (see this section), as well as the IUCN – World Conservation Union (see NGOs), in programmes of assistance for developing countries.

Over the past decade, MEL's expertise has been applied to many pressing international environmental challenges, such as:

- tracking the effects of ocean disposal of nuclear wastes;
- assessing and mitigating the marine impacts of the Gulf War;
- investigating the radiological consequences of nuclear weapons testing in the Pacific;
- analysing the greenhouse effect and the potential for global warming;
- studying the impacts of industrial and agro-chemical pollution on marine ecosystems.

MEL has been engaged in deepening scientific understanding of marine radioactivity since its beginnings. Over the decades, moreover, research has broadened to include analysis of a wide range of non-radioactive pollutants in the marine environment, using nuclear and isotopic techniques.

MEL examines the consequences of radioactive discharges and disposals by monitoring and assessing radionuclide levels and modelling their dispersion in the marine environment. The results then assist states in radiological assessments related to nuclear weapons test sites and nuclear waste disposal areas, and in emergency responses to accidents at sea. To facilitate this work, MEL has created a Global Marine Radioactivity Database (GLOMARD) to provide states with radioactivity baseline data on seawater, sediment, and biota for undertaking assessments.

In co-operation with the IAEA's Departments of Nuclear Sciences and Applications and Technical Co-operation, MEL provides support to developing states in obtaining high quality data on marine radioactivity and radioecology, while the non-nuclear contaminants are covered through close co-operation with other specialized agencies, including UNEP, the IOC of UNESCO, UNESCO (see this section) and the UN Development Programme (UNDP). The Laboratory also supports marine pollution monitoring and research in developing countries by conducting joint exercises and training courses as part of an integrated programme of quality assurance for states.

Radiotracer methods are used to study agrochemical compounds, such as pesticides, and their accumulation and effects in marine systems. They are also applied in establishing the pathways and accumulations of heavy metals and other toxic elements in the marine environment and their effects on people and the ecosystem.

MEL has had a long history of collaboration with UNEP's Regional Seas programme (see Agreements), notably through its quality assurance programmes and expertise in marine analytical chemistry. The laboratory has served to underpin the Regional Seas Programme, ensuring the acquisition of a database comprising reliable and comparable measurements for a wide range of marine pollutants, encompassing both organic and inorganic contaminants. Today MEL co-operates closely with the Mediterranean Action Plan, the Black Sea Environment Programme and the Kuwait Action Plan. The laboratory is now assisting the Caspian Environment Programme with a contaminant survey in sediments from that region.

MEL conducts regional exercises for quality assurance in the Mediterranean, the Persian Gulf area, the western and south-east Pacific, west and central Africa, east Africa, South-East Asia, the Caribbean, the south-west Atlantic, the Arctic, the Baltic, and the Black Sea.

Together with experts from the Russian Federation, Norway, and the USA, MEL has been undertaking five expeditions to and laboratory analysis of samples collected in the Kara and Barents Seas to determine potential hazards to humans and the marine environment from dumped wastes, including reactors. Computer models have also been developed to predict the dispersion of any future leakage, and laboratory studies of concentration factors and distribution coefficients in Arctic conditions have been carried out.

Nuclear weapons test in the south Pacific. At the request of the French government, MEL has participated in an in-depth analysis of the radiological consequences of several decades of weapons testing on the Mururoa and Fangataufa atolls in French Polynesia. The study was directed by a special international advisory committee convened by IAEA's Director-General, and its findings were discussed at an international conference in Vienna from 30 June to 3 July 1998. The study found that the terrestrial and aquatic environments of the atolls that are accessible to people contain residual radioactive material attributable to the nuclear tests, but at generally very low concentrations which the study concluded were of no radiological significance.

Rising waters of the Caspian Sea. In collaboration with the Isotope Hydrology Section in IAEA headquarters, UNEP, and governments from affected zones, MEL is conducting studies to understand better the causes of the dramatically rising levels of the Caspian Sea. By employing isotopic techniques to study the water cycle, the investigation will provide a new platform for the affected countries to co-operate in solving this environmental crisis.

Pollution of the Black Sea. In collaboration with the IAEA's Technical Co-operation Department and UNDP, MEL is at the centre of a combined research and capacity-building initiative that addresses the rapidly deteriorating condition of Black Sea waters. Isotope tracers are being used to investigate water circulation and pollutant behaviour, while equipping and training activities ensure an improved regional ability to monitor and control the quality of the marine environment.

The IAEA provides extensive support to member States in their endeavour to understand better the origin and replenishment of their groundwater resources by integrating isotope techniques into water resource assessment approaches. In 1998 environmental ministers signed the *Black Sea Declaration*, which stresses the important role played by the IAEA in upgrading the capabilities of member States in the region to assess the marine environment. In this connection, a cruise was also organized to sample sea water, sediments, and biota in the Black Sea with the participation of member State laboratories in the region.

Shortage of water is a key development issue in much of Africa. In 1998 technical co-operation activities aimed at promoting the use of isotope hydrology in combination with other techniques to improve the development and management of water resources were under implementation in 16 countries. Activities of a regional model project were completed with tangible achievements in the four countries concerned (Egypt, Ethiopia, Morocco, and Senegal). In Egypt, for example, the IAEA's support was connected to national efforts for reclamation of new lands on the fringes of the Nile flood plain. The project enabled the preparation of a comprehensive hydrogeological map to be used in the future management of water resources of the areas investigated at Wadi Qena and Esna.

Building upon the management experience and promising results of this project, a new regional programme was formulated for countries in eastern and southern Africa (Kenya, Madagascar, Namibia, South Africa, United Republic of Tanzania, Uganda, and Zimbabwe). The aim of the programme is to foster regional co-operation in water resource assessment and management, and to enable national water sector authorities and end-users to devise appropriate policies and strategies for optimum management of existing resources. In South Africa, for example, the IAEA's assistance will help in the assessment of the recharge and storage capacity of fractured-rock aquifer systems in the Northern Province which constitute the main water supply for the 3.6 million inhabitants of the region.

Today it is generally accepted that global budgeting of atmospheric carbon is a prerequisite for projections of future atmospheric levels and their impact on the climate. For more than 35 years the IAEA/WMO Global Network for Isotopes in Precipitation (GNIP) has provided the basic isotopic data necessary for the use of hydrogen and oxygen isotopes in hydrological investigations relating to water resources assessment. In recent years the GNIP database, which at present comprises more than 250,000 isotopic and meteorological data from more than 500 locations, has also proved essential in palaeoclimatology and in the verification and further improvement of atmospheric circulation models to be used for the prediction of the global climate change and its impact on the water cycle. The scientific achievements made by the IAEA during the last decade include a review of the GNIP database through which the relationship between surface air temperature and the stable isotopic composition of precipitation has been refined.

Considerable efforts have been directed towards improving predictions of climate changes induced by human activities and their impact on the global environment. One promising approach is the study of past climate changes through isotope investigations of climate archives. Isotope techniques have proved to be indispensable as proxy indicators of the climate and a dating tool for past climatic events. Substantial progress has been made in this field through the Co-ordinated Research Programme (CRP) of IAEA on the use of isotope techniques in palaeoclimatology, with special reference to continental isotope indicators of palaeoclimate.

A significant part of the Agency's overall programme in the field of environmental protection is played by the joint FAO/IAEA Division of Nuclear Techniques in Food and Agriculture, almost entirely devoted to increasing food production while reducing the environmental impact of fertilizer and pesticide use.

The IAEA's laboratory at Seibersdorf acts as a sample collection, data acquisition, and distribution centre in the Background Air Pollution Monitoring Network (BAPMON) of the WMO (see this section).

Under the IAEA's Radioactive Waste Management Advisory Programme (WAMAP), advisory services are available to member States needing advice on establishing national waste-management programmes and technical assistance on specific waste-management issues or problems.

The IAEA provides various services to member States in the field of safe operation of nuclear power plants and nuclear facilities to protect the environment from contamination.

Decision-making bodies

The policy-making organs of the IAEA are the Board of Governors and the General Conference. The General Conference is composed of representatives of all the IAEA member States and meets once a year. The Board of Governors, IAEA's executive body, is composed of representatives of 35 governments, of which 13 are designated by the Board itself for a period of one year and

22 are elected by the General Conference for a period of two years. The Board meets five times a year. The Secretariat is headed by a Director-General appointed by the Board with the approval of the General Conference.

Finance

IAEA financial resources fall into two categories—the regular budget and the voluntary contributions. The regular budget provides for the normal administrative expenses of the IAEA (safeguard inspections, safety services, environmental activities, publications, research conferences, and information services). It is funded by contributions based on annual assessments of member States and by miscellaneous income. The Technical Assistance and Co-operation Fund consists of voluntary contributions used for financing the IAEA's technical co-operation programme. It is funded by contributions from member States and the UN.

Budget
The regular budget was US$226.3 million in 2000 and $230 million in 2001, and is $245 million in 2002.

Main contributors
Main contributors in 2000 were the USA (25.636 per cent), Japan (20.241 per cent), Germany (9.934 per cent), France (6.624 per cent), Italy (5.501 per cent), and the United Kingdom (5.156 per cent).

Special funds
The target for voluntary contributions for the IAEA Technical Co-operation Fund was set at $73 million in 2001 and is set at $73 million in 2002.

Publications and databases

The IAEA publishes books, reports, proceedings, safety manuals, statistics, etc. Regular publications are:

- *IAEA Bulletin* (quarterly);
- *IAEA Newsbriefs* (bi-monthly);
- *International Nuclear Information System (INIS) Atomindex*;
- *Nuclear Fusion* (monthly);
- *Meetings on Atomic Energy* (quarterly).

Regular IAEA on-line databases are:

- *International Nuclear Information System (INIS)*;
- *Power Reactor Information System (PRIS)*;
- *International Information System for the Agricultural Sciences and Technology (AGRIS)*.

Sources on the Internet

<http://www.iaea.org>

International Council for the Exploration of the Sea (ICES)

Objectives

• to promote and encourage research and investigation for the study of the marine environment and its living resources in the North Atlantic and adjacent seas;
• to publish or disseminate the results of this research, including the provision of scientific information and advice, to national governments, regional fishery management, and pollution control commissions.

Organization

Type
Intergovernmental organization (IGO).

Membership
Open to any State upon approval by three-quarters of its member States. Not open to regional integration organizations. 19 member States by 1 April 2002. Four states, the European Commission, 28 IGOs, and one NGO have observer status.

Founded
22 July 1902.

Secretariat

ICES, Palægade 2–4,
DK-1261 Copenhagen K, Denmark
Telephone: +45-33-154225
Telefax: +45-33-934215
E-mail: ices.info@ices.dk

General Secretary
Mr David de G. Griffith.

Environment Adviser
Dr Janet Pawlak.

Number of staff
13 professionals and 24 support staff (February 2002).

Activities

Much of the work of ICES is conducted under approximately 90 working groups or study groups, approximately one-third of which cover assessment of the stocks of various species of commercial fish and shellfish. Other groups are concerned with physical, chemical, and biological oceanography, issues related to the study of marine contaminants and their effects, mariculture issues, and methods of measurement and assessment. This work is co-ordinated by seven Science Committees (Oceanography, Marine Habitat, Fisheries Technology, Living Resources, Resource Management, Mariculture, and Baltic) and three Advisory Committees, the Advisory Committee on Fishery Management (ACFM), the Advisory Committee on Ecosystems (ACE), and the Advisory Committee on the Marine Environment (ACME). The overall scientific work is co-ordinated by the Consultative Committee, while the overall advisory work is co-ordinated by the Management Committee on the Advisory Process.

In support of these activities, ICES maintains databases on oceanographic conditions in the North Atlantic, and for the North-East Atlantic (including the Baltic Sea and Arctic waters) on contaminants in marine media (biota, sea water, and sediments, including in particular data on biological effects of contaminants), fish diseases, and fisheries statistics.

In mid-1996 ICES established a project office to co-ordinate the North Atlantic Regional Programme of GLOBEC (Global Ocean Ecosystem Dynamics). GLOBEC will provide an enhanced understanding of oceanic mesoscale physical and biological interactions, contributing to the international global change research effort.

Decision-making bodies

The ICES Council, composed of two delegates appointed by each member government, elects the Bureau. The Council holds statutory meetings, termed the Annual Science Conference.

Finance

Budget
The administrative budget was Dkr.22.7 million for the financial year 1999/2000 and Dkr.23.2 million in 2001, and is Dkr.23.8 million in 2002.

Publications

• *ICES Annual Report*;
• *ICES/CIEM Information* (bi-annual).

Sources on the Internet

<http://www.ices.dk>

International Fund for Agricultural Development (IFAD)

Objectives

• to mobilize additional resources to be made available on concessional terms for agricultural development in developing countries;
• to focus attention on the needs of the poorest rural communities, in particular small farmers, the landless, fishermen, livestock herders, and impoverished rural women;
• to pay special attention to grassroots development and innovative approaches which build on local participation and the preservation of the natural resource base;
• to provide financing primarily for projects and programmes specifically designed to introduce, expand, or improve food production systems and to strengthen related policies and institutions within the framework of national priorities and strategies, taking into consideration: the need to increase food production in the poorest food-deficient countries, the potential for increasing food production in other developing countries, and the importance of improving the nutritional level and living conditions of the poorest populations in developing countries.

Organization

Type
Intergovernmental organization (IGO). International financing institution which is a specialized agency of the UN.

Membership
States. The Fund was established as a partnership of industrialized countries, oil-producing and -exporting countries, and other developing countries which joined together to raise funds and share in the governance arrangements. The Fund's member States are classified as follows: List A (primarily OECD members); List B (primarily OPEC members); and List C (developing countries). List C is further divided into sub-list C1 (countries in Africa); sub-list C2 (countries in Europe, Asia, and the Pacific); and sub-list C3 (countries in Latin America and the Caribbean). (See also Decision-making bodies, below.)

Countries not original members of IFAD may join after approval of their membership by the Governing Council and accession to the IFAD agreement. Not open to regional integration organizations. Total of 162 member States by 5 June 2002.

Founded
11 December 1977.

Secretariat

International Fund for Agricultural Development (IFAD),
107 via del Serafico,
I-00142 Rome,
Italy
Telephone: +39-06-54592215
Telefax: +39-06-54592143
E-mail: communications@ifad.org

President and Chairman of the Executive Board
Mr Lennart Båge (2001–05).

Co-ordinator, External Communications
Mr Taysir Al-Ghanem.

Number of staff
134 professionals and 181 general service staff (June 2002). The Fund has no field, regional, or country offices.

Activities

IFAD projects range from provision of farming inputs and services (seed, fertilizer, tools, and agricultural research and extension) to irrigation, storage facilities, access roads, and credit to poor farmers and workers who would have no other source of loans.

IFAD lends money, most of which is on highly concessional or low-interest terms, and is concerned not only with raising agricultural production but also with improving local prospects for employment, nutrition, and income distribution.

Between 1978 and 2002, IFAD had committed a total of $US7.3 billion in loans and grants for financing 603 projects in 115 recipient countries and independent territories. The total cost of these projects amounts to about $21.7 billion, which includes contributions from external co-financiers ($6.4 billion) and from governments of recipient countries ($7.6 billion).

Environmental activities

In 1997 IFAD was given the responsibility of hosting the Global Mechanism of the Convention to Combat Desertification (CCD) (see Agreements). Following an agreement in April 1997, the Fund and the World Bank (see this section) initiated a joint Global Environment Facility (GEF) 'accelerated learning programme' to assist dryland countries in controlling land degradation, alleviating poverty, and addressing global environmental objectives. It is intended that the development of a demonstration pipeline of GEF land-degradation projects will allow the GEF to play a useful role in countering land degradation in the context of the CCD.

Decision-making bodies

The highest directing body of IFAD is the Governing Council, where all the member States are represented by a Governor and an Alternate Governor. The Council meets annually and elects the President of the Fund by a two-thirds majority for a four-year term.

Under the new voting system approved in February 1997, member States have two types of vote: a membership vote (equal votes for all members) and votes based on the size of contributions to the Fund's resources. (Under the old system all three categories had equal voting powers.)

Current operations are supervised by an Executive Board composed of 18 Members and 18 Alternate Members. The Board is elected by the Council for a three-year period. In addition to the conduct and general operation of IFAD, it approves loans and grants for projects and holds three regular sessions a year.

The secretariat is headed by the President of IFAD and is responsible for the management of the Fund. It has three main administrative departments:

- External Affairs Department;
- Programme Management Department, with five regional divisions, as well as a Technical Advisory Division;
- Treasury, Controller, Finance, and Administrative Department, including Personnel Division, Management of Information Services, and Administrative Services Unit.

Other units are: offices of Evaluation and Studies, Internal Audit, and Legal Services.

Finance

The Fund is financed by contributions from its member States. Its initial resources, in 1977, amounted to $US899 million. The First Replenishment (effective on 18 June 1982) amounted to $992 million. The Second Replenishment (effective on 27 November 1986) amounted to $473 million. The Third Replenishment (effective on 24 December 1990) amounted to $543 million. The Fourth Replenishment (effective on 29 August 1997) amounted to $460 million. The Fifth Replenishment (effective on 13 September 2001) amounts to $451 million.

Budget

The administrative budget was $54.0 million in 2000, including a contingency of $6.9 million, and $53.6 million in 2001, including a contingency of $250,000, and is $41.7 million in 2002, including a contingency of $165,000.

Publications

- annual reports;
- *Reports of the Sessions of Governing Council* (annual);
- *IFAD Update Bulletin* (quarterly);
- IFAD Operations by country (IFAD in India, Indonesia, the Philippines, Uganda, Argentina, Chile, Venezuela, Tanzania, Zimbabwe, and Kenya);
- The State of World Rural Poverty (series);
- *Meeting the Challenge of Hunger and Poverty*;
- *Providing Food Security for All.*

Sources on the Internet

<http://www.ifad.org>

International Labour Organization (ILO)

Objectives

To establish social justice as the foundation for universal and lasting peace, by unifying governments, employers, and workers in common action to promote fundamental principles and rights at work, generate employment, and improve living and working conditions.

Organization

Type

Intergovernmental organization (IGO). A specialized agency within the UN system. The tripartite structure of the ILO, whose organs involve organizations representing employers and workers along with governments, is unique in the UN system.

Membership

Open to members of the UN. Non-members of the UN must be approved by the General Conference by a two-thirds majority. 175 members by 1 January 2002.

Founded

11 April 1919.

Secretariat

International Labour Office,
4 route des Morillons,
CH-1211 Geneva,
Switzerland

Telephone:	+41-22-7997912
Telefax:	+41-22-7998577
E-mail:	communication@ilo.org

Director General

Mr Juan Somavia.

Director of Communication

Ms Zohrek Tabatabai.

Number of staff

The staff of the Office, at headquarters, and at field, regional, and country offices totals 2254 (November 2001).

Activities

One of the oldest and most important functions of the ILO is the adoption, by the tripartite International Labour Conference, of conventions and recommendations which set international labour standards. The ILO has adopted 184 conventions and 192 recommendations, forming an international labour code as a guideline for national law and practice in all spheres of labour activities. Through ratification by member States, conventions create binding obligations to put their provisions into effect. More than 6600 ratifications have been registered. Recommendations provide guidance on policy, legislation, and practice.

International technical co-operation is carried out in the major fields of standards, employment, training, working conditions, labour administration and labour relations, enterprise development, and social security.

Main conventions on environment under the auspices of ILO

- *Convention No. 115 Concerning the Protection of Workers against Ionizing Radiations*, 1960;
- *Convention No. 136 Concerning Protection against Hazards of Poisoning Arising from Benzene*, 1971;
- *Convention No. 139 Concerning Prevention and Control of Occupational Hazards Caused by Carcinogenic Substances and Agents*, 1974;
- *Convention No. 148 Concerning the Protection of Workers against Occupational Hazards in the Working Environment Due to Air Pollution, Noise, and Vibration*, 1977;
- *Convention No. 155 Concerning Occupational Safety and Health and the Working Environment*, 1981;
- *Convention No. 162 Concerning Safety in the Use of Asbestos, Geneva*, 1986;
- *Convention No. 170 on Safety in the Use of Chemicals at Work*, 1990;
- *Convention No. 174 Concerning the Prevention of Major Industrial Accidents*, 1993.

Environmental activities

In the area of the environment, the ILO's actions have been extended beyond the traditional emphasis on occupational safety and health and the working environment to include: strengthening the role of trade unions and employers' organizations in securing sustainable development; environment and development training; employment, poverty, and development issues; and environmental concerns related to women and indigenous and tribal peoples.

Decision-making bodies

The International Labour Conference, which meets annually, is composed of national delegations comprising two government delegates, one delegate representing employers and one representing workers. The Governing Body, composed of 56 members (28 governments, 14 employers, and 14 workers), meets three times a year and supervises the work of the ILO. It takes decisions on ILO policy, decides the agenda of the International Labour Conference, adopts the draft programme and budget of ILO for submission to the Conference, and elects the Director-General. The International Labour Office acts as secretariat to the Organization.

Finance

Apportioned among member governments according to a scale of contributions approved by the Conference.

Budget

The administrative budget was $US481 million for the years 1998–99 and $467 million for 2000–01, and is $474 million for 2002–03.

Publications

- *World of Work Magazine* (five times a year);
- *International Labour Review* (quarterly);
- *Yearbook of Labour Statistics*;
- *World Labour Report*;
- *World Employment Report*.

Sources on the Internet

<http://www.ilo.org>

International Maritime Organization (IMO)

Objectives

• to provide machinery for co-operation among governments on technical matters affecting international merchant shipping, with special responsibility for safety at sea;
• to ensure that the highest possible standards of safety at sea and of efficient navigation are achieved;
• to prevent pollution of the sea caused by ships and other craft operating in the marine environment;
• to be responsible for convening international maritime conferences and drafting international maritime conventions.

Organization

Type
Intergovernmental organization (IGO). A specialized agency brought into relationship with the UN and the UN Economic and Social Council (ECOSOC) through an agreement with the UN.

Membership
Governments of 162 states and two associate members by June 2002. Not open to regional integration organizations.

Consultative status with 37 intergovernmental bodies (June 2002). 61 non-governmental organizations (NGOs) enjoy consultative status with IMO (June 2002).

Founded
6 March 1948, Geneva. The original name was Inter-Governmental Maritime Consultative Organization (IMCO). This was changed to International Maritime Organization (IMO) on 22 May 1982.

Secretariat

International Maritime Organization (IMO),
4 Albert Embankment,
London SE1 7SR,
United Kingdom
Telephone: +44-20-77357611
Telefax: +44-20-75873210
E-mail: info@imo.org

Secretary-General
Mr William A. O'Neil (Canada)
(1 January 2002–31 December 2003).

Public Information Manager
Mr Lee Adamson.

Number of staff
114 professionals and 158 support staff (31 March 2001).

Activities

IMO has drawn up and promoted the adoption of 40 conventions and protocols, nearly all of which are now in force. Conventions and protocols are binding legal instruments and, upon entry into force, their requirements must be implemented by all States Parties.

Main conventions on the environment under the auspices of IMO (see Agreements)
• *International Convention on Civil Liability for Oil Pollution Damage 1969 (1969 CLC)*, Brussels, 1969, 1976, and 1984;
• *International Convention Relating to Intervention on the High Seas in Cases of Oil Pollution Casualties (Intervention Convention)*, Brussels, 1969;
• *International Convention on the Establishment of an International Fund for Compensation for Oil Pollution Damage 1971 (1971 Fund Convention)*, Brussels, 1971;
• *Convention on the Prevention of Marine Pollution by Dumping of Wastes and Other Matter (London Convention 1972)*, London, 1972;
• *International Convention for the Prevention of Pollution from Ships, 1973, as modified by the Protocol of 1978 relating thereto (MARPOL 73/78)*, London, 1973 and 1978;
• *International Convention on Oil Pollution Preparedness, Response, and Co-operation (OPRC)*, London, 1990;
• *International Convention on Liability and Compensation for Damage in Connection with the Carriage of Hazardous and Noxious Substances by Sea (HNS Convention)*, London, 1996;
• *International Convention on Civil Liability for Bunker Oil Pollution Damage (Bunkers Convention)*, London, 2001.

In addition IMO adopts numerous non-treaty instruments, such as codes of practice and recommendations, which, although not mandatory, provide a basis for legislation in member States. This helps prevent unilateral, unco-ordinated, and possibly conflicting standards.

An important function of IMO is to facilitate technical co-operation within the scope of its mandate. Through a biennial Integrated Technical Co-operation Programme (ITCP), IMO provides advice and assistance to developing countries in the technical, legal, and administrative fields, assigning the highest priority to capacity building and institutional development. It provides opportunities in national and regional maritime training institutions, including specialized training at the World Maritime University in Malmö, Sweden (information available on the Internet at <www.wmu.se>), the International Maritime Training Institute in Msida, Malta, and the International Maritime Academy in Trieste, Italy.

Decision-making bodies

Political
The IMO Assembly is the supreme governing body and meets biennially. It is open to all member States as well as representatives of the intergovernmental and non-governmental organizations in consultative status with IMO. One of the Assembly's most important tasks is to adopt the numerous resolutions and recommendations that have been prepared during the previous two years by subsidiary bodies.

It also elects the members of the IMO Council for the next two years. The Council is IMO's only elective body and consists of 32 member States (40 member States from 7 November 2002, see below). In electing the members of the Council the Assembly shall observe the following criteria:
(*a*) eight shall be states with the largest interest in providing international shipping services;
(*b*) eight shall be other states with the largest interest in international seaborne trade;
(*c*) 16 shall be states not elected under (*a*) or (*b*) above which have special interests in maritime transport or navigation, and whose election to the Council will ensure the representation of all major geographic areas of the world.

In November 1993 the Assembly adopted an amendment to the IMO Convention which, upon entry into force, will increase the size of the Council to 40. Groups (*a*) and (*b*) will be increased to ten members and group (*c*) to 20. The amendment will enter into force on 7 November 2002.

The Council normally meets twice a year and acts as the governing body of IMO between sessions of the Assembly. It is also responsible for preparing for the Assembly's consideration the budget and work programme that it is to handle.

Scientific/technical

There are five main committees consisting of all member States:

• The Maritime Safety Committee (MSC), the highest technical body for the Organization, was set up in 1973. It is composed of government experts and observers from organizations which have been granted consultative status with IMO. All members of IMO are entitled to take part, together with representatives of non-IMO states which are parties to treaties in respect of which the Committee exercises functions;

• The Legal Committee, composed of government experts and observers from organizations which have been granted consultative status with IMO, was set up after the Torrey Canyon disaster in 1967. Its functions are to consider any legal matters falling within the scope of IMO;

• The Marine Environment Protection Committee (MEPC), composed of government experts and observers from organizations which have been granted consultative status with IMO, and set up in 1973, is responsible for co-ordinating and administering the activities of the organization concerning the prevention and control of pollution;

• The Technical Co-operation Committee is composed of representatives from member States and observer organizations which have been granted consultative status with IMO. It is responsible for establishing directives and guidelines for the execution of IMO's comprehensive programme of assistance to developing countries in the maritime field, for monitoring its progressive development, and for reviewing its results. Through this programme, IMO assists in helping governments to implement IMO conventions and other instruments through various forms of global, regional, and national projects;

• The Facilitation Committee, a subsidiary body of the IMO Council and composed of government experts and experts from organizations which have been granted consultative status with IMO, has the main function of directing IMO efforts to reduce unnecessary formalities and obstructions to allied trade.

There are nine IMO Sub-Committees, dealing with Bulk Liquids and Gases; Carriage of Dangerous Goods, Solid Cargoes, and Containers; Fire Protection; Radiocommunications and Search and Rescue; Safety of Navigation; Ship Design and Equipment; Stability and Load Lines and Fishing Vessels Safety; Standards of Training and Watchkeeping; and Flag State Implementation.

Finance

Contributions to the IMO budget are based on a formula which is different from that used in other United Nations agencies. The amount paid by each member State depends primarily on the gross tonnage of its merchant fleet.

Budget

The total approved regular budget by appropriation for the years 2000–01 was £36,612,200 (£18,104,700 for 2000 and £18,507,500 for 2001) and is £39,531,100 for the years 2002–03.

Assessments on member States amounted to £18,326,100 in 1999 and £17,764,700 in 2000.

The actual administrative costs at headquarters were £18,574,434 in 1999 and £18,300,259 in 2000.

Main contributors

The top ten contributors for 2000 were Panama (15.8 per cent), Liberia (10.17 per cent), Japan (5.23 per cent), the Bahamas (4.36 per cent), Greece (4.32 per cent), the USA (4.12 per cent), Malta (3.96 per cent), Cyprus (3.91 per cent), Norway (3.86 per cent), and Singapore (3.31 per cent).

Special funds

Major changes in funding sources over the last decade have prompted the development of new technical co-operation policies and long-term strategies under the new framework of the Integrated Technical Co-operation Programme (ITCP). The largest traditional funding source, the UN Development Programme (UNDP), registered a severe downward trend from $US5.6 million in 1990, through to some $0.5 million in 1996, and dropping further until 1999. This had a negative impact upon the total level of donor funds, which plummeted to a low of $5,435,000 in 1994 for total disbursements.

Since 1996 this has been offset by the strengthening of links with other traditional donor bodies and the establishment of new partnerships enabling a broader donor base. This includes, *inter alia*, the Global Environment Facility (GEF), the UN Environment Programme (UNEP), the International Trade Workers Federation (ITF), the European Community (EC), Norway, France, the Netherlands, and the United Kingdom as major donors. A significant impact has been registered through the introduction in 1996 of IMO's own Technical Co-operation Fund, with the approval by Council of biennial allocations for the ITCP. In 1999 the Technical Co-operation Fund made up more than 30 per cent of total disbursed funds, the latter reaching almost $7 million.

The new approach through the ITCP (originally introduced 30 years ago) has strengthened the main goal of bridging the gap between the developed and the developing maritime nations in matters concerning sea transport and related activities. Prominent among the aims of the Programme are improving safety at sea, reducing marine pollution, and mitigating effects of pollution. The ITCP, with the support of donor countries and agencies, contributes directly to environment- and development-motivated projects within the thematic priorities of the technical co-operation subprogrammes, including the MEPC.

Publications

IMO has about 250 titles (conventions, codes, regulations, recommendations, guidelines, etc.) and nine electronic publications on CD-ROM, which cover the majority of the titles. A catalogue is available from the secretariat.

IMO News, the magazine of IMO, is published quarterly.

Sources on the Internet

<http://www.imo.org>

International Monetary Fund (IMF)

Objectives

• to promote international monetary co-operation through a permanent institution which provides the machinery for consultation and collaboration on international monetary problems;
• to facilitate the expansion and balanced growth of international trade;
• to promote exchange stability and maintain orderly exchange agreements among members and avoid competitive exchange depreciation.

Organization

Type
Intergovernmental organization (IGO). An agreement of relationship concluded with the UN outlines a programme of mutual assistance between the UN and the Fund as an independent international organization and a UN specialized agency. The IMF co-operates particularly with the UN Conference on Trade and Development (UNCTAD), the World Trade Organization (WTO), and the International Bank for Reconstruction and Development of the World Bank (IBRD) (see this section).

Membership
Open to all countries. Not open to regional international organizations. Ratification of the articles and acceptance of conditions laid down by the Fund are conditions of membership. Total of 183 members as of 1 April 2002.

Founded
27 December 1945.

Secretariat

International Monetary Fund (IMF),
700 19th Street NW,
Washington, DC 20431,
USA
Telephone: +1-202-6237000
Telefax: +1-202-6236278
E-mail: publicaffairs@imf.org

Managing Director
Mr Horst Köhler (2000–05).

Director of External Relations
Mr Thomas Dawson.

Number of staff
1727 professionals and 728 support staff at headquarters and in field, regional, and country offices. In addition, the IMF had 380 contractual employees in different staff categories (August 2001).

Activities

The Fund offers a range of financial facilities to help member countries in balance-of-payments difficulties resolve their problems in return for sound policy changes. The facilities include Stand-By and Extended Fund arrangements, which provide financing to support reform programmes; a Compensatory Financing Facility, which makes additional resources available to compensate for unexpected temporary shortfalls in export earnings for commodities; and a Poverty Reduction and Growth Facility (PRGF), which provides highly concessional loans to low-income developing members facing protracted balance-of-payments problems.

The IMF, together with the IBRD, has developed an Initiative to resolve the debt problems of the Heavily Indebted Poor Countries (HIPCs). It was designed to provide assistance to HIPCs that follow sound policies but for which traditional debt-relief mechanisms are inadequate to secure a sustainable external debt position over the medium term. The IMF has recently released a substantial amount of information in hard copy and on its website in the interest of greater 'transparency' (see Sources on the Internet, below). In April 1997, for example, in the wake of discussions on the value of transparency in enhancing effective surveillance, the Board agreed to the voluntary issuance of public information notices following the conclusion of Article IV consultation discussions for those members seeking to make known the IMF's views about their economies. It has also released the full text of Article IV consultation papers, with the agreement of the member countries.

Environmental activities
The Fund's mandate is to promote international monetary co-operation and stability. Fund staff seek to develop greater understanding of the interplay between economic

policies, economic activity, and environmental change, drawing upon the expertise of other institutions with environmental competence and responsibilities. This work enables Fund staff to conduct better-informed discussions with national authorities who face macro-economic policy choices entailing major environmental implications.

Decision-making bodies

The IMF operates through a Board of Governors, a Board of Executive Directors, an International Monetary and Financial Committee, a Managing Director, three Deputy Managing Directors, and staff. The Board of Governors consists of one Governor and one Alternate Governor appointed by each member country—typically the minister of finance or governor of the central bank. A meeting of the Board, in conjunction with that of the World Bank Group, is held each autumn. All powers of the Fund are vested in the Board. The Executive Board is responsible for the day-to-day business of the Fund. It consists of the Managing Director as Chair and 24 Executive Directors, who are appointed or elected by individual member countries or by groups of countries. Each member has an assessed quota, which is subscribed and determines voting power. As of January 2002 the USA, as the largest contributor, had 17.2 per cent of the voting power, while the smallest contributors held considerably less than 1 per cent each. Access to use of the Fund's resources is also determined in relation to quota, taking account of the balance-of-payments needs of the member and the policies it agrees to implement to restore balance-of-payments viability. The USA, Japan, Germany, France, and the United Kingdom, in that order, have the largest quotas (with the quotas of France and the United Kingdom equal). The total of members' quotas, as of January 2002, was, in Special Drawing Rights (SDR), about SDR212.4 billion.

Finance

The general resources of the Fund can be supplemented by borrowing from member countries in strong balance-of-payments positions. These borrowed resources are made available to member countries under a variety of facilities and policies.

Administrative budget

IMF's administrative budget was $US585.1 million for the financial year 1999/2000 and $649.8 million for 2000/01, and is $695.4 million for 2001/02.

Use of Fund resources

The total of stand-by and extended arrangements approved as of 4 January 2002 was SDR53.5 billion, of which SDR25.6 billion was undrawn. The total approved under PRGF arrangements was SDR4.2 billion, of which SDR2.7 billion was undrawn. As of the same date the IMF had credit and loans outstanding for an amount of SDR59.8 billion.

Publications

- annual reports (including the IMF Annual Report and the Annual Report on Exchange Arrangements and Exchange Restrictions);
- *IMF Survey* (23 times a year);
- *Finance and Development* (quarterly);
- *World Economic Outlook* (bi-annual in World Economic and Financial Surveys (WEFS) series);
- *International Capital Markets* (annual in WEFS series);
- *IMF Staff Papers* (quarterly scholarly journal);
- Economic Issues series;
- Occasional Papers series;
- working papers;
- policy discussion papers;
- staff country reports;
- books and manuals.

Sources on the Internet

<http://www.imf.org>

International Oil Pollution Compensation Funds (IOPC Funds)

Objectives

International Oil Pollution Compensation Fund 1971 (1971 Fund)

To administer the system of additional compensation created by the International Convention on the Establishment of an International Fund for Compensation for Oil Pollution Damage 1971 (1971 Fund Convention, i.e. to provide supplementary compensation to victims of oil pollution damage in states which are Parties to the 1971 Fund Convention who, cannot obtain full compensation for the proven damage under the International Convention on Civil Liability for Oil Pollution Damage 1969 (1969 CLC) (see Agreements).

International Oil Pollution Compensation Fund 1992 (1992 Fund)

To administer the regime of compensation created by the 1971 Fund Convention as amended by the 1992 Protocol thereto, known as the International Convention on the Establishment of an International Fund for Compensation for Oil Pollution Damage 1992 (1992 Fund Convention) (see Agreements), i.e. to provide supplementary compensation to victims of oil pollution damage in states which are Parties to the 1992 Fund Convention who, cannot obtain full compensation for the proven damage under the 1969 CLC as amended by the 1992 Protocol thereto, known as the International Convention on Civil Liability for Oil Pollution Damage 1992 (1992 CLC).

Organization

Type

Intergovernmental organizations (IGOs).

Membership

The 1971 Fund Convention ceased to be in force on 24 May 2002, and therefore the 1971 Fund has no members. However, the 1971 Fund will continue to exist until all outstanding claims have been resolved and any remaining assets have been distributed among the former member States.

Members of the 1992 Fund are states which have ratified, acceded to, approved, or accepted the 1992 Fund Convention (76 members by 1 March 2002). Observer status is granted former members of the 1971Fund and to States which have notified the Secretariat that they are considering ratification of the 1992 Fund Convention. Such status has also been granted to seven IGOs and 14 NGOs.

Founded

The 1992 Fund was established in London on 30 May 1996. The 1971 Fund, established in London on 17 October 1978, has no members since the 1971 Fund Convention ceased to be in force on 24 May 2002.

Secretariat

International Oil Pollution Compensation Funds (IOPC Funds),
23rd Floor,
Portland House,
Stag Place,
London SW1E 5PN,
United Kingdom

Telephone: +44-20-75927100
Telefax: +44-20-75927111
E-mail: info@iopcfund.org

Director

Mr Måns Jacobsson
(1 January 1985–31 December 2004).

Number of staff

14 professionals and 13 support staff (March 2002).

Activities

The major activities at the 1992 Fund are:

• to administer the system of compensation established under the 1992 Fund Convention;
• to handle claims for compensation arising out of oil pollution incidents and pay compensation to victims;
• to levy contributions to finance the activities of the 1992 Fund;
• to promote ratification of the 1992 Fund Convention.

Decision-making bodies

The 1992 Fund has an Assembly as the supreme governing body which meets annually. Sessions of the Assembly are open to the governments of all respective member States. States and organizations which have observer status with the Fund are invited as observers.

Decisions of the Assembly and of its subsidiary bodies shall be made, elections shall be determined, and reports, resolutions, and recommendations shall be adopted by a majority of the members present and voting. Each member has one vote.

The 1992 Fund has an Executive Committee, comprising 15 member States elected by the Assembly, which meets several times a year. The main function of the Executive Committee is to approve settlements of claims, to the extent that the Director is not authorized to do so. Voting rules are similar to the rules of the Assembly.

The 1971 Fund has an Administrative Council which takes decisions on outstanding claims and issues relating to the winding up of the 1971 Fund.

Finance

The 1992 Fund and the 1971 Fund are financed by contributions of persons who receive more than 150,000 tonnes of crude or heavy fuel oil after sea transport in a member State during a calendar year. Contributions are determined in proportion to the quantity of oil received.

Budget

Annual joint secretariat costs amount to approximately £UK2.2 million.

Publications

• annual reports;
• claims manuals;
• texts of conventions on liability and compensation for oil pollution damage.

Sources on the Internet

<http://www.iopcfund.org>

Organization for Economic Co-operation and Development (OECD), Environment Policy Committee (EPOC)

Objectives

• to contribute to sustainable development at the global, regional, and national level;
• to contribute to the advancement of integrated policies for the management of the environment of OECD member countries and selected non-member countries, individually or in an international context;
• to provide and disseminate high-quality and reliable environmental information and data;
• to provide a platform for discussion on environmental issues for governments, NGOs, business, trade unions, and scientific institutions.

Organization

Type
Intergovernmental organization (IGO).

Membership
Open to states and regional integration organizations. 30 member countries and the Commission of the European Communities with full membership by July 2002. The UN Environment Programme (UNEP) (see this section), the Council of Europe, the UN Economic Commission for Europe (UNECE), and the UN Commission on Sustainable Development (CSD) (see this section) hold observer status.

Founded
• OEEC: 1948, OECD: 1960.
• OECD Environment Committee: 1970, replaced by the Environment Policy Committee (EPOC): 1992.

Secretariat

OECD, Environment Directorate,
2 rue André Pascal,
F-75775 Paris Cedex 16,
France

Telephone:	+33-1-45248200
Telefax:	+33-1-44306399
E-mail:	env.contact@oecd.org

Secretary-General (OECD)
Mr Donald Johnston.

Director for the Environment
Mr Kenneth Ruffing (Acting Director).

Executive Secretary, EPOC
Ms Amy Plantin.

Number of staff
118 at the Environment Directorate, including professional and support staff (May 2002), all located at headquarters. There are approximately 700 professionals and 1150 support staff at the OECD headquarters (May 2002).

Activities

EPOC has a work programme for 2001–02 that is composed of 6 main clusters of activities:

• *Outlook and Strategy*. OECD published in 2001 its first *OECD Environmental Outlook*. It provides an economy-based vision of environmental conditions in OECD member countries up to 2020, including quantitative projections and qualitative assessments of environmental changes. The *Outlook* was the analytical basis for the development of an *OECD Environmental Strategy for the First Decade of the 21st Century*, which was adopted by OECD Environment Ministers in May 2001. The *Environmental Strategy* identifies the actions OECD countries agree to take towards achieving environmental sustainability, the indicators that can be used to measure their progress, and the work OECD can undertake to support them in these efforts.

In a follow-up to the *Environmental Outlook* and *Strategy*, OECD will examine the use of key environmental policy principles and guidelines, and monitoring the implementation of the *Environmental Strategy* by OECD countries;

• *Policies and Instruments for Integration*. OECD promotes the compatibility and mutual reinforcement of economic, social, and sectoral policies and provides policy analysis and recommendations regarding the use of a range of policies which can be used to help foster such policy integration, such as taxes, charges, and tradable permits. Under EPOC's Working Party on National Environmental Policies, OECD looks into the design and implementation of environmentally effective and economically efficient policy instruments. The social implications of environmental policies and mechanisms are also identified, and OECD continues to examine the policy tools that can be used to overcome social (e.g. on employment or incomes) and competitiveness impacts of environmental policies.

In many cases, environmental policies need to be applied at the sectoral level. OECD has specific programmes for examining sectoral integration of environmental concerns, in particular for agriculture and transport. Through a Joint Working Party with the OECD Committee for Agriculture, EPOC continues its work on such issues as sustainable agriculture, the development of agri-environmental indicators, climate change and agriculture, and eco-labelling of agricultural produce. Transport is another area of concern, for which OECD is now looking at the practical implementation of the *Guidelines for Environmentally Sustainable Transport* in specific regions;

• *Sustainable Management of Natural Resources*. The sustainable management of natural resources is becoming ever more important, both for OECD and for non-OECD countries, as the focus of environmental concern shifts away from pollution-related problems towards resource-based ones. Under EPOC's Working Group on Economic Aspects of Biodiversity, considerable work is being undertaken on the design and use of incentive measures for biodiversity protection and sustainable use, particularly on the use of valuation and the development of markets for biodiversity goods and services.

Global climate change is one of the most serious and complex environmental challenges facing the world today. OECD's work on climate change emphasizes linkages with economic development, the direct and indirect benefits of policies to respond to climate change, including technological responses, and technological options for responding. The Annex I Experts Group of the UNFCCC provides a platform for discussing issues related to the negotiation of

climate change agreements. For example, work is under way in this context on emissions trading, the clean development mechanism, and joint implementation (see Agreements, UN Framework Convention on Climate Change).

Technical, social, and economic changes can contribute to major improvements in the efficient use of resources, helping to break the link between economic growth and the growth in resource use and pollution. To improve understanding of how resource efficiency can contribute to sustainable development, OECD has established a cross-cutting work programme in this area. Work is also being undertaken on how governments can generate both direct and indirect environmental benefits through green public purchasing programmes, with particular attention paid to financial, budgeting, and accounting issues. In addition, a project on sustainable consumption patterns—especially in the areas of tourism, food, energy, and water consumption, waste generation, and sustainable construction—seeks to provide governments with the most effective application of a broad range of policy instruments to reduce the environmental impacts arising from current consumption patterns.

OECD recently completed a reference manual on *Strategic Waste Prevention*, and has been working on various projects relating to the use of economic incentives for waste minimization and increased reuse and recycling. Work in this area includes the identification of market barriers and failures in secondary material markets, the waste reduction implications of different types of waste service contracts, and continuing work on extended producer responsibility. A series of OECD Council Acts establish a broad framework for the control of transboundary movements of wastes, such as the toxic residues from chemical and manufacturing industries. To ensure the appropriate management and recovery of wastes, work is underway to develop international guidelines for environmentally sound management (ESM) of recoverable wastes in the receiving facility. Procedures for the management of the transboundary movement of wastes exist additionally under the Basel Convention (see Agreements) and within the European Union (see this section), and harmonization of the procedures and requirements of the different systems is now almost completed;

• *Globalization and the Environment*. The opening up of the world's trade and investment regimes, an important element of globalization, is likely to have a substantial effect on the environment—nationally, regionally, and globally. OECD has been examining the interaction between trade and the environment for over a decade. Since agreement in 1995 on a set of OECD Procedural Guidelines on Trade and the Environment, the focus has been on the environmental effects of trade liberalization, the trade dimensions of sustainable product policies, and the development of methodologies for assessing the environmental effects of trade agreements. This work is discussed in a Joint Working Party on Trade and Environment, and supports discussions in the World Trade Organization (see this section).

A second significant feature of globalization has been growth in the flow of private capital, including foreign direct investment (FDI). FDI is the most significant type of capital flow for the environment, although the impacts of portfolio flows of investment are also of interest. The OECD Guidelines for Multinational Enterprises, agreed in 2000, incorporated recommendations aimed at ensuring that multinational enterprises' activities are undertaken in an environmentally sustainable manner;

• *Accountability for Environmental Performance*. The OECD has long been an authoritative source of environmental data on its member countries. These data are essential, since they provide a strong factual and quantitative basis for much of the rest of the work of the Environment Programme. Ensuring that the public has easy access to environmental information is a high priority, and to this end work is continuing in support of OECD countries' efforts, which are spurred on in part by the 1998 *OECD Council Recommendation on Environmental Information*.

Environmental progress across the

OECD is monitored with the help of the environmental indicators developed under the Programme. The widely used 'Pressure-State-Response' framework helps decision makers and the public to see how environmental, economic, and social indicators are interconnected. The OECD regularly publishes a core set of such indicators, covering both environmental and socio-economic issues—including sectoral trends in transport and energy consumption, agricultural activity, climate change and biodiversity, and spending by OECD countries to achieve their environmental goals. In 2001 the OECD published a set of key environmental indicators which are intended to give a broad overview of environmental issues in OECD countries. These indicators were endorsed by environment ministers as a tool for use in OECD work and for public information and communication by OECD.

The OECD's Environmental Performance Reviews scrutinize the efforts of its member countries to reach their environmental goals—both domestic objectives and international commitments—and recommend changes that could lead to better performance. The process is one of 'peer review' in which experts from the governments of several OECD countries and the OECD secretariat spend two weeks in a given country reviewing its performance. Their report is discussed in depth in EPOC's Working Party on Environmental Performance before it is finalized. Four or five OECD countries are examined in this way each year. A first cycle of reviews has been completed, and a second cycle was started in 2000 which places more emphasis on the use of indicators to measure performance, the integration of environmental, economic, and social policies to achieve sustainable development, and reviewing progress with respect to previous OECD recommendations;

• *Chemicals and Biotechnology.* The OECD Chemicals Programme, now the Environment, Health, and Safety (EHS) Programme, was established in 1971 to increase the OECD's capacity to foster international co-operation in order to help ensure the safety of the products of this massive industry. The work on chemicals and other topics in the field of environmental health and safety is intended to assist member countries by developing high-quality instruments for use in the protection of health and the environment, avoiding the duplication of effort among countries, and minimizing non-tariff barriers to trade.

The OECD has developed a set of test guidelines and laid down agreed principles of good laboratory practice so that safety tests undertaken in one member country do not have to be needlessly repeated elsewhere. The OECD is also assisting its member countries in developing risk-management approaches such as analysis of socio-economic factors and risk communication. The OECD has developed harmonized criteria for classifying hazardous chemicals which will be applied globally through the United Nations. The EHS Programme allows member countries to share the burden of testing existing chemicals that are produced in high volumes (defined as more than 1000 tons in any one country). This massive workload is divided up among the participating countries, which share the data they generate and then make a co-operative hazard assessment. The savings made possible by this OECD work on the mutual acceptance of data are conservatively estimated to be around US$60 million a year. The registration by public authorities of potentially harmful releases of pollutants into air, water, and soil, as well as of wastes transferred elsewhere for treatment and disposal, allows a database to be built up. This is a Pollutant Release and Transfer Register (PRTR). The OECD provides countries with guidance on how to develop a PRTR system.

The EHS Programme is also developing harmonized methodologies for assessing the safety of the products of modern biotechnology, such as genetically modified crops and micro-organisms. There is intense public interest in these, and the OECD data are made widely available through the 'Bio-Track On-Line' system on the Internet. The Pesticide Programme is helping OECD countries share the work of pesticide registration by harmonizing both the way in which the industry submits data (electronically) to the regulatory authorities, and the way in which regulators produce review reports. The Pesticide Programme also helps member countries to find ways of reducing the risks associated with pesticide use and enables them to stay informed about other countries' activities. In addition, the OECD provides a forum where government and industry experts, worker representatives, international organizations, and environmental interest groups can exchange information and experience on chemical accidents.

Co-operation with non-member countries on environment

Sharing analysis and knowledge and engaging non-member countries in a constructive dialogue is essential for OECD countries in an era of global interdependence. The OECD Environment Directorate houses the secretariat for a Task Force for the Implementation of the Environmental Action Programme in Central and Eastern Europe (EAP). The Task Force provides a forum for dialogue and co-operation between countries in transition and the members of the OECD, as well as international organizations active in the region and partners from business, labour, and non-governmental organizations.

EPOC works with the Committee on Co-operation with Non-Members (CCNM), which organizes its programme around two main areas. The first concerns Global Forums. Eight of these have been established to promote the development of networks for policy dialogue among policy makers from member and non-member countries and to address policy co-ordination issues. EPOC takes an active role in a number of these forums and in particular the Global Forums on Sustainable Development, International Investment, and Knowledge Economy: Biotechnology. The second area concerns country and regional activities. In 2002 there is an environmental component for work in Europe and Central Asia and in Asia.

Decision-making bodies

The supreme body of the OECD is its Council, composed of one representative from each member State as well as a representative of the European Commission. The Council meets either at permanent representative level (about once a fortnight) under the chairmanship of the Secretary-General, or at ministerial level (usually once a year) under the chairmanship of a minister elected annually. Decisions and recommendations are adopted by mutual agreement of all members of the Council. The Council is assisted by an Executive Committee, which is comprised of all member countries. The major part of the OECD's work is, however, prepared and carried out by numerous specialized committees and working parties.

The Environmental Policy Committee, which is composed of high-level government officials, is serviced by the Environment Directorate. The Environment Directorate works closely with many other bodies, particularly those of the UN and the European Community—as well as other sectoral directorates in OECD.

Finance

The OECD is funded by contributions from its member countries on the basis of an agreed scale of contributions. The scale is calculated essentially in terms of the capacity of the member countries to contribute as determined by reference to their 'taxable' income. Each country's contribution represents between 0.1 per cent and 25 per cent of the total budget.

Budget
The OECD budget amounted to about FFr.1.2 billion in 2001 and amounts to about €EUR187.5 million in 2002, of which approximately 80 per cent finances the cost of staff.

Special funds
Grants from the member countries to promote specific projects.

Publications

- *OECD Environmental Outlook*;
- *Handbook of Biodiversity Valuation: A Guide for Policy Makers*;
- *Saving Biological Diversity: Harnessing Markets for Conservation and Sustainable Use*;
- *Towards Sustainable Household Consumption?: Trends and Policies in OECD Countries*;
- *Working Together Towards Sustainable Development*;
- *Implementing Domestic Tradable Permits: Recent Development and Future Challenges*;
- *Environmentally Related Taxation in OECD Member Countries: Issues and Strategies*;
- *Domestic Transferable Permits for Environmental Management: Design and Implementation*;
- *Extended Producer Responsibility: Guidance Manual for Governments*;
- *Strategic Waste Prevention: Core Messages from the OECD Reference Manual*;
- *Greener Public Purchasing: Issues and Practical Solutions*;
- *Assessing the Environmental Effects of Trade Liberalisation Agreements: Methodologies*;
- *Towards Sustainable Development: Environmental Indicators 2001*;
- *Environmental Information: Performance and Challenges in OECD Countries*;
- *Environmental Performance Reviews: Achievements in OECD Countries*;
- Environmental Performance Reviews (series); countries reviewed in 2001–02 include Germany, Iceland, Italy, Japan, Norway, Portugal, the Slovak Republic, and the United Kingdom;
- *Ancillary Benefits and Costs of Greenhouse Gas Mitigation*;
- *Emission Baselines: Estimating the Unknown*;
- *Harmonised Integrated Classification System for Human Health and Environmental; Effects of Chemical Substances and Mixtures*;
- *OECD Guidelines for the Testing of Chemicals.*

Sources on the Internet

<http://www.oecd.org>

United Nations Children's Fund (UNICEF)

Objectives

UNICEF is mandated by the UN General Assembly to advocate the protection of children's rights, to help meet their basic needs, and to expand their opportunities to reach their full potential.

Guided by the Convention on the Rights of the Child, UNICEF strives to establish children's rights as enduring ethical principles and international standards of behaviour towards children.

UNICEF insists that the survival, protection, and development of children are universal development imperatives that are integral to human progress.

UNICEF is part of a growing global movement for children, a collective global force devoted to creating a world where every child's right to dignity, security, and self-fulfilment is achieved.

Over the next few years, UNICEF activities will focus on:

- girl's education;
- early childhood development and immunization 'plus' (strengthening health system and outreach);
- HIV/AIDS;
- the improved protection of children against violence, exploitation, and abuse.

Organization

Type

An integral part of the UN system. UNICEF is a subsidiary body of the UN General Assembly, to which it reports through the UN Economic and Social Council (ECOSOC).

Membership

UNICEF has no membership and relies entirely upon voluntary contributions to finance its activities. The ECOSOC elects states to sit on the UNICEF Executive Board (see Decision-making bodies, below), from states, which are members of the UN, or any of its specialized agencies, or of the International Atomic Energy Agency (see this section).

Founded

11 December 1946.

Secretariat

UNICEF House,
3 United Nations Plaza,
New York, NY 10017,
USA

Telephone:	+1-212-3267000
Telefax:	+1-212-888-7465/7454
E-mail:	netmaster@unicef.org

Executive Director
Ms Carol Bellamy.

Media Chief
Ms Liza Barrie.

Number of staff

1739 international professionals, 1524 national professionals, and 4625 general service staff serving world-wide (July 2002). Of these, 423 professionals and 312 general service staff were employed at New York headquarters.

Activities

UNICEF was originally created to meet the emergency needs of children in war-ravaged countries in the aftermath of the Second World War. Since 1953 the organization has carried out long-term programmes to benefit children in developing countries. With an extensive field network, and in partnership with governments, local communities, non-governmental organizations, and other UN agencies, UNICEF supports community-based programmes in primary health care and immunization, nutrition, education, HIV/AIDS, water supply, environmental sanitation, and gender and development. UNICEF also seeks to improve the lives of children in special need of protection, including working children, street children, abused children, children with disabilities, and children affected by war and HIV/AIDS, and works increasingly to promote equality for girls and the empowerment of women. UNICEF country programmes are based on the Convention on the Rights of the Child and other international human rights standards.

Priorities are set according to need. Almost all resources are therefore invested in the least-developed countries, especially in sub-Saharan Africa, with the greatest share going to children in the high-risk early years, up to the age of five.

Since 2000, UNICEF has helped in galvanizing major support for the Global Movement for Children (a collection of people and organizations around the world dedicated to promoting the rights of the child). Through the 'Say Yes for Children' campaign, launched in April 2001, nearly 100 million people all over the world pledged their support for children.

UNICEF served as the substantive secretariat for the UN General Assembly Special Session on Children held in New York from 8 to 10 May 2002, and supported a wide range of consultations and events around the world to ensure that children and young people had a voice in the process and in the session itself. The Special Session adopted the outcome document *A World Fit For Children*, setting 21 concrete time-bound goals for children on four key priorities: promoting healthy lives; providing quality education for all; protecting children against abuse, exploitation, and violence; and combating HIV/AIDS. Over 400 young delegates participated in the Children's Forum and unanimously agreed to a message calling for a world fit for children, which was delivered to world leaders at the Special Session.

UNICEF co-sponsored the second World Congress Against Commercial Sexual Exploitation of Children, held in Yokohama from 17 to 20 December 2001, together with the Government of Japan, End Child Prostitution in Asian Tourism (ECPAT) International, and the NGO Group on the Convention on the Rights of the Child.

Environmental activities

UNICEF has long focused on supporting community-based programmes in safe drinking-water supply and environmental sanitation, including hygiene promotion. These interventions aim to improve hygiene and environmental conditions around children's daily life, so as to increase their survival rates and ensure their healthy growth and development. UNICEF presently supports water and sanitation programmes and activities in over 80 developing countries.

Great efforts have been made to promote and support low-cost water and sanitation technologies, such as hand pumps installed on boreholes and hand-dug wells, rainwater harvesting and gravity-flow systems, and improved toilets. In recent years, UNICEF has strengthened its work in East, South, and South-East Asia on support for water-quality monitoring efforts in co-ordination with WHO. It has supported school sanitation and hygiene education activities in over 40 countries in recent years, linking these efforts with the inter-agency initiative Focusing Resources on Effective School Health (FRESH). Water and sanitation interventions also constitute a major component in UNICEF's humanitarian responses to emergencies.

UNICEF, together with WHO, has been in the forefront of monitoring global progress in expanding people's access to water supply and sanitation. The latest report from this joint monitoring programme is a global assessment for the year 2000.

UNICEF is increasing advocacy and monitoring efforts on selected major children's environmental health issues, such as unsafe water and sanitation, lead poisoning, indoor smoke, and exposure to pesticides. UNICEF participated actively in the UN Conference on Environment and Development (UNCED) in 1992 and, together with its UN, government, and NGO partners, made successful efforts to incorporate children's concerns, needs, and interests in Agenda 21. UNICEF is working closely with its partners to promote policy attention to children's environmental health issues through various forums, including the World Summit on Sustainable Development in 2002 and the Third World Water Forum in 2003.

Decision-making bodies

The Executive Board is the UNICEF governing body. It comprises 36 states, representing all major regions (eight from African states, seven from Asian and Pacific states, four from Eastern European states, five from Latin American and Caribbean states, and 12 from Western European and other states). The Board, in turn, reports to the UN General Assembly through ECOSOC. Its members serve three-year terms, with approximately one-third of the terms expiring annually.

The Board meets in one annual session to discuss major policy issues and introduce new initiatives. Two additional sessions yearly deal with programme, budget, organizational, and other issues.

The officers of the Board, constituting the Bureau, are elected by the Board from among its members at its first regular session of each calendar year. There are five officers—the President and four Vice-Presidents—representing the five regional groups at the UN. Officers of the Board are elected for a one-year term.

The secretariat is headed by the Executive Director, appointed by the Secretary-General of the UN in consultation with the Board. The Executive Director is responsible for the administration of UNICEF as well as for the appointment and direction of UNICEF staff. Regional offices in Abidjan, Amman, Bangkok, Panama City, Bogotá, Geneva, Kathmandu, and Nairobi provide and co-ordinate specialized support for the 126 field offices world-wide, which are the key operational units for advocacy, advisory services, programming, and logistics.

Headquarters in New York develops and directs policy, manages resources, and deals with donor governments and NGOs. UNICEF also has offices in Tokyo, Brussels, Copenhagen, and Florence. There are 37 National Committees for UNICEF, mostly in industrialized countries, which help in fund-raising and advocacy.

Finance

UNICEF had a total income of $US1118 million in 1999, $1139 million in 2000, and $1218 million in 2001; 33 per cent of the 2001 income came from non-governmental/private-sector sources, 64 per cent from governments/intergovernmental organizations, and 3 per cent from other sources.

UNICEF supports programmes for children in 162 developing countries, areas, and territories. The total expenditure was $1064 million in 1999, $1111 million in 2000, and $1246 million in 2001 (including write-offs).

Budget

The approved support budget was $266.4 million for the years 2000–01 for headquarters (New York, Geneva, Copenhagen, Florence, and Tokyo), $55.3 million for regional offices, and $223.8 million for field offices. The approved support budget is $270.5 million for the years 2002–03 for headquarters, $58.9 million for regional offices, and $236.7 million for field offices.

Main contributors

The top ten contributors (governments) to UNICEF's regular resources for 2000 were the USA ($248 million/1.09 per capita), the United Kingdom ($84 million/1.78 per capita), Japan ($72 million/1.16 per capita), Sweden ($56 million/6.76 per capita), Norway ($54 million/12.30 per capita), the Netherlands ($51 million/5.48 per capita), Denmark ($29 million/5.76 per capita), Australia ($20 million/1.32 per capita), Canada ($20 million/0.89 per capita), and Italy (17 million/0.70 per capita).

The top ten contributors (governments) to UNICEF's regular resources for 2001 were the USA ($110 million/0.39 per capita), Norway ($35 million/7.72 per capita), the Netherlands ($32 million/2.00 per capita), Sweden ($30 million/3.36 per capita), Japan ($26 million/0.20 per capita), the United Kingdom ($25 million/0.41 per capita), Denmark ($22 million/4.22 per capita), Italy (12 million/0.20 per capita), Finland ($10 million/2.03 per capita), and Switzerland ($10 million/1.33 per capita).

Publications

- *The State of the World's Children* (annual);
- *UNICEF Annual Report*;
- *UNICEF Facts and Figures* (annual);
- sectoral studies and newsletters.

Sources on the Internet

<http://www.unicef.org>

United Nations Development Programme (UNDP)

Objectives

UNDP is the UN's global development network, advocating for change and connecting countries to knowledge, experience, and resources to help people build a better life.

Organization

Type

Intergovernmental organization (IGO). An organ of the UN. Linked to the UN General Assembly through UN Economic and Social Council (ECOSOC).

Membership

Open to all members and observers of the UN, of its specialized agencies, and of the International Atomic Energy Agency (IAEA) (see this section). 195 member States by June 2002.

Founded

November 1965, through a merger of two predecessor programmes for UN technical co-operation.

Secretariat

UN Development Programme (UNDP),
1 United Nations Plaza,
New York, NY 10017, USA
Telephone: +1-212-9065000
Telefax: +1-212-9066663
E-mail: aboutundp@undp.org

Administrator

Mr Mark Malloch Brown.

Director, Communications Office

Mr Djibril Diallo.

Number of staff

1782 serving world-wide (May 2001). Of these, 977 staff members were at headquarters; 103 were at other headquarters offices; and 702 were at country offices.

Activities

UNDP is on the ground in 166 countries, working with them on their own solutions to global and national development challenges. As they develop local capacity, they draw on the people of UNDP and its wide range of partners.

World leaders have pledged to achieve the Millennium Development Goals (MDGs), including the overarching goal of cutting poverty in half by 2015. UNDP's network links and co-ordinates global and national efforts to reach these goals. Its focus is helping countries build and share solutions to the challenges of:

• *Democratic Governance*. More countries than ever before are working to build democratic governance. Their challenge is to develop institutions and processes that are more responsive to the needs of ordinary citizens, including the poor. UNDP brings people together within nations and around the world, building partnerships and sharing ways to promote participation, accountability, and effectiveness at all levels. It helps countries strengthen their electoral and legislative systems, improve access to justice and public administration, and develop a greater capacity to deliver basic services to those most in need.

• *Poverty Reduction*. Through the MDGs, the world is addressing the many dimensions of human development, including the halving by 2015 of the proportion of people living in extreme poverty. Developing countries are working to create their own national poverty eradication strategies based on local needs and priorities. UNDP advocates for these nationally-owned solutions and helps ensure their effectiveness. It sponsors innovative pilot projects; connect countries to global best practices and resources; promote the role of women in development; and bring governments, civil society, and outside funders together to coordinate their efforts.

• *Crisis Prevention and Recovery*. Many countries are increasingly vulnerable to violent conflicts or natural disasters that can erase decades of development and further entrench poverty and inequality. Through its global network, UNDP seeks out and shares innovative approaches to crisis prevention, early warning, and conflict resolution. As UNDP is on the ground in almost every developing country it will also be present to help bridge the gap between emergency relief and long-term development, wherever the crisis occurs.

• *Energy and Environment*. Energy and environment are essential for sustainable development. The poor are disproportionately affected by environmental degradation and lack of access to clean affordable energy services. These issues are also global as climate change, loss of biodiversity, and ozone-layer depletion cannot be addressed by countries acting alone. UNDP helps countries strengthen their capacity to address these challenges at global, national, and community levels, seeking out and sharing best practices, providing innovative policy advice, and linking partners through pilot projects that help poor people build sustainable livelihoods.

• *Information and Communications Technology*. Information and Communications Technology (ICT) is an increasingly powerful tool for participating in global markets; promoting political accountability; improving the delivery of basic services; and enhancing local development opportunities. But without innovative ICT policies, many people in developing countries—especially the poor—will be left behind. UNDP helps countries draw on expertise and best practices from around the world to develop strategies that expand access to ICT and harness it for development. Working in 166 countries, UNDP also relies on ICT solutions to make the most effective use of its own global network.

• *HIV/AIDS*. To prevent the spread of HIV/AIDS and reduce its impact, developing countries need to mobilize all levels of government and civil society. As a trusted development partner, UNDP advocates for placing HIV/AIDS at the centre of national planning and budgets; helps build national capacity to manage initiatives that include people and institutions not usually involved with public heath; and promotes decentralized responses that support community-level action. Because HIV/AIDS is a worldwide problem, UNDP supports these national efforts by offering knowledge, resources, and best practices from around the world.

• *Energy and Environment Policy*. UNDP promotes environmentally sound development policies to improve the livelihoods of the poor, sustain economic growth, and protect the global environment. This involves strengthening polices and institutions for the development of clean, affordable energy and the sustainable management of natural resources, including water, land, and biodiversity.

A *Human Development Report*, published yearly for UNDP since 1990 and drafted by a team of independent consultants, assists the international community in developing new, practical, and pragmatic concepts, measures, and policy instruments for promoting more people-oriented development.

Environmental activities
Environment and energy were among the main themes for UNDP's 1997–2001 programming cycle. Environmental objectives were reflected in over 90 per cent of the country programmes approved for the year 2000. Programmes to build capacities for sustainable development and natural resource management are supported in such areas as:

• mainstreaming environment in national development planning and policy frameworks;
• improving access to and management of national resource assets and environment services;
• promoting access to sustainable energy services for poverty reduction and sustainable development;
• reducing the vulnerability of the poor to climate change and other environmental shocks and stresses.

As a follow-up to the 1992 UN Conference on Environment and Development (UNCED), UNDP has assisted developing countries in integrating environmental concerns into national development plans and providing support in strengthening capacity for management of environment and sustainable development programmes as called for in Agenda 21, UNCED's blueprint for action. For this purpose UNDP launched Capacity 21 in 1993. Experience in sustainable development gained around the world through Capacity 21 programmes has been fed into the preparations for the World Summit on Sustainable Development (WSSD).

Capacity 21 embarked on a new beginning in 2002. An independent evaluation concluded that Capacity 21 provided a unique type of assistance to developing countries seeking to ensure that local capabilities are generated to catalyze processes that lead to sustainable outcomes. The evaluation recommended that UNDP and donors, including the Global Environment Facility, the World Bank, and private sector organizations, should establish a trust fund mechanism in partnership with the Group of 77, building on the experience of Capacity 21. UNDP decided to re-launch the initiative, expanding and renewing its mandate under the more precise focus of the MDGs and the challenges of globalization for the sustainability of local communities.

In 2001, Capacity 21 also assumed the role of co-ordinating UNDP activities for the World Summit on Sustainable Development and elaborated a corporate strategy that included supporting 140 countries financially and technically in preparing the national assessments of Agenda 21 implementation, supporting civil society participation in the regional and global preparatory committees and preparing technical inputs into major meetings.

UNDP promotes and supports environmental programmes in co-operation with a wide variety of partners in government, NGOs, community-based groups, UN organizations, and academic and research institutions. It participate in various global environmental programmes:

• The *Global Environment Facility (GEF)* (see this section) is a financial mechanism that provides grant and concessional funds to recipient countries for projects and activities that aim to protect the global environment. The GEF is jointly managed by UNDP, the UN Environment Programme (UNEP), and the World Bank. GEF resources are available for projects and other activities that address biological diversity, climate change, international waters, and depletion of the ozone layer. Activities addressing land degradation, primarily desertification and deforestation, as they relate to the four focal areas, are also eligible for funding. In its GEF activities, UNDP has concentrated on capacity-building programmes, technical assistance, and training. In 2001, GEF supported close to \$US156 million worth of projects in all parts of the developing world and the Commonwealth of Independent States: \$42 million for biodiversity management; \$57 million to mitigate climate change; \$33 million to protect international waters, \$0.270 million to fight ozone depletion; \$23.1 million to address multisectoral issues, including land degradation; and \$1.4 million to combat persistent organic pollutants, an emerging focal area for GEF. New partnerships have been launched with regional development banks, the International Fund for Agricultural Development, the private-sector, and some major NGOs. In this regard, a portfolio of about 20 projects is currently under development, preparation, or implementation;
• The *Multilateral Fund of the Montreal Protocol* (see Agreements). To assist governments in implementing fully the country-driven approach advocated by the Multilateral Fund, the Montreal Protocol intensified its role in advising governments on key issues of legislation and policy measures, taxation policies, licensing, and quota systems that encourage the use of alternative technologies to achieve the various Montreal Protocol reduction targets during the compliance period that started in 2000. UNDP received funding from the Multilateral Fund to initiate 186 new activities worth \$37 million, which will result in the phasing-out of 4,050 tonnes/year of ozone-depleting substances. The project activities covered 34 different countries, nine of which are in Africa. Six projects will strengthen the capacity of the national ozone units and provide support to national policy-makers;
• The *Office to Combat Desertification and Drought (UNSO)* is the central entity within UNDP for spearheading work on desertification control and drought preparedness in all affected UNDP programme countries world-wide. UNSO concentrates its work on the root causes of dryland degradation in supporting the implementation of the UN Convention to Combat Desertification (CCD) (see Agreements). UNSO's activities focus have focused on working with/through UNDP's country offices in providing conceptual, technical, and financial support to national and Subregional Action Programme processes to combat desertification, with emphasis on effective participatory planning processes and partnership building among all stakeholders. Moreover, UNSO has been involved in cross-cutting support activities critical for the implementation of the CCD at national, subregional, and regional levels, such as national desertification funds, drought preparedness and mitigation, assessment, and monitoring of desertification/environmental information systems, promotion of exchange of experiences and know-how in dryland management, building on indigenous knowledge and livelihood systems. UNSO has also developed advocacy materials and collaborates with other UN agencies and NGOs to generate improved knowledge of linkages between desertification and other development challenges, such as food security, poverty, rural–urban migration, biodiversity, and climate change.

The operations and location of UNSO underwent marked changes in 2001. At the end of June 2001, UNSO relocated from New York to Nairobi and has undergone radical reforms. In line with the overall management changes within UNDP, UNSO now provides policy level advice and programme support to countries through country offices. A new Drylands Development Centre has been established that links UNSO to the overall UNDP practice network;

- *Sustainable Energy Programme.* Since 1990 UNDP has been working to transform global energy systems through increased energy efficiency and use of renewable energy systems, as well as through cleaner conventional energy. The objective is to promote overall economic and social development, while at the same time addressing the threats of climate change. UNDP's approach to energy is supported by the policy and analytic work of the Sustainable Energy Programme within the Bureaux for Development Policy (BDP).

UNDP policy support services focus on: integration of sustainable energy objectives in national development and poverty-reduction strategies; capacity building for energy planners; market-based energy policy innovations; cross-sectoral dialogue and participatory processes for national energy planning; new energy financing mechanisms and public–private partnerships.

UNDP's country support includes the following activities:

- cutting-edge analysis of energy trends, technology innovations, and policy options such as the recent *World Energy Assessment: Energy and the Challenge of Sustainability* (2000), produced with UN Department of Economic and Social Affairs (DESA) and the World Energy Council;
- advocacy on the important energy linkages with economic growth, environmental protection, trade, security, social services provision, and debt through publications, including *Energy After Rio: Prospects and Challenges* (1997);
- UNDP core-funded energy activities in 58 UNDP country programmes, focusing on renewable energy and energy efficiency (60%), and energy polices (26%) amounting to $60 million in the 1991–2000 period. An additional $317 million of emergency programme assistance for Iraq supported the rehabilitation of the electricity sector;
- energy account activities of over $9 million, focusing on rural renewable energy services provision and leveraging investments from the banking and private sector;
- training materials such as *Sustainable Energy Strategies: Tools for Decision Makers* (2000), covering topics and policy issues related to energy efficiency, renewable energy, new technologies, energy and gender, environment, micro-credit financing, and institutional change;
- case-studies and training materials on policies to promote income generation and healthy, labour-saving technology with respect to (1) women and energy linkages and (2) modernized biomass use;
- analysis and piloting approaches under the Clean Development Mechanism to support the implementation of the UN Framework Convention on Climate Change (UNFCCC) (see Agreements);
- support and capacity building for developing-country negotiators participating in the UNFCCC process and Kyoto mechanisms;

- *Poverty and Environment Initiative (PEI).* Since 1998, UNDP and the European Commission have pioneered an initiative that aims to identify practical, concrete policy measures that simultaneously advance the twin goals of poverty eradication and environmental regeneration. Through research, electronic conferences, a website and knowledge network, expert-group meetings, the collection of good practices from around the world, a publication series, and an international forum of ministers, the PEI has explored the relationship between poverty and the environment, challenged widespread myths about poor people and the environments in which they live, made practical recommendations, and championed 'win–win' strategies. Starting in 2001, the emphasis will be on operationalizing those recommendations and strategies at the country level.

Decision-making bodies

The UNDP is headed by an Administrator, who is responsible to a 36-nation Executive Board, representing all major regions (eight from African states, seven from Asian and Pacific states, four from Eastern European states, five from Latin American and Caribbean states, and 12 from Western European and other states) and both donor and recipient countries. The Board, in turn, reports to the UN General Assembly through the Economic and Social Council (ECOSOC). In addition to setting policy guidelines, the Board approves the volume of assistance allocated to each country, as well as all country programmes.

Finance

The UNDP is financed by yearly voluntary contributions from member States of the UN or its related agencies.

Budget

Country contributions to UNDP totalled $US652 million in 2001 (core resources). In 2001, UNDP received additional non-core (earmarked) financial resources (see below), raising the total amount to $2.6 billion ($2.1 billion in 2000). In its decision 98/23, the Board adopted an annual funding target of $1.1 billion for contributors to UNDP regular core resources. The Executive Board decision also highlighted the importance of annual increases in volume of core contributions until the target is met, as well as the need for enhanced predictability of income through multi-year pledges and fixed income schedules.

Total expenditures were $2 billion in 2000. The support expenditures were $311.1 million in 2000. Total expenditures were $2 billion in 2001. The gross support budget was estimated to be $585 million for the years 2000–01, and is estimated to be $567 million for the years 2002–03.

Main contributors

For 2001 Japan was the largest donor to UNDP (14.73 per cent); followed by USA (12.16 per cent); Norway (10.56 per cent); the Netherlands (10.17 per cent); Sweden (8.14 per cent); the United Kingdom (8.12 per cent); Denmark (7.56 per cent); Switzerland (4.48 per cent); Canada (4.13 per cent); and Germany (3.3 per cent).

Main recipients

In line with Executive Board decision 95/23, 60 per cent of target for resource assignment from the core (TRAC) resources are allocated to least-developed countries and 88 per cent to low-income countries

Associated funds

The UNDP manages several associated funds, which received an estimated $48.6 million in voluntary contributions in 2001. Among them are the UN Capital Development Fund (UNCDF), the UN Volunteers (UNV), and the UN Development Fund for Women (UNIFEM). UNDP also provides management support services for bilateral projects and programmes financed through multilateral financing institutions.

Publications

- annual reports;
- *Human Development Report* (annual);
- *Choices* (quarterly magazine covering development issues).

Sources on the Internet

<http://www.undp.org>

United Nations Educational, Scientific, and Cultural Organization (UNESCO)

Objectives

To contribute to peace and security in the world by promoting collaboration among nations through education, science, culture, and communication in order to further universal respect for democracy, for justice, for the rule of law, and for the human rights and fundamental freedoms which are affirmed by the Charter of the UN for the peoples of the world, without distinction of race, sex, language, or religion.

Organization

Type
Intergovernmental organization (IGO). A specialized agency of the UN.

Membership
Member States of the UN. Non-members of the UN may be admitted as members by a two-thirds vote in the General Conference. Not open to regional integration organizations. 188 member States and six associate members by June 2002.

Founded
4 November 1946.

Secretariat

UNESCO,
7 place de Fontenoy,
F-75352 Paris 07 SP,
France

Telephone: +33-1-45681000
Telefax: +33-1-45671690
E-mail: opi.opdoc@unesco.org

Director-General
Mr Koïchiro Matsuura (12 November 1999–11 November 2005).

Director, Bureau of Public Information
Mr Michel Barton.

Number of staff
2160 professionals and general staff, of which approximately 645 work outside headquarters in one of 56 UNESCO field offices and units world-wide (April 2002).

Activities

UNESCO's five main functions are:
• to conduct prospective studies in order fully to understand the origins and consequences of the profound changes taking place today, along with the place occupied by education, science, culture, and communication;
• to contribute to the advancement, transfer, and universal sharing of knowledge. To this end, UNESCO initiates and co-ordinates regional or world-wide networks which have a triple vocation: research, exchange of research results, and training;
• to participate in the efforts of member States in order to set international standards;
• to respond to requests for technical assistance from member States;
• to collect and distribute world-wide specialized information.

Main conventions on environment under the auspices of UNESCO:
• *Convention Concerning the Protection of the World Cultural and Natural Heritage (World Heritage Convention)*, Paris, 1972 (see Agreements);
• *Convention on Wetlands of International Importance especially as Waterfowl Habitat (Ramsar Convention)*, Ramsar, 1971 (see Agreements).

UNESCO has also adopted a statutory framework for the World Biosphere Reserves Network which sets definitions and criteria and regulates the functioning of this network at the international level.

Environmental activities
UNESCO's role in the environmental field is: to improve understanding of the natural and human environment and of complex environmental and development issues; to contribute to problem solving by providing policy-relevant information to decision makers; to increase scientific and technical expertise; to foster institutional development and change; to provide the public with the knowledge and skills needed for sustainable development through both formal education programmes and public awareness activities; and to promote international co-operation and exchange, with emphasis on

addressing the needs of developing countries.

UNESCO is actively involved in the implementation of Agenda 21, the Convention on Biological Diversity, and the UN Framework Convention on Climate Change (see Agreements). UNESCO's activities to follow up the UN Conference on Environment and Development (UNCED) cut across all its areas of competence, and include the following: Man and the Biosphere Programme; Intergovernmental Oceanographic Commission and programmes on marine-science-related issues; International Hydrological Programme, Earth Sciences and Natural Hazards programmes, including the International Geological Correlation Programme; Network of Microbial Resources Centres; UNESCO–UNEP International Environmental Education Programme; Management of Social Transformations Programme.

Decision-making bodies

The General Conference, composed of representatives from member States, meets biennially to decide the policy, programme, and budget of UNESCO. The Executive Board consists of representatives of 58 member States elected for a four-year term; elections are held every two years on a rotation basis. The General Conference elects board members on the basis of balanced geographical distribution, allocating one seat for every three member States in each of UNESCO's five electoral groups. The Board meets twice a year and is responsible for the execution of the programme adopted by the Conference.

Finance

Each member State contributes according to the scale of assessments adopted by the UN General Assembly.

Budget

The budget was $US544,367,250 for the years 2000–01 and is $544,367,250 for 2002–03.

Main contributors

Extra-budgetary resources, which amounted to $250 million for the years 2000–01 and are expected to amount to $334 million for 2002–03, are used mostly to implement operational projects. A major part of these resources comes from governments and institutions under funds-in-trust arrangements by the World Bank and regional development banks and funds, institutions, and individuals. Operational activities are also financed by UN agencies, particularly the UN Development Programme (UNDP) and the UN Population Fund (UNFPA) (see this section).

Publications

There are no periodicals dealing explicitly with environment and development issues. However, UNESCO Publishing's catalogue has more than 1000 titles, several of which deal with science and these issues. A publication catalogue is available on UNESCO's website (see below).

Sources on the Internet

<http://www.unesco.org>
<http://mirror-us.unesco.org>

United Nations Environment Programme (UNEP)

Objectives

To provide leadership and encourage partnership in caring for the environment by inspiring, informing, and enabling nations and peoples to improve their quality of life without compromising that of future generations.

Organization

Type
Intergovernmental organization (IGO). Subsidiary to the UN General Assembly and the Economic and Social Council (ECOSOC).

Membership
Not applicable. See Decision-making bodies, below.

Founded
15 December 1972 by the UN General Assembly. Established as a result of the UN Conference on the Human Environment in Stockholm, June 1972.

Secretariat

UN Environment Programme (UNEP),
PO Box 30552,
United Nations Avenue, Gigiri,
Nairobi,
Kenya

Telephone:	+254-2-621234
Telefax:	+254-2-62-3927/3692
E-mail:	cpiinfo@unep.org

Executive Director
Mr Klaus Töpfer
(February 2002–January 2006).

Chief, Communications and Public Information
Mr Nick Nuttall (Officer-in-Charge).

Number of staff
157 professionals and 186 support staff at headquarters (31 March 2002). 254 professionals and 185 support staff at regional and other offices (31 March 2002).

Information on environmental conventions is also available through:
UN Environment Programme (UNEP),
Information Unit for Conventions,
International Environment House,
15 chemin des Anémones,
CH-1292 Châtelaine,
Switzerland

Telephone:	+41-22-9178-244/196/242
Telefax:	+41-22-7973464
E-mail:	iuc@unep.ch
Internet:	<http://www.unep.ch/iuc>

Activities

UNEP's most important function is to serve as a forum for addressing existing and emerging environmental issues at the global and regional levels. Since it was established, it has served as the primary means of bringing environmental experts together to share experiences and address global environmental issues collectively.

UNEP's programme is implemented through eight divisions:

- the *Division of Early Warning and Assessment (DEWA)* performs the function of bringing better information into the decision-making process in order to link analysis with decisions and to obtain the best available description of the implications of policy choices. Early warning and assessment gives substance to the ecological insight that 'everything is connected'. The Global Environment Outlook (GEO) process and report series relies on a network of collaborating centres, advisory groups, scientists and policy makers, and linkages with other UN bodies. The main output of the process is the GEO report series, which aims to reflect the best information and perspectives available on the global environment.

In February 2001 DEWA launched the UNEP.Net (see Sources on the Internet, below) to ensure better public access to environmental information, while supporting environmental assessment for well-informed decision making. UNEP.Net is an Internet-based interactive catalogue and multifaceted portal that offers access to environmentally relevant geographic, textual, and pictorial information. It also provides a platform for UN national focal points, UNEP partners, and collaborating institutions and centres, e.g. GEO collaborating centres, national consortia, UNEP's global environmental information exchange network INFOTERRA, and UNEP's Global Resource Information Database (GRID) to share among themselves and with the public the environmental information they possess. The design of UNEP.Net supports global reporting processes and ensure that these processes are mutually supportive. UNEP.Net is the result of a partnership with two leading institutions from the private sector in the field of environment information, the Environment Systems Research Institute (ESRI) and the National Geographic.

DEWA also incorporates the UNEP World Conservation Monitoring Centre (UNEP-WCMC), which was established in June 2000 as the key biodiversity assessment centre of UNEP;

• the *Division of Policy Development and Law (DPDL)* is responsible for promoting constructive and structured dialogue on strategic policy issues, while drawing on the creativity and expertise of a range of UNEP divisions and working towards common corporate objectives. DPDL was actively involved in the preparation of the first Global Ministerial Environment Forum in May 2000 in Malmö, Sweden. The Malmö Declaration, which was the principal output of this forum, acknowledged that the central challenge is to work out how the global ambitions contained in the increasing number of international environmental agreements can be turned into concrete local action and implementation. The impetus provided by the Declaration can be seen in the various activities of the Division;

• the *Division of Policy Implementation (DEPI)* provides technical and advisory services to partners around the globe and implements capacity- and institution-building activities. It also develops and implements pilot projects and participates in the identification and dissemination of best practices. In addition to these technical co-operation activities, the Division spearheads UNEP's response to environmental emergencies and promotes the enforcement of, and compliance with, multilateral environmental agreements (MEAs) and streamlines the implementation of the Global Programme of Action for the Protection of the Marine Environment from Land-based Activities (GPA). A priority task of DEPI has been to develop draft framework guidelines on compliance and enforcement of environmental agreements and prevention of environmental crime. The guidelines will not be legally binding, but they will provide general guidance to countries in their efforts to improve on their compliance with and the enforcement of environmental agreements and to prevent and combat environmental crime;

• the *Division of Technology, Industry, and Economics (DTIE)* works as a catalyst and encourages decision makers in government, industry, and business to develop and adopt environmentally sound policies, strategies, practices, and technologies. This involves raising awareness, building international consensus, codes of practice, and economic instruments, strengthening capabilities, exchanging information, and initiating demonstration projects;

• the *Division of Regional Co-operation and Representation (DRCR)* is focused on harmonization of regional environmental actions by strengthening intergovernmental policy dialogue through ministerial forums and increased regional and subregional co-operation. These developments are underpinned by enhanced information exchange within regions and the building of public environmental awareness on environmental issues;

• the main priority of the *Division of Environmental Conventions (DEC)* is to promote collaboration among environmental conventions and related international agreements. Within the Division's scope the second Global Meeting of Regional Seas Conventions and Action Plans, held at The Hague in July 1999, made several decisions on closer ties by laying the blueprint for the revitalization of regional seas conventions (see Agreements, Conventions within the UNEP Regional Seas Programme) and proposed a closer collaboration between the regional seas conventions, the Convention on Biological Diversity (CBD), and the Convention on International Trade in Endangered Species of Wild Fauna and Flora (CITES) (see Agreements). The Fourth Global Meeting of Regional Seas Conventions and Action Plans, which was held in Montreal, Canada in November 2001, focused on initiating dialogue between regional seas programmes and the private sector, specifically the shipping, oil, and chemicals industries.

DEC actively supports the negotiations of new legally binding instruments. It is facilitating the on-going negotiations of a convention for the protection and sustainable development of the marine and coastal area of the North-East Pacific and the negotiation of a framework convention for the protection of the marine environment of the Caspian Sea. DEC is also assisting in the revision of the Protocol Concerning Protected Areas and Wild Fauna and Flora to the Convention for the Protection, Management, and Development of the Marine and Coastal Environment of the Eastern African Region. DEC provided substantial programmatic and logistical support to intergovernmental meetings of UNEP-administered environmental conventions.

In 2001 the Division developed a project on the streamlining of national reporting of biodiversity-related conventions. For many countries, the national reporting process for these conventions is an excessive burden, funnelling funds away from conservation work. Often countries have to prepare several reports for different conventions using the same information. UNEP believes that if the wildlife-related conventions can be streamlined it would be a blueprint for improving the efficiency of other environmental conventions, such as those covering climate and chemicals. The project's findings will be reported at the World Summit on Sustainable Development (WSSD).

Through the UNEP/Global Environment Facility (GEF) (see this section) Pilot Biosafety Enabling Activity Project, DEC has been supporting developing countries and countries with economies in transition to prepare effective national biosafety frameworks in the context of the Biosafety Protocol, consistent with article 8 (g) of the CBD. The Project's National Level Component encompassed the preparation of National Biosafety Frameworks using the *UNEP International Technical Guidelines for Safety in Biotechnology* as a guide. Under the Global Level Component, eight regional workshops on biosafety were organized in Africa (Nairobi, Kenya), Asia/Pacific (New Delhi, India), Central/Eastern Europe (Bled, Slovenia), and Latin America and the Caribbean (Havana, Cuba). The workshops covered capacity-building requirements to enhance safety in biotechnology in respect of issues related to risk assessment and risk management of living modified organisms (LMOs), including their environmental impact assessment, for enhancement of biosafety. They also addressed issues related to the transboundary transfer of LMOs, including appropriate mechanisms and modalities for the supply and exchange of information.

DEC has initiated an activity to develop a harmonized customs code system for MEAs which will bring together disparate conventions that are linked by shared operational concerns. UNEP has commenced preparations in collaboration with the World Customs Organization on the need to develop such a harmonized customs code system.

DEC has jointly with DTIE worked closely to organize a series of meetings addressing trade issues under MEAs. Meetings with selected environmental conventions were held in 2000 to discuss potential synergies and mutual support of trade and environment rules and institutions. These meetings contributed to the solidification of the positions of MEAs in their presentations to the Committee on Trade and Environment of the World Trade Organization (WTO) (see IGOs). A UNEP/WTO meeting was held in October 2000 on enhancing synergies and mutual support of environmental conventions and World Trade Organization secretariats.

DEC and DTIE are also working with the UN University and the Massachusetts Institute of Technology (MIT), focusing on linkages between the Convention for the Protection of the Ozone Layer and the Framework Convention on Climate Change (see Agreements).

Through its Information Unit on Conventions (IUC), and in collaboration with the UNEP's Division of Communications and Public Information (see below), DEC provides support in the area of public awareness and information, including the provision of media services, to environmental conventions. Its special outputs include, *inter alia*, the launch of:

- the regional seas website at <www.unep.ch/seas>;
- the environmental conventions website at <www.unep.ch/conventions>, which includes the newsletter *Synergies*. The latter disseminates information on collaboration among conventions;

• the *Division of Global Environment Facility (GEF)* (see this section) *Co-ordination* catalyzes the development of scientific and technical analysis and advancing environmental management in GEF-financed activities. UNEP provides guidance on relating the GEF-financed activities to global, regional, and national environmental assessments, policy frameworks and plans, and to international environmental agreements. As trustee for the environment, UNEP plays a distinctive and strategic role in the GEF by:

- co-operating with UNDP and the World Bank (see this section) as a full partner;
- advancing greater responsiveness of the GEF to global environmental priorities through informed decision making, by providing strategic inputs, and fostering complementarity between actions in each focal area, so that GEF activities are consistent with global and regional assessments, conventions and agreements, action plans, and policy frameworks in the development context;
- providing necessary scientific and technical inputs at all levels so as to ensure the scientific and technical integrity of the GEF process, and contributing effectively to the formulation of GEF operational strategies;
- providing the perspective of global and regional frameworks and strategies which UNEP has helped to develop, so as to strengthen the GEF operations;
- executing projects of a strategic nature and importance that directly contribute to increased understanding, knowledge, and awareness of critical aspects of global environmental issues addressed by the GEF, and contributing to the execution of projects of the partner agencies at their request;
- assisting countries, when so requested by governments, and relevant organizations, to assess their needs and develop project ideas.

UNEP provides also the secretariat of the Scientific and Technical Advisory Panel (STAP) of the GEF, comprising 12 world-renowned experts in the fields relevant to the GEF activities and designated by the Executive Director of UNEP;

• the *Division of Communications and Public Information* communicates UNEP's core messages to all stakeholders and partners, raising environmental awareness and enhancing the profile of UNEP world-wide.

Main conventions on the environment under the auspices of UNEP (see Agreements)

- *Convention on International Trade in Endangered Species of Wild Fauna and Flora (CITES)*, Washington, DC, 1973;
- *Convention on the Conservation of Migratory Species of Wild Animals (CMS)*, Bonn, 1979;
- *Vienna Convention for the Protection of the Ozone Layer*, Vienna, 1985, including the *Montreal Protocol on Substances that Deplete the Ozone Layer*, Montreal, 1987;
- *Convention on the Control of Transboundary Movements of Hazardous Wastes and their Disposal (Basel Convention)*, Basel, 1989;
- *Convention on Biological Diversity (CBD)*, adopted in Nairobi and opened for signature in Rio de Janeiro, 1992;
- the following conventions within the *UNEP Regional Seas Programme*:
  - *Convention for the Protection, Management, and Development of the Marine and Coastal Environment of the Eastern African Region*, Nairobi, 1985;
  - *Convention for the Protection of the Marine Environment and the Coastal Region of the Mediterranean (Barcelona Convention)*, Barcelona, 1976;
  - *Convention for Co-operation in the Protection and Development of the Marine and Coastal Environment of the West and Central African Region*, Abidjan, 1981;
  - *Convention for the Protection and Development of the Marine Environment of the Wider Caribbean Region*, Cartagena de Indias, 1983;
- *Lusaka Agreement on Co-operative Enforcement Operations Directed at Illegal Trade in Wild Fauna and Flora*, Lusaka, 1994;
- *Convention on the Prior Informed Consent Procedure for Certain Hazardous Chemicals and Pesticides in International Trade (Rotterdam Convention on PIC)*, Rotterdam, 1998 (see Agreements). Operated jointly with the Food and Agriculture Organization (FAO);
- *Stockholm Convention on Persistent Organic Pollution (Stockholm Convention on POPs)*, Stockholm, 2001.

Decision-making bodies

The UNEP Governing Council is composed of 58 members of the UN elected by the UN General Assembly for three years terms. It reports to the UN General Assembly through ECOSOC. The Council assesses the state of the world environment, establishes UNEP's programme priorities, and approves the budget. The membership of the Governing Council is made up on the following geographical basis: Africa (16), Asia (13), Latin America and the Caribbean (10), Eastern Europe (6), Western Europe, North America, and other (13).

A High-Level Committee of Ministers and Officials (HLCOMO) was established by a decision of the Governing Council in April 1997 as a subsidiary body of the Council. It has the mandate to consider the international environmental agenda and to make reform and policy recommendations to the Governing Council. It also provides guidance and advice to UNEP's Executive Director on emerging environmental issues; enhances the collaboration and co-operation of UNEP with other relevant multilateral bodies as well as with the environmental conventions and their secretariats; and supports the Executive Director in mobilizing adequate and predictable financial resources for UNEP's implementation of the global environmental agenda approved by the Council. The Committee consists of 36 members elected from among members of the UN and its specialized agencies. Members serve for two years, taking into account the principle of equitable regional representation as reflected in the composition of the Council.

The Committee of Permanent Representatives, the other subsidiary organ of the Governing Council, whose membership is open to Permanent Representatives accredited to UNEP from among members of the UN and its specialized agencies, has the mandate to: review, monitor, and assess the implementation of decisions of the Council; review reports on the effectiveness, efficiency, and transparency of the functions and work of the secretariat and make recommendations thereon to the Council; and prepare draft decisions for consideration by the Council.

The Secretariat, headed by the Executive Director, supports the Governing Council, co-ordinates environmental programmes within the UN system, and administers the Environment Fund.

Finance

UNEP is financed through the regular budget of the UN, the Environment Fund, Trust Funds, and counterpart contributions.

Budget

The budget for the Environment Fund for financing UNEP's programme activities was $US119.4 million for 2000–01 and is $119.9 million for 2002–3.

Main contributors

Main contributors in 2000 were the USA ($7.2 million), the United Kingdom ($6.3 million), Germany ($4.9 million), Japan ($4.5 million), Finland ($2.5 million), the Netherlands ($2.5 million), Switzerland ($2.1 million), Norway ($1.8 million), Denmark ($1.6 million), and Sweden ($1.5 million).

Main contributors in 2001 were the USA ($6.5 million), the United Kingdom ($6.0 million), Germany ($4.8 million), Japan ($4.5 million), the Netherlands ($4.5 million), Finland ($2.5 million), Switzerland ($2.3 million), Sweden ($2.1 million), Denmark ($1.8 million), and Norway ($1.7 million).

Special funds

The Environment Fund is a voluntary fund used to finance the costs of the implementation of UNEP's programme of work. Some programmes are financed totally by the Environment Fund, but most are funded from more than one source, including the Trust Funds and counterpart contributions.

Publications

In addition to studies, reports, legal texts, technical guidelines, etc.:

- *Environment in Print 2000* (UNEP's publications catalogue);
- *Annual Report of the Executive Director*;
- *Our Planet* (quarterly);
- *Industry and Environment Review* (quarterly);
- Technical Reports (series);
- Environment and Trade (series) (25 publications);
- *Environmental Law Bulletin* (bi-annually);
- *Global Environment Outlook Report* (every two years) (GEO 3 was due in early 2002);
- *Earth Views* (quarterly newsletter of the Environment Assessment Division);
- *Synergies* (quarterly newsletter of the Information Unit on Conventions (IUC))
- *OzonAction*;
- *APELL* (Awareness and Preparedness for Emergencies at the Local Level) (newsletter);
- *UNEP Chemicals*;
- International Environmental Technical Centre's newsletter *IETC's Insight*.

Sources on the Internet

<http://www.unep.org>
<http://www.unep.net>

United Nations Industrial Development Organization (UNIDO)

Objectives

Within the UN system, UNIDO has the lead role in industrial development. It is mandated by its constitution to promote and accelerate industrial development in developing countries and encourage industrial co-operation. The ultimate aim is to create a better life for people by laying the industrial foundations for long-term prosperity and economic strength. Acting as a global forum for industrial development, UNIDO brings together representatives of government, industry, and the public and private sector, as well as civil society from developed and developing countries and countries with economies in transition. UNIDO is also a service organization, supporting the industrial development efforts of its clients through its technical co-operation programmes and putting into practice the principles developed at the global forum level.

Organization

Type

Intergovernmental organization (IGO). A specialized agency of the UN. Linked to UN Economic and Social Council (ECOSOC) on matters of UN-wide concern.

Membership

Open to members of the UN and its specialized agencies. 169 member States by 1 June 2002.

Founded

1 January 1967. Status as a UN specialized agency since 17 December 1985.

Secretariat

UNIDO,
PO Box 300,
A-1400 Vienna,
Austria

Telephone:	+43-1-260260
Telefax:	+43-1-2692669
E-mail:	unido@unido.org

Director-General

Mr Carlos Alfredo Magariños
(December 2001–December 2005).

Communication and Information Office

Mr Agustin Stellatelli.

Number of staff

545 staff at headquarters and 105 in the field (May 2002).

Activities

The *Business Plan on the Future Role and Functions of UNIDO*, approved by the seventh session of the General Conference in Vienna from 1 to 5 December 1997, sets the basis for UNIDO's programme and structure. It regroups activities into two main areas:

• the strengthening of industrial capacities, comprising: the promotion of both investment and related technologies and programmes in support of the global forum function, together with policy advice, including that relating to industrial policy based on action-oriented research; institutional capacity building at the country and sectoral levels; quality, standardization, and metrology; industrial information through networking, in particular information on the transfer of technology; industrial statistics.

• cleaner and sustainable industrial development, comprising: support programmes on environmentally sustainable industrial development strategies and technologies, including transfer of environmental technologies within industrial subsectors assigned a high priority; and development of specific norms and standards relating to environmentally sustainable industrial development strategies and technologies, and implementation of international protocols, agreements, and conventions.

Since an increasing part of UNIDO's activities were covered by, or developed in direct response to, international conventions and agreements, the Medium Term Framework 2002–05, submitted to the ninth session of the UNIDO General Conference in December 2001, regrouped activities by adding a third area: International Conventions and Agreements. This comprises: The Montreal Protocol on Substances that Deplete the Ozone Layer; the Stockholm Convention on Persistent Organic Pollutants; the Kyoto Protocol to the UN Framework Convention on Climate Change; the Cartagena Protocol on Biosafety to the Convention on Biological Diversity (see this section); and WTO's Agreement on Technical Barriers to Trade (TBT Agreement) and Agreement on the Application of Sanitary and Phytosanitary Measures (SPS Agreement).

While maintaining its universal character and vocation, UNIDO pursues a geographical, sectoral, and thematic concentration of its activities as follows: services to least developed countries (LDCs), in particular in Africa, with special attention to the regional and subregional level; services in support of agro-based industries and their integration through subsectoral linkages into national industrial structures; services in support of small- and medium-scale enterprises (SMEs) and their integration into national industrial structures.

UNIDO technical co-operation activities are formulated as integrated programmes (IP) (or country service frameworks (CSF) for larger countries), based on the following eight service modules: Industrial Governance and Statistics; Investment and Technology Promotion; Quality and Productivity; Small Business Development; Agro-industries; Industrial Energy and the Kyoto Protocol; the Montreal Protocol; and Environmental Management. Integration in UNIDO programmes is not only at the level of the service modules selected for a particular programme, but also at the level of donor mechanisms, national counterparts, and other development activities in the country or region.

At the end of 2001, there were 44 approved integrated programmes (not including the country service frameworks for China and India), with a total value of $US257.1 million, of which $81.3 million had been mobilized, in addition to 'stand-alone' projects. In line with the priorities set by the Millennium Declaration and the Business Plan, UNIDO has paid special attention to the needs of Africa and the least developed countries. Africa accounted for 39.5 per cent of the countries covered by integrated programmes, of which 75 per cent are in sub-Saharan Africa.

Environmental activities

Within the UN, UNIDO has the responsibility to ensure that cleaner industrialization is at the centre of the development agenda. It helps governments integrate environmentally sustainable industrial development (ESID) concepts at the policy level and build up national capacity to acquire cleaner technologies, and deals with environmental concerns related to health and safety in the workplace. UNIDO integrates environmental considerations into its technical assistance projects, which include cleaner industrial production and pollution-control measures for air and water emissions. In co-operation with the UN Environment Programme (UNEP) (see this section), UNIDO promotes national cleaner production centres (NCPs) and supports their roles in providing technical information and advice on cleaner production, demonstrating cleaner production techniques and technologies, and training industry and government professionals. July 2002 is the tenth anniversary of UNIDO as an active implementing agency of the Montreal Protocol, providing technical assistance and support services at the plant level for phasing out ozone-depleting substances in the refrigerants, solvents, foams, halons, and fumigants sectors. Under the Stockholm Convention on POPs, UNIDO's focus includes measures to reduce or eliminate production outright, as by-products in other production processes or as releases from stockpiles and wastes. Under the Kyoto Protocol, UNIDO is active in assisting the Parties in mobilizing and strengthening national capacities to participate in the implementation of the Protocol, particularly through the clean development mechanism (CDM) and joint implementation (JI) (see Agreements).

Decision-making bodies

The General Conference, comprising all member States, reviews UNIDO strategies and policy concepts on industrial development. The Industrial Development Board, consisting of 53 member States, reviews implementation of the approved work programme, the corresponding regular and operational budgets, and the implementation of the General Conference decisions. The Programme and Budget Committee, comprising 27 member States, assists the Board in preparing its work programmes and budget.

Finance

Contributions from member States, UN system funds, government funds, development finance institutions, trust funds, and voluntary contributions through the Industrial Development Fund (IDF) (see below).

Budget

The regular budget, consisting of assessed contributions by member States, was €EUR155.8 million for the years 2000–01 and is €133.7 million for the years 2002–03.

Main contributors

The five largest donors to the regular budget for the year 2002 were Japan (22 per cent), Germany (14 per cent), France (9.3 per cent), the United Kingdom (7.9 per cent), and Italy (7.3 per cent).

The five largest donors to the regular budget for the year 2003 are Japan (22 per cent), Germany (13.9 per cent), France (9.2 per cent), the United Kingdom (7.8 per cent), and Italy (7.2 per cent).

Special funds

UNIDO administers the UN Industrial Development Fund (IDF), a voluntary fund aimed at enhancing UNIDO's ability to meet the needs of developing countries. In addition, several donors provide funds for individual projects on the basis of trust funds. Taking into account both categories, the main contributors in 2001 were Italy, Japan, Denmark, Austria, and Norway. Net contributions agreed with donor governments amounted to •39 million.

Publications

In addition to various publications related to industrial development, UNIDO publishes:

- annual reports;
- Industrial Development Report;
- *International Yearbook of Industrial Statistics*;
- Emerging Technology Series;
- *Industrial Africa* (newsletter);
- *UNIDOScope* (weekly electronic newsletter on the UNIDO website (see below).

Sources on the Internet

<http://www.unido.org>

United Nations Population Fund (UNFPA)

Objectives

- to assist countries: in providing reproductive health and family-planning services on the basis of individual choice; in formulating population strategies in support of sustainable development; and in advocacy for issues related to population, reproductive health, and the empowerment of women;
- to advance the strategy endorsed by the 1994 International Conference on Population and Development (ICPD), which emphasized the inseparability of population and development and focused on meeting individuals' needs rather than demographic targets;
- to promote co-operation and co-ordination among UN system organizations, bilateral agencies, governments, non-governmental organizations, and the private sector in addressing issues of population and development, reproductive health and family planning, and gender equality and women's empowerment.

Organization

Type
Intergovernmental organization (IGO). Co-ordination with other UN agencies and organizations is maintained through the mechanism of the Administrative Committee on Co-ordination and through meetings of a Joint Consultative Group on Policy composed of the following five funding agencies: the UN Development Programme (UNDP), UNFPA, UNICEF, the World Food Programme (WFP), and the International Fund for Agricultural Development (IFAD) (see this section).

Membership
Not applicable.

Founded
1969.

Secretariat

UN Population Fund (UNFPA),
220 East 42nd Street,
New York, NY 10017, USA
Telephone: +1-212-2975020
Telefax: +1-212-5576416
E-mail: hq@unfpa.org

Executive Director
Ms Thoraya Ahmed Obaid.

Director, Information and External Relations
Mr Stirling D. Scruggs.

Number of staff
1020 staff in authorized budget posts at its headquarters in New York and its regional and field offices world-wide. Fifty per cent of the professional staff members are women. 76 per cent of staff is located in the field. (June 2002).

Activities

UNFPA has three main programme areas: reproductive health, including family planning and sexual health; population and development strategy; and advocacy.

In reproductive health, UNFPA supports the provision of a wide range of family-planning methods and related information within a constellation of integrated services, which also includes, among others: safe motherhood; counselling; and prevention of infertility, abortion, reproductive tract infections, and sexually transmitted diseases, including HIV-AIDS. It also helps to meet the reproductive health needs of adolescents and of women in emergency situations such as natural disasters and armed conflicts. UNFPA supports technical assistance, training, and research in these areas.

UNFPA is an advocate for the goals of the International Conference on People and Development (ICPD), including better reproductive health, longer life expectancy, lower infant and maternal mortality, closing the gender gap in education, and strengthening national capacity to formulate and implement population and development strategies.

Environmental activities
UNFPA adopted policy guidelines on population and environment in 1989 to promote the integration of environmental concerns into population activities. In line with these guidelines and Agenda 21, UNFPA supports a range of projects dealing with the impact on the environment and vice versa of population factors such as growth, distribution, age structure, and migration in particular. The Programme of Action of the ICPD emphasized the close links between population issues, sustainable development, and environmental protection. As an integral part of the implementation of the Programme of Action, UNFPA will take new initiatives in many fields, including the field of population and environment.

Decision-making bodies

The Executive Board of the UNDP (see this section) and UNFPA acts as the governing body, under the policy supervision of the UN Economic and Social Council (ECOSOC).

Finance

Voluntary contributions from governments and private donors, the majority of which pledge on a yearly basis.

Budget
Expenditure was $US255.6 million in 2000, of which $134.2 million was for country and regional programmes, $84.8 million was expenditure on administrative and programme support services. Total expenditure was $377.8 million in 2001, of which $317.7 million was on programming.

Total income was $367.4 million in 2000, of which $264.0 million was from regular income (general/core resources) and $103.4 million was provided through multi- and bilateral co-financing. Total (provisional) income was $297.4 million in 2001, of which $268.7 million was from regular income (general/core resources) and $123.5 million was provided through multi- and bilateral co-financing.

Main contributors
The five largest donors in 2001 were the Netherlands, the United Kingdom, Japan, Norway, and Denmark. The total number of donors in 2001 consisted of 120 governments.

Publications

- *Dispatches: News from UNFPA* (six issues a year);
- *State of World Population Report* (annual);
- *Population in the 21st Century: UNFPA and Agenda 21*;
- *Population, Environment and Poverty Linkages; Operational Challenges.*

Sources on the Internet

<http://www.unfpa.org>

World Bank

Objectives

• to help raise standards of living in developing countries by channelling financial resources to them from industrialized countries;
• to provide capital for productive purposes, particularly the development of productive facilities and resources in developing countries;
• to promote private foreign investment for productive purposes and, where necessary, supplement private investment by providing finance;
• to identify the more useful and urgent projects required to support economic and social development;
• to ensure that such projects are given appropriate priority by arranging or guaranteeing finance.

Organization

The World Bank includes the International Bank for Reconstruction and Development (IBRD) and the International Development Association (IDA). IBRD was established on 27 December 1945 when representatives of 28 countries signed the Articles of Agreement which had been drawn up at the Bretton Woods Conference in July 1944. IDA was established on 24 September 1960 in Washington, DC. The name 'World Bank' is generally taken to mean the IBRD and IDA together.

Type
Intergovernmental organization (IGO). IBRD and IDA are both UN specialized agencies. Besides IBRD and IDA, the World Bank Group includes the International Finance Corporation (IFC) and the Multilateral Investment Guarantee Agency (MIGA).

Membership
Membership is open to all members of the International Monetary Fund (IMF) (see this section). Not open to regional integration organizations. IBRD had 183 member States and IDA had 162 member States by 15 June 2002. A country must be a member of the IBRD before it can join the IDA.

Founded
27 December 1945 (IBRD); 24 September 1960 (IDA).

Secretariat

The World Bank,
1818 H Street NW,
Washington, DC 20433,
USA
Telephone: +1-202-4771234
Telefax: +1-202-4776391
E-mail: askus@worldbank.org

The World Bank had offices in 100 countries, in addition to East Timor, Hong Kong SAR, and the West Bank and Gaza (see illustration), by January 2002.

President
Mr James D. Wolfensohn.

Director, Environment Department
Ms Kristalina Georgieva.

Number of staff
Approximately 8000 at headquarters and 2500 at country offices (January 2002).

Activities

The World Bank finances infrastructure facilities such as roads, railways, and power facilities as well as small-scale projects such as providing credits to micro-entrepreneurs and farmers. It has increased emphasis on investments which can directly affect the well-being of the masses of poor people, e.g. in developing countries, by making them more productive and by including them as active participants in the development process.

Environmental activities
Policy and research work on the environment is conducted in all the Bank's sectors, but especially in energy, industry, urban infrastructure, and agriculture.

Central to integrating environmental concerns into the Bank's activities is the Operational Directive on Environmental Assessment, approved in October 1989. The Directive mandates an environmental assessment for all projects that may have a significant impact on the environment. In

the financial year 1991/92 the Directive was revised to require that people affected by Bank-supported projects have access to the information contained in the assessment.

The Bank works closely with the UN Development Programme (UNDP) (see this section) and often serves as executing agency for UNDP projects.

The Bank co-operated with UNDP and the UN Environment Programme (UNEP) in the three-year pilot programme Global Environment Facility (GEF) (see this section) adopted in 1991. The restructured GEF was established by the same implementing agencies in 1994.

At the end of the financial year 2000/01, there were 95 active environment projects amounting to $US5.1 billion. In addition, there were numerous sector projects with primarily environmental objectives amounting to $11 billion. This 'broad' environmental portfolio, which totals $16 billion in lending, consists of projects with clear environmental objectives in the area of pollution management and urban environmental priorities, natural resource management, environmental capacity building, and global environmental issues.

In the financial year 2000/01, seven new stand-alone environment projects were approved, totalling $516 million. (In the same year 11 stand-alone environmental projects were closed.) In addition, there were eight new projects in other sectors with primarily environmental objectives amounting to over $525.4 million. Thus, environmental lending for projects approved in the financial year 2000/01 amounted to more than $1 billion. Each loan is disbursed usually over a five- to ten-year period.

After two years of consultations across the globe and through the Internet, the World Bank's Board of Governors (see Decision-making bodies below) approved a new environmental strategy in July 2001. This new strategy places emphasis on developing country priorities with three objectives:

• to improve the quality of life—people's health, livelihood ,and vulnerability—affected by environmental conditions;
• to improve the quality of growth—by supporting policy, regulatory, and institutional frameworks for sustainable environmental management and by promoting sustainable private development;
• to protect the quality of the regional and global commons such as climate change, forests, water resources, and biodiversity.

The new strategy builds on a stocktaking of several decades of work in the environmental area. This work began with a series of safeguard policies designed to limit damage to the environment. More recently, the focus has shifted to the positive contribution that environmental policy can bring to the quality of life in developing nations.

Decision-making bodies

All powers of the Bank are vested in a Board of Governors, which consists of one Governor appointed by each member State. The Governors have delegated most of their powers to the Executive Directors responsible for matters of policy and approval of all the loans made by the Bank. The Bank's operation is the responsibility of a President selected by the Executive Directors, who is, *ex officio*, their Chairman.

IDA is a separate legal entity with its own financial resources. It has the same Board of Governors and the same Executive Directors representing countries that are members of both IBRD and IDA. The President of the Bank is *ex officio* President of IDA and the officers and staff of the Bank also serve IDA. Each member has an assessed quota, which is subscribed and determines voting-power in IDA and IBRD. By September 2001 the USA, as the largest contributor, had 14.37 per cent of the voting power in IDA. Japan (10.90 per cent), Germany (7.04 per cent), the United Kingdom (4.94 per cent), and France (4.32 per cent) have, together with the USA, the largest share of voting-power. By September 2001 the voting-power in IBRD of the five largest shareholders was as follows: USA (16.41 per cent), Japan (7.87 per cent), Germany (4.49 per cent), France (4.31 per cent), and the UK (4.31 per cent).

Finance

The IBRD, which accounts for about three-quarters of all World Bank lending, raises most of its money on the world's financial markets. It sells bonds and other debt securities to pension funds, insurance companies, corporations, other banks, and individuals around the world. In the financial year 2000/01, IBRD raised $US17 billion in international debt capital markets. Borrowings and shareholder equity fund IBRD's loans and investments.

IDA, however, depends almost entirely on the wealthier member governments for its financial resources. Donors are asked every three years to replenish IDA funds. The Twelfth Replenishment (IDA12) is financing projects from 1 July 1999 to 1 July 2002. Funding for IDA12 will allow IDA to lend about $20 billion, of which donors' contributions will provide a little over half. Additional funds come from IBRD's profits and from borrowers' repayments of earlier IDA credits.

Budget

The approved administrative budget for the World Bank was $1467.9 million for the financial year 1999/2000, $1442.2 million for 2000/01, and $1589.7 million for 2001/02.

Main contributors

The largest pledges to IDA12 were made by the USA, Japan, Germany, France, the United Kingdom, Italy, and Canada. IDA12 donors also included developing countries such as Turkey and the Republic of Korea.

Lending

Developing countries borrow from the Bank because they need capital, technical assistance, and policy advice. There are two types of Bank lending. The first type is for developing countries that are able to pay near-market interest rates. The money for these loans comes from investors around the world. These investors buy bonds issued by the World Bank.

The second type of loan goes to the poorest countries, which are usually not creditworthy in the international financial markets and are unable to pay near-market interest rates on the money they borrow. IDA loans (known as credits) have maturities of 35 or 40 years with a ten-year grace period on repayment of principal. There is no interest charge, but credits do carry a small service charge, currently 0.75 per cent.

IDA funds are allocated to the borrowing countries in relation to their size, income level, and track record of success in managing their economies and their ongoing IDA projects. During the IDA12 period, IDA intends to increase Africa's share of IDA resources with the aim of reaching 50 per cent of IDA12. Most of the rest will go to Asian countries such as Bangladesh, India, Vietnam, Pakistan, and Nepal, with smaller amounts allocated to China and the poorer nations of Latin America and the Caribbean, the Middle East, Europe, and Central Asia.

Publications

- numerous research studies, country reports, etc.;
- annual reports;
- *Annual Report on the Environment*;
- *World Development Report* (annual);
- *Environment Matters* (newsletter of the World Bank Environment Community);
- *Global Development Finance*;
- *Trends in Developing Countries*;
- *World Bank Atlas*.

Sources on the Internet

<http://www.worldbank.org>

World Food Programme (WFP)

Objectives

• to use food aid to support economic and social development;
• to meet refugee and other emergency food needs, and the associated logistics support;
• to promote world food security in accordance with the recommendations of the United Nations and FAO.

The core policies and strategies that govern WFP activities are to provide food aid:

• to save lives in refugee and other emergency situations;
• to improve the nutrition and quality of life of the most vulnerable people at critical times in their lives;
• to help build assets and promote the self-reliance of poor people and communities, particularly through labour-intensive works programmes.

Organization

Type
Intergovernmental organization (IGO).

Membership
No general members (see Decision-making bodies, below).

Founded
24 November 1961.

Secretariat

World Food Programme (WFP),
68/70 via Cesare Giulio Viola,
Parco dei Medici,
I-00148 Rome,
Italy
Telephone: +39-06-65132628
Telefax: +39-06-65132840
E-mail: wfpinfo@wfp.org

Executive Director
Ms Catherine Bertini.

Head of Information
Mr Trevor Rowe.

Number of staff
298 professionals and 296 general service staff at headquarters; 976 professionals and 963 general service staff are in the field, delivering food and monitoring its use (December 2000). 5544 temporary staff (with contracts of less than one year) are engaged in emergency operations.

Activities

In 2000, WFP assisted 83 million of the poorest people in 83 countries. 97 new operational activities world-wide were approved in 2000. WFP operational activities in 2000 were: 19 countries with country programmes, representing an approved resource level of $US1.5 billion; 189 development activities in 59 countries with operational expenditure of $215.2 million; 185 emergency operations in 64 countries with an operational expenditure of $697.0 million; 93 protracted relief operations and protracted relief and recovery operations in 39 countries with an operational expenditure of $424.9 million.

WFP's development portfolio has been declining continually since the late 1980s, when it had reached more than $3.5 billion. In 2000 operational expenditure for development accounted for only 14 per cent of WFP's overall expenditures. This is the lowest level of development funding in 23 years.

WFP-assisted development projects have traditionally fallen almost exclusively within two broad categories: (1) agricultural and rural development and (2) human resource development. WFP's expenditures for projects aimed at assisting agricultural and rural development totalled $119.3 million in 2000. Expenditures for human resource development projects, mainly for mothers and pre-school and primary-school children, in 2000 were valued at $95.9 million. Well over 50 per cent of WFP development assistance directly supports women's advancement.

Environmental activities
WFP spends US$230 million a year on forestation, soil conservation, and other activities to promote environmentally sustainable agricultural production.

WFP's ongoing projects that have natural resource and environmental components totalled 84 in 1998. They include forestry activities, land and water development activities, rangeland development, and forestry and agricultural training.

WFP has taken a number of initiatives to address environmental concerns in both its relief and development interventions, including collaboration with the UN High Commissioner for Refugees (UNHCR) in 1998 to identify sustainable environmental management practices in areas hosting large numbers of refugees.

Based on these experiences, WFP has adopted a policy to ensure that environmental issues are systematically considered in the design and implementation of all interventions and programmes.

WFP's environmental policy identifies the main elements required for formulating an environmentally sound programming response. These include:

• ensuring that the energy and environmental implications of the WFP-provided food basket are taken into account. For example, assessing the fuel requirements to cook different types of foods when determining the composition of the food basket and identifying mitigation measures (such as providing cooking fuel or training in fuel-saving techniques) to help reduce the rate of deforestation;
• undertaking environmental reviews in selected types of interventions. Environmental reviews will be required for development activities implemented in the areas of natural resources or creation of assets, such as road improvements, irrigation, and water works. Technical assistance will be sought from government counterparts, NGOs, and staff of specialized agencies;
• ensuring sound procurement, storage, use and disposal of hazardous chemicals required for WFP operations. WFP will minimize or, where possible, phase out the use of the most hazardous chemicals, including certain pesticides and fumigants. Work has been undertaken in collaboration with the Food and Agriculture Organization (FAO) and the World Health Organization (WHO) (see this section) to identify best practices for the use of hazardous chemicals;
• developing partnerships to effectively strengthen WFP's capacities to address environmental issues.

Decision-making bodies

The Executive Board, comprising 36 members, is WFP's governing body. It consists of members elected by the FAO Council (see this section) and the UN Economic and Social Council (ECOSOC) who serve three-year terms and are eligible for re-election. The Board provides a forum for intergovernmental consultation on national food aid programmes and policies; reviews trends in food aid requirements and availability, and formulates proposals for effective co-ordination of multilateral, bilateral, and non-governmental food aid programmes, including emergency aid.

Finance

WFP is funded by voluntary contributions from donor countries and intergovernmental bodies made in commodities, cash, and services.

Budget
WFP's annual expenditure amounted to \$1.2 billion in 1998, \$1.4 billion in 1999, and \$1.5 billion in 2000; 9 per cent of the budget has been devoted to administration.

Main contributors
In 2000: the USA (47 per cent), Japan (15 per cent), the EU (7 per cent), the Netherlands (4 per cent), the United Kingdom (4 per cent), Australia (3 per cent), Canada (3 per cent), Germany (3 per cent), Denmark (2 per cent), and Norway (2 per cent).

Special funds
WFP has special funds for dealing with emergency situations such as the International Emergency Food Reserve (IEFR) and the Intermediate Response Account (IRA). In 1995 the IRA was redesigned to be both a revolving and a replenishment fund.

Contributions for 2000 to the IEFR totalled \$1030 million. Contributions to the IRA totalled \$18 million, well below the \$35 million annual target.

Publications

• annual reports;
• *Tackling Hunger in a World of Plenty: Tasks for Food Aid*;
• *Ending the Inheritance of Hunger: Food Aid for Human Growth*;
• *Enabling Development*;
• *Into School, Out of Hunger, WFP School Feeding*.

Sources on the Internet

<http://www.wfp.org>

World Health Organization (WHO)

Following the reorganization of the WHO in 1998–99, the outcome at headquarters in Geneva is an organizational structure around eight clusters. The cluster concerned mainly with international co-operation on environment and development is the Sustainable Development and Healthy Environments (SDE) cluster. SDE consists of five departments: (1) Emergency and Humanitarian Action (EHA); (2) Co-operation and Co-ordination; (3) Nutrition for Health and Development (NHD); (4) Iraq Programme; and (5) Protection of the Human Environment (PHE). For the purpose of this *Yearbook*, we limit our attention to thelast of these, which embodies five departments: (a) Water, Sanitation, and Health; (b) Occupational and Environmental Health; (c) Food Safety; (d) Chemical Safety; and (e) Radiation and Environmental Health.

Objectives

The role of PHE is to advocate, promote, co-ordinate, and carry out international work in health and environment, including the development and promotion of evidence-based guidelines; the monitoring and assessment of environmental quality; the environmental and health impact assessment; support for national capacity building in environmental health; and the provision of advice, guidance, and technical assistance to WHO member States.

PHE's mandate encompasses global-, regional-, and country-level environmental management, as well as health protection from environmental hazards, including water and sanitation; health aspects of water resources management; control of air and water quality; pollution control; occupational health, radiation protection, electromagnetic fields, ultraviolet radiation, and hazardous wastes management; chemical hazards; poisonings and food safety; and environmental settings supportive of health.

Organization

Type
Intergovernmental organization (IGO). A specialized agency of the UN, linked to the UN Economic and Social Council (ECOSOC).

Membership
All member States of the UN may become members of WHO by accepting its Constitution. Other countries may be admitted as members on approval of their application by a simple majority vote of the World Health Assembly. Territories not responsible for the conduct of their own international relations may become associate members. There were 191 member States by 30 June 2002.

Founded
7 April 1948.

Secretariat

World Health Organization (WHO),
20 avenue Appia,
CH-1211 Geneva,
Switzerland

Telephone:	+41-22-7912111
Telefax:	+41-22-7913111
E-mail:	info@who.int pfistera@who.int

Director-General
Dr Gro Harlem Brundtland
(21 July 1998–20 July 2003).

Co-ordinator, Office of the Spokesperson of WHO
Mr Jon Lidén.

Executive Director, SDE
Dr David Naborro.

PHE Documentation and Information Centre
Ms Nada Osseiran.

Director, PHE
Dr Richard Helmer.

Number of staff
Approximately 150 professionals in the global health and environment area. WHO world-wide has about 4500 staff in both professional and service staff categories, working at WHO headquarters (20 per cent), in the six regional offices (40 per cent), and in country offices (40 per cent) (July 2001).

Activities

Current environmental activities of WHO
WHO has adopted a two-track approach to preparation for the World Summit on Sustainable Development (WSSD). Track 1 focuses on the overall, long-term benefits for social, economic, and environmental development that result from investment in people's health. Track 2 reflects the environmental health aspects of specific issues on the summit agenda.

Key emphases are:

- the positive impact of health, both as a good in its own right and as a means of advancing economic development and poverty reduction;
- the direct impact of environmental degradation and unsustainable use of natural resources on people's health, and their indirect impact on the livelihoods of the poor;
- the need to assess the impact on people's health of national and international development policies and practices;
- the importance of partnerships and alliances as a means of addressing environmental threats to health and promoting sustainable development.

In relation to both tracks, WHO's strategy is to strengthen the evidence base for the different links between health and sustainable development. By drawing on data derived from country experiences, synthesized either within WHO or by centres of excellence collaborating with the Organization. An important source of information has been the work of the Commission on Macroeconomics and Health, which presented its report to WHO in December 2001.

A series of consultations has taken place to help define issues, strategies, and policy positions on health and sustainable development. The positions will be advocated before, during, and after the summit. The consultations have been hosted by national governments and international organizations, in co-operation with WHO, and have involved, in addition, academic groups, private entities, NGOs, voluntary bodies, and other parties.

Protection of the Human Environment (PHE)
PHE's programmes focus on:

- building evidence base and normative function (assessment of physical, chemical, and biological health risks) for the environment and health;

• assessing relevant global and regional status and trends;

• identifying and promoting good practices in health risk management (including evidence for the effectiveness of technical, strategic, and policy interventions);

• providing support to WHO member States in national and local capacity development and implementation in specific settings, including support to international legal and regulatory initiatives and agreements;

• estimation of the global and national environmental burden of disease;

• health impact assessment of major economic sectors.

PHE has extensive co-operation with WHO regional offices and environment centres; and network building through WHO collaborating centres, facilitating their substantive inputs to all major programme areas.

Due to the pervasive nature of both environmental health problems and solutions, PHE takes an intersectoral approach to its work, integrating concerns such as global climate change, public participation, freedom of information, and environmental equity into its overall programmes structure.

Decision-making bodies

The World Health Assembly is the policy-making body of WHO and meets in annual session. The Executive Board, which meets at least twice a year, acts as the executive organ of the Assembly. The Board is composed of 32 persons technically qualified in the field of health, each one designated by a member State elected to do so by the Assembly. Member States are elected for three-year terms.

Six regional offices have been established as integral parts of the organization, each consisting of a regional committee and a regional office. Regional committees meet in annual sessions. The Secretariat is headed by the Director-General, who is appointed by the Assembly on the nomination of the Board.

Finance

The budget is made up of assessed contributions from member States and associate members. This is known as the regular budget. WHO also receives voluntary contributions from member States and from other sources, often referred to as extra-budgetary contributions.

Budget

The regular WHO administrative budget was $US842.7 million for the years 2000–01 and the same for the years 2002–03. Extra-budgetary contributions were $1.1 billion for 2000–01 and are estimated to be $1.38 billion for 2002–03.

The regular SDE budget was $46.2 million for 2000–01 and is $47.4 million for 2002–03. Extra-budgetary contributions were $81 million in 2000–01 and are estimated at $93 million in 2002–3.

Publications

• *Bulletin of the World Health Organization* (monthly).

Sources on the Internet

WHO:
<http://www.who.int>
SDE/EHA:
<http://www.who.int/disasters>
SDE/NHD:
<http://www.who.int/nut>
SDE/PHE:
<http://www.who.int/peh>

World Meteorological Organization (WMO)

Objectives

• to facilitate international co-operation in the establishment of networks of stations for the making of meteorological observations as well as hydrological and other geophysical observations related to meteorology and to promote the establishment and maintenance of centres charged with the provision of meteorological and related services;
• to promote the establishment and maintenance of systems for rapid exchange of meteorological and related information;
• to promote standardization of meteorological and related observations and ensure the uniform publication of observations and statistics;
• to further the application of meteorology to aviation, shipping, water problems, agriculture, and other human activities;
• to promote activities in operational hydrology and further close co-operation between Meteorological and Hydrometeorological Services;
• to encourage research and training in meteorology, and, as appropriate, in related fields, and to assist in co-ordinating the international aspects of such research and training.

Organization

Type
Intergovernmental organization (IGO). A specialized agency of the UN. Agreements and working arrangements with governmental and non-governmental organizations (NGOs), other national, regional, and international scientific organizations, and UN agencies.

Membership
States and territories. 179 member States and six Territories by 1 June 2002.

Founded
23 March 1950.

Secretariat

World Meterological Organization (WMO),
7 bis, avenue de la Paix,
PO Box 2300,
CH-1211 Geneva 2,
Switzerland

Telephone: +41-22-7308111
Telefax: +41-22-7308181
E-mail: wmo@gateway.wmo.ch

Secretary-General
Professor Godwin O. P. Obasi.

Chief Information and Public Affairs Officer
Vacant.

Number of staff
109 professionals and 141 support staff at headquarters (June 2002). Ten professionals and 1 support staff at field, regional, or country offices.

Activities

WMO carries out its work through eight major scientific and technical programmes which have strong components in each region: the World Weather Watch Programme, World Climate Programme, Atmospheric Research and Environment Programme, Applications of Meteorology Programme, Hydrology and Water Resource Programme, Education and Training Programme, Regional Programme, and Technical Co-operation Programme.

Environmental activities
The WMO works through its members to provide authoritative scientific measurements, as well as assessments and predictions of the state and the composition of the global atmosphere and of the Earth's freshwater resources, as well as oceanic state.

The WMO promotes increasingly effective application of meteorological, hydrological, and related geophysical information in seeking environmentally sound and sustainable development.

With climate change as an issue of growing concern, the World Climate Programme provides an inter-agency interdisciplinary framework to address the full range of climate and climate change issues.

It calls attention to the need for global action for the reduction of ozone-depleting chemicals and to reduce pollution of the atmosphere, on the basis of available scientific information.

It has several programmes and activities operated jointly with other IGOs and NGOs. These include the Intergovernmental Panel on Climate Change (IPCC) to provide assessments of available scientific information on climate change and the resulting environmental and socio-economic impacts, the Global Climate Observing System (GCOS) to provide observations for monitoring climate and detecting climate change and to support climatological applications for national economic development and research, and the World Climate Research Programme (WCRP), which aims to develop an improved understanding of climate and predictions of global and regional climate changes on all time-frames.

WMO is also actively involved in the work of the Conference of the Parties to the UN Framework Convention on Climate Change (UNFCCC), Convention to Combat Desertification (CCD), the Montreal Protocol on Substances that Deplete the Ozone Layer (see Agreements), and several aspects of Agenda 21 of the UN Conference on Environment and Development (UNCED).

The Atmospheric Research and Environment Programme (AREP) co-ordinates and fosters research on the structure and composition of the atmosphere and its related physical characteristics; the physics of weather processes; and weather forecasting on various time- and space-scales in particular for meteorological events with high socio-economic impact. The Programme consists of four major components: the Global Atmospheric Watch, the World Weather Research programme (WWRP), Tropical Meteorology Research and Physics and Chemistry of Clouds, and Weather Modification Research.

A majority of natural disasters are weather- or climate-related, such as tropical cyclone, tornado, storm surge, flood, and drought. WMO, through its members and their National Meteorological and Hydrological Services, and in co-operation with other UN agencies and international organizations, is contributing to disaster preparedness and mitigation by means of prediction and warnings.

Following UNCED, WMO considered specific follow-up actions. In view of its long-standing experience in addressing environmental issues relevant to the atmospheric, oceanic, and hydrological sciences, WMO took actions to strengthen its related programmes, including taking new initiatives to highlight further the environmental issues of the ozone layer deletion, climate change, desertification, mitigation of natural disasters, and water resources management. Through these efforts, many of these issues were brought to the forefront of the world's scientific and political agenda. Additionally, major efforts were made for an integrated approach to the atmospheric and oceanic monitoring and research. Some of these are carried out in collaboration with a number of partner organizations.

Weather, climate, and water application and services are essential in many socio-economic sectors and for the protection of the environment. WMO therefore urges the Johannesburg Summit to address weather, climate, and water related aspects in the context of key areas of the Summit's deliberations, including: poverty eradication, sustainable consumption and protection, and sustainable development of natural resources.

Decision-making bodies

The main bodies of WMO are the World Meteorological Congress, which meets every four years and in which all member States and Territories are represented, and the Executive Council, composed of 36 directors of National Meteorological and Hydrological Services, which meets at least once a year to review the activities of the Organization and to implement the programmes approved by the Congress. The six regional associations (Africa, Asia, South America, North and Central America and the Caribbean, South-West Pacific, and Europe) are composed of member governments, and work to co-ordinate meteorological and related activities within their respective regions. The eight technical commissions, composed of experts designated by member States, study matters within their specific areas of competence. These are the commissions for:

- aeronautical meteorology;
- agricultural meteorology;
- atmospheric sciences;
- basic systems;
- climatology;
- hydrology;
- instruments and methods of observations;
- oceanography and marine meteorology (jointly with the Intergovernmental Oceanographic Commission (IOC).

The Secretariat, headed by a Secretary-General, serves as the administrative, documentation, and information centre of the Organization.

Finance

Contributions of members according to a proportional scale adopted by percentage assessment of total contribution.

Budget

The approved budget was SFr.255 million for the years 1996–9 and is SFr.252.3 million for 2000–03.

Special funds

In addition to the extra-budgetary funds for activities in respect of technical co-operation projects, WMO administers several trust funds and special accounts financed by various member States and international organizations.

Publications

- *WMO Bulletin* (quarterly);
- *World Climate News* (quarterly);
- *El Niño Update* (monhtly since November 1997);
- mandatory publications;
- programme-supporting publications;
- special environmental reports.

Sources on the Internet

<http://www.wmo.ch>

World Trade Organization (WTO)

Objectives

The main objectives of the World Trade Organization (WTO) are:

- to supervise and liberalize international trade;
- to supervise the settlements of commercial conflicts.

The WTO shall facilitate the implementation, administration, and operation, and further the objectives of the General Agreement on Tariffs and Trade (GATT) 1994 and the Multilateral Trade Agreements (which are binding on all members), including the General Agreement on Trade in Services and the Agreement on Trade-Related Aspects of Intellectual Property Rights (TRIPS), and shall also provide the framework for the implementation, administration, and operation of the Plurilateral Trade Agreements (which are binding on the members that have accepted them, but which do not create either obligations or rights for members that have not accepted them).

The main objectives of the GATT 1994 are:

- to enter into reciprocal and mutually advantageous arrangements directed to the substantial reduction of tariffs and other barriers to trade;
- to eliminate discriminatory treatment in international trade relations.

WTO members recognize that their relations in the field of trade and economic endeavour should be conducted with a view to contributing to the following objectives:

- to raise standards of living, ensuring full employment and a large and steadily growing volume of real income and effective demand;
- to expand the production of and trade in goods and services, while allowing for the optimal use of the world's resources in accordance with the objective of sustainable development, seeking both to protect and to preserve the environment and to enhance the means for doing so in a manner consistent with the member's respective needs and concerns at different levels of economic development;
- to ensure that developing countries, and especially the least developed among them, secure a share in the growth in international trade commensurate with the needs of their economic development.

Organization

Type

Intergovernmental organization (IGO).

Membership

Any state or separate customs territory possessing full autonomy in the conduct of external trade may apply for WTO membership. Membership entails accepting all the results of the Uruguay Round of Multilateral Trade Negotiations (1986–94) without exception and the submission of national tariff schedules on goods and initial commitments on services. The WTO had 144 members, including the European Union, and more than 30 observer countries, by June 2002.

Founded

1 January 1995.

Secretariat

World Trade Organization,
Centre William Rappard,
154 rue de Lausanne,
CH-1211 Geneva 21, Switzerland
Telephone: +41-22-7395111
Telefax: +41-22-7395458
E-mail: enquiries@wto.org

Director-General

Dr Supachai Panitchpakdi
(1 September 2002–31 August 2005).

Director of Information

Mr Keith Rockwell.

Number of staff

Approximately 560 at the WTO Secretariat (June 2002).

Activities

Environmental activities

The WTO has no specific agreement dealing with the environment, although a number of the WTO agreements include provisions dealing with environmental concerns. The objectives of sustainable development and environmental protection are stated in the preamble to the Agreement Establishing the WTO.

The increased emphasis on environmental policies is relatively recent. At the end of the Uruguay Round in 1994, trade ministers from participating countries decided in Marrakech to begin a comprehensive work programme on trade and environment in the WTO. The WTO's Committee on Trade and Environment (CTE) was created following the adoption of the 1994 Ministerial Decision on Trade and Environment. The CTE is open to the entire membership, and a number of intergovernmental organizations have observer status in its meetings. With its broad-based mandate, covering all areas of the multilateral trading system—goods, services, and intellectual property—the CTE has contributed to bring environmental and sustainable development issues into the mainstream of the WTO's work. Its mandate is:

- to identify the relationship between trade measures and environmental measures in order to promote sustainable development;
- to make appropriate recommendations on whether any modifications of the provisions of the multilateral trading system are required, compatible with the open, equitable, and non-discriminatory nature of the system.

The committee's work is based on two important principles:

- The WTO is competent to deal only with trade. In other words, in environmental issues its sole task is to study questions that arise when environmental policies have a significant impact on trade. Its members do not want it to intervene in national or international environmental policies or to set environmental standards. Other agencies that specialize in environmental issues are better qualified to undertake those tasks.
- If the committee does identify problems, the solutions must continue to uphold the principles of the WTO trading system.

More generally—and this was recognized in the results of the UN Conference on Environment and Development in Rio in 1992—WTO members are convinced that an open, equitable, and non-discriminatory multilateral trading system has a key contribution to make to national and international efforts to protect and conserve environmental resources better and to promote sustainable development.

The committee's work programme focuses on ten areas. Its agenda is driven by proposals from individual WTO members on issues of importance to them.

About 20 multilateral environmental agreements (MEAs) include provisions that can affect trade, for example by banning trade in certain products, or by allowing countries to restrict trade in certain circumstances. Among them are the Montreal Protocol on Substances that Deplete the Ozone Layer, the Convention on the Control of Transboundary Movements of hazardous Wastes and their Disposal (Basel Convention), and the Convention on International Trade in Endangered Species (CITES) (see Agreements).

Briefly, the CTE says the basic WTO principles of non-discrimination and transparency do not conflict with trade measures needed to protect the environment, including actions taken under the environmental agreements. It also notes that clauses in the agreements on goods, services, and intellectual property allow governments to give priority to their domestic environmental policies.

The CTE says the most effective way to deal with international environmental problems is through the environmental agreements. It says this approach complements the WTO's work in seeking internationally agreed solutions for trade problems. In other words, using the provisions of an international environmental agreement is better than one country trying on its own to change other countries' environmental policies.

The Committee notes that actions taken to protect the environment and having an impact on trade can play an important role in some environmental agreements, particularly when trade is a direct cause of the environmental problems. But it also points out that trade restrictions are not the only actions that can be taken, and they are not necessarily the most effective. Alternatives include helping countries to acquire environmentally friendly technology, giving them financial assistance, providing training, etc.

So far, no action affecting trade and taken under an international agreement has been challenged in the GATT-WTO system.

Like non-discrimination, 'transparency: information without too much paperwork' is an important WTO principle. Here, WTO members should provide as much information as possible about the environmental policies they have adopted or actions they may take, when these can have a significant impact on trade. They should do this by notifying the WTO, but the task should not be more of a burden than is normally required for other policies affecting trade.

The CTE says WTO rules do not need changing for this purpose. The WTO Secretariat compiles from its Central Registry of Notifications all information on trade-related environmental measures that members have submitted. These are put in a single database, which all WTO members can access.

At the fourth Ministerial Conference in Doha, Qatar, in November 2001, ministers agreed to launch negotiations on certain aspects of the trade and environment linkage. These negotiations aim at clarifying the relationship between the multilateral trade and environment regimes, and also cover information exchange between WTO committees and MEA secretariats and the liberalization of trade in environmental goods and services.

At the first meeting of the Trade Negotiations Committee on 1 February 2002, it was agreed that negotiations on trade and environment would take place in special sessions of the CTE.

In the context of the work on trade and environment, the GATT and subsequently the WTO have undertaken a number of initiatives aiming to promote greater coherence and mutual supportiveness of trade and environmental policies.

Increasingly, the CTE and the WTO Secretariat have been collaborating with UNEP and MEA Secretariats, as well as other international organizations dealing with trade and environment and trade and development issues, such as UN Conference on Trade and Development (UNCTAD).

A number of MEA information sessions have been held, where MEA Secretariats made presentations on various aspects of their work. These sessions have contributed to stimulate a constructive, open, and informal dialogue between the WTO, trade and environment officials, and intergovernmental organizations.

The WTO Secretariat has also begun to organize side-events at certain MEA high-level meetings. These events are aimed at increasing developing-country participants' awareness of the links between rules and work regarding environmental issues at the WTO.

Decision-making bodies

The Ministerial Conference, comprising all members, is the main governing body of the WTO, and meets at least every two years. The fourth Conference was held in Doha, Qatar, from 9 to 13 November 2001, and the fifth Conference will be held in Mexico in 2003. A General Council, composed of all members, oversees operation of the WTO between meetings of the Ministerial Conference, including acting as a dispute-settlement body and administering the trade policy review mechanism.

The Council has established subsidiary bodies such as the Council for Trade in Goods, the Council for Trade in Services, the Trade-Related Aspects of Intellectual Property Rights (TRIPs) Council, and the Committee on Trade and the Environment (CTE).

Decision making is by consensus. If a decision cannot be arrived at by consensus, the matter at issue shall be decided by voting at meetings of the Ministerial Conference and the General Council. Each member of the WTO has one vote.

Finance

Each member contributes its share in the expenses of the WTO in accordance with the financial regulations adopted by the General Council. Contributions by members reflect shares in international trade in goods, services, and intellectual property.

Budget

The administrative budget of the WTO was SFr.127 million in 2000 and Fr.131 million in 2001, and is Fr.143 million in 2002.

Main contributors

Main contributors in 2001 were the USA (15.6 per cent), Japan (7.2 per cent), the United Kingdom (6.0 per cent), France (5.8 per cent), Italy (4.7 per cent), Canada (3.9 per cent), Hong Kong SAR (3.6 per cent), the Netherlands (3.4 per cent), and Belgium (2.8 per cent).

Publications

- annual reports;
- *WTO Focus* (10 times a year);
- *Trade and Environment Bulletin* (following each meetings of the CTE);
- *International Trade* (annual);
- *Trade and Environment* (1999).

Sources on the Internet

<http://www.wto.org>

Non-Governmental Organizations (NGOs)

Note:
The NGOs have mainly been selected using the following criteria:

- that they should be *member organizations* (with membership made up of individuals and/or organizations);
- that they should be *multinational* (with member organizations, national affiliates, or offices in several countries);
- that they should be *active over a period*, i.e. *ad hoc* organizations are not included;
- that a substantial part of their activities are within the fields of *environment* and *development*. For organizations with a main focus on development, an environmental component is also required;
- that they should be reasonably *independent of governments* (an exception has been made for IUCN);
- that they should *not be a foundation* or *research organization.*

A few exceptions have been made, largely for organizations grouped in the Other NGO Networks, Instruments, and Resources subsection.

The Editors

Basel Action Network (BAN)

Objectives

• to prevent the globalization of the toxic crisis due to the trade in toxic products, toxic technologies, and toxic wastes;
• to promote the ratification and implementation of the Basel Convention and the Basel Ban Amendment.

Organization

Type
Non-governmental organization (NGO). Regular observer at meetings of the Conferences of the Parties to the Basel Convention (see Agreements) and its subsidiary bodies.

Membership
Membership open to non-profit NGOs only. 25 member organizations in 18 countries by January 2002.

Founded
1997.

Secretariat

Basel Action Network,
c/o Asia Pacific Environmental Exchange,
1305 Fourth Avenue, Suite 606,
Seattle,
Washington 98101,
USA

Telephone:	+1-206-6525555
Telefax:	+1-206-6525750
E-mail:	info@ban.org

Number of staff
Three professionals and contracted assistance (January 2002).

Activities

In order to reach its objectives, BAN works as follows:
• it operates a website on the transboundary movements of hazardous waste;
• it actively investigates and researches toxic trade incidences around the world;
• it maintains a clearing-house function for academics, journalists, and others regarding the transboundary movements of hazardous waste;
• it attends key Basel meetings, including all Conferences of Parties, and works as an advocacy observer to end toxic trade of all kinds;
• it prepares detailed submissions regarding Basel Convention policy and positions;
• it participates in bilateral and multilateral campaigns against key waste trade activities, such as the Formosa Plastics dumping in Cambodia, shipbreaking etc.;
• it co-operates with and co-ordinates member groups and others to ensure ratification of the Basel Convention and the Basel Ban Amendment;
• it works to prevent the trade organizations from impeding or eroding the mandates of the Basel Convention, or countries' rights to ban the import or export of hazardous wastes, products, or technologies.

Decision-making bodies

The Secretariat serves the member organizations. Votes are called by members when seen as necessary to change the activities or policies of the Secretariat.

Finance

BAN is funded primarily by American and European foundation grants. The main contributors in 2001 were the Kapor Foundation and the Rausing Family Trust.

Budget
No information available.

Sources on the Internet

<http://www.ban.org>

Climate Action Network (CAN)

Objectives

• to promote government and individual action to limit human-induced climate change to ecologically sustainable levels;
• to co-ordinate information exchange on international, regional, and national climate policies and issues;
• to formulate policy options and position papers on climate-related issues;
• to undertake further collaborative action to promote effective non-governmental organizations' (NGOs) involvement in efforts to avert the threat of global warming.

Organization

Type
Non-governmental organization (NGO). Observer status at UN negotiations under the UN Framework Convention on Climate Change (UNFCCC) (see Agreements).

Membership
Non-governmental, citizen-based organizations with a special interest in climate-related issues. Seven regional offices covering 331 member organizations in 83 countries by January 2002.

Founded
March 1989.

Secretariat

CAN has the following regional focal points:

Climate Network Africa (CNA),
PO Box 76479,
Nairobi,
Kenya

Telephone:	+254-2-564040
Telefax:	+254-2-573737
E-mail:	cna@lion.meteo.go.ke

Climate Action Network South Asia (CANSA),
Bangladesh Centre for Advanced Studies,
House 23, Road 10 A,
Dhanmondi R/A,
Dhaka-1209,
Bangladesh

Telephone:	+880-2-8115829
Telefax:	+880-2-8111344
E-mail:	atiq.r@bdcom.com

Climate Action Network South-East Asia (CANSEA),
Centre for Environment, Technology and Development (CETDEM),
17 JLN SS2/53,
Petaling Jaya 47300,
Malaysia

Telephone:	+60-3-78757767
Telefax:	+60-3-78754039
E-mail:	cetdem@po.jaring.my

Climate Action Network Central and Eastern Europe (CANCEE),
Terra Mileniul III,
Brasov 19,
773691 Bucharest,
Romania

Telephone:	+40-1-4402487
Telefax:	+40-1-7452487
E-mail:	terra@fx.ro

Climate Action Network Europe (CAN Europe),
48 rue de la charité,
B-1210-Brussels,
Belgium
Telephone: +32-2-2295220
Telefax: +32-2-2295229
E-mail: info@climnet.org

Climate Action Network Latin America (CANLA),
Casilla 16749 Correo 9,
Santiago,
Chile
Telephone: +56-2-2777104
Telefax: +56-2-2777104
E-mail: relac@terra.cl

US Climate Action Network (USCAN),
1367 Connecticut Avenue, NW,
Suite 300,
Washington, DC 20036-1860,
USA
Telephone: +1-202-7858702
Telefax: +1-202-7858701
E-mail: info@climatenetwork.org

Number of staff (all regional offices)
Ten professionals and 15 support staff (January 2002).

Activities

Activities are organized through the regional focal points:

- Climate Network Africa (CNA) is an African NGO focal point on climate change activities. It acts as a resource centre for climate change, desertification, and ozone depletion issues. Networking is an important part of CNA's activities, as is information dissemination through *IMPACT Newsletter*;
- CAN South Asia (CANSA) research activities include climate change and poverty; climate, environment, and population; and climate change and natural disasters;
- CAN South-East Asia (CANSEA) has established core groups in the Philippines, Indonesia, and Malaysia, and others are being sought in Thailand and other Indo-Chinese countries;
- Climate Action Network Central and Eastern Europe (CANCEE) has 24 NGOs affiliated in 16 countries;
- Climate Action Network Europe (CAN Europe), previously the Climate Network Europe (CNE), was the first Climate Network node. It was created as an NGO service on climate change issues managed by the Stockholm Environment Institute (SEI). It has regularly co-ordinated activities between 84 European NGOs in 19 countries and also acts as a resource centre for climate change information. It has a regularly updated website at <http://www.climnet.org> and produces a newsletter on climate and energy policy in Europe five times a year.
- CAN Latin America (CANLA) consists of organizations in most countries of the region;
- USCAN is the focal point of global warming research and advocacy by American NGOs. It has contributed to the scientific capacity of the NGOs within the UN climate convention negotiations and has benefited from interaction with southern NGOs on the complexities of development issues in the South. USCAN is expanding its domestic efforts at the state and local level by pursuing several legislative and administrative initiatives designed to reduce emissions of CO2 and other greenhouse gases.

The main CAN global publication is the *ECO Climate Change Newsletter*, which is produced during UNFCCC meetings and is posted on the website at <http://www.climatenetwork.org/eco>.

Decision-making bodies

The regional co-ordinators convene meetings depending on the number of sessions held under the UN Framework Convention on Climate Change. They convened several meetings in July and again in November 2001.

Finance

Each regional group raises its own finances. Sources include foundations and national governments. Additional financing comes through projects.

Budget
No information available.

Sources on the Internet

<http://www.climnet.org>
<http://www.climatenetwork.org>

Consumers International (CI)

Objectives

Consumers International supports, links, and represents consumer groups and agencies all over the world. It strives to promote a fairer society through defending the rights of all consumers, including poor, marginalized, and disadvantaged people, by:

- supporting and strengthening member organizations and the consumer movement in general
- campaigning at the international level for policies which respect consumer concerns.

Organization

Type
Non-governmental organization (NGO). Consultative status with IAEA, the UN Economic and Social Council (ECOSOC), UNESCO, FAO, WHO, UNICEF, UNIDO (see IGOs), ISO, and the International Civil Aviation Organization (ICAO).

Membership
287 member organizations—mostly non-governmental consumer associations and government-financed consumer councils—in 117 countries and six territories as of January 2002.

Founded
International Organization of Consumers Unions (IOCU): 1 April 1960.

Secretariat

Consumers International (CI),
Head Office,
24 Highbury Crescent,
London N5 1RX,
United Kingdom
Telephone: +44-20-72266663
Telefax: +44-20-73540607
E-mail: consint@consint.org

Number of staff
70 (January 2002).

CI also has three regional offices, in Chile, Zimbabwe, and Malaysia, and its Office for Developed & Transition Economies is based in London.

Activities

Through its regional offices and programmes, CI promotes an exchange of skills and experiences between consumer groups throughout the world. It has developed expertise in a number of key areas that support the work of its member organizations. These include: model consumer-protection legislation, consumer magazine development, product-testing support, media and communications support, consumer education, and national and international advocacy guidelines.

CI links the work of its member organizations through information networks, regular publications, seminars, workshops, and a triennial world congress. It initiates research and action and publishes briefings on many international issues.

Decision-making bodies

The General Assembly, the governing body, consists of one voting delegate from each full member organization. The Council, composed of 20 full members elected by the Assembly, designates the eight-member Executive Committee.

Finance

Membership dues, sale of publications, and grants from governments, UN agencies, development organizations, development aid agencies, and donor institutions.

Budget

The total core budget was £UK1,166,000 in 1999, £1,145,000 in 2000, and £1,147,000 in 2001.

Sources on the Internet

<http://www.consumersinternational.org>

Earth Council

Objectives

The mission of the Earth Council is to support and empower people in building a more secure, equitable, and sustainable future. It has the following main objectives:

- to promote the alleviation of poverty as an ethical imperative and as an important component of building a more secure and conflict-free global society;
- to provide bridges for partnership and collaboration between individuals, governments, organizations, and institutions, so as to ensure the full participation of civil societies in the processes of globalization and provide an active voice to those that will experience the changes produced by global processes;
- to encourage informed public participation and capacity building, in accessible and transparent decision-making processes, at all levels of governmental, institutional, and private planning and development decisions;
- to provide creative, inclusive, and accessible alternative dispute resolution in transnational disputes involving natural resources;
- to promote and implement a common values framework as a guide for the multiple nations and actors impacting upon sustainability and to insert the principle of the 'common good' as an integral component of our global future;
- to promote awareness, and provide education and training to achieve more sustainable, equitable, and enduring development and communities of life.

Organization

Type

Non-governmental organization (NGO). Accredited to UN Economic and Social Council (ECOSOC).

Membership

In addition to the governing body of 17 members, drawn from the world's political, business, scientific, and non-governmental communities, there are 14 people who are honorary members. By January 2002, the Earth Council had 80 partner organizations working with sustainable development.

Founded

September 1992.

Secretariat

Earth Council,
University for Peace Campus,
PO Box 319-6100,
San José,
Costa Rica
Telephone: +506-2051600
Telefax: +506-2493500
E-mail: fvanharen@ecouncil.ac.cr

Number of staff

Five professionals and 11 support staff at headquarters, and six representatives outside headquarters (January 2002).

Activities

The National Councils for Sustainable Development Program consults, manages, and collaborates with NCSDs and similar entities in over 80 countries to create a platform for dialogue between the civil society, economic sector, and government.

The Earth Charter is a declaration of fundamental principles for building a just, sustainable, and peaceful global society in the twenty-first century. It seeks to inspire in all peoples a new sense of global interdependence and shared responsibility for the well-being of the human family and the larger living world. It is an expression of hope and a call to help create a global partnership at a critical juncture in history. The Earth Charter is the product of a decade-long, worldwide, cross-cultural conversation about common goals and shared values.

The Van Lennep Program of Economic for Sustainable Development was created to promote economic reforms required for sustainable development, including improved economic instruments, the removal of inefficient subsidies, and the integration of sustainable criteria into economic policies.

The Indigenous and Tribal Peoples Centre (ITP Centre) of the Earth Council and its partners are working to enhance the capacity of its constituencies to contribute to the construction of a sustainable, equitable, and peaceful future for all by generating concrete actions and results. An important aspect of our work is to find ways to perpetuate the traditional values, knowledge, and practices with modern science and technology. The production of education tools, the development of education programs, and sharing research findings on the views and recommendation of Indigenous and Tribal Peoples are some of the results that we are generating.

The International Ombudsman Centre for the Environment and Development (OmCED): On 5 July 2000 the Earth Council Foundation signed a Memorandum of Agreement establishing the International Ombudsman Centre for the Environment and Development, OmCED. With this recent initiative the two organizations are responding to a long-perceived need for a non-adversarial, non-judicial, and agile mechanism to deal authoritatively with potential and actual conflictive issues pertaining to environment and sustainable development.

Main publications include *Earth Charter*

Bulletin (bi-monthly) and the *Earth Charter Handbook*.

Decision-making bodies

The Board members of the Earth Council Foundation meet once a year to discuss, review, and take necessary action for implementation of the Earth Council programmes. It has been supported, since its inauguration, by the Earth Council Secretariat.

Finance

The Earth Council receives support from governments, foundations, corporations, and individuals.

Main contributors

Sponsoring institutions include the principal world federations of organizations dealing with development, environment, and science, among them the International Council of Scientific Unions (ICSU); the International Development Research Centre (IDRC); the Society for International Development (SID) (see this section); IUCN (see this section); the Danish Ministry of Foreign Affairs; the Ford Foundation; and the Minister for Development Cooperation in the Netherlands. Small grants are also received from the Netherlands and Switzerland representations in Costa Rica.

Budget

The budget was $US2,700,000 in 2000 and $2,500,000 in 2001.

Sources on the Internet

<http://www.ecouncil.ac.cr>
<http://www.earthcharter.org>
<http://www.ncsdnetwork.org>
<http://www.itpcentre.org>

Earthwatch Institute

Objectives

To promote sustainable conservation of our natural resources and cultural heritage by creating partnerships between scientists, educators, and the general public.

Organization

Type

Non-governmental organization (NGO). Consultative status with IUCN.

Membership

Individuals, organizations, corporations, and schools. About 30,000 individual members and 65,000 past volunteers, with four Earthwatch Institute offices in four countries as of March 2002.

Founded

1971.

Secretariat

Earthwatch Institute,
57 Woodstock Road,
Oxford, OX2 6HJ,
United Kingdom
Telephone: 44-1865-318831
Telefax: 44-1865-311383
E-mail: info@earthwatch.org.uk

In addition, Earthwatch Institute has offices in Melbourne (Australia), Maynard, MA (USA), and Tokyo (Japan).

Number of staff

Around 100 professionals (world-wide) as of January 2002.

Activities

Earthwatch Institute sponsors around 130 projects in 45 countries. Projects are year-round and each volunteer pays a share of the cost to cover field-work, food, and lodging. The volunteers must be 16 years or older and no special skills are needed. Projects are 2–3 weeks in length.

Volunteer tasks can range from observing snow leopards in Nepal, to excavating Mayan ruins in Mexico, to surveying one of the last remaining freshwater lakes in Kenya. Volunteers are an invaluable resource to scientists in collecting data pertaining to critical environmental issues.

Since 1971 more than 65,000 volunteers have contributed over $US43 million to search for solutions to important environmental problems world-wide.

The Centre for Field Research receives more than 400 proposals each year from scholars who need the help of volunteers. The Centre, with its academic advisory board, is responsible for peer review, screening, and selection of projects for Earthwatch Institute support.

Earthwatch Institute also arranges human resource capacity building and training programs through hands-on field-work, especially for nationals from non-industrialized countries.

Main publications include *Earthwatch Journal* (quarterly) and *Earthwatch Research and Exploration Guide* (annual).

Decision-making bodies

Board of Trustees (meets quarterly), Board of Science Advisers and a Special Adviser (p.t. Sir Crispin Tickell).

Finance

Grants provided by foundations, corporations, and individual donors, as well as by national governments and the European Union. More than three-quarters of its income is derived from subscribers and volunteers, who share the cost and labour of the field research.

Budget

The world-wide budget was $US10.0 million in 1999, $9.7 million in 2000, and $10.1 million in 2001.

Sources on the Internet

<http://www.earthwatch.org>

Environment Liaison Centre International (ELCI)

Objectives

To make information a useful tool to improve the environment measurably.

Organization

Type

Non-governmental organization (NGO). ELCI is a networking instrument for NGOs. Consultative status with the Commission on Sustainable Development (CSD), UNEP, and the Food and Agriculture Organization (FAO) (see IGOs) and the UN Economic and Social Council (ECOSOC). Accredited to, among others, the Intergovernmental Negotiating Committee on Desertification (see Agreements, Convention to Combat Desertification (CCD)), the Meetings of the Conference of the Parties to the Convention on Biological Diversity (see Agreements), the Montreal Protocol (see Agreements, the Vienna Convention for the Protection of the Ozone Layer), the UN Commission on Human Settlements (UNCHS)/Habitat II, and UNESCO (see IGOs).

Membership
92 non-governmental and community-based organizations in 22 countries by February 2002.

Founded
1974.

Secretariat

Environment Liaison Centre International (ELCI),
PO Box 72461,
Nairobi,
Kenya
Telephone: +254-2-576114/576119
Telefax: +254-2-576125
E-mail: info@elci.org

Number of staff
Eleven professionals and seven support staff (February 2002).

Activities

ELCI activities are concentrated in five thematic areas: forests, water, energy, agriculture, and environmental governance. For each thematic area, a variety of approaches and projects are implemented. These are based at the local, national, and regional levels, with cross-cutting initiatives concentrated at international fora.

ELCI focuses on the local-global linkages, especially with those initiatives that bring policy or ideas to the grassroots levels or 'on the ground' case studies or lessons learned to the decision-making people. The main aspects of this work are communication, information generation, and dissemination aimed at environmental conservation and sustainable use of natural resources.

In addition, ELCI focuses on the link between civil society and UNEP, encouraging a stronger advisory role of NGOs in UNEP decision-making.

Recent and ongoing activities include:

• *RIO +10 Review: NGO participation in Sustainable Development (Chapter 27 of Agenda 21)*. Participation in the regional preparation process for the Johannesburg World Summit on Sustainable Development.

• The *Information Exchange Mechanisms* project has conducted a participatory review of the information and communication needs of NGOs in eight countries in Eastern and Southern Africa.

• *Mandate the Future* is a project which seeks to empower youth to speak on issues of sustainable development. ELCI is co-ordinating a youth network within Kenya, and in the past six months has continued to develop regional focal points and training on information access through the Internet, as well as general awareness raising of environmental issues while reviewing local solutions.

• *Public Access to Environmental Information, Decision making, and Justice in Kenya* is a project aiming to increase the role of civil society in promoting good environmental governance and sustainable development in Kenya.

• Preparing joint Kenyan NGO/government proposals and input for the upcoming sixth Meeting of the Conference of the Parties to the Convention on Biological Diversity.

• *Managing Agricultural Resources for Biodiversity Conservation*. This programme has reviewed published material on planning for agrobiodiversity conservation, and has conducted case studies of regional experiences in integrating biodiversity conservation into agricultural planning (in Ethiopia, Kenya, Zimbabwe, South Africa, West Africa, Russia and the CIS region, China, Cuba, Mexico, Brazil, India, Vietnam, and the Philippines). Seven expert reviews have been completed on the areas of pollination, soil biodiversity, biodiversity that provides mitigation of pests and diseases, crop and livestock genetic resources, diversity at the landscape level, wild biodiversity in agro-ecosystems, and support for traditional knowledge of agrobiodiversity resources. An international Managing Agricultural Resources for Biodiversity Conservation Workshop was held in Nairobi in July 2001 to develop guidelines for incorporation of agrobiodiversity concerns in national agricultural planning.

• A study has been conducted for the Institute for Cultural Affairs (ICA) Ghana regarding local initiatives in building community ownership systems for sustainable forest management.

• The *Forest Campaign* is aiming to put pressure on the Kenyan government to stop further excision of forest land.

• In the *Magoroto Forest* project, ELCI has developed a proposal to conserve the unique Magoroto Forest of the East Usambara forest region in Tanzania. This project attempts a multi-pronged approach to address the issues of reducing the communities' reliance on the forest through introducing alternatives to forest products and income-generating activities, while attempting to achieve biological and financial sustainability for the continuation of the forest in perpetuity.

Main ELCI publications include *Ecoforum* (four times a year) and various newsletters on conservation and biological diversity.

Decision-making bodies

ELCI's main decision-making body is the Board of Directors, which meets annually to determine policy directives. The regionally balanced Board of Directors consists of 14 elected and up to five co-opted members. Directors are elected by the members in their own region.

Under a new constitution adopted in 1995, a Triennial Congress of members is convened in order to solicit advice from the general membership on policies and programme strategies. The first Congress was held in 1997 in India.

Finance

The main sources of income are bilateral and multilateral donors, private foundations, members' fees, and the sale of publications.

Budget
The administrative budget was $US495,000 in 1999, $500,000 in 2000, and $600,000 in 2001.

Main contributors
Main contributors are development agencies in the Netherlands, Sweden, Canada, and UNEP.

Sources on the Internet

<http://www.elci.org>

European Environmental Bureau (EEB)

Objectives

• environmentally sustainable development in the European Union, providing for protection and restoration of biodiversity, a clean and safe environment for human beings, and the prevention of depletion of natural resources;

• external policies of the European Union that contribute to environmentally sustainable development in other countries and globally;
• achieving this by:
  • ensuring that the environmental movement in EU member States and candidate countries is informed about environmentally relevant policy making at EU level;
  • organizing substantial input from environmental organizations in the preparations for, decision making about, and implementation of such environmentally related policies.

Organization

Type

Non-governmental organization (NGO). Consultative status at the Council of Europe and the United Nations, and working relations with the Commission of the European Union, the Economic and Social Committee of the European Union, and the OECD (see IGOs).

Membership

NGOs dealing with environmental conservation and protection, based in the EU, in European Economic Area (EEA) countries, or in official EU candidate countries, can become full members. NGOs that are active in the field of environmental protection or related fields, but who do not meet the criteria for becoming full members, may become associate members. By January 2002, there were 123 full member organizations in 25 countries and 11 associate member organizations in seven countries.

Founded

13 December 1974.

Secretariat

European Environmental Bureau (EEB), Federation of Environmental Citizens' Organizations,
34 boulevard de Waterloo,
B-1000 Brussels,
Belgium

Telephone:	+32-2-2891090
Telefax:	+32-2-2891099
E-mail:	info@eeb.org

Number of staff

Seven full-time professionals, one part-time professional, and three support staff in Brussels (January 2002).

Activities

The activities of the EEB focus on the EU's role in the field of environment, both within and beyond the EU's borders.

The EEB monitors the European institutions' respect for the principles of the European Treaty, according to which EU legislation is to meet a high level of environmental protection; environmental protection requirements are to be a component of the Union's other policies.

The EEB is active within the following areas: agriculture, chemicals, energy, integrated product policy (IPP), land-use planning, biodiversity, pollution control, standardization, tourism, transport, air pollution, waste, water, and specific areas of EU environmental policy such as the Århus Convention and the EU Sustainable Development Strategy. In addition, it works with the environmental aspects of EU relations with Central and Eastern Europe.

It has also created a number of working groups in order to facilitate close co-operation and exchange of information among EEB member organizations and their experts. At present, these comprise ten main groups: Agriculture, Air, Biodiversity, Chemicals, Ecolabel, Enlargement, Industry, Noise, Waste, and Water. These groups play an important role in the formulation of EEB positions and policies.

The four main challenges for EEB for the first few years of the twenty-first century are: environmental policy integration and sustainable development; enlargement of the EU; a new generation of environmental policies; and regional co-operation in the EU on steps forward; while simultaneously strengthening the environmental debate in countries where currently it is weak.

The EEB continues to pressure the EU for effective, transparent, decisive, and sufficient environmental legislation and for its implementation. It works to improve the EU's environmental policies on realizing sustainable development by effectively integrating environmental objectives into the horizontal and sectoral policies of the EU, and ensuring compliance with effective strategies to achieve these objectives. It also pushes for the improvement of the environment and sustainable development to be realized in the enlargement of the EU, and promotes green leadership of the EU in the global arena.

The EEB works with European institutions to encourage them in their decision making towards a sustainable Europe, in order to make a high level of environmental protection the basis for all programmes, plans, and policies. It aims to achieve its objectives through a mixture of advocacy and general and specific publications. It holds between five and seven seminars or conferences a year, and a similar number of workshops or round tables.

Main publications include *Metamorphosis* (tri-monthly newsletter), *Memoranda to the EU Presidencies*, and the EEB's *Annual Report*.

Decision-making bodies

The Annual General Meeting, where each full member organization has one vote, elects the Executive Committee (Board) for a two-year term (for reasons of continuity, half the board is elected each year). The Executive Committee normally consists of one member per country. Each member organization may attend the meetings. In each of the EU Member States, and in some Accession Countries, national conferences of EEB members are also organized at least once a year.

Finance

Grants from the European Commission and national governments, members' dues, and contributions from other organizations.

Budget

The budget was €EUR1,204,000 in 1999, €1,269,00 in 2000, and €1,149,000 in 2001, and is €1,327,000 in 2002.

Main contributors

The European Commission and the governments of (alphabetically): Austria, Denmark, Finland, France, Germany, Greece, Italy, Luxembourg, the Netherlands, Norway, Sweden, and the UK.

Sources on Internet

<http://www.eeb.org>
<http://www.participate.org>

Forest Stewardship Council (FSC)

Objectives

To support environmentally appropriate, socially beneficial, and economically viable management of the world's forests.

Organization

Type

Non-governmental organization (NGO). Non-profit/membership organization.

Membership

Individuals as well as representatives from environmental institutions, the timber trade, the forestry profession, indigenous peoples' organizations, community forestry groups, and forest product certification organizations. The FSC had 531 members in 60 countries by January 2002.

Founded

October 1993, Toronto.

Secretariat

Forest Stewardship Council (FSC),
Avenida Hidalgo 502,
68000 Oaxaca,
Mexico
Telephone: +52-951-5146905/5163244
Telefax: +52-951-5162110
E-mail: fscoax@fscoax.org

Number of staff

14 professionals and 11 support staff at the Secretariat (February 2002).

Activities

The mission of FSC is to support environmentally appropriate, socially beneficial, and economically viable stewardship of the world's forests. The organization hopes to accomplish this goal by evaluating, accrediting, and monitoring certification bodies, and by strengthening national certification and forest management capacity through training, education, and the development of national certification initiatives.

The FSC does not certify products itself; rather it ensures consumers that certification organizations have the highest level of credibility and integrity. The FSC provides this assurance by evaluating, accrediting, and monitoring certifiers of forest and forest products based on their adherence to the FSC principles, criteria, and guidelines for certifiers.

The FSC principles and criteria are intended to apply to all types of forests. They are designated to allow flexibility in their application through the development of national and regional standards, which fit ecological, social, and economic circumstances. The principles and criteria provide consistency among certifiers and their standards by supplying an overall framework for developing and evaluating local and national forest management standards.

The FSC also promotes forest stewardship by encouraging the development of local forest management standards world-wide. It encourages the formation of national and regional working groups to develop forest management standards. FSC provides guidelines and technical assistance to working groups and interested stakeholders for developing national and regional standards. To ensure that certification is based on realistic and locally defined forest management practices, and to secure the consistency and integrity of standards in different countries around the world, FSC formally endorses those standards which clearly meet all FSC requirements, including the process leading to their development.

Main publications include the *FSC News+Notes* newsletter.

Decision-making bodies

The General Assembly of members is the final authority of the association. For voting purposes it is divided into three chambers, environmental, social, and economic, each with one-third voting weight. It meets every three years. Within each chamber, 'northern' and 'southern' members each hold half of the voting weight.

The same balance is reflected in the composition of the Board, which is elected by the members.

Finance

FSC is funded by charitable foundations, government donors, membership subscriptions, and accreditation fees. Funding has been received from the Austrian, Dutch, and Mexican governments, the European Commission, the Ford Foundation, the MacArthur Foundation, WWF-Netherlands, IUCN-Netherlands, the Swedish Society for Nature Conservation (SSNC), the Wallace Global Fund, the Flora Family Foundation, the Summit Foundation, WWF Sweden, the Rockefeller Brothers Fund, WWF International, WWF USA/World Bank Alliance, and GTZ.

Budget

The total budget was $US1,982,000 in 2000 and $2,854,000 in 2001, and is $3,767,000 in 2002.

Sources on the Internet

<http://www.fscoax.org>

Friends of the Earth International (FoEI)

Objectives

- to protect the Earth against deterioration and repair damage inflicted upon the environment as a result of human activity and negligence;
- to preserve the Earth's ecological, cultural, and ethnic diversity;
- to increase public participation and democratic decision making in the protection of the environment and the management of natural resources, first and foremost by the people most directly affected;
- to achieve social, economic, and political justice and equal access to resources and opportunities on a local, national, and international level;
- to promote environmentally sustainable development on a local, national, and global level.

Organization

Type

Non-governmental organization (NGO). Observer status at FAO, IMO, the London Convention 1972, the International Oil Pollution Compensation Fund (see IGOs), the Barcelona Convention (see Agreements, UNEP Regional Seas Programme), the International Whaling Commission (IWC) (see Agreements, ICRW), the Ramsar Convention, and the International Tropical Timber Agreement (ITTA) (see Agreements). Consultative status at UNESCO, the UN Economic and Social Council (ECOSOC), and the UN Economic Commission for Europe (UNECE). Participates in the meetings of the International Atomic Energy Agency (IAEA), the Intergovernmental Panel on Climate Change (IPCC) (see Agreements, UN Framework Convention on Climate Change), the Montreal Protocol (see Agreements, Vienna Convention for the Protection of the Ozone Layer), and others. Member of ELCI and IUCN.

Membership

National member groups and NGOs. Each national member group is an autonomous body with its own funding and strategy. Total of 66 member groups

Friends of the Earth International (FoEI)

in 64 countries and one territory, with about 1 million individual members, by January 2002. 12 affiliated NGOs.

Founded
1971.

Secretariat
Friends of the Earth International (FoEI),
PO Box 19199,
1000 GD Amsterdam,
The Netherlands
Telephone: +31-20-6221369
Telefax: +31-20-6392181
E-mail: foei@foei.org

Number of staff
Nine professionals and four volunteers at the International Secretariat (January 2002).

Activities
FoEI works to create networks of environmental, consumer, and human-rights organizations world-wide.

It co-ordinates their activities at the international level through campaigns led by national member groups. Main international co-ordinating areas are political lobbying, the flow of information through the FoEI network, and citizen action. In 2001/02 FoEI had campaigns and projects running on energy/climate change, mining, wetlands, international financial institutions, genetically modified organisms, forests, ecological debt, desertification, Rio+10, transnational corporations, and environmentally sustainable trade. In addition it lobbies on subjects such as Antarctica and maritime issues.

The organization keeps an eye especially on sustainability, and looks at ways in which the North can reduce its consumption of natural resources and the environmental space of the South can be increased.

Main FoEI publications include the quarterly *Link* magazine.

Decision-making bodies
A bi-annual General Meeting of the national organizations elects the FoEI Executive Committee. The International Secretariat in Amsterdam is crucial in the co-ordination of information exchange and joint campaigns, the development of the network, and fund raising.

Finance
Each national group is responsible for its own budget and makes annual contributions to the FoEI Secretariat. Main sources are fees, donations, and subsidies. Main contributors in 2000 were the Dutch donor agencies ICCO, HIVOS, and NOVIB, the Dutch Committee for IUCN, the Goldman, CS Mott, and Rockefeller Brothers Foundations, the Wallace Global Fund, and the Swedish Society for Nature Conservation.

Budget
FoEI's total budget was $US724,000 in 2000 and €EUR1,110,000 in 2001, and is estimated to be €1,167,000 in 2002.

Sources on the Internet
<http://www.foei.org>

Yearbook reference
See Keith Suter (2002), 'Friends of the Earth International', *Yearbook of International Co-operation on Environment and Development 2002/03*, 69–75.

Greenpeace International
Objectives
• to stop the chemicalization of the planet and the trade in toxic waste and dirty technology;
• to protect the Earth's biological diversity of species in the ocean and on land;
• to end the threat of nuclear weapons, nuclear weapons testing, nuclear power, and nuclear waste;
• to protect the Earth's atmosphere from ozone depletion and build-up of greenhouse gases and to push for clean and alternative energy and refrigeration technologies.

Greenpeace International

Organization

Type
Non-governmental organization (NGO), with offices world-wide. Consultative status with the UN Economic and Social Council (ECOSOC). Accredited to more than 30 international and regional organizations dealing with environmental issues.

Membership
World-wide individual membership of approximately 2.5 million supporters. Presence in 41 countries by January 2002.

Founded
1971.

Secretariat

Greenpeace International,
Keizersgracht 176,
1016 DW Amsterdam,
The Netherlands
Telephone: +31-20-5236222
Telefax: +31-20-5236200
E-mail:
supporter.services@ams.greenpeace.org

Number of staff
About 1100 world-wide (December 2001). There are about 120 professionals at the International Secretariat.

Activities

In 2001 Greenpeace focused campaign resources in a number of areas. These included special efforts:

- to protect the planet's climate and ozone layer by ensuring that governments of industrialized countries radically cut emissions of polluting greenhouse and ozone-depleting gases;
- to protect the marine environment from over-fishing, pollution, and dumping of waste and other hazardous substances;
- to transform refrigeration, air-conditioning, and other industries in order to eliminate the use of ozone-depleting chemicals;
- to monitor and ensure enforcement of global controls on the international waste trade;
- to stop clearcutting and protect ancient forests, and to promote economic alternatives to intensive logging;
- to eliminate the use of hazardous chemicals, in particular chlorine, which is still used widely for paper bleaching, PVC, and other industrial applications, in spite of mounting evidence of their devastating impacts on human and animal health;
- to stop commercial whaling;
- to eliminate the use of drift-nets;
- to halt the nuclear threat.

Decision-making bodies

The Greenpeace Council, consisting of one representative from each member country, defines objectives and strategies at the annual meeting. The Council elects seven members to the Greenpeace International Board, which appoints a chairperson and an administrative executive. The International Board is responsible for the supervision of the organization during the year. The national offices are autonomous in their daily activities.

Finance

Financed by voluntary contributions from the public and from the sale of merchandise. In 2000, 94 per cent of funding for Greenpeace International came from individual supporters.

Budget
The budget of Greenpeace International was €EUR26,937,000 in 1999, €34,824,000 in 2000, and €34,824,000 in 2001.

Sources on the Internet

<http://www.greenpeace.org>

International Chamber of Commerce (ICC)

Objectives

- to serve world business by promoting trade and investment and the market economy system;
- to represent business and promote the interests of the private sector in devel-

oped and developing countries and in the economies in transition;
• to facilitate commerce among nations through the provision of practical services and training for business people.

Organization

Type
Non-governmental organization (NGO). The ICC has first-class consultative status with the UN and its specialized agencies.

Membership
National committees or groups in 80 countries and one territory by January 2002. More than 7000 individual company members in over 140 countries around the world.

Founded
The ICC in June 1919, the Commission on Environment in 1978.

Secretariat

ICC,
38 Cours Albert 1er,
F-75008 Paris,
France
Telephone: +33-1-49532828
Telefax: +33-1-49532859
E-mail: webmaster@iccwbo.org

Number of staff
120 professionals (January 2002).

Activities

The ICC Commission on Energy & Environment, with members drawn from a wide cross-section of global industry, develops policy positions in four core areas of interest:
• *trade and environment*;
• *sustainable development*;
• *climate change*;
• *biosociety*.
The Commission also has expert groups on environmental management systems (EMS) and waste management. The Commission works to formulate policy positions which are presented to all key UN agencies and conventions, as well as the World Trade Organization (WTO) (see IGOs).

The ICC is joint co-ordinator of the Business Action for Sustainable Development (BASD) which will spearhead business preparations for—and presence at—the World Summit on Sustainable Development in Johannesburg in September 2002.

Main publications include the *ICC Handbook* and the *ICC Annual Report*.

Decision-making bodies

The ICC World Council, the supreme governing body, meets twice yearly. Members of the Executive Board are appointed by the Council on the recommendation of the president, who is elected by the Council and holds office for two years.

Finance

The ICC derives its income from services, publications, contributions from the national committees, and groups.

Budget
No information available.

Sources on the Internet

<http://www.iccwbo.org>
<http://www.basd-action.net>

International Confederation of Free Trade Unions (ICFTU)

Objectives

• to maintain and develop a powerful and effective international organization at world-wide and regional levels composed of free and democratic trade unions independent of any external domination and pledged to the task of promoting the interests of working people throughout the world and of enhancing the dignity of labour;
• to promote fair and just economic development on the basis that this development can ultimately be fair and socially just only if it is at the same time sustainable;
• to defend the right of individuals to mutual protection of their interests through forming and joining trade unions;
• to promote equality of opportunity for all people.

Organization

Type
Non-governmental organization (NGO). Consultative status with the UN system. Accredited to the UN Economic and Social Council (ECOSOC), ILO, IMF, UNESCO, FAO, UNIDO, IAEA, the World Bank, WTO, and WHO (see IGOs).

Membership
Trade unions world-wide. 225 affiliated organizations in 139 countries and nine territories representing 157 million working people by December 2001.

Founded
December 1949.

Secretariat

International Confederation of Free Trade Unions (ICFTU),
5 Blvd. du Roi Albert II, Bte 1,
B-1210 Brussels,
Belgium
Telephone: +32-2-2240211
Telefax: +32-2-2015815
E-mail: internetpo@icftu.org

Number of staff
25 professionals and 46 support staff at Head Office (December 2001).

Activities

ICFTU made environment and development one of the main themes at its World Congress in 1996 and focused particularly on the international aspects of sustainable development.

It stressed the importance of involving workers in the decision-making process as the only means of ensuring that the necessary changes are carried out fairly, efficiently, and with the minimum amount of social disruption commensurate with achieving the goal of sustainable development.

It further stressed the need for resources to be made available in and to developing countries in order to ensure that they have the wherewithal to be able to undertake the sometimes costly activities that will be necessary to protect the environment.

The ICFTU sends a large delegation each year to the UN Commission for Sustainable Development (CSD) (see IGOs) in New York, with a particular focus on the Agenda 21 follow-up to the Rio Summit. The ICFTU is also involved in preparations for the Johannesburg Earth II Summit. The ICFTU provided trade union input into the climate change meetings, e.g. the sixth Conference of the Parties (COP) to the UN Framework Convention on Climate Change in The Hague, the sixth COP bis in Bonn (July 2001), and the seventh COP in Morocco (November 2001).

In April 2000 it organized its 17th ICFTU congress, on the subject of globalization of social justice. A statement was adopted on 'Employment, Sustainable Development and Social Justice: ICFTU Programme for Sustainable Economic Growth', recognizing issues that pertain to the three pillars of sustainable development: the economic, environmental, and social dimensions. The ICFTU has just produced a statement/publication: *Fashioning a New Deal: Workers and Trade Unions for the World Summit on Sustainable Development 2002*.

Main publications include *Trade Union World* (12 times a year), *Survey on Violations of Trade Union Rights* (annually), and *ICFTU Online* (daily, by e-mail).

Decision-making bodies

The Congress, which meets every fourth year, elects the Executive Board and the General Secretary. The Executive Board meets at least once a year and elects the President, Vice-Presidents, and a Steering Committee, which meets twice a year and consists of 17 members.

Finance

Affiliation fees and voluntary contributions.

Budget

The total budget was €EUR10,123,972 in 2000 and €10,322,286 in 2001, and is expected to be €10, 537,000 in 2002.

Sources on the Internet

<http://www.icftu.org>

International Organization for Standardization (ISO)

Objectives

To promote the development of standardization and related activities in the world with a view to facilitating the international exchange of goods and services, and to developing co-operation in the spheres of intellectual, scientific, technological, and economic activity.

ISO's work results in international agreements, which are published as International Standards.

Organization

Type

Non-governmental organization (NGO). Member organization. ISO collaborates with the International Electrotechnical Commission (IEC), whose scope of activities complements that of ISO. In turn, ISO and the IEC co-operate on a joint basis with the International Telecommunication Union (ITU). ISO is building a strategic partnership with the World Trade Organization (WTO) (see IGOs) with the common goal of promoting a free and fair global trading system. The political agreements reached within the framework of the WTO require underpinning by technical agreements. ISO is recognized as providing a special technical support role to the new and expanded WTO programmes.

Membership

ISO is made up of its members, which are divided into three categories (only one body in each country/territory may be admitted to membership of ISO):

- a *member body*, the national body 'most representative of standardization in its country';
- a *correspondent member*, usually an organization in a country which does not yet have a fully developed national standards activity;
- *subscriber membership*, for countries with very small economies.

ISO had 143 members in 140 countries and three territories, comprising 93 member bodies, 36 correspondent members, and 14 subscriber members, by January 2002.

Founded

23 February 1947.

Secretariat

International Organization for Standardization (ISO),
Central Secretariat,
1, rue de Varembé,
Case postale 56,
CH-1211 Geneva 20,
Switzerland

Telephone:	+41-22-7490111
Telefax:	+41-22-7333430
E-mail:	central@iso.org

Number of staff

165 at the central Secretariat (January 2002).

Activities

Most of ISO's work is decentralized, carried out within some 2850 technical committees, subcommittees, and working groups. These are manned by experts on loan from the industrial, technical, and business sectors which have asked for the standards, and which subsequently put them to use. These experts may be joined by others with relevant knowledge, such as representatives of government agencies and testing laboratories.

Within the ISO technical committees and subcommittees, International Standards are developed by a six-step process: proposal stage; preparatory stage; committee stage; enquiry stage; approval stage; and publication stage. The Standards are developed according to the principles of:

- *consensus*, where the views of all interests are taken into account: manufacturers, vendors and users, consumer groups, testing laboratories, governments, engineering professions, and research organizations;
- being *industry-wide*, seeking global solutions to satisfy industries and customers world-wide;
- being *voluntary*, that is market-driven and therefore based on voluntary involvement of all interests in the market-place.

While the major responsibility for administrating a standards committee is assumed by one of the national standards bodies that make up the ISO membership, the Central Secretariat in Geneva acts to ensure the flow of documentation in all directions, to clarify technical points with secretariats and chairmen, and to ensure that the agreements approved by the technical committees are edited, printed, submitted as draft International Standards to ISO member bodies for voting, and published. Meetings of technical committees and subcommittees are convened by the Central Secretariat, which co-ordinates all such meetings with the committee secretariats before setting the date and place.

Main ISO publications include *International Standards*, *ISO Bulletin* (monthly), *ISO Management Systems* (bi-monthly), and *ISO in figures* (annual).

Environmental activities

The ISO 14000 family of standards addresses environmental management and is among ISO's most widely known standards. The objective of ISO 14000 is to help organizations to meet their environmental challenges. Environmental management means what the organization does to minimize harmful effects on the environment caused by its activities, and continually to improve its environmental performance.

The ISO 14000 standards have been developed with the aim of providing a framework for an overall, strategic approach to the environmental policy, plans, and actions of all types of organizations. The underlying philosophy is that the requirements of an effective environmental management system are the same, whatever the business sector. The ISO 14000 standards do not specify levels of environmental performance, thus allowing the standards to be implemented by a wide variety of organizations, whatever their current level of environmental maturity. However, a commitment to compliance with applicable environmental legislation and regulations is required, along with a commitment to continuous improvement—for which the environmental management system provides the framework.

Decision-making bodies

The highest organ of ISO is the General Assembly, which is constituted by the officers (President, Policy and Technical Management Vice-Presidents, Treasurer, and Secretary-General) and delegates nominated by the member bodies. Correspondent members and subscriber members may attend as observers. As a general rule, the General Assembly meets once a year. Its agenda includes, inter alia, actions relating to the ISO annual report, an ISO multi-year strategic plan with financial implications, and the Treasurer's annual financial status report on the Central Secretariat. The President is Chairman of the General Assembly.

The operations of ISO are governed by the Council, consisting of the officers and 18 elected member bodies. The Council appoints the Treasurer, the 12 members of the Technical Management Board, and the Chairmen of the policy development committees. It also decides on the annual budget of the Central Secretariat.

Finance

The financing of the Central Secretariat derives from member subscriptions (65 per cent) and revenues from the sale of the organization's standards and other publications (35 per cent). The subscriptions required of members for financing the operations of the Central Secretariat are expressed in units and calculated in Swiss francs. The number of units that each member is invited to pay is calculated on the basis of economic indicators: gross national product (GNP) and the value of imports and exports. The value of the subscription unit is set each year by the ISO Council.

Budget

Annual operational expenditure for the ISO work is currently estimated at SFr.150 million. Operating expenditure of the Central Secretariat represents about one-fifth of the total cost of financing the ISO administrative operations.

Sources on the Internet

<http://www.iso.org>

International Solar Energy Society (ISES)

Objectives

• to provide a common meeting-ground for all those concerned with the nature and utilization of renewable energy;
• to foster science and technology relating to the applications of renewable energy;
• to promote education and encourage research and development;
• to gather, compile, and disseminate information in these fields.

Organization

Type

Non-governmental organization (NGO). Non-profit organization. Consultative status (category C) with UNESCO. Member of the UN Economic and Social Council (ECOSOC).

Membership

Organizations, companies, and individuals with a special interest in renewable energy. The current (January 2002) network consists of some 30,000 members (organizations, companies, and individuals with a special interest in renewable energy) in over 110 countries, including 48 national and multinational Sections organized in 4 Regional Offices and the Headquarters.

Founded

24 December 1954.

Secretariat

International Solar Energy Society (ISES),
Villa Tannheim,
Wiesentalstrasse 50,
79115 Freiburg,
Germany

Telephone: +49-761-459060
Telefax: +49-761-4590699
E-mail: hq@ises.org

Number of staff

Ten professionals and three support staff at the secretariat (January 2002).

Activities

The Society's interests embrace all aspects of solar energy, including characteristics, effects, and methods of use.

It organizes major international congresses on renewable energy at which numerous scientific and technical papers are presented and discussed. These congresses are held every two years in different countries. The next ISES Solar World Congress will be in Adelaide in 2001. Its national sections and regional offices arrange conferences and workshops.

ISES has projects running in several countries on various aspects of renewable energy technology. Currently they are working on a utility initiative for Africa, on solar co-operatives, on solar cities, rural energy supply models (RESuM) and sustainable energy policy concepts (SEPCo).

Main publications include *Solar Energy Journal* (12 issues per year, paper and electronic versions), and *Refocus* magazine (6 issues per year).

Decision-making bodies

The Society is administered by a Board of Directors, elected by and representative of the world-wide membership. The Board meets annually, normally just before to the Annual General Meeting of the Society's members. Day-to-day administration is provided by the Executive Director in the Society's headquarters office.

Finance

No information available.

Budget

No information available.

Sources on the Internet

<http://www.ises.org>
<http://wire.ises.org>

IUCN – The World Conservation Union

IUCN – The World Conservation Union

Objectives

The vision of IUCN is 'a just world that values and conserves nature'. The mission of IUCN is to influence, encourage, and assist societies throughout the world to conserve the integrity and diversity of nature. The objectives are:
• to secure the conservation of nature, and especially of biological diversity, as an essential foundation for the future;
• to ensure that, where the Earth's natural resources are used, this is done in a wise, equitable way;
• to guide the development of human communities towards ways of life that are both of good quality and in enduring harmony with other components of the biosphere.

Organization

Type
Non-governmental organization (NGO). Observer to the UN. Consultative status with the UN Economic and Social Council (ECOSOC), FAO, IMO, and UNESCO.

Membership
States (71), government agencies (107), national NGOs (675), international NGOs (68). Total by January 2002 of 955 members in 139 countries and eight territories, including 34 non-voting affiliates.

Founded
5 October 1948.

Secretariat

IUCN – The World Conservation Union,
28 rue Mauverney,
CH-1196 Gland,
Switzerland
Telephone: +41-22-9990000
Telefax: +41-22-9990002
E-mail: mail@hq.iucn.org

In addition, IUCN has an Environmental Law Centre in Bonn, Germany, and regional offices in South and South-East Asia, Europe, North America, Central America, South America, Eastern Africa, Central Africa, Southern Africa, and Western Africa, and numerous country and project offices, found mostly in developing countries.

Number of staff
A total of approximately 1000, of which approximately 100 are based at headquarters and some 900 are outposted in IUCN offices world-wide.

Activities

IUCN carries out a single integrated programme. Approved by the triennial World Conservation Congress (previously General Assembly) (see below), the programme is co-ordinated by the central Secretariat (both at headquarters and in the regional and country offices) and implemented with assistance from the network of volunteer experts in the IUCN Commissions, consultants, and a wide range of IUCN members and collaborating agencies. The Union's activities include:
• harnessing the strengths of its members, Commissions, and other constituents to build global partnerships for conservation;
• catalyzing action by the Union's members, Secretariat, and Commissions in order to achieve more effective conservation of nature and natural resources in keeping with the principles set out in *Caring for the Earth*, the 1991 follow-up to the World Conservation Strategy (1980);
• providing a forum for government and NGO members to discuss global and regional conservation issues, including their scientific, educational, legal, economic, social, cultural, and political dimensions;

• contributing to an increased global awareness of the interrelationships between conservation, long-term survival, and human well-being, through publications, information dissemination, and education;
• communicating authoritative statements on conservation, drawing on the expertise of its members, Commissions, and Secretariat;
• developing national and regional strategies for sustainability, capacity building, and institutional support, a process often led by IUCN regional and country offices, in collaboration with governments and NGOs;
• influencing national and international legal and administrative instruments to safeguard the environmental rights of future generations;
• participating actively in the preparation of international conventions relevant to the conservation of nature and natural resources and equitable and sustainable resource use.

The IUCN Commissions (see below) constitute a global network of more than 10,000 scientists and professionals.

Main IUCN publications include *The IUCN Red List of Threatened Species*, *Species Action Plans*, *United Nations List of National Parks and Protected Areas*, *World Conservation* (quarterly), and *Global Biodiversity Strategy*.

Decision-making bodies

Political

The World Conservation Congress (previously General Assembly) in principle meets every three years and consists of delegates from the member bodies. In October 2000 the IUCN held its World Conservation Congress in Amman. The Congress elects the President, the Regional Councillors, and the Commission Chairs. The Council, which meets at least annually, consists of the President, up to four Vice-Presidents, 24 Regional Councillors, five appointed Councillors, and six Chairs of Commissions.

Scientific/technical

The six IUCN Commissions are:
• the *Commission on Ecosystem Management (CEM)*, which provides expert guidance on integrated ecosystem approaches to the management of natural and modified ecosystems. CEM's focus is on a range of issues, including ecosystem restoration; climate change impacts on ecosystems; participation in the Millennium Ecosystem Assessment; development of indices of ecosystem status; and support to IUCN's Water and Nature Initiative and the Global Peatland Action Plan;
• the *Commission on Education and Communication (CEC)*, which brings together experts in environmental and sustainable development education and communication. CEC members are volunteers contributing their expertise to guide IUCN policy and advocacy for education and communication, as well as on the effective management and evaluation of educational programmes. CEC develops capacity-building programmes in environmental communication;
• the *Commission on Environmental Law*, which implements the legal aspects of the IUCN Law Programme. The main goals of the Environmental Law Programme are to promote the creation of sound international and national environmental legal instruments, to monitor developments in the field of environmental law, and to provide assistance and service in this field, especially to developing countries. It has been instrumental in the development of several conservation conventions, and, in addition to practice-oriented legal analysis and studies, carries out specific projects in more than 20 countries. Its Environmental Law Information System (ELIS) comprises a comprehensive collection of material on international and national environmental law;
• the *Commission on Environmental, Economic & Social Policy (CEESP)*, which is an interdisciplinary network of professionals whose mission is to act as a source of advice on the environmental, economic, social, and cultural factors that affect natural resources and biological diversity and to provide guidance and support towards effective policies and practices in environmental conservation and sustainable development. CEESP focuses on four themes: collaborative management of natural resources; sustainable livelihoods; environment and security; and environment, trade, and investment;
• the *Species Survival Commission (SSC)*, which is a knowledge network of some 7000 volunteer members working in almost every country of the world. Most of SSC's members are deployed in more than 120 Specialist Groups and Task Forces. The SSC produces the IUCN Red List of Threatened Species (see <http://www.redlist.org>); provides advice to governments on the status and protection of species; shares knowledge and information; implements conservation projects; and carries out research;
• the *World Commission on Protected Areas (WCPA)*, which is the world's leading global network of protected area specialists. The WCPA has more than 1000 members who aim to promote the establishment and effective management of a world-wide representative network of terrestrial and marine protected areas as an integral contribution to the IUCN mission. WCPA helps governments plan protected areas; strengthens the capacity of managers through guidance, tools, and information; and promotes investment in protected areas and the capacity of its members to implement the programme.

Finance

IUCN membership dues constitute a basic source of discretionary funds. Specific financing of programmes and projects is also provided by individual governments and aid agencies, multilateral organizations (including UN agencies such as UNESCO and UNEP (see IGOs) and the Commission of the European Union), international NGOs (such as the World Wide Fund For Nature (WWF)), foundations, the corporate sector, and individual donors.

Budget

The total expenditure was SFr.96 million in 2000 and approximately Fr.120 million in 2001, and is approximately Fr.140 million in 2002.

Main sources

IUCN receives its income from government sources, foundations, corporations, membership, and others. The largest government supporters have been the Netherlands, Sweden, and Switzerland.

Sources on the Internet

<http://iucn.org>

Pesticide Action Network International (PAN)

Objectives

• to advocate the adoption of ecologically sound practices in place of pesticide use;
• to encourage citizen action to challenge the global proliferation of pesticides;
• to defend basic rights to health and environmental quality;
• to ensure the transition to a just and viable society.

Organization

Type
International coalition of non-governmental organizations (NGOs).

Membership
PAN is a regionally based organization, with five regional centres: Africa, Asia and the Pacific, Europe, North America, and South America. It is a network of over 600 NGOs in more than 60 countries.

Founded
1982.

Secretariat

The Pesticide Action Network has five regional centres:

Pesticide Action Network North America (PANNA),
49 Powell Street, Suite 500,
San Francisco,
CA 94102,
USA
Telephone: +1-415-981 1771
Telefax: +1-415-981 1991
E-mail: panna@panna.org

Pesticide Action Network Asia and the Pacific (PAN AP),
PO Box 1170,
10850 Penang,
Malaysia
Telephone: +60-4-6560381
Telefax: +60-4-6577445
E-mail: panap@panap.po.my

Pesticide Action Network Latin America,
Red de Acción en Alternativas al Uso de Agroquímicos,
Apartado Postal 11-0581,
Julio Rodavero 682,
Lima,
Peru
Telephone: +51-1-3375170
Telefax: +51-1-4257955
E-mail: rapalpe@terra.com.pe

Pesticide Action Network Africa (PAN Africa),
BP 15938,
Dakar-Fann,
Senegal
Telephone: +221-825-4914
Telefax: +221-825-1443
E-mail: panafric@sentoo.sn

Pesticide Action Network Europe, *jointly co-ordinated by PAN UK and PAN Germany*

Pesticide Action Network United Kingdom (PAN UK),
Eurolink Centre,
49 Effra Road,
London SW2 1BZ,
United Kingdom
Telephone: +44-20-72748895
Telefax: +44-20-72749084
E-mail: admin@pan-uk.org

Pesticide Action Network Germany (PAN Germany),
Nernstweg 32,
D-22765 Hamburg,
Germany
Telephone: +49-40-399191022
Telefax: +49-40-3907520
E-mail: coordinator@pan-europe.de

Activities

Each PAN centre works towards the same goals, and, while there are different regional priorities, there are many areas of collaboration and shared focus.

PAN attends selected international events and processes, such as the revision of the FAO International Code of Conduct on the Distribution and Use of Pesticides, the Rotterdam Convention on Prior Informed Consent, the Stockholm Convention on Persistent Organic Pollutants, and the Convention on Biological Diversity (see Agreements). PAN's participants bring research results on the adverse impacts of pesticide use and provide briefings for governments.

PAN monitors and studies the health impacts of pesticide use and provides information to the general public on the pesticide strategies of agrochemical companies.

In addition to various research and campaigning activities, PAN groups aim to demonstrate viable sustainable agricultural alternatives to pesticides.

Main PAN publications include *Global Pesticide Campaigner* (three times a year – PANNA), *Panups* (weekly e-mail newsletter – PANNA), *Pesticides News* (quarterly – PAN UK), *Pesticides and Alternatives* (three times a year – PAN Africa), and *Pesticide Monitor* (PAN AP).

Decision-making bodies

PAN decision making is regionally based through each Regional Centre. Each centre is autonomous and has its own board. The regional co-ordinators meet at least once a year, and the three-yearly international conference guides priorities and strategies.

Finance

The PAN centres are financed through foundation grants, individual donations, and membership fees.

Budget
The PAN centres each have their own budget. No information available.

Sources on the Internet

<http://www.pan-international.org>

Sierra Club

Objectives

• to explore, enjoy, and protect the wild places of the earth;
• to practice and promote the responsible use of the earth's ecosystems and resources;
• to educate and enlist humanity to protect and restore the quality of the natural and human environment.

Organization

Type
Non-governmental organization (NGO). Consultative status with the UN Economic and Social Council (ECOSOC) and observer status with the International Whaling Commission (IWC) (see Agreements, International Convention for the Regulation of Whaling). Member of IUCN and the Forest Stewardship Council (FSC).

Membership
Individuals and groups, primarily in North America. More than 700,000 members in 27 countries, 67 chapters

in two countries (63 in the USA and four in Canada), and 27 offices (including one in Canada) by January 2002.

The Club is also assisted by the Sierra Club Foundation (which has its own budget and staff).

Founded
The Sierra Club in 1892, the International Program, as the international arm of the Sierra Club, in 1972.

Secretariat
Sierra Club,
85 Second Street, Second Floor,
San Francisco,
CA 94105-3441,
USA
Telephone: +1-415-9775500
Telefax: +1-415-9775799
E-mail: information@sierraclub.org

The Washington Legislative Office is located at:
Sierra Club, International Program,
408 C Street, NE,
Washington, DC 20002,
USA
Telephone: +1-202-5471141
Telefax: +1-202-5476009
E-mail: information@sierraclub.org

Number of staff
Approximately 250 professionals and 100 support staff (January 2002).

Activities
The Sierra Club is currently working for legislation that guarantees clean air and water; to regulate the use and disposal of poisonous toxic chemicals; to set aside the most special places for parks and wilderness; to protect tropical forests; to ensure that environmental trade agreements do not override US environmental laws; and to increase support for stabilizing population growth.

The Club pursues its aims through programmes to influence public policy, education, and litigation, and to provide assistance to environmentally minded candidates for public office. One programme aims to strengthen the safety of environmental activists in developing countries. The Club also runs campaigns on human rights and the environment and on global warming.

Main Sierra Club publications include *Sierra Magazine* (six issues a year) and *The Planet* (10 issues a year).

Decision-making bodies
The Sierra Club is guided by a Board of Directors with 15 members elected by the membership. It meets five times a year. Dozens of standing committees assist the directors. Volunteer activity within the states is guided by 67 chapters (63 in the USA, four in Canada), which in turn oversee work by more than 400 groups.

Finance
Membership dues are the basic source of funding.

Budget
The total budget was approximately $US52 million in 1999 and approximately $60 million in 2000.

Associated funds
The non-legislative work of the Club is funded by the *Sierra Club Foundation*, with net assets totaling $US75 million (end 2000) and 2000 program grants totaling $26 million. Main contributors are Sierra Club members and foundations.

Sources on the Internet
<http://www.sierraclub.org>

Society for International Development (SID)

Objectives
SID is a global network of individuals and institutions concerned with participatory, pluralistic, and sustainable development. It seeks:

• to support development innovation at all levels—local, national, global—in order to contribute to the search for solutions to poverty, injustice, gender inequity, and the lack of sustainability;
• to encourage, support, and facilitate the creation of a sense of community among individuals and organizations committed to social justice at the local, national, regional, and international levels;
• to promote the sharing of knowledge, dialogue, understanding, and co-operation for social and economic development that furthers the well-being of all peoples.

In pursuing this purpose, SID sees its role as:

• a bridge between diverse constituencies, including grass-roots movements, academia, policy makers, the progressive business sector, and multilateral institutions, as well as between local and global constituencies;
• a global catalyst for civil society: SID aims to mobilize and strengthen civil society groups by actively building partnerships among them and with other sectors;
• a knowledge broker: SID supports the generation of knowledge on innovative development initiatives, concepts, and practices, and stimulates exchanges and dissemination at all levels and across sectors.

Organization
Type
Non-governmental organization (NGO). Consultative status (category I) with the UN Economic and Social Council (ECOSOC), UNESCO, FAO, ILO, IFAD, UNEP, UNFPA, UNICEF (see IGOs), the UN Conference on Trade and Development (UNCTAD), and the Council of Europe.

Membership
Individual and corporate members, as well as associated institutional and international sponsors. More than 3000 members in 125 countries by September 2001. Institutional presence through chapters and/or institutional members in 51 countries and one territory. It works with more than 200 associations, networks, and institutions, involving academia, parliamentarians, students, political leaders, and development experts, both at local and international levels.

Founded
19 October 1957.

Secretariat
Society for International Development,
207 via Panisperna,
I-00184 Rome,
Italy
Telephone: +39-06-4872172
Telefax: +39-06-4872170
E-mail: info@sidint.org

Number of staff
15 professionals and two interns (January 2002).

Activities

SID's international programmes provide the framework for the engagement of chapters and institutional members. Each programme, which combines substantive research with organizational development, is led by a small resource group composed of experts on the particular theme, from SID and other networks. The 2001–03 portfolio includes the following programmes:

• *Conflicts Over Access to Natural Resources.* Since June 1997, this programme has aimed to strengthen the capacity of rural communities to defend their rights over natural resources by fostering greater co-ordination and synergy among different groups and by facilitating the striking of new alliances for sustainable and equal use of natural resources. SID has launched an information sharing system to facilitate the exchange of knowledge and experience among its members;

• *Futures Search Programme: Supporting Societies in Transition.* This programme seeks to support the transitions to democracy in selected African countries through a process of scenario building that catalyzes debates and discussions at various levels of society on what sort of future the countries should be working towards. By so doing, it seeks to contribute to the development of a greater sense of collective vision of the future in these countries;

• *Health and Globalization.* The programme looks at how to tackle the specific health problems linked to new patterns of global consumption, distribution, and migration. It aims to elaborate alternative policy interventions in areas of chronic disease, nutrition, mental health, violence, and the marketing of unhealthy products. It focuses on: 1) gathering knowledge on the impact of global processes on public health; 2) creating partnerships among public health professionals, the UN, the public sector, the private sector, and community health networks for the prevention of non-communicable disease; and 3) contributing to positive change within the World Health Organization (WHO);

• *Knowledge, Information and Communication Technologies for Development: Women on the Net (WoN).* The Women on the Net project works to assist the ways women are using the Internet for their empowerment. The project aims to open up possibilities for women to engage with this new information technology with a comprehensive understanding of the medium in both its technological capacity and political context;

• *Participatory Action for Capacity Building and Food Security.* Based on a sustainable livelihoods approach to food security, this programme explores through participatory actions: (a) the establishment of efficient partnerships between governments and civil society in the pursuit of food security, and (b) the increase in the bearing of local perspectives on national policy making related to food security. The project adopts a process-oriented approach, aiming to build a shared understanding among stakeholders at the national level about the need and challenges of capacity mobilization for food security. It puts forward concrete strategies for the attainment of food security and influences international development agencies towards capacity mobilization for food security;

• *Power, Culture, Identity: Women and the Politics of Place.* This programme brings together activists and intellectuals from around the world to analyse women's place-based political engagement around the body, environment, and public space in response to globalization. The programme gathers together a series of empirical studies on how women's groups are often at the forefront of the process of reconstructing the world from 'below';

• *Reproductive Health, Women's Empowerment & Population Policy.* The programme facilitates strategic network building, lobbying, and advocacy aims for women's reproductive rights and health beyond the traditional 'population policy' spheres. Working with SID's established network in this field, the programme advocates a supportive political and economic environment for reproductive rights and health policy at the national and international level. The programme's main strategy is to build alliances across sectoral interests to ensure that reproductive health and rights enter into broader development policy arenas;

• *Responsible Europe in a Global Society.* SID's Responsible Europe initiative focuses on key questions related to Europe's actual and potential role in the process of globalization that derives from its economic and financial power. The initiative aims to raise public debate on Europe–South relations in the changing global environment that challenges traditional parameters of development thinking and calls for more responsible policies and practices.

Main SID publications include *Development* (quarterly journal), and *Bridges* (bimonthly newsletter).

Decision-making bodies

The General Assembly (which convenes every three years, at the World Conference) is composed of all members. The Governing Council (which meets annually) is elected by the membership for three-year terms: it consists of the three most recent presidents, the Secretary-General, and a minimum of 24 and a maximum of 36 elected members from each of the major regions of the world. The Executive Committee consists of six to nine members elected by the Council from among its membership and the SID Secretary-General as an ex-officio member.

Chapters, organized at national and local levels, function autonomously under the broad guidelines of the Society. The International Secretariat has operated in Rome since 1978.

Finance

Members' dues (income-rated). Contributions from private, public, and international governmental and non-governmental organizations. Main sources of funding are governmental.

Budget

The budget was €EUR1,264,000 in 2000 and €1,200,000 in 2001, and is expected to be €1,600,000 in 2002.

Main contributors

Main contributors to SID's programmes in 2000–01 were the Canadian International Development Agency (CIDA), the Ministry of Development Co-operation of the Netherlands (DGIS), the Ministry of Foreign Affairs of Finland, the Ministry of Foreign Affairs of Italy (DGCS), the Rockefeller Foundation, UNFPA, WHO, and WFP.

Sources on the Internet

<http://www.sidint.org>

Third World Network (TWN)

Objectives

• to promote a greater articulation of the needs and rights of people of the Third World;
• to encourage a fair distribution of world resources and forms of development which fulfil people's needs and are ecologically and humanely harmonious;
• to exchange information and present Third World perspectives to the industrialized countries as well as within the Third World itself.

Organization

Type
Non-governmental organization (NGO). Consultative status with the UN Conference on Trade and Development (UNCTAD) and the UN Economic and Social Council (ECOSOC). Accredited to the CSD (see IGOs).

Membership
NGOs and individuals. Active affiliated member organizations in 12 countries. Offices in five countries by January 2002.

Founded
14 November 1984.

Secretariat

Third World Network (TWN),
228 Macalister Road,
10400 Penang,
Malaysia

Telephone:	+60-4-2266-159/728
Telefax:	+60-4-2264505
E-mail:	twn@igc.apc.org twnet@po.jaring.my

Number of staff
12 professionals and 13 support staff (January 2002).

Activities

The activities of TWN include:
• participation and involvement in global and regional processes related to the Convention on Biological Diversity (see Agreements), CSD, WTO, World Bank (see IGOs), UNCTAD, etc.;
• networking with NGOs on development and the environment;
• research activities, the publication of books and magazines, and a news features service in the area of economics, the environment, health, and other development issues;
• organizing seminars, conferences, and workshops.

Main TWN publications include *Third World Resurgence* (monthly), *Third World Economics* (fortnightly), and *South–North Development Monitor (SUNS)* (daily bulletin from Geneva).

Decision-making bodies

The decision-making structure of TWN consists of an International Board, with affiliated and collaborating NGOs forming a separate part of the structure.

Finance

Membership dues are the basic source of funding.

Budget
No information available.

Sources on the Internet

<http://www.twnside.org.sg>

Water Environment Federation (WEF)

Objectives

• to preserve and enhance the global water environment;
• to guide technological developments in water quality and provide technical information to a world-wide audience;
• to review and comment on environmental regulations and legislation;
• to build alliances with other organizations;
• to export quality services to its members.

Organization

Type
Non-governmental organization (NGO). Consultative status with the UN Economic and Social Council (ECOSOC).

Membership
WEF is a federation of 79 member associations in 31 countries and two territories (representing 42,000 individual members) (January 2002). It has six corresponding associations in six countries, and members in 88 countries.

Founded
1928.

Secretariat

Water Environment Federation,
601 Wythe Street,
Alexandria,
VA 22314-1994,
USA

Telephone:	+1-703-6842452
Telefax:	+1-703-6842492
E-mail:	beisenberg@wef.org

Number of staff
109 professionals (January 2002).

Activities

For nearly 75 years WEF has guided technological developments in water quality and provided its members and the public with the latest information on waste-water treatment and water quality protection. Federation representatives testify before government bodies, and they review and comment on environmental regulations and legislation. The Federation also provides expertise on issues ranging from non-point source pollution and hazardous waste to biosolids reuse and groundwater contamination.

In co-operation with the US Agency for International Development (USAID), the Federation is working to strengthen environmental professional associations in Asia.

WEF sponsors technical meetings of representatives from Pacific Rim countries to discuss environmental problems in the Pacific area and has sponsored regional conferences in Asia and in Latin America. The Federation is active in efforts such as the Stockholm Water Prize and Symposium, Water Associations World-Wide, and the Global Water Network. In addition, it arranges several conferences and training programmes on water quality and pollution control technology and issues. As a result, the Federation has published widely on these subjects. While the majority of WEF's technical publications are available in English only, a number have been translated into Spanish and/or other languages.

Main WEF publications include *Water Environment and Technology* (monthly), *Water Environment Research* (bi-monthly), *Water Environment Regulation Watch* (monthly), *Biosolids Technical Bulletin* (bi-monthly), *WEF Highlights* (monthly), and *Operations Forum* (monthly).

Decision-making bodies

The Board of Directors, where each member association is represented, is the organization's policy-making group. The Board meets twice a year.

Finance
WEF finances its activities through membership dues, grants, and income from advertising, the annual conference, and publication sales.

Budget
The total budget was $US18 million in 1999, $18 million in 2000, and $18.5 million in 2001.

Sources on the Internet
<http://www.wef.org>

Women's Environment and Development Organization (WEDO)

Objectives
WEDO is an international advocacy organization that seeks to increase the power of women world-wide as policy makers in governance and in policy-making institutions, forums, and processes, at all levels, to achieve economic and social justice, a peaceful and healthy planet, and human rights for all.

Organization
Type
Non-governmental organization (NGO). Consultative status with the UN Economic and Social Council (ECOSOC) and the UN Department of Public Information. Affiliated with the Earth Charter, the World Civil Society Conference, the Microcredit Summit, International POPs Elimination Network, Diverse Women for Diversity, and the Millennium NGO Forum. Accredited to CSD and WTO (see IGOs), the International Conference on Population and Development (ICPD), the World Summit on Social Development (WSSD), the Fourth World Conference on Women (FWCW), Habitat II, the Commission on Status of Women (CSW), and the World Food Summit.

Membership
Although not a membership organization, WEDO maintains a network comprising several thousand individuals and groups in more than 100 countries across all the regions of the world.

Founded
1990.

Secretariat
Women's Environment and Development Organization,
355 Lexington Avenue, 3rd Floor,
New York,
NY 10017-6603,
USA

Telephone:	+1-212-9730325
Telefax:	+1-212-9730335
E-mail:	wedo@wedo.org

Number of staff
Ten professional full-time staff, one consultant, and a varying number of interns (January 2002).

Activities
WEDO brings together women of diverse backgrounds from all regions of the world to share experiences and expertise and to take action on common agendas in the United Nations and other international policy-making forums.

WEDO organized the 1991 Women's Congress for a Healthy Planet in Miami, Florida, USA, at which the *Women's Action Agenda 21* was formulated and adopted in the lead up to the 1992 UN Conference on Environment and Development. Armed with this powerful tool, women successfully lobbied for sections on gender equality in the official UNCED documents, *Agenda 21*, and the *Rio Declaration.*

At UNCED, WEDO established the Women's Caucus, and through this mechanism organized and facilitated a women's perspective at all the major UN conferences on development during the 1990s and in the subsequent Review sessions. In the lead up to the World Summit on Sustainable Development 2002, WEDO has again been active in bringing women of the world together to produce an updated women's platform, *Women's Action Agenda for a Healthy and Peaceful Planet 2015.*

WEDO has three programme areas. The Gender and Governance Program seeks women's full and equal access to all areas of public life and runs a global campaign, *50/50 by 2005: Get the Balance Right!* The Sustainable Development Program fosters development that is ecologically sound, economically viable, and socially just. The Economic and Social Justice Program promotes a gender-sensitive framework and analysis in all global processes of economic decision making.

Main WEDO publications include *News and Views* and a WEDO primer series on gender, environment, and international economic issues. WEDO also publishes periodic in-depth global monitoring reports on the progress that governments are making to implement the commitments they have made to women in UN global conferences over the last decade.

Decision-making bodies
WEDO's seven-member International Board is made up of national and regional experts and meets three times a year.

Finance
The main sources of income are donations from foundations, UN agencies, international development agencies, and individuals.

Budget
No information available.

Sources on the Internet
<http://www.wedo.org>

World Business Council for Sustainable Development (WBCSD)

Objectives
- to be the leading business advocate on issues connected with sustainable development;
- to participate in policy development in order to create a framework that allows business to contribute effectively to sustainable development;
- to demonstrate business progress in environmental and resource management and corporate social responsibility and to share leading-edge practices among our members;
- to contribute to a sustainable future for developing nations and nations in transition.

Organization
Type
Non-governmental organization (NGO). Member organization. Advocacy group for business and sustainable development. The Council was formed through a merger between the Business Council for Sustainable Development (BCSD) in Geneva and the World Industry Council for the Environment (WICE) in Paris. It maintains close links

with the International Chamber of Commerce (ICC) (see this section). WBCSD is accredited to the main UN offices in Geneva and New York.

Membership
By January 2002, WBCSD's Regional Network consisted of a total of 34 national and regional business councils and partner organizations located in 31 countries.

WBCSD membership is by invitation to companies from around the world. As of November 2001, there were 160 international companies in more than 30 countries and 20 major industrial sectors.

Founded
January 1995.

Secretariat
World Business Council for Sustainable Development,
4 chemin de Conches,
CH-1231 Conches-Genève,
Switzerland
Telephone: +41-22-8393100
Telefax: +41-22-8393131
E-mail: info@wbcsd.org

Number of staff
46 professionals (January 2002).

Activities
The WBCSD follows the specific objectives and strategic directions of business leadership, policy development, best practice, and global outreach.

It offers a platform to look at areas of sustainable development where industry's voice can make a difference, and throughout 2001 it positioned itself for input into the World Summit for Sustainable Development in Johannesburg in 2002.

The organization released in 2001 a document offering new views to a sustainable society: *The Business Case for Sustainable Development – Making a difference toward the Johannesburg Summit 2002 and beyond.* This document is part of a programme for the World Summit; two other documents are planned for release for the summit: a *WorkBook*, complete with case studies; and a collection of facts and trends, undertaken in co-operation with the World Resources Institute (WRI), the UN Environmental Programme (UNEP), and the International Herald Tribune (IHT).

Also published in 2001 was the GHG Protocol report, developed by the GHG Protocol Initiative, a broad coalition of businesses, NGOs, governments, and intergovernmental organizations and managed jointly by the WBCSD and the World Resources Institute (WRI). The GHG Protocol offers practical guidance to help companies understand, calculate, and manage their GHG emissions.

In 2001 the WBCSD issued a study on sustainable mobility, *Mobility 2001*, which identifies the major threats to the future of mobility world-wide.

Several Multi-Stakeholder Dialogues were held world-wide in 2002 on topics such as corporate social responsibility and sustainability through the market. In 2001 extensive research and stakeholder dialogues were undertaken in the sectors of finance, mobility, cement, mining and minerals, forestry, and electric utilities. The organization captured these experiences in a publication, *Stakeholder Dialogue: The WBCSD's Approach to Engagement.*

Two new council projects were launched in 2001: Sustainable Livelihoods: the Business Connection and Digital Opportunities.

The WBCSD continues its work on sustainable development reporting, innovation and technology, climate and energy, and natural resources.

The WBCSD's Regional Network was also much expanded in 2001, reaching over to Egypt, Peru, and Portugal, and the creation of a BCSD in China is planned for 2002.

The WBCSD continues to promote and disseminate eco-efficiency, both at the practical level (through the encouragement of hands-on involvement with member companies and by publishing case-studies) and at the communications level.

In co-operation with UNCTAD, the WBCSD in 1999 helped to set up the International Emissions Trading Association (IETA), and in 2000 it joined with UNEP to facilitate private-sector investments under the Clean Development Mechanism (CDM).

Main WBCSD publications include the quarterly newsletter *Sustain* and the *Annual Review*.

Decision-making bodies
The WBCSD is governed by its Council. This meets annually to discuss strategic issues and decide the priorities and direction of the organization.

Each member company is represented on the Council through its Chief Executive Officer (CEO), or a business leader of equivalent rank, who appoints a Liaison Delegate. An Executive Committee composed of a Chairman, four Vice-Chairmen from different regions, and up to nine CEOs oversees the work of the organization.

The President and a secretariat in Geneva are responsible for managing the activities of the WBCSD.

Finance
The WBCSD is financed by membership fees, financial support for individual working groups, and in-kind support through the active participation of members in the work programme.

Budget
No information available.

Sources on the Internet
<http://www.wbcsd.org>

World Wide Fund For Nature (WWF)

Objectives
WWF's mission is to stop the degradation of the planet's natural environment and to build a future in which humans live in harmony with nature, by:
• conserving the world's biological diversity;
• ensuring that the use of renewable natural resources is sustainable;
• promoting the reduction of pollution and wasteful consumption.

Organization
Type
Non-governmental organization (NGO). Works in conjunction with governments, other NGOs, scientists, business and industry, the world's major religions, and people at the local level. Consultative status (category i) with UN Economic and Social Council (ECOSOC).

Membership
Nearly 5 million regular supporters world-wide by January 2002. The WWF network operates in more than 90 countries, with 52 country or regional offices located in 47 countries and one territory. In addition, four associate organizations promote shared conservation objectives.

Founded
11 September 1961. Formerly known as World Wildlife Fund, it continues

WWF International

to be known under its former name in Canada and the USA.

Secretariat

WWF International,
Avenue du Mont-Blanc,
CH-1196 Gland,
Switzerland
Telephone: +41-22-3649111
Telefax: +41-22-3645358
E-mail: infobox@wwfint.org

Number of staff
110 core positions (January 2002).

Activities

WWF actively supports and operates biodiversity conservation programmes on the ground in Africa, Asia, Europe, and Latin America. World-wide, WWF undertakes more than 1300 projects every year, employing more than 3800 people and investing some $US270 million in its global conservation programme and campaigns.

The six major areas of the organization's long-term conservation work are: forests; fresh water; oceans and coasts; species; climate change; and toxic chemicals. Recognizing that local conservation problems often have their roots in wider social and economic issues which influence how people use and consume resources and affect the environment, WWF has adopted an ecoregion conservation approach. WWF has identified more the 200 ecoregions—the Global 200—which are the most representative of the world's biological diversity and which must be preserved if we are to leave a living planet to future generations. It is in these areas that WWF is working hardest to make a difference. WWF also reinforces the effectiveness of wildlife trade monitoring through the TRAFFIC Network (the wildlife trade monitoring programme of WWF) and IUCN – The World Conservation Union. WWF is emphasizing capacity building through such grant schemes as 'Across the Waters' and the WWF Prince Bernhard Scholarships for Nature Conservation.

Main WWF publications include *WWF's Global Conservation Programme* (annual), and *Living Planet Magazine* (quarterly).

Decision-making bodies

Board of Trustees (meets twice a year), Executive Committee, and Programme Committee (twice a year).

Finance

Sources of income in 2001 were individuals (47 per cent), governments and aid agencies (20 per cent), trusts and legacies (16 per cent), and others (17 per cent). WWF International benefits from substantial endowments, such as The 1001: A Nature Trust, to meet its basic running costs. This ensures that all contributions go directly to WWF's conservation programmes.

Budget
The overall income of WWF International, including all national organizations, was SFr.575 million in 1999/2000 and Fr.574.8 million in 2000/01. The income of WWF International alone was Fr.104 million in 1999/2000.

Sources on the Internet
<http://www.panda.org>

Other NGO Networks, Instruments, and Resources

Arab Network for Environment and Development (RAED)

Objectives

- to gather, disseminate, and exchange regional and international data on different environmental and developmental problems;
- to co-ordinate between regional community organizations in the exchange of skills and information;
- to mobilize already existing grass-roots organizations to have a share in this information and to partake in the problem-solving process;
- to create new grass-roots activities to be implemented by RAED's member organizations;
- to encourage the inclusion of community participation projects in government programmes.

Organization

NGO network of 260 NGOs from Mauritania, Morocco, Algeria, Tunisia, Libya, Sudan, Egypt, Jordan, Palestine, Lebanon, Syria, Kuwait, Qatar, Bahrain, Oman, Saudi Arabia, and Yemen.

Secretariat

Arab Network for Environment and Development,
c/o The Arab Office for Youth and Environment (AOYE),
PO Box 2,
Magles El Shaab,
Cairo,
Egypt
Telephone: +20-2-3041634
Telefax: +20-2-3041635
E-mail: aoye@link.net
Internet: http://www.aoye.org/raed.htm

Both ENDS

Objectives

The main role of Both ENDS is to be a go-between to support the work of environmental organizations, primarily in the so-called South (developing countries) and the Central and Eastern European (CEE) countries. The organization's principal focus is the realization of sustainable forms of natural resource management and to promote policy making in the Netherlands as well as world-wide. The organization produces funding guides and research and lobby documents, supports campaigns, and helps build coalitions. For the years 2001–03 its specific objectives are:

- to offer direct services to basic groups and NGOs who support an integrated approach of sustainable development and social justice;
- to facilitate, strengthen, and support innovative initiatives—alternatives—in the area of sustainable environmental management in collaboration with local environmental groups;
- to facilitate and initiate policy making in the Netherlands and world-wide by collaboration and dialogue;
- to continue adaptation of the organization to be able to execute these services now and in the future in a reliable, adequate, and efficient manner.

Organization

Dutch non-profit NGO foundation, founded in 1986. Receives financial contributions on a project base from various private charity foundations and development institutions.

Secretariat

Both ENDS,
Damrak 28–30,
1012 LJ Amsterdam,
The Netherlands
Telephone: +31-20-6230823
Telefax: +31-20-6208049
E-mail: info@bothends.org
Internet: http://www.bothends.org

Genetic Resources Action International (GRAIN)

Objectives

GRAIN's main objective is to promote the sustainable management and use of agricultural biodiversity based on people's control over genetic resources and local knowledge. GRAIN works to achieve this by:

- protecting and strengthening community control of agricultural biodiversity: GRAIN monitors, researches, and lobbies against pressures that undermine the rights of farmers and local communities to use, and benefit from, biodiversity. GRAIN also works with organizations in the South to build mechanisms that enhance community control over local genetic resources and associated knowledge;
- promoting agriculture rich in biodiversity: all over the world there are livelihood systems rich in biological and cultural diversity. With other NGOs, GRAIN works to support farmers and communities in strengthening people-driven sustainable agricultural approaches that serve food security. GRAIN also explores how agricultural research programmes can better serve these approaches;
- stopping the destruction of genetic diversity: agricultural policies and trade liberalization have led to a more industrialized and vulnerable food system. Through research, information, and strategy work, GRAIN aims to help those involved in various activities to stop further privatization and loss of agricultural biodiversity.

Organization

GRAIN is a non-profit international NGO foundation, established in 1990. It is financed by grants from NGOs, governments, and IGOs.

Secretariat
Genetic Resources Action International (GRAIN),
Girona 25, pral.,
E-08010 Barcelona,
Spain
Telephone: +34-933-011381
Telefax: +34 933-011627
E-mail: grain@grain.org
Internet: http://www.grain.org

In addition, GRAIN has permanent staff/offices in Argentina, Benin, France, India, the Philippines, Uruguay, and the USA.

Global Legislators Organization for a Balanced Environment (GLOBE)

Objectives and activities
- to enhance international co-operation between parliamentarians on global environmental issues;
- to highlight environmental problems and urge effective action by governments and private sector leaders, and to suggest alternative approaches;
- to develop common environmental policy for sustainability across the planet.

Organization
International network NGO, with membership open to democratically elected parliamentarians. Founded 1989. GLOBE had more than 800 members in 100 countries by January 2002, with six regional affiliate offices in Belgium (EU and Europe), South Africa, Russia, Japan, and the USA, and additional offices in parliaments throughout the regional networks.

Secretariat
GLOBE International,
1636 R Street NW, Third Floor,
Washington, DC 20009,
USA
Telephone: +1-202-2939090
Telefax: +1-202-2939098
E-mail: info@globeinternational.org
Internet:
http://www.globeinternational.org

International Institute for Sustainable Development (IISD)

Objectives
IISD's overall mission is to champion innovation, enabling societies to live sustainably. More specifically, over the next five years (2001–2006), IISD intends:
- to promote government expenditure and taxation policies that encourage the transition to sustainable development;
- to design and advocate trade and investment policies that advance sustainable development;
- to develop and promote creative responses to climate change and its impacts;
- to encourage more sustainable forms of agriculture and other natural resource use through the development of incentives and increased community participation in decision making; and
- to develop robust sets of indicators for public- and private-sector decision makers to measure progress towards sustainable development, and to build an international consensus to promote their use.

IISD's main products are:
- action recommendations based on careful analysis;
- knowledge networks to build the capacity of civil society and other organizations in both South and North;
- timely reporting of international negotiations critical to the sustainability of the planet, using Internet technology.

Organization
IISD is a non-profit NGO foundation, funded by the governments of Canada and Manitoba, other national governments, UN agencies, foundations, and the private sector.

Secretariat
International Institute for Sustainable Development,
161 Portage Avenue East, 6th Floor,
Winnipeg,
Manitoba,
Canada R3B 0Y4
Telephone: +1 204-9587700
Telefax: +1 204-9587710
E-mail: info@iisd.ca
Internet: http://www.iisd.org
http://www.iisd.ca
http://www.iisd.ca/wssd/portal.html

Regional Environmental Center for Central and Eastern Europe (REC)

Objectives
REC's mission is to assist in solving environmental problems in Central and Eastern Europe through the promotion of co-operation among NGOs, governments, business, and other environmental stakeholders, and to promote free exchange of information and public participation in environmental decision making.

Organization
Non-profit, non-advocacy NGO. Founded in 1990. Headquartered in Hungary, with additional offices in 14 Central and Eastern European countries (Albania, Bosnia and Herzegovina, Bulgaria, Croatia, the Czech Republic, Estonia, Latvia, Lithuania, FYR Macedonia, Poland, Romania, Slovakia, Slovenia, and Yugoslavia). Most funds contributed by Japan, the European Commission, the USA, various European states, and UNEP.

Secretariat
Regional Environmental Center for Central and Eastern Europe (REC),
Head Office,
Ady Endre ut 9–11,
H-2000 Szentendre,
Hungary
Telephone: +36-26-504000
Telefax: +36-26-311294
E-mail: info@rec.org
Internet: http://www.rec.org

Stakeholder Forum for Our Common Future

Objectives
The primary objective of the Stakeholder Forum (formerly known as UNED Forum) is to promote sustainable development through facilitating the involvement of major groups and stakeholders in the policy work of the United Nations and other intergovernmental institutions. At its creation in 1993, the focus was on promoting the outcomes from the first Earth Summit in Rio 1992, but since 1998 Stakeholder Forum's work has been built around preparing the 2002 Earth Summit in Johannesburg, mainly through its 'Towards Earth Summit 2002' project, with

its main activities being the organization of multi-stakeholder dialogues and information dissemination.

Organization

Stakeholder Forum is organized and staffed by the United Nations Environment & Development – UK Committee (UNED-UK). UNED-UK is an UK membership NGO, independent, but with close ties to UNEP, UNDP, and CSD. Founded in 1993, most of its funds come from UK and European government agencies, private companies and foundations, and the European Union. While being directed by an Executive Committee of UK stakeholders, the 'Towards Earth Summit 2002' project has been guided by an international advisory board reflecting the stakeholder groups outlined in Agenda 21.

Secretariat

Stakeholder Forum,
c/o UN Association of Great Britain and Northern Ireland,
3 Whitehall Court,
London SW1A 2EL,
UK
Telephone: +44-20-78391784
Telefax: +44-20-79305893
E-mail: info@earthsummit2002.org
Internet:
http://www.stakeholderforum.org
http://www.earthsummit2002.org

United Nations Non-Governmental Liaison Service (UN-NGLS)

Objectives

• to promote increased UN–NGO dialogue, understanding, and co-operation on international sustainable development issues;
• to bring important development and environment activities and issues of the UN system to the attention of NGOs;
• to work with southern and northern NGOs seeking access to UN system events, processes, and resources.

Organization

NGLS is an inter-agency programme of the UN system established in 1975.

Secretariat

UN-NGLS,
Palais des Nations,
CH-1211 Geneva 10,
Switzerland
Telephone: +41-22-9172076
Telefax: +41-22-9170049
E-mail: ngls@unctad.org

UN-NGLS,
Room DC1-1106,
United Nations,
New York,
NY 10017,
USA
Telephone: +1-212-9633125
Telefax: +1-212-9638712
E-mail: ngls@un.org
Internet:
http://www.unsystem.org/ngls

Tables of International Organizations and Degrees of Participation, by Country and Territory

Intergovernmental Organizations (IGOs)

International Council for the Exploration of the Sea (ICES)
OECD, Environment Policy Committee (EPOC)

Key

○ States with observer status

● Member States

Non-Governmental Organizations (NGOs)

Basel Action Network (BAN)
Climate Action Network (CAN)
Consumers International (CI)
Environmental Liaison Centre International (ELCI)
European Environmental Bureau (EEB)
Forest Stewardship Council (FSC)
Friends of the Earth International (FoEI)
Greenpeace International
International Chamber of Commerce (ICC)
International Confederation of Free Trade Unions (ICFTU)
International Organization for Standardization (ISO)
International Solar Energy Society (ISES)
IUCN - The World Conservation Union
Pesticide Action Network (PAN)
Sierra Club
Society for International Development (SID)
Third World Network (TWN)
Water Environment Federation (WEF)
World Business Council for Sustainable Development (WBCSD)
World Wide Fund For Nature (WWF)

Key

General

○ Associate or corresponding member organizations

● Member organizations, national affiliates, and offices

IUCN - The World Conservation Union

● Members

Note: Most of the IGOs are not included, as the degree of participation is almost universal. For the degree of participation regarding the European Union (EU) and the Commission on Sustainable Development (CSD), see entries in the IGO subsection.

	Intern. Council for the Exploration of the Sea (ICES)	OECD, Environment Policy Committee (EPOC)	Basel Action Network (BAN)	Climate Action Network (CAN)	Consumers International (CI)	Environm. Liaison Centre International (ELCI)	European Environmental Bureau (EEB)	Forest Stewardship Council (FSC)	Friends of the Earth International (FoEI)	Greenpeace International	Intern. Chamber of Commerce (ICC)	Intern. Confederation of Free Trade Unions (ICFTU)	Intern. Organization for Standardization (ISO)	Intern. Solar Energy Society (ISES)	IUCN - The World Conservation Union	Pesticide Action Network (PAN)	Sierra Club	Society for International Development (SID)	Third World Network (TWN)	Water Environment Federation (WEF)	World Business Council for Sust. Devel. (WBCSD)	World Wide Fund for Nature (WWF)
Afghanistan															●							
Albania				●	●								○									
Algeria				●		●	○				●	●	●		●						●	
Andorra															●							
Angola												●			●							
Antigua & Barbuda												●	○									
Argentina				●	●			●	●	●	●	●	●	●	●			●		●	●	○
Armenia					●								●									
Australia	○	●		●	●			●	●	●	●	●	●	●	●			●		●	●	●
Austria		●		●	●		●	●	●	●	●	●	●	●	●			●			●	●
Azerbaijan					●							●	○									
Bahamas												●			●							
Bahrain											●		○	●								
Bangladesh				●	●				●		●	●	●		●			●	○			
Barbados												●	●		●							
Belarus				●	●								●									
Belgium	●	●		●	●		●	●	●	●	●	●	●	●	●			●				●
Belize												●			●							
Benin					●				●			●	○					●				
Bhutan																						●
Bolivia				●	●			●					○		●			●				●
Bosnia & Herzegovina													●									
Botswana					●							●	●		●							
Brazil			●	●	●			●	●	●	●	●	●		●			●	○	●	●	●
Brunei Darussalam													○		●							
Bulgaria			●	●	●		●		●			●	●	●	●					○		
Burkina Faso				●	●	●					●	●	○		●							
Burundi					●																	
Cambodia			●										○									
Cameroon				●	●			●	●		●	●	○		●			●				●
Canada	●	●	●	●	●			●	●	●	●	●	●	●	●		●	●		●		●
Cape Verde				●								●										

	Intern. Council for the Exploration of the Sea (ICES)	OECD, Environment Policy Committee (EPOC)	Basel Action Network (BAN)	Climate Action Network (CAN)	Consumers International (CI)	Environm. Liaison Centre International (ELCI)	European Environmental Bureau (EEB)	Forest Stewardship Council (FSC)	Friends of the Earth International (FoEI)	Greenpeace International	Intern. Chamber of Commerce (ICC)	Intern. Confederation of Free Trade Unions (ICFTU)	Intern. Organization for Standardization (ISO)	Intern. Solar Energy Society (ISES)	IUCN - The World Conservation Union	Pesticide Action Network (PAN)	Sierra Club	Society for International Development (SID)	Third World Network (TWN)	Water Environment Federation (WEF)	World Business Council for Sust. Devel. (WBCSD)	World Wide Fund for Nature (WWF)
Central African Rep.												●										
Chad					●							●										
Chile	○			●	●			●	●	●	●	●	●		●					●		
China					●			●		●	●		●	●	●			●		●		●
Colombia					●			●	●		●	●	●		●			●	○	●	●	●
Comoros													○									
Congo												●			●							
Congo (DR of)									●			●	○		●			●				
Cook Islands												●										
Costa Rica				●	●			●	●			●	●	●	●						●	●
Côte d'Ivoire				●	●							●	○									●
Croatia			●	●	●				●			●	●	●	●						●	
Cuba				●	●						●		●		●							
Cyprus					●		●		●	●	●	●	●	●	●							
Czech Republic		●		●	●		●	●	●	●	●	●	●	●	●						●	
Denmark	●	●		●	●		●	●	●	●	●	●	●	●	●							●
Djibouti												●										
Dominica												●	○									
Dominican Republic					●							●	○		●							
East Timor																						
Ecuador				●	●			●	●		●	●	●		●			●	○			○
Egypt					●						●		●	●	●			●		●	●	
El Salvador					●				●			●	○		●			●			●	
Equatorial Guinea																						
Eritrea												●										
Estonia	●			●			●	●	●			●	○		●							
Ethiopia													●		●				○			
Fiji					●					●		●	○	●	●			●				●
Finland	●	●		●	●		●	●	●	●	●	●	●	●	●					○		●
France	●	●	●	●	●		●	●	●	●	●	●	●	●	●						●	●
Gabon					●			●				●										●
Gambia						●						●						●				

	Intern. Council for the Exploration of the Sea (ICES)	OECD, Environment Policy Committee (EPOC)	Basel Action Network (BAN)	Climate Action Network (CAN)	Consumers International (CI)	Environm. Liaison Centre International (ELCI)	European Environmental Bureau (EEB)	Forest Stewardship Council (FSC)	Friends of the Earth International (FoEI)	Greenpeace International	Intern. Chamber of Commerce (ICC)	Intern. Confederation of Free Trade Unions (ICFTU)	Intern. Organization for Standardization (ISO)	Intern. Solar Energy Society (ISES)	IUCN - The World Conservation Union	Pesticide Action Network (PAN)	Sierra Club	Society for International Development (SID)	Third World Network (TWN)	Water Environment Federation (WEF)	World Business Council for Sust. Devel. (WBCSD)	World Wide Fund for Nature (WWF)
Georgia					●				●			●		●	●							
Germany	●	●		●	●	●	●	●	●	●	●	●	●	●	●	●		●		○		●
Ghana				●	●	●		●	●		●	●	●	●	●			●	●			
Greece	○	●		●	●		●		●	●	●	●	●	●	●			●				●
Grenada									●			●	○									
Guatemala				●	●			●		●		●	○		●							
Guinea				●								●						●				
Guinea-Bissau												●			●							
Guyana					●			●				●	○									
Haiti			●						●									●				
Holy See (Vatican)												●										
Honduras					●			●				●	○		●						●	
Hungary		●		●	●		●		●		●	●	●	●	●					●		●
Iceland	●	●		●	●						●	●	●		●							
India			●	●	●	●		●		●	●	●	●	●	●			●	●	●	●	●
Indonesia			●	●	●			●	●		●	●	●		●				○	○		●
Iran (Islamic Rep. of)											●		●		●							
Iraq													●									
Ireland	●	●		●	●		●	●	●		●	●	●		●							
Israel					●	●		●		●	●	●	●	●	●			●		●		
Italy		●		●	●		●	●	●	●	●	●	●	●	●			●		●		●
Jamaica					●							●	●		●							
Japan		●		●	●	●		●	●	●	●	●	●	●	●			●		●		●
Jordan					●	●			●		●	●	●		●							
Kazakhstan					●								●		●							
Kenya				●	●	●						●	●		●			●				●
Kiribati					●							●										
Korea (DPR of)													●		●							
Korea (Rep. of)		●		●	●						●	●	●	●	●					●		
Kuwait											●		●		●			●				
Kyrgyz Republic													○		●							
Laos															●							

	Intern. Council for the Exploration of the Sea (ICES)	OECD, Environment Policy Committee (EPOC)	Basel Action Network (BAN)	Climate Action Network (CAN)	Consumers International (CI)	Environm. Liaison Centre International (ELCI)	European Environmental Bureau (EEB)	Forest Stewardship Council (FSC)	Friends of the Earth International (FoEI)	Greenpeace International	Intern. Chamber of Commerce (ICC)	Intern. Confederation of Free Trade Unions (ICFTU)	Intern. Organization for Standardization (ISO)	Intern. Solar Energy Society (ISES)	IUCN - The World Conservation Union	Pesticide Action Network (PAN)	Sierra Club	Society for International Development (SID)	Third World Network (TWN)	Water Environment Federation (WEF)	World Business Council for Sust. Devel. (WBCSD)	World Wide Fund for Nature (WWF)
Latvia	●			●	●			●	●			●	○		●							
Lebanon										●	●	●	○		●							
Lesotho					●								○									
Liberia					●							●										
Libyan Arab Jamah.													●		●							
Liechtenstein															●							
Lithuania				●	●		●		●		●	●	○		●			●				
Luxembourg		●		●	●		●		●	●	●	●	●		●							
Macedonia (FYR of)					●				●				●									
Madagascar												●	○		●							●
Malawi					●							●	○		●							
Malaysia			●	●	●	●		●	●			●	●	●	●	●			●	●	●	●
Maldives																						
Mali				●	●				●			●	○		●			●				
Malta				●	●		●		●	●		●	●		●							
Marshall Islands																						
Mauritania				●								●			●							
Mauritius					●	●			●			●	●		●			●				
Mexico		●		●	●			●		●	●	●	●	●	●			●		●	●	●
Micronesia (FS of)																						
Moldova (Rep. of)				●								●	○		●							
Monaco											●				●							
Mongolia					●							●	●		●						●	
Morocco				●	●						●	●	●		●							
Mozambique			●		●							●	○		●							
Myanmar								●														
Namibia					●							●	○		●							
Nauru																						
Nepal				●	●						●	●	○	●	●			●				●
Netherlands	●	●	●	●	●	●	●	●	●	●	●	●	●	●	●			●		●		●
New Zealand		●		●	●			●	●	●	●	●	●		●					●	●	●
Nicaragua					●			●	●			●	○		●							

	Intern. Council for the Exploration of the Sea (ICES)	OECD, Environment Policy Committee (EPOC)	Basel Action Network (BAN)	Climate Action Network (CAN)	Consumers International (CI)	Environm. Liaison Centre International (ELCI)	European Environmental Bureau (EEB)	Forest Stewardship Council (FSC)	Friends of the Earth International (FoEI)	Greenpeace International	Intern. Chamber of Commerce (ICC)	Intern. Confederation of Free Trade Unions (ICFTU)	Intern. Organization for Standardization (ISO)	Intern. Solar Energy Society (ISES)	IUCN - The World Conservation Union	Pesticide Action Network (PAN)	Sierra Club	Society for International Development (SID)	Third World Network (TWN)	Water Environment Federation (WEF)	World Business Council for Sust. Devel. (WBCSD)	World Wide Fund for Nature (WWF)
Niger				●								●			●			●				
Nigeria					●			●	●		●	●	●		●			●		●		○
Niue																						
Norway	●	●	●	●	●		●	●	●	●	●	●	●	●	●					○		●
Oman													○		●							
Pakistan			●	●	●						●	●	●	●	●			●				●
Palau																						
Panama				●	●			●				●	●		●							
Papua New Guinea					●			●		●		●	○		●							
Paraguay				●				●	●			●	○		●							
Peru				●	●			●	●		●	●	○		●	●					●	●
Philippines				●	●				●	●	●	●	●	●	●			●	○	●	●	●
Poland	●	●		●	●			●	●		●	●	●	●	●						●	
Portugal	●	●		●	●		●	●			●	●	●	●	●					●	●	
Qatar											●		○									
Romania				●	●			●			●	●	●	●	●							
Russian Federation	●			●	●			●		●	●	●	●	●	●						●	●
Rwanda												●	○									
St Kitts & Nevis												●										
St Lucia												●	○		●							
St Vinc. & Grenadines												●										
Samoa (Western)					●	●		●				●			●							
San Marino												●										
São Tomé & Príncipe																						
Saudi Arabia											●		●		●							
Senegal				●	●	●					●	●			●	●		●				
Seychelles					●							●	○		●							
Sierra Leone									●			●			●							
Singapore											●	●	●		●					●		
Slovakia		●		●	●			●	●	●	●	●	●		●							
Slovenia			●	●	●		●				●		●	●	●							
Solomon Islands								●		●												

	Intern. Council for the Exploration of the Sea (ICES)	OECD, Environment Policy Committee (EPOC)	Basel Action Network (BAN)	Climate Action Network (CAN)	Consumers International (CI)	Environm. Liaison Centre International (ELCI)	European Environmental Bureau (EEB)	Forest Stewardship Council (FSC)	Friends of the Earth International (FoEI)	Greenpeace International	Intern. Chamber of Commerce (ICC)	Intern. Confederation of Free Trade Unions (ICFTU)	Intern. Organization for Standardization (ISO)	Intern. Solar Energy Society (ISES)	IUCN - The World Conservation Union	Pesticide Action Network (PAN)	Sierra Club	Society for International Development (SID)	Third World Network (TWN)	Water Environment Federation (WEF)	World Business Council for Sust. Devel. (WBCSD)	World Wide Fund for Nature (WWF)
Somalia																						
South Africa	○		●	●	●			●			●	●	●	●	●			●		●	●	●
Spain	●	●		●	●		●	●	●	●	●	●	●	●	●			●		●	●	●
Sri Lanka				●	●	●			●		●	●	●		●			●				
Sudan													○		●							
Suriname												●										
Swaziland												●	○		●							
Sweden	●	●		●	●		●	●	●	●	●	●	●	●	●					●		●
Switzerland		●		●	●	●		●	●	●	●	●	●	●	●			●	●	○		●
Syrian Arab Rep.											●		●		●							
Taiwan			●	●	●						●	●						●		●	●	
Tajikistan															●							
Tanzania (UR of)				●	●	●					●	●	●		●			●				●
Thailand					●			●		●	●	●	●		●			●	○	●	●	●
Togo				●	●	●			●		●	●										
Tonga												●										
Trinidad & Tobago					●						●	●	●									
Tunisia				●	●				●	●	●	●	●		●			●				
Turkey		●			●		●			●	●	●	●	●	●					●		●
Turkmenistan					●								○		●							
Tuvalu																						
Uganda					●	●						●	○		●							
Ukraine				●	●				●		●		●	●	●							
United Arab Emirates					●								●		●							
United Kingdom	●	●		●	●		●	●	●	●	●	●	●	●	●	●		●		●	●	●
USA	●	●	●	●	●	●		●	●	●	●	●	●	●	●	●	●	●		●	●	●
Uruguay				●	●			●	●		●		●		●			●	●			
Uzbekistan													●		●							
Vanuatu												●										
Vatican (see Holy See)																						
Venezuela				●	●			●			●	●	●		●					●	●	○
Viet Nam					●								●		●							●

	Intern. Council for the Exploration of the Sea (ICES)	OECD, Environment Policy Committee (EPOC)	Basel Action Network (BAN)	Climate Action Network (CAN)	Consumers International (CI)	Environm. Liaison Centre International (ELCI)	European Environmental Bureau (EEB)	Forest Stewardship Council (FSC)	Friends of the Earth International (FoEI)	Greenpeace International	Intern. Chamber of Commerce (ICC)	Intern. Confederation of Free Trade Unions (ICFTU)	Intern. Organization for Standardization (ISO)	Intern. Solar Energy Society (ISES)	IUCN - The World Conservation Union	Pesticide Action Network (PAN)	Sierra Club	Society for International Development (SID)	Third World Network (TWN)	Water Environment Federation (WEF)	World Business Council for Sust. Devel. (WBCSD)	World Wide Fund for Nature (WWF)
Yemen												●			●							
Yugoslavia											●	●	●		●							
Zambia				●	●							●			●			●				
Zimbabwe				●	●	●		●				●	●	●	●				○		●	●
European Union	○	●																				
Bermuda												●										
Falkland Islands												●			●							
French Polynesia												●										
Gibraltar															●							
Greenland															●							
Hong Kong SAR					●						●	●	○		●							●
Macau SAR					●								○									
Martinique					●										●							
Montserrat												●										
Neth. Antilles					●				●			●			●							
New Caledonia						●						●			●							
Puerto Rico					●	●						●								●		
Réunion															●							
St Helena												●										
Samoa (American)					●	●																
West Bank and Gaza													○					●		●		

Index

Entries in the reference sections are denoted in italics

List of Articles in 1992–2002/03 Volumes

Please note that the title of the 1992–7 volumes was *Green Globe Yearbook* (published by Oxford University Press).

Agreements on environment and development

General

The Johannesburg Summit and Sustainable Development: How Effective Are Environmental Mega-Conferences?, Gill Seyfang and Andrew Jordan (2002/03)

Global Environmental Governance: UN Fragmentation and Co-ordination, Steinar Andresen (2001/02)

Twenty Years On and Five Years In, Richard Sandbrook (1998/9)

Russia and International Environmental Co-operation, Vladimir Kotov and Elena Nikitina (1995)

International Environmental Treaty Secretariats: Stage-Hands or Actors?, Rosemary Sandford (1994)

Atmosphere

The Global Climate Change Regime: Taking Stock and Looking Ahead, Benito Müller (2002/03)

The 1999 Multi-Pollutant Protocol: A Neglected Break-Through in Solving Europe's Air Pollution Problems?, Jørgen Wettestad (2001/02)

Evaluation of the Climate Change Regime and Related Developments, Joyeeta Gupta (1999/2000)

International Protection of the Ozone Layer, Edward A. Parson (1996)

A Global Climate Regime: Mission Impossible?, Helge Ole Bergesen (1995)

European Climate Change Policy in a Global Context, Michael Grubb (1995)

International Co-operation to Combat Acid Rain, Marc A. Levy (1995)

The Role of Science in the Global Climate Negotiations, John Lanchbery and David Victor (1995)

Protection of the Global Climate: Ecological Utopia or Just a Long Way to Go?, Helge Ole Bergesen and Anne Kristin Sydnes (1992)

Stratospheric Ozone Depletion: Can we Save the Sky?, Alan Miller and Irving Mintzer (1992)

Hazardous substances

The Basel Convention and the International Trade in Hazardous Wastes, Jonathan Krueger (2001/02)

The Success of a Voluntary Code in Reducing Pesticide Hazards in Developing Countries, Barbara Dinham (1996)

Dumping on Our World Neighbours: The International Trade in Hazardous Wastes, and the Case for an Immediate Ban on All Hazardous Waste Exports from Industrialized to Less-Industrialized Countries, Jim Puckett (1992)

Marine environment

Environmental Protection in the South Pacific: The Effectiveness of SPREP and its Conventions, Richard Herr (2002/03)

The United Nations Fish Stocks Agreement, Lawrence Juda (2001/02)

Liability and Compensation for Ship-Source Marine Pollution: The International System, Edgar Gold (1999/2000)

Beyond Dumping? The Effectiveness of the London Convention, Olav Schram Stokke (1998/9)

The International Convention for the Regulation of Whaling: From Over-Exploitation to Total Prohibition, Sebastian Oberthür (1998/9)

Protecting the Marine Environment of the Wider Caribbean Region: The Challenge of Institution-Building, Marian A. L. Miller (1996)

The 20th Anniversary of the Mediterranean Action Plan: Reason to Celebrate?, Jon Birger Skjærseth (1996)

Deep Seabed Mining and the Environment: Consequences, Perceptions, and Regulations, Jan Magne Markussen (1994)

International Co-operation to Prevent Oil Spills at Sea: Not Quite the Success it should Be, Gerard Peet (1994)

International Efforts to Combat Marine Pollution: Achievements of North Sea Co-operation and Challenges Ahead, Steinar Andresen, Jon Birger Skjærseth, and Jørgen Wettestad (1993)

Nature conservation and terrestrial living resources

The Ramsar Convention on Wetlands: Has it Made a Difference?, Michael Bowman (2002/03)

The Protocol on Environmental Protection to the Antarctic Treaty: A Ten-Year Review, Davor Vidas (2002/03)

Biodiversity: Between Diverse International Arenas, G. Kristin Rosendal (1999/2000)

Commodity or Taboo? International Regulation of Trade in Endangered Species, Peter H. Sand (1997)

The Convention on Biological Diversity: A Viable Instrument for Conservation and Sustainable Use?, G. Kristin Rosendal (1995)

Combating Desertification: Encouraging Local Action within a Global Framework, Camilla Toulmin (1994)

Combating the Illegal Timber Trade: Is there a Role for ITTO?, Clare Barden (1994)

The Problem of Migratory Species in International Law, Cyrille de Klemm (1994)

Biological Diversity in a North–South Context, Cary Fowler (1993)

International Controversy over Sustainable Forestry, Vandana Shiva (1993)

Protecting the Frozen South, Olav Schram Stokke (1992)

Trade with Endangered Species, Joanna Boddens Hosang (1992)

Nuclear safety

International Co-operation in Nuclear Safety, Roland Timerbaev and Abram Iorysh (1999/2000)

International Co-operation to Promote Nuclear Reactor Safety in the Former USSR and Eastern Europe, Michael Herttrich, Rolf Janke, and Peter Kelm (1994)

Intergovernmental organizations (IGOs)

The World Bank: A Lighter Shade of Green?, David Hunter (2001/02)

The Treatment of Environmental Considerations in the World Trade Organization, Beatrice Chaytor and James Cameron (1999/2000)

The CSD Reporting Process: A Quiet Step Forward for Sustainable Development, Farhana Yamin (1998/9)

The Global Environment Facility: International Waters Coming into its Own, Lisa Jorgenson (1997)

UNDP and Global Environmental Problems: The Need for Capacity Development at Country Level, Poul Engberg-Pedersen and Claus Hvashøj Jørgensen (1997)

From 'Lead Agency' to 'Integrated Programming': The Global Response to AIDS in the Third World, Christer Jönsson (1996)

Why UNEP Matters, Konrad von Moltke (1996)

The Commission on Sustainable Development: Paper Tiger or Agency to Save the Earth?, Martin Khor (1994)

Can GATT Survive the Environmental Challenge?, David Pearce (1993)

Has the World Bank Greened?, Amulya K. N. Reddy (1993)

The Global Challenges of Aids, Christer Jönsson (1992)

Non-governmental organizations (NGOs) and civil society

Friends of the Earth International, Keith Suter (2002/03)

ISO Environmental Standards: Industry's Gift to a Polluted Globe or the Developed World's Competition-Killing Strategy?, Jennifer Clapp (2001/02)

The Forest Stewardship Council: Using the Market to Promote Responsible Forestry, Eleonore Schmidt (1998/9)

IUCN: A Bridge-Builder for Nature Conservation, Leif E. Christoffersen (1997)

The World Wide Fund for Nature: Financing a New Noah's Ark, Jacob Park (1997)

Greenpeace: Storm-Tossed on the High Seas, Fred Pearce (1996)

Building an Environmental Protection Framework for North America: The Role of the Non-governmental Community, Betty Ferber, Lynn Fischer, and Janine Ferretti (1995)

International Attitudes towards Environment and Development, Riley E. Dunlap (1994)

Non-governmental Organizations at UNCED: Another Successful Failure?, Elin Enge and Runar I. Malkenes (1993)

Non-governmental Organizations: The Third Force in the Third World, Bill Hinchberger (1993)

Democracy, Development, and Environmental Sustainability, Jeanette Hartmann (1992)

Indigenous People's Role in Achieving Sustainability, Russel Barsh (1992)

The Inside Out, the Outside In, Pros and Cons of Foreign Influence on Brazilian Environmentalism, Ricardo Arnt (1992)

Environment and sustainable development

Development Assistance and the Integration of Environmental Concerns: Current Status and Future Challenges, Torunn Laugen and Leiv Lunde (1996)

An Overview of Follow-up of Agenda 21 at the National Level, Alicia Bárcena (1994)

Promoting International Transfer of Environmentally Sound Technologies: The Case for National Incentive Schemes, Calestous Juma (1994)

Energy for Sustainable Development in the Third World, Amulya K. N. Reddy (1992)

International business and industry

World Business Council for Sustainable Development: The Greening of Business or a Greenwash?, Adil Najam (1999/2000)

Transnational Corporations' Strategic Responses to 'Sustainable Development', Harris Gleckman (1995)

International Business and Sustainable Development, Alex Trisoglio (1993)